The GASP IV Simulation Language

The GASP IV Simulation Language

A. ALAN B. PRITSKER

School of Industrial Engineering
Purdue University

A WILEY-INTERSCIENCE PUBLICATION

JOHN WILEY & SONS, New York • London • Sydney • Toronto

Library of Congress Cataloging in Publication Data:

Pritsker, A Alan B 1933–
The GASP IV simulation language.

"A Wiley-Interscience publication."
Bibliography: p.
1. GASP (Computer program language) I. Title.

QA76.73.G15P74 001.6'424 74-3281

ISBN 0-471-70045-2

Printed in the United States of America

10 9 8 7 6 5 4

To my parents

GERTRUDE and ROBERT

PREFACE

The need for a combined simulation language resulted from the author's interest in societal systems analysis. To orient engineering education to the problems of society (through the establishment of the Center for Large-Scale Systems at Purdue), fundamental differences in system goals, analysis objectives, and methods of approach were perceived. The level of aggregation and the data base available for such problems are fundamentally different from those of industrial problems. This necessitates that a large amount of flexibility be designed into the techniques developed to model and analyze such systems. Based on this premise GASP IV has been designed and developed.

This book provides engineers, ecologists, management scientists, and systems analysts with the necessary information to use GASP IV: A Combined Continuous/Discrete FORTRAN based Simulation Language. GASP IV is practical and useful. Being FORTRAN based it is also relatively easy to learn. The simulation concepts included within GASP IV can be quickly grasped because they are presented in the familiar framework of FORTRAN. Since GASP IV is a combined language, methods for writing discrete (next event) simulation programs or simulation programs involving continuous variables are available. The procedures for obtaining either a discrete or a continuous simulation program using GASP IV are detailed in this book. Combining discrete and continuous simulations into a single program is most important. GASP IV provides the conceptual basis for accomplishing this and provides the supporting routines that facilitate the development of combined simulation programs.

The conceptual and programming bases for GASP IV are presented in Chapters 1 and 2. The design of GASP IV is based on the material presented in these chapters. Chapter 3 describes the GASP IV subprograms, the user required subprograms, and data input formats. Chapter 3 can be considered as a user's manual which provides all the necessary information to write programs using GASP IV.

Chapter 4 documents each subprogram of GASP IV. The FORTRAN listings and the coding used in each subprogram are described.

Since simulation modeling is an art, it is necessary to have examples and case studies that demonstrate the use of a simulation language. For this reason, 11 complete simulation studies are included in this book. A standard format that includes a problem statement, objectives in solving the problem, special GASP IV features illustrated by the example, procedures used in modeling and writing the GASP IV program, and a discussion of simulation reports is used for each example. Since the emphasis is on simulation using GASP IV, the procedure section of each study is stressed. FORTRAN listings for all system models are presented with a listing of input data cards. Flow charts and final output reports are presented where appropriate.

Chapter 5 includes five discrete simulation examples. An inventory situation, two queueing systems, the simulation of a PERT network, and the allocation of resources to tasks are involved in these examples. In Chapter 6 two examples of the use of GASP IV for simulating systems involving continuous variables are presented. The examples involve a pilot ejection system and an analysis of a slip clutch used in a business machine. In these examples differential equations are used to model the system behavior.

In Chapter 7 two examples of combined simulation are presented. A fleet of tankers that provides crude oil input to a refinery is modeled. The input to the refinery is deposited in a storage tank, which is modeled as a continuous variable. The interactions between discrete events and a continuous demand for crude oil by the refinery makes this an interesting combined simulation example. The second combined simulation example involves a system of four chemical reactors. Maintenance events that discretely change the status of the system are included in the example.

The last chapter describes how GASP IV can be used to analyze Systems Dynamics models. Forrester's World Model and Industrial Dynamics model are programmed in GASP IV and analyzed. Procedures for including discrete events and those based on the status of the system are described. The modeling of systems using both differential and difference equations is illustrated. GASP IV provides extensive capabilities for analyzing Systems Dynamics as well as econometric models.

GASP IV is the only well-documented combined simulation language currently available. Since GASP IV is FORTRAN based, it can be used on a variety of computing machines. The program has been distributed and is currently operational in computer installations throughout the country.

The program is maintained by Pritsker & Associates, Inc., 1201 Wiley Drive, West Lafayette, Indiana 47906, from whom copies of the source deck may be purchased.

GASP IV has been developed over the past three years at Purdue University and is based on GASP II, which was developed at Arizona State University, which in turn was based on the original GASP developed at U.S. Steel by Mr. Philip J. Kiviat. Mr. Kiviat's contributions to the field of discrete simulation are well known, and my association with him has influenced my research activities, for which I am most grateful.

Many individuals assisted me in the design and development of GASP IV. Foremost is Dr. Nicholas R. Hurst, who did his dissertation research on GASP IV. Without Dr. Hurst's efforts GASP IV would not be a reality, and I consider him to be a codeveloper of the GASP IV language. During the past two years, Mr. C. Elliott Sigal contributed to the development of GASP IV by his applications of the language and suggestions for ways to improve it. Mr. Sigal reviewed the manuscript of this book and I thank him for his critical comments. My thanks also go to Dr. Clifford C. Petersen for reviewing the manuscript and making numerous suggestions of both a technical and editorial nature that helped me to clarify important aspects of the language.

In preparing this manuscript, Mr. Joseph Golan assisted in the revamping, debugging, and running of GASP IV and the eleven examples. Mr. Golan's tireless efforts are sincerely appreciated and gratefully acknowledged. It is a pleasure to record my appreciation to Mrs. Connie L. Houston who typed the major portion of the manuscript, and to my wife, Anne, for her "inspirational" support and for assisting in the typing effort.

Although GASP IV has been developed with the assistance of many individuals, I assume full responsibility for GASP IV and the material presented in this book.

A. ALAN B. PRITSKER

West Lafayette, Indiana
November, 1973

CONTENTS

The GASP IV Simulation Language

Chapter One

GASP IV

Models, Systems, and Simulation

Simulation is a problem solving procedure for defining and analyzing a model of a system. In this book, only digital computer simulation is of interest, and a more restrictive definition is used: *simulation is the establishment of a mathematical-logical model of a system and the experimental manipulation of it on a digital computer.*

A simulation language provides the structure and the terminology to facilitate the building of simulations. GASP IV is such a computer language; it helps the user to build computer simulation programs that can be both the model of the system and the analysis vehicle. Thus this program can be thought of as a model of a system and as a generator of statistical data about the model of the system. After gaining familiarity with simulation through use, this dual designation seems natural and simplifies communication.

This book documents the GASP IV simulation language. It describes the philosophy and world view embodied in GASP IV and emphasizes details of the language so that its structure may readily be used for building simulation programs. Since building such a program is an art, and the best way to obtain confidence in an art form is through experience, many detailed examples of the use of GASP IV are presented.

The reasons for building and using simulation programs stem from the observation that a simulator is an artificial laboratory. Once a system is modeled and programmed, experiments can be performed using the model. These experiments, or simulations, permit inferences to be drawn about systems

- Without building them, if they are only proposed systems.
- Without disturbing them, if they are operating systems that are costly or unsafe to experiment with.
- Without destroying them, if the object of an experiment is to determine their limits of stress.

In this way, simulation programs can be used for design, procedural analysis, and performance assessment (107).

Simulation can be applied to problems that are large or small, simple or complex, statistical or deterministic. They can be performed when mathematical analyses fail or cannot be performed at all and are used by various disciplines in diverse ways (19,46,98). Bibliographies (8,94) about simulation are available, and many reference and textbooks have been published on simulation methods and applications in the past five years (19,20,27,29,33,46,47,85,89,91,94,95,118,121).

SIMULATION METHODOLOGY

Given that a system and its associated performance measures have been defined and that a problem is posed within the system definition, four basic tasks should be performed in a simulation project:

1. Determine that the problem requires simulation. The crucial factors are the cost, the feasibility of conducting real world experiments, and the possibility of mathematical analysis.
2. Build a model to solve the problem.
3. Write a computer program that converts the model into an operating simulation program.
4. Use the computer simulation program as an experimental device to resolve the problem.

If simulation is to be employed successfully tools are needed to make these four tasks easier. GASP IV addresses tasks (2) and (3) directly, but pertains to (1) and (4) more by its presence than by direct technical contributions. GASP IV enables statistical experiments to be conducted, but it does not deal with actual experimental design. GASP IV can make simulation economical and technically feasible, but it does not provide information that makes the "simulate or not" decision any easier.

ADVANTAGES OF GASP IV

GASP IV provides a view of the world that simplifies model building. As a philosophy, it embodies concepts that facilitate the representation of the relevant aspects of system behavior (task 2). As a programming language, GASP IV gives the computer programmer a set of FORTRAN statements designed to carry out the most important functions in simulation programming (task 3). Modeling concepts are translated by GASP IV into FORTRAN routines that can be easily used. This provides the link between the modeling and programming activities that is so important to a successful simulation study. Thus, when using GASP IV, tasks (2) and (3) are integrated, which greatly simplifies the design and analysis activities required of the problem solver. This simulation power accelerates the pace of going from task (1) to task (4), and in many cases allows tasks (1) through (4) to be performed repeatedly.

GASP IV has five distinct features that make it particularly attractive as a simulation language:

1. *GASP IV is FORTRAN* based and requires no separate compiling system. It is easily maintained and can be implemented on new computing systems and on the computing systems of different manufacturers.
2. *GASP IV is modular* and can be made to fit on all machines that have a FORTRAN IV compiler.
3. *GASP IV is easy to learn* since the host programming language is usually known and only the simulation concepts need to be mastered. The implementation of these concepts is apparent to the user.
4. *GASP IV is used for discrete, continuous, and combined modeling*, and is the only well-documented simulation language with this capability.
5. *GASP IV is easily modified and extended* to meet the needs of particular applications.

CHARACTERISTICS OF SYSTEMS AND MODELS (68,107)

A system is a collection of items from a circumscribed sector of reality that is the object of study or interest. Therefore, a system is a relative thing. In one situation a particular collection of objects may be only a small part of a larger system—a subsystem; in another situation that same collection of objects may be the primary focus of interest and would be considered as the system. The scope of every system, and every model of a system, is determined solely by its reason for being identified and isolated. The scope of every simulation model is determined by the particular problems the model is designed to solve.

To consider the scope of a system, one must contemplate its boundaries and contents. The boundary of a system may be physical; however, it is better to think of a boundary in terms of cause and effect. Given a tentative system definition, some external factors may affect the system. If they completely govern its behavior, there is no merit in experimenting with the defined system. If they partially influence the system, there are several possibilities:

The system definition may be enlarged to include them.
They may be ignored.
They may be treated as inputs to the system.

If treated as inputs, it is assumed that the factors are functionally specified by prescribed values, tables, or equations. For example, when defining the model of a company's manufacturing system, if the sales of the company's product are considered as inputs to the manufacturing system, the model will not contain elements that influence sales. The model of the manufacturing system does not contain a cause and effect sales relation; it only includes a statistical description of historical or predicted sales, which is used as an input. In such a model of the manufacturing system, the sales organization is outside the boundaries of the "defined" system. In systems terminology, objects that are outside the boundaries of the system, but which can influence it, constitute the *environment* of the system.

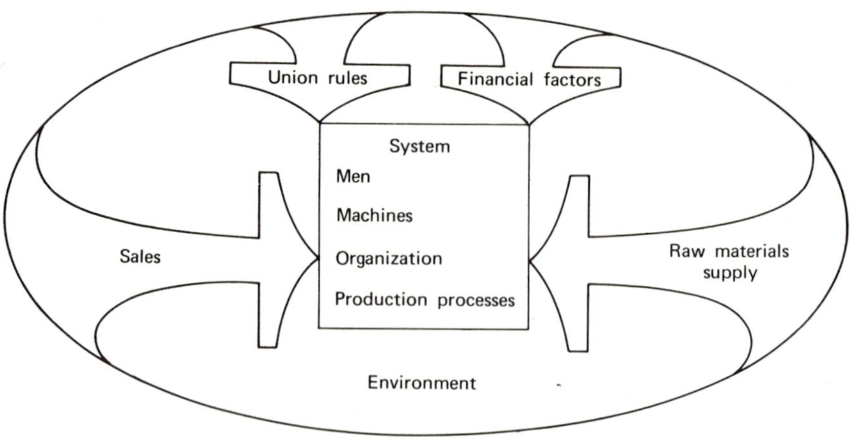

Figure 1-1 Manufacturing system model showing external influences.

Thus systems are collections of mutually interacting objects that are affected by outside forces. Figure 1-1 shows such a system.

The objects within the boundaries of a system, such as people, equipment, orders, and raw materials, are called *entities*. There are many types of entities and each has various characteristics or *attributes*. Although they engage in different types of activities, entities may have a common attribute requiring that they be grouped together. Groupings of entities are called *files* in GASP IV. Inserting an entity into a file implies that it has some relation with other entities in the file.

The aim of a simulation model is to reproduce the activities that the entities engage in and thereby learn something about the behavior and performance potential of the system. This is done by defining the states of the system and constructing activities that move it from state to state. The *state of a system* is defined in terms of the numeric values assigned to the attributes of the entities. A system is said to be in a *particular* state when all of its entities are in states consonant with the range of attributes values that define that state. Simulation is the dynamic portrayal of the states of a system over time.

Two of the most important modeling activities associated with simulation are the identification of entities and their attributes and the coding of attribute values for the characterization of system states. As an example, consider an elevator system. In Table 1-1, a list of the entities that could be defined for such a system and some of the attributes needed to characterize them is presented (107,128).

Table 1-1 Definition of an Elevator System and Its Entities and Attributes

System	Entities	Attributes
Elevator in building	Building	Number of floors
		Distance between floors
	Elevator	Passenger capacity
		Speed
		Minimum stopping time at a floor
		Current floor location
	Floor	Number of people waiting for elevator
		Probability that people will want to go to other floors, given that they are on this floor.
	People	Arrival rate at building
		Preference for floors
		Arrival rate of people on floor waiting to go up or down.

The important characteristics of this definition of the system are:

1. There are different entity types. For each type, the number of entities varies. For example, a particular model (simulation) might consider one building, with three elevators, serving 15 floors, with a population of 500 people.
2. The attributes chosen to characterize each entity type are rather arbitrary and certainly do not describe them exhaustively. Each entity needs only the attributes necessary to perform a realistic simulation and analysis of its activities. If the activity of entering an elevator somehow depends on a person's age, this information has to be included as an attribute; if it does not, age need not be included.
3. Certain system activities are implied in the entity-attribute description. Furthermore, the logic of these activities influences the selection of attributes.

Some activities that might be represented in an elevator simulation are listed in Table 1-2.

Table 1-2 Some Activities Associated with an Elevator Simulation

Elevator discharges passengers
Elevator loads passengers
Elevator travels to next floor
Person travels to elevator position

A model moves from state to state as its entities engage in activities that change their states. In a discrete model, an elevator moves up one floor and changes from the state "at floor 2" to the state "at floor 3." In a continuous model, an elevator's position changes continuously from the state "at the twelve foot level" to the state "at the twenty-four foot level." With GASP IV, either may be conveniently modeled.

Activities rarely have an instantaneous effect on a system. Instead, as indicated in Table 1-2, they take place over a period of time and may create a new system state at the end of that time.

Events mark the start and completion of activities.* Table 1-3 lists some events that might be represented in an elevator simulation. Consider the events "elevator starts travel" and "elevator arrives at next floor." In a

* A formal definition and discussion of events is given in Chapter 2.

Table 1-3 Events Associated with Activities of an Elevator Simulation

Elevator door starts to open
Elevator door fully open
Passengers start to leave elevator
Passengers gone from elevator
Passengers start to enter elevator
Passengers in elevator
Elevator door starts to close
Elevator door shut
Elevator starts travel
Elevator arrives at next floor
Person starts for elevator
Person reaches elevator position

discrete model, the time of travel between floors would be known either deterministically or stochastically. Thus the processing of the event "elevator starts travel" would include scheduling the event "elevator arrives at next floor" to occur at the current simulated time plus the "known" travel time. In a continuous model, the travel time beween floors would not have an explicit value. Instead, the equation of motion of the elevator would be prescribed. The parameters of the equation may be functions of many things, for example, direction of travel, the number of people on the elevator, the number of operational elevators, and so forth. In this case, the processing of the event "elevator starts travel" would require the determination of these parameters. The event "elevator arrives at the next floor" cannot be scheduled, but must be detected from an examination of elevator position as time progresses. It would, therefore, be an event based on the value of the attribute, position of elevator. Attributes that define an entity's status or the system's status, based on a continuous representation of the dynamics associated with the attribute, are defined as *state variables*. With this example as background, the concepts of discrete and continuous simulation can be explored.

DISCRETE, CONTINUOUS, AND COMBINED SIMULATION

In practice, in the literature, in texts, in professional conferences, in virtually every way, simulation is divided into two categories: discrete change and continuous change. Note that these terms describe the model, not the real system. In fact, as indicated in the preceding example, it may be possible to model the same system with either a discrete change (hereafter referred to simply as discrete) or a continuous change (continuous) model. GASP IV is designed to accommodate both categories of models, separately or combined. In most simulations, time is the major independent variable. Other variables included in a simulation are functions of time and are the dependent variables. The adjectives discrete and continuous refer to the behavior of the dependent variables.

Discrete simulation occurs when the dependent variables of the model change discretely at specified points in simulated time. The time variable may be either continuous or discrete in such a model, depending on whether the discrete changes in the dependent variables can occur at any point in time or only at specified points. Variable time increment (including next-event) procedures result in a continuous time variable, whereas fixed time increment procedures are normally discrete in time. An example of a discrete simulation is shown in Fig. 1-2.

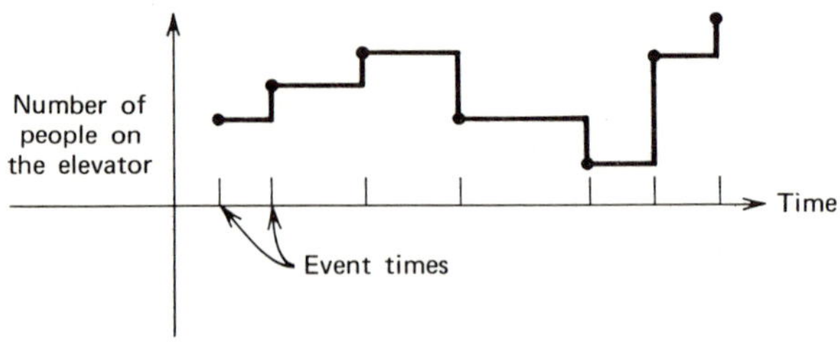

Figure 1-2 Response measurement from a discrete time simulator.

GASP II is a discrete simulation language (107). Other commonly used discrete simulation languages are SIMSCRIPT (71,84,140) and GPSS (46,59,122). Kiviat (67,69,70) and Fishman (33) present excellent reviews of discrete simulation languages and their development. In addition, Fishman compares the event scheduling approach as used in GASP II and SIMSCRIPT with the activity scanning approach and the process interaction approach employed in other languages. Other reviews have been written (15,65,119,129,131,132,137) and the reader interested in language comparisons is referred to the literature.

It is necessary to recognize that a digital computer is technically discrete in its operation. As a practical matter, however, any variable whose possible values are limited only by the inherent capabilities of a computer is considered continuous.

In *continuous simulation* the dependent variables of the model may change continuously over simulated time. A continuous model may be either continuous or discrete in time, depending on whether the values of the dependent variables are available at any point in simulated time or only at specified points in simulated time. Figures 1-3 and 1-4 illustrate examples of these models.

During the 1950s and early 1960s, analog computers were the primary means for performing continuous simulations. Continuous simulation languages such as CSMP (58), MIMIC (23), and CSSL (123) were specifically designed for digital computers. Review articles (10,57) and texts (15,20) that discuss continuous simulation in detail are available.

In *combined simulation* the dependent variables of a model may change discretely, continuously, or continuously with discrete jumps superimposed. The time variable may be discrete or continuous. One of the primary advocates of combined simulation has been Schoeffler. Fahrland (30,31) and Golden (42–44) worked with Schoeffler and developed combined languages. Hixson, another advocate of combined simulation, has been actively involved in the design and development of CLASS (51,52).

GASP IV is a language that can be used for discrete, continuous, or combined simulation (54,106,109). In GASP IV the most important characteristics of combined simulation, which arise from the interaction be-

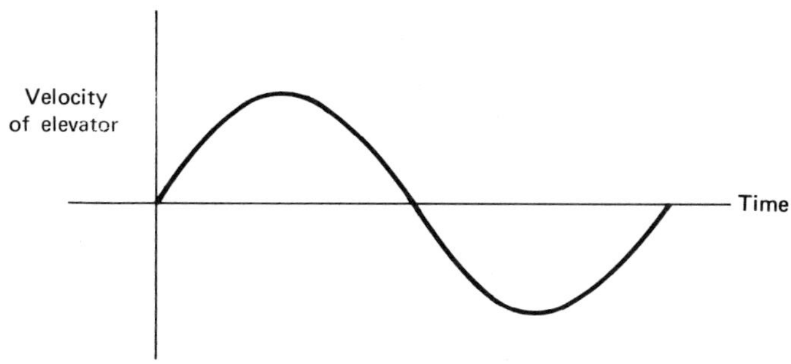

Figure 1-3 Response measurement from a continuous simulator.

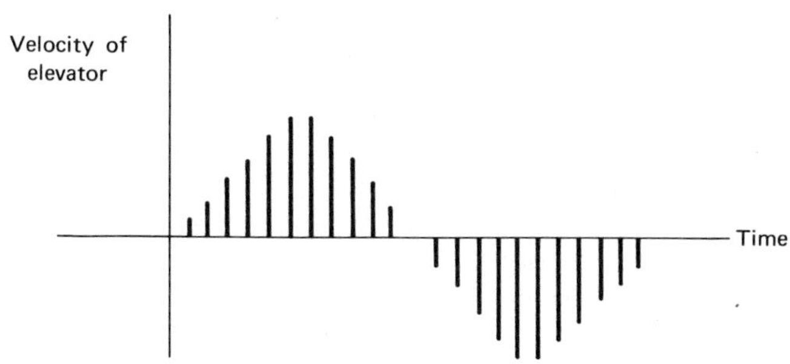

Figure 1-4 Response measurement from a continuous simulator using discrete time steps.

tween discretely and continuously changing variables, are easily modeled. In general, this interaction takes one of three forms. First, discrete changes may be applied to "continuous" variables. Examples of this type of interaction are the completion of a new power station, which would discretely increase the, total energy available within a system, or the chemical spraying of a lake, which could instantaneously decrease the population of particular species in the lake (127). Second, achieving specified conditions for a state variable may cause an event to occur or to be scheduled. For example, when a chemical process is completed because a prescribed concentration level is obtained, the process may be shut down for cleaning and maintenance activities (55). When the level of crude oil available for input to a refinery is below a prescribed value, the refinery must be shut down (109). Third, the functional description of continuous variables may be changed discretely. For example, discharging a pollutant into an ecosystem may immediately alter the growth relationships governing species populations, or completing the docking operation of a space vehicle would require the use of new equations for simulating its motion.

The GASP IV philosophy and language enhances a modeler's capability to design and develop models involving both discrete and continuous concepts. In the next chapter, the philosophy of GASP IV is presented. The language and its use are presented in subsequent chapters.

EXERCISES

1-1. What are the differences between a simulation model and an analytical model?

1-2. A system is composed of a pair of standard six-sided dice. What are the possible states of the system?

1-3. List three advantages that make a simulation model of a chemical plant superior to a pilot plant for studying plant design. List three disadvantages.

1-4. What is a simulation programming language?

1-5. A system with which we are all familiar is a supermarket or neighborhood grocery. Specify the boundary of one such system, and describe its operations in terms of entities, attributes, relationships, and activities. Prepare a model of the supermarket system.

1-6. Define several states of the supermarket system of Exercise 1-5 and illustrate them numerically.

1-7. Characterize a university problem in terms of discrete and continuous variables. Describe activities that invoke interactions between the variables.

1-8. Model a water softener processing unit.

1-9. Model an elevator system serving five floors, assuming an equation for the rate of arrival of passengers at each floor and equations for elevator velocity (128).

Chapter Two

GASP IV

Philosophy

The philosophical basis for the design of GASP IV is the concept of modeling a system in two dimensions: the time dimension and the state-space dimension. Fundamental to building a GASP IV simulation model is the decomposition of time and the state space into manageable elements. The decomposition in the time dimension involves the defining of events and the potential changes to the system when an event occurs. The GASP IV philosophy requires that the user specify the causal mechanisms by which events can occur, but relieves him completely of the need for sequencing the events. Thus the user must only define the mathematical-logical relations that transpire at an event occurrence and is not required to model the timing of events during a simulation. This decomposition of the time axis into points at which events could occur is a huge reduction in the size of the modeling effort.

In the state-space dimension GASP IV presumes that a system model can be decomposed into its entities, which are described by attributes. These are further classified as discrete or continuous.* The value of a discrete attribute remains constant between event times. The value of a continuous attribute may change between events according to a prescribed

* The use of the adjectives discrete and continuous is motivated by the definitions as used in discrete and continuous simulation. More descriptive adjectives would be static and dynamic.

dynamic behavior. Because of the special nature of continuous attributes and the need for the user to model their dynamic behavior, they are referred to as *state variables.* Special storage arrays are provided in GASP IV for storing values of state variables and, if required, their derivatives and immediate past values. To avoid confusion, the word attribute is used in this book to refer only to a discrete attribute.

GASP IV provides a formalized world view based on the above discussion. This world view specifies that the status of a system be described in terms of a *set of entities, their associated attributes*, and *state variables.* The GASP IV simulation philosophy is that a dynamic simulation can be obtained by modeling the events of the system and by advancing time from one event to the next. This philosophy presumes a broader definition of *event* than has normally been used in discrete-event languages:

> An event occurs at any point in time beyond which the status of a system cannot be projected with certainty.

Events usually cause changes in the status of the system or in the equations defining the state variables of the system. However, this definition does not necessarily relate an event to any change, either discrete or continuous, in the status of a system. Events could occur at decision points where the decision is *not* to change the status of the system. Conversely, the above definition allows the system status to change continuously without an event occurring, as long as the change has been prescribed in a well-defined manner.

In GASP IV it is useful to describe events in terms of the mechanism by which they are scheduled. Those that occur at a specified projected point in time are referred to as *time-events.* They are commonly thought of in conjunction with "next event" simulation. Those that occur when the system reaches a particular state are called *state-events.* Unlike time-events, they are not scheduled in the future but occur when state variables meet prescribed conditions. In GASP IV state-events can initiate time-events, and time-events can initiate state-events.

The behavior of a system model is simulated by computing the values of the state variables at small time steps and computing the values of the attributes at event times. The time step increment is automatically determined by GASP IV, based on the equation form for the state variables, the time of the next event, and accuracy and output requirements.

When an event occurs, it can change system status in three ways: by altering the value of state variables or the attributes of the entities; by altering relationships that exist among entities or state variables; and/or by changing the number of entities present. Methods are available in

GASP IV for accomplishing each type of change. Any of these changes can result from the occurrence of an event. *Between event times, only the values of the state variables can change.*

At each time step, the state variables are evaluated to determine if the conditions prescribing a state-event have occurred. If a state-event was passed, the step size was too large and is reduced. If a state-event occurs, the model status is updated according to the user's state-event subroutine. Step size is automatically set so that no time-event will occur within a step. This is accomplished by setting the step size so that the time-event ends the step.

Since time-events are scheduled happenings, certain attributes are associated with them. At the minimum, a time-event must have attributes that define its time of occurrence and its type. If the time-event is associated with an entity, either the attributes of that entity must be associated with it or the event must be able to refer to the attributes of the entity. For example, if there is an end-of-service event for an item, the attributes for that item must in some way be associated with the event.

EXAMPLE OF THE GASP MODELING PHILOSOPHY

Figure 2-1 illustrates a simple service system consisting of a server and customers who are seeking service (107). The entities in the system and their attributes and relationships to one another are shown. Note that although the type of entities present in the system is fixed (server and

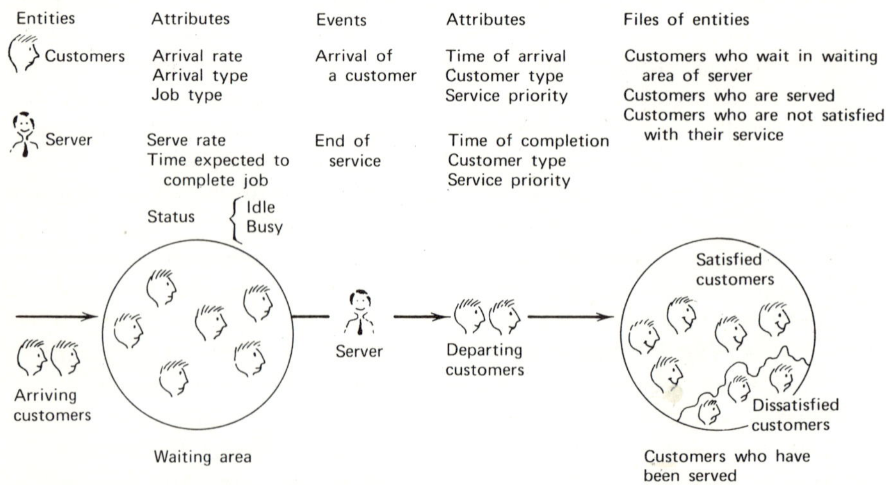

Figure 2-1 Single server queueing system.

customers), the number of entities present at any one time can vary, depending on how the customers arrive and how the server works. It should again be emphasized that the attributes defined for the server entity and for the customer entity are somewhat arbitrary. The definitions for the attributes and the files for grouping entities are, however, related to the objectives of the simulation model.

The operation of the system can be described in terms of events. The system shown might operate in the following manner: a customer (an entity) arrives (an event) at some specific time (an attribute of both the event and the customer). If the server (an entity) is free (an attribute of the server), a service time is determined, based on the service time distribution of the server (an attribute). A customer completes service at the time he enters service plus his service time; the completion time becomes an attribute of the customer and the server. An end-of-service event is "scheduled" to occur at this completion time. If the server is busy when the customer arrives, the customer joins the waiting line (a file *relating* customer entities waiting for service to the server) in a position based on the priority system assigned to customers. The priority system and the number in the waiting line are attributes of the line. The particular values used to rank the customers are attributes of the customers themselves.

This example illustrates the use of time-events. The model is easily altered to include a state-event. A state-event would be necessary if service time is a function of the amount of money the customer has and his rate of spending. A completion of service could occur when he spends 25% of his money. Since spending rate may be a function of other attributes, the time at which the event is to occur cannot be projected, thereby necessitating a state-event.

DATA STORAGE AND TIMING REQUIREMENTS

In GASP IV a system's file-entity-attribute structure is established by data declarations. Entities are represented by vectors and matrices, the elements of which are stored and represent attribute data. The FORTRAN statement DIMENSION SERVR(10,3) might represent 10 servers in a system, each of which has three attributes: (1) service status, (2) service rate, and (3) number of services completed. SERVR(2,1) represents the service status of the second server, SERVR(9,2) the servicing rate of the ninth server, and so forth.

The membership of entities in groups (such as a waiting line) is changeable, and the data that express them are stored differently. They are stored in computer lists called files. A single array NSET is used to store all files (NSET is equivalenced to QSET to allow real attributes and integer pointers). Special routines, such as FILEM (to put an entity in a file) and RMOVE (to take an entity from a file), are part of the GASP IV language. These routines are described in Chapters 3 and 4.

Entities, attributes, state variables, and file memberships comprise the static structure of a simulation model. They describe the state of a system model but not the operation of the system. The latter depends on event definitions and the equations defining the behavior of the state variables.

The key to event simulation is the ability to organize events so that they are executed within the computer in an order corresponding to that which would occur in the real system. This preserves the time relationship between simulated and real events. Ordinary programming languages are unsuited to this task because they operate in a strictly sequential manner; there is no way to tell a FORTRAN program to "do something later" without building special subprograms. GASP IV provides these subprograms.

Thus in simulation studies it has often been necessary to expend a considerable amount of time and effort designing programs that organize and schedule events so that a simulated system moves through time in a realistic manner. Such a program is often called a *timing mechanism*. Its use relieves the simulation programmer of the task of sequencing events in their proper chronological order.

A METHOD OF SIMULATION PROGRAMMING

Every GASP IV simulation model consists of: (1) a set of event programs or state variable equations, or both, that describe a system's dynamic behavior, (2) lists and matrices that store information, (3) an executive routine that directs the flow of information and control within the model, and (4) support routines. These form an operating computer program whose performance reflects that of a simulated system. A GASP IV program is made up of subprograms linked together by an executive routine that organizes and controls the performance of the subprograms.

Uniqueness in a simulation model is due to the description of the system and its rules of operation. Although it is possible to give some rather general rules or principles of model construction, the successful application of these principles is greatly dependent upon the experience of the model builder. One purpose of the extensive set of sample simulation problems contained in this book is to illustrate, by example, these rules and their application.

There is, however, a common structure for all GASP IV simulation programs, and GASP IV gives a simulation programmer a particular structural logic with which he can implement simulations. To understand the implementation mechanism, the functional capabilities inherent in the routines that comprise GASP IV must be understood.

Simulation programs contain routines for reading input data, performing record keeping tasks, advancing time, updating system status, producing reports of the simulated system's behavior, and so forth. A simulation program is said to be in a particular *mode* of operation when it is performing the corresponding function, for example, the input mode or the simulation mode. A mode can, when necessary, call upon many separate programs, each performing a task related to the general function of the mode.

GASP IV FUNCTIONAL CAPABILITIES

GASP IV is organized to provide eight specific functional capabilities:

1. Event control.
2. State variable updating using integration if necessary.
3. Information storage and retrieval.
4. System state initialization.
5. System performance data collection.
6. Program monitoring and event reporting.
7. Statistical computations and report generation.
8. Random deviate generation.

Four of these capabilities, (1), (2), (4), and (6) are primary functions. At the time a program is engaged in one of them it is not doing any of the others. The remaining four, (3), (5), (7), and (8) are support oriented; they provide a fundamental computational or data processing capability that is not control oriented.

The four primary capabilities constitute the basic modes of GASP IV, which are shown in Fig. 2-2.

In every simulation a crucial role is played by the program that advances time and decides when different subprograms should be executed. This program acts as "director" by guiding the flow of information in an orderly manner, according to the rules of the model.

Two forms of program control are required. One directs the program into its various modes: initialization, state variable updating, monitoring, and so forth. The other operates within the simulation model and sequences the execution of event routines. In GASP IV, the first function is called the *executive function* and the second is called the *event selection function.*

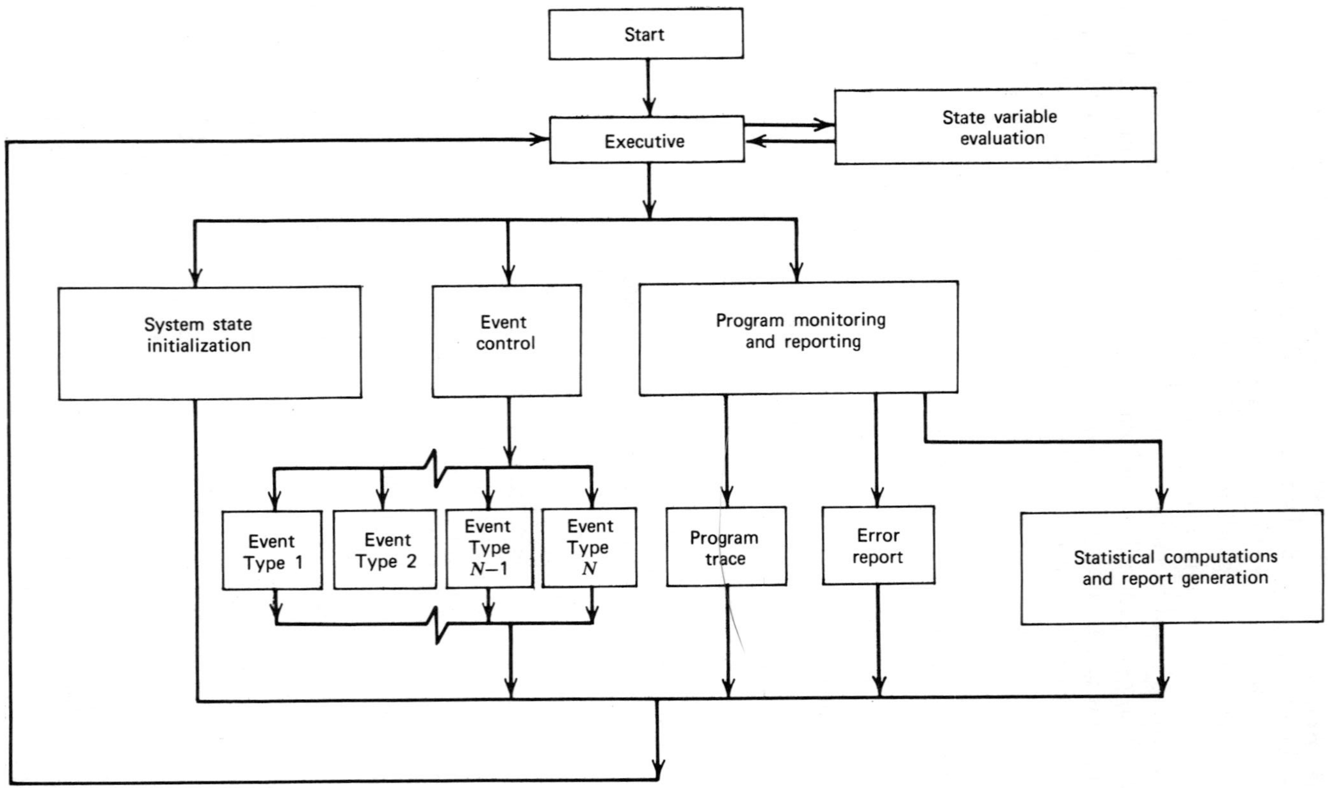

Figure 2-2 Basic modes of GASP IV control.

The executive function is computationally and logically oriented; it switches from mode to mode as the logic of a program dictates. It also updates state variables over time using a step-evaluate-step procedure. At each step, the state variables are updated and their values are checked against the conditions defining state-events. The event selection function is time-oriented; it switches to an event when an event occurs.

Additional simulation flexibility can be achieved by defining control events in addition to system activity events. These events are time oriented instructions to the executive that allow mode switching to be done on a time and a logic basis. One can schedule an event to "go into output mode" when the simulator clock reaches 1000 hours as well as when demand exceeds 100 units.

Many forms have been suggested for the mechanics of executive and event control programs. The choices made by various simulation languages in use today are documented in their programming manuals (23,44,59,71) and in survey literature (10,15,119,129).

The form of organization used in GASP IV is hierarchical; there are two levels of control, and each level has authority over its subordinate levels.

The highest level of program control, the executive level, determines what the program must do at each point in simulated time and directs control to the appropriate mode to perform the selected task. Control passes from executive level to mode and back again. Control is maintained within a mode until all computations and evaluations pertinent to that mode have been made. The sequencing of the computations and evaluations is accomplished as part of the function designed into the subprograms of the mode.

One of the most important uses of simulation is to investigate the effect of changes in a system on selected measures of system performance. This is true whether a simulation is being used for evaluation or design. The "hierarchical control-mode-data pool" concepts provide the needed flexibility in design and adaptation, since changes in simulation models usually require changes in input data, system elements, or event logic (22). A modular structure allows event logic to be changed quite simply, because each event is a separate subprogram. A data pool allows changes made in data inputs to be communicated throughout an entire simulation model by a change in a single data input. The preparation of reports summarizing the results of simulation runs is simplified by utilizing standard report programs that obtain their information from the common data pool. Perhaps most important of all, model debugging is simplified by providing access points at which program results can be sampled without interfering with the logic of particular events.

This chapter has presented the fundamental concepts underlying GASP IV. In Chapter 3 the GASP IV variables and subprograms are defined and the procedures for using GASP IV are detailed. Chapter 3 can be considered a user's manual for GASP IV.

EXERCISES

2-1. What is meant by the decomposition of time into events?

2-2. Graph a model of a system illustrating: (*a*) two state variables; (*b*) an entity with one attribute; (*c*) a time-event; (*d*) two state-events; and (*e*) the types of interactions between discrete and continuous variables.

2-3. GASP IV uses an event scheduling approach. For discrete events, other languages use a process interaction approach (33). Compare these approaches.

2-4. List the different ways in which you could model state variables.

2-5. Why would an attribute of an entity be more descriptively called a static variable than a discrete variable?

2-6. Model a rain barrel that has a leak in it to determine the average amount of water in the barrel. Define the state variables, the entities, and the events associated with the model. Specify the variables that define the status of the system.

2-7. Discuss the conditions under which the following would be events:
- (*a*) Arrival of an elevator at a floor.
- (*b*) Population of the world exceeding 10 billion.
- (*c*) A football coach deciding not to try a field goal.
- (*d*) Withdrawing from a class.
- (*e*) Accepting a budget limitation.
- (*f*) Reviewing inventory levels.
- (*g*) Spending $30.00.
- (*h*) Signing an order for a new car.

2-8. Discuss each of the eight GASP IV functional capabilities on an intuitive basis.

Chapter Three

GASP IV

Definitions and Procedures

A simulation program written in GASP IV consists of two parts: a user part and a GASP IV part. The user part contains subprograms for initialization (the main program and subroutine INTLC); equations for state variables and conditions defining state-events (subroutines STATE and SCOND); event code definitions (subroutine EVNTS); event processing (subroutines called by EVNTS); and special data collection and reporting procedures (subroutines SSAVE, OTPUT, and UERR). The GASP IV part contains subprograms that provide for the following functions: the executive or mode controller (subroutine GASP), data and event initialization (subroutine DATIN), data storage and retrieval, data collection, statistics computation and reporting, monitoring and error reporting, random deviate generation, and miscellaneous support. In this chapter sufficient detail is presented to enable the reader to develop simulation programs using GASP IV.

AN OVERVIEW OF GASP IV

A general descriptive flow chart illustrating a complete simulation program consisting of the GASP IV provided subprograms and user written subprograms is shown in Fig. 3-1. The main program initializes the non-GASP variables that are to remain constant for all simulation runs. Sub-

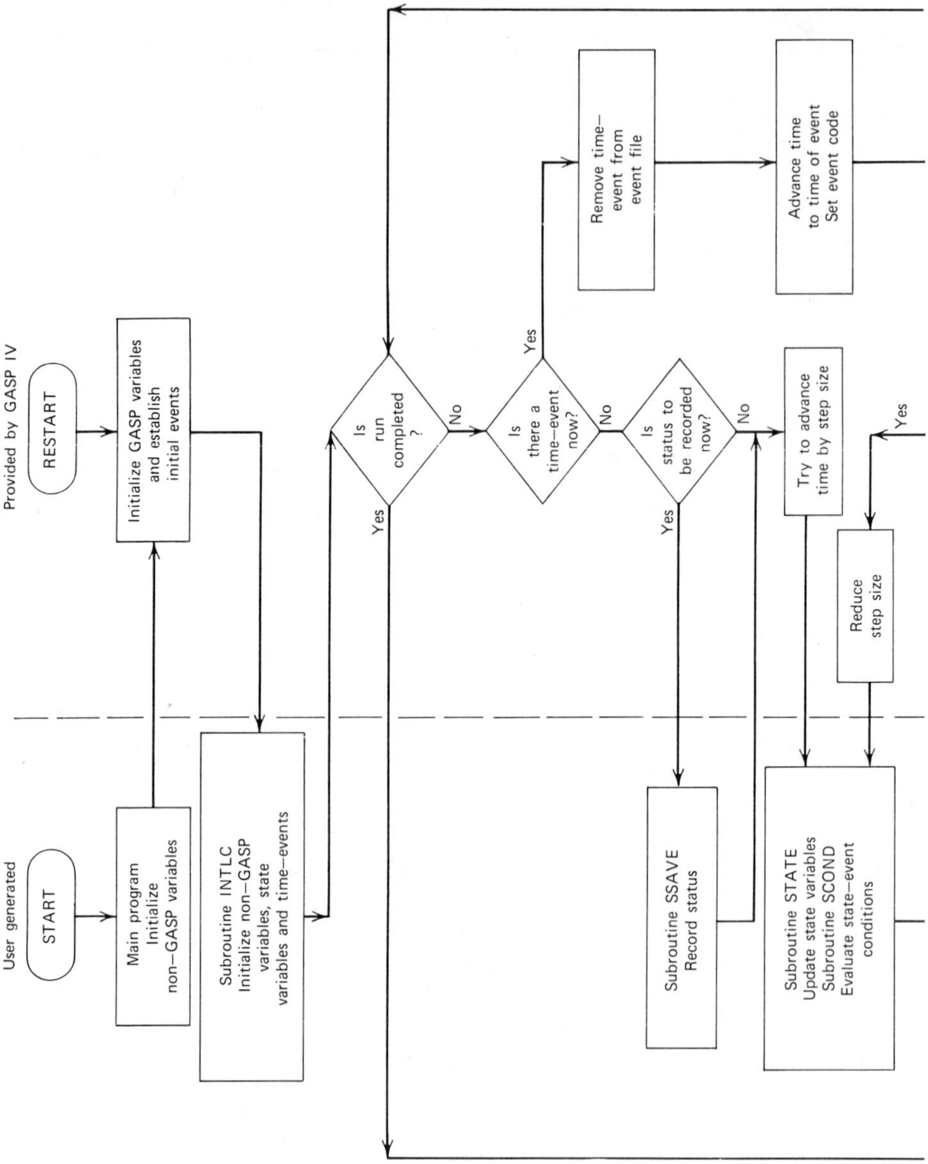
User generated
Provided by GASP IV
START
RESTART
Main program
Initialize
non–GASP variables
Initialize GASP variables
and establish
initial events
Subroutine INTLC
Initialize non–GASP
variables, state
variables and time–events
Is
run
completed
?
Yes
No
Is
there a
time–event
now?
Yes
No
Remove time–
event from
event file
Advance time
to time of event
Set event code
Is
status to
be recorded
now?
Yes
No
Subroutine SSAVE
Record status
Try to advance
time by step size
Reduce
step size
Yes
Subroutine STATE
Update state variables
Subroutine SCOND
Evaluate state–event
conditions

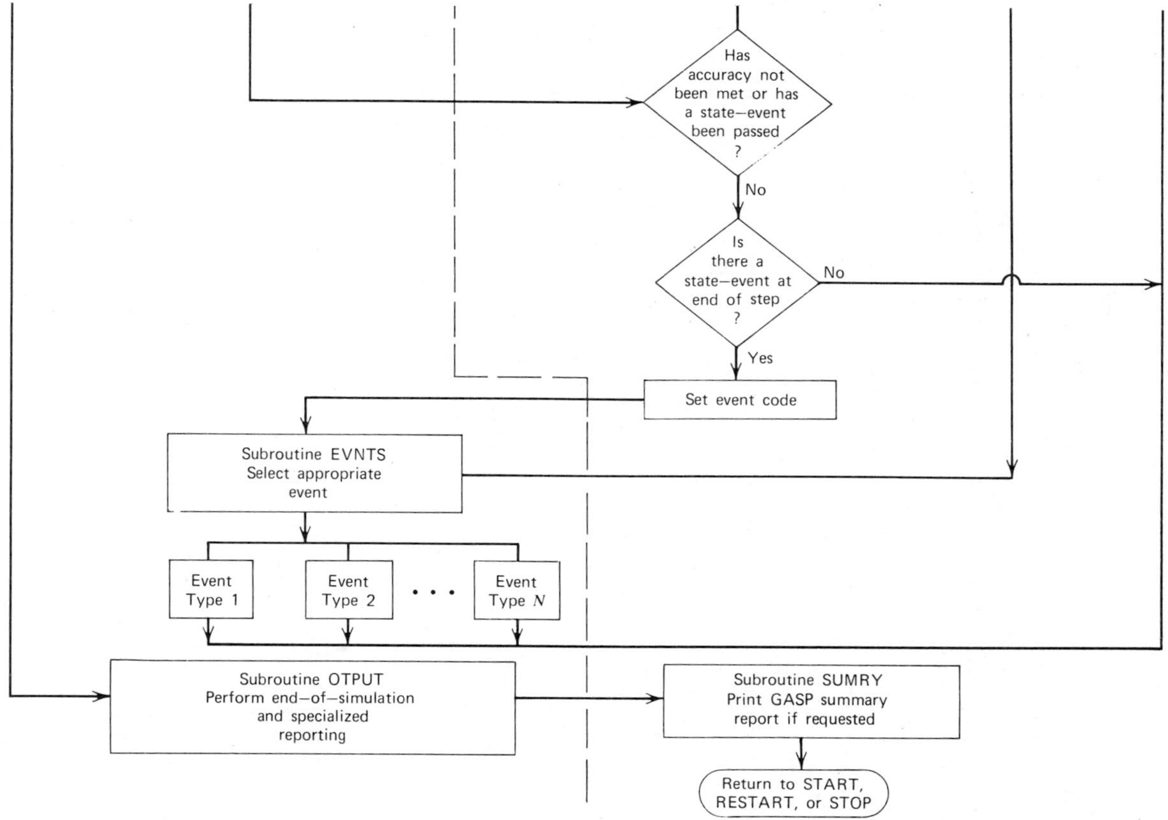

Figure 3-1 Functional flow chart of a GASP IV program.

routine GASP is then called from the main program. The general layout of the main program is shown in Fig. 3-2. Subroutine GASP's first action is to call subroutine DATIN, which initializes all GASP IV variables either through arithmetic statements or the reading of data cards. Either data cards or programming code can be used to establish the initial events and entities for the simulation. Subroutine DATIN calls the user generated subroutine INTLC, which is used to initialize non-GASP variables at the start of each run. Through the use of subroutine INTLC the user can perform sequential simulations with changes in the non-GASP variables. Initialization of state variables is accomplished by a call to subroutine STATE. This completes the initialization phase of the simulation.

During a simulation run, subroutine GASP determines if a time advance by a step or to the next event should be made. If the simulation only involves time-events, TNOW is set equal to the time of the next event. If only a continuous simulation is being performed, TNOW is advanced to the time at which the next evaluation of the state variables is to be made. If a combined simulation is being performed, the time advance occurs by steps, with the step size adjusted when necessary to end at an event. A run can be completed either by setting a time for completion or by having an end-of-simulation event. If a run is not completed, the clock for the simulation, as represented by the variable TNOW, is advanced.

In continuous and combined simulations, the updating of the state variables is performed in subroutine STATE. The vectors SS(·) and DD(·)

```
C     MAIN PROGRAM
      DIMENSION NSET (NNSET)
C     NNSET to be specified
      COMMON (GASP variables)
      COMMON (non-GASP variables. This must be a named
      COMMON Block)
      EQUIVALENCE (NSET(1), QSET(1))
C     Initialization of non-GASP variables
C     Initialize Card Reader Value, NCRDR and Printer Value,
C     NPRNT.
      CALL GASP
C     If more runs are desired, insert GO TO statement
C     to either reinitialize non-GASP variables or
C     to CALL GASP again
      STOP
      END
```

Figure 3-2 Layout of main program.

are used to define the state variable values and their derivatives, respectively. The user must code subroutine STATE in a manner that permits the calculation of SS(·) or DD(·). The options available for evaluating SS(·), based on equations for DD(·), are also presented in this chapter. Once the state variables are updated, their values are checked against user prescribed conditions that define state-events in subroutine SCOND. If no state-event has occurred, time is again advanced by subroutine GASP.

If time has advanced to a time-event, subroutine GASP obtains the attributes for the event by removing the first event stored in file 1, which is the event file or calendar of events. The user written subroutine EVNTS(IX) is then called to decipher the event code, IX, and to call the appropriate event subroutine.

A call to subroutine EVNTS is also made if a state-event occurs. In this case, IX is the state-event code indicating that a state-event has occurred. The general form of subroutine EVNTS is shown in Fig. 3-3, which indicates that event code 1 represents an arrival event (ARRIV), event code 2 represents an end-of-service event (ESERV), and event code 3 represents all state-events (SEVNT). In subroutines ARRIV and ESERV, the user codes the processes and decisions that would happen at the arrival and

```
      SUBROUTINE EVNTS(IX)
      DIMENSION NSET(1)
      COMMON QSET(1)
      COMMON (GASP variables)
      COMMON (non-GASP variables. This must be a named
      COMMON Block)
      EQUIVALENCE (NSET(1), QSET(1))
C     For this example, the user has specified the following.
C     If IX is 1 or 2, a time event has occurred. If IX is 3, a
C     state event has occurred.
      GO TO (1,2,3), IX
    1 CALL ARRIV
      GO TO 10
    2 CALL ESERV
      GO TO 10
    3 CALL SEVNT
   10 RETURN
      END
```

Figure 3-3 Layout of subroutine EVNTS.

end-of-service event times. In SEVNT the processes and decisions associated with all state-events would be coded. Following the processing of the statements contained in the specific event subroutines, a return to subroutine GASP is made and the above process is repeated.

When a simulation run is completed, subroutine OTPUT is called. Subroutine OTPUT provides the user with a mechanism to make final calculations for the simulation run and to print out any specific information that was collected during the run. Thus the call of subroutine OTPUT can be used as an end-of-simulation event. Following a return from subroutine OTPUT, subroutine GASP calls subroutine SUMRY, which prints out the final GASP IV summary report, including statistical information, tables of state variables, and plots of state variables. The user can also suppress the printing of the GASP IV summary report. Following the printing of the final summary report, tests are made to determine if other simulation runs are to be made. A new simulation run can be started by returning to the main program for complete reinitialization or to subroutine DATIN for partial reinitialization. If another run is to be made, the abovementioned process is repeated. If no further runs are required, the simulation program is terminated.

The description above represents an overview of the processing of a GASP IV simulation program from an overall design perspective. Since it is so important to understand how the GASP IV executive works, an overview from the perspective of subroutine GASP is also given. Hopefully, the redundancy included will help to clarify the executive processing procedure.

AN OVERVIEW OF SUBROUTINE GASP

Figure 3-4 presents a descriptive flow chart of subroutine GASP. GASP first calls subroutine DATIN, which initializes all GASP IV variables either directly or from reading data cards. Initial events and other file entries can also be established by DATIN. Besides initialization, DATIN also prints out the values of the input data. Events to occur at the beginning of the simulation are then processed.

A test is then made to determine if the simulation involves only time-events, that is, a discrete simulation. If this is the case, a next event time advance is used and the simulation proceeds from time-event to time-event until a signal is given to end the simulation. The method used in GASP IV to perform the next event portion of a simulation involves file 1,

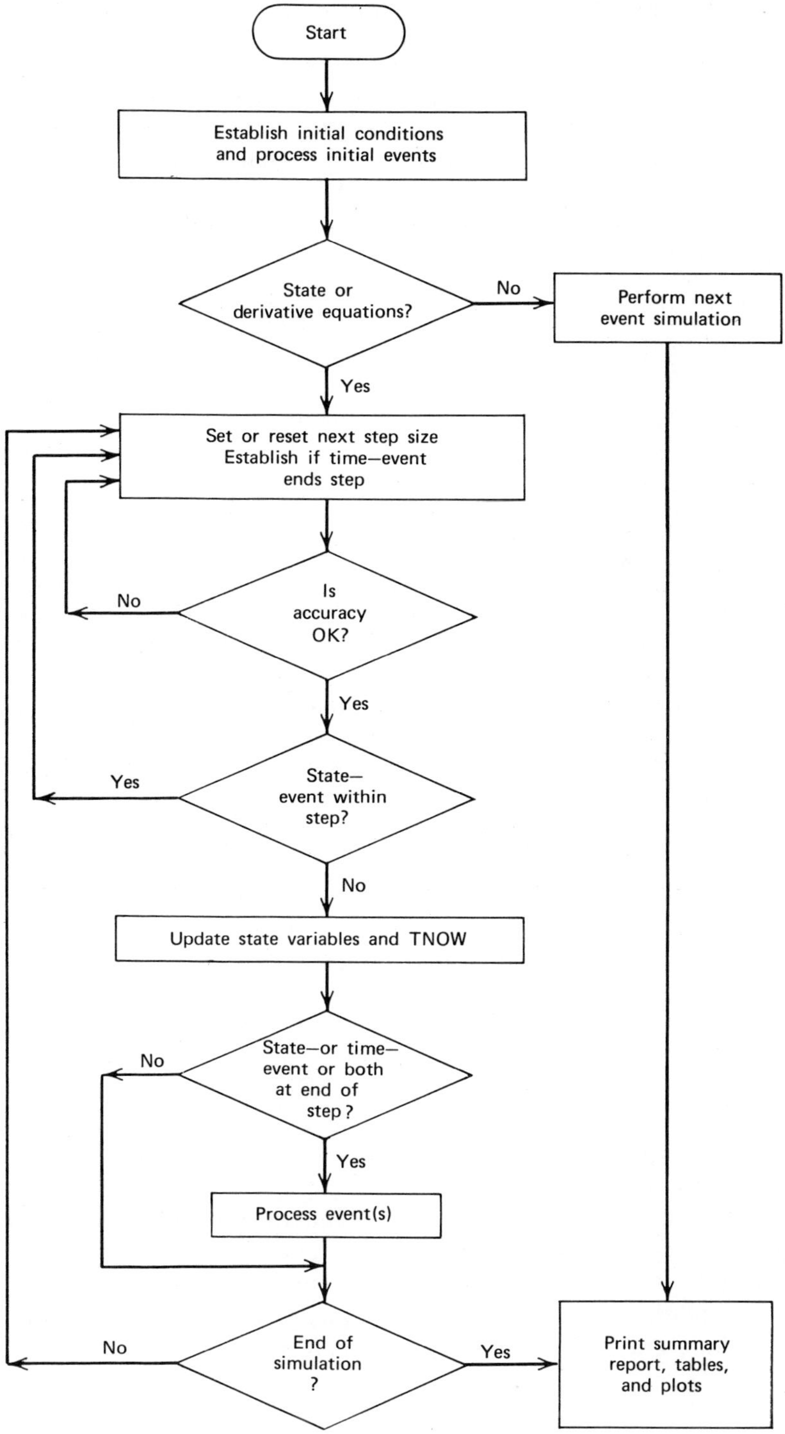

Figure 3-4 Descriptive flow chart of subroutine GASP.

the event file used to store attributes associated with events. Since events must be inserted in the file and removed from it in chronological order, it is necessary to have routines for these functions. The GASP IV subroutine FILEM puts events in the event file based on the time-of-event attribute. The subroutine RMOVE removes events from the event file. Thus GASP IV provides an information storage and retrieval system for events.

In addition to the calendar of events, other files of information must usually be maintained during simulation runs. All files are stored in the equivalenced arrays NSET/QSET and are processed by the subroutines FILEM and RMOVE.

To write a discrete event simulation program, it is necessary to specify the changes that occur at event times, and the future events that are generated by event occurrences. The user writes these event routines, such as ARRIV and ESERV, which specify what happens in the simulation model when these events occur.

To write a continuous simulation program, the equations governing the dynamics of the state variables must be defined, and state-event conditions must be specified if they exist. For a combined discrete-continuous simulation, all of these must be written. GASP IV has been designed to reduce, as much as possible, the amount of programming necessary beyond writing the event and state variable routines.

If the simulation involves "continuous" variables, a step-evaluate-step time advance procedure is used. The step size is variable to ensure that no events occur within the step and that desired accuracy in the calculation of state variables is maintained. The accuracy test is necessary only if state variables are described in terms of a derivative equation, where integration is required to obtain state variable values. To ensure that a time-event does not occur within a step, the step size is automatically adjusted so that the time-event occurs at the end of the step. For state-events the step size is reduced if such an event occurs within the step. The step size is set so that either no state-event occurs within it (but may occur at the end of the step) or the minimum step allowed is used. The minimum step allowed is specified as an input value by the user. A state-event occurring within the minimum step size is considered to occur at the end of the step.

The conditions for a state-event are defined by the user and would normally involve a state variable achieving a threshold with a prescribed tolerance. The user codes these conditions in subroutine SCOND. The equations defining the state variables are coded in subroutine STATE. Subroutine GASP establishes a step size by which it attempts to advance time. This is discussed in detail in the next section. Subroutine STATE is called to compute the values of the state variables at the end of the proposed step. For each derivative equation, intermediate calls to STATE are made to perform accuracy checks and to allow derivative equations to be functions of the state variables. If accuracy is not met, the step size is reduced accordingly and the process described above is reinitiated.

If accuracy conditions are met, subroutine SCOND is called to check whether a state-event occurred within the step. After a return from SCOND, GASP performs a test on the GASP IV variable, ISEES, to determine if a state-event has been passed (ISEES $< 0.$), if one occurs at the end of the step (ISEES > 0), or neither (ISEES $= 0$). In the first case, the step size is reduced and the abovementioned process is repeated. In the latter two cases, the step size is accepted and model status, including TNOW, is updated. GASP IV provides the subprogram KROSS, which automatically sets ISEES. Function KROSS detects the crossing of a variable beyond a threshold, or the crossing of one variable by another variable. If the user does not employ KROSS, he must set ISEES before returning from subroutine SCOND.

If the step ends with an event, this is processed by calling subroutine EVNTS, which calls the appropriate event based on the event code of the event occurring. A check is then made to determine if the simulation is to be ended. If not, a next step is processed.

At the end of the simulation run, a standard GASP IV summary report is printed, and tables and plots of the state variable values are printed as requested.

Based on these two overviews of GASP IV, the technical details of how to use the language are presented. Table 3-1 lists definitions for the GASP IV variables that are commonly used by the GASP IV programmer. Other important variables are established through data input and these are defined in Table 3-3. A complete glossary of GASP IV variables is presented in Appendix 2. Most variables in GASP COMMON have either the same first two letters or the first two letters as DT. There are 14 exceptions: ATRIB(·); ISEES; JEVNT; LFLAG(·); MFA; MFE(·); MLE(·); MSTOP; NCRDR; NFLAG; NPRNT; NSET(·); QSET(·), and TNOW. These variables are frequently used and the GASP IV user should have no problem avoiding designating his own variables with these names.

All GASP IV variables, with the exception of NSET, are in named COMMON blocks. Blank COMMON is only used for the array NSET. The GASP IV user must *not* use blank COMMON for non-GASP variables.

Table 3-1 Definitions of Commonly Used GASP IV Variables

Variable	Definition
ATRIB(I)	Buffer storage for the Ith attribute value to be stored in or removed from QSET
DD(I)	The value of the derivative of SS(I) at TNOW
DDL(I)	The value of the derivative of SS(I) at TTLAS
DTFUL	Full step size
DTNOW	TNOW-TTLAS
IIEVT	Code of state-events
IINN(I)	Priority ranking indicator for file I
ISEES	Internal indicator that a state-event ends current-step
JEVNT	Code of time-event to be processed, which is the second attribute of an event
KKRNK(I)	The attribute on which file I is ranked
LFLAG(I)	State condition flags
MFA	Relative address of the first cell of NSET/QSET available for storing a new entry
MFE(I)	The pointer to the first entry in file I
MLE(I)	The pointer to the last entry in file I
MSTOP	Indicator for specifying method of ending the simulation
NNATR	Number of attributes per entry
NCRDR	Number of the card reader (input tape number)
NFLAG	Number of state condition flags
NPRNT	Number of the printer (output tape number)
NNQ(I)	The current number of entries in file I
NSET(I)	Integer representation of filing array; used for pointers only
PPARM(I,J)	Array for storing parameter values
QSET(I)	Real valued representation of the file storage area; used for all attribute values
QQTIM(I)	Time of last use of file I
SS(I)	The value of the state variable SS(I) at TNOW
SSL(I)	The value of the state variable SS(I) at TTLAS
TTLAS	The last time at which an event could have occurred; when a step advance is in progress. TTLAS is the time at which acceptable values of SS(I) were computed
TNOW	Current time of simulation; when a step advance is in progress, TNOW is the time to which GASP is trying to advance

MODEL STATUS DEFINITION AND CONTROL

The status of a GASP IV simulation model is defined in terms of events, entities and their attributes, state variables, or a combination of the three. Entity definition and storage in GASP IV is accomplished through the use of the file storage arrays NSET/QSET and file processing routines. Events are scheduled to occur either at a future time (a time-event) or when state variables meet specified conditions (a state-event). Time-events and their associated attributes are stored in file 1. Entities and their associated attributes are stored in file 2 through file NNFIL. State variables and their derivatives are stored in the GASP IV arrays SS(·) and DD(·).

The GASP IV Filing System

The primary function of the GASP IV file storage array is to store time-events and entities with their associated attributes. *The word entry is used to denote either an event or an entity.* By the use of an equivalence statement, EQUIVALENCE(NSET(1),QSET(1)), it is possible to use the same storage array for either real or integer type data. This technique permits the file pointers to be stored as integers; all other values are stored as reals. To simplify reference to the storage array, the name NSET is used to denote it when either name applies. Whenever the user references an attribute value, the array QSET must be used. When a pointer is referenced, the array NSET must be used. NSET is one dimensional and resides in blank COMMON. Because NSET resides in COMMON storage, it is accessible to the GASP IV subroutines without having to be included as an argument in their calling sequence. Since NSET is in blank COMMON, the user can dimension NSET in the main program, and all subprograms can be precompiled with NSET dimensioned to one.

Entries in a file can be thought of as items on a list, customers in a queue, days on a calendar, and so forth. The entries stored in a file are considered by GASP IV in a logical order, not a physical order. The first and second entries in a file are not necessarily stored next to one another. Their order in the file is maintained by a pointing system. Each entry potentially has a predecessor and successor entry in the file. Pointers are used to keep track of each entry's predecessor and successor. The pointers establish the location in NSET where the entries are stored. A zero value for a pointer indicates that either no predecessor or no successor exists.

As an example, consider NSET to be a 16 cell storage array and let the entries in NSET have only two attributes. Four cells would be required to store the entry: the first cell stores the entry's predecessor pointer, the next two cells are for the attribute values, and the last cell stores the entry's successor pointer. Since there are only 16 cells and it takes four cells per entry, four entries, at most, could be stored in the 16 cells of NSET. This is shown below.

1	2	3	4	5	6	7	8	9	10	11	12	13	14	15	16	Cell number
																NSET

The pointer to an entry is the first cell number of the group of cells in which the entry is stored. Thus in the example above, the pointer to an entry stored in cells 1–4 is 1, cells 5–9 is 5, and so forth. At initialization, each group of cells is linked to a successor group using the pointers, as shown below.

1	2	3	4	5	6	7	8	9	10	11	12	13	14	15	16	Cell number
−1			5	−1			9	−1			13	−1			0	NSET

For a given group, the pointer to its successor group is stored in the last cell of the given group. Its first cell is used to store the pointer to the entry's predecessor. Zeros indicate that either no predecessor or no successor exists. On initialization a −1 is put in each cell normally used for the predecessor pointer. In the example above, if we name each group by its first cell number, group 1 has as its successor group 5. The successor of group 5 is group 9. After initialization, all groups of cells are available for storing attributes of entries. The way NSET is initialized, group 1 is the first available group. The variable MFA is used to point to this first available group and, at initialization, MFA = 1. The second available group is the successor to the first available group. The successor pointer stored in cell 4 shows that this is the group whose first cell number is five. The GASP IV variable NNATR defines the number of attributes per entry, and the variables NNAPO and NNAPT are equal to NNATR + 1 and NNATR + 2, respectively. For the example being considered, NNATR = 2. In general terms, the pointer to the successor group of the first available group (MFA) is stored in NSET(LC) where LC = MFA + NNAPO. By continuing in this manner, all groups that are available for storing entries can be determined.

Thus far only the available groups of cells for storing entries have been discussed. Suppose that an entry must be inserted into file 1. The user first defines the attribute values by using the buffer vector ATRIB. Since there are only two attributes, the user would define ATRIB(1) and ATRIB(2). These would be inserted into file 1, using the GASP IV subprogram FILEM, and the statement would be CALL FILEM(1). This entry, which consists of the above two attributes, would be stored in the first available group of NSET. Thus the two attribute values would be stored in cells 2 and 3 of QSET and the predecessor and successor pointers for group 1 would be changed to show that group 1 is in file 1 and is no longer a member of the file of groups available for storing entries. In this case, the pointers for the new entry would both be zero since there are no other entries in file 1. In GASP IV, the variables MFE(I) and MLE(I) are the values of the pointers to the first entry in file I and the last entry in file I, respectively. Whenever MFE(I) or MLE(I) is zero, there are no entries in file I. GASP IV automatically updates these pointers and keeps track of statistics on the number of entries in each file. Thus the variables MFE(1) and MLE(1) are assigned the value 1 to indicate that group 1 is the only entry in file 1.

Since an entry has been put into available group 1, group 1 is no longer the first available group for storing an entry. The new first available group is the successor of the old first available group. As a result, MFA is updated and given a value of five to indicate that cell 5 is the starting location of the new first available group. Note that by this procedure a consistent list of available groups is maintained and only the first one on the list has been deleted. As entries are removed from files, their storage cells become available for storing new entries, and the group of cells is placed at the top of the list by updating MFA and the successor pointer of the new group. If the value for MFA is zero, there is no longer a group of cells available for storing an entry. If the user attempts to store an entry when MFA is zero, error number 301 will result. (All GASP IV error codes are listed in Appendix 3.)

Ranking Entries in a File

We now consider how an entry is placed in a file. Since, by definition, the entries in a file are related, they have common attributes. One of these attributes establishes the ordering, or ranking, of the entries in the file. The ranking attribute might be time of arrival, dollar value, service time, or number of children. The GASP IV array KKRNK(·) defines the attribute used for ranking in file I except for file 1, the event file. For file 1, attribute 1 is the event time and attribute 2 is the event code. These two attributes for file 1 are the only prescribed attribute definitions used in GASP IV. The event file is always ranked on the time the event is to occur, attribute 1, with low-value-first. For other files, whether high values or low values have priority must also be stated. Thus if the ranking attribute is time of arrival, small values might be preferred, which would establish a low-value-first priority for the entries. On the other hand, if the ranking attribute is dollar value, it might be desirable to assign priority on a high-values-first basis.

The GASP IV array IINN(·) defines the ranking procedure. Four values are possible for IINN(I). If IINN(I) = 1, low values are given priority in file I; this is referred to as a low-value-first, or LVF, ranking procedure. If IINN(I) = 2, high values are given priority in file I; this is referred to as a high-value-first, or HVF, ranking procedure. A first-in, first-out (FIFO) procedure, or a last-in, first-out (LIFO) procedure, is specified by setting IINN(I) = 3 or IINN(I) = 4, respectively. When either a FIFO or a LIFO procedure is specified, the ranking attribute is not used.

As noted previously, file 1, the event file, is a special case in which the ranking attribute and priority method are established by its special nature. In this case, KKRNK(1) and IINN(1) are used to establish a secondary ranking procedure to determine priority if two events have the same time of occurrence.

Multiple Files in NSET

Entries for all files are stored in NSET. The number of files involved in a simulation is defined by the user, on input, as the variable NNFIL. Files are used to group entities. Thus all customers waiting for service could be considered as a group, in which case each customer's attributes could be stored as an entry in file 2. Keeping track of the entries that belong to a file is accomplished through the predecessor and successor pointers. The following diagram illustrates two files in NSET where each entry has one attribute.

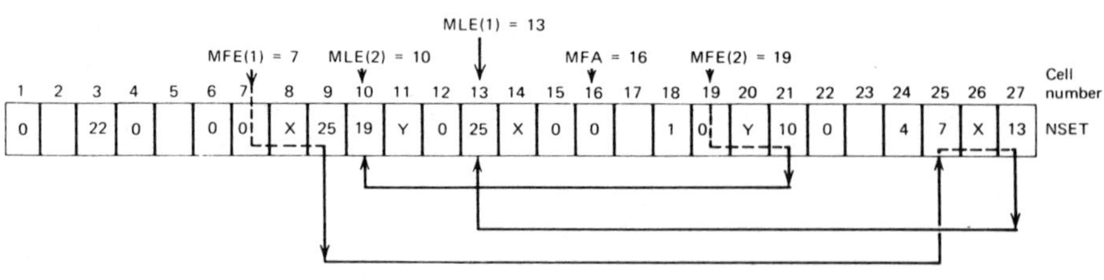

In the diagram, the entries in file 1 are stored in the groups whose first cell numbers are 7, 25, and 13, and the entries in file 2 start in cells 19 and 10.

Getting Entries In and Out of NSET

The filing system is maintained automatically by GASP IV. The programmer does not have to manipulate or use the pointing mechanisms.

Normally, the programmer does not even use the array NSET directly, but inserts attribute values into a file through the buffer storage vector ATRIB, which is a one dimensional array with NNATR elements, ATRIB(1), . . . , ATRIB(NNATR). The GASP IV statement, CALL FILEM(I) would place these values of ATRIB in QSET in the correct logical position of file I.

The values of the attributes of a particular entity in QSET are retrieved by the statement CALL RMOVE(NTRY,I) where NTRY is the first cell number of the group and I is the file number.

The attributes associated with the entry removed are placed in the buffer storage vector ATRIB. For example, the removal of the first entry of file 3 would be accomplished by using the statement CALL RMOVE (MFE(3),3). To find the first cell number of an entry in a file, GASP IV provides the function NFIND, which is discussed later in the book.

Example of File Operations

As an example of the use of the GASP IV filing system, consider the file storage area depicted in Fig. 3-5. The file storage area consists of 16 cells used for the storage of up to four entries of two attributes each (NNTRY = 4; NNATR = 2). There are two files (NNFIL = 2). Recall that the entries in file 1 are always ranked LVF (low-value-first) based on the first attribute of the entry, and KKRNK(1) and IINN(1) are used to specify secondary ranking for file 1. For this example, secondary ranking for file 1 is HVF (high-value-first), based on attribute 2 (IINN(1) = 2, KKRNK(1) = 2). File 2 is LIFO(IINN(2) = 4). The file storage area is normally initialized by subroutine DATIN through a CALL SET statement. After initialization, the pointers are as shown in Fig. 3-5, with each successor pointer pointing to the succeeding cell, except for the last one, zero, which indicates the end of the available storage area. Next consider what happens if the attribute values of 1.0 and 1.0 are placed in file 1. The first available group of cells for storing an entry is group 1 (MFA = 1), which consists of cells 1, 2, 3, and 4. When the entry is filed, cell 1, containing the predecessor pointer, is set at zero, indicating that there is no predecessor to the entry being filed. Cells 2 and 3 are set equal to the attribute values to be stored. Cell 4, the successor pointer, is set at zero to indicate there is no successor. The pointers to the first (MFE(1)) entry and last (MLE(1)) entry in file 1 are set equal to one. The number of entries in file 1 is also set equal to one. Similarly, the succeeding rows in Fig. 3-5 result from the indicated file operations.

In operation 5, CALL FILEM(1) with an ATRIB vector of (1,2), a

Operation	ATRIB Value before Operation		Cell Number of NSET/QSET																MFA	File Variables Values after Operations					
			1	2	3	4	5	6	7	8	9	10	11	12	13	14	15	16		NNQ(1)	MFE(1)	MLE(1)	NNQ(2)	MFE(2)	MLE(2)
1. CALL SET	—	—	−1	0.	0.	5	−1	0.	0.	9	−1	0.	0.	13	−1	0.	0.	0	1	0	0	0	0	0	0
2. CALL FILEM(1)	1.	1.	0	1.	1.	0	−1	0.	0.	9	−1	0.	0.	13	−1	0.	0.	0	5	1	1	1	0	0	0
3. CALL FILEM(1)	2.	2.	0	1.	1.	5	1	2.	2.	0	−1	0.	0.	13	−1	0.	0.	0	9	2	1	5	0	0	0
4. CALL FILEM(2)	3.	3.	0	1.	1.	5	1	2.	2.	0	0	3.	3.	0	−1	0.	0.	0	13	2	1	5	1	9	9
5. CALL FILEM(1)	1.	2.	13	1.	1.	5	1	2.	2.	0	0	3.	3.	0	0	1.	2.	1	0	3	13	5	1	9	9
6. CALL RMOVE (MFE(2),2)	1.	2.	13	1.	1.	5	1	2.	2.	0	0	3.	3.	0	0	1.	2.	1	9	3	13	5	0	0	0
7. CALL RMOVE (1,1)	3.	3.	0	1.	1.	9	13	2.	2.	0	0	3.	3.	0	0	1.	2.	5	1	2	13	5	0	0	0

Figure 3-5 Snapshots of filing array, NSET/QSET, with IINN(1) = 2, KKRNK(1) = 2, and IINN(2) = 4.

tie exists in the ranking attribute. Since the secondary rule is HVF based on ATRIB(2), the new entry has priority and is put in the first position of file 1. In operation 6, note that the RMOVE operation does not zero out the cells used to store attribute values. Cells of NSET that are not used for storing attribute values are not accessed by the GASP IV subprograms. Therefore, there is no need to reinitialize cell values. In operation 7, note that the first argument of the call to subroutine RMOVE is the first cell location of the event to be deleted from the event file.

State Variable Definition

The GASP IV variables SS(I), SSL(I), DD(I), and DDL(I) are used to define the state variables and their derivatives at times TNOW and TTLAS where

TNOW = time at which values of the state variables are being computed.
TTLAS = time at the beginning of the current step (the time at which the values for the state variables were last accepted).
SS(I) = value of state variable I at time TNOW.
SSL(I) = value of state variable I at time TTLAS.
DD(I) = value of the derivative of state variable I at time TNOW.
DDL(I) = value of the derivative of state variable I at time TTLAS.

The equations for calculating the values of SS(I) and DD(I) must be written by the user and included in subroutine STATE. The procedure for writing these equations is described in the section on user written subroutines. All state variables are in GASP IV common storage and are accessible to the user in any subprogram.

Time Advance Procedures

In GASP IV, the amount by which simulated time is advanced depends on the type of simulation being performed and the values of specific variables at the current point in time.

In a discrete simulation, time is advanced from one event to the next event. In this case the time interval between events is TTNEX − TNOW where TTNEX is the time of the next event. Time is advanced from TNOW to TTNEX by resetting TNOW equal to TTNEX and assuming that the system status has remained constant between events. Since status at TNOW is always accepted, there is no need to maintain values at

TTLAS, and TNOW can be used as both the last update point and then as the new event time, that is, TTLAS is neither required nor used.

For a continuous simulation, the variable DTFUL is the value for a full step size. If all the equations for state variables are written in terms of SS(·), the variable representing the time advance increment, DTNOW, would normally be set equal to DTFUL. The time at the beginning of the step is TTLAS and the time at the end of the proposed step is TNOW, that is, TNOW = TTLAS + DTNOW. DTFUL remains constant at the maximum step size prescribed by the user, DTMAX, unless an event occurs within the step.

The increment in time between the recording of the status of the system is specified through the variable DTSAV. For DTSAV > 0, subroutine GASP will call subroutine SSAVE every DTSAV time units. The variable TTSAV is used to define the next time at which the system status is to be recorded. These time points are called save times. If a save time occurs within an interval, that is, TTLAS + DTNOW is greater than TTSAV, the step size is reduced to TTSAV − TTLAS. In this way the status of the system is updated to TNOW = TTSAV. TTLAS is then updated and TTSAV is reset to TNOW + DTSAV. To avoid updating the status at save times that are very close to regular update points, a resolution factor is used. If the difference between an update point and a save time is 1/100th of DTSAV, the update point is used as the save time. The projection of the next save time is then made from TTSAV.

The size of a step is also decreased if a state-event is passed. Thus if the value of a state variable at time TTLAS + DTNOW results in the crossing of a threshold beyond allowable tolerances, the step size is reduced. In this case, DTFUL is halved. If the tolerance is still not met, halving of the step size continues until the value of DTFUL is set equal to a user prescribed minimum step size, DTMIN. Note that DTFUL can be less than DTMIN if either TTNEX − TTLAS < DTMIN or TTSAV − TTLAS < DTMIN. Further note that if a fixed step size is desired for a simulation involving only SS(·) variables in which there are no time-events, DTMIN = DTMAX will accomplish this objective.

The most complex time advance procedure occurs when there are variables defined by DD(·) equations included in a GASP IV simulation program. In this case, all the considerations described above pertain; in addition, the full step size, DTFUL, is divided into fourths so that the time advance increment, DTNOW, proceeds as one-fourth DTFUL. The SS(·) variables are evaluated at these intermediate points within the step and used by GASP IV in the integration of the equations for DD(·).

These intermediate values for SS(·) and DD(·) allow error estimates to be made and simultaneous differential equations to be evaluated.

The variable DTACC is defined as the next step size to be used, based on allowable error specifications. Initially, DTACC is set equal to DTMAX. Whenever the accuracy of the integration algorithm does not meet the user's prescribed accuracy, as defined by an absolute error value AAERR and a relative error value RRERR, the value of DTACC is halved. At the start of each step, DTFUL is set equal to DTACC. The halving of DTACC when accuracy is not met is only permitted until DTACC becomes less than DTMIN, at which time DTACC is set equal to DTMIN.

When all state variables are within the accuracy specifications to a significant extent, DTACC is doubled. At the current time, a significant extent has been defined as the error estimate obtained when the integration algorithm is within 2% of the allowed user's specified error. In this way, the step size is increased when good estimates for the state variables are obtained by the integration algorithm. In no case will GASP IV allow DTACC to become greater than DTMAX. When a state-event is passed, DTFUL is halved. If a state-event was passed at the half step point, DTFUL is reduced to one-fourth of its previous value.

It is obvious that the time advance procedures included within GASP IV involve many variables with many interactions between these variables. Subroutine GASP automatically advances time for the user based on the input values prescribed for DTMIN, DTMAX, DTSAV, and the accuracy requirements (AAERR and RRERR) when DD(·) equations are specified. The calculation of DTFUL, DTNOW, and DTACC as well as the next discrete event time, TTNEX, and the next save time, TTSAV, are internally computed in subroutine GASP.

A note of caution is in order regarding the use of DTNOW in subroutine STATE. DTNOW is the value of the time increment through which GASP updates the state variables over a full step of size DTFUL. In many cases, DTNOW = DTFUL. In other cases, this is not so. In fact, if two events occur at the same time, DTNOW will assume a value of zero for the second event processed. Thus DTNOW should not be used in the denominator of any equation in subroutine STATE. However, DTNOW should be used in any equation in subroutine STATE in which the state variable is updated by a rate multiplied by the increment in time for which the update is being performed.

The following is provided in an attempt to summarize the time advance procedures. If derivative equations are included (NNEQD > 0), then

DTFUL = min[DTACC; TTSAV − TTLAS; TTNEX − TTLAS; time to next state-event],
DTNOW = f(DTFUL),
TNOW = TTLAS + DTNOW,
max DTACC = DTMAX,
min DTACC = DTMIN,
min (full step size to next state-event) = DTMIN.

If derivative equations are not included (NNEQD = 0), but state equations are (NNEQS > 0), then

DTFUL = min [DTMAX; TTSAV − TTLAS; TTNEX − TTLAS, time to next state-event]
DTNOW = DTFUL,
TNOW = TTLAS + DTNOW,
min [full step size to next state-event] = DTMIN,
and DTACC is not used.

If NNEQD = 0 and NNEQS = 0, then DTFUL, DTNOW, DTACC, and TTLAS are not used and TNOW is the time of the current event being processed. Only time-events are possible.

GASP IV SUBPROGRAMS

Figure 3-6 diagramatically presents the relationship of the GASP IV subprograms and the user written subprograms. The lines in Fig. 3-6 represent calls of one subprogram by another. Each of the user written subprograms can call any of the GASP IV subprograms. Lines indicating such calls are problem specific and are not shown in the figure. Subprogram names that have both a solid box and a dashed box around them are usually written by the user. If no user version is written, GASP IV provides a "dummy" version. Descriptions of the GASP IV subprograms are listed in Table 3-2. Detailed information and the coding for these subprograms is given in Chapter 4. Examples of the use of these subprograms to illustrate their functions are given in this chapter.

EXAMPLES OF THE USE OF GASP IV SUBPROGRAMS

Each of the GASP IV subprograms is discussed below in the order it is presented in Table 3-2. Where appropriate, examples of the use of the GASP IV subprograms are given.

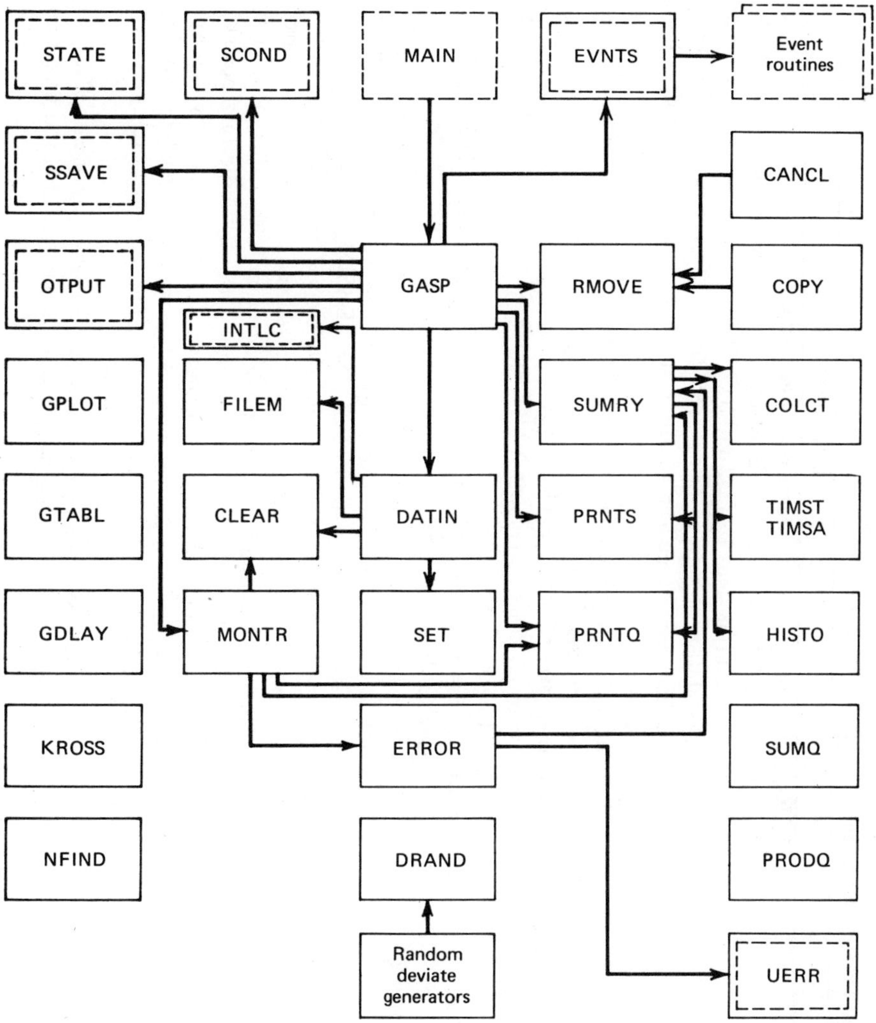

Figure 3-6 Relation of GASP IV and user subprograms. ☐ GASP IV subprogram. ⧈ Dummy subprogram. ⬚ User programs required. [A]→[B] Subprogram A calls subprogram B.

Subroutine GASP is the executive routine and is only called from the user's main program. Subroutine DATIN is called by subroutine GASP and is normally not referred to by the GASP IV user. Subroutine CLEAR is used to zero out the storage arrays that collect values of variables to be reported in the final summary report. For example, if the user wants to calculate statistics based on data collected after time 1000, the statement CALL CLEAR inserted into the program at time 1000 (possibly through

Table 3-2 Description of GASP IV Subprograms

Name	Description
SUBROUTINE GASP	Executive routine for advancing time and status
SUBROUTINE DATIN	Initializes GASP IV variables (see section on input formats) and calls user written functions INTLC and STATE
SUBROUTINE CLEAR	Initializes statistical storage arrays (SSOBV, SSTPV, and JJCEL) and allows the user to collect statistics starting at any time during the simulation
SUBROUTINE SET	Initializes file pointers and file statistics arrays
SUBROUTINE FILEM(IFILE)	Files an entry into IFILE
SUBROUTINE RMOVE(NTRY,IFILE)	Removes entry NTRY from file IFILE
SUBROUTINE CANCL(NTRY)	Cancels event stored as entry NTRY in file 1 by removing it without updating TNOW
SUBROUTINE COPY(NTRY)	Puts attributes of entry NTRY into buffer storage array ATRIB without removing the entry
FUNCTION KROSS(IKRSG,IKRSD, CMULT,CADD,LDIR,TOL)	Tests for a crossing during a proposed step of the value of state variable SS(IKRSG), (or its derivative if IKRSG is passed as a negative value) against the value of state variable, SS(IKRSD), (or its derivative) times CMULT plus CADD within a tolerance TOL; LDIR specifies the direction of the crossing; LDIR values can be +, 0, or − corresponding to a crossing in a positive direction, either direction, or a negative direction; KROSS values returned are: 2—indicating positive crossing exceeding tolerance, 1—indicating positive crossing within tolerance, 0—indicating no crossing, −1—indicating negative crossing within tolerance or −2—indicating negative crossing exceeding tolerance Function KROSS automatically sets the GASP IV variable ISEES to indicate if a state event has been passed or occurs within the time step

FUNCTION NFIND(XVAL, MCODE, IFILE, JATT, TOL)	Locates an entry in file IFILE whose JATT attribute is related to the value XVAL according to the specification given by MCODE as shown below: MCODE = 1: maximum value but greater than XVAL MCODE = 2: minimum value but greater than XVAL MCODE = 3: maximum value but less than XVAL MCODE = 4: minimum value but less than XVAL MCODE = 5: value equal to XVAL ± TOL NFIND is set equal to the first cell number of the entry desired; the Ith attribute of the entry is located in QSET(IC) where IC = NFIND + I; if no entry is found, NFIND is set to zero
SUBROUTINE COLCT(XX,ICLCT)	If ICLCT > 0, records value XX as an observation on variable number ICLCT; if ICLCT = 0, computes and reports statistics on all NNCLT variables; if ICLCT < 0, computes and reports statistics on variable −ICLCT
SUBROUTINE TIMST(XX,T,ISTAT)	IF ISTAT > 0, integrates variable number ISTAT assuming the value during the interval up to time T is the value of XX at the last call to TIMST for variable ISTAT; XX is the value variable ISTAT will have during the next interval; if ISTAT = 0, computes and reports statistics on all NNSTA variables; if ISTAT < 0, computes and reports statistics on variable −ISTAT
SUBROUTINE TIMSA(XX,T,ISTAT)	Integrates variable number ISTAT assuming that the value during the past interval is the average of XX and the value of XX at the last call to TIMSA for variable ISTAT; computation and reporting for variable ISTAT is performed by subroutine TIMST
SUBROUTINE HISTO(XX,IHIST)	If IHIST > 0, determines the cell number associated with the value XX for variable IHIST and increases the cell content by 1; if IHIST = 0,

Table 3-2 Description of GASP IV Subprograms (*continued*)

Name	Description
	prints and plots all NNHIS histograms; if IHIST < 0, prints and plots histogram $-$IHIST
SUBROUTINE GPLOT(XX,T,IPLOT)	If IPLOT > 0, IPLOT is the plot number and GPLOT stores values of the dependent variables XX (up to 10 values per plot) for a value of the independent variable T; if IPLOT = 0, prints table and/or graph for all plots as specified by input data; if IPLOT < 0, prints table and/or graph of plot $-$IPLOT
SUBROUTINE PRNTQ(IFILE)	Computes statistics and prints results and entries in files; if IFILE $\leqslant 0$, all files are printed; if IFILE > 0, a status report is only printed for file IFILE
SUBROUTINE PRNTS	Prints contents of the state storage vectors, SS(I) and DD(I)
SUBROUTINE SUMRY	Prints GASP IV summary report
SUBROUTINE MONTR	Allows for monitoring a simulation by printing information at monitor event times defined by the user; monitor event codes available are: 0 Start or stop tracing each event −1 Print file storage area −2 Reset file statistics and clear statistical arrays (CALL CLEAR) −3 Print state storage vectors −4 Print file storage area and state storage vector −5 Prints GASP IV summary report −6 Causes error exit
SUBROUTINE ERROR(KODE)	Prints reports and error messages
FUNCTION SUMQ(JATT,IFILE)	Sums the values of attribute JATT of all entries in file IFILE
FUNCTION PRODQ(JATT,IFILE)	Obtains the product of the values of attribute JATT of entries in file IFILE

FUNCTION GTABL(TAB,X,XLOW, XHIGH,XINCR)	Performs a table look-up to obtain a value of a dependent variable from discrete values stored in the vector TAB for a given value of the independent variable X; XLOW is the value of X corresponding to TAB(1) and XHIGH is the largest value for X; XINCR is the difference in the independent variable for successive values of the dependent variable
SUBROUTINE GDLAY(IFS,ILS,XIN,DEL)	Variable order exponential delay for Systems Dynamics problems, IFS and ILS are the first and last state variables used to maintain the delay; the order of the delay is ILS − IFS + 1. *NNEQD must be greater than ILS to use GDLAY*; XIN is the input to the delay and DEL to the delay constant
FUNCTION DRAND(ISTRM)	Pseudo-random number generator for stream ISTRM; initial seed values are specified in DATIN; *this routine is machine dependent*
FUNCTION UNFRM(ULO,UHI,ISTRM)	Uniform deviate generator using stream ISTRM; deviates are between ULO and UHI
FUNCTION TRIAG(IPAR,ISTRM)	Triangular deviate generator using stream ISTRM and parameters from parameter set IPAR
FUNCTION RNORM(IPAR,ISTRM)	Normal deviate generator using stream ISTRM and parameters from parameter set IPAR
FUNCTION RLOGN(IPAR,ISTRM)	Lognormal deviate generator using stream ISTRM and parameters of corresponding normal distribution stored in parameter set IPAR
FUNCTION ERLNG(IPAR,ISTRM)	Erlang deviate generator using stream ISTRM and parameters from parameter set IPAR
FUNCTION GAMA(IPAR,ISTRM)	Gamma deviate generator using stream ISTRM and parameters from parameter set IPAR
FUNCTION BETA(IPAR,ISTRM)	Beta deviate generator using stream ISTRM and parameters from parameter set IPAR
FUNCTION NPSSN(IPAR,ISTRM)	Poisson deviate generator using stream ISTRM and parameters from parameter set IPAR
FUNCTION GAM(AK,ISTRM)	Support routine for BETA and GAMA functions

a time-event) can be used to accomplish this. If file statistics as well as summary statistics are to be reinitialized, this can be accomplished using subroutine MONTR.

Subroutine SET initializes the filing array NSET and all variables associated with the filing array. This includes the following variables: number of entries in file I, NNQ(I); the time integrated number of entries in file I, EENQ(I); the second moment of the time integrated number of entries in file I, VVNQ(I); the largest number of entries that have been in file I, MMAXQ(I); and the last time an entry was either filed or removed from file I, QQTIM(I). A call to subroutine SET can be activated through the use of the GASP IV input cards. When subroutine SET is called, all events and entities stored in all files are deleted and the file structure is reinitialized.

To file an entry into a particular file, subroutine FILEM is used. Suppose that a user has to schedule an event of type 2 to occur 12 time units from the current time. Assume further that the third attribute associated with the event has a value of 7. The following four statements will accomplish the insertion of the event into file 1:

```
ATRIB(1) = TNOW + 12.
ATRIB(2) = 2.
ATRIB(3) = 7.
CALL FILEM(1)
```

To remove an entry from a file, subroutine RMOVE is used. Suppose that it is desired to remove the second entry of file 3. First the number of entries in file 3 should be tested to determine that there is a second entry. Then the cell number identifying the second entry should be determined. This cell number is defined by the successor pointer of the first entry. Once the cell number is established, subroutine RMOVE can be used to remove the entry. The GASP IV coding to accomplish this is shown below:

```
IF (NNQ(3).LT. 2) RETURN
INDXS = MFE(3) + NNAPO
LSFE = NSET(INDXS)
CALL RMOVE(LSFE, 3)
```

The pointer to the first entry of file 3 is MFE(3). The cell number in which its successor label is stored is the last cell of the group, that is, MFE(3) + NNAPO. The pointer to the successor to the first entry is stored in this cell of NSET. After removal, subroutine RMOVE automatically updates the pointers.

Subroutine CANCL is provided to remove events from the event file. The statement CALL CANCL(NTRY) is equivalent to CALL RMOVE (NTRY,1). Consider now the cancelling of the next to the last event in the event file. The pointer to the last event in the event file is stored as MLE(1). Since the pointer indicates the cell containing the predecessor value, the first cell number of the next to the last event is simply the value in the cell of the pointer to the last event, that is, INDXP = MLE(1). The first cell number for the next to the last event is then simply NSET (INDXP). The coding to cancel the next to the last event is shown below:

```
IF (NNQ(1) .LT. 2) RETURN
INDXP = MLE(1)
LPLE = NSET(INDXP)
CALL CANCL(LPLE)
```

CANCL removes the event from the event file and automatically updates the pointers.

Suppose that in the above example it was only desired to obtain attributes of the next to the last event in the event file. This could be accomplished by replacing the call to CANCL with a call to COPY. That is, the last statement of the above sequence of statements would be CALL COPY(LPLE). This call to COPY essentially performs the coding shown below:

```
   DO 10 I = 1, NNATR
   J = LPLE + I
10 ATRIB(I) = QSET(J)
```

Note that when dealing with the attributes stored in the filing array, reference is made to QSET, whereas when dealing with the pointers, reference is made to NSET. This is made possible through the EQUIVALENCE statement, as previously discussed. To insure proper program operation, QSET and NSET must be used in this manner.

Function KROSS can be used to test the crossing of one state variable by another state variable. Suppose that a user wants to determine if, for a proposed time step, SS(3) has crossed the value of 10.0 ⋆ SS(1) + 4.0 in the positive direction. Function KROSS would then be used in subroutine SCOND. If it is desired to detect this crossing within 0.25 units measured on the same scale as the state variables, the following statement should be used in SCOND:

```
LFLAG(1) = KROSS(3,1,10.0,4.,+1,0.25)
```

Through the above statement, LFLAG(1) is set to zero if no crossing occurs. LFLAG(1) is set equal to 1 if a crossing occurs and at the end of the step $10. \star SS(1) + 4. \leq SS(3) \leq 10. \star SS(1) + 4.0 + 0.25$. LFLAG(1) is set equal to 2 if a crossing occurs and at the end of the step $SS(3) > 10. \star SS(1) + 4. + 0.25$. In the last case, GASP IV automatically decreases the step size to obtain a crossing with SS(3) within the prescribed tolerance at the end of the step, if this is possible. It may not be possible because the minimum time step, DTMIN, was not made sufficiently small to permit the crossing within the specified tolerance. When this occurs, the variable LLERR is checked to determine if a warning message should be printed and if the simulation should continue even though the tolerance level could not be maintained. Other examples of the use of function KROSS are provided in the discussion of subroutine SCOND.

Function NFIND is used to locate entries in NSET. NFIND is set equal to the first cell number of the entry. As an example, consider finding the location of the entry in file 3 that has the largest value for attribute 2. Only entries with attribute 2 values greater than 50.0 are to be considered. The statement to obtain the first cell number of the entry that meets the prescribed conditions is shown below:

```
LVIF = NFIND(50.0,1,3,2,0.0)
```

The second argument of NFIND is the code for the type of search. Code 1 specifies that the entry to be located is to have the largest value of attribute 2 (argument 4) in file 3 (argument 3). If no entry has an attribute 2 value greater than 50.0 (argument 1), NFIND returns a zero value. The fifth argument is a tolerance for searches seeking equality (code 5). A zero value for the tolerance is arbitrarily used in the above example.

Subroutine COLCT is used to collect a sample value of a variable. The variables are given numeric codes that are communicated to subroutine COLCT by its second argument (ICLCT). The value of the sample is passed to COLCT by its first argument, XX. As an example of the use of subroutine COLCT, consider a queueing situation in which we have calculated the time spent in the system by a customer. Each of these calculated times represents a sample value that is determined in an end-of-service event for the customer. The GASP IV user assigns a numeric code to this variable, for example, 3, which identifies this as the variable for which statistics will be collected whenever subroutine COLCT is called with ICLCT = 3. In the end-of-service event the user would calculate the time in the system, TISYS, by subtracting the arrival time for the customer from the current time, TNOW. This particular sample of TISYS would then be added to all previous samples through the following statement: CALL COLCT(TISYS,3). This statement adds TISYS, which must be a real variable, to the sum of other values collected to date, adds the square of TISYS to the square of other values obtained, increases the number of observations by one, and keeps track of the minimum and maximum values of TISYS observed. These five quantities are stored in the array SSOBV(3,J), $J = 1, \cdots, 5$. In general, row ICLCT is used for values of variables with code ICLCT.

As indicated in Table 3-2, the user can obtain output statistics based on the values collected by calling COLCT with a zero or negative value for ICLCT. When this is done, GASP IV prints out estimates of the mean, standard deviation, standard deviation of the mean, coefficient of variation, the minimum and maximum values observed, and the number of observations on which these statistics were based. The values stored in SSOBV(ICLCT,J) are not altered when these statistics are reported. In the preparation of the GASP IV summary report, subroutine COLCT is called to print this information for each variable.

Subroutine TIMST is also used for collecting values of variables for which statistical estimates are desired. When TIMST is used, the variable in question is assumed to have maintained a constant value over a time interval. This type of variable is referred to as a time persistent variable. An example of a time persistent variable would be the number of customers in a queueing system. The number of customers in a queueing system has a constant value over a time interval before it is changed. The length of the time interval dictates the weight assigned to the value of the variable in computing its average over the entire simulation. Subroutine TIMST integrates the value of the variable over the time interval by multiplying these two quantities together. Suppose that XISYS represents the number in the system for the next interval of time, that is, from TNOW until the next event.* Furthermore, the user has specified that code 2 indicates a value of XISYS is being passed to subroutine TIMST. The statement CALL TIMST(XISYS,TNOW,2) would then be used to collect the integrated value. Note that the first two arguments to

* Subroutine TIMST differs from earlier versions in that the variable on which statistics are being collected must be updated prior to the call to TIMST.

TIMST must be real variables. This call to TIMST updates the following six quantities in the array SSTPV(2,J), J = 1, · · · , 6: the sum of the time integrated value; the sum of the time integrated values squared; the value of the second argument (TNOW), which is the time of the last computation; the minimum value observed; the maximum value observed; and the value of the first argument (XISYS). As with subroutine COLCT, subroutine TIMST can be used for printing out statistical estimates for the time persistent variables.

Subroutine TIMSA performs the same function as subroutine TIMST except that the average of the last value observed and the current value are used to integrate the time persistent variable. TIMSA is particularly useful for keeping statistics on state variables, since their values are permitted to change between events as well as at event times. The trapezoidal integration used in TIMSA yields better estimates for such variables than does TIMST. The statement CALL TIMSA(SS(2), TNOW,4) would maintain statistics on state variable 2. The numeric code assigned to the statistic is 4. The array SSTPV(4,J) is used to store these statistics for the variable SS(2). By data input, the number of variables for which TIMST and TIMSA are used is defined as the variable NNSTA. Clearly, since SSTPV is used by TIMST and TIMSA, different numeric codes must be assigned to variables using these two subroutines. Initial values of time persistent variables, for statistical calculations, must be set either by standard GASP IV input, by an initial call to TIMST or TIMSA, or by setting SSTPV(I,6) in the main program.

Subroutine HISTO is used to determine the relative frequency with which a variable falls within a set of prescribed limits. It is normally used for variables that have a prescribed value based on an observation, such as the time in the system for a customer, TISYS. The lower limit and width of each cell of the histogram are described by data input for each histogram. If histogram 1 is the code assigned for the TISYS variable, the statement CALL HISTO(TISYS,1) would be used to add one observation to the cell that covered the interval in which the TISYS value occurred. The array JJCEL is used to store the histogram. The number of cells for histogram I is specified by input and stored in the array NNCEL(I). The upper limit of the first cell and the width of each cell of histogram I is specified by input and stored in the arrays HHLOW(I) and HHWID(I), respectively. As with subroutines COLCT and TIMST, subroutine HISTO is used to print and to plot histograms and can be called by the user. Histograms are automatically printed at the end of a simulation run as part of the GASP IV summary report.

Subroutine GPLOT collects values for eventual plotting of up to 10 dependent variables for one independent variable. The independent variable must be monotonic. Many options are available with regard to the type and scaling for the plot, and these are defined by the input data on data card type 6. At most 10 plots, each with 10 dependent variables, can be stored on tape units. Significant reduction in computing time is obtained when the plot data are stored in core memory. GASP IV provides the capability for maintaining the values for one plot in core. It is strongly suggested that during the debugging phases of program development tape storage for plots not be used. If data for a plot is stored in core, only one plot is allowed for the program.

The first argument of GPLOT is a dimension variable that accepts up to 10 values. Since the dummy argument in the subroutine is dimensioned, there are various ways of passing the dependent variables to the plotting subroutine. Thus if state variables SS(3) through SS(7) were to be plotted versus time, the collection of data for eventual plotting could be accomplished by (1) passing the value of SS(3) as the first argument or (2) defining a five element array and setting the values of SS(3) through SS(7) into this newly defined array. These two alternatives are shown below:

Alternative 1

```
      CALL GPLOT(SS(3),TNOW,1)
```

Alternative 2

```
      DO 10 J = 3,7
   10 PLOT(J - 2) = SS(J)
      CALL GPLOT(PLOT,TNOW,1)
```

For either of these alternatives, the input data would have specified that there were five dependent values for each independent value, and the numeric code 1 is given for this plot. GPLOT is used for printing a table, plotting the values recorded, or both.

Subroutines PRNTQ and PRNTS are used to print the filing array and the state storage vectors, respectively. The statement CALL PRNTQ(2) would cause the computation and printing of the average number, standard deviation, and maximum number of entries in file 2, and would prepare a tabular listing of the contents of file 2. The statement CALL PRNTQ(0) would perform the procedure for all files. The statement CALL PRNTS would cause the state variables and their derivatives to be printed out.

Subroutine SUMRY causes the GASP IV final report to be prepared and printed. This is accomplished within SUMRY through calls to subroutines COLCT, TIMST, HISTO, PRNTQ, PRNTS, and GPLOT. (Values recorded through calls to TIMSA are obtained by the call to TIMST.) When the final report is produced with the statement CALL SUMRY, no changes are made to the GASP IV variables. Thus subroutine SUMRY can be called repeatedly throughout a simulation to obtain intermediate summary reports without altering the values used in the simulation. When a summary report is printed, statistics on the time persistent variables and the number in the file are calculated up to the time at which the summary report is requested. However, only the values printed are updated to the time of printing; the running totals, which provide the basis for the output, are not changed.

Subroutine MONTR provides capabilities for: selectively monitoring events; printing the file array, state storage vectors, or a summary report at a prescribed point in time; and reinitializing statistical storage areas. Calls to subroutine MONTR can be accomplished through events inserted into the event file at the beginning of the simulation or by calls to subroutine MONTR in the user's subprograms. The particular use of MONTR is specified through the value given to the event code indicator JEVNT. For example, to trace all events that occur from time 100 to time 200, two initial events would be included in the data initialization deck. The first event would be scheduled to occur at time 100 with the event code 0. The second would be scheduled to occur at time 200 also with the event code 0. Events with code 0 are used in pairs, and the first such event activates the tracing (printout) of each event as it occurs. The second event with code 0 halts the tracing.

If the event code is -1, all files will be printed when the event occurs. Similarly if the event code is -3, the state storage vectors will be printed. An event code of -4 prints both the file storage area and the state storage vectors. An event code of -5 causes a summary report to be printed. When ATRIB(3) $>$ 0.0 and the event code is -1, -3, -4, or -5, another monitor event with the same event code is scheduled to occur at TNOW + ATRIB(3). If, for example, the initial data contains an event with ATRIB(1) = 500.0, ATRIB(2) = -5.0, and ATRIB(3) = 100.0., summary reports will be printed at times 500.0, 600.0, 700.0, ...

An event code of -2 reinitializes file statistics and the statistical storage arrays. This can be done both through input data, if the time at which the reinitialization is to be performed is known, or through coding, as shown below:

```
JEVNT = - 2
CALL  MONTR
```

The statements could be included in an event in which it was determined that an average value had stabilized to the point where statistical collection should be reinitiated. It is also useful when statistical reports for time intervals are needed. An event code of −6 causes subroutine MONTR to make an error exit.

When an illogical condition occurs, or when GASP IV is asked to do something that it cannot, subroutine ERROR is called. Attempting to file an entry into NSET when no available storage space exists, or to remove an entry from a file that has no entries are examples of such situations. These errors are given the standard GASP IV error codes of 301 and 311, respectively. Appendix 3 contains a list of all standard GASP IV error codes. Subroutine ERROR can be called directly by the user, and additional error codes can be defined to indicate specific problems detected in the subprograms written by the user. No GASP IV error codes are less than 100; consequently, these error code values are available to the user. The statement CALL ERROR(23), for example, results in the message GASP ERROR EXIT, TYPE 23 ERROR AT TIME_____._______, with TNOW being inserted as the time. Following this, subroutine ERROR calls a user written program UERR, which allows the user to output specific information at the time of an error. A call to subroutine SUMRY is then made to obtain a summary report at the time of error. A deliberate FORTRAN error is then caused to obtain the FORTRAN error output and program termination.

The function SUMQ computes the sum of all attribute values for a given file. Suppose that the assets of a corporation are stored in file 2 with attribute 3 being used to define the value of an asset. The statement TASSC = SUMQ(3,2) computes the value of the total assets of the corporation as TASSC. The function PRODQ performs a similar function to SUMQ but multiplies the values of the attributes instead of summing them. Therefore, if the components logically in series in a system are stored as entries in file 3, and attribute 4 is the reliability of a component, the statement SREL = PRODQ(4,3) will compute the system reliability SREL.

The function GTABL provides a look-up function for a table in which the independent variable of the table has equal intervals. Given the table below, which relates values of FOFY to Y, a value of FY1 can be obtained for a given value Y1 by the statement

```
FY1 = GTABL(FOFY,Y1,0.0,5.0,1.0)
```

where the arguments are the name of the array storing the table defining the function, the value of the independent variable for which the function is to be evaluated, the values of the independent variable corresponding to the first and last tabulated value, and the interval of the independent variable corresponding to the interval between the tabulated values. The values of FY1 that would result for any value of Y1 are shown in Fig. 3-7. As can be seen from the figure, interpolation is used for values within the range of the table. Otherwise, the end point values are assigned.

Subroutine GDLAY provides a vehicle to obtain a variable order exponential delay for use in Systems Dynamics simulations. The statement CALL GDLAY(7,9,20.0,4.0), for example, causes the input value of 20. to be processed through a third order delay with a delay constant of 4. Viewing a third order delay as a three-stage process, the above statement would set DD(7), DD(8), and DD(9) to values that would drive the state variables SS(7), SS(8), and SS(9) to the value 20 from their current values. The delay constant 4 and the three-stage process prescribe that at each stage four-thirds of the delay is encountered. Thus the rate of change for SS(7) is the difference between the input value (20.) and SS(7) divided by 4./3. (or equivalently multiplying by 3./4.). That is, DD(7) = (20. − SS(7)) ⋆ 3./4. Similarly, the rates of change for SS(8) and

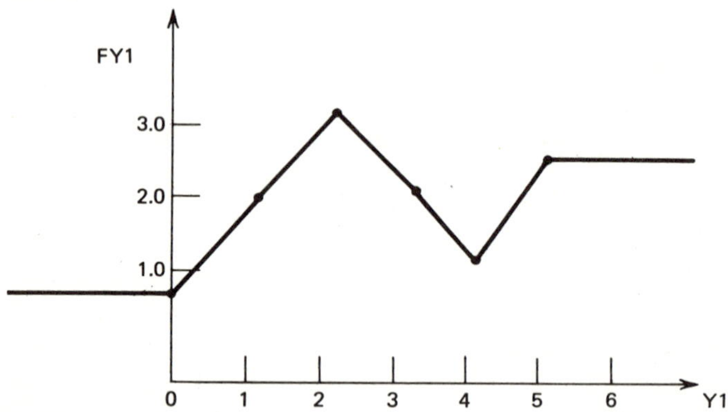

Figure 3-7 Interpolated values, FY1, obtained from function GTABL for values of Y1. Stored table of FOFY for specific values of Y:

Y	FOFY
0.0	0.8
1.0	2.0
2.0	3.0
3.0	2.0
4.0	1.0
5.0	2.5

SS(9) are: DD(8) = (SS(7) − SS(8)) ★ 3./4. and DD(9) = (SS(8) − SS(9)) ★ 3./4.

To use GDLAY, each stage must be represented by a DD(·) variable. In the above example, DD(7), DD(8), and DD(9) are used. GASP IV automatically updates corresponding SS(·) variables in subroutine GASP.

There are eight subprograms included in GASP IV for obtaining *random deviates*. Each of these functions calls DRAND(ISTRM) to obtain a pseudorandom number on the interval (0,1) from stream ISTRM. DRAND is the only machine specific function in GASP IV. In Chapter 4 three versions of DRAND are presented.

Seven of the subprograms use the array PPARM(·,·) to store parameters of the distribution from which a deviate is desired. The parameters are referred to as a parameter set with the set number corresponding to the first argument or row designator for the array PPARM. In general, PPARM(I,2) represents the minimum deviate obtainable when sampling using parameter set I, and PPARM(I,3) represents the maximum deviate obtainable. The values assigned to PPARM(I,1) and PPARM(I,4) are dependent on the distribution from which the deviate is to be sampled. The values of the PPARM array are part of the standard GASP IV input. When a parameter set is employed, the first and fourth values of PPARM are identified using the following notation:* μ = mean, σ = standard deviation, m = mode, a = minimum value, and b = maximum value.

TRIAG	PPARM(1,1) = m, PPARM(1,4) not used
RNORM	PPARM(2,1) = μ, PPARM(2,4) = σ
RLOGN	PPARM(3,1) = μ_N, PPARM(3,4) = σ_N where $\sigma_N^2 = \ln(\sigma^2/\mu^2 + 1)$ and $\mu_N = \ln \mu - \sigma_N^2/2$
ERLNG	PPARM(4,1) = σ^2/μ and PPARM(4,4) = μ^2/σ^2
GAMA	PPARM(5,1) = σ^2/μ and PPARM(5,4) = μ^2/σ^2
BETA	PPARM(6,1) = $\frac{(\mu - a)}{(b - a)}\left[\frac{(\mu - a)(b - \mu)}{\sigma^2} - 1\right]$ and PPARM(6,4) = PPARM(6,1) ★ $\frac{(b - \mu)}{\mu - a}$
NPSSN	PPARM(7,1) = $\mu - a$ and PPARM(7,4) not used

* The parameter values are specified in terms of means and variances. The parameters are more directly related to the parameters used in the functional form of the distributions.

Examples of the eight random deviate generators are shown below.

Statement	Deviate Form
Y = UNFRM(3.0,7.0,1)	Uniform distribution on the interval (3.0, 7.0) using stream 1
Y = TRIAG(1,2)	Triangular distribution with parameters from parameter set 1 using stream 2
Y = RNORM(2,3)	Normal distribution with parameters from parameter set 2 using stream 3
Y = RLOGN(3,3)	Lognormal distribution with parameters from parameter set 3 using stream 3
Y = ERLNG(4,2)	Erlang distribution with parameters from parameter set 4 using stream 2
Y = GAMA(5,1)	Gamma distribution with parameters from parameter set 5 using stream 1
Y = BETA(6,2)	Beta distribution with parameters from parameter set 6 using stream 2
N = NPSSN(7,5)	Poisson distribution with parameters from parameter set 7 using stream 5

The stream number is used to make different stochastic processes independent. Thus an arrival process could be generated using stream 1 and a service process using stream 2. In this manner, the order in which service events occur does not affect the arrival process.

USER WRITTEN SUBROUTINES

In addition to the main program, the user communicates with GASP IV through the subroutines described in Table 3-3.

The function of the main program, EVNTS, INTLC, and OTPUT were described in the GASP IV overview. Subroutine UERR allows the user the option of performing operations and printing specific information when a GASP IV error is detected. The programming for the main program and the above subroutines is normally straightforward. The examples presented in the last four chapters of this book clearly illustrate how to code these routines and demonstrate how the GASP IV subprograms are used within these routines. Attention is now focused on the procedures for writing subroutines STATE, SCOND, and SSAVE.

Table 3-3 Description of User Written Subroutines*

Name	Description
SUBROUTINE EVNTS(IX)	Called by subroutine GASP to process event IX. A computed GO TO statement with argument IX is used to transfer to the appropriate time-event processing subroutine; however if IX = IIEVT, a state-event is to be processed; determination of which state event when IX = IIEVT must be made by the user in EVNTS; normally, the vector LFLAG is used for this purpose where LFLAG(I) is set by the user in subroutine SCOND; the form of subroutine EVNTS is illustrated in Fig. 3-3
SUBROUTINE OTPUT	OTPUT provides a way for the user to obtain output in addition to the standard GASP IV summary report; OTPUT is called prior to subroutine SUMRY and can be used as an end-of-simulation event
SUBROUTINE UERR(KODE)	Called by subroutine ERROR to allow the user to print specific information if an error occurs
SUBROUTINE INTLC	Can be used to initialize state variables and non-GASP variables; called in subroutine DATIN after all GASP IV data cards have been read
SUBROUTINE STATE	Defines state variables through a listing of difference or derivative equations or both; called by subroutine DATIN (after INTLC is called) and then by subroutine GASP to compute current values of state variables; TTLAS is the time of the last accepted computation of state variables; TNOW is the time to which GASP IV is trying to advance when STATE is called; DTNOW is the increment involved in the current update
SUBROUTINE SCOND	Called by subroutine GASP to determine if a state-event has occurred; in SCOND, the user must make certain the value of the GASP IV variable ISEES is set to communicate if a state-event has been

* The user normally also writes a subroutine for each type of event included in a model.

Table 3-3 *(continued)*

Name	Description
	passed (ISEES < 0), if no state-event has been passed (ISEES = 0), or if no state-event has been passed but one does end the current step (ISEES > 0) When function KROSS is used, ISEES is automatically set; the user should indicate through the setting of a variable when a state-event occurs; the GASP IV vector LFLAG can be used for this purpose and the user can test LFLAG in the user written state-event routines; the LFLAG vector is not tested in GASP IV; after a return from EVNTS, subroutine GASP sets LFLAG(I) = 0 for I = 1,NFLAG
SUBROUTINE SSAVE	Called by subroutine GASP normally to record system status; the value of DTSAV specifies the frequency with which SSAVE is called as follows: DTSAV < 0 SSAVE called only at event times DTSAV = 0 SSAVE called at each accepted update point, that is, at the end of each time step (which includes all event times) DTSAV > 0 SSAVE called each DTSAV time units and at event times Through SSAVE the user collects the data desired for eventual printout

SUBROUTINE STATE: THE SUBPROGRAM FOR WRITING THE EQUATIONS DEFINING STATE VARIABLES

Subroutine STATE is written to compute the current value of each state variable or its derivative. GASP IV permits state variables to be defined by state equations or derivative equations in subroutine STATE. Subroutine STATE is frequently called, especially if there are active derivative equations, and, therefore, should contain only essential code. It is most efficient if the state variables are numbered sequentially.

There are several policies regarding the writing of state equations that must be followed. By definition, the largest subscript for a derivative equation is NNEQD. Therefore, equations defining the rate of change of state variables, that is, equations for DD(I), must satisfy the expression I $\leq$ NNEQD. Equations defining SS(I) must satisfy the expression NNEQD + 1 $\leq$ I $\leq$ NNEQT where NNEQT is the largest subscript I in the defining equations for SS(I). Thus if these are equations defining DD(M) and SS(N), then M $\leq$ NNEQD;M< N, and NNEQD + 1 $\leq$ N $\leq$ NNEQT. NNEQS = NNEQT − NNEQD is the largest possible number of equations written in terms of SS(I). NNEQD, NNEQS, or both can be zero. Since it is most efficient to have the DD(·) numbered sequentially, NNEQD is often referred to as the number of defining equations written for DD(·) variables. Similarly, NNEQS is often referred to as the number of defining equations written for SS(·)variables.

These equations specify the numbering procedure to be used for state variables. The order in which the equations are written in subroutine STATE is left to the user, that is, a statement defining SS(5) can precede one defining DD(3). Because GASP IV does not change the execution sequence of state equations, correct sequencing of state and derivative equations is the responsibility of the user. If the defining equations for DD(·) do not involve other DD(·) variables then any order is permitted and the integration procedure simultaneously solves for all DD(·) and corresponding SS(·) variables. Thus DD(1) = A ⋆ SS(1) + B ⋆ SS(2) and DD(2) = C ⋆ SS(1) + F ⋆ SS(2) can be written in either order and the values obtained for DD(1), DD(2), SS(1), and SS(2) would be the same.

If the defining equations for DD(·) do involve other DD(·) variables, ordering becomes important. For example, if DD(3) = f(DD(5)), the equation for DD(5) must precede the equation for DD(3) according to standard FORTRAN conventions. If there are simultaneous equations involving DD(·) variables, the user must develop an algorithm for solving the set of equations. This is also the case when a set of simultaneous state equations are written.

In subroutine STATE, the equations for DD(·) and SS(·) can be written in a variety of forms. The equations*

```
DD(M) = RATE
```

and

```
SS(M) = SSL(M) + DTNOW * RATE
```

* Equations that define both DD(M) and SS(M) at the same time instant are only permitted if M > NNEQD. In this case, DD(M) is *not* related to SS(M) by GASP IV and is processed as if it were an SS(·) variable.

are essentially equivalent (GASP IV sets DTNOW = TNOW − TTLAS). When an equation for DD(M) is written, values of SS(M) are obtained through the integration routine contained within subroutine GASP. Values of DDL(M) and SSL(M) are automatically maintained. The step size is automatically determined to meet specified accuracy requirements on the computation of SS(M) and tolerances on state-event occurrences. When the equation is written for SS(M), only SSL(M) is maintained by GASP IV. Accuracy requirements are not specified on SS(M) and the step size DTNOW for updating SS(M) is maintained at the maximum value specified by the user unless there is an intervening event. DTNOW is automatically reduced if there are intervening time-events, state-events, or a need to record a value of SS(M) for eventual communication (output).

The form of the equations for DD(·) and SS(·) is limited only by FORTRAN statement types. Thus the user has a great deal of flexibility in defining the state variables for the model. In fact, the user can make the description conditional on time or any model variable. For example, if a rate changes after TC time units have elapsed, it could be written as

```
IF(TNOW.LT.TC) DD(M) = RATE1
IF(TNOW.GE.TC) DD(M) = RATE2
```

State- or time-events could be used to trigger the change by resetting the rate values or by setting an indicator, possibly IND, equal to 1 at the time of the event. In the former case, DD(M) = RATE, where RATE is set equal to RATE1 or RATE2 in subroutine EVNTS or in an event routine. In the latter case, we could write the following in subroutine STATE:

```
DD(M) = RATE1
IF(IND.EQ.1) DD(M) = RATE2
```

Since the former case results in less code in subroutine STATE, it is the preferred method.

For documentation purposes, it is sometimes convenient to make use of EQUIVALENCE statements in subroutine STATE, so that the equations can be put in a more mnemonic form. An example of this using one state variable Y = SS(1), is shown in Fig. 3-8. The use of EQUIVALENCE statements is left to the discretion of the user.

Modeling Using Derivatives of State Variables

GASP IV uses a Runge-Kutta-England (RKE) algorithm (28,124) to integrate the equations of subroutine STATE written in terms of the DD(·)

Variables

C = Consumption
I = Investment
T = Taxes
G = Government Expenditure
Y = National Income
Z = National Income (lagged)

Model

$$I = 2 + 0.1Z$$
$$Y = 45.45 + 2.27(I + G)$$
$$T = 0.2Y$$
$$C = 20 + 0.7(Y - T)$$

GASP Subroutine STATE

```
REAL I
EQUIVALENCE (SS(1),Y),(SSL(1),Z)
I = 2.0 + 0.1 ★ Z
Y = 45.45 + 2.27 ★ (I + G)
T = 0.2 ★ Y
C = 20.0 + 0.7 ★ (Y – T)
```

Figure 3-8 A recursive model of the economy.

variables. The RKE algorithm is used to obtain a solution to a set of simultaneous first order ordinary differential equations of the form

$$y'_j(t) = f_j(y_1,y_2, \ldots, y_m,t), j = 1, 2, \ldots, m$$

where $$y'_j(t) = \frac{dy_j(t)}{dt}$$

In GASP IV, these equations would be expressed in the following form:

```
DD(J) = fJ(SS(1),SS(2), . . . , SS(M), TNOW), J = 1, 2, . . . M.
```

For example, if $$y'_1(t) = a_1y_1 + b_1y_2$$

and $$y'_2(t) = a_2y_1 + b_2y_2$$

the corresponding GASP IV coding would be

```
DD(1) = A1 ★ SS(1)+ B1 ★ SS(2)
```

and

```
DD(2) = A2 * SS(1) + B2 * SS(2).
```

Higher order differential equations can be modeled by putting the equations in canonical form. Thus if an nth order differential equation of the form

$$x^{(n)}(t) = f(x, x', x^{(2)}, \ldots, x^{(n-1)}, t)$$

is to be modeled in GASP IV, n variables, $x_j(t)$, $j = 1, 2, \ldots n$ must be defined as follows:

$$x_1(t) = x(t)$$
$$x_2(t) = x_1'(t)$$
$$x_3(t) = x_2'(t)$$

and

$$x_n(t) = x_{n-1}'(t).$$

By substitution, $x_j(t) = x^{(j-1)}(t)$ and $x_n'(t) = f(x_1, x_2, \ldots, x_{n-1}, x_n, t)$. With these equations, x_1 is the solution to the nth order differential equation.

As an example consider the second order equation

$$x^{(2)}(t) = Ax'(t) + Bx(t) + C.$$

Letting

$$x_1(t) = x(t)$$
$$x_2(t) = x'(t)$$
$$x_2'(t) = x^{(2)}(t)$$

results in the set of first order equations

$$x_1'(t) = x_2(t)$$

and

$$x_2'(t) = Ax_2(t) + Bx_1(t) + C.$$

In GASP IV symbolism, this would be coded as

```
DD(1) = SS(2)
DD(2) = A * SS(2) + B * SS(1) + C.
```

Modeling Using State Variables

Subroutine STATE can be used to model the state variables using any combination of DD($\cdot$) and SS($\cdot$) variables. The use of SS($\cdot$) to model difference equations is a straight translation of the difference equations, that is,

$$y_n = A \star y_{n-1} + B$$

is equivalent to the GASP statement

```
SS(1) = A ★ SSL(1) + B,
```

where SS(1) is used to represent the value of y at time n, that is, y_n, and SSL(1) is used to represent the value of y at time $n - 1$, that is, y_{n-1}. Generalization to allow A and B to be functions of time is also direct. Higher order difference equations can be modeled in a manner similar to that given for higher order differential equations. The translation of

$$y_n = A \star y_{n-1} + B \star y_{n-2} + C$$

is obtained by using two state equations,

```
SS(1) = SSL(2)
SS(2) = A ★ SSL(2) + B ★ SSL(1) + C.
```

State variables can also be used to model differential equations by using an Euler integration method (16,75). In this case the user must provide the integration method that consists of the appropriate equations for the SS(·) variables. Consider the differential equation

$$\frac{dy}{dt} + A \star y = B$$

or

$$y' = B - A \star y.$$

Suppose we know y at time point $n - 1$ and we call this value y°_{n-1}. Then

$$y'_{n-1} = B - A \star y^{\circ}_{n-1}.$$

If we assume y'_{n-1} is a good approximation of y' between $n - 1$ and n then

$$y_n = y^{\circ}_{n-1} + h \star y'_{n-1}$$

where h is the interval of time between points $n - 1$ and n.

Substituting yields

$$y_n = y^{\circ}_{n-1} + h \star (B - A \star y^{\circ}_{n-1})$$
$$y_n = y^{\circ}_{n-1} \star (1 - h \star A) + h \star B.$$

In terms of GASP IV variables this becomes

```
SS(1) = SSL(1) ★ (1. – DTNOW ★ A) + DTNOW ★ B
```

since DTNOW is the time interval between calculations of state variables. The GASP IV user can use more advanced Euler type integrators by coding such integrators in subroutine STATE.

If any sets of simultaneous equations involving the SS(·) variables are included in STATE, the user must provide the means for solving them.

Subroutine SCOND: The Subprogram for Defining and Detecting State-Events

State-events are normally defined in terms of state variables crossing a prescribed threshold or a prescribed variable with a tolerance specified for the allowed amount of over-crossing. Examples of state-event definitions are:

1. SS(1) crossed the value of 10.0 in the positive direction,
2. SS(2) crossed SS(1) in the negative direction,
3. SS(3) crossed C1 ⋆ SS(4) + C2 in either direction,
4. DD(2) crossed 5.0 in the negative direction.

When subroutine SCOND is called by subroutine GASP, tentative values for SS(I) at TNOW have been calculated. Since SSL(I) is the value of SS(I) at TTLAS, it is possible to determine if a crossing (or a state-event) occurred from TTLAS to TNOW. Function KROSS provides the user with the capability to do this.

When a return is made to subroutine GASP from SCOND, either the step size is reduced because a state-event was passed, or the values of SS(I) are acceptable and time can advance to TNOW. In the former case, the step size is reduced, a new and smaller value for TNOW is calculated, and new values for SS(I) are computed. In the latter case, when the step size is acceptable, two possibilities exist. If an event ends the step, subroutine EVNTS is called. If no event ends the step, another step is started. Either a time-event or a state-event can end a step. GASP IV compares the time at the end of a proposed step with the time of the next time-event (TTNEX). It automatically reduces the step size so that any time-event will occur only at the end of the step. When a time-event ends a step, subroutine GASP has set an indicator to record this information. However, when a state-event ends the step, subroutine GASP does not have this information. Subroutine SCOND is used to detect state-events and to transmit information concerning state-events to subroutine GASP. This is done through the variable ISEES (Indicator that State-Event Ends Step). ISEES is automatically set by function KROSS. If KROSS is not used to detect state-events the user has the responsibility for setting ISEES.

If a crossing beyond a prescribed tolerance occurred within TNOW − TTLAS, then KROSS sets the variable ISEES to a negative value, which causes subroutine GASP to reduce the step size, define a new value for TNOW, and recompute the state variables at the new value of TNOW. Recall that TTLAS is the time of the last accepted time advance and TNOW is the time to which GASP IV is trying to advance.

The use of function KROSS for detecting crossings is now illustrated (see Table 3-2 for a definition of KROSS arguments). For each of the four examples given at the beginning of this section, the following statements using the function KROSS can detect the prescribed crossings.

```
1.  LFLAG(1) = KROSS(1,0,0.0,10.0, + 1, TOL)
2.  LFLAG(2) = KROSS(2,1,1.0,0.0, − 1, TOL)
3.  LFLAG(3) = KROSS(3,4,C1,C2,0,TOL)
4.  LFLAG(4) = KROSS(− 2,0,0.0,5.0, − 1,TOL)
```

Function KROSS returns a value equal to −2, −1, 0, +1, or +2, depending on the direction of the crossing (− for negative, + for positive) and whether a crossing occurred (0 for none, 1 for crossing within tolerance, and 2 for crossings exceeding the tolerance). For statement (1), if $SS(1) < 10.0$ at TTLAS, at TNOW: $LFLAG(1) = 0$, if $SS(1) < 10.0$; $LFLAG(1) = 1$, if $10.0 \leq SS(1) \leq 10.0 + TOL$; and $LFLAG(1) = 2$, if $SS(1) > 10.0 + TOL$. Also for statement 1, if $SS(1) \geq 10.0$ at TTLAS, $LFLAG(1) = 0$ at TNOW.

If the crossing exceeded the tolerance, $ISEES < 0$, the step size is reduced. If a crossing within tolerance is detected, $ISEES > 0$, it is assumed that a state-event has occurred at the end of the step. Subroutine GASP calls subroutine EVNTS with event code IIEVT, the user defined code for all state-events. In subroutine EVNTS, the user should test the LFLAG vector to determine which state-events occurred. More than one state-event can occur at the same time instant, and sequential testing of the LFLAG(·) values should be performed. The state-events can then be processed either in subroutine EVNTS or in state-event subroutines written by the user.

Two aspects of KROSS warrant mention. First, KROSS can only detect an odd number of crossings in a given step interval. If a variable crosses and recrosses a threshold during a step, it will not be detected. By specifying a small value for the largest step size allowed (DTMAX), the chance of obtaining more than one crossing during a step is reduced. Also, if a state-event is defined for a combination of crossings, it is the user's responsibility to set the variable ISEES to its proper value, even though KROSS is called.

Subroutine EVNTS: The Subprogram for Decoding Events

Subroutine EVNTS is called by subroutine GASP whenever an event is detected. If the event is a time-event, the argument to subroutine EVNTS is the event code for the time-event. This event code can be used in a computed GO TO statement to transfer to the appropriate event. If EVNTS is called because a state-event occurred, the argument to subroutine EVNTS is the state-event code IIEVT established by the user as input data.

The determination of which state-event has occurred is normally accomplished by tests on the LFLAG(·) vector. The value of LFLAG(·) when a call is made to subroutine EVNTS will be either 0, specifying that the state-event has not occurred, or nonzero, specifying that the state-event has occurred. Subroutine SCOND, through the use of function KROSS, establishes a nonzero for at least one of the LFLAG(·) indicators when a state event occurs. The decoding of LFLAG(·) must be done by the user.

For example, if a rate is to be set equal to RATE1 when the value of the state variable 2 crosses the threshold 50 in the positive direction with a tolerance of 0.5, the following combination of statements would be used. First, in subroutine SCOND the following statement would be included: LFLAG(1) = KROSS(2,0.0,0.0,50.0,1,0.5). This statement sets LFLAG(1)=1 when SS(2) crosses the threshold 50, but is less than 50.5.

In subroutine EVNTS, the code required to specify what happens when this state-event occurs is written. In this case, the following statement would be used. If (LFLAG(1). GE. 1) RATE=RATE1. (This assumes a passed state-event should be processed as if the state-event occurred at the end of the step.) If more complex logic is required at the state-event time, a call to a specially designed state-event subroutine could be performed, that is, IF (LFLAG(1). GE. 1) CALL SEVT1, where SEVT1 is the state-event corresponding to LFLAG(1) having a value of 1. As previously discussed, multiple state events can occur at the same instant, and sequential testing of the LFLAG(·) vector is required in the coding for subroutine EVNTS.

Subroutine SSAVE: The Subprogram for Collecting Data on State Variables

Subroutine SSAVE provides a means to collect data on state variables and is called by GASP. The user can specify through input that subroutine SSAVE be called at uniformly spaced intervals, at the end of each step, or only at event times. This is accomplished by the proper setting of the variable DTSAV on input data card type 9. If DTSAV is negative, SSAVE will be called only at event times. If DTSAV is zero, SSAVE will be called at the end of each step. Event times are included when DTSAV = 0 since events occur only at the end of a step. If DTSAV is positive, SSAVE will be called each DTSAV time units and at each event time. When an event occurs, SSAVE is next called at the event time plus DTSAV.

As an example of the use of subroutine SSAVE, suppose that it is desired to obtain a plot of the variables X, Y, and Z as a function of time. The values of these variables are to be plotted every two time units and at each event time. To accomplish this, DTSAV would be set equal to 2 on input. The coding in SSAVE to obtain the plot information is shown below:

```
      SUBROUTINE SSAVE
C***** COMMON AND DIMENSION CARDS
      PLOT(1) = X
      PLOT(2) = Y
      PLOT(3)= Z
      CALL GPLOT(PLOT,TNOW,1)
      RETURN
      END
```

The array PLOT is defined by the user and is local to subroutine SSAVE. GPLOT is the GASP IV subroutine that contains the program for storing table and plot information. The value 1 as the third argument to GPLOT indicates that X, Y, and Z as a function of time are identified as plot 1. The information defining the plot scale, symbols, and plotting interval is specified through data input cards (specifically data card type 6). The resulting plot for the data collected in subroutine SSAVE is a standard part of the GASP IV summary report. However, the user can obtain the plot at any time by the following statement:

```
CALL GPLOT(PLOT, TNOW, - 1).
```

Whenever a plot is printed, the data for that plot are no longer maintained.

INPUT FORMATS

The formats and variable names for each GASP IV data card type are shown in Fig. 3-9. Definitions of the GASP IV variables for each card are then presented in Table 3-4. General information about each card is given below.

Card	1–5	6–10	11–15	16–20	21–25	26–30	31–35	36–40
1	NNAME			NNPRJ	MMON	NNDAY	NNYR	NNRNS
2	NNCLT	NNSTA	NNHIS	NNPRM	NNPLT	NNSTR	NNTRY	NNATR
3		I	LLABC(I)					
4		I	LLABT(I)		Initial Value			
5		I	LLABH(I)			NNCEL(I)	HHLOW(I)	
6		I	LLABP(11)			IITAP(I)	NNVAR(I)	LLPLT
		IJ	a* LLABP(IJ)		LLPLO(IJ)	LLPHI(IJ)	PPLO(IJ)	
7	KKRNK(1)	KKRNK(2)	KKRNK(3)	KKRNK(4)	KKRNK(5)	KKRNK(6)	KKRNK(7)	KKRNK(8)
8	IINN(1)	IINN(2)	IINN(3)	IINN(4)	IINN(5)	IINN(6)	IINN(7)	IINN(8)
9	IIEVT	LLERR	AAERR		RRERR		DTMIN	
10		J	PPARM(J,1)		PPARM(J,2)		PPARM(J,3)	
11	MSTOP	JJCLR	JJBEG	IICRD	TTBEG		TTFIN	
12		IFILE	ATRIB(1)		ATRIB(2)		ATRIB(3)	
0	LLSUP			IICRD				

*a—LLSYM(IJ).

Figure 3-9 GASP IV input data worksheet.

41–45	46–50	51–55	56–60	61–65	66–70	Format / Read if
LLSUP						(3A4,3X,5I5,15I1) IICRD.EQ.0.OR.IICRD.EQ.1
NNFIL	NNSET	NNEQD	NNEQS	NFLAG		**(15I5)** LLSUP(2).LE.1
						(5X,I5,2A4) **NNCLT.GT.0.AND.LLSUP(3).LE.1**
						(5X,I5,2A4,2X,E10.0) NNSTA.GT.0.AND.LLSUP(4).LE.1
HHWID(I)						**(5X,I5,2A4,7X,I5,2E10.0)** NNHIS.GT.0.AND.LLSUP(5).LE.1
DTPLT(I)						**(5X,I5,2A4,7X,3I5,E10.0)** NNPLT.GT.0.AND.LLSUP(6).LE.1
PPHI(IJ)						(5X,I5,A1,2A4,1X,2I5,2E10.0) **IJ.LE.NNVAR(I)**
KKRNK(9)	KKRNK(10)	KKRNK(11)	KKRNK(12)	KKRNK(13)	KKRNK(14)	**(14I5)** NNFIL.GT.0.AND.LLSUP(7).LE.1
IINN(9)	IINN(10)	IINN(11)	IINN(12)	IINN(13)	IINN(14)	**(14I5)** NNFIL.GT.0.AND.LLSUP(8).LE.1
DTMAX		DTSAV				(2I5,5E10.0) NNEQT.GT.0.AND.LLSUP(9).LE.1
PPARM(J,4)						**(5X,I5,4E10.0)** NNPRM.GT.0.AND.LLSUP(10).LE.1
JJFIL	IISED(1)	IISED(2)	IISED(3)	IISED(4)	IISED(5)	(4I5,2E10.0,I5,(6I5)) LLSUP(11).LE.1
ATRIB(4)		ATRIB(5)		ATRIB(6)		**(5X,I5,(6E10.0))** NNFIL.GT.0.AND.LLSUP(12).LE.1
						(15I1,I5) NNRNS.GT.1.AND.IICRD.EQ.0

Table 3-4 Definitions for GASP IV Variables Initialized by Data Inputs

Data Card Type	GASP IV Variable Initialized	Definition
1	NNAME	User's name
	NNPRJ	Project number
	MMON	Month number
	NNDAY	Day number
	NNYR	Year number
	NNRNS	Number of simulation runs to be made
	LLSUP(I),I = 1,12	Read and print suppression codes 0 → read and print card type I 1 → read card type I 2 → skip reading and printing of card type I
	LLSUP(13)	Print suppression key: 0 → print initial entries in files if any; 1 → skip printing
	LLSUP(14)	Print suppression key: 0 → print initial values of SS(·) and DD(·) if any; 1 → skip printing
	LLSUP(15)	Print suppression key: 0 → CALL SUMRY at end of simulation to obtain final report; 1 → skip printing of final report
2	NNCLT	Number of sets of statistics collected by COLCT
	NNSTA	Number of sets of statistics that can be collected by TIMST and TIMSA
	NNHIS	Number of histograms
	NNPRM	Number of parameter sets
	NNPLT	Number of plots or tables
	NNSTR	Number of random number streams
	NNTRY	Maximum allowable number of entries in NSET/QSET
	NNATR	Maximum number of attributes per entry in NSET/QSET
	NNFIL	Number of files in NSET/QSET

Card	Variable	Description
	NNSET	The dimension of NSET/QSET; available number of words for storing plot data is NNSET − NNTRY ★ (NNATR + 2)
	NNEQD	Number of derivative equations
	NNEQS	Number of equations defining state levels
	NFLAG	Number of state condition flags (LFLAG) employed
3	I	Index
	LLABC(I)	Label associated with Ith variable used in COLCT
4	I	Index
	LLABT(I)	Label associated with Ith variable used in TIMST or TIMSA
	SSTPV(I,6)	Initial value of time persistent variable I
5	I	Index
	LLABH(I)	Label associated with Ith histogram
	NNCEL(I)	Number of cells in Ith histogram
	HHLOW(I)	Upper limit of first cell of Ith histogram
	HHWID(I)	Width of a cell for Ith histogram
6A	I	Index
	LLABP(11)	Label associated with independent variable for Ith plot
	IITAP(I)	Index of the tape on which data for plot I are stored; if IITAP(I) = 0, data are stored in QSET
	NNVAR(I)	Number of variables to be plotted/tabled in plot/table I
	LLPLT	Key for specifying type of table/plot; values for LLPLT are: $< 0 \rightarrow$ quick plot; $0 \rightarrow$ plot only; $1 \rightarrow$ table only; $> 1 \rightarrow$ table and plot
	DTPLT(I)	The increment of the independent variable between successive plot points for plot I
6B	IJ	Index (there are NNVAR(I) cards of type 6B following a type 6A card with Index I)
	LLSYM(IJ)	Plot symbol for variable IJ for plot I

Table 3-4 Definitions for GASP IV Variables Initialized by Data Inputs *(continued)*

Data Card Type	GASP IV Variable Initialized	Definition
	LLABP(IJ)	Label associated with variable IJ of plot I
	LLPLO(IJ)	Key for specifying the lower limit of the scale for variable IJ of plot I; values for LLPLO(IJ) are: 0 → use minimum from simulation; 1 → use PPLO(IJ); 2 → use minimum from simulation rounded to nearest PPLO(IJ)
	LLPHI(IJ)	Key for specifying upper limit of the scale for variable IJ of plot I; keys are similar to LLPLO(IJ) above
	PPLO(IJ)	Value associated with lower limit of plot ordinate
	PPHI(IJ)	Value associated with upper limit of plot ordinate
7	KKRNK(I),I = 1,NNFIL	Ranking attribute for file I. (Secondary ranking attribute for file I.)
8	IINN(I),I = 1,NNFIL	Key for priority system to be used in file I; values for IINN(I) are: (1) low-value-first (LVF); (2) high-value-first (HVF); (3) first-in-first-out (FIFO); (4) last-in-first-out (LIFO). (Secondary ranking for file I.)
9	IIEVT	State-event code
	LLERR	Key to indicate severity of error when accuracy cannot be maintained by the Runge-Kutta integration package: −1 → proceed without warning message; 0 → proceed with warning message; +1 → fatal error Accuracy is required to be less than equal to AAERR + RRERR ★ SS(I) for all I
	AAERR	Absolute local truncation error allowed in Runge-Kutta integration
	RRERR	Relative error allowed in Runge-Kutta integration
	DTMIN	Minimum step size permitted
	DTMAX	Maximum step size permitted

	DTSAV	Time between communication points if positive; if DTSAV = 0, communication to occur at each accepted update point; if DTSAV < 0, communication only at event times
10	J	Parameter set number
	PPARM(J,K),K = 1,4	Parameter values; definitions depend on distribution type or user option
11	MSTOP	Key for specifying method of stopping: 0 → user to stop simulation by resetting MSTOP = − 1 1 → stop at TTFIN
	JJCLR	Key for specifying if statistic arrays should be cleared during initialization: 0 → do not clear 1 → clear
	JJBEG	Key for initializing DRAND, TNOW, state variables and initial conditions set in INTLC: 0 → do not initialize 1 → initialize
	IICRD	Key for specifying data card type at which reading should begin for the next run
	TTBEG	Initial value of TNOW
	TTFIN	Ending time of simulation if MSTOP > 0
	JJFIL	Key for initializing file system: 0 → do not initialize 1 → initialize
	IISED(I),I = 1,NNSTR	Initial random number seed for random number stream I
12	IFILE	File number for attributes; if negative, initialize file system; if 0, end of data card type 12
	ATRIB(I),I = 1,NNATR	Attributes for the entry to be filed
0	LLSUP(I),I = 1,15	Keys for suppressing reading and writing of data cards
	IICRD	Key for determining the data card type at which reading should begin for the next run

Data card type 1 contains heading, run identification, and data suppression information. If NNRNS is less than 1, the run terminates. On the right hand side of the input worksheet the use of LLSUP for suppressing the reading of input cards is indicated. As an example, consider data card type 3. If LLSUP(3) $>$ 1, data card type 3 will not be read. The worksheet specifies that both NNCLT $>$ 0 and LLSUP(3) $\leq$ 1 if data card type 3 is to be read. If either condition is not met, data card type 3 is not read. If NNCLT $>$ 0, then LLSUP(3) = 0 causes data card type 3 to be read and the data printed. No printing is performed if LLSUP(3) = 1.

Data card type 2 contains variables describing the size of the model being run. The variables defined are immediately used to control the number of subsequent data cards that will be read (see Table 3-4 for definitions).

Data card types 3, 4, 5, and 6 are similar in that each is associated with a specific form of data collection, computation, and reporting. On each card, the first five columns are skipped when reading a card. These columns are left for the user to identify the card type and are not read by GASP IV. Columns 6–10 are used to number the cards sequentially within each card type. The program expects the cards to be numbered sequentially. The sequence indicated by the value in columns 6–10 is used to compare to the expected number. If they do not agree, a warning is printed and reading continues. GASP IV accepts the value on the data card as the correct code number.

Data card types 3 and 4 contain labels that are used to identify the tabular output prepared by subroutine COLCT and subroutines TIMST and TIMSA. *There must be NNCLT data cards of type 3 and NNSTA data cards of type 4, even if no labels are desired.* If only code numbers are desired then the labels should be assigned the code values. The initial value of each time persistent variable must be initialized on data card type 4. The initial value is for statistics collection purposes only, and is used as the value during the first interval of time.

Data card type 5 contains a label, the number of cells, the upper limit for the first cell, and the cell width for each histogram. After reading and printing the values on the data cards, DATIN calculates the storage location of the last cell associated with each histogram. This index is then stored in NNCEL. (On input NNCEL equals the number of internal cells of the histogram.) *There must be NNHIS data cards of type 5.*

Data card type 6 provides information for plotting output through the use of subroutine GPLOT. For each plot two different types of data cards are required. The input is arranged in sets with the first card of a set defining the variables applicable to the plot or table. Succeeding data cards are associated with each of the variables to be plotted or tabled. Thus the type 6 data cards in a deck would consist of NNPLT cards of the first type, each followed by NNVAR(I) cards of the second type. If IITAP(I) = 0, only one plot is allowed and data for the plot will be saved in core storage in the array QSET. If IITAP(I) > 0 for any I, data for the plot will be saved on tape unit number IITAP(I). It is not permissible to use both core and tape storage for plots.

Data card types 7 and 8 are necessary only if the simulation requires files. Data card type 7 is used to define the ranking attribute for a file, KKRNK, and data card type 8 defines the priority rule for a file IINN. In GASP IV, KKRNK(1) and IINN(1) are defined as the attribute number and ranking rule for breaking ties in file 1.

Data card type 9 is associated with state variables. A negative value for the maximum step size DTMAX is not meaningful (backward integration is not allowed in GASP IV), so DTMAX is set equal to 0.1 if it is read in as a nonpositive number. Because a step can never be greater than DTSAV, DTMAX is equated to DTSAV if it is larger than a positive DTSAV. (The meaning of nonpositive values of DTSAV is described in the description of subroutine SSAVE.) Likewise, if DTMIN is not positive, it is set equal to 0.01 times DTMAX. If the sum of AAERR and RRERR is zero, they are each equated to 0.00001.

Data card type 10 is used if the number of parameters, NNPRM, is greater than zero. As with data card types 3, 4, and 5, the first two fields are designed for identification of card type and sequence. There must be NNPRM type 10 cards if their reading is not suppressed.

Data card type 11 contains basic run control variables. IICRD is the data card type for which data are to be read-in on the next run. Seed values for the random number generators are read as integers, but both real and integer seeds are made available. NNSTR defines the number of streams used in the simulation. The variables MSTOP, JJCLR, TTBEG, and TTFIN relate to the method of stopping the simulation, the clearing of statistics, the beginning time for the simulation, and the ending time for the simulation. JJFIL can be used to initialize the filing array NSET and statistics on the filing array.

The reading of data card type 12 is initiated if the number of files, NNFIL, is greater than zero and LLSUP (12) $\leq$ 1. The file storage area can be initialized by reading a data card type 12 with IFILE < 0. This is an alternate method to setting JJFIL = 1 on data card type 11. The number of type 12 data cards to be read is limited only by the storage available. Each type 12 card contains an entry that is filed into file IFILE. If there are more than six attributes per entry, additional cards are required (see format). The last data card of type 12 is indicated by IFILE = 0.

Data card type 0 is read only if the number of runs, NNRUN is greater than one and IICRD = 0. It may be used to set the values of LLSUP(·) and IICRD for the succeeding run. It is designated a type 0 card because its effect is upon the succeeding run, prior to the reading of data card type 1.

An example showing a completed input data worksheet is presented in Fig. 3-10. Most of the data initializes GASP IV variables. Data card type 6 specifies that values for plot 1 are to be stored in core (IITAP(1) = 0). Storing plot data in core rather than on tape can result in significant computer time reduction. Space in NSET was allocated for this purpose on data card type 2 through the setting of the variable NNSET. NNSET is specified as 20,000 (in the main program, NSET would be dimensioned to 20,000) but a maximum of 30 entries in NSET were prescribed (NNTRY = 30) with five attributes per entry (NNATR = 5). Therefore, only 30 ★ 7 = 210 cells of NSET will be allocated to the filing structure. (Recall that 2 cells are used for pointers.) The remaining 19,790 cells will be used to store data for the plot requested. For data card type 12, the cards with IFILE = 1 cause events to be put into file 1. The card with IFILE = 0 indicates that there are no more initial entries for the files.

GASP IV STORAGE REQUIREMENTS AND LIMITATIONS

Named (labeled) COMMON is used for all GASP IV variables except for the file storage array NSET. Named COMMON is to be used for all non-GASP variables defined by the user. Blank COMMON is reserved for the array NSET. *The GASP IV user must not use blank COMMON except for NSET.*

The COMMON, DIMENSION, and EQUIVALENCE cards for GASP IV are:

```
 DIMENSION NSET(1)
 COMMON QSET(1)
 COMMON /GCOM1/ ATRIB(25),JEVNT,MFA,MFE(100),MLE(100),MSTOP,NCRDR,NGCOM1   1
1NAPO,NNAPT,NNATR,NNFIL,NNQ(100),NNTRY,NPRNT,PPARM(50,4),TNOW,TTBEGGCOM1   2
2,TTCLR,TTFIN,TTRIB(25),TTSET                                      GCOM1   3
 COMMON /GCOM2/ DD(100),DDL(100),DTFUL,DTNOW,ISEES,LFLAG(50),NFLAG,GCOM2   1
1NNEQD,NNEQS,NNEQT,SS(100),SSL(100),TTNEX                          GCOM2   2
 COMMON /GCOM3/ AAERR,DTMAX,DTMIN,DTSAV,IITES,LLERR,LLSAV,LLSEV,RREGCOM3   1
1PR,TTLAS,TTSAV                                                    GCOM3   2
 COMMON /GCOM4/ DTPLT(10),HHLOW(25),HHWID(25),IICRD,IITAP(10),JJCELGCOM4   1
1(500),LLABC(25,2),LLABH(25,2),LLABP(11,2),LLABT(25,2),LLPHI(10),LLGCOM4   2
2PLO(10),LLPLT,LLSUP(15),LLSYM(10),MMPTS,NNCEL(25),NNCLT,NNHIS,NNPLGCOM4   3
3T,NNPTS(10),NNSTA,NNVAR(10),PPHI(10),PPLO(10)                     GCOM4   4
 COMMON /GCOM5/ IIEVT,IISED(6),JJBEG,JJCLR,MMNIT,MMON,NNAME(3),NNCFGCOM5   1
1I,NNDAY,NNPT,NNSET,NNPRJ,NNPRM,NNRNS,NNRUN,NNSTR,NNYR,SSEED(6)    GCOM5   2
 COMMON /GCOM6/ EENQ(100),IINN(100),KKRNK(100),MMAXQ(100),QQTIM(100GCOM6   1
1),SSOBV(25,5),SSTPV(25,6),VVNQ(100)                               GCOM6   2
 EQUIVALENCE(NSET(1),QSET(1))
```

The organization of the named COMMON blocks was designed to minimize the number of COMMON blocks required in the user subprograms. A gross description of the variables for each common block is given below:

GCOM1 Variables associated with discrete simulations.
GCOM2 Variables associated with continuous simulations.
GCOM3 Variables associated with a step time advance procedure.
GCOM4 Variables associated with data collection and reporting.
GCOM5 Variables associated with run conditions and description.
GCOM6 Variables associated with filing system and statistical storage arrays.

All variables in GCOM3 through GCOM6 either have the same first two letters or begin with the letters DT. The 14 exceptions to this rule involve NSET and QSET and 12 variables included in GCOM1 and GCOM2.

The array sizes selected are those that have been found to satisfy most GASP IV users without requiring an excessive amount of core storage. With the above array sizes, the GASP IV subroutine package requires about 50K words octal (20K words decimal) on the CDC 6500 computer.

The limitations imposed by array size and the variables causing the limitation are presented below. A DATA statement is included in subroutine DATIN, which specifies the largest value for each limitation. A check is made in subroutine DATIN to ensure that these array sizes are not exceeded.

Number of state variables $\leq$ 100; (DD, DDL, SS, SSL).
Number of histograms $\leq$ 25; (LLABH, HHLOW, HHWID, NNCEL).
Total number of cells for all histograms $\leq$ 500; (JJCEL).
Number of variables for which statistics are collected $\leq$ 25; (LLABC, SSOBV).
Number of variables for which statistics are collected over time $\leq$ 25; (LLABT, SSTPV).
Number of attributes describing an event $\leq$ 25; (ATRIB, TTRIB).
Number of files $\leq$ 100; (EENQ, QQTIM, VVNQ, IINN, KKRNK, MMAXQ, MFE, MLE, NNQ).
Number of parameter sets $\leq$ 50; (PPARM).
Number of plots $\leq$ 10; (DTPLT, IITAP, NNPTS).
Number of variables per plot $\leq$ 10; (PPHI, PPLO, LLABP, LLPHI, LLPLO, LLSYM, NNVAR).
Number of random number streams $\leq$ 6; (IISED, SSEED, local Variable L in DRAND).

Card	5	10	15	20	25	30	35	40
1	NNAME			NNPRJ	MMON	NNDAY	NNYR	NNRNS
	PRITSKER			8	6	30	1973	1
2	NNCLT	NNSTA	NNHIS	NNPRM	NNPLT	NNSTR	NNTRY	NNATR
	2	4	2	2	1	5	30	5

Card		I	LLABC(I)	
3		I	LLABC(I)	
	3	1	WAIT TIM	
	3	2	TRIP TIM	
				No blank card

Card		I	LLABT(I)		Initial Value
4		I	LLABT(I)		Initial Value
	4	1	UNL UTIL		0.0
	4	2	LDR UTIL		0.0
	4	3	REFIN UP		1.0

Card		I	LLABH(I)		NNCEL(I)	HHLOW(I)
5		I	LLABH(I)		NNCEL(I)	HHLOW(I)
	5	1	WAIT TIM		10	0.0
	5	2	TRIP TIM		10	6.0

Card		I	LLABP(11)		IITAP(I)	NNVAR(I)	LLPLT
6		I	LLABP(11)		IITAP(I)	NNVAR(I)	LLPLT
	6A	1	TIME		0	2	0

Card		IJ	a*	LLABP(IJ)	LLPLO(IJ)	LLPHI(IJ)	PPLO(IJ)
		IJ	a*	LLABP(IJ)	LLPLO(IJ)	LLPHI(IJ)	PPLO(IJ)
	6B	1	T	TANKER	1	1	0.0
	6B	2	S	STORAGE	1	1	0.0

Card								
7	KKRNK(1)	KKRNK(2)	KKRNK(3)	KKRNK(4)	KKRNK(5)	KKRNK(6)	KKRNK(7)	KKRNK(8)
	1	1	3					
8	IINN(1)	IINN(2)	IINN(3)	IINN(4)	IINN(5)	IINN(6)	IINN(7)	IINN(8)
	1	1	3					

Card					
9	IIEVT	LLERR	AAERR	RRERR	DTMIN
	4	0	0.00001	0.00001	0.25
10		J	PPARM(J,1)	PPARM(J,2)	PPARM(J,3)
	10	1	5.0	3.5	8.0
	10	2	4.0	3.0	7.0

Card						
11	MSTOP	JJCLR	JJBEG	IICRD	TTBEG	TTFIN
	1	1	1	0	0.0	365.0

Card					
12		IFILE	ATRIB(1)	ATRIB(2)	ATRIB(3)
	12	1	0.0	1.0	
	12	1	0.16666	5.0	
	12	0			

Card			
0	LLSUP	IICRD	
			No blank card

*a—LLSYM(IJ).

Figure 3-10 Sample data worksheet.

45	50	55	60	65	70	Format / Read if
	LLSUP					(3A4,3X,5I5,15I1) IICRD.EQ.0.OR.IICRD.EQ.1
NNFIL	NNSET	NNEQD	NNEQS	NFLAG		(15I5) LLSUP(2).LE.1
3	20000	0	2	5		
						(5X,I5,2A4) NNCLT.GT.0.AND.LLSUP(3).LE.1
		No blank card				
						(5X,I5,2A4,2X,E10.0) NNSTA.GT.0.AND.LLSUP(4).LE.1
HHWID(I)						(5X,I5,2A4,7X,I5,2E10.0) NNHIS.GT.0.AND.LLSUP(5).LE.1
	0.25					
	2.00					
			No blank card			
DTPLT(I)						(5X,I5,2A4,7X,3I5,E10.0) NNPLT.GT.0.AND.LLSUP(6).LE.1
	0.25					
PPHI(IJ)						(5X,I5,A1,2A4,1X,2I5,2E10.0) IJ.LE.NNVAR(I)
	300.0					
	2000.0					
			No blank card			
KKRNK(9)	KKRNK(10)	KKRNK(11)	KKRNK(12)	KKRNK(13)	KKRNK(14)	(14I5) NNFIL.GT.0.AND.LLSUP(7).LE.1
IINN(9)	IINN(10)	IINN(11)	IINN(12)	IINN(13)	IINN(14)	(14I5) NNFIL.GT.0.AND.LLSUP(8).LE.1
DTMAX		DTSAV				(2I5,5E10.0) NNEQT.GT.0.AND.LLSUP(9).LE.1
	0.25		0.25			
PPARM(J,4)						(5X,I5,4E10.0) NNPRM.GT.0.AND.LLSUP(10).LE.1
	1.5					
	1.0					
				No blank card		
JJFIL	IISED(II)	IISED(2)	IISED(3)	IISED(4)	IISED(5)	(4I5,2E10.0,I5,(6I5)) LLSUP(11).LE.1
1	65397	43183	19249	45212	15893	
ATRIB(4)		ATRIB(5)		ATRIB(6)		(5X,I5,(6E10.0)) NNFIL.GT.0.AND.LLSUP(12).LE.1
						(15I1,I5) NNRNS.GT.1.AND.IICRD.EQ.0

Number of state conditions ≤ 50; (LFLAG).
Number of entries per file limited only by available core storage.

THE NEXT STEP

Chapter 3 presented the procedures required to prepare a GASP IV simulation program. Chapter 4 presents detailed information on the GASP IV subprograms. Examples illustrating the use of GASP IV begin in Chapter 5. Chapter 3 should provide sufficient background for the reader to go directly to Chapter 5, and this is recommended. However, one of the beauties of GASP IV is the flexibility provided the user because he is able to understand, manipulate, and extend the GASP IV package. Therefore, it is strongly recommended that if Chapter 4 is by-passed, it should be returned to after application experience is obtained.

EXERCISES

3-1. Events in a simulation are known to occur at times 7, 9, and 13. A fixed step size of 3 has been specified to evaluate continuous variables. A communications interval of 4 is also desired. The simulation is to begin at time 0 and to end at time 20. What values have been given to the following variables: TTBEG, TTFIN, DTMIN, DTMAX, and DTSAV? List the points in time at which the state variables will be evaluated by the above conditions.

3-2. A simulation program requires the use of three files. There are two events in the simulation: an arrival event that has been designated by the event code 1 and an end-of-service event that has been designated with an event code 2. If an arrival and an end-of-service occur at the same time, it is desired to process the arrival event first. Four attributes are to be maintained for each entry in each file. At most, there will be six entries in files 1, 2, and 3 at the same time. File 2 is to be ranked on attribute 3 with high values first. File 3 is a first-in, first-out file. Define all the GASP IV variables that can be set by the information provided above.

3-3. For the conditions specified in Exercise 3-2, prepare snapshots of the filing array NSET for the following operations. Specify the values of the variables associated with NSET, as was done in Fig. 3-5.

(*a*) Initialize NSET.
(*b*) File the buffer storage vector.
(*c*) Remove the first entry from file 1.
(*d*) Insert an entry with attribute values (2.0,3.0,4.0,5.0) into file 2.
(*e*) Insert an entry into file 2 with the attribute values (3.0,4.0,5.0,6.0)

(*f*) Insert an entry into file 1 with attribute values (1.0,1.0,1.0,1.0).
(*g*) Insert an entry into file 1 with attribute values (1.0,2.0,3.0,4.0).
(*h*) Insert an entry into file 1 with attribute values (2.0,4.0,4.0,4.0).
(*i*) Remove from file 1 the entry whose second attribute equals 2.
(*j*) Remove the last entry from file 2.
(*k*) Remove the first entry from file 2.
(*l*) Insert an entry into file 1 with attribute values (1.5,1.0,0.0,0.0).

3-5. Write the GASP IV statement corresponding to each operation listed in Exercise 3-3.

3-6. Write the statements necessary to obtain the attribute values associated with the second event in the event file. Specify the values of the variables that would be obtained from your statement if NSET contains the entries shown on the last line in Fig. 3-5.

3-7. Write the statements required to determine the location of the entry that satisfies the following conditions:
(*a*) The entry in file 2 that has attribute 3 equal to 10.
(*b*) The entry with the largest value of attribute 4 greater than 0 in file 1. What subroutine should be used to remove this entry from file 1?
(*c*) The entry whose third attribute is closest to 10 but does not exceed 10 in file 3.
(*d*) In file 3, the entry whose third attribute is closest to 10 but is not less than 10.
(*e*) The entry in file 4 whose second attribute is the largest. Entries with the value of attribute 2 less than 3 cannot be used.

3-8. Specify whether you would use subroutine COLCT, TIMST, or TIMSA to collect statistics on each of the following variables. Give an explanation for your decision.
(*a*) The age of individuals going to a barber shop.
(*b*) The time it takes a secretary to type a letter.
(*c*) The amount of time devoted by employees to breaks.
(*d*) The amount of water in a reservoir.
(*e*) The price of a stock during a given day.
(*f*) The price of a stock over the last 100 days.
(*g*) The dollars in your bank account.

3-9. Given that a histogram has 10 cells, the lower limit is specified as 5, and the width of each cell is specified as 1, determine the cell number into which each of the following values would be inserted: 7.2, 9.1, 5.0, 4.1, 22.7, and 3.3.

3-10. Write a program to compute 400 samples from a normal distribution with a mean of 50, a standard deviation of 10, a minimum value of 0, and a maximum value of 100. In this program, compute the average and standard deviation of the samples, the minimum and maximum value obtained from the samples, and a histogram of the sample values between 30 and 70 with a cell width equal to 4. Obtain a plot of the sample values versus the sample number.

3-11. Write a GASP IV statement to generate a sample from the following regression equation:

$$T = a_0 + a_1x_1 + a_2x_1{}^2 + \mu$$

when μ is normally distributed and has parameters stored in the third row of the array PPARM.

3-12. The items that a company sells are stored as the entries of file 4. Attribute 1 for this file gives the price of the item and attribute 4 gives the quantity sold. Write the GASP IV statement necessary to obtain the total sales for the company.

3-13. The components of a system are stored as entries in file 3; attribute 4 of each entry is the reliability of the component. Assuming that the system reliability is the product of the component reliabilities, write a GASP IV statement to determine the reliability of the system.

3-14. In a user written subprogram, the following variables are required: TNOW, ATRIB(·), and SS(·). Also used in the subprogram are the following user defined variables, which are in COMMON: TOTAL, BOILER, DEVIL. Assuming these three variables are the only variables in the user's COMMON, write out the DIMENSION and COMMON statements for the subprogram.

3-15. The equation for the current i in a series electrical system is shown below.

$$L\frac{d^2i}{dt^2} + R\frac{di}{dt} + \frac{i}{c} = \omega E \sin \omega t.$$

Develop the equations for simulating the current i in GASP IV form. When the current exceeds the value A, a fuse is blown. Develop the statements that would have to be put in subroutine SCOND to detect the time at which the fuse would be blown. Assume that the tolerance on the current is 0.1 ★ A. Write the statements for subroutine SCOND, first using function KROSS and then without using function KROSS. In the latter case, the variable ISEES must be set directly.

3-16. Develop an Euler integration procedure for solving the differential equation presented in Exercise 3-15.

3-17. The amount of wheat stored in the United States is equal to the amount stored from the previous year, plus the amount harvested, minus the amount sold. A similar equation can be written for the amount of soy beans in storage. If the amount of wheat exceeds W bushels, there is a probability P_W that the government will sell 50% of the wheat to China. If the amount of soy beans exceeds B, there is a probability P_B that the government will sell three-fourths of the soy beans to Japan. Write the statements that would be included in subroutines STATE, SCOND, and EVNTS which would simulate the above conditions.

3-18. Prepare a data worksheet for the input to the simulation program for which there are 2 files with a maximum number of 25 entries in the file and a maximum of 4 attributes for any entry. File 2 is a high-value-first file with priority based on attribute 4. Statistics on 5 variables are to be collected in subroutine COLCT and the labels for these variables are HT, WT, TOL, SIZE, and GRADE. Statistics on 2 variables are to be collected in subroutine TIMST; these are BAL and POL with initial values of 2,000 and .2E − 5, respectively. Statistics on 1 variable are to be collected using subroutine TIMSA, which has the label LEVEL and initial value of 0. There will be 1 histogram collected on the variable GRADE, and it is desired to have 15 cells in the histogram, not including the end cells. The lower limit for the histogram is 10 and a cell width of 5 is desired. There are no parameter values associated with this program. There are three equations written in terms of the DD(·) variables and two written in terms of the SS(·) variables. Four values of LFLAG(·) are used to define state conditions. The state event code is 1. If accuracy cannot be met or tolerance on the state-event conditions cannot be satisfied, a warning is to be printed but the simulation is to be continued. The absolute error and relative error for accuracy computation are specified as 1.E − 4 and 1.E − 5, respectively. The minimum step size allowed is .001 and the maximum step size permitted is 1.0. The values of the state variables are to be recorded at the end of each step and at event times. One plot is to be obtained using core storage and 5000 words of core are to be allocated for the file. The independent variable of the plot will be TIME and there will be 3 dependent variables for the plot. Plot points should be obtained every 2 time units and both a table and a plot are desired. The minimum and maximum values obtained from the simulation are to be rounded to the nearest integer and used for scaling. The symbols X, Y, and Z are to be plotted and the labels for these variables are XPOS, YPOS, and ZPOS, respectively.

The beginning time for the simulation is 10 and the simulation will be completed by an end-of-simulation event. Statistical storage areas are to be cleared. Only one random number stream is to be used and the initial random number seed is 56747. The filing array is to be initialized and an event of type 2 is to occur at time 11. An end-of-simulation event with event code 3 is to occur at time 225. An entry with ATRIB(1) = 3 and ATRIB(2) = 5 is to be stored in file 2. Events occurring between time 50 and 100 are to be monitored. Summary reports are desired, starting at time 100 and for every 25 time units thereafter, until the end of the simulation. Only one simulation run is to be made.

3-19. Specify the values for the LLSUP(·) vector that suppress the printing of the filing array and summary report. Specify the values of LLSUP(·) in order that the ranking attribute for a file can be changed on a second run and only new initial entries in the file are to be included in the data for the second run.

Chapter Four

GASP IV

Subprograms*

The GASP IV subprograms are FORTRAN coded subprograms organized to assist the user in the preparation of simulation models. As discussed in Chapters 1 and 2, these GASP IV subprograms provide a world view that emphasizes the commonality among simulation problems and allows full flexibility for handling the peculiarities of individual problems.

To fully document the GASP IV language, the FORTRAN listing for each subprogram is presented and described individually. The description outlines its basic function and its salient features. Prior to the presentation of the subprograms, a few sections on coding practices are given.

GASP IV COMMON

GASP IV uses both named and blank COMMON storage. Variables are stored in COMMON for one of two reasons: (1) to make their values accessible to other subprograms or (2) to prevent their undefinition upon execution of a RETURN in the subprogram in which they are defined. (ANSI FORTRAN(3) permits a local variable in a subprogram

* This chapter presents a detailed discussion of each GASP IV subprogram and may be bypassed on first reading by the reader interested mainly in applications.

to become undefined upon execution of the RETURN statement in the subprogram.)

Blank COMMON is only used for the array, NSET. *The GASP IV user must not use blank COMMON for non-GASP variables.*

NSET is placed in blank COMMON storage so that it can be dimensioned to the required size in the main program and nominally dimensioned to one in all the GASP IV subprograms. This takes advantage of the fact that the size of blank COMMON in the various subprograms comprising an executable program need not be the same. Thus precompiled GASP IV subprograms with NSET dimensioned at one can be maintained on the computing system, and the dimension of NSET can be set in the user's main program.

Named COMMON is used for all GASP IV variables other than NSET, which require COMMON storage. The composition of the GASP IV named COMMON blocks has evolved during coding of the example problems for which GASP IV has been used. The basic objective of the selected organization is to provide convenience of use in both the GASP IV subprograms and the user subprograms. The final design consists of six blocks labeled (named) GCOM1 through GCOM6. Normally only GCOM1 or GCOM2, or both, need be included in a user subprogram. Dimensioning of arrays in GASP IV is based on those dimensions that were found to be convenient when using GASP II.

MACHINE INDEPENDENCE

One of the primary advantages of GASP II is its degree of machine independence. Great care has been taken to ensure that GASP IV is also machine independent. ANSI Coding (2,3) has been used for all GASP IV subprograms except the system specific function DRAND.

Three specific tests have been made to confirm that GASP IV does comply with the provisions of ANSI FORTRAN. GASP IV has been compiled under the ANSI option of the Minnesota FORTRAN Compiler, the Control Data FORTRAN Extended compiler, and CLEAN. No nonstandard coding was detected.

Additional coding restrictions were self-imposed during the coding of GASP IV to make it easier to learn, to implement on a wide range of systems, and to modify and extend. These additional coding restrictions are:

1. A maximum of five continuation cards are used.
2. A maximum of five characters are used in a variable name.

3. The symbol $ is not used.
4. No complex or double precision variables or constants are used.
5. No EXTERNAL statements are used.
6. Only one and two dimensional arrays and subscripts are used.
7. No ASSIGN or assigned GO TO statements are used.
8. No PAUSE statements are used.
9. Only F, E, I, A, H, and X field descriptors are used. The largest A field used is A4. No scale factors are used.
10. All DIMENSION statements precede all COMMON statements, which precede all EQUIVALENCE statements, which precede all DATA statements, which precede all executable statements.
11. No type statements are used. All GASP IV variables retain their implicit type.
12. No adjustable dimensions are used.
13. No GASP IV subprogram names are the same as commonly used function names.
14. Only one variable per word is used, that is, no packing of words is performed.

The GASP IV user is in no way restricted in his coding by the above. *He can employ any coding practice acceptable to the FORTRAN compiler available to him in the writing of his subprograms.*

Compilation and execution experience has been accumulated for many example models using seven different compilers on three operating systems.

The vast majority of experience has been on the Purdue University Computing Center CDC 6500 MACE operating system using the RUN compiler. The GASP IV program has been compiled, and at least one combined example successfully executed on the FUN, RUM, FTN, and MNF compilers on the same system. The program has been compiled on the University of Illinois IBM 360/75 under OS/MVT (20.6) using FORTRAN IVG. The program has also been compiled and executed on the Purdue University Administrative Data Processing Center IBM 370/155 under OS/MVT (20.7) using FORTRAN IVG.

FUNCTIONAL BREAKDOWN OF GASP IV

The functional breakdown of the GASP IV subprograms is shown in Table 4-1. In addition to listing the general functions included in simulation programs, Table 4-1 categorizes each subprogram according to whether it is GASP IV provided or user written. Each of the subprograms is now described.

Table 4-1. Functional Breakdown of GASP IV and User Subprograms

Function	Subprograms Supporting Function	
	Provided by GASP IV	Provided by the User
Time advance and status update	Subroutine GASP	Subroutine STATE Subroutine SCOND Subroutine EVNTS Event subroutines
Initialization	Subroutine DATIN Subroutine CLEAR Subroutine SET	Main program Subroutine INTLC Input data
Data storage and retrieval	Subroutine FILEM Subroutine RMOVE Subroutine CANCL Subroutine COPY	
Location of conditions and entries	Function KROSS Function NFIND	
Data collection, computation, and reporting	Subroutine COLCT Subroutine TIMST Subroutine TIMSA Subroutine HISTO Subroutine GPLOT Subroutine PRNTQ Subroutine PRNTS Subroutine SUMRY	Subroutine SSAVE Subroutine OTPUT
Program monitoring and error reporting	Subroutine MONTR Subroutine ERROR	Subroutine UERR
Random deviate generation	Function DRAND Function UNFRM Function TRIAG Function RNORM Function RLOGN Function ERLNG Function GAMA Function BETA Function NPSSN Function GAM	
Miscellaneous support	Function SUMQ Function PRODQ Function GTABL Subroutine GDLAY	

Time Advance and Status Update

The GASP IV function of status advance includes the sequencing of time-events, identification of state-events, and state variable integration if needed. It is the heart of the executive process.

Subroutine GASP. As discussed in Chapter 3, subroutine GASP is the GASP IV executive routine. It selects the appropriate mode of control and calls the necessary subroutines to process a simulation from initialization of the first run through output of the final run. Subroutine GASP is called only by the user written main program, and control is not returned to the main program until the requested number of runs has been completed.

Since subroutine GASP has a large number of statements, it is difficult to grasp the sequence in which operations are performed. Figure 3-4 provided a descriptive flow chart of subroutine GASP. In this section a statement-by-statement analysis of subroutine GASP is provided. To facilitate the presentation, a detailed flow chart of subroutine GASP is given in Fig. 4-1. The discussion of the subroutine, however, will reference the FORTRAN listing directly. Before reading the following paragraphs, it is suggested that the flow chart be analyzed to gain a familiarity with the GASP IV variables. This will assist in understanding the statement-by-statement description of the subroutine. Although a detailed description of the flow chart is not presented here, it is anticipated that the flow chart will be extremely useful to the user in answering questions related to processing technique or executive control sequencing.

Figure 4-2 gives the FORTRAN listing of subroutine GASP. The significant features of subroutine GASP are described in the order of their appearance in the FORTRAN listing. Abbreviations of sequence numbers or statement numbers are given in parentheses to indicate the approximate location of the code being described. For example, (G-3) is the abbreviation for sequence number GSP 3, and (S-101) is the abbreviation for statement number 101. Both refer to the statement: 101 CALL DATIN. When either reference can be used, the statement number is referenced.

First, IICRD is set equal to zero (G-2), causing DATIN to perform complete initialization. Next, DATIN is called, and a successful return from DATIN is indicated by writing "INTERMEDIATE RESULTS" on the output file. The allowed deviation (RESLS) from the fixed interval between save times (TTSAV) is then set equal to 1% of the interval between save times (DTSAV). (A save time is the time at which sub-

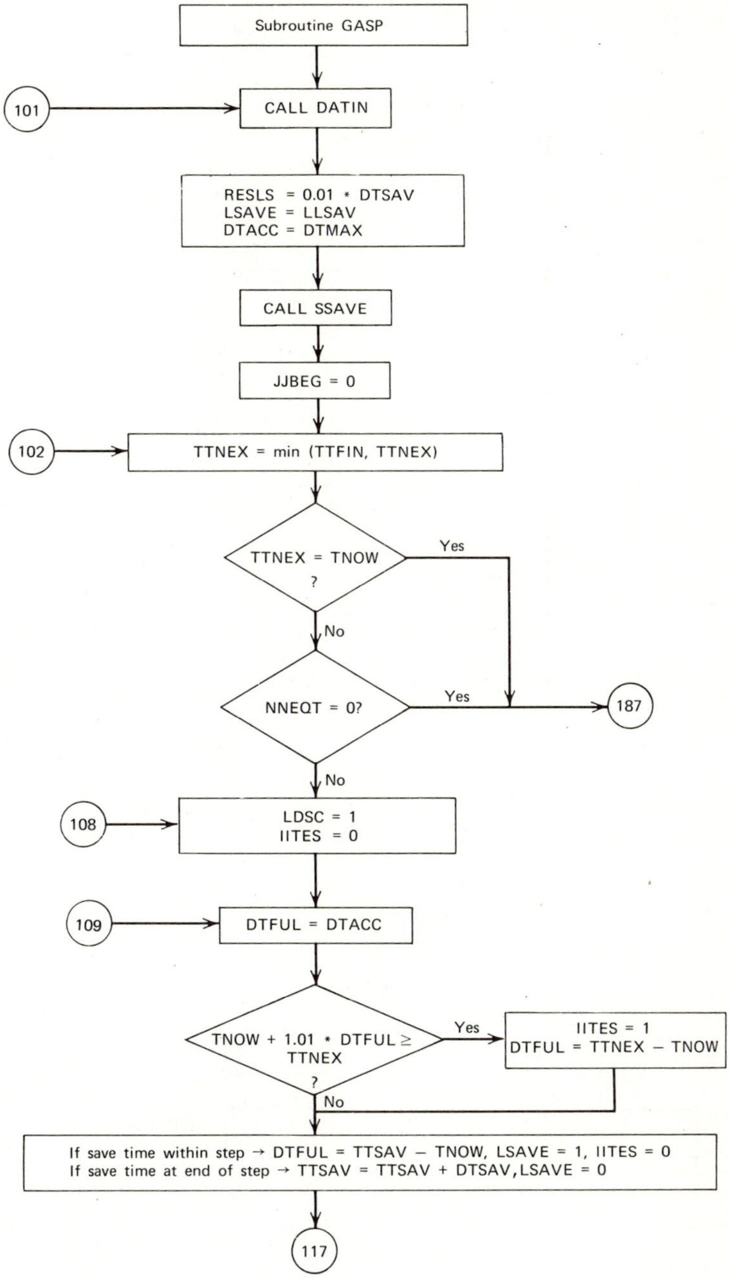

(a)

Figure 4-1*a* Flow chart of subroutine GASP.

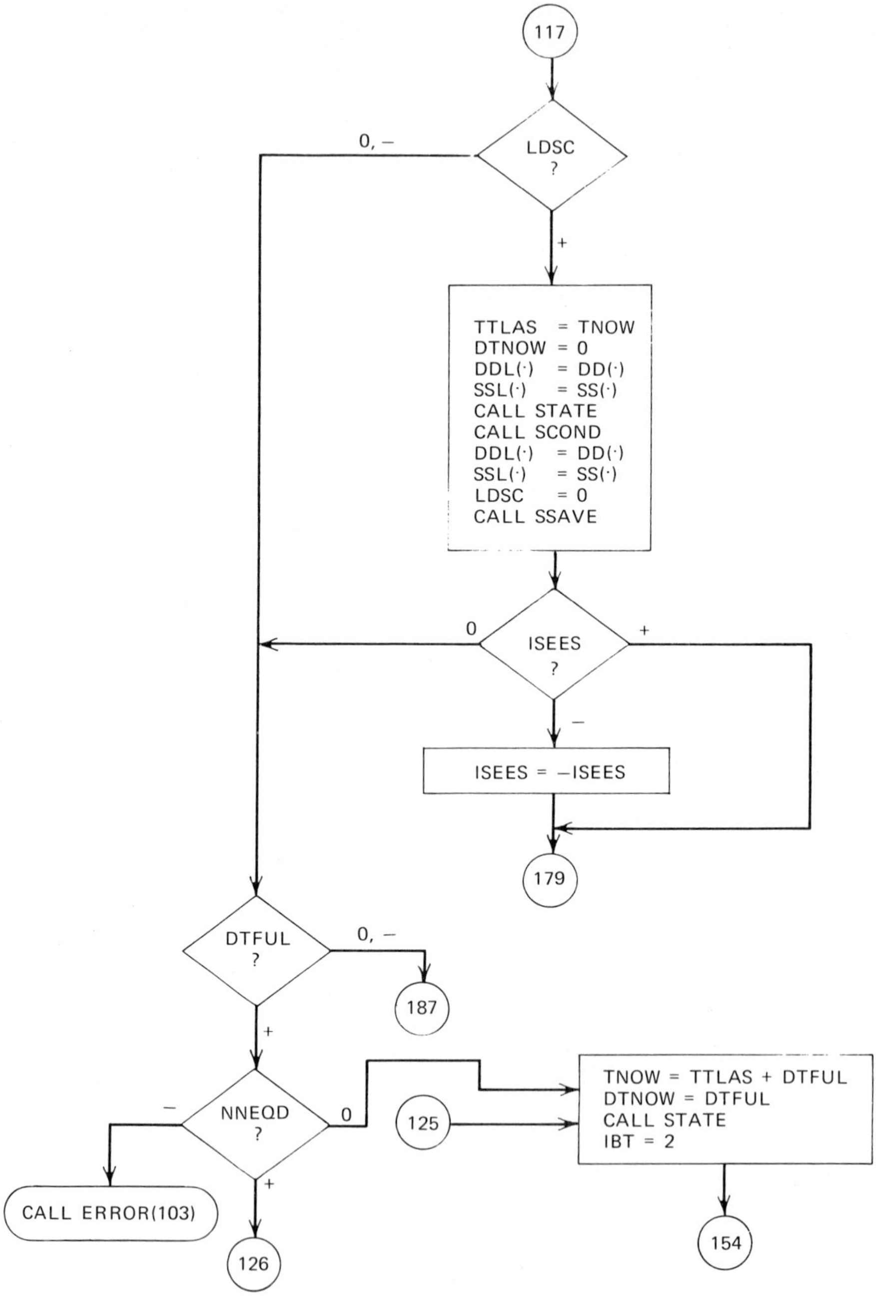

(b)

Figure 4-1*b* *(continued)*

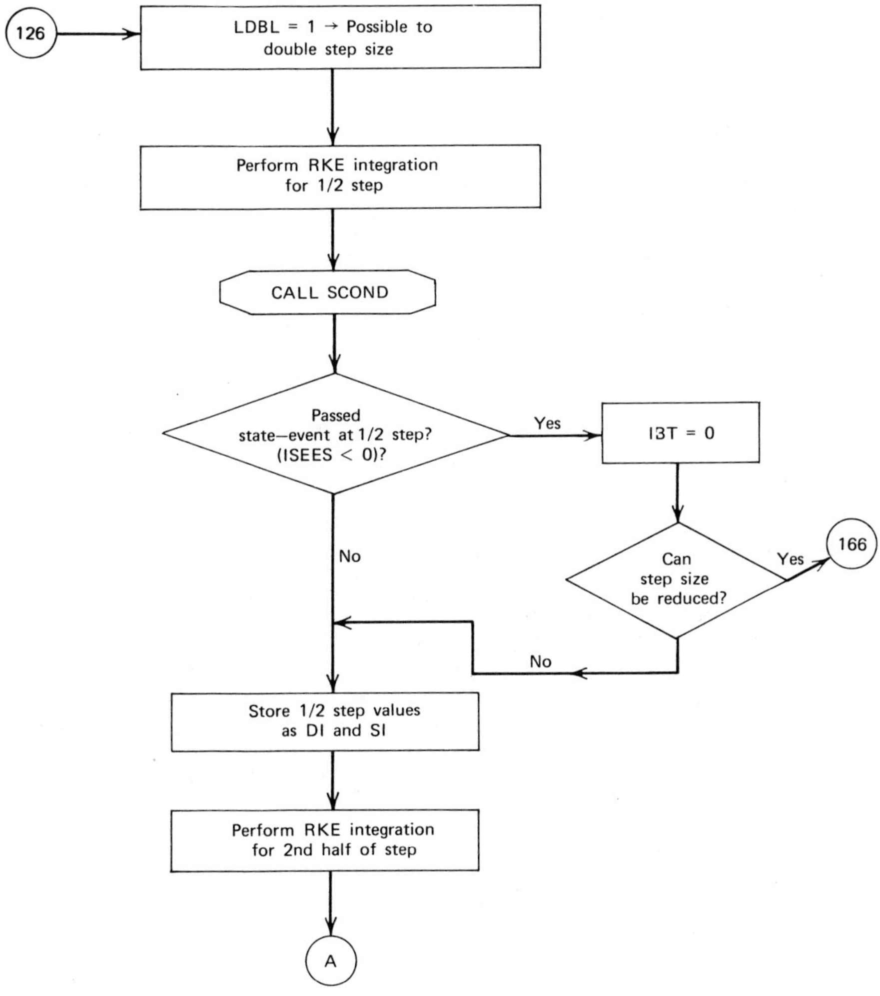

(c)

Figure 4-1*c* *(continued)*

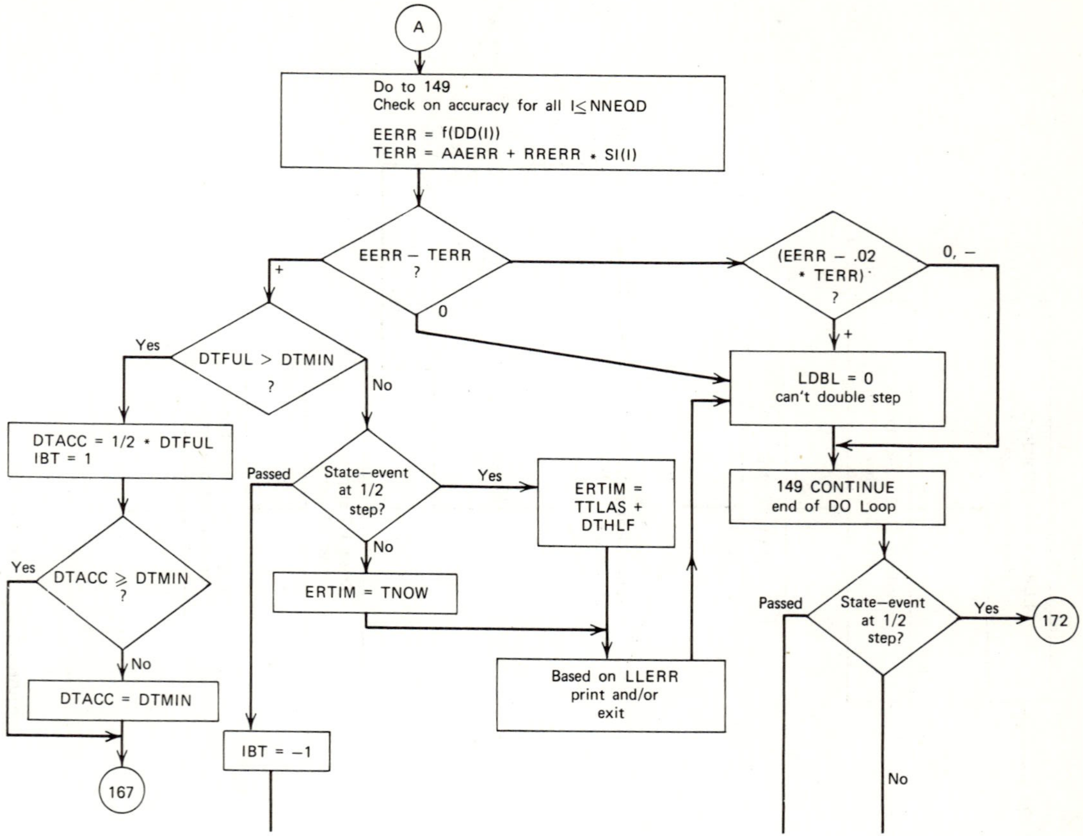
A
Do to 149
Check on accuracy for all I≤NNEQD
EERR = f(DD(I))
TERR = AAERR + RRERR * SI(I)
EERR – TERR ?
+
0
(EERR – .02 * TERR) ?
0, –
+
DTFUL > DTMIN ?
Yes
No
LDBL = 0
can't double step
DTACC = 1/2 * DTFUL
IBT = 1
Passed
State–event at 1/2 step?
Yes
No
ERTIM = TTLAS + DTHLF
149 CONTINUE
end of DO Loop
DTACC ≥ DTMIN ?
Yes
No
ERTIM = TNOW
DTACC = DTMIN
Based on LLERR print and/or exit
IBT = –1
167
Passed
State–event at 1/2 step?
Yes
No
172

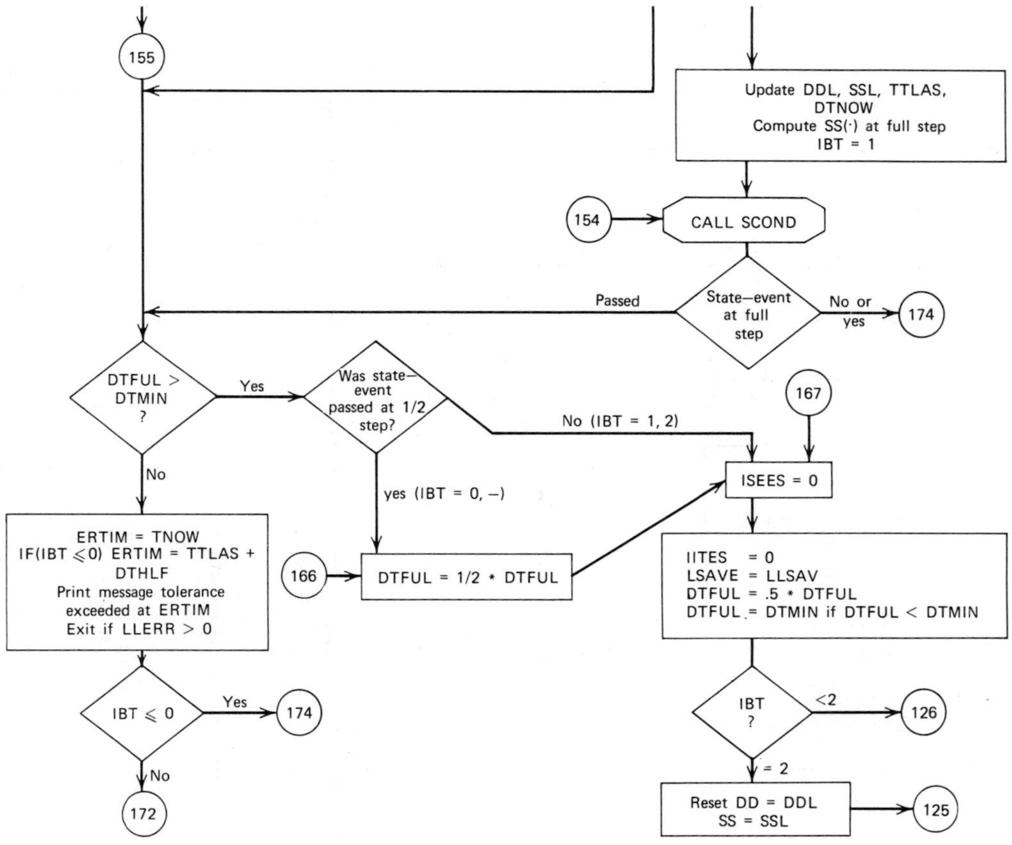

Figure 4-1*d* *(continued)*

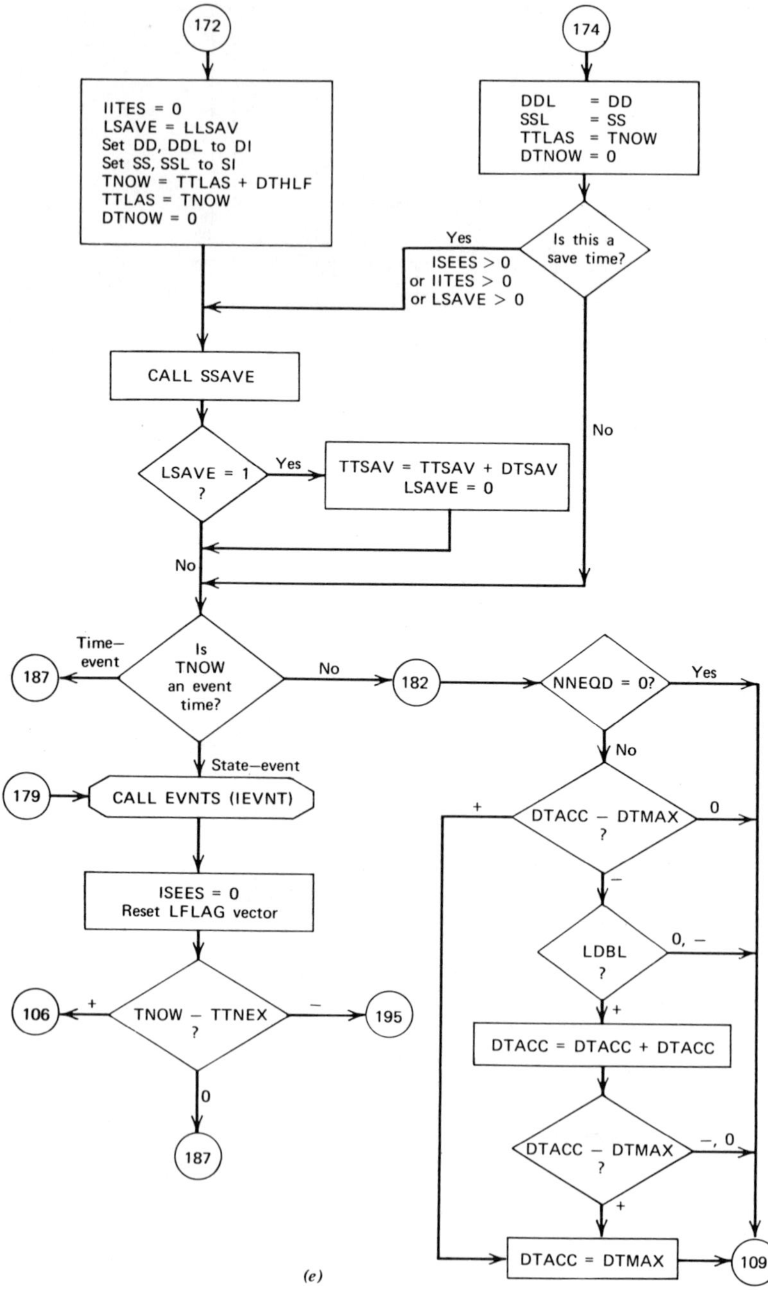

(e)

Figure 4-1*e* *(continued)*

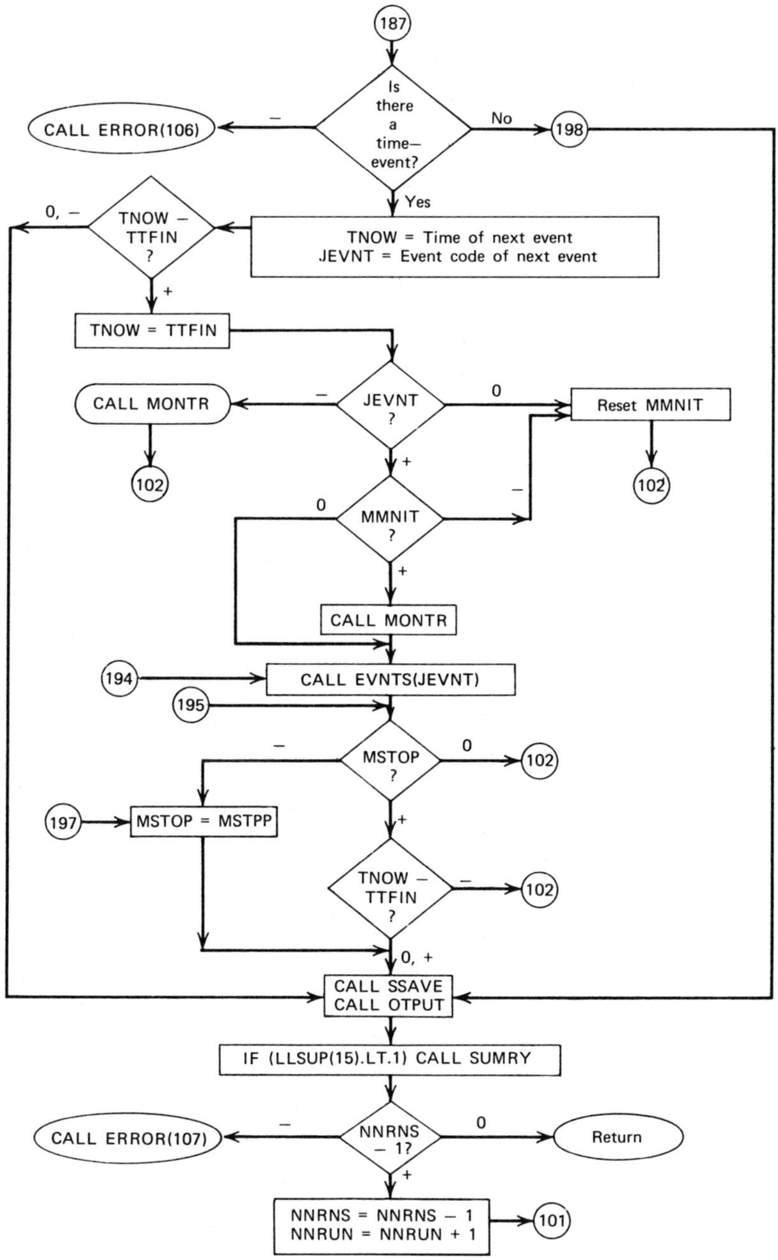

(f)

Figure 4-1*f* *(continued)*

```
      SUBROUTINE GASP                                                   GSP
      DIMENSION SI(100), DI(100), A1(100), A2(100), A3(100), A4(100), A5GSP
     1(100), A6(100), A7(100)                                           GSP
      DIMENSION NSET(1)                                                 GSP
      COMMON QSET(1)                                                    GSP
      COMMON /GCOM1/ ATRIB(25),JEVNT,MFA,MFE(100),MLE(100),MSTOP,NCRDR,NGSP
     1NAPO,NNAPT,NNATR,NNFIL,NNQ(100),NNTRY,NPRNT,PPARM(50,4),TNOW,TTBEGGSP
     2,TTCLR,TTFIN,TTRIB(25),TTSET                                      GSP
      COMMON /GCOM2/ DD(100),DDL(100),DTFUL,DTNOW,ISEES,LFLAG(50),NFLAG,GSP
     1NNEQD,NNEQS,NNEQT,SS(100),SSL(100),TTNEX                          GSP
      COMMON /GCOM3/ AAERR,DTMAX,DTMIN,DTSAV,IITES,LLERR,LLSAV,LLSEV,RREGSP
     1RR,TTLAS,TTSAV                                                    GSP
      COMMON /GCOM4/ DTPLT(10),HHLOW(25),HHWID(25),IICRD,IITAP(10),JJCELGSP
     1(500),LLABC(25,2),LLABH(25,2),LLABP(11,2),LLABT(25,2),LLPHI(10),LLGSP
     2PLO(10),LLPLT,LLSUP(15),LLSYM(10),MMPTS,NNCEL(25),NNCLT,NNHIS,NNPLGSP
     3T,NNPTS(10),NNSTA,NNVAR(10),PPHI(10),PPLO(10)                     GSP
      COMMON /GCOM5/ IIEVT,IISED(6),JJBEG,JJCLR,MMNIT,MMON,NNAME(3),NNCFGSP
     1I,NNDAY,NNPT,NNSET,NNPRJ,NNPRM,NNRNS,NNRUN,NNSTR,NNYR,SSEED(6)    GSP
      EQUIVALENCE (NSET(1),QSET(1))                                     GSP
      IICRD=0                                                           GSP
  101 CALL DATIN                                                        GSP
      MSTPP=MSTOP                                                       GSP
      IF (LLSUP(1).NE.-1) WRITE (NPRNT,207)                             GSP
      RESLS=0.01*DTSAV                                                  GSP
      LSAVE=LLSAV                                                       GSP
      DTACC=DTMAX                                                       GSP
      CALL SSAVE                                                        GSP
      JJBEG=0                                                           GSP
C                                                                       GSP
C*****IF TNOW=TTNEX, PROCESS NEXT TIME EVENT.  IF TNOW.LT.TTNEX,        GSP
C*****ADVANCE TNOW TO TTNEX, TTFIN, OR THE FIRST STATE EVENT.           GSP
C                                                                       GSP
  102 IF (TTFIN-TTNEX) 103,104,104                                      GSP
  103 TTNEX=TTFIN                                                       GSP
  104 IF (TTNEX-TNOW) 106,185,105                                       GSP
  105 IF (NNEQT) 107,185,108                                            GSP
  106 WRITE (NPRNT,208) TTNEX,TNOW                                      GSP
      CALL ERROR (101)                                                  GSP
  107 CALL ERROR (102)                                                  GSP
  108 DTFUL=DTACC                                                       GSP
      IITES=0                                                           GSP
      TTLAS=TNOW                                                        GSP
      DTNOW=0.0                                                         GSP
      CALL SCOND                                                        GSP
      DO 109 I=1,NNEQT                                                  GSP
      DDL(I)=DD(I)                                                      GSP
  109 SSL(I)=SS(I)                                                      GSP
      CALL STATE                                                        GSP
      CALL SSAVE                                                        GSP
      IF (ISEES) 112,110,177                                            GSP
  110 CALL SCOND                                                        GSP
      DO 111 I=1,NNEQT                                                  GSP
      DDL(I)=DD(I)                                                      GSP
  111 SSL(I)=SS(I)                                                      GSP
      IF (ISEES) 112,113,177                                            GSP
  112 ISEES=-ISEES                                                      GSP
      GO TO 177                                                         GSP
C                                                                       GSP
C*****PREPARE FOR NEW STEP.                                             GSP
C                                                                       GSP
  113 DTFUL=DTACC                                                       GSP
  114 IF (TNOW+1.01*DTFUL-TTNEX) 117,115,115                            GSP
  115 IITES=1                                                           GSP
      IF (TTNEX-TNOW) 106,185,116                                       GSP
  116 DTFUL=TTNEX-TNOW                                                  GSP
  117 IF (TNOW+DTFUL+RESLS-TTSAV) 123,122,118                           GSP
  118 IF (TNOW+DTFUL-RESLS-TTSAV) 122,122,119                           GSP
  119 IF (ABS(TNOW-TTSAV)-RESLS) 120,120,121                            GSP
  120 TTSAV=TTSAV+DTSAV                                                 GSP
      LSAVE=0                                                           GSP
      GO TO 117                                                         GSP
  121 DTFUL=TTSAV-TNOW                                                  GSP
```

Figure 4-2 FORTRAN listing of subroutine GASP.

```
      IITES=0
  122 LSAVE=1
C
C*****CHECK TO SEE IF RUNGE-KUTTA INTEGRATION IS REQUIRED.
C
  123 IF (NNEQD) 124,125,126
  124 CALL ERROR (103)
  125 TNOW=TTLAS+DTFUL
      DTNOW=DTFUL
      CALL STATE
      IBT=2
      GO TO 154
C
C*****BEGIN NEW STEP.
C
  126 LDBL=1
      DTHLF=0.5*DTFUL
      DTQRT=0.5*DTHLF
      DO 127 I=1,NNEQD
      A1(I)=DTHLF*DDL(I)
  127 SS(I)=SSL(I)+0.5*A1(I)
      TNOW=TTLAS+DTQRT
      DTNOW=TNOW-TTLAS
      CALL STATE
      DO 128 I=1,NNEQD
      A2(I)=DTHLF*DD(I)
  128 SS(I)=SSL(I)+0.25*(A1(I)+A2(I))
      CALL STATE
      DO 129 I=1,NNEQD
      A3(I)=DTHLF*DD(I)
  129 SS(I)=SSL(I)-A2(I)+A3(I)+A3(I)
      TNOW=TTLAS+DTHLF
      DTNOW=TNOW-TTLAS
      CALL STATE
      DO 130 I=1,NNEQD
      A4(I)=DTHLF*DD(I)
  130 SS(I)=SSL(I)+(A1(I)+4.0*A3(I)+A4(I))/6.0
C
C*****CHECK FOR STATE EVENTS AT HALF STEP.
C
      CALL SCOND
      IF (ISEES) 131,132,132
  131 IBT=0
      IF (DTFUL-DTMIN) 132,132,164
C
C*****STORE HALF STEP VALUES.
C
  132 DO 133 I=1,NNEQT
      DI(I)=DD(I)
  133 SI(I)=SS(I)
      CALL STATE
      DO 134 I=1,NNEQD
      A5(I)=DTHLF*DD(I)
  134 SS(I)=SI(I)+0.5*A5(I)
      TNOW=TTLAS+DTHLF+DTQRT
      DTNOW=TNOW-TTLAS
      CALL STATE
      DO 135 I=1,NNEQD
      A6(I)=DTHLF*DD(I)
  135 SS(I)=SI(I)+0.25*(A5(I)+A6(I))
      CALL STATE
      DO 136 I=1,NNEQD
      A7(I)=DTHLF*DD(I)
  136 SS(I)=SSL(I)+(-A1(I)-96.0*A2(I)+92.0*A3(I)-121.0*A4(I)+144.0*A5(I)
     1+6.0*A6(I)-12.0*A7(I))/6.0
      TNOW=TTLAS+DTFUL
      DTNOW=DTFUL
      CALL STATE
C
C*****CHECK FOR ACCEPTABLE ACCURACY AT FULL STEP.
C
      DO 149 I=1,NNEQD
```

Figure 4-2 *(continued)*

```
      EERR=ABS((-A1(I)+4.0*A3(I)+17.0*A4(I)-23.0*A5(I)+4.0*A7(I)-DTHLF*D
     1D(I))/90.0)
      TERR=AAERR+ABS(FRERR*SI(I))
      IF (EERR-TERR) 137,148,138
  137 IF (EERR-0.02*TERR) 149,149,148
  138 IF (DTFUL-DTMIN) 141,141,139
  139 DTACC=0.5*DTFUL
      IBT=1
      IF (DTACC-DTMIN) 140,165,165
  140 DTACC=DTMIN
      GO TO 165
  141 IF (ISEES) 142,144,143
  142 IBT=-1
      GO TO 155
  143 ERTIM=TTLAS+DTHLF
      GO TO 145
  144 ERTIM=TNOW
  145 IF (LLERR) 148,147,146
  146 WRITE (NPRNT,209) I,ERTIM
      CALL ERROR (104)
  147 WRITE (NPRNT,209) I,ERTIM
  148 LDBL=0
  149 CONTINUE
C
C*****ACCURACY IS ACCEPTABLE.  CHECK FOR STATE EVENT AT HALF STEP.
C
      IF (ISEES) 155,150,170
C
C*****NO STATE EVENT AT HALF STEP.  UPDATE STATUS TO HALF STEP AND
C*****CONTINUE.
C
  150 DO 151 I=1,NNEQT
      DDL(I)=DI(I)
  151 SSL(I)=SI(I)
      TTLAS=TTLAS+DTHLF
      DTNOW=TNOW-TTLAS
      DO 152 I=1,NNEQD
  152 SS(I)=SI(I)-A6(I)+A7(I)+A7(I)
      CALL STATE
      DO 153 I=1,NNEQD
  153 SS(I)=SI(I)+(A5(I)+4.0*A7(I)+DTHLF*DD(I))/6.0
      IF (NNEQS.GT.0) CALL STATE
C
C*****CHECK FOR STATE EVENTS AT FULL STEP.
C
      IBT=1
  154 CALL SCOND
      IF (ISEES) 155,172,172
C
C*****PASSED STATE EVENT.
C
  155 IF (DTFUL-DTMIN) 157,157,156
  156 IF (IBT-1) 164,165,165
  157 ERTIM=TNOW
      IF (IBT.LE.0) ERTIM=TTLAS+DTHLF
      IF (LLERR) 161,158,158
  158 IF (ISEES+1000) 160,159,159
  159 I=-ISEES
      WRITE (NPRNT,210) I,ERTIM
      GO TO 161
  160 I=-ISEES-1000
      WRITE (NPRNT,211) I,ERTIM
  161 ISEES=-ISEES
      IF (LLERR) 162,162,163
  162 IF (IBT) 170,170,172
  163 CALL ERROR (105)
  164 DTFUL=0.5*DTFUL
  165 ISEES=0
C
C*****REDUCE STEP SIZE, RETURN TO TTLAS, AND CONTINUE.
C
      IITES=0
```

Figure 4-2 *(continued)*

```
      LSAVE=LLSAV
      TNOW=TTLAS
      DTFUL=0.5*DTFUL
      IF (DTFUL-DTMIN) 166,167,167
  166 DTFUL=DTMIN
  167 IF (IIET-1) 126,114,168
  168 DO 169 I=1,NNEQT
      DD(I)=DDL(I)
  169 SS(I)=SSL(I)
      GO TO 125
C
C*****STATE EVENT AT HALF STEP. UPDATE STATUS TO HALF STEP.
C
  170 IITES=0
      LSAVE=LLSAV
      DO 171 I=1,NNEQT
      DD(I)=DI(I)
      DDL(I)=DD(I)
      SS(I)=SI(I)
  171 SSL(I)=SS(I)
      TNOW=TTLAS+DTHLF
      TTLAS=TNOW
      DTNOW=0.0
      GO TO 174
C
C*****FULL STEP VALUES ARE GOOD.  UPDATE STATUS TO FULL STEP AND
C*****CONTINUE.
C
  172 DO 173 I=1,NNEQT
      DDL(I)=DD(I)
  173 SSL(I)=SS(I)
      TTLAS=TNOW
      DTNOW=0.0
C
C*****CHECK TO SEE IF TNOW IS A SAVE TIME.
C
      IF (LSAVE+IITES+ISEES) 176,176,174
C
C*****SAVE VALUES.
C
  174 CALL SSAVE
      IF (LSAVE-1) 176,175,176
  175 TTSAV=TTSAV+DTSAV
      LSAVE=0
C
C*****IF TNOW IS NOT AN EVENT TIME, START NEW STEP. IF TNOW IS A
C*****STATE EVENT TIME, PROCESS STATE EVENT. IF TNOW IS A TIME EVENT
C*****TIME BUT NOT A STATE EVENT TIME, PROCESS TIME EVENT.
C
  176 IF (ISEES+ISEES+IITES-1) 180,185,177
C
C*****TNOW IS A STATE EVENT TIME. PROCESS STATE EVENT.
C
  177 IF (MMNIT.GT.0) CALL MONTR
      CALL EVNTS (IIEVT)
      ISEES=0
      IITES=1
      IF (NFLAG) 194,194,178
  178 DO 179 I=1,NFLAG
  179 LFLAG(I)=0
      IF (TNOW-TTNEX) 194,185,106
C
C*****TNOW IS NOT AN EVENT TIME.  CHECK TO SEE IF STEP SIZE CAN BE
C*****INCREASED.  CONTINUE.
C
  180 IF (NNEQD) 113,113,181
  181 IF (DTACC-DTMAX) 182,113,184
  182 IF (LDBL) 113,113,183
  183 DTACC=DTACC+DTACC
      IF (DTACC-DTMAX) 113,113,184
  184 DTACC=DTMAX
      GO TO 113
C
C*****FIRST ENTRY IN FILE 1 IS NEXT EVENT. IF FILE 1 IS EMPTY,
C*****TNOW=TTNEX=TTFIN, RUN IS COMPLETED.
```

Figure 4-2 *(continued)*

```
C
  185 IF (NNQ(1)) 187,186,188
  186 WRITE (NPRNT,212) TNOW
      GO TO 197
  187 CALL ERROR (106)
C
C*****SET TNOW=ATRIB(1) AND JEVNT=ATRIB(2) AND CALL RMOVE TO LOAD ENTRY
C*****INTO ATRIB.
C
  188 NEXTE=MFE(1)
      TNOW=QSET(NEXTE+1)
      JEVNT=QSET(NEXTE+2)
      IF (TNOW-TTFIN) 190,190,189
  189 TNOW=TTFIN
      GO TO 197
  190 CALL RMOVE (NEXTE,1)
C
C*****TEST TO SEE IF THIS EVENT IS A MONITOR EVENT.
C
      IF (JEVNT) 202,203,191
  191 IF (MMNIT) 204,193,192
  192 CALL MONTR
C
C*****CALL PROGRAMMERS EVENT ROUTINES.
C
  193 CALL EVNTS (JEVNT)
C
C*****TEST METHOD FOR STOPPING.
C
  194 IF (MSTOP) 196,195,195
  195 IF (TNOW-TTFIN) 102,197,197
  196 MSTOP=MSTPP
C
C*****TEST FOR NO SUMMARY REPORT.
C
  197 CALL SSAVE
      CALL OTPUT
      IF (LLSUP(15)) 198,198,199
  198 CALL SUMRY
C
C*****TEST NUMBER OF RUNS REMAINING.
C
  199 IF (NNRNS-1) 201,206,200
  200 NNRNS=NNRNS-1
      NNRUN=NNRUN+1
      GO TO 101
  201 CALL ERROR (107)
  202 CALL MONTR
      GO TO 102
C
C*****RESET MMNIT.
C
  203 IF (MMNIT) 204,204,205
  204 MMNIT=1
      GO TO 102
  205 MMNIT=0
      GO TO 102
C
C*****ALL RUNS ARE COMPLETED.  RETURN TO MAIN PROGRAM.
C
  206 RETURN
C
  207 FORMAT (1H1,45X,24H**INTERMEDIATE RESULTS**//)
  208 FORMAT (///36X,6HTTNEX=,E17.9,5X,5HTNOW=,E17.9)
  209 FORMAT (/2X,38HSPECIFIED LOCAL ERROR EXCEEDED FOR SS(,I3,9H) AT TI
     1ME,E12.4)
  210 FORMAT (/2X,38HSPECIFIED  TOLERANCE  EXCEEDED FOR SS(,I3,9H) AT TI
     1ME,E12.4)
  211 FORMAT (/2X,38HSPECIFIED  TOLERANCE  EXCEEDED FOR DD(,I3,9H) AT TI
     1ME,E12.4)
  212 FORMAT (12X,24HSIMULATION ENDED AT TIME,F14.4,2X,28HWITH NO EVENTS
     1 IN EVENT FILE)
C
      END
```

Figure 4-2 *(continued)*

routine SSAVE is called to record values of prescribed variables.) This is used to eliminate integrating to a save time if a step ends within RESLS of the save time. The time increment required for numeric accuracy, DTACC, is set to its initial value, DTMAX. The initial model status is recorded by a call to subroutine SSAVE and initialization is completed by setting JJBEG equal to zero. JJBEG is read in DATIN to initialize TNOW and the random number streams. JJBEG is only allowed to be nonzero during initialization.

The value of the next time-event, TTNEX, is then compared to the ending time of the simulation, TTFIN, so that the simulation will end at TTFIN if TTFIN $<$ TTNEX. (If TTFIN is not used, i.e., MSTOP = 0, TTFIN is set to 10^{20} in DATIN.) A check is then made to determine if there is a time-event to be processed. If not, a check is made to determine if there are any active state or derivative equations. Assuming that there are no time-events scheduled at TNOW and that there are active state or derivative equations, preparations are made to advance status (S-108). The variable LDSC is set equal to one, indicating that there may have been a discrete state change at TNOW. Next, the full step size DTFUL is set to the smallest value of the time to the next time-event; the step size required for numeric accuracy, and the time to the next save point. Two facts deserve note. First, the step size is set to be greater (by a maximum of 1%) than the maximum specified by DTMAX if it will advance time exactly to the next time-event. Second, the actual time at a save point may differ from the computed time by as much as 1% of DTSAV. Concurrent with the setting of the step size, two indicators are set. IITES is set to one if the step will terminate at a time-event, and LSAVE is set equal to one if the step will terminate at a save time. Otherwise, these variables are set to zero.

If discrete state changes could have occurred at the present time, status is updated (S-118) and an evaluation of status to detect the occurrence of state-events is made (G-47). Subroutine SSAVE is called to record status. A check for the occurrence of a state-event is then made. This evaluation is slightly different than normal. If subroutine SCOND returns a negative value of ISEES, at least one specified state condition has usually been passed by an amount exceeding the specified tolerance. If no specified state conditions have occurred or been passed, ISEES is made zero. Since the current time is an update point (TNOW = TTLAS), a negative value of ISEES indicates that the specified state conditions were not met within tolerance because of an instantaneous discrete change. Consequently, the specified state conditions are located exactly in time, and the negative value of ISEES has the same meaning normally associated with a positive value of ISEES. In this case a transfer is made to statement 179.

A check is then made to assure that the step size DTFUL is positive (S-122) since it may be zero in the case of simultaneous events. If DTFUL is zero, a time-event must be processed and a transfer to statement 187 is made.

Consider next the situation in which only equations in SS(·) are included in STATE (S-125). The time to which GASP IV is trying to project is TNOW = TTLAS + DTFUL, and the step size DTNOW equals DTFUL. Subroutine STATE is called (G-64) to obtain projected values of SS(·) at TNOW. An indicator IBT is set at 2 to indicate that only SS(·) equations are being processed. A transfer to statement 154 is then made to evaluate the projected values of SS(·) at TNOW in order to determine if the step size is acceptable. Since this evaluation is also performed when DD(·) equations are included in the program, discussion of the evaluation procedure is presented later.

When NNEQD > 0, a new step begins with the setting of LDBL at 1 to indicate that the doubling of the step size is possible (S-126). The coding from statement number 126 (S-126) to statement number 153 (S-153) contains the appropriate equations for the RKE integration algorithm. The computational procedure associated with the RKE algorithm is presented in Appendix 1.

Values for the half step and quarter step size are set, and the RKE integration procedure begins (G-73). At the half step point a check is made for state-events (G-96). The action taken if any state-events have been passed is described later. If none have been passed, the half step value is stored and processing of the step continues until it is possible to test numeric accuracy. The test for numeric accuracy (114,125) is then made (G-130). If accuracy is satisfactory for all of the state variables, processing continues. If accuracy is at least 50 times better than that required for each variable, LDBL retains its value of one, which may later allow the step size to be doubled. If accuracy is not acceptable but the step size can be reduced (G-139), DTACC is reduced (S-139) and IBT is set at 1. Conditions for restarting the step are established by transferring to statement 167.

If accuracy is not acceptable and the step size cannot be reduced, either a fatal error has occurred (if LLERR > 0), a warning will be printed and processing will continue (if LLERR = 0), or processing will continue with no warning printed (if LLERR < 0).

If accuracy is acceptable at the end of the full step, a check is made to determine if a state-event occurred at the half step (G-153). If so, time is advanced to the half step and the event is processed (S-172).

If not, values of the state variables at the end of the full step are computed (S-150 to S-153).

At statement 154, the evaluation of state conditions is made. (Recall a transfer is also made to statement 154 when only SS(·) equations are involved.) If a state-event was passed at the half step (S-166), the step size is reduced to one-fourth of its value, or to half of its value if the state-event was passed at the full step (S-167). The procedure is then repeated with the new step size. If the step size cannot be reduced, a warning message is printed, a fatal error occurs, or both, depending on the value of LLERR (S-159 to S-165). If the step size is acceptable, status is updated (S-172 or S-174) and saved if necessary (S-176). A check is then made to determine if the current time is an event time (S-178). If the current time is a state-event time, the state-event is processed by a call to subroutine EVNTS(IIEVT) at statement 179. State condition flags are reset (S-181), and a check for run termination is made by transferring to statement 195.

If the current time is not an event time, a check is made to determine if the step size can be doubled (LDBL $>$ 0 at S-184), and a new step is started by transferring to statement 109.

The code for the processing of time-events begins at statement 187 where a test is made on the number of entries in the event file. If there are none, GASP IV assumes that the time-event being processed must be the final event ending the simulation run at time TTFIN. The start of a run and the end of a run are the only time-events not requiring an entry in the event file. If the event file is not empty, TNOW is set equal to attribute 1 of the first event in file 1 (G-284), and JEVNT is set equal to attribute 2 (G-285). If the event occurs after TTFIN, TNOW is set equal to TTFIN (S-190) and the run is terminated (S-198). Otherwise, the event is removed from the event file by a call to subroutine RMOVE (S-191). The event code is tested (G-293) and if it is zero or negative, a monitoring action has been requested. The normal situation is that JEVNT is positive, and a transfer is made to statement 192 where a test is made to determine if tracing of events is being performed. If event tracing is being performed, subroutine MONTR is called to perform the trace (S-193). A call is then made to subroutine EVNTS to process the event with the code JEVNT (S-194). The user must write subroutine EVNTS to decode JEVNT and to call the appropriate subroutine representing the event to be processed.

Following a return from EVNTS, a test is made on the key that specifies the method for stopping, MSTOP (S-195). If MSTOP is negative, the user has indicated that the simulation run is completed. If MSTOP is zero, the run is to be continued and a transfer is made to statement 102.

If MSTOP is positive, the method of stopping is based on time, and TNOW is compared to TTFIN (S-196).

When the simulation run is completed, a call is made to subroutine SSAVE to update any state variables to the end-of-simulation time (S-198). A call is then made to subroutine OTPUT to allow the user to perform any end-of-simulation processing or to print out any values that he desires at the end of the simulation. Next, the suppression code for the GASP IV summary report is tested (G-311); if it is zero, the GASP IV summary report is obtained by a call to subroutine SUMRY (S-199). The number of runs remaining is tested (S-200) and the run number is increased. A transfer to statement 101 is then made so that DATIN can be called for the next simulation run.

At statement 203 a call is made to subroutine MONTR since the event code was negative. Following the MONTR event another pass through subroutine GASP is made. At statement 205 the switch for tracing events as they occur is either set or reset. At statement 207 a return from subroutine GASP to the main program is made.

Initialization

Initialization of variables prior to the execution of a GASP IV simulation run occurs in phases. Some variables are initialized during program compilation by DATA statements. Others are assigned values obtained directly from the reading of GASP IV input data cards. Finally, some variables are assigned initial values after all GASP IV input data cards have been read. In general, each phase is associated with specific elements of the executable program. DATA statements in individual subprograms assign values to variables local to those subprograms. The main program must initialize two GASP IV variables: the card reader number, NCRDR; and the printer number, NPRNT.* The user may employ the main program to initialize non-GASP variables prior to the assumption of executive control by subroutine GASP. The preceding phases occur before the first run but not prior to subsequent runs if multiple runs are made. The last phases of initialization are controlled by subroutine DATIN; they are discussed in conjunction with the description of that subprogram.

* The use of DATA statements to assign values to variables in named COMMON is not allowed by IBM 360 FORTRAN compilers. Employing BLOCK DATA was ruled out because of a conflict with the use of the name on a particular library of the CDC 6500 at Purdue.

Subroutine DATIN. This subroutine provides for the selective initialization of GASP IV variables through four mechanisms. Some GASP IV variables are initialized to standard or default values; some are assigned values equal to or computed from GASP IV input data; some are assigned values derived from the user provided subroutines INTLC and STATE; and some are assigned values (or left unchanged) from a previous run. Subroutine DATIN accomplishes this initialization in the proper sequence to facilitate either single or multiple runs. The FORTRAN listing of subroutine DATIN is shown in Fig. 4-3.

Subroutine DATIN also performs error checking and provides a printout (echo check) of the input data that may be selectively suppressed. The GASP IV echo check may not always print the values read in. For example, if a zero value is read in for a variable having a default value, this value will be printed in the echo check. In most cases the values read in and the ones printed are the same; therefore, the echo check enables the user to verify the values of his input data.

Subroutine DATIN is called only by subroutine GASP and only during the initialization phase of a simulation run. To provide selective initialization, allowing the user full flexibility with respect to the variables to be initialized and echo checked, the control variables IICRD and LLSUP(·) are used. IICRD indicates the type of the first data card to be read for the succeeding run. IICRD is set equal to zero in subroutine GASP prior to initialization of the first run; it may subsequently be set by either a type 11 or a type 0 data card. When IICRD equals zero, data card type 1 is read first. This is the normal case except for multiple runs. When IICRD is greater than zero, subroutine DATIN begins reading data cards with the data card type indicated. For example, if IICRD equals seven, data card type 7 and all subsequent data card types will be read if they are not suppressed. If IICRD equals 13, 14, or 15, no data cards are read. For IICRD equal to 13 or 14, the random number generators and the time variable are reset if JJBEG = 1. Also, NSET is initialized if JJFIL = 1. If IICRD is 13 but not 14, subroutine INTLC is called, state variables are initialized, subroutine CLEAR is called if JJCLR > 0, and subroutine STATE is called if JJBEG = 1. For IICRD = 15, the echo check heading is printed and a return is made from DATIN.

LLSUP(·) is used in conjunction with IICRD to control the reading and error checking of data cards as well as the output of a standard summary report. LLSUP(·) is a 15 element array in which each of the first 12 elements corresponds to a specific data card type. If LLSUP(I), for I = 1, 12 is less than or equal to zero, the type I data card will be read and echo checked. If LLSUP(I) equals one, the type I data card

```
      SUBROUTINE DATIN
      COMMON /GCOM1/ ATRIB(25),JEVNT,MFA,MFE(100),MLE(100),MSTOP,NCRDR,N
     1NAPO,NNAPT,NNATR,NNFIL,NNQ(100),NNTRY,NPRNT,PPARM(50,4),TNOW,TTBEG
     2,TTCLR,TTFIN,TTRIB(25),TTSET
      COMMON /GCOM2/ DD(100),DDL(100),DTFUL,DTNOW,ISEES,LFLAG(50),NFLAG,
     1NNEQD,NNEQS,NNEQT,SS(100),SSL(100),TTNEX
      COMMON /GCOM3/ AAERR,DTMAX,DTMIN,DTSAV,IITES,LLERR,LLSAV,LLSEV,RRE
     1RR,TTLAS,TTSAV
      COMMON /GCOM4/ DTPLT(10),HHLOW(25),HHWID(25),IICRD,IITAP(10),JJCEL
     1(500),LLABC(25,2),LLABH(25,2),LLABP(11,2),LLABT(25,2),LLPHI(10),LL
     2PLO(10),LLPLT,LLSUP(15),LLSYM(10),MMPTS,NNCEL(25),NNCLT,NNHIS,NNPL
     3T,NNPTS(10),NNSTA,NNVAR(10),PPHI(10),PPLO(10)
      COMMON /GCOM5/ IIEVT,IISED(6),JJBEG,JJCLR,MMNIT,MMON,NNAME(3),NNCF
     1I,NNDAY,NNPT,NNSET,NNPRJ,NNPRM,NNRNS,NNRUN,NNSTR,NNYR,SSEED(6)
      COMMON /GCOM6/ EENQ(100),IINN(100),KKRNK(100),MMAXQ(100),QQTIM(100
     1),SSOBV(25,5),SSTPV(25,6),VVNQ(100)
      DATA MEQT,MHIST,MCELS,MCLCT,MSTAT,MATRB,MFILS,MPRMS,MPLOT,MSTRM,MF
     1LAG/100,25,500,25,25,25,100,50,10,6,50/
      DATA JBEGG/0/
      NEPG=IICRD
      IF (IICRD) 102,103,101
C
C*****IICRD IS A CONTROL VARIABLE FOR DETERMINING THE STARTING CARD
C*****TYPE FOR MULTIPLE RUN PROBLEMS.  THE VALUE OF IICRD SPECIFIES THE
C*****STARTING CARD TYPE.
C
  101 JJBEG=JBEGG
      NRTOT=NNRNS+NNRUN-1
      IF (LLSUP(1).LT.1.AND.IICRD.NE.1) WRITE (NPRNT,213) NNPRJ,NNAME,MM
     1ON,NNDAY,NNYR,NNRUN,NRTOT,LLSUP
      GO TO (103,109,114,121,128,137,150,154,158,171,178,182,182,182,211
     1), NEPG
  102 CALL ERROR (201)
  103 NNRUN=1
C
C*****DATA CARD TYPE ONE
C
      READ (NCRDR,214) NNAME,NNPRJ,MMON,NNDAY,NNYR,NNRNS,LLSUP
      DO 105 I=1,15
      IF (LLSUP(I)) 104,104,105
  104 LLSUP(I)=0
  105 CONTINUE
C
C*****PRINT OUT PROGRAM IDENTIFICATION INFORMATION
C
      IF (LLSUP(1)-1) 106,107,107
  106 WRITE (NPRNT,213) NNPRJ,NNAME,MMON,NNDAY,NNYR,NNRUN,NNRNS,LLSUP
  107 IF (NNRNS) 108,108,109
  108 WRITE (NPRNT,215)
      STOP
C
C*****DATA CARD TYPE TWO
C
  109 IF (LLSUP(2)-1) 110,110,114
  110 READ (NCRDR,216) NNCLT,NNSTA,NNHIS,NNPRM,NNPLT,NNSTR,NNTRY,NNATR,N
     1NFIL,NNSET,NNEQD,NNEQS,NFLAG
      IF (NNSTR.EQ.0) NNSTR=1
      IF (NNCLT.GT.MCLCT) CALL ERROR (204)
      IF (NNSTA.GT.MSTAT) CALL ERROR (205)
      IF (NNHIS.GT.MHIST) CALL ERROR (206)
      IF (NNPLT.GT.MPLOT) CALL ERROR (207)
      IF (NNATR.GT.MATRB) CALL ERROR (208)
      IF (NNFIL.GT.MFILS) CALL ERROR (209)
      IF (NFLAG.GT.MFLAG) CALL ERROR (200)
      IF (NNPRM.GT.MPRMS) CALL ERROR (199)
      IF (LLSUP(2)-1) 111,112,112
  111 WRITE (NPRNT,217) NNCLT,NNSTA,NNHIS,NNPRM,NNPLT,NNSTR,NNTRY,NNATR,
     1NNFIL,NNSET,NNEQD,NNEQS,NFLAG
  112 NNEQT=NNEQD+NNEQS
      IF (NNEQT.GT.MEQT) CALL ERROR (198)
      NNAPO=NNATR+1
      NNAPT=NNATR+2
```

Figure 4-3 FORTRAN listing of subroutine DATIN.

```
      NNCFI=NNTRY*NNAPT
      IF (NNCFI.GT.NNSET) CALL ERROR (202)
      NNPT=0
      DO 113 I=1,10
  113 NNPTS(I)=0
C
C*****DATA CARD TYPE THREE IS USED ONLY IF NNCLT IS GREATER THAN ZERO,
C
  114 IF (NNCLT) 121,121,115
  115 IF (LLSUP(3)-1) 116,117,121
  116 WRITE (NPRNT,233)
  117 DO 120 J=1,NNCLT
      READ (NCRDR,218) I,LLABC(I,1),LLABC(I,2)
      IF (LLSUP(3)-1) 118,120,121
  118 WRITE (NPRNT,220) I,LLABC(I,1),LLABC(I,2)
      IF (I-J) 119,120,119
  119 WRITE (NPRNT,221)
  120 CONTINUE
C
C*****DATA CARD TYPE FOUR IS USED ONLY IF NNSTA IS GREATER THAN ZERO.
C
  121 IF (NNSTA) 128,128,122
  122 IF (LLSUP(4)-1) 123,124,128
  123 WRITE (NPRNT,233)
  124 DO 127 J=1,NNSTA
      READ (NCRDR,219) I,LLABT(I,1),LLABT(I,2),SSTPV(I,6)
      IF (LLSUP(4)-1) 125,127,128
  125 WRITE (NPRNT,222) I,LLABT(I,1),LLABT(I,2),SSTPV(I,6)
      IF (I-J) 126,127,126
  126 WRITE (NPRNT,221)
  127 CONTINUE
C
C*****DATA CARD TYPE FIVE IS USED ONLY IF NNHIS IS GREATER THAN ZERO.
C
  128 IF (NNHIS) 137,137,129
  129 IF (LLSUP(5)-1) 130,131,137
  130 WRITE (NPRNT,233)
  131 DO 134 J=1,NNHIS
      READ (NCRDR,218) I,LLABH(I,1),LLABH(I,2),NNCEL(I),HHLOW(I),HHWID(I
     1)
      IF (HHWID(I).EQ.0) HHWID(I)=1.
      IF (LLSUP(5)-1) 132,134,137
  132 WRITE (NPRNT,223) I,LLABH(I,1),LLABH(I.2),NNCEL(I),HHLOW(I),HHWID(
     1I)
      IF (I-J) 133,134,133
  133 WRITE (NPRNT,221)
  134 CONTINUE
      NNCEL(1)=NNCEL(1)+2
      IF (NNHIS-1) 137,137,135
  135 DO 136 I=2,NNHIS
  136 NNCEL(I)=NNCEL(I)+NNCEL(I-1)+2
      IF (NNCEL(NNHIS).GT.MCELS) CALL ERROR (196)
C
C*****DATA CARD TYPE SIX IS USED ONLY IF NNPLT IS GREATER THAN ZERO.
C
  137 IF (NNPLT) 150,150,138
  138 IF (LLSUP(6)-1) 139,140,150
  139 WRITE (NPRNT,233)
  140 DO 149 J=1,NNPLT
      READ (NCRDR,224) I,LLABP(11,1),LLABP(11,2),IITAP(I),NNVAR(I),LLPLT
     1,DTPLT(I)
      IF (LLSUP(6)-1) 141,143,150
  141 WRITE (NPRNT,226) I,LLABP(11,1),LLAEP(11,2),IITAP(I),NNVAR(I),LLPL
     1T,DTPLT(I)
      IF (I-J) 142,143,142
  142 WRITE (NPRNT,221)
  143 NVAR=NNVAR(I)
      DO 146 JI=1,NVAR
      READ (NCRDR,225) IJ,LLSYM(IJ),LLABP(IJ,1),LLABP(IJ,2),LLPLO(IJ),LL
     1PHI(IJ),PPLO(IJ),PPHI(IJ)
      IF (LLSUP(6)-1) 144,146,150
  144 WRITE (NPRNT,227) IJ,LLSYM(IJ),LLABP(IJ,1),LLABP(IJ,2),LLPLO(IJ),L
     1LPHI(IJ),PPLO(IJ),PPHI(IJ)
      IF (IJ-JI) 145,146,145
```

Figure 4-3 *(continued)*

```
  145 WRITE (NPRNT,221)
  146 CONTINUE
      IT=IITAP(I)
      IF (IT) 147,147,148
  147 MMPTS=(NNSET-NNCFI)/(NNVAR(I)+1)
      GO TO 149
  148 REWIND IT
      WRITE (IT) LLPLT,LLSYM,LLABP,LLPLO,PPLO,LLPHI,PPHI
  149 CONTINUE
C
C*****DATA CARD TYPE SEVEN IS USED ONLY IF NNFIL IS GREATER THAN ZERO.
C*****SPECIFY KKRNK=RANKING ATTRIBUTE.
C
  150 IF (NNFIL) 158,158,151
  151 IF (LLSUP(7)-1) 152,152,154
  152 READ (NCRDR,216) (KKRNK(I),I=1,NNFIL)
      IF (LLSUP(7)-1) 153,155,155
  153 WRITE (NPRNT,228) (KKRNK(I),I=1,NNFIL)
C
C*****DATA CARD TYPE EIGHT IS USED ONLY IF NNFIL IS GREATER THAN ZERO.
C*****SPECIFY IINN=1 FOR LVF, IINN=2 FOR HVF, IINN=3 FOR FIFO,
C*****IINN=4 FOR LIFO.
C
  154 IF (NNFIL) 158,158,155
  155 IF (LLSUP(8)-1) 156,156,158
  156 READ (NCRDR,216) (IINN(I),I=1,NNFIL)
      IF (LLSUP(8)-1) 157,158,158
  157 WRITE (NPRNT,229) (IINN(K),K=1,NNFIL)
C
C*****DATA CARD TYPE NINE IS USED ONLY IF NNEQT IS GREATER THAN ZERO.
C
  158 IF (NNEQT) 159,159,160
  159 DTSAV=0.0
      DTMAX=0.0
      LLSAV=2
      GO TO 171
  160 IF (LLSUP(9)-1) 161,161,171
  161 READ (NCRDR,230) IIEVT,LLERR,AAERR,RRERR,DTMIN,DTMAX,DTSAV
      IF (DTMAX) 162,162,163
  162 DTMAX=0.1
  163 IF (DTSAV.GT.0.0.AND.DTMAX.GT.DTSAV) DTMAX=DTSAV
      IF (DTMIN) 164,164,165
  164 DTMIN=0.01*DTMAX
  165 IF (DTMAX-DTMIN) 166,166,167
  166 DTMIN=DTMAX
  167 IF (AAERR+RRERR) 168,168,169
  168 AAERR=0.00001
      RRERR=0.00001
  169 IF (LLSUP(9)-1) 170,171,171
  170 WRITE (NPRNT,231) IIEVT,LLERR,AAERR,RRERR,DTMIN,DTMAX,DTSAV
C
C*****DATA CARD TYPE TEN IS USED ONLY IF NNPRM IS GREATER THAN ZERO.
C
  171 IF (NNPRM) 178,178,172
  172 IF (LLSUP(10)-1) 173,174,178
  173 WRITE (NPRNT,233)
  174 DO 177 K=1,NNPRM
      READ (NCRDR,232) I,(PPARM(I,J),J=1,4)
      IF (LLSUP(10)-1) 175,177,178
  175 WRITE (NPRNT,234) I,(PPARM(I,J),J=1,4)
      IF (I-K) 176,177,176
  176 WRITE (NPRNT,221)
  177 CONTINUE
C
C*****DATA CARD TYPE ELEVEN. THE IICRD VALUE IS FOR THE NEXT RUN.  SET
C*****JJBEG NOT EQUAL TO ZERO TO SET TNOW EQUAL TO TTBEG.
C
  178 IF (LLSUP(11)-1) 179,179,182
  179 READ (NCRDR,235) MSTOP,JJCLR,JJBEG,IICRD,TTBEG,TTFIN,JJFIL,(IISED(
     1I),I=1,NNSTR)
      IF (NNSTR.GT.MSTRM) CALL ERROR (197)
```

Figure 4-3 *(continued)*

```
      DO 180 I=1,NNSTR
  180 SSEED(I)=IISED(I)
      JBEGG=JJBEG
      IF (LLSUP(11)-1) 181,182,182
  181 WRITE (NPRNT,236) MSTOP,JJCLR,JJBEG,IICRD,TTBEG,TTFIN,JJFIL,(IISED
     1(I),I=1,NNSTR)
C
C*****IF JJBEG IS NOT EQUAL TO ZERO, INITIALIZE DRAND AND TIME.
C
  182 IF (JJBEG) 183,189,183
  183 DO 184 I=1,NNSTR
      NI=-I
  184 RNUM=DRAND(NI)
      TNOW=TTBEG
      TTLAS=TNOW
      IF (TTFIN.LE.0.0) TTFIN=1.E20
      IF (MSTOP.LE.0) TTFIN=1.E20
      TTNEX=TTFIN
      IF (DTSAV) 186,187,185
  185 LLSAV=0
      TTSAV=TTBEG+DTSAV
      GO TO 189
  186 LLSAV=0
      GO TO 188
  187 LLSAV=2
  188 TTSAV=1.E20
  189 IF (JJFIL) 191,191,190
  190 CALL SET
  191 IF (NEPG-13) 192,199,211
C
C*****DATA CARD TYPE TWELVE IS USED ONLY IF NNFIL IS GREATER THAN ZERO.
C*****INITIALIZE FILE STORAGE AREA IF IFILE=-1 FOR FIRST ENTRY.
C*****READ IN INITIAL ENTRIES.
C*****END INITIAL ENTRIES WITH IFILE=0
C
  192 IF (NNFIL) 198,198,193
  193 IF (LLSUP(12)-1) 194,194,198
  194 IDD=NNTRY+2
      DO 197 JS=1,IDD
      READ (NCRDR,238) IFILE,(ATRIB(JK),JK=1,NNATR)
      IF (IFILE) 195,198,196
  195 CALL SET
      GO TO 197
  196 CALL FILEM (IFILE)
  197 CONTINUE
      CALL ERROR (203)
C
C*****DATA CARD TYPE ZERO IS USED ONLY IF NNRNS IS GREATER THAN
C*****ONE AND IICRD EQUALS ZERO.
C
  198 IF (NNRNS.LT.2.OR.IICRD.NE.0) GO TO 199
      READ (NCRDR,212) LLSUP,IICRD
      WRITE (NPRNT,237) LLSUP,IICRD
C
C*****IF JJCLR.GT.0, INITIALIZE SSOBV, SSTPV, AND JJCEL
C
  199 IF (JJCLR) 201,201,200
  200 CALL CLEAR
C
C*****IF JBEG IS GREATER THAN ZERO, CONTINUE INITIALIZATION.
C
  201 IF (JJBEG) 210,210,202
  202 IF (NNEQT.EQ.0) GO TO 204
      DO 203 I=1,NNEQT
      SS(I)=0.0
  203 DD(I)=0.0
  204 CALL INTLC
      IF (NNEQT) 210,210,205
  205 DTFUL=DTMAX
      DTNOW=0.
      ISEES=0
      DO 206 I=1,NNEQT
      DDL(I)=DD(I)
  206 SSL(I)=SS(I)
      CALL STATE
      DO 207 I=1,NNEQT
      DDL(I)=DD(I)
  207 SSL(I)=SS(I)
      IF (NFLAG) 210,210,208
```

Figure 4-3 *(continued)*

```
  208 DO 209 I=1,NFLAG
  209 LFLAG(I)=0
  210 MMNIT=0
C
C*****PRINT STORAGE AREA DUMPS.
C
      IF (LLSUP(13).LT.1.AND.NNFIL.GT.0) CALL PRNTQ (0)
      IF (LLSUP(14).LT.1.AND.NNEQT.GT.0) CALL PRNTS
  211 RETURN
C
  212 FORMAT (15I1,I5)
  213 FORMAT (1H1,33X,25HSIMULATION PROJECT NUMBER,I4,2X,2HBY,2X,3A4//34
     1X,4HDATE,I3,1H/,I3,1H/,I5,7X,10HRUN NUMBER,I5,3H OF,I5/34X,6HLLSUP
     2=,15I1,3X,23HGASP IV VERSION 23JUN73)
  214 FORMAT (3A4,3X,5I5,15I1)
  215 FORMAT (///47X,18HNO OUTPUT, NNRNS=0)
  216 FORMAT (14I5)
  217 FORMAT (//2X,6HNNCLT=,I6,4X,6HNNSTA=,I6,4X,6HNNHIS=,I6,4X,6HNNPRM=
     1,I6,4X,6HNNPLT=,I6,4X,6HNNSTR=,I6,4X,6HNNTRY=,I6/2X,6HNNATR=,I6,4X
     2,6HNNFIL=,I6,4X,6HNNSET=,I6,4X,6HNNEQD=,I6,4X,6HNNEQS=,I6,4X,6HNFL
     3AG=,I6)
  218 FORMAT (5X,I5,2A4,7X,I5,2E10.0)
  219 FORMAT (5X,I5,2A4,2X,E10.0)
  220 FORMAT (2X,9HCOLCT NO.,I3,4X,6HLLABC=,2A4)
  221 FORMAT (1X,46HINPUT WARNING, PRECEDING CARD NOT IN SEQUENCE.)
  222 FORMAT (2X,9HTIMST NO.,I3,4X,6HLLABT=,2A4,2X,6HI.C. =,3X,E12.4)
  223 FORMAT (2X,9HHISTO NO.,I3,4X,6HLLABH=,2A4,18X,6HNNCEL=,I6,4X,6HHHL
     1OW=,3X,E12.4,3X,6HHHWID=,3X,E12.4)
  224 FORMAT (5X,I5,2A4,7X,3I5,E10.0)
  225 FORMAT (5X,I5,A1,2A4,1X,2I5,2E10.0)
  226 FORMAT (2X,9HGPLOT NO.,I3,4X,6HLLABP=,2A4,2X,6HIITAP=,I6,4X,6HNNVA
     1R=,I6,4X,6HLLPLT=,I6,12X,6HDTPLT=,3X,E12.4)
  227 FORMAT (4X,7HVAR NO.,I3,8X,A1,1H=,2A4,2X,6HLLPLO=,I6,4X,6HLLPHI=,I
     16,4X,6HPPLO =,3X,E12.4,3X,6HPPHI =,3X,E12.4)
  228 FORMAT (/2X,6HKKRNK=,2H (,I4,1H),1X,I6,12I7/(6X,14I7))
  229 FORMAT (/2X,6HIINN =,2H (,I4,1H),1X,I6,12I7/(6X,14I7))
  230 FORMAT (2I5,5E10.0)
  231 FORMAT (/2X,6HIIEVT=,I6,4X,6HLLERR=,I6,4X,6HAAERR=,3X,E12.4,11X,6H
     1RRERR=,3X,E12.4/2X,6HDTMIN=,3X,E12.4,11X,6HDTMAX=,3X,E12.4,11X,6HD
     2TSAV=,3X,E12.4)
  232 FORMAT (5X,I5,4E10.0)
  233 FORMAT (1X)
  234 FORMAT (2X,13HPARAMETER SET,I7,2H =,4(3X,E12.4,1X))
  235 FORMAT (4I5,2E10.0,I5,(6I5))
  236 FORMAT (/2X,6HMSTOP=,I6,4X,6HJJCLR=,I6,4X,6HJJBEG=,I6,4X,6HIICRD=,
     1I6,4X,6HTTBEG=,3X,E12.4,3X,6HTTFIN=,3X,E12.4/2X,6HJJFIL=,I6,/(2X,6
     2HIISED=,6(I6,10X)))
  237 FORMAT (/2X,6HLLSUP=,5X,15I1,6X,6HIICRD=,I6)
  238 FORMAT (5X,I5,(6E10.0))
C
      END
```

Figure 4-3 *(continued)*

will be read but not echo checked. If LLSUP(I) is greater than or equal to two, the type I data card will be neither read nor echo checked. For I = 13, 14, or 15, LLSUP ≥ 1 suppresses the printing of the initial entries in the files, the initial values of the state variables, and the GASP IV summary report, respectively.

Since most of the code involves the reading of data cards, as described in Chapter 3, only the significant statements that do not reflect input or output formats are discussed here. On data card type 1, if NNRNS is less than one, the run terminates. This is one method for terminating a series of runs (S-107).

Data card type 2 contains variables describing the size of the model being run. The variables defined are used immediately to control the number of subsequent data cards that will be read (S-110).

Data card types 3, 4, 5, and 6 are similar in that each is associated with a specific form of data collection, computation, and reporting. On each card, the first five columns are skipped when reading a card. These columns are left for the user to identify the card type. They are not read by GASP IV. Columns 6–10 are used to number the cards sequentially within each card type. *The program expects the cards to be numbered sequentially.* The sequence indicated by the value in columns 6–10 is compared to the expected number (D-70). If they do not agree, a warning is printed (S-118). The number on the input data card is assumed to be correct.

Data card type 3 contains the labels used to identify the tabular output prepared by subroutine COLCT. Data card type 4 contains labels and initial values for the time persistent variables processed by subroutines TIMST and TIMSA. The initial values are used in the calculations for the first interval over which statistics are collected in TIMST and TIMSA. *The values do not initialize the variables to which they correspond.* Data card type 5 contains a label, the number of cells, the upper limit for the first cell, and the cell width for each histogram. After reading data card type 5 (D-93), DATIN calculates the storage location of the last cell associated with each histogram (S-135). This index is then stored in NNCEL. (On input NNCEL equals the number of internal cells of the histogram.)

Following the reading of type 6 data cards (D-114), DATIN either calculates the maximum number of points that can be saved in core (S-146) or writes the plot specific data on tape (D-133), depending on the storage location specified by the user in the variable IITAP(·). If IITAP(·) = 0, only one plot is permitted and the data for the plot will be saved in core storage in the array QSET. If IITAP(·) > 0, data will be saved on tape unit number IITAP(·).

Data card type 7 is used to define the ranking attribute for a file (S-151) and data card type 8 defines the priority rule for a file (S-155).

Data card type 9 is associated with state variables. There are several variables on this card that have default values. IIEVT is the code assigned by the user to identify *all* state-events.

A negative value for DTMAX is not meaningful (backward integration is not allowed in GASP IV), therefore, DTMAX is set equal to 0.1 if it is read in as a nonpositive number (S-160). Because a step can never be greater than DTSAV, DTMAX is equated to DTSAV if it is larger than a positive DTSAV (S-161). Likewise, if DTMIN is not positive, it is set equal to 0.01 times DTMAX. If the sum of absolute allowed error AAERR and the relative error RRERR is zero, they are each equated to 0.00001. These values are only used if the RKE integration algorithm is used.

Data card type 10 is used if NNPRM is greater than zero. As with data card types 3, 4, and 5, the first two fields are designed for identification of card type and sequence.

Data card type 11 contains basic run control variables. The value of JJBEG is saved as the local variable JBEGG so that it can be recovered in case of multiple runs. If JJBEG is nonzero, the random number generator, TNOW, TTLAS, and TTNEX are initialized. The random number generator is initialized by calling DRAND with negative stream indices. TNOW and TTLAS are set to the value read in as the beginning time for the simulation (TTBEG). If TTFIN was not set or if MSTOP ≤ 0, TTFIN is set to a large value, 10^{20} (D-211). TTNEX is the time for the next time event, which is initialized as TTFIN. Initialization of LLSAV, the indicator for the communication interval type, and TTSAV, the time of the next communication point, is performed based on the values of DTSAV (D-214).

The reading of data card type 12 is initiated if NNFIL is greater than zero. The number of type 12 data cards to be read is limited only by the storage available. The format for reading entries into files is given by statement 234. Note that six attributes per card are specified. Therefore, if 15 attributes per entry are specified, it requires three cards per entry. (The last card will have three attributes on it).

Data card type 0 is read only if NNRNS > 1 and IICRD $= 0$. It may be used to set the values of LLSUP and IICRD for the succeeding run. It is designated a type 0 card because its effect is on the succeeding run, prior to the reading of data card type 1.

If JJCLR is greater than zero, subroutine CLEAR is called to initialize the statistical storage arrays (S-197).

Next, if JJBEG is positive, subroutine INTLC is called to enable the user to initialize the state variables (S-200). Subroutine INTLC may also be used to initialize other GASP IV variables. For example, multiple runs differing only in the value of KKRNK(25) could be run with one set of data cards and a read statement in INTLC, which reads a value for KKRNK(25). Initialization of the state variables is then completed by calling STATE (D-266) and setting the state variable values associated with time TTLAS(SSL(·)) equal to those associated with TNOW (SS(·)).

The final function of subroutine DATIN is to print the values stored in the file storage area (D-277) and the state storage area (D-278) if requested.

Subroutine CLEAR. This subroutine initializes the statistical storage arrays SSOBV, SSTPV, and JJCEL. The FORTRAN listing of CLEAR is given in Fig. 4-4. Note that for the Ith variable using subroutine COLCT, the initial minimum SSOBV(I,4) and maximum SSOBV(I,5) values are 10^{20} and -10^{20}, respectively. This presumes that some observed value will be greater than -10^{20} and less than 10^{20}. The minimum and maximum value for a time persistent variable is the initial value.

Subroutine CLEAR is normally called by subroutine DATIN during initialization. In addition, the user may employ CLEAR at any time by a direct call or by scheduling a time-event (a monitor event) with an event code of -2. Monitor events are discussed in conjunction with subroutine MONTR. The time at which subroutine CLEAR is called is stored as the variable TTCLR. Statistical calculations performed in subroutine TIMST use the value of TTCLR.

Subroutine SET. This subroutine initializes the pointers and statistics associated with the file storage array NSET. The FORTRAN listing of SET is given in Fig. 4-5. Each group of cells for storing an entry has NNATR + 2 = NNAPT cells. Therefore, the location of the last cell of the Ith group is I ⋆ NNAPT. This cell contains a successor pointer. Subroutine SET defines ICSUC = I ⋆ NNAPT, and sets NSET (ICSUC) =

```
      SUBROUTINE CLEAR                                                  CLR      1
      COMMON /GCOM1/ ATRIB(25),JEVNT,MFA,MFE(100),MLE(100),MSTOP,NCRDR,NGCOM1    1
     1NAPO,NNAPT,NNATR,NNFIL,NNQ(100),NNTRY,NPRNT,PPARM(50,4),TNOW,TTBEGGCOM1    2
     2,TTCLR,TTFIN,TTRIB(25),TTSET                                      GCOM1    3
      COMMON /GCOM4/ DTPLT(10),HHLOW(25),HHWID(25),IICRD,IITAP(10),JJCELGCOM4    1
     1(500),LLABC(25,2),LLABH(25,2),LLABP(11,2),LLABT(25,2),LLPHI(10),LLGCOM4    2
     2PLO(10),LLPLT,LLSUP(15),LLSYM(10),MMPTS,NNCEL(25),NNCLT,NNHIS,NNPLGCOM4    3
     3T,NNPTS(10),NNSTA,NNVAR(10),PPHI(10),PPLO(10)                     GCOM4    4
      COMMON /GCOM6/ EENQ(100),IINN(100),KKRNK(100),MMAXQ(100),QQTIM(100GCOM6    1
     1),SSOBV(25,5),SSTPV(25,6),VVNQ(100)                               GCOM6    2
      KODE=211                                                          CLR      2
      TTCLR=TNOW                                                        CLR      3
      IF (NNCLT) 101,105,102                                            CLR      4
  101 CALL ERROR (KODE)                                                 CLR      5
  102 DO 104 J=1,NNCLT                                                  CLR      6
      DO 103 I=1,3                                                      CLR      7
  103 SSOBV(J,I)=0.                                                     CLR      8
      SSOBV(J,4)=1.0E20                                                 CLR      9
  104 SSOBV(J,5)=-1.0E20                                                CLR     10
  105 KODE=212                                                          CLR     11
      IF (NNSTA) 101,108,106                                            CLR     12
  106 DO 107 J=1,NNSTA                                                  CLR     13
      SSTPV(J,1)=0.0                                                    CLR     14
      SSTPV(J,2)=0.0                                                    CLR     15
      SSTPV(J,3)=TNOW                                                   CLR     16
      SSTPV(J,4)=SSTPV(J,6)                                             CLR     17
  107 SSTPV(J,5)=SSTPV(J,6)                                             CLR     18
  108 KODE=213                                                          CLR     19
      IF (NNHIS) 101,111,109                                            CLR     20
  109 NCELT=NNCEL(NNHIS)                                                CLR     21
      DO 110 I=1,NCELT                                                  CLR     22
  110 JJCEL(I)=0                                                        CLR     23
  111 RETURN                                                            CLR     24
C                                                                       CLR     25
      END                                                               CLR     26
```

Figure 4-4 FORTRAN listing of subroutine CLEAR.

```
      SUBROUTINE SET
      DIMENSION NSET(1)
      COMMON QSET(1)
      COMMON /GCOM1/ ATRIB(25),JEVNT,MFA,MFE(100),MLE(100),MSTOP,NCRDR,N
     1NAPO,NNAPT,NNATR,NNFIL,NNQ(100),NNTRY,NPRNT,PPARM(50,4),TNOW,TTBEG
     2,TTCLR,TTFIN,TTRIB(25),TTSET
      COMMON /GCOM6/ EENQ(100),IINN(100),KKRNK(100),MMAXQ(100),QQTIM(100
     1),SSOBV(25,5),SSTPV(25,6),VVNQ(100)
      EQUIVALENCE (NSET(1),QSET(1))
      IF (NNTRY.LE.0) CALL ERROR (221)
      TTSET=TNOW
      MFA=1
C
C*****INITIALIZE POINTING CELLS OF NSET.
C
      DO 101 I=1,NNTRY
      ICSUC=I*NNAPT
      ICPRD=ICSUC-NNAPO
      NSET(ICPRD)=-1
  101 NSET(ICSUC)=ICSUC+1
      NSET(ICSUC)=0
      DO 102 K=1,NNFIL
      NNQ(K)=0
      MFE(K)=0
      MMAXQ(K)=0
      MLE(K)=0
      EENQ(K)=0.0
      VVNQ(K)=0.0
  102 QQTIM(K)=TNOW
      RETURN
C
      END
```

Figure 4-5 FORTRAN listing of subroutine SET.

ICSUC + 1 since each successor pointer must initially point to the next cell. All predecessor pointers are set at −1 and the last cell of NSET is assigned a zero value.

Subroutine SET is called by subroutine DATIN during initialization, upon request by the user. In addition, the user may use SET at any time by a direct call. The time at which subroutine SET is called is stored as the variable TTSET.

Data Storage and Retrieval

The data storage and retrieval subprograms provide the mechanisms through which entries with their associated attributes are maintained. In GASP IV entries are stored in a doubly linked list maintained in the filing array NSET. NSET is a one dimensional array that is equivalenced to the one dimensional array QSET, which is in COMMON storage. This enables each of the attribute values to be stored as a real and pointers to be stored as integers.

Priority in a file is based on a ranking attribute and a priority method. Any attribute number can be used as the ranking attribute for a file. The ranking attribute number for file I is established by data input and is stored as the GASP IV variable KKRNK(I).

Four priority codes are available in GASP IV.

1. Low-value-first (LVF).
2. High-value-first (HVF).
3. First-in-first-out (FIFO).
4. Last-in-first-out (LIFO).

Secondary ranking for LVF and HVF procedures is FIFO. The GASP IV variable IINN(I) is used to indicate the priority method for file I. If IINN(2) = 2 and KKRNK(2) = 3, file 2 orders its entries in the order of high values for attribute 3. The first entry in the file has the highest value of attribute 3. The KKRNK(·) and IINN(·) variables are accessible to the user and can be changed during a simulation run. When this is done, it is the user's responsibility to rerank the entries existing in the file at the time of the change.

Subroutine FILEM(IFILE). This subroutine stores the attributes of an entry in a file, updates statistics for the file, and maintains the time for the next discrete event TTNEX if the new entry is an event. Subroutine FILEM is a long subroutine since it contains the coding for inserting any entry into any file under any of the four priority methods. Figure 4-6 gives the FORTRAN listing of FILEM, which is now described.

The first test is made to see if there is space to store the new entry (F-5). If no space is available, MFA is zero and error code 301 results (S-101). If space is available, the new entry is identified with the first cell number MFA and the attributes are stored in cells MFA + 1 to MFA + NNATR (S-102). MFA is then updated to be the successor of the group used to store the new entry.

Subroutine FILEM now performs the task of inserting the new entry (NEW) into its proper sequence in file IFILE by updating its pointers and the pointers to the first (MFE) and last (MLE) entries of the file, if necessary. A test is made to see if there are any entries in IFILE (F-21). If not (NNQ = 0), NEW has neither a predecessor nor a successor, and its pointers are set at zero (F-26, F-32). The first entry and last entry pointer are then set to NEW. File statistics are updated and if NEW is an event, TTNEX is set equal to the first attribute of the first event in the event file (F-50).

If there are entries in IFILE, a transfer is made to statement 112. MFEX is the pointer to the first entry in the file, and MLEX is the pointer to the entry against which NEW is tested to determine its proper position in the file. MLEX is initially set to the pointer to the last entry. If NEW is an event (S-113), the ranking attribute is identified as attribute 1 (S-114) and the LVF priority method is established (F-67). The

```
      SUBROUTINE FILEM (IFILE)                                          FLM
      DIMENSION NSET(1)                                                 FLM
      COMMON QSET(1)                                                    FLM
      COMMON /GCOM1/ ATRIB(25),JEVNT,MFA,MFE(100),MLE(100),MSTOP,NCRDR,NFLM
     1NAPO,NNAPT,NNATR,NNFIL,NNQ(100),NNTRY,NPRNT,PPARM(50,4),TNOW,TTBEGFLM
     2,TTCLR,TTFIN,TTRIB(25),TTSET                                      FLM
      COMMON /GCOM2/ DD(100),DDL(100),DTFUL,DTNOW,ISEES,LFLAG(50),NFLAG,FLM
     1NNEQD,NNEQS,NNEQT,SS(100),SSL(100),TTNEX                          FLM
      COMMON /GCOM6/ EENQ(100),IINN(100),KKRNK(100),MMAXQ(100),QQTIM(100FLM
     1),SSOBV(25,5),SSTPV(25,6),VVNQ(100)                               FLM
      EQUIVALENCE (NSET(1),QSET(1))                                     FLM
C                                                                       FLM
C*****TEST TO SEE IF THERE IS SPACE AVAILABLE FOR ANOTHER ENTRY.        FLM
C                                                                       FLM
      IF (MFA) 101,101,102                                              FLM
  101 CALL ERROR (301)                                                  FLM
C                                                                       FLM
C*****PUT ATTRIBUTE VALUES INTO FILE AS ENTRY MFA.                      FLM
C                                                                       FLM
  102 DO 103 I=1,NNATR                                                  FLM
      NSISA=MFA+I                                                       FLM
  103 QSET(NSISA)=ATRIB(I)                                              FLM
C                                                                       FLM
C*****NEW IS ENTRY BEING FILED                                          FLM
C                                                                       FLM
      NEW=MFA                                                           FLM
      MFA=NSET(NSISA+1)                                                 FLM
C                                                                       FLM
C*****TEST WHETHER THERE ARE ENTRIES IN FILE IFILE.                     FLM
C                                                                       FLM
      IF (NNQ(IFILE)) 103,104,112                                       FLM
C                                                                       FLM
C*****NEW HAS NO PREDECESSOR. FIRST ENTRY IN FILE IS MFA.               FLM
C                                                                       FLM
  104 NSET(NEW)=0                                                       FLM
      MFE(IFILE)=NEW                                                    FLM
C                                                                       FLM
C*****NEW HAS NO SUCCESSOR. LAST ENTRY IN FILE IS NEW.                  FLM
C                                                                       FLM
  105 NSISB=NNAPO+NEW                                                   FLM
      NSET(NSISB)=0                                                     FLM
      MLE(IFILE)=NEW                                                    FLM
C                                                                       FLM
C*****UPDATE STATISTICS FOR FILE IFILE.                                 FLM
C                                                                       FLM
  106 XNQ=NNQ(IFILE)                                                    FLM
      EENQ(IFILE)=EENQ(IFILE)+XNQ*(TNOW-QQTIM(IFILE))                   FLM
      VVNQ(IFILE)=VVNQ(IFILE)+XNQ*XNQ*(TNOW-QQTIM(IFILE))               FLM
      QQTIM(IFILE)=TNOW                                                 FLM
      NNQ(IFILE)=NNQ(IFILE)+1                                           FLM
      IF (NNQ(IFILE)-MMAXQ(IFILE)) 108,108,107                          FLM
  107 MMAXQ(IFILE)=NNQ(IFILE)                                           FLM
C                                                                       FLM
C*****IF IFILE.EQ.1, UPDATE TTNEX.                                      FLM
C                                                                       FLM
  108 IF (IFILE-1) 109,110,111                                          FLM
  109 CALL ERROR (302)                                                  FLM
  110 NEXTE=MFE(1)                                                      FLM
      TTNEX=QSET(NEXTE+1)                                               FLM
  111 RETURN                                                            FLM
C                                                                       FLM
C*****MFEX AND MLEX ARE FIRST AND LAST ENTRIES IN FILE IFILE WHICH HAVE FLM
C*****NOT BEEN TESTED AGAINST NEW.                                      FLM
C                                                                       FLM
  112 MFEX=MFE(IFILE)                                                   FLM
      MLEX=MLE(IFILE)                                                   FLM
      IF (IFILE-1) 109,113,114                                          FLM
  113 KS=1                                                              FLM
      INNS=1                                                            FLM
      QQIND=1.                                                          FLM
```

Figure 4-6 FORTRAN listing of subroutine FILEM.

```
      IF (IINN(1).EQ.2) QQIND=-1.
      GO TO 117
C
C*****KS IS RANKING ATTRIBUTE OF ENTRY.
C
  114 KS=KKRNK(IFILE)
      INNS=IINN(IFILE)
C
C*****CHECK TO SEE HOW FILE IS RANKED.
C
      IF (INNS-2) 117,116,115
  115 IF (INNS-4) 124,127,101
C
C*****TEST RANKING ATTRIBUTE OF NEW AGAINST MLEX.
C
  116 QIND=-1.
      GO TO 118
  117 QIND=+1.
  118 NSISA=KS+NEW
  119 NSISB=KS+MLEX
      IF ((QSET(NSISA)-QSET(NSISB))*QIND) 126,120,124
C
C*****A TIE EXISTS. IF IFILE=1, SWITCH TO SECONDARY
C*****RANKING, OTHERWISE, BREAK TIE BY FIFO.
C
  120 IF (IFILE-1) 109,121,124
  121 IF (IINN(1)-3) 122,124,123
  122 NSISA=KKRNK(1)+NEW
      NSISB=KKRNK(1)+MLEX
C
C*****TEST RANKING ATTRIBUTE OF NEW AGAINST MLEX.
C
      IF ((QSET(NSISA)-QSET(NSISB))*QQIND) 123,124,124
  123 MLEX=NSET(MLEX)
      IF (MLEX) 127,127,118
C
C*****MSU IS OLD SUCCESSOR OF MLEX. NEW SUCCESSOR OF MLEX IS NEW.
C*****PREDECESSOR OF NEW IS MLEX.
C
  124 NSISA=NNAPO+MLEX
      MSU=NSET(NSISA)
      NSET(NSISA)=NEW
      NSET(NEW)=MLEX
      IF (MSU) 105,105,125
C
C*****SUCCESSOR OF NEW IS MSU. PREDECESSOR OF MSU IS NEW.
C
  125 NSISA=NNAPO+NEW
      NSET(NSISA)=MSU
      NSET(MSU)=NEW
      GO TO 106
C
C*****NEW MLEX IS PREDECESSOR OF OLD MLEX.
C
  126 MLEX=NSET(MLEX)
      IF (MLEX) 127,127,119
C
C*****NEW HAS NO PREDECESSOR. FIRST ENTRY IN FILE IS NEW.
C
  127 NSET(NEW)=0
      MFE(IFILE)=NEW
C
C*****SUCCESSOR OF NEW IS MFEX. PREDECESSOR OF NEW IS MFEX.
C
      NSISA=NNAPO+NEW
      NSET(NSISA)=MFEX
      NSET(MFEX)=NEW
      GO TO 106
C
      END
```

Figure 4-6 *(continued)*

position of NEW is determined by comparing its ranking attribute value against the corresponding value of entry MLEX. If NEW has priority over MLEX, the predecessor to MLEX is considered. This is continued until an entry currently in the file has a value of the ranking attribute that has a higher or equal priority than the corresponding attribute for the new entry, or NEW is determined to be the first in the file. When the first alternative occurs, NEW is inserted at this point in the file unless a tie exists *and* it is the event file. When this happens, the secondary ranking method and attribute for the event file are used to break ties.

To establish the position of NEW, a test of the ranking attribute of NEW against the ranking attribute of MLEX is performed (F-86). The priority methods LVF (low-value-first) and HVF (high-value-first) are tested by the same statement through the use of the indicator QIND, which is set at +1 (LVF) or −1 (HVF). NEW has priority if the difference in the ranking attributes of NEW and MLEX times QIND is positive. If NEW has a lower priority than MLEX, we have found its place in the file (S-125). If a tie exists and NEW is not being put into file 1, it is placed after the entry in the file that has the same value for its ranking attribute. Thus a FIFO tie breaking rule is used for both LVF and HVF procedures. If the entry is an event, the secondary ranking rule is put into effect (S-121); if NEW has a lower or equal priority based on the secondary ranking procedure, it is placed after the entry with which it is tied (F-103). If NEW is preferred according to the secondary ranking rule, a transfer is made to statement 127 where the next entry to be tested is obtained, that is, the predecessor to MLEX. If no predecessor entry to MLEX exists, NEW becomes the first in the file (S-128). Otherwise, the testing process is repeated (S-113).

When the proper location for NEW is established (S-125), the successor and predecessor entries are established. If NEW is to be the last in the file, a transfer to statement 105 is made where MLE is set equal to NEW. If NEW has a successor MSU, the pointers are established so that the successor of NEW is MSU and the predecessor of MSU is NEW (S-126). A transfer is then made to statement 106 where statistics are collected.

For a FIFO file (IINN = 3), NEW is the last entry and no comparison of attribute values need be made (S-125). For a LIFO file (IINN = 4), NEW is the first entry and no comparison of attribute values is necessary (S-128). This completes the description of subroutine FILEM.

Subroutine RMOVE(NTRY,IFILE). This subroutine is called to remove the entry whose first cell number is NTRY(1) from file IFILE. The local variable NTRYG is set equal to NTRY(1). RMOVE may also be used to cancel an entry. Discussions of this capability are presented in later sections. Subroutine RMOVE is called by subroutine GASP to process the next time-event. RMOVE may also be called directly by the user. The FORTRAN listing of subroutine RMOVE is given in Fig. 4-7. The first function performed by subroutine RMOVE is to load the attribute buffer ATRIB with the attribute values for the entry that is being removed or cancelled. The cells of NSET that contain the attribute values are NTRYG + 1, NTRYG + 2, . . . , NTRYG + NNATR (S-103). Subroutine CANCL calls RMOVE with a file number of −1. The file number is converted to a positive value (S-104).

Since NTRYG is being removed, it becomes the first in line for filing

```
      SUBROUTINE RMOVE (NTRY,IFILE)
      DIMENSION NSET(1)
      COMMON QSET(1)
      COMMON /GCOM1/ ATRIB(25),JEVNT,MFA,MFE(100),MLE(100),MSTOP,NCRDR,N
     1NAPO,NNAPT,NNATR,NNFIL,NNQ(100),NNTRY,NPRNT,PPARM(50,4),TNOW,TTBEG
     2,TTCLR,TTFIN,TTRIB(25),TTSET
      COMMON /GCOM2/ DD(100),DDL(100),DTFUL,DTNOW,ISEES,LFLAG(50),NFLAG,
     1NNEQD,NNEQS,NNEQT,SS(100),SSL(100),TTNEX
      COMMON /GCOM3/ AAERR,DTMAX,DTMIN,DTSAV,IITES,LLEPR,LLSAV,LLSEV,RRE
     1RR,TTLAS,TTSAV
      COMMON /GCOM6/ EENQ(100),IINN(100),KKRNK(100),MMAXQ(100),QQTIM(100
     1),SSOBV(25,5),SSTPV(25,6),VVNQ(100)
      EQUIVALENCE (NSET(1),QSET(1))
      DIMENSION NTRY(1)
      NTRYG=NTRY(1)
      IF (NTRYG) 101,101,102
  101 CALL ERROR (311)
C
C*****PUT VALUES OF NTRY IN ATRIB
C
  102 DO 103 I=1,NNATR
      NSISA=NTRYG+I
  103 ATRIB(I)=QSET(NSISA)
      IFILG=IFILE
      IF (IFILE) 104,101,105
  104 IFILG=-IFILE
C
C*****REMOVAL OF AN ENTRY FROM IFILE.
C*****UPDATE POINTERS TO ACCOUNT FOR REMOVAL OF NTRY.
C*****LET JL EQUAL SUCCESSOR OF NTRY AND JK EQUAL PREDECESSOR OF NTRY.
C*****IF JL=0, NTRY WAS LAST ENTRY. IF JK=0, NTRY WAS FIRST ENTRY.
C
  105 NSISA=NNAPO+NTRYG
      JL=NSET(NSISA)
      JK=NSET(NTRYG)
      NSET(NSISA)=MFA
      MFA=NTRYG
      NSISA=NNAPO+JK
      IF (JL) 107,107,106
  106 IF (JK) 109,109,108
  107 IF (JK) 111,111,110
C
C*****NTRY WAS NOT FIRST OR LAST ENTRY. UPDATE POINTERS SO THAT
C*****JL IS SUCCESSOR OF JK AND JK IS PREDECESSOR OF JL.
C
  108 NSET(NSISA)=JL
      NSET(JL)=JK
      GO TO 112
C
C*****NTRY WAS FIRST ENTRY BUT NOT LAST ENTRY. UPDATE POINTERS.
C
  109 NSET(JL)=0
      MFE(IFILG)=JL
      GO TO 112
```

Figure 4-7 FORTRAN listing of subroutine RMOVE.

```
C
C*****NTRY WAS LAST ENTRY BUT NOT FIRST ENTRY. UPDATE POINTERS.
C
  110 NSET(NSISA)=0
      MLE(IFILG)=JK
      GO TO 112
C
C*****NTRY WAS ONLY ENTRY. UPDATE POINTERS.
C
  111 MFE(IFILG)=0
      MLE(IFILG)=0
C
C*****IF IFILG=1 UPDATE TTNEX
C
  112 IF (IFILG-1) 114,113,117
  113 NEXTE=MFE(1)
      IF (NEXTE) 114,116,115
  114 WRITE (NPRNT,118)
      CALL ERROR (312)
  115 TTNEX=QSET(NEXTE+1)
      IF (TTNEX-TTFIN) 117,117,116
  116 TTNEX=TTFIN
C
C*****UPDATE FILE STATISTICS.
C
  117 XNQ=NNQ(IFILG)
      ENQ(IFILG)=EENQ(IFILG)+XNQ*(TNOW-QQTIM(IFILG))
      VVNQ(IFILG)=VVNQ(IFILG)+XNQ*XNQ*(TNOW-QQTIM(IFILG))
      QQTIM(IFILG)=TNOW
      NNQ(IFILG)=NNQ(IFILG)-1
      RETURN
C
  118 FORMAT (//5X,44HPOSSIBLE CAUSE OF ERROR IS USER BLANK COMMON)
C
      END
```

Figure 4-7 *(continued)*

an entry, that is, MFA. The local variable JL is used to store the successor of NTRYG, and JK is used to store the predecessor of NTRYG. NTRYG is then put into the list of available groups for filing entries by setting its successor to the old first available (MFA) and setting MFA to NTRYG (R-25).

NSISA is set equal to the cell number containing the successor pointer of the predecessor of NTRYG (R-26). Special conditions are then checked to determine whether NTRYG had no successor (R-27), no predecessor (S-106), or no predecessor and no successor (S-107). In the last case, NTRYG was the only entry in the file and only the first entry pointer (MFE) and last entry pointer (MLE) need to be updated. This is done at statement 111. If NTRYG had both a predecessor and a successor, these are made to point to one another (S-108). If NTRYG was the first entry but not the last entry, then NTRYG's successor has no predecessor and the pointer to the first entry in the file MFE is set equal to JL, the successor of NTRYG (S-109). If NTRYG was the last entry in the file but not the first, NTRYG's predecessor does not point to an entry and the pointer to the last entry in the file MLE is set equal to JK, that is, the last entry in the file is now the predecessor of NTRYG (S-110).

If an event is being removed, that is, IFILG = 1, TTNEX is established as the smaller of the time of the next event in the event file and TTFIN (S-113 to S-116).

File statistics are then updated (S-117). The maximum number of entries in the file is not updated since a maximum cannot be obtained when an entry is being removed.

Subroutine CANCL(NTRY). This subroutine is used to cancel an entry in the event file whose first cell is NTRY. Cancellation of an event consists of removing it from the file storage array, updating TTNEX if the event was the next event, loading the buffer ATRIB, and updating file statistics. In other words, cancellation consists of the same functions as removal. The FORTRAN listing of subroutine CANCL is given in Fig. 4-8.

Subroutine CANCL is included only for its mnemonic value and is equivalent to the direct use of the statement CALL RMOVE(NTRY, + 1).

Subroutine COPY(NTRY). This subroutine is called to copy the values of the attributes of entry NTRY to the buffer ATRIB. Copying an entry does not change the file storage area or its associated statistics in any way. The FORTRAN listing of subroutine COPY is given in Fig. 4-9.

Location of State Conditions and Entities

Two functions, KROSS and NFIND, are included in GASP IV for location purposes. Function KROSS assists in locating the time at which specified state conditions are met. NFIND is used to identify the first cell of an entry having an attribute with a specified value in a particular file.

Function KROSS(IKRSG,IKRSD,CMULT,CADD,LDIR,TOL). This function locates specified state conditions and returns a coded value indi-

```
      SUBROUTINE CANCL (NTRY)
      DIMENSION NTRY(1)
C
C*****REMOVE NTRY FROM EVENT FILE, UPDATE TTNEX , DO NOT UPDATE TNOW OR
C*****JEVNT.
C
      CALL RMOVE (NTRY(1),-1)
      RETURN
C
      END
```

Figure 4-8 FORTRAN listing of subroutine CANCL.

```
      SUBROUTINE COPY (NTRY)                                            CPY    1
      DIMENSION NTRY(1)                                                 CPY    2
      DIMENSION NSET(1)                                                 DIM    1
      COMMON QSET(1)                                                    COM    1
      COMMON /GCOM1/ ATRIB(25),JEVNT,MFA,MFE(100),MLE(100),MSTOP,NCRDR,NGCOM1    1
     1NAPO,NNAPT,NNATR,NNFIL,NNQ(100),NNTRY,NPRNT,PPARM(50,4),TNOW,TTBEGGCOM1    2
     2,TTCLR,TTFIN,TTRIB(25),TTSET                                      GCOM1  3
      EQUIVALENCE (NSET(1),QSET(1))                                     EQUIV  1
C                                                                       CPY    3
      NTRYG=NTRY(1)                                                     CPY    4
      IF (NTRYG) 101,101,102                                            CPY    5
  101 CALL ERROR (313)                                                  CPY    6
  102 DO 103 I=1,NNATR                                                  CPY    7
      NSISA=NTRYG+I                                                     CPY    8
  103 ATRIB(I)=QSET(NSISA)                                              CPY    9
      RETURN                                                            CPY   10
C                                                                       CPY   11
      END                                                               CPY   12
```

Figure 4-9 FORTRAN listing of subroutine COPY.

cating whether the conditions have been met, not met, or exceeded. The definition of the arguments for KROSS are:

Argument	Definition
IKRSG	Index of the crossing variable; the crossing variable is: SS(I) if $I > 0$ DD(−I) if $-I > 0$ None if $I = 0$
IKRSD	Index of the crossed variable; the crossed variable is: SS(I) if $I > 0$ DD(−I) if $-I > 0$ None if $I = 0$
CMULT	A multiplicative constant associated with the crossed variable
CADD	An additive constant associated with the crossed variable
LDIR	A user specified code indicating the direction of crossing of interest: Positive crossings only if LDIR > 0 All crossings if LDIR $= 0$ Negative crossings only if LDIR < 0
TOL	The tolerance associated with the crossing

Function KROSS is used primarily in subroutine SCOND and performs the dual functions of causing subroutine GASP (through its calls to SCOND) to "search" for specified state conditions and marking the satisfaction of those conditions. The first function is accomplished through use of the GASP IV control variable ISEES. The second is accomplished by returning a coded value of KROSS, indicating that a crossing has occurred.

A crossing may be either positive or negative. A positive crossing occurs when a variable (the crossing variable) increases in value from less than to greater than or equal to a second variable (the crossed variable), times a multiplicative constant, plus an additive constant. Both the crossing and crossed variables must be state variables when using KROSS, and they are identified by their subscripts. A zero value for the subscript of the crossed variable or a zero value of the multiplicative constant reduces the crossing description to one of a variable crossing a constant. The concept of a negative crossing is analogous to that of a positive crossing.

A crossing is defined as being located with sufficient precision if (1) a discrete change caused the crossing, in which case the crossing is located exactly in time or (2) a time advance caused the crossing *and* the difference at the end of the step between the crossing variable and the crossed function is less than or equal to the prescribed tolerance. Figure 4-10 illustrates the tolerance concept in determining crossings. The "X" points on the SS(1) curve indicate where SS(1) is evaluated.

At TTLAS, SS(1) $<$ 10.0 and at TNOW, SS(1) $>$ 10.5. If in SCOND the statement LFLAG(2) = KROSS(1,0,0.0,10.0, + 1,0.5) is written, GASP IV would attempt to reduce TNOW and reevaluate the state variables to make SS(1) $\leq$ 10.5. If DTNOW = DTMIN, no reduction is possible and either the simulation is halted (LLERR = +1) or the state-

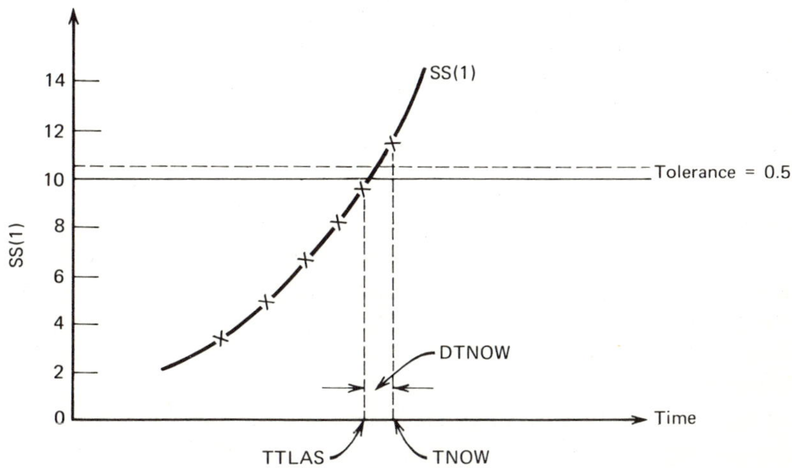

Figure 4-10 Illustration of tolerance concepts in determining a crossing.

event defined by LFLAG(2) is assumed to occur at TNOW (LLERR < 1). If DTNOW > DTMIN, DTNOW is reduced and SS(1) is recomputed at the new smaller value of TNOW. If $10.0 \leq$ SS(1) ≤ 10.5, it is assumed that the state-event occurs at TNOW. The direct relationship between the value of the tolerance and the value assigned to DTMIN should be noted. The tolerance value should be in the range of DTMIN times the maximum rate of change between the crossing variable and the function to be crossed. It is the user's responsibility to make these values consistent.

The user specifies not only the state conditions and tolerances defining a crossing but also the direction of crossing. Thus it is possible to search for and identify either negative or positive crossings or both. This flexibility permits, for example, the location of a local maximum (or point of inflection) by defining a negative crossing of zero by the derivative of the variable of interest.

The flow chart and FORTRAN listing for function KROSS are given in Figs. 4-11 and 4-12, respectively. The coding of function KROSS begins with a calculation of the value of both the crossing variable at time TTLAS and time TNOW (CRSGL and CRSGN, respectively) and the crossed function at TTLAS and TNOW (CRSDL and CRSDN, respectively). A check is made to determine if a crossing has occurred in the direction of interest (S-107). Note that an even number of crossings during the same time step would not be detected. KROSS is then assigned the appropriate value as defined in the following table:

KROSS	Condition
+2	Positive crossing exceeding the specified tolerance
+1	Positive crossing within tolerance
0	No crossing in the specified direction of interest
−1	Negative crossing within tolerance
−2	Negative crossing exceeding the specified tolerance

Function KROSS also sets the control variable ISEES thereby causing GASP IV to "search" for specified state conditions. The value to which ISEES is set depends on the previous value of ISEES. The reason for this can best be illustrated by an example. If subroutine SCOND contains two statements that use KROSS, and the first sets ISEES < 0 (indicating that specified state conditions were passed in excess of tolerance), the second use of KROSS must not reset ISEES even though the second set of state conditions may not have occurred. In subroutine SCOND, ISEES should not be reset unless a combination of crossings is programmed by the user.

Upon return from SCOND, subroutine GASP resets ISEES after taking appropriate action based on the value of ISEES. On input to function KROSS, the value of ISEES would be zero if no previous calls to KROSS were made, or it could have any value associated with a crossing if previous calls to KROSS were made. Based on the value of ISEES on input, KROSS sets ISEES as follows for the conditions indicated.

Condition	Input Value of ISEES	Output Value of ISEES
Crossing by SS(I) exceeding tolerance	>0	−I
	=0	−I
	<0	Input value
Crossing by SS(I) within tolerance	>0	Input value
	=0	I
	<0	Input value
Crossing by DD(I) exceeding tolerance	>0	−I − 1000
	=0	−I − 1000
	<0	Input value
Crossing by DD(I) within tolerance	>0	Input value
	=0	I + 1000
	<0	Input value
No crossing in specified direction of interest	>0	Input value
	=0	Input value
	<0	Input value

Function KROSS is normally used in conjunction with the GASP IV state condition flags (LFLAG). The reason is that these state condition flag indicators are automatically reset within subroutine GASP whenever an event is processed. It should be recognized, however, that KROSS need not always be used with LFLAG. For example, KROSS may be used in conjunction with MSTOP to terminate a run.

Function NFIND(XVAL,MCODE,IFILE,JATT,TOL). Function NFIND locates an entry called NFIND in file IFILE, which contains a value for attribute JATT that bears a relationship designated by the user to a specified value, XVAL. Definitions of the arguments to NFIND are:

1. XVAL—A value used to locate an entry in NSET containing an attribute value having a specified relationship to XVAL.

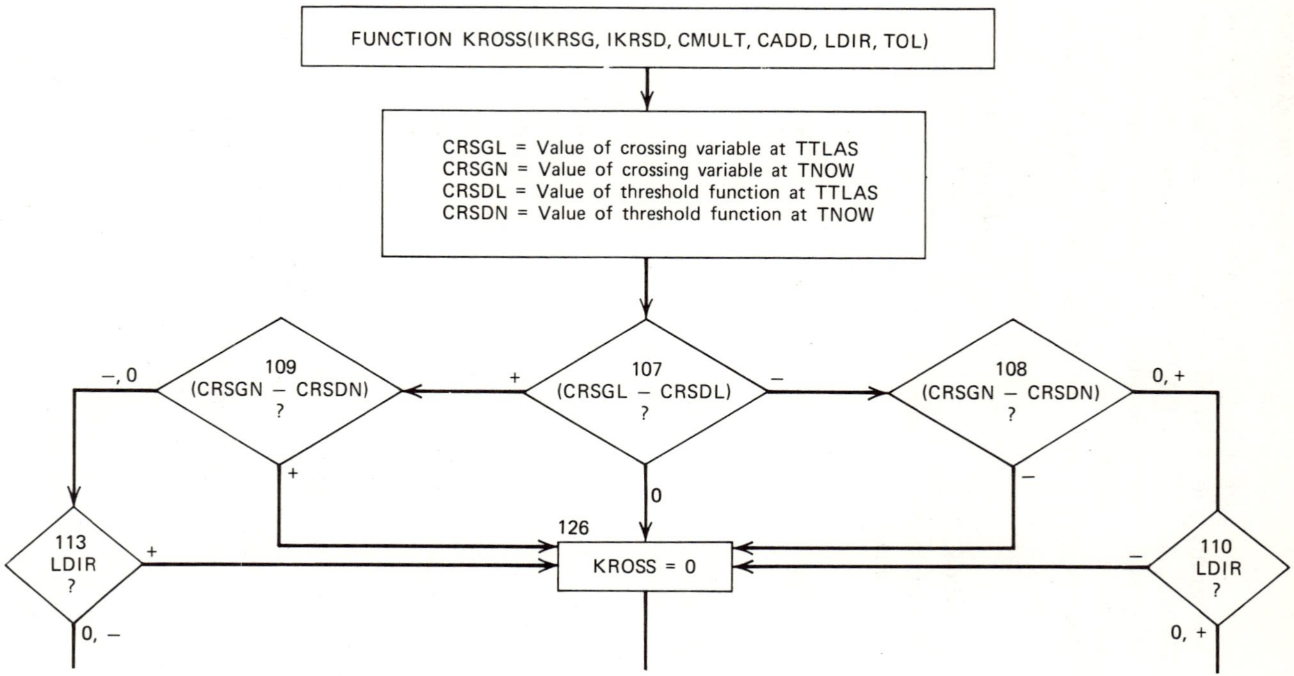
FUNCTION KROSS(IKRSG, IKRSD, CMULT, CADD, LDIR, TOL)
CRSGL = Value of crossing variable at TTLAS
CRSGN = Value of crossing variable at TNOW
CRSDL = Value of threshold function at TTLAS
CRSDN = Value of threshold function at TNOW
107 (CRSGL − CRSDL) ?
108 (CRSGN − CRSDN) ?
109 (CRSGN − CRSDN) ?
110 LDIR ?
113 LDIR ?
126
KROSS = 0
−, 0
0, +
0, −
+
−
0

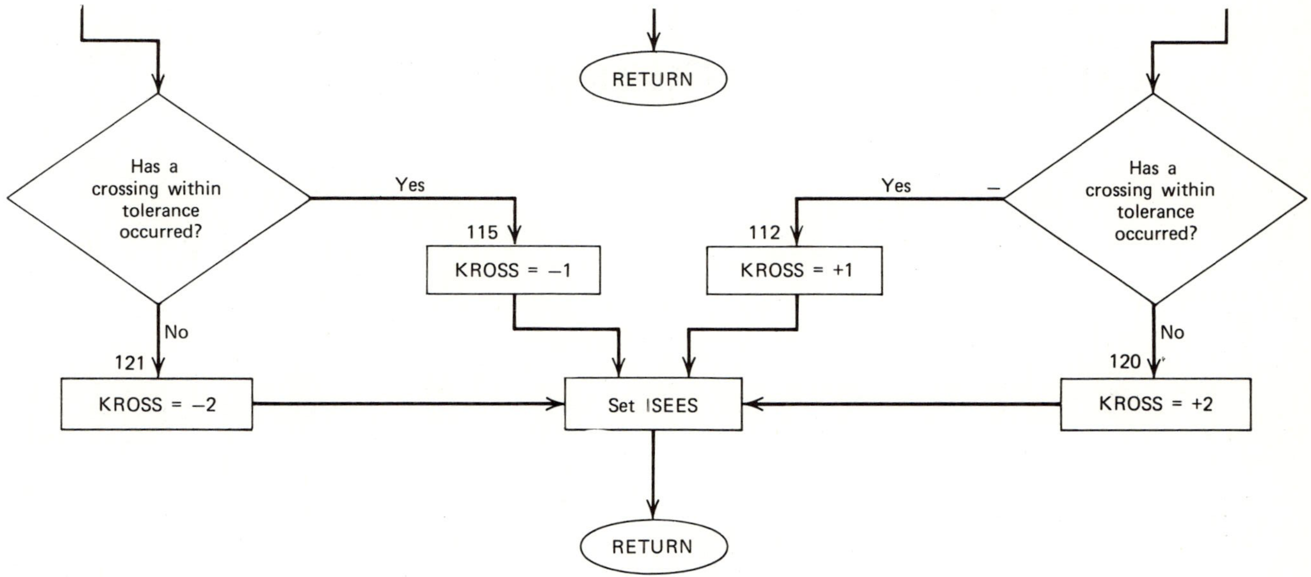

Figure 4-11 Flow chart of function KROSS.

```
      FUNCTION KROSS(IKRSG,IKRSD,CMULT,CADD,LDIR,TOL)
      COMMON /GCOM2/ DD(100),DDL(100),DTFUL,DTNOW,ISEES,LFLAG(50),NFLAG,
     1NNEQD,NNEQS,NNEQT,SS(100),SSL(100),TTNEX
      JKRSG=IKRSG
      JKRSD=IKRSD
      IF (JKRSG) 101,126,102
  101 JKRSG=-JKRSG
      CRSGL=DDL(JKRSG)
      CRSGN=DD(JKRSG)
      GO TO 103
  102 CRSGL=SSL(JKRSG)
      CRSGN=SS(JKRSG)
  103 IF (JKRSD) 104,105,106
  104 JKRSD=-JKRSD
      CRSDL=DDL(JKRSD)*CMULT+CADD
      CRSDN=DD(JKRSD)*CMULT+CADD
      GO TO 107
  105 CRSDL=CADD
      CRSDN=CADD
      GO TO 107
  106 CRSDL=SSL(JKRSD)*CMULT+CADD
      CRSDN=SS(JKRSD)*CMULT+CADD
  107 IF (CRSGL-CRSDL) 108,126,109
  108 IF (CRSGN-CRSDN) 126,110,110
  109 IF (CRSGN-CRSDN) 113,113,126
  110 IF (LDIR) 126,111,111
  111 IF (CRSGN-CRSDN-TOL) 112,112,120
  112 KROSS=1
      GO TO 116
  113 IF (LDIR) 114,114,126
  114 IF (CRSGN-CRSDN+TOL) 121,115,115
  115 KROSS=-1
  116 IF (ISEES) 127,117,127
  117 IF (IKRSG) 118,127,119
  118 ISEES=JKRSG+1000
      GO TO 127
  119 ISEES=JKRSG
      GO TO 127
  120 KROSS=2
      GO TO 122
  121 KROSS=-2
  122 IF (ISEES) 127,123,123
  123 IF (IKRSG) 124,127,125
  124 ISEES=-JKRSG-1000
      GO TO 127
  125 ISEES=-JKRSG
      GO TO 127
  126 KROSS=0
  127 RETURN
C
      END
```

Figure 4-12 FORTRAN listing of function KROSS.

2. MCODE—A code specifying the relationship between XVAL and the attribute value. The following five options are available: (a) MCODE = 1; maximum value greater than XVAL; (b) MCODE = 2; minimum value greater than XVAL; (c) MCODE = 3; maximum value less than XVAL; (d) MCODE = 4; minimum value less than XVAL; and (e) MCODE = 5; value equal to XVAL ± TOL.

3. IFILE—The file containing the entry to be located. IFILE can be 1, 2, . . . , NNFIL.

4. JATT—The attribute number specified to find the entry meeting the conditions specified by MCODE. The user specifies a value for JATT from 1 to NNATR.

5. TOL—A value that is used when MCODE = 5 (see 2(e) above).

The flow chart and FORTRAN listing for function NFIND are given in Figs. 4-13 and 4-14. The search for an entry that meets the conditions specified by MCODE starts with the first entry. Each entry in the file is then examined in turn for feasibility (satisfying the prescribed conditions) and optimality (being the entry with the largest or smallest value). Each search code specifies a combination of values for XGRNV and XMAMN

where XGRNV = +1 if search requires entry to have attribute value greater than XVAL
−1 if search requires entry to have attribute value smaller than XVAL,
and XMAMN = +1 if largest value is desired
−1 if smallest value is desired.

All tests for feasibility compare the attribute of the entry with XVAL. If the entry is feasible, the test for optimality is performed (N-49). When an entry is preferred to the current best entry KBEST, it becomes KBEST (S-116). If in the test for feasibility equality is found within a tolerance, and if an equality search is being performed (MCODE = 5), the appropriate entry has been found. Specifically, the entry with the highest ranking in the file that has attribute JATT in the interval (XVAL − TOL, XVAL + TOL) is specified as the desired entry. For MCODE values other than 5, all entries in the file are compared and the best one is specified as the desired entry NFIND. If no entry meets the feasibility criterion, NFIND is set equal to zero and a return is made to the calling routine.

Data Collection, Computation, and Reporting

GASP IV includes eight subroutines that support data collection, computation, and reporting. Subroutines COLCT, TIMST, HISTO, and GPLOT each perform all three functions. The user normally employs only the collection mode since the computation and reporting mode are automatically used during the preparation of a GASP IV summary report. Subroutine TIMSA is used only for data collection. Subroutines PRNTQ and PRNTS perform only computation and reporting. They are normally used during the preparation of the echo check and again during the preparation of the summary report. Subroutine SUMRY performs only a reporting function. It is normally called by subroutine GASP to provide

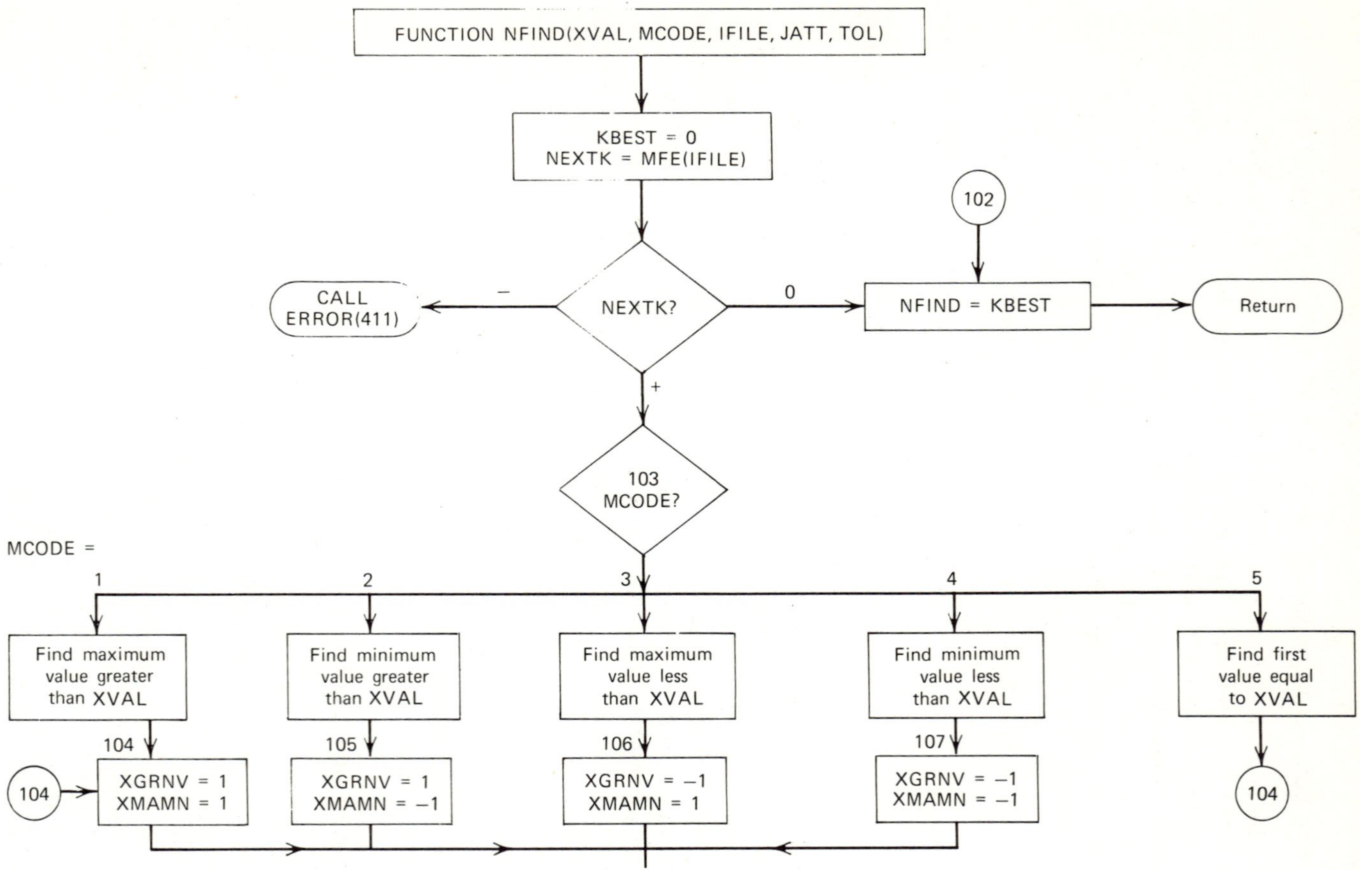
FUNCTION NFIND(XVAL, MCODE, IFILE, JATT, TOL)
KBEST = 0
NEXTK = MFE(IFILE)
102
CALL ERROR(411)
–
NEXTK?
0
NFIND = KBEST
Return
+
103
MCODE?
MCODE =
1
2
3
4
5
Find maximum value greater than XVAL
Find minimum value greater than XVAL
Find maximum value less than XVAL
Find minimum value less than XVAL
Find first value equal to XVAL
104
105
106
107
104
XGRNV = 1
XMAMN = 1
XGRNV = 1
XMAMN = –1
XGRNV = –1
XMAMN = 1
XGRNV = –1
XMAMN = –1
104

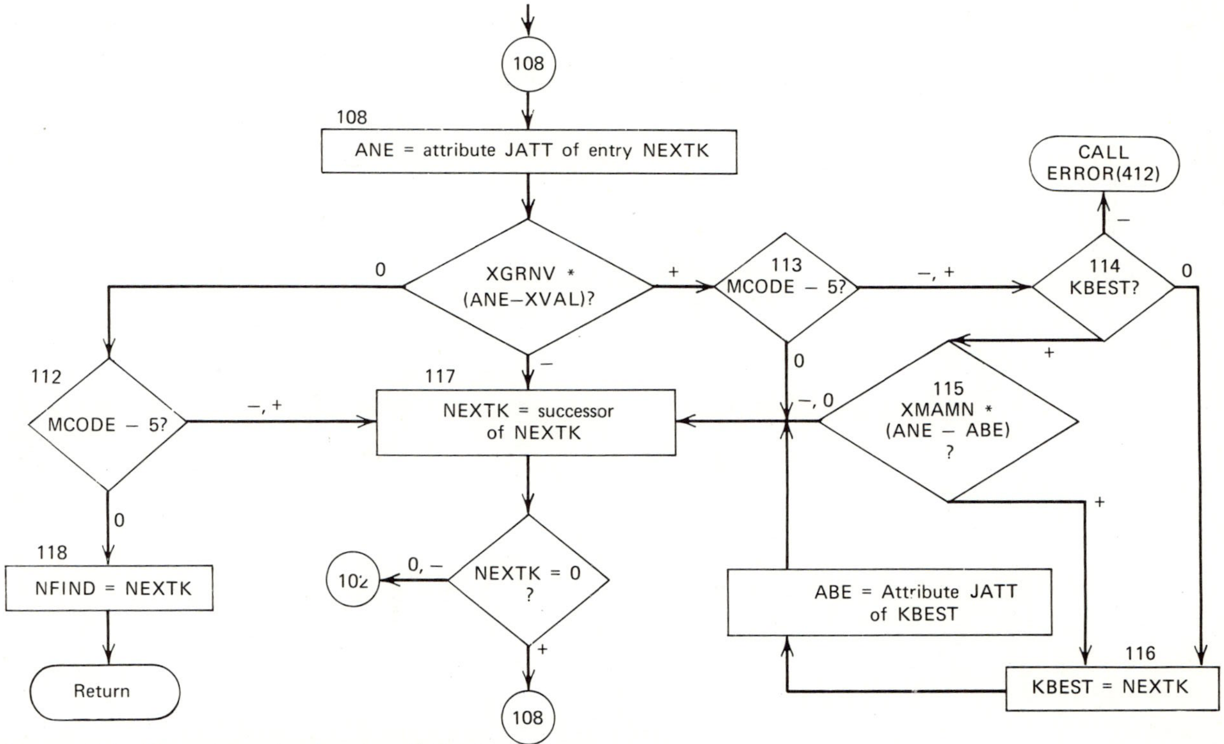

Figure 4-13 Flow chart of subroutine NFIND.

```
      FUNCTION NFIND(XVAL,MCODE,IFILE,JATT,TOL)
      DIMENSION XVAL(1)
      DIMENSION NSET(1)
      COMMON QSET(1)
      COMMON /GCOM1/ ATRIB(25),JEVNT,MFA,MFE(100),MLE(100),MSTOP,NCRDR,NN
     1NAPO,NNAPT,NNATR,NNFIL,NNQ(100),NNTRY,NPRNT,PPARM(50,4),TNOW,TTBEG
     2,TTCLR,TTFIN,TTRIB(25),TTSET
      EQUIVALENCE (NSET(1),QSET(1))
C
C*****THE ENTRY WHICH IS THE BEST CANDIDATE IS KBEST
C
      KBEST=0
C
C*****THE NEXT ENTRY TO BE CONSIDERED IS NEXTK.
C
      NEXTK=MFE(IFILE)
      KODE=411
      IF (NEXTK) 101,102,103
  101 CALL ERROR (KODE)
  102 NFIND=KBEST
      GO TO 119
C
C*****XGRNV IS +1 FOR GREATER THAN SEARCH AND -1 FOR LESS THAN SEARCH
C*****XMAMN IS +1 FOR MAXIMUM AND -1 FOR MINIMUM
C*****FOR SEARCH FOR EQUALITY THE SIGN OF XGRNV AND XMAMN ARE NOT USED.
C
  103 GO TO (104,105,106,107,104), MCODE
  104 XGRNV=1.
      XMAMN=1.
      GO TO 108
  105 XGRNV=1.
      XMAMN=-1.
      GO TO 108
  106 XGRNV=-1.
      XMAMN=1.
      GO TO 108
  107 XGRNV=-1.
      XMAMN=-1.
  108 NSISA=JATT+NEXTK
      TEMP=XGRNV*(QSET(NSISA)-XVAL(1))
      TEM=TEMP
      IF (TEMP) 109,110,110
  109 TEM=-TEMP
  110 IF (TEM-TOL) 112,112,111
  111 IF (TEMP) 117,112,113
C
C*****WHEN EQUALITY IS OBTAINED TEST FOR MCODE=5, THE SEARCH FOR A
C*****SPECIFIED VALUE.
C
  112 IF (MCODE-5) 117,118,117
  113 IF (MCODE-5) 114,117,114
  114 KODE=412
      IF (KBEST) 101,116,115
  115 NSISB=JATT+KBEST
      IF (XMAMN*(QSET(NSISA)-QSET(NSISB))) 117,117,116
  116 KBEST=NEXTK
  117 NSISA=NNAPO+NEXTK
      NEXTK=NSET(NSISA)
      IF (NEXTK) 102,102,108
  118 NFIND=NEXTK
  119 RETURN
C
      END
```

Figure 4-14 FORTRAN listing of function NFIND.

a complete summary report. However, SUMRY can be called by the user at any time without altering any GASP IV variables.

Subroutine COLCT(XX,ICLCT). This subroutine collects sample data for variables based on an observation of the variable when used in the collection mode. In the computation and reporting mode, it calculates the mean, standard deviation, standard deviation of the mean (assuming independent observations), coefficient of variation, minimum, maximum, and number of observations. It also provides tabular output of the calculated statistics. The arguments are:

Argument	Definition
XX	If ICLCT > 0, the value of the variable collected; if ICLCT ≤ 0, not used
ICLCT	The code identifying both the variable for which data is collected and the mode in which COLCT is being used. The modes and ICLCT values identifying the modes are:

Condition	Mode
ICLCT > 0	Collect on XX
ICLCT = 0	Compute and report on all variables identified by I = 1, NNCLT
ICLCT < 0	Compute and report on variable identified by −ICLCT

The FORTRAN listing of subroutine COLCT is given in Fig. 4-15. Statements 105 through 108 provide the data collection calculations.

When called, COLCT adds the value XX to the sum of all previous observations with code ICLCT, adds XX^2 to the sum of the square of the previous observations, adds 1 to the number of observations, and determines if XX is either the maximum or the minimum value observed so far.

In GASP IV data can be collected for a maximum of NNCLT different variables. Values calculated in COLCT are stored in the array SSOBV (ICLCT,J), J = 1,2,3,4,5. The statement CALL COLCT(10.0,2) adds 10.0 to SSOBV(2,1), 100.0 to SSOBV(2,2), and 1.0 to SSOBV(2,3). SSOBV(2,4) is set equal to the minimum of SSOBV(2,4) and 10.0. SSOBV(2,5) is set equal to the maximum of SSOBV(2,5) and 10.

Since the sum of the observations are stored in SSOBV(ICLCT,1) and the number of observations in SSOBV(ICLCT,3), the average is the ratio of these quantities (C-29). The calculations of all statistical quantities

```
      SUBROUTINE COLCT (XX,ICLCT)                                       CLC    1
      DIMENSION XX(1)                                                   CLC    2
      COMMON /GCOM1/ ATRIB(25),JEVNT,MFA,MFE(100),MLE(100),MSTOP,NCRDR,NGCOM1  1
     1NAPO,NNAPT,NNATR,NNFIL,NNQ(100),NNTRY,NPRNT,PPARM(50,4),TNOW,TTBEGGCOM1  2
     2,TTCLR,TTFIN,TTRIB(25),TTSET                                      GCOM1  3
      COMMON /GCOM4/ DTPLT(10),HHLOW(25),HHWID(25),IICRD,IITAP(10),JJCELGCOM4  1
     1(500),LLABC(25,2),LLABH(25,2),LLABP(11,2),LLABT(25,2),LLPHI(10),LLGCOM4  2
     2PLO(10),LLPLT,LLSUP(15),LLSYM(10),MMPTS,NNCEL(25),NNCLT,NNHIS,NNPLGCOM4  3
     3T,NNPTS(10),NNSTA,NNVAR(10),PPHI(10),PPLO(10)                     GCOM4  4
      COMMON /GCOM6/ EENQ(100),IINN(100),KKRNK(100),MMAXQ(100),QQTIM(100GCOM6  1
     1),SSOBV(25,5),SSTPV(25,6),VVNQ(100)                               GCOM6  2
      IF (ICLCT) 101,102,103                                            CLC    3
  101 IFC=-ICLCT                                                        CLC    4
      ILC=IFC                                                           CLC    5
      GO TO 109                                                         CLC    6
  102 IFC=1                                                             CLC    7
      ILC=NNCLT                                                         CLC    8
      GO TO 109                                                         CLC    9
  103 IF (ICLCT-NNCLT) 105,105,104                                      CLC   10
  104 CALL ERROR (501)                                                  CLC   11
  105 SSOBV(ICLCT,1)=SSOBV(ICLCT,1)+XX(1)                               CLC   12
      SSOBV(ICLCT,2)=SSOBV(ICLCT,2)+XX(1)*XX(1)                         CLC   13
      SSOBV(ICLCT,3)=SSOBV(ICLCT,3)+1.                                  CLC   14
      IF (XX(1)-SSOBV(ICLCT,4)) 106,107,107                             CLC   15
  106 SSOBV(ICLCT,4)=XX(1)                                              CLC   16
  107 IF (XX(1)-SSOBV(ICLCT,5)) 117,117,108                             CLC   17
  108 SSOBV(ICLCT,5)=XX(1)                                              CLC   18
      GO TO 117                                                         CLC   19
  109 WRITE (NPRNT,118)                                                 CLC   20
      DO 116 J=IFC,ILC                                                  CLC   21
      IF (SSOBV(J,3)) 110,111,112                                       CLC   22
  110 CALL ERROR (502)                                                  CLC   23
  111 WRITE (NPRNT,119) LLABC(J,1),LLABC(J,2)                           CLC   24
      GO TO 116                                                         CLC   25
  112 XS=SSOBV(J,1)                                                     CLC   26
      XSS=SSOBV(J,2)                                                    CLC   27
      XN=SSOBV(J,3)                                                     CLC   28
      AVG=XS/XN                                                         CLC   29
      NXN=XN+.000001                                                    CLC   30
      IF (NXN-1) 113,113,114                                            CLC   31
  113 STD=0.                                                            CLC   32
      GO TO 115                                                         CLC   33
  114 STD=SQRT((XSS-XS*XS/XN)/(XN-1.))                                  CLC   34
  115 STDM=STD/SQRT(XN)                                                 CLC   35
      CV=99999.                                                         CLC   36
      IF (AVG.NE.0.0) CV=STD/AVG                                        CLC   37
      WRITE (NPRNT,120) LLABC(J,1),LLABC(J,2),AVG,STD,STDM,CV,SSOBV(J,4)CLC   38
     1,SSOBV(J,5),NXN                                                   CLC   39
  116 CONTINUE                                                          CLC   40
  117 RETURN                                                            CLC   41
C                                                                       CLC   42
  118 FORMAT (//33X,49H**STATISTICS FOR VARIABLES BASED ON OBSERVATION**CLC   43
     1/16X,4HMEAN,10X,7HSTD DEV,8X,10HSD OF MEAN,10X,2HCV,11X,7HMINIMUM,CLC   44
     29X,7HMAXIMUM,6X,3HOBS/)                                           CLC   45
  119 FORMAT (2X,2A4,39X,18HNO VALUES RECORDED)                         CLC   46
  120 FORMAT (2X,2A4,1X,E12.4,1X,5(3X,E12.4,1X),I6)                     CLC   47
C                                                                       CLC   48
      END                                                               CLC   49
```

Figure 4-15 FORTRAN listing of subroutine COLCT.

are made by statements 112–116. The array SSOBV is a GASP IV vector and is accessible to the user in any subprogram that includes the GCOM6 named COMMON block.

Subroutine TIMST(XX,T,ISTAT). This subroutine collects sample data for time persistent variables when used in the collection mode. In the computation and reporting mode it calculates the mean, standard deviation, and maximum and minimum of the sampled values. It also provides tabular output of the calculated statistics. The arguments are:

Argument	Definition
XX	If ISTAT > 0, the value of the variable computed at time T and which persists over the time interval that starts with T; if ISTAT ≤ 0, not used
T	The time at which the value of XX is changed and up to which integration is to be performed
ISTAT	The code identifying both the variable for which data is collected and the mode in which TIMST is being used. The modes and ISTAT values identifying the modes are:

Condition	Mode
ISTAT > 0	Integrate SSTPV(ISTAT,6) from SSTPV (ISTAT,3) to T; store XX as SSTPV (ISTAT,6)
ISTAT = 0	Compute and report on all variables identified by I = 1,NNSTA
ISTAT < 0	Compute and report on variable identified by −ISTAT

The FORTRAN listing of subroutine TIMST is given in Fig. 4-16.

Assuming that a variable has a constant value during an interval, the relative frequency with which the variable has a given value can be considered as the proportion of time during the simulation that it has that value. When this is the case, the average value of the variable can be computed as

$$\text{Average value} = \sum_x \frac{x \star t(x)}{\text{TOT}}$$

where x is a value of the variable; $t(x)$ is the time during the simulation that the value of the variable is x; and TOT is the total simulation time. For simulation runs, it is desirable to compute $x \star t(x)$ as the simulation progresses. Letting x_{j-1} be the value of x during the time interval (t_{j-1},t_j), where t_j is the point in time at which the jth change in x occurs,

$$\sum_j x_{j-1} \star (t_j - t_{j-1}) = \sum_j x \star t(x).$$

By storing x_{j-1} and t_{j-1} and then calling TIMST at t_j with the value

```
      SUBROUTINE TIMST (XX,T,ISTAT)
      DIMENSION XX(1)
      COMMON /GCOM1/ ATRIB(25),JEVNT,MFA,MFE(100),MLE(100),MSTOP,NCRDR,N
     1NAPO,NNAPT,NNATR,NNFIL,NNQ(100),NNTRY,NPRNT,PPARM(50,4),TNOW,TTBEG
     2,TTCLR,TTFIN,TTRIB(25),TTSET
      COMMON /GCOM4/ DTPLT(10),HHLOW(25),HHWID(25),IICRD,IITAP(10),JJCEL
     1(500),LLABC(25,2),LLABH(25,2),LLABP(11,2),LLABT(25,2),LLPHI(10),LL
     2PLO(10),LLPLT,LLSUP(15),LLSYM(10),MMPTS,NNCEL(25),NNCLT,NNHIS,NNPL
     3T,NNPTS(10),NNSTA,NNVAR(10),PPHI(10),PPLO(10)
      COMMON /GCOM6/ EENQ(100),IINN(100),KKRNK(100),MMAXQ(100),QQTIM(100
     1),SSOBV(25,5),SSTPV(25,6),VVNQ(100)
      IF (ISTAT) 101,102,103
  101 IFC=-ISTAT
      ILC=IFC
      GO TO 109
  102 IFC=1
      ILC=NNSTA
      GO TO 109
  103 IF (ISTAT-NNSTA) 105,105,104
  104 CALL ERROR (511)
  105 TT=T-SSTPV(ISTAT,3)
      YY=SSTPV(ISTAT,6)
      SSTPV(ISTAT,1)=SSTPV(ISTAT,1)+YY*TT
      SSTPV(ISTAT,2)=SSTPV(ISTAT,2)+YY*YY*TT
      SSTPV(ISTAT,6)=XX(1)
      SSTPV(ISTAT,3)=T
      IF (XX(1)-SSTPV(ISTAT,4)) 106,107,107
  106 SSTPV(ISTAT,4)=XX(1)
  107 IF (XX(1)-SSTPV(ISTAT,5)) 114,114,108
  108 SSTPV(ISTAT,5)=XX(1)
      GO TO 114
  109 WRITE (NPRNT,115)
      T=TNOW
      DO 113 J=IFC,ILC
      IF (SSTPV(J,3)-TTCLR) 110,111,112
  110 CALL ERROR (512)
  111 WRITE (NPRNT,116) LLABT(J,1),LLABT(J,2)
      GO TO 113
  112 XS=SSTPV(J,1)+SSTPV(J,6)*(T-SSTPV(J,3))
      XSS=SSTPV(J,2)+SSTPV(J,6)*SSTPV(J,6)*(T-SSTPV(J,3))
      XT=T-TTCLR
      AVG=XS/XT
      STD=(XSS/XT-AVG*AVG)
      IF(STD.LT.0.0) STD=0.0
      STD=SQRT(STD)
      WRITE (NPRNT,117) LLABT(J,1),LLABT(J,2),AVG,STD,SSTPV(J,4),SSTPV(J
     1,5),XT,SSTPV(J,6)
  113 CONTINUE
  114 RETURN

  115 FORMAT (/36X,44H**STATISTICS FOR TIME-PERSISTENT VARIABLES**/16X,4
     1HMEAN,10X,7HSTD DEV,9X,7HMINIMUM,9X,7HMAXIMUM,7X,13HTIME INTERVAL,
     23X,10HCUR. VALUE/)
  116 FORMAT (2X,2A4,39X,18HNO VALUES RECORDED)
  117 FORMAT (2X,2A4,1X,6(E12.4,4X))

      END
```

Figure 4-16 FORTRAN listing of subroutine TIMST.

x_j, the quantity on the left-hand side of the equation can be computed. Thus the statement CALL TIMST(x_j,t_j,I) causes $x_{j-1} \star (t_j - t_{j-1})$ to be collected, and x_j is stored in order to make the next computation.

Row ISTAT of the array SSTPV is used to store information on the variable with code ISTAT. The arguments of TIMST(XX, T, and ISTAT) are used in the following manner. The time interval between collection points TT is computed as TT = T − SSTPV(ISTAT,3). T is stored in SSTPV(ISTAT,3). SSTPV(ISTAT,6) contains the last (or initial) value of XX. Call this value XXL. XXL ★ TT is computed and added to SSTPV(ISTAT,1). In addition, $\text{XXL}^2 \star \text{TT}$ is computed and added to SSTPV(ISTAT,2). Then it is determined whether XX (the new value) is the minimum or the maximum value observed up to the current time. SSTPV(ISTAT,4) and SSTPV(ISTAT,5) are used to store these minimum and maximum values, respectively. The value XX is then stored in SSTPV(ISTAT,6). Whenever TIMST is called for reporting purposes ($\text{ISTAT} \leq 0$), the statistical quantities of interest include values for the interval between SSTPV(ISTAT,3) and the time TIMST is called. SSTPV(ISTAT,6) is used for this purpose (T-30).

The data stored in SSTPV are used to compute and print: (1) estimates of the mean and standard deviation of the variables with respect to time,* (2) total time over which the statistics were collected, and (3) the minimum and maximum values of the variables observed during the simulation. Data can be collected for a maximum of NNSTA time persistent variables. The statement CALL TIMST(4.,TNOW,3) causes TT = TNOW − SSTPV(3,3), adds TT ★ SSTPV(3,6) to SSTPV(3,1), and performs the other calculations indicated above. The value of XX used as an argument for TIMST should be the value of a variable after it is changed by a simulation event. For multiple runs, the resetting of the value of SSTPV(I,6) is the responsibility of the user.

Subroutine TIMSA(XX,T,ISTAT). This subroutine collects sample data for time persistent variables that may change value during the time interval between statistical collection points. It also collects information identical to the information discussed in the section on subroutine TIMST, except that an average value during the past interval is assumed as an approximation to the value during the interval. Since SSTPV (ISTAT,6) contains the value of XX at the beginning of the interval and XX is the new value,

$$\frac{\text{XX} + \text{SSTPV(ISTAT,6)}}{2}$$

approximates the average value during the interval. The FORTRAN listing for subroutine TIMSA is given in Fig. 4-17. Subroutine TIMST is used for calculating and reporting statistics for the values collected in TIMSA. The code ISTAT must be different for TIMST and TIMSA

* Since successive values of these variables are not independent, the equivalent number of independent observations is not easily obtained. This complicated the design of simulation experiments (53,56) and hypothesis testing. Fishman (32–35) and Mihram (89) have written extensively on this subject.

```
      SUBROUTINE TIMSA (XX,T,ISTAT)
      DIMENSION XX(1)
      DIMENSION NSET(1)
      COMMON QSET(1)
      COMMON /GCOM4/ DTPLT(10),HHLOW(25),HHWID(25),IICRD,IITAP(10),JJCEL
     1(500),LLABC(25,2),LLABH(25,2),LLABP(11,2),LLABT(25,2),LLPHI(10),LL
     2PLO(10),LLPLT,LLSUP(15),LLSYM(10),MMPTS,NNCEL(25),NNCLT,NNHIS,NNPL
     3T,NNPTS(10),NNSTA,NNVAR(10),PPHI(10),PPLO(10)
      COMMON /GCOM6/ EENQ(100),IINN(100),KKRNK(100),MMAXQ(100),QQTIM(100
     1),SSOBV(25,5),SSTPV(25,6),VVNQ(100)
      EQUIVALENCE (NSET(1),QSET(1))
      X=(SSTPV(ISTAT,6)+XX(1))*0.5
      SSTPV(ISTAT,6)=XX(1)
      IF (ISTAT-NNSTA) 102,102,101
  101 CALL ERROR (511)
  102 TT=T-SSTPV(ISTAT,3)
      SSTPV(ISTAT,1)=SSTPV(ISTAT,1)+X*TT
      SSTPV(ISTAT,2)=SSTPV(ISTAT,2)+X*X*TT
      SSTPV(ISTAT,3)=T
      IF (XX(1)-SSTPV(ISTAT,4)) 103,104,104
  103 SSTPV(ISTAT,4)=XX(1)
  104 IF (XX(1)-SSTPV(ISTAT,5)) 106,106,105
  105 SSTPV(ISTAT,5)=XX(1)
  106 RETURN
C
      END
```

Figure 4-17 FORTRAN listing of subroutine TIMSA.

variables and the total number of all time persistent variables must be NNSTA.

***Subroutine HISTO*(*XX,IHIST*).** When used in the collection mode, this subroutine tabulates the number of times a variable is within prescribed cell limits. In the computation and reporting mode, it calculates the observed, relative, and cumulative frequency for each cell. It also provides a plotted histogram of the relative and cumulative frequency of observations. The arguments are:

Argument	Definition
XX	The value of the variable collected
IHIST	The code identifying both the variable for which data is collected and the mode in which HISTO is being used. The modes and IHIST values identifying the modes are:

Condition	Mode
IHIST > 0	Determine proper cell position of XX in histogram identified by IHIST; increase number in cell by one
IHIST = 0	Compute and report on all histograms identified by I = 1, NNHIS
IHIST < 0	Compute and report on histogram identified by −IHIST.

The label, number of cells, upper limit of the first cell, and cell width associated with each histogram are given on data card type 5. The FORTRAN listing of subroutine HISTO is given in Fig. 4-18. The array NNCEL(I) identifies the location in JJCEL(·) where the value for the last cell of the Ith histogram is stored. Thus the location in JJCEL(·) of the first cell is

$$\text{NFCX} = \begin{cases} \text{NNCEL(IHIST} - 1) + 1 & \text{if IHIST} > 1, \\ 1 & \text{if IHIST} = 1. \end{cases}$$

The first cell of each histogram keeps a count of the number of observations less than or equal to HHLOW. The ICth cell counts the number of observations XX in the following range:

$$\text{HHLOW} + (\text{IC} - 1) \star \text{HHWID} < \text{XX} \leq \text{HHLOW} + \text{IC} \star \text{HHWID}.$$

The FORTRAN statement that uses this result is given in statement 112 where the proper cell number IC is calculated and includes a correction for the first cell and truncation.

Following statement 115, the code deals with the preparation and printing of the table and plot for the histogram. Figure 4-19 is an example of the histogram output. The symbol ⋆ is used to plot the relative frequency and the letter C is used to plot the cumulative frequency. For the first cell containing data, only the ⋆ is plotted. The cells of the histogram are open at the lower end and closed at the upper end. For example, in Fig. 4-19 there were 71 observations in the interval (9,11], that is, values greater than 9 but less than or equal to 11.

Subroutine GPLOT(XX,T,IPLOT). When used in the collection mode, this subroutine collects values of up to 10 dependent variables and one independent variable. In the computation and reporting mode, it provides a table or plot of the collected data or both. The FORTRAN listing of subroutine GPLOT is given in Fig. 4-20. The arguments are:

Argument	Definition
XX	The value of the dependent variable collected; XX is a one dimensional array of 10 or less elements.
T	The independent variable collected (must be monotonic nondecreasing or nonincreasing).
IPLOT	The code identifying both the dependent variables for which data is collected and the mode in which GPLOT is being used. The modes and IPLOT values identifying the modes are:

```
      SUBROUTINE HISTO (XX,IHIST)
      DIMENSION XX(1), NOUT(50)
      COMMON /GCOM1/ ATRIB(25),JEVNT,MFA,MFE(100),MLE(100),MSTOP,NCRDR,N
     1NAPO,NNAPT,NNATR,NNFIL,NNQ(100),NNTRY,NPRNT,PPARM(50,4),TNOW,TTBEG
     2,TTCLR,TTFIN,TTRIB(25),TTSET
      COMMON /GCOM4/ DTPLT(10),HHLOW(25),HHWID(25),IICRD,IITAP(10),JJCEL
     1(500),LLABC(25,2),LLABH(25,2),LLABP(11,2),LLABT(25,2),LLPHI(10),LL
     2PLO(10),LLPLT,LLSUP(15),LLSYM(10),MMPTS,NNCEL(25),NNCLT,NNHIS,NNPL
     3T,NNPTS(10),NNSTA,NNVAR(10),PPHI(10),PPLO(10)
      DATA IPLUS,IBLNK,IAST,ICEE/1H+,1H ,1H*,1HC/
      IF (IHIST) 101,103,105
  101 IFH=-IHIST
      ILH=IFH
      IF (IFH-1) 104,104,102
  102 NFCX=NNCEL(IFH-1)+1
      GO TO 115
  103 IFH=1
      ILH=NNHIS
  104 NFCX=1
      GO TO 115
  105 IF (IHIST-NNHIS) 107,107,106
  106 CALL ERROR (571)
  107 IF (IHIST-1) 108,108,109
  108 FXX=0.
      GO TO 110
  109 FXX=NNCEL(IHIST-1)
C
C*****TRANSLATE XX BY SUBTRACTING HHLOW(IHIST)
C
  110 X=XX(1)-HHLOW(IHIST)
      IF (X) 111,111,112
  111 IC=FXX+1.
      GO TO 114
C
C*****DETERMINE CELL NUMBER IC. ADD 1 FOR LOWER LIMIT CELL AND 1 FOR
C*****TRUNCATION.
C
  112 IC=X/HHWID(IHIST)+1.999999+FXX
      IF (IC-NNCEL(IHIST)) 114,114,113
  113 IC=NNCEL(IHIST)
  114 JJCEL(IC)=JJCEL(IC)+1
      GO TO 128
  115 DO 127 I=IFH,ILH
      XLOW=HHLOW(I)
      NLCX=NNCEL(I)
      NTOT=0
      DO 116 K=NFCX,NLCX
  116 NTOT=NTOT+JJCEL(K)
      XTOT=NTOT
      WRITE (NPRNT,129) I,LLABH(I,1),LLABH(I,2)
      IF (NTOT) 117,117,118
  117 WRITE (NPRNT,130)
      GO TO 126
  118 CUML=0.
      DO 125 J=NFCX,NLCX
      RELA=FLOAT(JJCEL(J))/XTOT
      CUML=CUML+RELA
      MR=RELA*50.+.5
      MC=CUML*50.+.5
      DO 119 N=1,50
  119 NOUT(N)=IBLNK
      NOUT(50)=IPLUS
      IF (MC.GE.1) NOUT(MC)=ICEE
      IF (MR) 122,122,120
  120 DO 121 N=1,MR
  121 NOUT(N)=IAST
  122 IF (J-NLCX) 123,124,125
  123 WRITE (NPRNT,132) JJCEL(J),RELA,CUML,XLOW,NOUT
      XLOW=XLOW+HHWID(I)
      GO TO 125
  124 WRITE (NPRNT,131) JJCEL(J),RELA,CUML,NOUT
  125 CONTINUE
```

Figure 4-18 FORTRAN listing of subroutine HISTO.

```
      WRITE (NPRNT,133) NTOT
  126 NFCX=NLCX+1
  127 CONTINUE
  128 RETURN
C
  129 FORMAT (1H1,54X,13H**HISTOGRAM NUMBER,I3,2H**//61X,2A4///20X,4HOBS
     1V,5X,4HRELA,5X,4HCUML,6X,11H   UPPER   /20X,3(4HFREQ,5X),1X,10HCELL
     2 LIMIT,6X,1H0,8X,2H20,8X,2H40,8X,2H60,8X,2H80,7X,3H100/60X,11(4X,1
     3H+))
  130 FORMAT (///20X,19HNO VALUES RECORDED.)
  131 FORMAT (19X,I5,2(4X,F5.3),9X,3HINF,10X,1H+,50A1)
  132 FORMAT (19X,I5,2(4X,F5.3),5X,E11.4,6X,1H+,50A1)
  133 FORMAT (21X,3H---,40X,1H+,10(4X,1H+)/19X,I5,40X,1H0,8X,2H20,8X,2H4
     10,8X,2H60,8X,2H80,7X,3H100)
C
      END
```

Figure 4-18 *(continued)*

Condition	Mode
IPLOT > 0	Store the values of XX for future tabular output and plotting for plot IPLOT.
IPLOT $= 0$	Print a table and/or plot for all plots identified by I = 1, NNPLT
IPLOT < 0	Print a table and/or plot for the plot identified by −IPLOT

The additional variables necessary for the preparation of plots or tables are given on data card type 6.

Subroutine GPLOT stores the collected data either in core (in the array QSET) or on auxiliary tape. When the data is stored in QSET, only one plot and/or associated table with up to 10 variables can be prepared. If tape is used, up to 10 plots and/or tables with as many as 10 variables per plot may be prepared. The appearance of the plotted output is very similar to other line printer plots, such as those produced by FORDYN (80), MIMIC (23), and DYNAMO (115).

```
                                     **HISTOGRAM NUMBER  2**

                                            TRIP TIM

OBSV     RELA     CUML        UPPER
FREQ     FREQ     FREQ     CELL LIMIT      0        20        40        60        80       100
                                           +    +    +    +    +    +    +    +    +    +    +
   0    0.000    0.000     5.0000E+00      +                                                  +
   0    0.000    0.000     7.0000E+00      +                                                  +
  14     .036     .036     9.0000E+00      +**                                                +
  71     .181     .216     1.1000E+01      +********* C                                       +
 110     .280     .496     1.3000E+01      +**************          C                         +
  94     .239     .735     1.5000E+01      +************                       C              +
  54     .137     .873     1.7000E+01      +*******                                   C       +
  24     .061     .934     1.9000E+01      +***                                          C    +
  14     .036     .969     2.1000E+01      +**                                            C   +
   8     .020     .990     2.3000E+01      +*                                              C+
   2     .005     .995     2.5000E+01      +                                                  C
   2     .005    1.000        INF          +                                                  C
 ---                                       +    +    +    +    +    +    +    +    +    +    +
 393                                       0        20        40        60        80       100
```

Figure 4-19 Example of histogram output.

```
      SUBROUTINE GPLOT (XX,T,IPLOT)
      DIMENSION XX(10), PLOG(10), PHIG(10), NCUT(117), RANGE(10)
      DIMENSION NSET(1)
      COMMON QSET(1)
      COMMON /GCOM1/ ATRIB(25),JEVNT,MFA,MFE(100),MLE(100),ISTOP,NCRDR,N
     1NAPC,NNAPT,NNATR,NNFIL,NNQ(100),NNTRY,NPRNT,PPARM(50,4),TNOW,TTBEG
     2,TTCLR,TTFIN,TTRIB(25),TTSET
      COMMON /GCOM4/ DTPLT(10),HHLOW(25),HHWID(25),IICRD,IITAP(10),JJCEL
     1(500),LLABC(25,2),LLABH(25,2),LLABP(11,2),LLABT(25,2),LLPHI(10),LL
     2PLO(10),LLPLT,LLSUP(15),LLSYM(10),MMPTS,NNCEL(25),NNCLT,NNHIS,NNPL
     3T,NNPTS(10),NNSTA,NNVAR(10),PPHI(10),PPLO(10)
      COMMON /GCOM5/ IIEVT,IISED(6),JJBEG,JJCLR,MMNIT,MMON,NNAME(3),NNCF
     1I,NNDAY,NNPT,NNSET,NNPRJ,NNPRM,NNRNS,NNRUN,NNSTR,NNYR,SSEED(6)
      EQUIVALENCE (NSET(1),QSET(1))
      DATA IPLUS,IBLNK,IAST,IPRD/1H+,1H ,1H*,1H./
      IF (IPLOT) 108,109,101
  101 IT=IITAP(IPLOT)
      NVAR=NNVAR(IPLOT)
      IF (IT) 102,102,106
  102 IF (NNPTS(IPLOT)-MMPTS) 104,103,103
  103 NNPT=NNPT+1
      GO TO 187
  104 IP=NNPTS(IPLOT)*(NVAR+1)+NNCFI
      DO 105 I=1,NVAR
      J=IP+I
  105 QSET(J)=XX(I)
      QSET(J+1)=T
      GO TO 107
  106 WRITE (IT) T,(XX(I),I=1,NVAR)
  107 NNPTS(IPLOT)=NNPTS(IPLOT)+1
      GO TO 187
  108 IFP=-IPLOT
      ILP=IFP
      GO TO 110
  109 IFP=1
      ILP=NNPLT
  110 DO 186 N=IFP,ILP
      DTPLG=DTPLT(N)
      DTPLP=ABS(DTPLG)
      IT=IITAP(N)
      NVAR=NNVAR(N)
      IF (IT) 112,112,111
  111 REWIND IT
      READ (IT) LLPLT,LLSYM,LLABP,LLPLO,PPLO,LLPHI,PPHI
  112 NPT=NNPTS(N)
      IF (LLPLT) 128,113,113
  113 WRITE (NPRNT,194) N,NNRUN
      WRITE (NPRNT,192) LLABP(11,1),LLABP(11,2),(LLABP(I,1),LLABP(I,2),I
     1=1,NVAR)
      DO 114 I=1,NVAR
      PLOG(I)=1.E20
  114 PHIG(I)=-1.E20
      DO 127 J=1,NPT
      IF (IT) 115,115,121
  115 IP=(J-1)*(NVAR+1)+NNCFI
      DO 119 I=1,NVAR
      JJ=IP+I
      IF (QSET(JJ)-PLOG(I)) 116,117,117
  116 PLOG(I)=QSET(JJ)
  117 IF (QSET(JJ)-PHIG(I)) 119,119,118
  118 PHIG(I)=QSET(JJ)
  119 CONTINUE
      IF (LLPLT-1) 127,120,120
  120 IL=IP+NVAR
      IP=IP+1
      WRITE (NPRNT,193) QSET(IL+1),(QSET(I),I=IP,IL)
      GO TO 127
  121 READ (IT) XTIME,(XX(I),I=1,NVAR)
      DO 123 IP=1,NVAR
      IF (XX(IP)-PLOG(IP)) 122,123,123
  122 PLOG(IP)=XX(IP)
  123 IF (XX(IP)-PHIG(IP)) 125,125,124
  124 PHIG(IP)=XX(IP)
```

Figure 4-20 FORTRAN listing of subroutine GPLOT.

```
125 CONTINUE
    IF (LLPLT-1) 127,126,126
126 WRITE (NPRNT,193) XTIME,(XX(I),I=1,NVAR)
127 CONTINUE
    WRITE (NPRNT,195) (PLOG(I),I=1,NVAR)
    WRITE (NPRNT,196) (PHIG(I),I=1,NVAR)
    IF (LLPLT-1) 128,183,128
128 WRITE (NPRNT,198) N,NNRUN
    DO 139 I=1,NVAR
    IF (LLPLO(I)-1) 133,132,129
129 IF (PLOG(I)) 130,131,131
130 PLOG(I)=PPLO(I)*FLOAT(IFIX((PLOG(I)-PPLO(I)+1.E-20)/PPLO(I)))
    GO TO 133
131 PLOG(I)=PPLO(I)*FLOAT(IFIX(PLOG(I)/PPLO(I)))
    GO TO 133
132 PLOG(I)=PPLO(I)
133 IF (LLPHI(I)-1) 138,137,134
134 IF (PHIG(I)) 135,135,136
135 PHIG(I)=PPHI(I)*FLOAT(IFIX(PHIG(I)/PPHI(I)))
    GO TO 138
136 PHIG(I)=PPHI(I)*FLOAT(IFIX((PHIG(I)+PPHI(I)-1.E-20)/PPHI(I)))
    GO TO 138
137 PHIG(I)=PPHI(I)
138 RANGE(I)=PHIG(I)-PLOG(I)
    QR=RANGE(I)*.25
    Q1=PLOG(I)+QR
    Q2=Q1+QR
    Q3=Q2+QR
139 WRITE (NPRNT,189) LLSYM(I),LLABP(I,1),LLABP(I,2),PLOG(I),Q1,Q2,Q3,
   1PHIG(I)
    WRITE (NPRNT,190) LLABP(11,1),LLABP(11,2)
    IF (IT) 140,140,142
140 IP=NNTRY*NNAPT
    DO 141 I=1,NVAR
    JJ=IP+I
141 XX(I)=QSET(JJ)
    XTIME=QSET(JJ+1)
    GO TO 143
142 REWIND IT
    READ (IT) LLPLT
    READ (IT) XTIME,(XX(I),I=1,NVAR)
143 IPT=1
    IDIF=1
    IF (DTPLG) 145,144,146
144 ISN=0
    TSN=XTIME
    TSL=TSN
    GO TO 148
145 ISN=((XTIME-TTBEG)/DTPLP)-0.499999
    GO TO 147
146 ISN=((XTIME-TTBEG)/DTPLP)+0.5
147 TSN=TTBEG+FLOAT(ISN)*DTPLP
148 DO 149 J=1,117
    NOUT(J)=IBLNK
149 CONTINUE
    DO 150 J=1,101,25
150 NOUT(J)=IPLUS
    NCOUN=103
    IF (IDIF-1) 151,154,152
151 CALL ERROR (531)
152 DO 153 J=2,IDIF
    TSL=TSL+DTPLG
    WRITE (NPRNT,191) TSL,NOUT
153 CONTINUE
154 DO 168 IP=1,NVAR
    PLIP=XX(IP)
    IF (PLIP-PLOG(IP)) 168,155,155
155 IF (PLIP-PHIG(IP)) 156,156,168
156 IF (RANGE(IP)) 168,168,157
157 NPCT=(PLIP-PLOG(IP))*100./RANGE(IP)+1.5
    NONP=NOUT(NPCT)
    IF (NONP-IBLNK) 158,166,158
158 IF (NONP-LLSYM(IP)) 159,168,159
```

Figure 4-20 *(continued)*

```
159 IF (NONP-IPLUS) 160,166,160
160 IF (NONP-IPRD) 161,166,161
161 IF (LLSYM(IF)-IPRD) 162,168,162
162 IF (NCOUN-117) 163,167,167
163 DO 165 J=103,NCOUN,3
    IF (NOUT(J+1)-LLSYM(IF)) 165,164,165
164 IF (NOUT(J)-NONP) 165,168,165
165 CONTINUE
    NOUT(NCOUN)=NOUT(NPCT)
    NOUT(NCOUN+1)=LLSYM(IF)
    NCOUN=NCOUN+3
    GO TO 168
166 NOUT(NPCT)=LLSYM(IP)
    GO TO 168
167 NOUT(117)=IAST
168 CONTINUE
    TSL=TSN
    ISL=ISN
    IF (IPT-NPT) 169,182,182
169 IF (IT) 170,170,172
170 IP=IPT*(NVAR+1)+NNOFI
    DO 171 I=1,NVAR
    JJ=IP+I
171 XX(I)=QSET(JJ)
    XTIME=QSET(JJ+1)
    GO TO 173
172 READ (IT) XTIME,(XX(I),I=1,NVAR)
173 IPT=IPT+1
    IF (DTPLG) 175,174,176
174 TSN=XTIME
    GO TO 181
175 ISN=((XTIME-TTBEG)/DTPLP)-0.499999
    GO TO 177
176 ISN=((XTIME-TTBEG)/DTPLP)+0.5
177 TSN=TTBEG+FLOAT(ISN)*DTPLP
    IF (DTPLG) 178,181,179
178 IDIF=ISL-ISN
    GO TO 180
179 IDIF=ISN-ISL
180 IF (IDIF) 151,154,181
181 WRITE (NPRNT,191) TSL,NOUT
    GO TO 148
182 WRITE (NPRNT,191) TSL,NOUT
    WRITE (NPRNT,190) LLABF(11,1),LLABF(11,2)
183 I=NPT*NVAR
    WRITE (NPRNT,197) NPT,I
    NNPTS(N)=0
    IF (IT) 184,184,185
184 I=MMPTS*(NVAR+1)
    J=NPT+NNPT
    JJ=J*(NVAR+1)
    WRITE (NPRNT,198) MMPTS,I,J,JJ
    NNPT=0
    GO TO 187
185 REWIND IT
    READ (IT) LLPLT
    IF (IPLOT) 187,185,187
186 CONTINUE
187 RETURN
C
188 FORMAT (1H1,55X,13H**PLOT NUMBER,I3,2H**/59X,11HRUN  NUMBER,I3//59GPT
   1X,14HSCALES OF PLOT)
189 FORMAT (2X,A1,1H=,2A4,2X,E11.4,4(14X,E11.4))
190 FORMAT (1H0,3X,2A4,7X,1H0,4X,1H5,3X,2H10,3X,2H15,3X,2H20,3X,2H25,3
   1X,2H30,3X,2H35,3X,2H40,3X,2H45,3X,2H50,3X,2H55,3X,2H60,3X,2H65,3X,
   22H70,3X,2H75,3X,2H80,3X,2H85,3X,2H90,3X,2H95,2X,3H100,1X,10HDUPLIC
   3ATES/)
191 FORMAT (1X,E12.4,2X,117A1)
192 FORMAT (3X,2A4,10(4X,2A4)/)
193 FORMAT (11(1X,E11.4))
194 FORMAT (1H1,48X,14H**TABLE NUMBER,I3,2H**/51X,12HRUN  NUMBER ,I3/)
195 FORMAT (/5X,7HMINIMUM,10E12.4)
196 FORMAT (5X,7HMAXIMUM,10E12.4)
197 FORMAT (///5X,21HOUTPUT  CONSISTS  OF ,I6,13H POINT SETS (,I6,8H P
   1OINTS))
198 FORMAT (5X,21HSTORAGE ALLOCATED FOR,I6,13H POINT SETS (,I6,8H WORD
   1S )/5X,21HSTORAGE  NEEDED   FOR,I6,13H POINT SETS (,I6,8H WORDS ))
C
    END
```

Figure 4-20 *(continued)*

During the collection mode, subroutine GPLOT first determines the storage medium to be used. If tape, the point set (values of the independent variable and dependent variables being collected) is written on the appropriate tape and the point set count is incremented by one. If the storage medium is core, a check is made to see if sufficient allocated space remains. (Space allocated for saving plot values in QSET is that portion of QSET from QSET(NNCFI + 1) to QSET(MMPTS) inclusive.) If there is not sufficient space, the counter indicating the number of point sets for which there is insufficient space is incremented by one and control is returned to the calling subprogram. (Note that this condition does not cause an error. A descriptive message is given at the end of the plot.) If there is sufficient space, the point set is stored and the point set count is incremented by one.

Subroutine GPLOT provides a quick plot option (indicated by LLPLT < 0). With this option no table is prepared, no data maxima or minima are found, and the user must specify the maximum and minimum ordinate values for each of the plotted variables.

If the quick plot option is not used, there are three options for determining the maximum and minimum ordinate values for each variable. An example for determining the maximum ordinate value for the first variable of a plot illustrates the available options. If LLPHI(1) < 1, the maximum ordinate value will be the maximum collected value for the associated variable. If LLPHI(1) $= 1$, the maximum ordinate value will be the user specified PPHI(1). If LLPHI(1) > 1, the maximum ordinate value will be the maximum collected value rounded outward (up for maximum values, down for minimum values) to the nearest multiple of PPHI(1).

The preparation of a plot progresses line by line with each line consisting of three components. The first is the value of the independent variable associated with that line. The second component of a plotted line contains the 101 print positions corresponding to the plot points themselves. The third component of a plotted line is a duplicates column that indicates any instances in which two different plot symbols occupied the same plot position. If this happens, the first symbol processed is plotted and the duplicates column contains a symbol pair showing the plotted symbol followed by the symbol that should occupy the same plot position. As many as five duplicates may be printed per plot line. If there are more, the first five are printed, followed by an asterisk.

Any character in the FORTRAN character set can be used as a plot symbol, but three are treated in a special manner. The symbols plus (+), period (.), and blank(   ) can be replaced in the plot vector by any plot symbol and no duplicates information will be maintained. Normally, plus and blank are used only by GPLOT. The symbol period may be used by the programmer for cursors or in any other case in which it is desired that the symbol appear only if no other symbol plots at the same point.

There are three situations in which a plot symbol will not appear on a plot. First, if it exceeds the range on the ordinate, it is not printed. Second, if the range on the ordinate is zero, it is not printed. Third, if it is a duplicate it will appear in the duplicates column, but only if it is one of the first five duplicates associated with a plotted line. An example of the output of subroutine GPLOT is shown in Fig. 4-21. Note that separate scales are used for each dependent variable. For the variable T = TANKER, the scale is 0 for the 0% cursor, 75 for the 25% cursor, 150 for the 50% cursor, 225 for the 75% cursor, and 300 for the 100% cursor. Information describing the number of point sets and, if it is stored in core, the number of words of storage used and needed are printed following a plot. An example of this is shown below for the plot given in Fig. 4-21.

```
OUTPUT   CONSISTS   OF    1200 POINT SETS (   2400 POINTS)
STORAGE ALLOCATED FOR    1200 POINT SETS (   3600 WORDS )
STORAGE   NEEDED    FOR    6055 POINT SETS ( 18165 WORDS )
```

The number of points in the plot is 2400 since there are 1200 point sets and two dependent variables per point. The number of words of QSET allocated for plotting was 3600. For the entire simulation, 6055 points could have been recorded. GPLOT prints the plot for the storage allocated (3600 words) and notifies the user that more storage must be allocated if a plot for the entire simulation is desired. Following the printing of a table or plot, the table and plot storage areas and counters are prepared for a new plot. Unlike the other data collection subroutines, subroutine GPLOT reinitializes automatically after it has been called in the computation and reporting mode.

Subroutine PRNTQ(IFILE). This subroutine computes and prints file statistics and a tabular listing of the contents of the entire file storage area (if IFILE ≤ 0) or file IFILE. The FORTRAN listing of subroutine PRNTQ is given in Fig. 4-22.

When the entire file storage area is requested, subroutine PRNTQ computes and prints the maximum number of entries stored in the file storage array since it was last initialized. This information is obtained from a sequential search of predecessor pointers. The first entry having a negative predecessor pointer is the first entry that has not been used. The normal listing for each file includes the current simulated time, the time the file was last used, the time-integrated average and standard deviation of the number of entries in the file (not included if current time is equal to file initialization time), the maximum number of entries in the file since last initialization (not included if current time is equal to initialization time), and a sequential listing of the entries currently in the file.

Subroutine PRNTS. PRNTS prints the contents of the state storage area. The FORTRAN listing of subroutine PRNTS is given in Fig. 4-23.

Subroutine SUMRY. SUMRY provides all standard GASP IV output by either printing or causing all of the following to be printed:

1. A heading.
2. All parameter sets.
3. All statistics for variables based on observation.
4. All statistics for time persistent variables.
5. All files and file statistics.
6. All state and derivative values.
7. All histograms.
8. All tables and plots.

The FORTRAN listing of subroutine SUMRY is given in Fig. 4-24.

Subroutine SUMRY is normally called by subroutine GASP during the output sequence. It may be suppressed, however, by setting LLSUP(15) greater than zero.

Monitoring and Error Reporting

The functions of monitoring and error reporting are supported by subroutines MONTR and ERROR. These subroutines are good candidates for user modification to obtain specific information for use during the debugging of a simulation program.

Subroutine MONTR. This subroutine selectively provides any of the following functions during a simulation run:

0. Start or stop tracing each event.
1. Print contents of files.
2. Reset file statistics and clear statistical storage arrays.

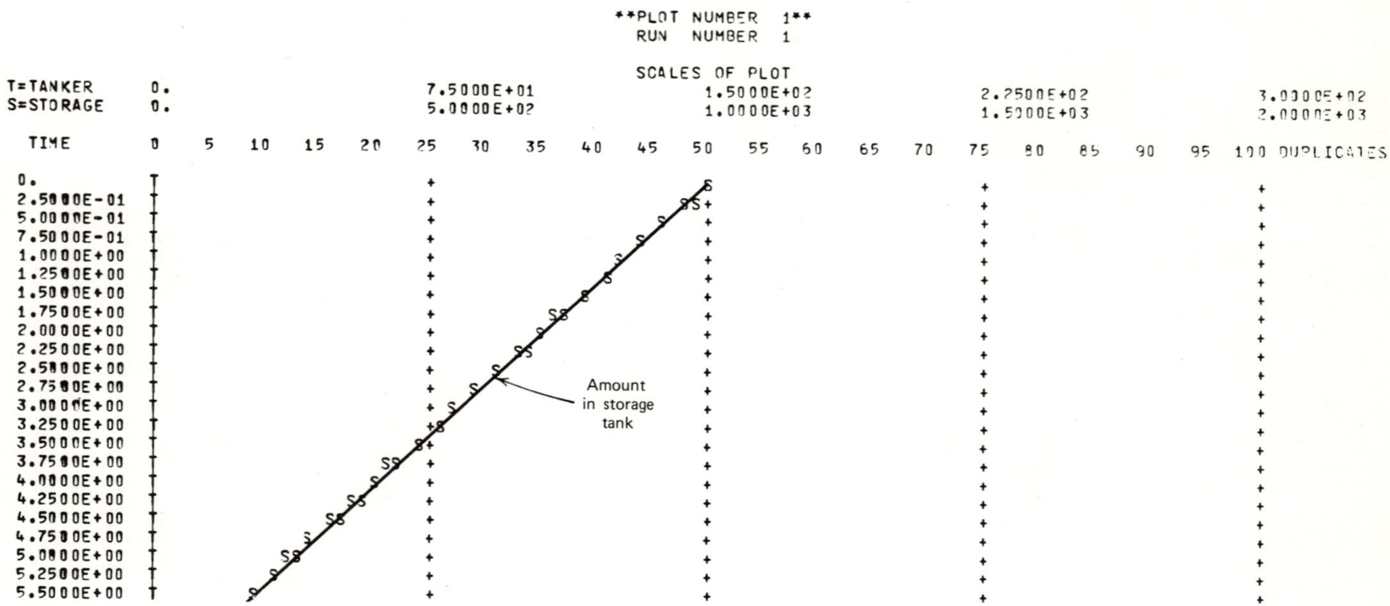
PLOT NUMBER 1
RUN NUMBER 1
SCALES OF PLOT
T=TANKER 0. 7.5000E+01 1.5000E+02 2.2500E+02 3.0000E+02
S=STORAGE 0. 5.0000E+02 1.0000E+03 1.5000E+03 2.0000E+03
TIME 0 5 10 15 20 25 30 35 40 45 50 55 60 65 70 75 80 85 90 95 100 DUPLICATES
0.
2.5000E-01
5.0000E-01
7.5000E-01
1.0000E+00
1.2500E+00
1.5000E+00
1.7500E+00
2.0000E+00
2.2500E+00
2.5000E+00
2.7500E+00
3.0000E+00
3.2500E+00
3.5000E+00
3.7500E+00
4.0000E+00
4.2500E+00
4.5000E+00
4.7500E+00
5.0000E+00
5.2500E+00
5.5000E+00
Amount in storage tank

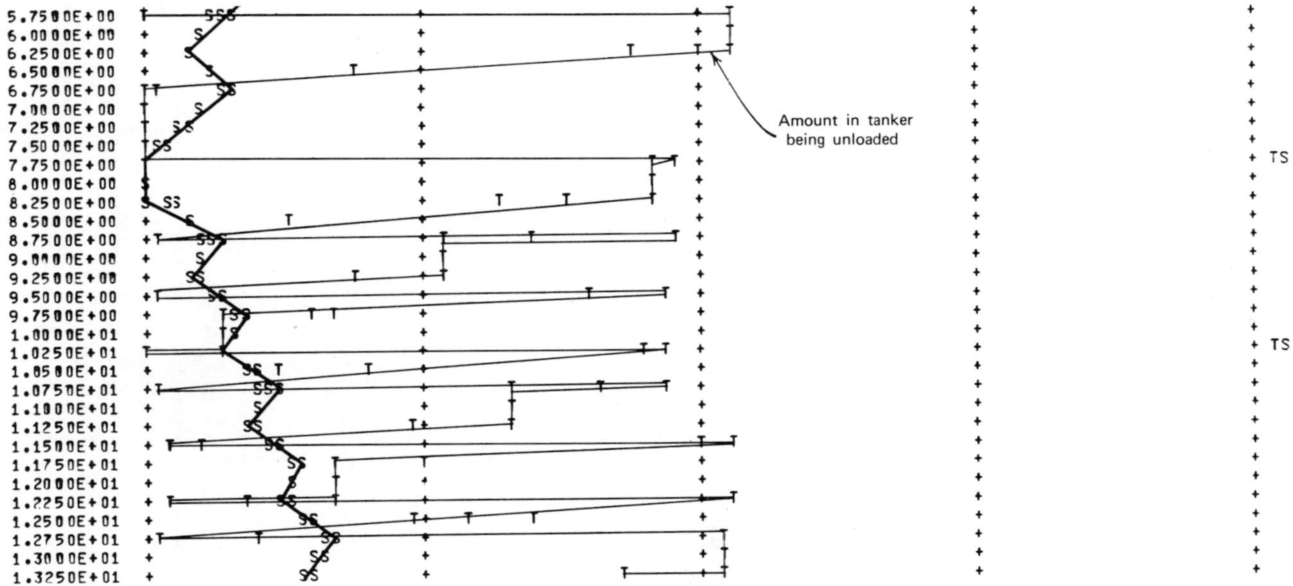

Figure 4-21 Sample output from subroutine GPLOT.

```
      SUBROUTINE PRNTQ (IFILE)
      DIMENSION NSET(1)
      COMMON QSET(1)
      COMMON /GCOM1/ ATRIB(25),JEVNT,MFA,MFE(100),MLE(100),MSTOP,NCRDR,N
     1NAPO,NNAPT,NNATR,NNFIL,NNQ(100),NNTRY,NPRNT,PPARM(50,4),TNOW,TTBEG
     2,TTCLR,TTFIN,TTRIB(25),TTSET
      COMMON /GCOM2/ DD(100),DDL(100),DTFUL,DTNOW,ISEES,LFLAG(50),NFLAG,
     1NNEQD,NNEQS,NNEOT,SS(100),SSL(100),TTNEX
      COMMON /GCOM6/ EENQ(100),IINN(100),KKRNK(100),MMAXQ(100),QQTIM(100
     1),SSOBV(25,5),SSTPV(25,6),VVNQ(100)
      EQUIVALENCE (NSET(1),QSET(1))
      IF (IFILE) 101,101,107
  101 WRITE (NPRNT,124) TNOW
      IF (NNFIL) 102,102,103
  102 WRITE (NPRNT,126)
      GO TO 117
  103 DO 104 I=1,NNTRY
      IXX=(I-1)*NNAPT+1
      IF (NSET(IXX)) 105,104,104
  104 CONTINUE
      I=NNTRY
      GO TO 106
  105 I=IXX/NNAPT
  106 WRITE (NPRNT,125) I
      IFF=1
      ILF=NNFIL
      GO TO 108
  107 IFF=IFILE
      ILF=IFF
  108 DO 116 JQG=IFF,ILF
      WRITE (NPRNT,119) JQG,TNOW,QQTIM(JQG)
      TPFS=TNOW-TTSET
      IF (TPFS) 110,110,109
C
C*****COMPUTE FILE STATISTICS
C
  109 XNQ=NNQ(JQG)
      X=(EENQ(JQG)+XNQ*(TNOW-QQTIM(JQG)))/TPFS
      STD=((VVNQ(JQG)+XNQ*XNQ*(TNOW-QQTIM(JQG)))/TPFS-X*X)
      STD=SIGN(SQRT(ABS(STD)),STD)
      WRITE (NPRNT,123) TPFS,X,STD,MMAXQ(JQG)
C
C*****PRINT FILE IN PROPER ORDER REQUIRES TRACING THROUGH THE POINTERS
C*****OF THE FILE
C
  110 LINE=MFE(JQG)
      IF (LINE) 111,111,112
  111 WRITE (NPRNT,121)
      GO TO 116
  112 WRITE (NPRNT,120)
      IXX=0
  113 IXX=IXX+1
      DO 114 I=1,NNATR
      NSISA=I+LINE
  114 TTRIB(I)=QSET(NSISA)
      WRITE (NPRNT,122) IXX,(TTRIB(I),I=1,NNATR)
      NSISA=NNAPO+LINE
      LINE=NSET(NSISA)
      IF (LINE) 115,116,113
  115 WRITE (NPRNT,118)
      STOP
  116 CONTINUE
  117 RETURN
C
  118 FORMAT (///45X,27HERROR EXIT, TYPE 541 ERROR.)
  119 FORMAT (//45X,23HPRINTOUT OF FILE NUMBER,I4/49X,6HTNOW =,E12.4/49X
     1,6HQQTIM=,E12.4)
  120 FORMAT (/51X,13HFILE CONTENTS)
  121 FORMAT (/49X,17HTHE FILE IS EMPTY)
  122 FORMAT (2X,5HENTRY,I4,4X,1H=,6(3X,E12.4,1X)/(16X,6(3X,E12.4,1X)))
  123 FORMAT (/39X,25HTIME PERIOD FOR STATISTICS,E11.4/39X,22HAVERAGE NU
     1MBER IN FILE,4X,F11.4/39X,18HSTANDARD DEVIATION,8X,F11.4/39X,22HMA
     2XIMUM NUMBER IN FILE,6X,I4)
  124 FORMAT (1H1,32X,37H**GASP FILE STORAGE AREA DUMP AT TIME,E12.4,2H*
     1*)
  125 FORMAT (//33X,48HMAXIMUM NUMBER OF ENTRIES IN FILE STORAGE AREA =,
     1I3)
  126 FORMAT (//41X,33HFILE STORAGE AREA NOT USED, NNFIL=0)
C
      END
```

Figure 4-22 FORTRAN listing of subroutine PRNTQ.

```
      SUBROUTINE PRNTS                                                  PTS       1
      COMMON /GCOM1/ ATRIB(25),JEVNT,MFA,MFE(100),MLE(100),MSTOP,NCRDR,NGCOM1     1
     1NAPO,NNAPT,NNATR,NNFIL,NNQ(100),NNTRY,NPRNT,PPARM(50,4),TNOW,TTBEGGCOM1     2
     2,TTCLR,TTFIN,TTRIB(25),TTSET                                      GCOM1     3
      COMMON /GCOM2/ DD(100),DDL(100),DTFUL,DTNOW,ISEES,LFLAG(50),NFLAG,GCOM2     1
     1NNEQD,NNEQS,NNEQT,SS(100),SSL(100),TTNEX                          GCOM2     2
      WRITE (NPRNT,105) TNOW                                            PTS       2
      IF (NNEQT) 101,102,103                                            PTS       3
  101 CALL ERROR (551)                                                  PTS       4
  102 WRITE (NPRNT,106)                                                 PTS       5
      GO TO 104                                                         PTS       6
  103 WRITE (NPRNT,107)                                                 PTS       7
      WRITE (NPRNT,108) (I,SS(I),DD(I),I=1,NNEQT)                       PTS       8
  104 RETURN                                                            PTS       9
C                                                                       PTS      10
  105 FORMAT (1H1,32X,38H**GASP STATE STORAGE AREA DUMP AT TIME,E12.4,2HPTS      11
     1**)                                                               PTS      12
  106 FORMAT (//41X,36HSTATE STORAGE AREA NOT USED, NNEQT=0)            PTS      13
  107 FORMAT (//43X,3H(I),8X,5HSS(I),12X,5HDD(I),13X)                   PTS      14
  108 FORMAT (41X,I4,5X,E12.4,4X,E12.4)                                 PTS      15
C                                                                       PTS      16
      END                                                               PTS      17
```

Figure 4-23 FORTRAN listing of subroutine PRNTS.

3. Print contents of state storage arrays.
4. Print information on state variables *and* files.
5. Print summary report.
6. Cause error exit.

Subroutine MONTR may be called directly by the user (after assigning an appropriate value to the event code, JEVNT), or by the occurrence of a monitor event (any time-event with an event code less than zero).

Functions 1–6 above are executed by calling MONTR with JEVNT equal to -1, -2, -3, -4, -5, and -6, respectively. These monitor events can be established as initial events by setting ATRIB(1) = time of monitoring, ATRIB(2) = event code, and ATRIB(3) = time between monitor events. By using ATRIB(3) sequential monitoring events can be established (except for code -2). Since three attributes are used for monitor events, NNATR ≥ 3 is required when subroutine MONTR is called. Monitoring of time-events is accomplished in subroutine GASP by setting JEVNT equal to zero and calling MONTR. Events with zero code cause GASP IV to either start tracing or stop tracing, if tracing is being performed. The FORTRAN listing of subroutine MONTR is given in Fig. 4-25. The FORTRAN code of MONTR is straightforward and involves testing JEVNT and performing the desired function based on the value of JEVNT. During the debugging, verification, or validation phases of a project, subroutine MONTR should be used. Statements should be added to MONTR to print problem specific information. Thus while tracing events, values of attributes and variables could be printed to allow a detailed analysis of the component behavior of the model.

```
      SUBROUTINE SUMRY
      DIMENSION XXXX(10)
      COMMON /GCOM1/ ATRIB(25),JEVNT,MFA,MFE(100),MLE(100),MSTOP,NCRDR,N
     1NAPO,NNAPT,NNATR,NNFIL,NNQ(100),NNTRY,NPRNT,PPARM(50,4),TNOW,TTBEG
     2,TTCLR,TTFIN,TTRIB(25),TTSET
      COMMON /GCOM2/ DD(100),DDL(100),DTFUL,DTNOW,ISEES,LFLAG(50),NFLAG,
     1NNEQD,NNEQS,NNEQT,SS(100),SSL(100),TTNEX
      COMMON /GCOM4/ DTPLT(10),HHLOW(25),HHWID(25),IICRD,IITAP(10),JJCEL
     1(500),LLABC(25,2),LLABH(25,2),LLABP(11,2),LLABT(25,2),LLPHI(10),LL
     2PLO(10),LLPLT,LLSUP(15),LLSYM(10),MMPTS,NNCFL(25),NNCLT,NNHIS,NNPL
     3T,NNPTS(10),NNSTA,NNVAR(10),PPHI(10),PPLO(10)
      COMMON /GCOM5/ IIEVT,IISED(6),JJBEG,JJCLR,MMNIT,MMON,NNAME(3),NNCF
     1I,NNDAY,NNPT,NNSET,NNPRJ,NNPRM,NNRNS,NNRUN,NNSTR,NNYR,SSEED(6)
      DATA XXX,XXXX(1)/2*0./
      WRITE (NPRNT,117)
      NRTCT=NNRNS+NNRUN-1
      WRITE (NPRNT,118) NNPRJ,NNAME,MMON,NNDAY,NNYR,NNRUN,NRTCT,TNOW
C
C*****PRINT PARAMETER SETS.
C
      KODE=561
      IF (NNPRM) 104,103,101
  101 DO 102 I=1,NNPRM
  102 WRITE (NPRNT,119) I,(PPARM(I,J),J=1,4)
C
C*****PRINT STATISTICS GATHERED BY COLCT.
C
  103 KODE=562
      IF (NNCLT) 104,106,105
  104 CALL ERROR (KODE)
  105 CALL COLCT (XXXX(1),0)
C
C*****PRINT STATISTICS GATHERED BY TIMST.
C
  106 KODE=563
      IF (NNSTA) 104,108,107
  107 CALL TIMST (XXXX(1),TNOW,0)
C
C*****PRINT FILES AND FILE STATISTICS.
C
  108 KODE=564
      IF (NNFIL) 104,110,109
  109 CALL PRNTQ (0)
C
C*****PRINT STATE STORAGE ARRAY.
C
  110 KODE=565
      IF (NNEQT) 104,112,111
  111 CALL PRNTS
C
C******PRINT HISTOGRAMS.
C
  112 KODE=566
      IF (NNHIS) 104,114,113
  113 CALL HISTO (XXXX(1),0)
C
C*****PRINT TABLES AND PLOTS.
C
  114 KODE=567
      IF (NNPLT) 104,116,115
  115 CALL GPLOT (XXXX(1),XXX,0)
  116 RETURN
C
  117 FORMAT (1H1,45X,23H**GASP SUMMARY REPORT**/)
  118 FORMAT (34X,25HSIMULATION PROJECT NUMBER,I4,2X,2HBY,2X,3A4//34X,4H
     1DATE,I3,1H/,I3,1H/,I5,7X,10HRUN NUMBER,I5,3H OF,I5//,34X,14HCURREN
     2T TIME =,E12.4,//)
  119 FORMAT (2X,13HPARAMETER SET,I7,2H =,4(3X,E12.4,1X))
C
      END
```

Figure 4-24 FORTRAN listing of subroutine SUMRY.

```
      SUBROUTINE MONTR
      DIMENSION NSET(1)
      COMMON QSET(1)
      COMMON /GCOM1/ ATRIB(25),JEVNT,MFA,MFE(100),MLE(100),MSTOP,NCRDR,N
     1NAPO,NNAPT,NNATR,NNFIL,NNQ(100),NNTRY,NPRNT,PPARM(50,4),TNOW,TTBEG
     2,TTCLR,TTFIN,TTRIB(25),TTSET
      COMMON /GCOM2/ DD(100),DDL(100),DTFUL,DTNOW,ISEES,LFLAG(50),NFLAG,
     1NNEQD,NNEQS,NNEQT,SS(100),SSL(100),TTNEX
      COMMON /GCOM6/ EENQ(100),IINN(100),KKRNK(100),MMAXQ(100),QQTIM(100
     1),SSOBV(25,5),SSTPV(25,6),VVNQ(100)
      EQUIVALENCE (NSET(1),QSET(1))
      DATA IX/1/
      IF (JEVNT) 101,103,103
  101 JX=-JEVNT
      IF (JX.EQ.2) GO TO 108
      IF (ATRIB(3).LE.0.0) GO TO 102
      ATRIB(1)=TNOW+ATRIB(3)
      ATRIB(2)=JEVNT
      CALL FILEM (1)
  102 GO TO (107,108,110,107,111,112), JX
  103 CALL UMONT (IX)
      IF (IX.EQ.0) GO TO 113
      IF (MFE(1)) 106,105,104
C
C*****JMNIT.EQ.1 AND JEVNT.GE.1: PRINT TNOW, ATTRIBUTES OF CURRENT
C*****EVENT, TTNEX, AND ATTRIBUTES OF NEXT EVENT.
C
  104 IFA=MFE(1)+1
      ILA=MFE(1)+NNATR
      WRITE (NPRNT,114) TNOW,(ATRIB(I),I=1,NNATR)
      WRITE (NPRNT,115) TTNEX,(QSET(I),I=IFA,ILA)
      GO TO 113
  105 WRITE (NPRNT,114) TNOW,(ATRIB(I),I=1,NNATR)
      WRITE (NPRNT,116) TTFIN
      GO TO 113
  106 CALL ERROR (602)
C
C*****JEVNT.EQ.-1, PRINT FILE STORAGE AREA DUMP.
C
  107 CALL PRNTQ (0)
      IF (JEVNT+3) 110,113,113
C
C*****JEVNT.EQ.-2, RESET FILE STATISTICS AND CLEAR STATISTICAL
C*****STORAGE ARRAYS.
C
  108 DO 109 J=1,NNFIL
      QQTIM(J)=TNOW
      EENQ(J)=0.0
      VVNQ(J)=0.0
  109 MMAXQ(J)=NNQ(J)
      TTSET=TNOW
      CALL CLEAR
      GO TO 113
C
C*****JEVNT.EQ.-3, PRINT STATE STORAGE AREA DUMP.
C
  110 CALL PRNTS
      GO TO 113
C
C***** IF JEVNT EQUALS -4 --- PRINT FILES AND STATE STORAGE.
C
C
C*****IF JEVNT= -5   PRINT SUMMARY REPORT.
C
  111 CALL SUMRY
      GO TO 113
C
C*****JEVNT.LE.-6, CAUSE ERROR EXIT, TYPE 601 ERROR.
C
  112 CALL ERROR (601)
  113 RETURN
C
  114 FORMAT (/2X,23HCURRENT EVENT.....TNOW=,E11.4/(7(3X,E12.4,1X)))
  115 FORMAT (2X,23HNEXT EVENT......TTNEX=,E11.4/(7(3X,E12.4,1X)))
  116 FORMAT (2X,23HNEXT EVENT......TTNEX=,E11.4/7X,36HTTNEX=TTFIN, THE
     1 EVENT FILE IS EMPTY)
C
      END
```

Figure 4-25 FORTRAN listing of subroutine MONTR.

Subroutine ERROR(KODE). ERROR is called when an error is detected in a GASP IV subprogram. The error message provides the programmer with a code (KODE) that indicates the condition causing the error and the location of its detection. Appendix 3 lists the error codes with their corresponding condition and location. The FORTRAN listing of subroutine ERROR is given in Fig. 4-26.

Because ERROR may be called by subroutines that are called by ERROR, a loop protection variable (NERR) is used to assure that a loop does not persist.

Subroutine ERROR provides useful diagnostic information by listing the error code, simulated time, and current values in the file storage buffer. Next, a call to the user provided subroutine UERR (S-103) permits any specific information to be output. A complete summary report is then prepared (if possible) and the error message is repeated (S-104). Finally, ERROR causes a FORTRAN error (S-105) to take advantage of FORTRAN provided diagnostic and traceback information.

Miscellaneous Support

The miscellaneous support subroutines included with GASP IV are functions SUMQ, PRODQ, and GTABL and subroutine GDLAY. These subprograms are sufficiently useful to be included in GASP IV. Many other functions (e.g., clips, switches, steps, and sampling routines for probabil-

```
      SUBROUTINE ERROR (KODE)
      COMMON /GCOM1/ ATRIB(25),JEVNT,MFA,MFE(100),MLE(100),MSTOP,NCRDR,N
     1NAPO,NNAPT,NNATR,NNFIL,NNQ(100),NNTRY,NPRNT,PPARM(50,4),TNOW,TTBEG
     2,TTCLR,TTFIN,TTRIB(25),TTSET
      DATA NERR,XX/0,-1.0/
      IF (NERR) 104,101,104
  101 NERR=NERR+1
      WRITE (NPRNT,107) KODE,TNOW
      IF (NNATR) 103,103,102
  102 WRITE (NPRNT,108) (ATRIB(I),I=1,NNATR)
  103 CALL UERR (KODE)
C
C*****PRINT SUMMARY REPORT UP TO PRESENT
C
      CALL SUMRY
  104 WRITE (NPRNT,109) KODE
      IF (XX) 105,106,106
  105 XX=SQRT(XX)
      STOP
  106 RETURN
C
  107 FORMAT (1H1,37X,23H**GASP ERROR EXIT, TYPE,I4,14H ERROR AT TIME,E1
     12.4,2H**)
  108 FORMAT (/46X,38HTHE CURRENT VALUES IN THE BUFFER ATRIB/(1X,E14.4,6
     1E16.4))
  109 FORMAT (///44X,16HERROR EXIT, TYPE,I4,7H ERROR.)
C
      END
```

Figure 4-26. FORTRAN listing of subroutine ERROR.

```
      FUNCTION SUMQ(JATT,IFILE)                                         SMQ    1
      DIMENSION NSET(1)                                                 DIM    1
      COMMON QSET(1)                                                    COM    1
      COMMON /GCOM1/ ATRIB(25),JEVNT,MFA,MFE(100),MLE(100),MSTOP,NCRDR,NGCOM1  1
     1NAPO,NNAPT,NNATR,NNFIL,NNQ(100),NNTRY,NPRNT,PPARM(50,4),TNOW,TTBEGGCOM1  2
     2,TTCLR,TTFIN,TTRIB(25),TTSET                                      GCOM1  3
      EQUIVALENCE (NSET(1),QSET(1))                                     EQUIV  1
      SUMQ=0.0                                                          SMQ    2
      IF (IFILE-NNFIL) 102,102,101                                      SMQ    3
  101 CALL ERROR (801)                                                  SMQ    4
  102 IF (NNQ(IFILE)) 103,103,104                                       SMQ    5
  103 RETURN                                                            SMQ    6
  104 MTEM=MFE(IFILE)                                                   SMQ    7
  105 NSISA=JATT+MTEM                                                   SMQ    8
      SUMQ=SUMQ+QSET(NSISA)                                             SMQ    9
      NSISA=NNAPO+MTEM                                                  SMQ   10
      MTEM=NSET(NSISA)                                                  SMQ   11
      IF (MTEM) 106,106,105                                             SMQ   12
  106 RETURN                                                            SMQ   13
C                                                                       SMQ   14
      END                                                               SMQ   15
```

Figure 4-27 FORTRAN listing of function SUMQ.

ity mass functions) could be included but are sufficiently simple to code in FORTRAN that they are not included in GASP IV.

***Function SUMQ*(*JATT,IFILE*).** SUMQ returns the sum of all values of attribute number JATT currently in file IFILE. The FORTRAN listing of SUMQ is shown in Fig. 4-27. As can be seen from Fig. 4-27, SUMQ weaves through a file adding the value of attribute JATT to SUMQ for each entry until the end of the file is reached.

***Function PRODQ*(*JATT,IFILE*).** PRODQ returns the product of all values of attribute number JATT currently in file IFILE. The FORTRAN listing of PRODQ is shown in Fig. 4-28. The coding for PRODQ is identical to SUMQ except for statements P-2 and P-10.

```
      FUNCTION PRODQ(JATT,IFILE)                                        PDQ    1
      DIMENSION NSET(1)                                                 DIM    1
      COMMON QSET(1)                                                    COM    1
      COMMON /GCOM1/ ATRIB(25),JEVNT,MFA,MFE(100),MLE(100),MSTOP,NCRDR,NGCOM1  1
     1NAPO,NNAPT,NNATR,NNFIL,NNQ(100),NNTRY,NPRNT,PPARM(50,4),TNOW,TTBEGGCOM1  2
     2,TTCLR,TTFIN,TTRIB(25),TTSET                                      GCOM1  3
      EQUIVALENCE (NSET(1),QSET(1))                                     EQUIV  1
      PRODQ=1.                                                          PDQ    2
      IF (IFILE-NNFIL) 102,102,101                                      PDQ    3
  101 CALL ERROR (811)                                                  PDQ    4
  102 IF (NNQ(IFILE)) 103,103,104                                       PDQ    5
  103 PRODQ=0.                                                          PDQ    6
      RETURN                                                            PDQ    7
  104 MTEM=MFE(IFILE)                                                   PDQ    8
  105 NSISA=JATT+MTEM                                                   PDQ    9
      PRODQ=PRODQ*QSET(NSISA)                                           PDQ   10
      NSISA=NNAPO+MTEM                                                  PDQ   11
      MTEM=NSET(NSISA)                                                  PDQ   12
      IF (MTEM) 106,106,105                                             PDQ   13
  106 RETURN                                                            PDQ   14
C                                                                       PDQ   15
      END                                                               PDQ   16
```

Figure 4-28 FORTRAN listing of function PRODQ.

```
      FUNCTION GTABL(TAB,X,XLOW,XHIGH,XINCR)
      DIMENSION TAB(1)
      IF (X-XLOW) 103,103,101
  101 IF (X-XHIGH) 102,104,104
  102 INTVL=((X-XLOW)/XINCR)+1.
      XINT=INTVL-1
      XLOI=XINCR*XINT+XLOW
      GTABL=TAB(INTVL)+(TAB(INTVL+1)-TAB(INTVL))*(X-XLOI)/XINCR
      GO TO 105
  103 GTABL=TAB(1)
      GO TO 105
  104 INTMX=((XHIGH-XLOW)/XINCR)+1.5
      GTABL=TAB(INTMX)
  105 RETURN
C
      END
```

Figure 4-29 FORTRAN listing of function GTABL.

Function GTABL(TAB,X,XLOW,XHIGH,XINCR). GTABL is the GASP IV table look-up function. The FORTRAN listing of function GTABL is shown in Fig. 4-29. The arguments are:

Argument	Definition
TAB	The array containing the values of the dependent variable
X	The independent variable
XLOW	The lowest value of the independent variable for which TAB contains a value for the dependent variable
XHIGH	The highest value of the independent variable for which TAB contains a value for the dependent variable
XINCR	The increment of the independent variable between corresponding values for the dependent variable

To use GTABL the programmer must provide an array and store the appropriate values for the dependent variable in the array. The values must correspond to the equally spaced values of the independent variable between XLOW and XHIGH in increments of XINCR.

The value of the dependent variable returned by GTABL is computed by linear interpolation within the defined range of the independent variable. If the independent variable is outside the range given, the appropriate end point value of the dependent variable is returned.

Subroutine GDLAY(IFS,ILS,XIN,DEL). GDLAY computes a variable order exponential information delay of the type commonly used in Systems Dynamics models (39). The FORTRAN listing of subroutine GDLAY is given in Fig. 4-30. The arguments are:

```
      SUBROUTINE GDLAY (IFS,ILS,XIN,DEL)
      COMMON /GCOM2/ DD(100),DDL(100),DTFUL,DTNOW,ISEES,LFLAG(50),NFLAG,
     1NNEQD,NNEQS,NNEQT,SS(100),SSL(100),TTNEX
      COMMON /GCOM5/ IIEVT,IISED(6),JJBEG,JJCLR,MMNIT,MMON,NNAME(3),NNCF
     1I,NNDAY,NNPT,NNSET,NNPRJ,NNPRM,NNRNS,NNRUN,NNSTP,NNYR,SSEED(6)
      DELXR=FLOAT(ILS-IFS+1)/DEL
      IF (JJBEG) 104,104,101
  101 IF (ILS-IFS) 105,102,102
  102 DO 103 I=IFS,ILS
  103 SS(I)=SS(ILS)
  104 DD(IFS)=(XIN-SS(IFS))*DELXR
      IF (ILS-IFS) 105,108,106
  105 CALL ERROR (831)
  106 ISS=IFS+1
      DO 107 I=ISS,ILS
  107 DD(I)=(SS(I-1)-SS(I))*DELXR
  108 RETURN
C
      END
```

Figure 4-30 FORTRAN listing of subroutine GDLAY.

Argument	Definition
IFS	Index (subscript) of the first state variable (corresponding to the first order delay)
ILS	Index (subscript) of the last state variable (corresponding to the ILS − IFS + 1 order delay)
XIN	The input to the delay
DEL	The magnitude of the delay constant

Subroutine GDLAY is a GASP IV routine for accomplishing the functions performed by DYNAMO built-in macros, SMOOTH, DLINFI, DLINF3, and DELAY3 (115). GDLAY involves derivative equations and permits the use of any order delay (the order of the delay equals ILS − IFS + 1). A comparison between GDLAY and DYNAMO delay functions is presented in Chapter 8.

The equations for the delayed variables are obtained by defining the rates of change for the variables. The statement CALL GDLAY(7,9,20.,4.) would result in the following equations:

DD(7) = (20. − SS(7)) ⋆ 3./4.
DD(8) = (SS(7) − SS(8)) ⋆ 3./4.

and

DD(9) = (SS(8) − SS(9)) ⋆ 3./4.

These equations would remain constant until changed by the user or until another call is made to GDLAY.

Subroutine GDLAY is self-initializing, therefore, the user need not be concerned with initialization of the associated state variables. The values of DD(I) and SS(I) for I = IFS to ILS are available to the user and are the respective values for the various orders of delay specified. When using GDLAY, NNEQD must be set greater than or equal to the largest value of ILS used.

Dummy Subroutines

Dummy subroutines for all the user written subroutines are included in the GASP IV package. Their inclusion permits the user to code only those subroutines that are needed for a given simulation. The executable statement in each of the dummy subroutines is to comply with the requirement of ANSI FORTRAN that every subprogram have at least one executable statement (3). The FORTRAN listing of the dummy subroutines is shown in Fig. 4-31.

Random Deviate Generators

To write general purpose subprograms for generating random deviates (samples), one must be able to reference parameter values for the dis-

```
      SUBROUTINE OTPUT                                    OTP
      I=1                                                 OTP
      RETURN                                              OTP
C                                                         OTP
      END                                                 OTP
      SUBROUTINE UERR (KODE)                              UER
      I=KODE                                              UER
      RETURN                                              UER
C                                                         UER
      END                                                 UER
      SUBROUTINE INTLC                                    ICG
      I=1                                                 ICG
      RETURN                                              ICG
C                                                         ICG
      END                                                 ICG
      SUBROUTINE STATE                                    STT
      I=1                                                 STT
      RETURN                                              STT
C                                                         STT
      END                                                 STT
      SUBROUTINE SCOND                                    SCD
      I=1                                                 SCD
      RETURN                                              SCD
C                                                         SCD
      END                                                 SCD
      SUBROUTINE EVNTS (IX)                               EVN
      I=IX                                                EVN
      RETURN                                              EVN
C                                                         EVN
      END                                                 EVN
      SUBROUTINE SSAVE                                    SSV
      I=1                                                 SSV
      RETURN                                              SSV
C                                                         SSV
      END                                                 SSV
```

Figure 4-31 FORTRAN listing of dummy subroutines.

tributions to be sampled within various subprograms. This is accomplished in GASP IV through a two dimensional array, PPARM. Each row of PPARM contains a set of values that are used as the parameters of a distribution. Since the parameters are stored in rows of PPARM, it is only necessary to designate the row number when calling a subprogram that requires parameter values. PPARM is initialized in subroutine DATIN through data cards, and the values of PPARM are printed to ensure that the values used in a simulation are recorded.

GASP IV provides the mechanism to obtain deviates given a distribution type and parameters for the distribution. The data collection, statistical analysis (including goodness-of-fit testing), and modeling to describe the inputs to a simulation must be performed by the user. Phillips has developed a procedure and a program to assist in this process (102).

Before discussing each particular subprogram, several common features of the subprograms are considered. The subprograms, as written, prohibit a random deviate from exceeding a minimum or a maximum value. If the value of a deviate is less than a prescribed minimum value, the minimum value is used as the random deviate. If the value is greater than a prescribed maximum value, the maximum value is used as the random deviate. This is not sampling from a truncated distribution but sampling from a distribution having a discrete probability of obtaining extreme values. By proper choice of the minimum parameter and the maximum parameter, the probability of obtaining the extreme values can be made sufficiently low to approximate sampling from a given distribution. To sample from truncated distributions, the programmer should rewrite the GASP IV subprograms to generate another deviate if the generated deviate is not between the minimum and the maximum values; that is, he should use a rejection method. If a rejection method is used, care must be taken that the minimum and maximum values specified do not cause very long running times due to excessive rejections of random deviates.

GASP IV provides subprograms for generating deviates from the following distribution types: uniform or rectangular, triangular, normal, lognormal, Erlang (gamma with an integer parameter), Gamma, Beta, and Poisson. The uniform, triangular, Erlang, and Poisson types employ the probability-integral-transformation approach (sometimes called the inverse-transformation approach) to random deviate generation. The normal generator sums 12 random numbers to obtain a deviate. This is an application of the central limit theorem. The Beta and Gamma generators use a derived analytic result in conjunction with a rejection technique. A deviate from the exponential distribution can be obtained from the Erlang function or through the writing of a single statement.

The probability-integral-transformation method for generating deviates from continuous distributions uses the result of the following theorem (1,33).

Theorem. Let X be a continuous random variable that has the cumulative distribution function $F_X(x) = \text{Prob}\,[X \leqq x]$. Let Y be a random variable defined by $Y = F_X(x)$. Then Y is uniformly distributed over the interval 0 to 1.

Proof. By the definition of $F_X(x)$, it is a nondecreasing function; consequently an inverse function* may be defined, say $F_X^{-1}(x)$. Let $G_Y(y)$ be the cumulative distribution function of Y; namely, $G_Y(y) = \text{Prob}[Y \leqq y]$ where $0 \leqq y \leqq 1$ since the range of $Y = F_X(x)$ is [0,1]. Thus $G_Y(y) = 0$ for $y < 0$ and $G_Y(y) = 1$ for $y > 1$. Substituting $Y = F_X(x)$ yields

$$G_Y(y) = \text{Prob}[F_X(x) \leqq y].$$

Taking the inverse of $F_X(x)$ yields

$$G_Y(y) = \text{Prob}[X \leqq F_X^{-1}(y)].$$

The right hand side of the above equation is in the form of the cumulative distribution function and can be written as

$$G_Y(y) = F_X[F_X^{-1}(y)] = y, \qquad 0 \leqq y \leqq 1$$

with $G_Y(y) = 0$ for $y < 0$ and $G_Y(y) = 1$ for $y > 1$.

From the above equations it is recognized that $G_Y(y)$ is the cumulative distribution function of a random variable, Y, uniformly distributed over the interval 0 to 1. Thus to obtain a random sample, x_s, of a random variable X, it is sufficient to obtain a random sample, y_s, of the random variable Y and to solve for x_s from $x_s = F_X^{-1}(y_s)$.

The probability-integral-transformation theorem is easy to see graphically. Figure 4-32 shows a cumulative distribution function. From Fig. 4-32, it is seen that

$$P[Y \leq y] = P[X \leq x].$$

But y is the cumulative distribution function of X, that is, $y = P[X \leq x]$, therefore,

$$P[Y \leq y] = y, \qquad 0 \leq y \leq 1,$$

* An inverse function specifies values of x for given values of y when the function given relates values of y to given values of x. Notationally, if we are given $y=f(x)$, the inverse function is $x=f^{-1}(y)$.

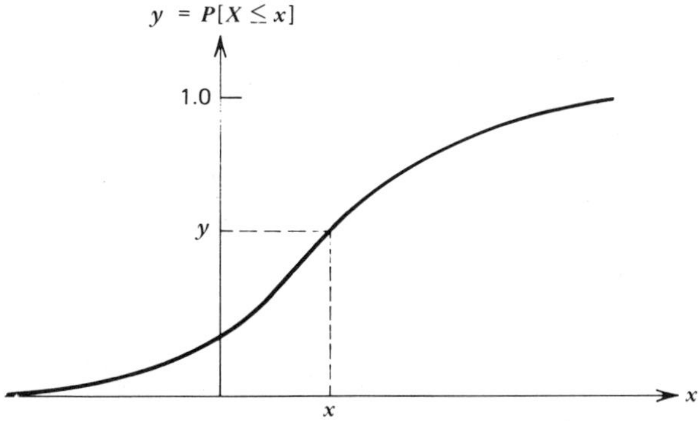

Figure 4-32 A cumulative distribution function.

which is recognized as the cumulative distribution for the uniform distribution.

The above result demonstrates the importance of sampling from a uniform distribution in the interval [0,1] since these samples can be used to obtain samples from other distributions. Samples from a uniformly distributed random variable in the interval 0 to 1 are called *random numbers*. When such samples are generated by deterministic numerical methods, they are called *pseudorandom numbers* (1,50,73,82,117). Intuitively, each pseudorandom number is equally likely to occur and there is no statistical dependence between random numbers. In GASP IV, the function DRAND is designed to generate pseudorandom numbers. Samples from all other distributions are obtained through the use of DRAND.

Function DRAND(ISTRM). This function generates a uniformly distributed random deviate in the interval 0 to 1, that is, a pseudorandom number. The argument ISTRM is used to indicate a different sequence or stream of random numbers. In GASP IV each stream is obtained from the same random number generator but the sequence is made to be different by starting the stream with a different initial value.

To obtain a random number generator with the desired properties (uniform distribution and independence), DRAND must be tailored to the computer being used. DRAND is the only machine dependent subprogram in GASP IV. Three versions of DRAND are presented; each uses a multiplicative congruence scheme for generating a random number (73,77). In Fig. 4-33, a "generalized" DRAND is shown (25) in which the user must insert only the number of bits per word of his machine in the DATA statement (D-11). In Fig. 4-34 the DRAND coding of the CDC 6500 random number generator is shown, and in Fig. 4-35

```
      FUNCTION DRAND(ISTRM)
C
C*****IF NSTRM IS GREATER THAN 6, THEN DIMENSION AND DATA STATEMENTS
C*****MUST REFLECT THE INCREASE
C
      DIMENSION L(6)
      COMMON /GCOM5/ IIEVT,IISED(6),JJBEG,JJCLR,MMNIT,MMON,NNAME(3),NNCF
     1I,NNDAY,NNPT,NNSET,NNFRJ,NNFRM,NNRNS,NNRUN,NNSTR,NNYR,SSEED(6)
C
C*****NBITS SHOULD BE SET EQUAL TO THE NUMBER OF BITS IN A FIXED POINT
C*****NUMBER FOR THE HOST COMPUTING SYSTEM
C
      DATA NBITS/60/
      IF (ISTRM) 102,101,104
  101 CALL ERROR (701)
  102 ISTRG=-ISTRM
      IF (ISTRG-NNSTR) 103,103,101
  103 L(ISTRG)=SSEED(ISTRG)
      L(ISTRG)=IABS(L(ISTRG))
      L(ISTRG)=(L(ISTRG)/2)*2+1
      IF (((L(ISTRG)/5)*5).EQ.L(ISTRG)) L(ISTRG)=L(ISTRG)-2
      GO TO 105
  104 ISTRG=ISTRM
      IF (ISTRG-NNSTR) 105,105,101
  105 IOPT=IABS(L(ISTRG))
      IF (IOPT.EQ.0) IOPT=1
      IF (NBITS) 106,106,107
  106 IOPT=IOPT*MULT
      IOPT=IOPT-(IOPT/NBASE)*NBASE
      L(ISTRG)=IOPT
      DRAND=FLOAT(IOPT)/BASE
      RETURN
  107 XBITS=NBITS-1
      N6=XBITS/3.0
      NBASE=2.0**(2*N6)
      BASE=NBASE
      MX=2.0**N6
      MULT=(MX/8)*8-3
      IF ((MULT/5)*5.EQ.MULT) MULT=MULT-2
      NBITS=-1
      GO TO 106
C
      END
```

Figure 4-33 FORTRAN listing of generalized function DRAND for computers with NBIT bits per word.

the DRAND coding of the IBM 360 and 370 random number generator is shown. For the IBM 360, Lewis, Goodman, and Miller (79) recommend a multiplicative constant of 16807, that is, K = 16807, rather than the K value of 65539 shown. *The author recommends using a random number generator that is either familiar to the user or which is in common use at the computer facility he is using.*

In GASP IV the random number seeds are initialized in DATIN by a call to DRAND with a negative stream number. The user may employ this technique to reinitialize the seed values. If no seed values are made available, those given in the DATA statement of DRAND are used. For the versions of DRAND shown in Figs. 4-33 to 4-35, NNSTR streams are permitted with a maximum value of 6 because of the dimensions of selected arrays. If additional streams are desired, the size of the arrays

```
      FUNCTION DRAND(ISTRM)                                             DRN    1
C                                                                       DRN    2
C***** IF NNSTR IS GREATER THAN 6, THEN DIMENSION AND DATA STATEMENTS   DRN    3
C***** MUST REFLECT THIS INCREASE.                                      DRN    4
C                                                                       DRN    5
      DIMENSION L(6)                                                    DRN    6
      COMMON /GCOM5/ IIEVT,IISED(6),JJBEG,JJCLR,MMNIT,MMON,NNAME(3),NNCF GCOM5  1
     1I,NNDAY,NNPT,NNSET,NNPRJ,NNPRM,NNRNS,NNRUN,NNSTR,NNYR,SSEED(6)    GCOM5  2
      DATA K/5536458/                                                   DRN    7
      DATA (L(M),M=1,6)/12743214774131558,34276135124613238,531743251541 DRN    8
     136213,53241624217672478,14632574324561578,70213677423225018/      DRN    9
      IF (ISTRM) 102,101,105                                            DRN   10
  101 CALL ERROR (701)                                                  DRN   11
  102 ISTRG=-ISTRM                                                      DRN   12
      IF (ISTRG-NNSTR) 103,103,101                                      DRN   13
  103 X=SSEED(ISTRG)                                                    DRN   14
      IF (X) 107,108,104                                                DRN   15
  108 SSEED(ISTRG)=L(ISTRG)                                             DRN  115
      GO TO 103                                                         DRN  215
  104 L(ISTRG)=(X.A.77777777777777778).O.1                              DRN   16
      GO TO 107                                                         DRN   17
  105 ISTRG=ISTRM                                                       DRN   18
      IF (ISTRG-NNSTR) 106,106,101                                      DRN   19
  106 L(ISTRG)=L(ISTRG)*K                                               DRN   20
  107 DRAND=(L(ISTRG).O.17170000000000000000B)+0.0                      DRN   21
      RETURN                                                            DRN   22
C                                                                       DRN   23
      END                                                               DRN   24
```

Figure 4-34 FORTRAN listing of function DRAND for the CDC 6000 Series System.

```
      FUNCTION DRAND(ISTRM)                                             DRN    1
C                                                                       DRN    2
C***** IF NSTRM IS GREATER THAN 6, THEN DIMENSION AND DATA STATEMENTS   DRN    3
C***** MUST REFLECT THIS INCREASE.                                      DRN    4
C                                                                       DRN    5
      DIMENSION L(6)                                                    DRN    6
      COMMON /GCOM5/ IIEVT,IISED(6),JJBEG,JJCLR,MMNIT,MMON,NNAME(3),NNCFGCOM5  1
     1T,NNDAY,NNPT,NNSET,NNPRJ,NNPRM,NNRNS,NNRUN,NNSTR,NNYR,SSEED(6)    GCOM5  2
      DATA K/65539/                                                     DRN    7
      DATA (L(M),M=1,6)/2135621899,1956987325,2060189406,1980776232,2095DRN    8
     1230059,1976924637/                                                DRN    9
      IF (ISTRM) 102,101,105                                            DRN   10
  101 CALL ERROR (701)                                                  DRN   11
  102 ISTRG=-ISTRM                                                      DRN   12
      IF (ISTRG-NNSTR) 103,103,101                                      DRN   13
  103 IX=SSEED(ISTRG)                                                   DRN   14
      IF (IX) 109,106,104                                               DRN   15
  104 L(ISTRG)=IX*K                                                     DRN   16
      GO TO 107                                                         DRN   17
  105 ISTRG=ISTRM                                                       DRN   18
      IF (ISTRG-NNSTR) 106,106,101                                      DRN   19
  106 L(ISTRG)=L(ISTRG)*K                                               DRN   20
  107 IF (L(ISTRG)) 108,101,109                                         DRN   21
  108 L(ISTRG)=L(ISTRG)+2147483647+1                                    DRN   22
  109 DRAND=L(ISTRG)                                                    DRN   23
      DRAND=DRAND*0.465661 3E-9                                         DRN   24
      RETURN                                                            DRN   25
C                                                                       DRN   26
      END                                                               DRN   27
```

Figure 4-35 FORTRAN listing of function DRAND for the IBM 360/370 Systems.

IISED, SSEED, and L must be increased. The number of initial values given in the DATA statement must also be increased.

Function UNFRM(ULO,UHI,ISTRM). The function UNFRM generates a deviate from a uniform distribution in the interval (ULO,UHI) using stream ISTRM, and returns the deviate value as the variable UNFRM. This function changes the range of a pseudorandom number from (0,1) to (ULO,UHI).

A uniform random variable X has the probability density function

$$f_X(x) = \begin{cases} \dfrac{1}{\text{UHI} - \text{ULO}} & \text{ULO} \leq x \leq \text{UHI}, \\ 0 & \text{otherwise}; \end{cases}$$

and cumulative distribution function

$$F_X(x) = \frac{x - \text{ULO}}{\text{UHI} - \text{ULO}} \qquad \text{ULO} \leq x \leq \text{UHI}.$$

The expected value and variance are $E[X] = (\text{UHI} + \text{ULO})/2$ and $\text{Var}\,[X] = [(\text{UHI} - \text{ULO})^2]/12$. Setting a random number $RN = F_X(x)$ as specified by the probability-integral-transformation and solving for a sample, say x_u, yields

$$x_u = \text{ULO} + RN \star (\text{UHI} - \text{ULO}).$$

Figure 4-36 is the FORTRAN listing of the function UNFRM in which the sample value has been given the name UNFRM and the random number, RN, is obtained by using the function DRAND. The random number stream is used as an argument to UNFRM and is passed directly to DRAND.

```
      FUNCTION UNFRM(ULO,UHI,ISTRM)
      UNFRM=ULO+(UHI-JLO)*DRAND(ISTRM)
      RETURN
C
      END
```

Figure 4-36 FORTRAN listing of function UNFRM.

Function TRIAG(IPAR,ISTRM). The function TRIAG generates a deviate from a triangular distribution using stream ISTRM and the parameter values in PPARM(IPAR,J) for J = 1,3. The definition of the parameters are

Column J	1	2	3	4
PPARM(IPAR,J)	Mode(b)	Minimum(a)	Maximum(c)	Not used

A triangular random variable X has the probability density function

$$f_X(x) = \begin{cases} \dfrac{2(x-a)}{(b-a)(c-a)} & a \le x \le b, \\ \dfrac{2(c-x)}{(c-b)(c-a)} & b \le x \le c, \\ 0 & \text{otherwise.} \end{cases}$$

The cumulative distribution function, expected value, and variance are

$$F_X(x) = \begin{cases} \dfrac{(x-a)^2}{(b-a)(c-a)} & a \le x \le b, \\ \dfrac{b-a}{c-a} + \dfrac{(c-b)^2 - (c-x)^2}{(c-b)(c-a)} & b \le x \le c, \end{cases}$$

$$E[X] = \frac{a+b+c}{3},$$

and

$$\text{Var}[X] = \frac{a(a-b) + c(c-a) + b(b-c)}{18}.$$

To use the probability-integral-transformation to obtain a deviate, a random number RN is equated to $F_X(x)$ and the above equations are solved for x. The sample value of x obtained in this manner is given the name TRIAG. This results in the equations

$$\text{TRIAG} = \begin{cases} a + \sqrt{(b-a) \star (c-a) \star RN} & 0 \le RN \le \dfrac{b-a}{c-a} \\ c - \sqrt{(c-b) \star (c-a) \star (1-RN)} & \dfrac{b-a}{c-a} \le RN \le 1. \end{cases}$$

The FORTRAN listing of the function TRIAG is given in Fig. 4-37.

Function RNORM (IPAR,ISTRM). The function RNORM generates a deviate from a normal distribution. The parameters for the distribution are specified by IPAR, which designates a row of the array PPARM. The parameter values in row IPAR to obtain a sample from a normal distribution are:

```
      FUNCTION TRIAG(IPAR,ISTRM)
      COMMON /GCOM1/ ATRIB(25),JEVNT,MFA,MFE(100),MLE(100),MSTOP,NCRDR,NGCOM1
     1NAPO,NNAPT,NNATR,NNFIL,NNQ(100),NNTRY,NPRNT,PPARM(50,4),TNOW,TTBEGGCOM1
     2,TTCLR,TTFIN,TTRIB(25),TTSET
      RN=DRAND(ISTRM)
      BMA=PPARM(IPAR,1)-PPARM(IPAR,2)
      CMA=PPARM(IPAR,3)-PPARM(IPAR,2)
      IF (RN-BMA/CMA) 101,101,102
  101 TRIAG=PPARM(IPAR,2)+SQRT(BMA*CMA*RN)
      GO TO 103
  102 TRIAG=PPARM(IPAR,3)-SQRT(CMA*(1.-RN)*(PPARM(IPAR,3)-PPARM(IPAR,1))
     1)
  103 RETURN
C
      END
```

Figure 4-37 FORTRAN listing of function TRIAG.

Column J	1	2	3	4
PPARM(IPAR,J)	Mean(μ)	Minimum	Maximum	Standard deviation(σ)

The density function of a random variable X, which is normally distributed with mean μ and variance σ^2, is

$$f_X(x) = \frac{1}{\sigma\sqrt{2\pi}} \exp\left[-\frac{1}{2}\left(\frac{x-\mu}{\sigma}\right)^2\right] \qquad -\infty < x < \infty, \sigma > 0$$

The technique used to obtain a normal deviate is to sum 12 pseudorandom numbers. This procedure makes use of the asymptotic result of the central limit theorem, that the distribution of the sum of random variables approaches a normal distribution. In function RNORM 12 random numbers are summed. The distribution of this sum is approximately normal with mean 6 and variance 1. A standardized normal deviate ($\mu = 0$, $\sigma^2 = 1$) is then the sum minus 6. Transforming to a normal deviate with mean μ and standard deviation σ involves multiplying by σ and adding μ. These calculations are shown in Fig. 4-38 where the FORTRAN listing for the function RNORM is given.

```
      FUNCTION RNORM(IPAR,ISTRM)
      COMMON /GCOM1/ ATRIB(25),JEVNT,MFA,MFE(100),MLE(100),MSTOP,NCRDR,NGCOM1
     1NAPO,NNAPT,NNATR,NNFIL,NNQ(100),NNTRY,NPRNT,PPARM(50,4),TNOW,TTBEGGCOM1
     2,TTCLR,TTFIN,TTRIB(25),TTSET
      SUM=0.0
      DO 101 I=1,12
  101 SUM=SUM+DRAND(ISTRM)
      V=SUM-6.0
      RNORM=V*PPARM(IPAR,4)+PPARM(IPAR,1)
      IF (RNORM-PPARM(IPAR,2)) 102,105,103
  102 RNORM=PPARM(IPAR,2)
      GO TO 105
  103 IF (RNORM-PPARM(IPAR,3)) 105,105,104
  104 RNORM=PPARM(IPAR,3)
  105 RETURN
C
      END
```

Figure 4-38 FORTRAN listing of function RNORM.

Experimental results have shown that for most applications this approximation is a good one. An alternate analytic approach, suggested by Box and Muller (9), is more aesthetically pleasing but requires more computer time and has not performed well when used with multiplicative congruential pseudorandom number generators.

Function RLOGN(IPAR,ISTRM). The function RLOGN generates a deviate from a lognormal distribution. The lognormal distribution is so named because the natural logarithm of a lognormal random variable is normally distributed (33,63). Thus if Q is a lognormally distributed random variable and X is a normally distributed random variable, the relationship between Q and X is

$$X = \ln Q \text{ or } Q = e^X$$

where
$$f_X(x) = \frac{1}{\sigma\sqrt{2\pi}} \exp\left[-\frac{1}{2}\left(\frac{x-\mu_X}{\sigma_X}\right)^2\right], \quad -\infty < x < \infty.$$

Random deviates from the lognormal distribution can be obtained from RNORM by specifying the μ_X and σ_X^2 corresponding to given values of μ_Q and σ_Q^2. The relationships are given by the equations

$$\mu_X = \ln \mu_Q - \frac{1}{2}\ln\left[\frac{\sigma_Q^2}{\mu_Q^2} + 1\right] = \ln \mu_Q - \frac{1}{2}\sigma_X^2$$

and
$$\sigma_X^2 = \ln\left[\frac{\sigma_Q^2}{\mu_Q^2} + 1\right].$$

The minimum and maximum values of Q can be translated into the corresponding minimum and maximum values of X by

$$\min X = \ln(\min Q)$$

and
$$\max X = \ln(\max Q).$$

(If the minimum value of Q is 0, set min X equal to a large negative value.) The table below specifies the parameters for a row of PPARM used to sample from a lognormal distribution whose associated normal random variable is X:

Column J	1	2	3	4
PPARM(IPAR,J)	μ_X	min X	max X	σ_X

The FORTRAN listing of function RLOGN is given in Fig. 4-39.

Conversion from the parameters of a lognormal distribution to the

```
      FUNCTION RLOGN(IPAR,ISTRM)
C
C*****THE PARAMETERS USED WITH RLOGN ARE THE MEAN AND STANDARD DEVIATION
C*****OF A NORMAL DISTRIBUTION
C
      VA=RNORM(IPAR,ISTRM)
      RLOGN=EXP(VA)
      RETURN
C
      END
```

Figure 4-39 FORTRAN listing of function RLOGN.

parameters of a normal distribution can be done either prior to the GASP IV simulation or in subroutine INTLC.

Function ERLNG(IPAR,ISTRM). The function ERLNG generates a deviate from an Erlang distribution (Gamma distribution with an integer α parameter). The density function for the ERLNG distribution is:

$$f_X(X) = \begin{cases} \dfrac{1}{(\alpha-1)!\beta^\alpha} e^{-x/\beta} x^{\alpha-1} & x > 0, \\ 0 & \text{otherwise;} \end{cases}$$

and

$$E[X] = \alpha\beta$$

$$\text{Var}[X] = \alpha\beta^2.$$

In the table below, the definitions of the parameter values that must be stored in a row of PPARM for use with function ERLNG are given:

Column J	1	2	3	4
PPARM(IPAR,J)	β	Minimum	Maximum	α

Note that the value in column 1 is β, not the mean of the Erlang distribution, which is $\alpha\beta$.

The exponential distribution is a special case of the Erlang distribution, when α equals 1. Function ERLNG generates samples from an exponential distribution with mean time β when α is set at 1, that is,

$$f_X(x) = \begin{cases} \dfrac{1}{\beta} \exp(-x/\beta) & x > 0, \beta > 0, \\ 0 & \text{otherwise.} \end{cases}$$

A sample from an exponential distribution can also be generated using the probability-integral-transformation. The distribution function for the exponential is

$$F_X(x) = \int_0^x 1/\beta \exp\left(-\frac{z}{\beta}\right) dz = 1 - \exp\left(-\frac{x}{\beta}\right)$$

Then, to obtain a sample value x_s, equate a random number, y_s, to the distribution function as follows:

$$y_s = 1 - \exp\left(-x_s/\beta\right)$$

and

$$x_s = -\beta \ln(1 - y_s)$$

Since $(1 - y_s)$ is also a random number $(1 - y_s)$ can be replaced by y_s, and

$$x_s = -\beta \ln y_s.$$

The corresponding GASP IV statement that generates a deviate, DEV, from an exponential distribution with a mean time of 10.0 ($\beta = 10.0$), using stream 1 is

DEV = − 10.0 ★ ALOG(DRAND(1)).

An Erlang distributed random variable is the sum of α independent and identically distributed exponential random variables. The FORTRAN listing of function ERLNG is given in Fig. 4-40. The coding of ERLNG involves summing K exponential deviates (K is used in place of α due to FORTRAN considerations) each with a mean time of β. The coding uses the derived form given below in order that the logarithm function only be used once.

```
      FUNCTION ERLNG(IPAR,ISTRM)
      COMMON /GCOM1/ ATRIB(25),JEVNT,MFA,MFE(100),MLE(100),MSTOP,NCRDR,NGCOM1
     1NAPO,NNAPT,NNATR,NNFIL,NNQ(100),NNTRY,NPRNT,PPARM(50,4),TNOW,TTBEGGCOM1
     2,TTCLR,TTFIN,TTRIB(25),TTSET
      K=PPARM(IPAR,4)
      IF (K-1) 101,102,102
  101 CALL ERROR (741)
  102 R=1
      DO 103 I=1,K
  103 R=R*DRAND(ISTRM)
      ERLNG=-PPARM(IPAR,1)*ALOG(R)
      IF (ERLNG-PPARM(IPAR,2)) 104,107,105
  104 ERLNG=PPARM(IPAR,2)
      GO TO 107
  105 IF (ERLNG-PPARM(IPAR,3)) 107,107,106
  106 ERLNG=PPARM(IPAR,3)
  107 RETURN
C
      END
```

Figure 4-40 FORTRAN listing of function ERLNG.

$$E = \sum_{i=1}^{K} -\beta \ln(r_i) = -\beta \sum_{i=1}^{K} \ln r_i = -\beta \ln \prod_{i=1}^{K} r_i.$$

Function NPSSN(IPAR,ISTRM). This function generates a deviate, NPSSN, from a Poisson distribution. The Poisson distribution is a discrete distribution that has the following form:

$$p(N = n) = p(n) = \begin{cases} \dfrac{\lambda^{(n-n_0)} e^{-\lambda}}{(n - n_0)!} & \lambda > 0 \\ & n = n_0, n_0 + 1, \ldots, \\ 0 & \text{otherwise;} \end{cases}$$

where λ is the expected value and n_0 is the minimum value. The values that must be stored in a row of the array PPARM for use as the parameters of a Poisson distribution are given in the following table:

Column J	1	2	3	4
PPARM(IPAR,J)	$\lambda - n_0$	n_0	Maximum	Not used

To generate a deviate from the Poisson distribution, a test is first made on the value stored in PPARM(IPAR,1) that contains the difference between the mean value and the lowest value. If this value is greater than 9, the Poisson deviate is obtained from the normal distribution. For large values, the normal distribution provides a good approximation to the Poisson distribution. If the normal approximation is not used, the Poisson deviate is obtained through the following analysis.

Consider that $p(n)$ represents the probability that the random variable N has occurred n times in one unit of time. (Assume the parameter of the Poisson distribution to be $\lambda\tau$ with $\tau = 1$.) It follows from probability theory that if events occur one at a time, and the number of occurrences of an event is Poisson-distributed with a mean number per unit time of λ, the time between occurrences of the event is distributed according to the exponential distribution with a mean time of $1/\lambda$. Thus the number of deviates obtained from an exponential distribution required to cause the sum of the deviates to exceed the unit interval must be Poisson-distributed. The distribution of the values of n will be Poisson-distributed if computed from the equation

$$\sum_{i=1}^{n} t_i \leq 1 < \sum_{i=1}^{n+1} t_i$$

where each t_i is exponentially distributed with a mean time of $1/\lambda$, that is,

$$t_i = -1/\lambda \ln (y_i)$$

and y_i is a random number.

Substituting in the above equation yields

$$\sum_{i=1}^{n} (-1/\lambda) \ln y_i \leq 1 < \sum_{i=1}^{n+1} (-1/\lambda) \ln y_i.$$

Multiplying by $(-\lambda)$, yields

$$\sum_{i=1}^{n} \ln y_i \geq -\lambda > \sum_{i=1}^{n+1} \ln y_i.$$

This can be replaced by the equivalent relationships

$$\exp\left[\sum_{i=1}^{u} \ln y_i\right] \geq \exp(-\lambda) > \exp\left[\sum_{i=1}^{n+1} \ln y_i\right],$$

$$\prod_{i=1}^{n} \exp[\ln y_i] \geq \exp(-\lambda) > \prod_{i=1}^{n+1} \exp[\ln y_i],$$

and

$$\prod_{i=1}^{n} y_i \geq \exp(-\lambda) > \prod_{i=1}^{n+1} y_i.$$

Thus the product of pseudorandom numbers is formed until it is less than the value $\exp(-\lambda)$. If the number of pseudorandom numbers required is $(n + 1)$, n is Poisson-distributed. The coding to accomplish the above calculations is given in Fig. 4-41, statements 101–104, where NPSSN is the variable equivalent to n.

Function GAM(AK,ISTRM). Function GAM is a support routine used by function GAMA to obtain a sample from a Gamma distribution, and by

```
      FUNCTION NPSSN(IPAR,ISTRM)
      COMMON /GCOM1/ ATRIB(25),JEVNT,MFA,MFE(100),MLE(100),MSTOP,NCRDR,N
     1NAPO,NNAPT,NNATR,NNFIL,NNQ(100),NNTRY,NPRNT,PPARM(50,4),TNOW,TTBEG
     2,TTCLR,TTFIN,TTRIB(25),TTSET
      NPSSN=0
      P=PPARM(IPAR,1)
      IF (P-9.0) 101,101,104
  101 Y=EXP(-P)
      X=1.0
  102 X=X*DRAND(ISTRM)
      IF (X-Y) 105,103,103
  103 NPSSN=NPSSN+1
      GO TO 102
  104 TEMP=PPARM(IPAR,4)
      PPARM(IPAR,4)=SQRT(PPARM(IPAR,1))
      NPSSN=RNORM(IPAR,ISTRM)+.5
      PPARM(IPAR,4)=TEMP
      IF (NPSSN) 104,105,105
  105 KK=PPARM(IPAR,2)
      KKK=PPARM(IPAR,3)
      NPSSN=KK+NPSSN
      IF (NPSSN-KKK) 107,107,106
  106 NPSSN=PPARM(IPAR,3)
  107 RETURN
C
      END
```

Figure 4-41 FORTRAN listing of function NPSSN.

function BETA to obtain a sample from a Beta distribution. Function GAM obtains a sample from a Gamma distribution with scale parameter 1 using a procedure proposed by Jöhnk (61) and Fox (7,41). The arguments of GAM are a shape parameter of the Gamma distribution AK and the stream number ISTRM.

It can be shown that the following relation holds

$$G = G_I + W \star E$$

where G, G_I, W, and E are random variables with the following distributions:

G is Gamma with shape parameter *AK* and scale parameter 1.

G_I is Gamma (Erlang) with integer shape parameter [AK] and scale parameter 1.

W is Beta with parameters θ = DG and $\phi = 1 -$ DG where DG = AK − [AK].

E is Exponential with a mean 1.

Procedures for generating G_I and E deviates have been previously discussed and only samples of W are required to obtain a value for G. The Beta density function is

$$f_W(w) = \begin{cases} \dfrac{\Gamma(\theta + \phi)}{\Gamma(\theta)\Gamma(\phi)} w^{\theta-1} (1 - w)^{\phi-1} & 0 \leq w \leq 1, \\ 0 & \text{otherwise.} \end{cases}$$

A sample from the Beta distribution is obtained as follows.

Let $$X = r_1^{1/\theta},$$

and $$Y = r_2^{1/\phi},$$

where r_i is a random number. If $X + Y \leq 1$, $W = X/(X + Y)$ is distributed according to the Beta distribution with parameters θ and ϕ.

Combining these results, deviates from the Gamma distribution can be obtained. The FORTRAN listing for function GAM is given in Fig. 4-42.

A sample from an Erlang distribution is obtained (S-101) and stored as the variable GAM. Next, the parameter DG to be used in obtaining the Beta deviate W is computed. If DG is within .015 of zero or one, it is assumed that the shape parameter is sufficiently close to an integer to use an Erlang deviate as the Gamma deviate. (If this is not done, an overflow or underflow may occur when raising the random number to the power 1./DG.) If DG $\leq$ .015, the value of GAM computed as the sum of [AK] exponentials is returned as the Gamma deviate. If DG $\geq$ .985, one more exponential sample is added to GAM (S-109) so that the Gamma deviate

```
GAM 1        FUNCTION GAM(AK,ISTRM)
GAM 2        K=AK
GAM 3        FK=K
GAM 4        GAM=0.
GAM 5        IF (K) 103,103,101
GAM 6    101 PROD=1.0
GAM 7        DO 102 I=1,K
GAM 8    102 PROD=PROD*DRAND(ISTRM)
GAM 9        GAM=-ALOG(PROD)
GAM 10   103 DG=AK-FK
GAM 11       IF (DG-.015) 110,110,104
GAM 12   104 IF (DG-.985) 106,105,105
GAM 13   105 W=1.
GAM 14       GO TO 109
GAM 15   106 A=1./DG
GAM 16       B=1./(1.-DG)
GAM 17   107 X=DRAND(ISTRM)**A
GAM 18       Y=DRAND(ISTRM)**B+X
GAM 19       IF (Y-1.) 108,108,107
GAM 20   108 W=X/Y
GAM 21   109 Y=-ALOG(DRAND(ISTRM))
GAM 22       GAM=GAM+W*Y
GAM 23   110 RETURN
GAM 24 C
GAM 25       END
```

Figure 4-42 FORTRAN listing of function GAM.

is the sum of [AK] + 1 exponentials. If $0.015 < DG < 0.985$, the procedure for obtaining a deviate from the Beta distribution is used. A rejection procedure is used if the specified condition is not met (G-19), that is, the values are rejected and new ones are generated until the condition is satisfied. The appropriate Beta deviate is obtained (S-108), an exponential deviate is computed (S-109), and the Gamma deviate is calculated (G-22).

Function GAMA(IPAR,ISTRM). This function generates a deviate, GAMA, from a Gamma distribution. The density function of the Gamma distribution is

$$f_X(x) = \begin{cases} \dfrac{1}{\Gamma(\alpha)\beta^\alpha} e^{-x/\beta} x^{\alpha-1} & x > 0, \\ 0 & \text{otherwise,} \end{cases}$$

with $E[X] = \alpha\beta$ and $\text{Var}[X] = \alpha\beta^2$. The values that must be stored in a row of PPARM when using function GAMA are

Column J	1	2	3	4
PPARM(IPAR,J)	β	Minimum	Maximum	α

If the mean and variance are known, α and β can be computed since the ratio of the variance to the mean is

$$\frac{\mathrm{Var}[x]}{E[x]} = \frac{\alpha\beta^2}{\alpha\beta} = \beta.$$

Using this value of β and the given mean, α can be computed as

$$E[x] = \alpha\beta$$

and

$$\alpha = \frac{E[x]}{\beta} = \frac{E^2[x]}{\mathrm{Var}[x]}.$$

The FORTRAN listing for function GAMA is shown in Fig. 4-43 and involves scaling by the value of PPARM(IPAR,1), a deviate obtained from function GAM. Tests against minimum and maximum allowed values are then made. The name GAMA was used instead of GAMMA to preclude a name conflict with the function GAMMA included in scientific packages. A new approach to obtaining GAMMA deviates by Phillips and Beightler (101) involves an approximation to the cumulative distribution function and then the application of the probability-integral-transformation. This proposed procedure is currently under test and preliminary results are promising.

Function BETA(IPAR,ISTRM). This function generates a deviate, BETA, from a Beta distribution that has the following form:

$$f_X(x) = \begin{cases} \dfrac{\Gamma(\theta+\phi)}{\Gamma(\theta)\Gamma(\phi)}\, x^{\theta-1}(1-x)^{\phi-1} & 0 \le x \le 1, \\ 0 & \text{otherwise,} \end{cases}$$

with $E[X] = \theta/(\theta+\phi)$ and $\mathrm{Var}[X] = \theta\phi/[(\theta+\phi)^2(\theta+\phi+1)]$. Values in the interval $[x_1, x_2]$ are obtained through the transformation $x = (x' - x_1)/(x_2 - x_1)$, where x' has a Beta distribution in the interval $[x_1, x_2]$.

Deviates from a Beta distribution can be obtained by the rejection

```
      FUNCTION GAMA(IPAR,ISTRM)                                         GMA    1
      COMMON /GCOM1/ ATRIB(25),JEVNT,MFA,MFE(100),MLE(100),MSTOP,NCRDR,NGCOM1  1
     1NAPO,NNAPT,NNATR,NNFIL,NNQ(100),NNTRY,NPRNT,PPARM(50,4),TNOW,TTBEGGCOM1  2
     2,TTCLR,TTFIN,TTRIB(25),TTSET                                      GCOM1  3
      A=PPARM(IPAR,4)                                                   GMA    2
      GAMA=GAM(A,ISTRM)*PPARM(IPAR,1)                                   GMA    3
      IF (GAMA-PPARM(IPAR,2)) 101,104,102                               GMA    4
  101 GAMA=PPARM(IPAR,2)                                                GMA    5
      GO TO 104                                                         GMA    6
  102 IF (GAMA-PPARM(IPAR,3)) 104,104,103                               GMA    7
  103 GAMA=PPARM(IPAR,3)                                                GMA    8
  104 RETURN                                                            GMA    9
C                                                                       GMA   10
      END                                                               GMA   11
```

Figure 4-43 FORTRAN listing of function GAMA.

procedure described and used in function GAM. However, it has been shown (40,41) that a more efficient method is to obtain a Beta deviate as the ratio of two unscaled Gamma deviates using the following equation:

$$\text{BETA} = \frac{G_\theta}{G_\theta + G_\phi}$$

where

$$G_\theta = \text{GAM}\ (\theta, \text{ISTRM})$$

and

$$G_\phi = \text{GAM}\ (\phi, \text{ISTRM}),$$

The values that must be stored in a row of PPARM when using function BETA are

Column J	1	2	3	4
PPARM(IPAR,J)	θ	x_1	x_2	ϕ

where x_1 and x_2 are the minimum and maximum values as described above. The values of θ and ϕ are computed from the equations for the mean and variance as follows:

$$\theta = E[X]\left\{\frac{E[X] - E^2[X]}{\text{Var}[X]} - 1\right\},$$

and

$$\phi = \theta\left\{\frac{1 - E[X]}{E[X]}\right\},$$

where $E[X] = (E[X'] - x_1)/(x_2 - x_1)$, and $\text{Var}[X] = \text{Var}[X']/[(x_2 - x_1)^2]$. The FORTRAN listing for function BETA is given in Fig. 4-44. The deviate BETA is a sample of x', hence it will have a value in the interval $[x_1, x_2]$.

```
      FUNCTION BETA(IPAR,ISTRM)                                         BET    1
      COMMON /GCOM1/ ATRIB(25),JEVNT,MFA,MFE(100),MLE(100),MSTOP,NCRDR,NGCOM1  1
     1NAPO,NNAPT,NNATR,NNFIL,NNQ(100),NNTRY,NPRNT,PPARM(50,4),TNOW,TTBEGGCOM1  2
     2,TTCLR,TTFIN,TTRIB(25),TTSET                                      GCOM1  3
      A=PPARM(IPAR,1)                                                   BET    2
      B=PPARM(IPAR,4)                                                   BET    3
      X=GAM(A,ISTRM)                                                    BET    4
      BETA=X/(X+GAM(B,ISTRM))                                           BET    5
      BETA=BETA*(PPARM(IPAR,3)-PPARM(IPAR,2))+PPARM(IPAR,2)             BET    6
      RETURN                                                            BET    7
C                                                                       BET    8
      END                                                               BET    9
```

Figure 4-44 FORTRAN listing of function BETA.

EXERCISES

4-1. Modify subroutine GASP to print the item and event code of every event. Specify the location of the added statements by giving them sequence numbers.

4-2. Indicate the changes in subroutine GASP required to eliminate the recording of state variables before and after an event occurs.

4-3. Develop a function subprogram that determines the total number of entires in all files. Define the function name as NTOTE.

4-4. If equations for DD(·) were not permitted in GASP IV, indicate the statements that could be deleted from subroutine GASP. Would this result in any data input changes?

4-5. Design a file system so that all files could have secondary ranking attributes.

4-6. Change function KROSS so that a crossing is defined if a crossing variable is within ±TOL of the function to be crossed.

4-7. Develop a procedure by which function KROSS returns a suggested time value at which a crossing might occur when a state-event is passed.

4-8. Write a subroutine called FIND3 that locates an entry NTRY in file J such that the value of ATRIB(1) is less than X(1), the value of ATRIB(2) is less than X(2), and the value of ATRIB(3) is greater than or equal to X(3). If no entry in file J satisfies the above conditions, return a negative value to the calling routine. Write a statement using FIND3 that locates an entry in file 4 whose first two attributes are less than three and whose third attribute is greater than five.

4-9. Modify subroutine TIMST so that the change to be made to the variable is included as an argument to the subroutine so that TIMST can update the value of the variable.

4-10. Write a subprogram that will compute the sum of the product of two attributes of a given file.

4-11. Develop a function subprogram for inclusion in GASP IV that performs a table look-up function for a table whose independent variable is not specified in equal increments.

4-12. Modify subroutine RNORM to obtain samples from a truncated normal distribution.

4-13. Specify the data for a type 6 data card so that samples from a Poisson distribution can be generated with a mean value of 50, a minimum of 40, and a maximum value of 70.

4-14. Specify the data values for a type 6 data card for sampling from an Erlang distribution having a mean of 50, an α value of 5, a minimum of 30, and a maximum of 70.

4-15. Develop a subroutine for GASP IV called RGRES that will generate samples from any desired regression equation involving terms in x with the exponents ½, 1, 2, and 3, and terms of the forms e^X and ln(X). Assume that the random portion of the regression sample is normally distributed and the coefficients are arguments to the subroutine.

4-16. Write a function subprogram to obtain random deviates of a random variable that is described by the following function (the Weibull distribution).

$$f_X(x) = \begin{cases} \alpha\lambda x^{\alpha-1} \exp\ (-\ \lambda x^{\alpha}) & x > 0, \lambda > 0, \alpha > 1, \\ 0 & \text{otherwise.} \end{cases}$$

[Hint: $F_X(x) = 1 - \exp\ (-\ \lambda x^{\alpha})$.]

4-17. Develop a function for inclusion in GASP IV for sampling from a probability mass function (see Example 4, Chapter 5).

4-18. Show that the ratio of Gamma-distributed random variables is Beta-distributed.

4-19. Show that the procedure described for generating Beta deviates is valid.

4-20. Derive the equations that are used to obtain deviates from the triangular distribution.

4-21. Many procedures are available for performing the integration required in the continuous simulations. Compare three such procedures for possible inclusion in GASP IV (16, 18, 62, 72, 75).

4-22. Rewrite subroutine GPLOT to allow multiple plots to be stored in QSET. (Hint: use subroutines FILEM and RMOVE).

4-23. Design a filing system that allows an entry to be a member of two files without storing the entry twice. Generalize the above. (Hint: use two pointing systems, one for files and one for each entry.)

Chapter Five

GASP IV

Discrete Simulation

This chapter presents five examples of GASP IV programs that analyze situations that can be modeled using discrete event concepts. An inventory situation, two queueing systems, and two network models are developed. For each problem type, the general approach to obtain a simulation model using a next event philosophy is presented. Each example demonstrates the procedures involved in using the general approach and in developing a computer program in the GASP IV language.

The inventory example involves the simulation of customers' demands for goods from a discount store. The store's policy is to periodically review its inventory position and to order more goods only when its inventory position falls below a prescribed value. The purpose of the simulation is to evaluate the stores policy on when to order more goods and how much to order.

The first queueing example involves a fleet of tankers being loaded in Valdez, Alaska, and carrying crude oil to Seattle, Washington. Each tanker is unloaded in Seattle and then returns to Valdez for reloading. The purpose of the simulation is to evaluate the utilization of the unloading dock and to determine the round trip and waiting times of the tankers (64). The second queueing example presents a simulation of a drive-in bank system that has two tellers, limited waiting space for cars seeking service from the tellers, and permits the jockeying of cars between the queues of the tellers (107). Balking by potential customers if the queues of the tellers are full is also simulated. The simulation is used to obtain estimates of the working time of the tellers and the waiting time of the customers. Both queueing examples illustrate the ease with which complex situations can be analyzed using simulation.

The fourth example of this chapter involves the simulation of a PERT network and compares the results of the simulation with the results obtained from a PERT analysis (107). How to obtain additional information about a PERT network through simulation is shown. The fifth and last example also involves the simulation of a network of activities but with the added consideration that each activity requires specific resources (107). The available resources are limited and the activities compete for the use of the resources. Thus the resources must be allocated to the activities before they can be started. Different rules for allocating the resources are simulated and an evaluation of the schedules that result is performed.

All of the examples in this book employ a standard format to express the simulation approach to problem solving. The standard format contains the following sections:

1. *Statement of the Problem.* A description of the system to be studied, including the parameter values of the system.
2. *Simulation Objectives.* A statement of the aspects of the problem to be evaluated from the simulation.
3. *Special Features.* The features and concepts of GASP IV that are illustrated by the example for the purpose of promoting understanding of simulation concepts and GASP IV techniques and procedures.
4. *Procedure.* The method of modeling the situation including the definitions of events, entities, attributes, files, and state variables. Flow charts, FORTRAN listings, and input data are included.
5. *Simulation Reports.* Reproductions of the reports generated by the GASP IV simulation are presented. Discussion of the simulation reports is limited to describing the meaning of various outputs. Statistical testing of the results is not included since this book deals only with the development and use of a language. The verification, validation, and detailed analysis of simulation results is beyond the scope of this book.

In this chapter the examples do not contain state variables and only involve time-events (discrete events). Therefore, subroutines STATE and SCOND are not required, and the dummy versions included in GASP IV will eliminate any loading messages or errors due to the inability of the computing system monitor to locate subroutines that are referred to by GASP IV even though they are not used.

SIMULATION OF INVENTORY SYSTEMS

Inventory situations continually attract great attention from practitioners and theoreticians in the industrial engineering—management science field. This interest is justified on the basis of the potential cost savings possible from improved decision making in inventory problems. Since solutions to such problems can be improved through the use of quantitative methods, there has been increased demand for studies on inventory theory. The published literature is extensive (11, 48, 130).

All inventory systems involve the storage of particular items for future sale or use. Demands are imposed on an inventory by customers seeking supplies of an individual item. A company must establish an inventory policy that specifies (1) when an order for additional items should be placed (or manufactured) and (2) how many of the items should be ordered at each order time. Inventory theory attempts to obtain optimal answers to these two questions. The solutions depend on the revenues and costs associated with the inventory situation. Revenue is a function of the number of units sold and the selling price per unit. Costs are more complex and include information processing and ordering costs, inventory carrying charges, opportunity cost due to loss of the use of capital tied up in inventory, and stock-out costs. Stock-out costs can be considered as either the cost associated with *backorders* (an order that is satisfied when inventory becomes available) or the cost associated with *lost sales.* Inventory theory deals with the determination of the best inventory policy in specified situations and the parameters of the policy to maximize profit or expected profit (or in some cases, minimize cost or expected cost).

In this book the prime concern is with methods for simulating inventory situations and not with methods for finding optimal solutions to inventory problems. Finding optimal solutions by simulation involves the use of search techniques that are beyond the scope of this book. However, the effects of different parameters of an inventory policy are examined.

When the items stored in inventory are discrete units, simulation of the inventory system using the next event philosophy is quite natural. The primary system variables are the number of units in storage, called the *inventory-on-hand*, and the number of units that are theoretically on the books of the company, called the *inventory position.* The inventory position is equal to the inventory-on-hand, plus the number of units on order (the number due in), minus the number of units that have been backordered by customers (the number due out). The inventory-on-hand represents the number of units available to be sold to customers. The inventory position represents the number of units that is or will be available to the company for potential sale. Inventory decisions regarding when to place an order and how much to order are normally based on the inventory position. Other attributes associated with inventory situations are: the number of units sold, the number of orders placed, the number of lost sales and/or the number of backorders, and the number of times the inventory position is reviewed to make a decision whether to place an order.

The events associated with an inventory situation at which these attributes could change their value are: a demand by a customer for the items in inventory, a review of the status of the inventory position to determine if an order should be placed, the receipt of goods from the distributor to be placed in inventory, and the satisfying of the customers demand for the item. Each of these events could be modeled as a simulation event. However, several of the above will always occur at the same point in time. When this happens, it is efficient to combine the events into a single event. For example, the satisfying of a customer demand would normally take place either when the customer demand is placed or when a shipment of units is received from the distributor. When this is done, the modeler assumes that the time delay in delivering a unit to a customer has an insignificant effect on the expected cost or profit associated with the inventory situation.

Customer demand events are normally modeled by specifying the time between customer demands. In this way, each demand event can be used to specify the time of the next demand. Then only the first demand event, which starts the demand process, and the time between demands would need to be specified.

Two types of review procedures to determine if an order should be placed are common in industry. A *periodic review procedure* specifies that a review should be performed at equally spaced points in time, for example, every month. The other review procedure involves the examination of the inventory position every time it decreases. This type of review is called *transaction reporting* and involves keeping a running log of the inventory position. When a transaction reporting review procedure is being studied, no separate review event is required since the inventory position can only be decreased when a customer demand occurs. Thus the review procedure can be incorporated into the customer demand event.

The event involving the receipt of units from the distributor does not change the inventory position since the inventory position was increased when these units were ordered. However, the inventory-on-hand and the number of backorders could change when the receipt event occurs. The time at which the receipt event occurs is based on the time at which it was decided to place an order (at a review time) plus the time for processing the order and shipping the units. The time from the placing of the order to the receipt of the units is called the *lead time*.

The above general discussion of events that can occur in an inventory situation provides a general framework for simulating any inventory system. To obtain a simulation using GASP IV, it would only be necessary to write subroutines for each of the events required by the specific inventory situation. The point in time at which the individual events occur would automatically be handled by GASP IV using the time between events as specified by the user in the appropriate event routines. The user would schedule the next demand event (in his subroutine representing the demand event) and the receipt of units to occur, at the review time plus the lead time, if it was decided that an order was to be placed. Of significant importance in the simulation of inventory systems is the complete absence of the need to specify the interdemand time distribution, the lead time distribution, the number of units requested by a customer at a demand point, and so forth, when discussing the overall procedure for simulating an inventory system. This information is only important when simulating a specific system. A specific example of the use of GASP IV to simulate an inventory situation is now given.

EXAMPLE 1—SIMULATION OF AN INVENTORY SYSTEM WITH LOST SALES

Statement of the Problem

A large discount house is planning to install a system to control the inventory of a particular radio. The number of units demanded is Poisson distributed with a mean of five radios per week, that is, the time between demands is exponentially distributed with a mean time of 0.2 weeks. The procurement lead time (the time from the placement of an order to its receipt) is constant and requires three weeks. The radio sells for $65.00 and costs the store $40.00. An inventory carrying charge of $0.20 per dollar year (or $0.003846 per dollar week) is used. If a customer demands the radio when it is not in stock, he will go to another nearby discount store to find it rather than select a different radio or wait until a new shipment arrives. The store has decided that each such unfilled request costs the store a loss of $20.00 in goodwill. The total cost of placing an order for radios from the supplier is estimated to be $50.00. Store policy is to review the inventory position every four weeks to decide if an order should be placed. The cost of this review is $30.00.

Assume that the initial inventory position is 36 radios in stock and that no orders are outstanding. Company policy is to order up to the stock control level (SCL) whenever the inventory position (POS) is found to be less than or equal to the reorder point (R). Several values for SCL and R are tested and the effect of changing the review period is explored.

Simulation Objective

The objective of this example is the simulation of an inventory system over a period of six years (312 weeks) to obtain the average values per week for the following quantities: (1) profit, (2) total sales, (3) inventory-on-hand, (4) safety stock, (5) number of orders, and (6) number of lost sales.

Special Features

This example illustrates how simulation is used to evaluate an inventory policy. First, a single policy is evaluated. Second, multiple runs using subroutine INTLC are made. Each run tests different parameter values for the inventory policy. The code is then modified to demonstrate the use of subroutine GPLOT to graphically portray important variables of the model.

Procedure

The events of the simulation are (1) a demand for a radio (DMAND), (2) the receipt of an order (RECPT), and (3) a periodic review of inventory (REVIEW). In this problem only an event file is necessary. In this file attribute 1 is the time of the event, and attribute 2 is the event code. The event code is either 1, 2, or 3, depending on whether the event is a demand, a receipt, or a review.

The non-GASP variables associated with this simulation are:

Variable	Definition	Initial Value
AVIN	Average inventory on hand (units/week)	Output
AVSS	Average safety stock	Output
CCHG	Inventory carrying charge ($/$-week)	0.003846
CPO	Cost per order ($/order)	50
CPR	Cost per review ($/review)	30
P	Average profit per week	Output
PCOU	Purchase cost of unit ($/unit)	40
POS	Inventory position	36
R	Reorder point	Read in
SALE	Total number of sales	0
SCL	Stock control level when an order is placed, SCL − POS is the amount ordered	Read in
SLOST	Number of lost sales	0
SPOU	Selling price of unit ($/unit)	65
STOCK	Inventory-on-hand	36
TBR	Time between reviews	Read in
TIIN	Time integrated inventory for the simulation period	Output
TLEAD	Time between placement and receipt of order (weeks)	3
TORD	Total number of orders	0
TREV	Total number of reviews	0
ULOSE	Cost due to loss in goodwill ($/lost sale)	20
XL	Mean time between demands (weeks)	0.2

With these definitions the average profit per week in a simulation run of T weeks can be computed as:

```
P = [(SPOU − PCOU) * SALE − (CPO * TORD + CPR * TREV +
    CCHG * PCOU * TIIN + ULOSE * SLOST)]/T
```

The main program first sets the card reader number NCRDR and printer number NPRNT. It then reads the values for the cost variables and the time between demands XL and the lead time TLEAD. The FORTRAN listing of the main program for this example is shown in Fig. 5-1.

Subroutine INTLC is used to initialize non-GASP variables that may change value from run to run. In this example such variables are the reorder point (R), the stock control level (SCL), and the time between

```
      PROGRAM MAIN (INPUT,OUTPUT,TAPE5=INPUT,TAPE6=OUTPUT)
      DIMENSION NSET(4000)
      COMMON QSET(4000)
      COMMON /GCOM1/ ATRIB(25),JEVNT,MFA,MFE(100),MLE(100),MSTOP,NCRDR,N
     1NAPO,NNAPT,NNATR,NNFIL,NNQ(100),NNTRY,NPRNT,PPARM(50,4),TNOW,TTBEG
     2,TTCLR,TTFIN,TTRIB(25),TTSET
      COMMON /UCOM1/XL,POS,STOCK,TLEAD,CPO,CCHG,ULOSE,SLOST,TREV,TORD,SA
     1LE,SPOU,PCOU,R,SCL,TBR,CPR
      EQUIVALENCE(NSET(1),QSET(1))
C
C*****LOST SALES
C
C
C*****SET VALUES FOR CARD READER AND PRINTER
C
      NCRDR=5
      NPRNT=6
C
C*****READ IN VALUES FOR INITIAL CONDITIONS.  INITIALIZE THE PRICE
C*****OF AN ITEM, THE NUMBER OF LOST SALES, THE TOTAL ORDERS AND THE
C*****NUMBER OF SALES.
C
      READ (NCRDR,101) SPOU,PCOU,CPO,CCHG,ULOSE,XL,TLEAD,CPR
      WRITE (NPRNT,102) SPOU,PCOU,CPO,CCHG,ULOSE,XL,TLEAD,CPR
C
C*****CONVERT CARRYING CHARGE TO WEEKLY RATE
C
      CCHG=CCHG/52.0
C
C     START THE SIMULATION
C
      CALL GASP
C
  101 FORMAT (8F5.2)
  102 FORMAT (41H         SPOU          PCOU          CPO          CCHG,40H          ULOSE
     1          XL        TLEAD          CPR/1X,8F10.2)
C
      END
```

Figure 5-1 FORTRAN listing of main program (Example 1).

reviews (TBR). Also, initial conditions are established in INTLC. The number of lost sales, orders, reviews, and sales are all set at zero. The initial stock and inventory position values are set at 36.0. By using INTLC, multiple runs can be made without returning to the main program. The FORTRAN listing of INTLC is given in Fig. 5-2. Note the insertion of the initial events into file 1 to occur at time zero.

Subroutine EVNTS transfers control to one of the three user written subroutines: DMAND, RECPT, or REVIEW.* The FORTRAN listing of subroutine EVNTS is given in Fig. 5-3.

The flow chart of subroutine DMAND is shown in Fig. 5-4. When a demand occurs, the next demand is scheduled to occur at TNOW plus a time drawn from an exponential distribution with mean XL. The disposition of the current demand is then determined. If there is no radio in inventory to meet the demand, the number of lost sales is increased by

* Although GASP IV subprograms were limited to five-character names, the user subprograms are only limited by the FORTRAN compiler used by their computer center.

```
      SUBROUTINE INTLC
      COMMON /GCOM1/ ATRIB(25),JEVNT,MFA,MFE(100),MLE(100),MSTOP,NCRDR,NGCOM1
     1NAPO,NNAPT,NNATR,NNFIL,NNQ(100),NNTRY,NPRNT,PPARM(50,4),TNOW,TTBEG
     2,TTCLR,TTFIN,TTRIB(25),TTSET
      COMMON /UCOM1/XL,POS,STOCK,TLEAD,CPO,CCHG,ULOSE,SLOST,TREV,TORD,SA
     1LE,SPOU,PCOU,R,SCL,TBR,CPR
      READ (NCRDR,101) R,SCL,TBR
      SLOST=0.0
      TORD=0.0
      TREV=0.0
      SALE=0.0
      STOCK=36.0
      POS=36.0
      CALL TIMST (STOCK,TNOW,1)
      ATRIB(1)=0.
      ATRIB(2)=1.0
      CALL FILEM (1)
      ATRIB(1)=0.
      ATRIB(2)=3.0
      CALL FILEM (1)
      RETURN
C
  101 FORMAT (3F5.2)
C
      END
```

Figure 5-2 FORTRAN listing of subroutine INTLC (Example 1).

one, and a return is made to the calling routine (EVNTS). If a radio is in stock, sales are increased by one, statistics are collected on the number of units in inventory, and the inventory-on-hand and inventory position are decreased by one. This completes the computations and decisions that are made at a demand time. The FORTRAN listing for DMAND is given in Fig. 5-5. Note how the isolation of the demand event simplifies the modeling logic required.

A review event occurs every TBR weeks. Through initialization the first review is scheduled to occur at time 0.0. Subroutine REVIEW models what occurs at the review event time. The FORTRAN listing is given in Fig. 5-6. First, the next review event is scheduled to occur at the current time TNOW plus the time between reviews TBR. The inventory position is then checked against the reorder point. If the inventory position is greater than the reorder point, no action is taken at this review time. If the inventory position is less than or equal to the reorder point, an order is made for Q units where Q = SCL−POS. A RECPT event is

```
      SUBROUTINE EVNTS (IX)
      GO TO (101,102,103), IX
  101 CALL DMAND
      GO TO 104
  102 CALL RECPT
      GO TO 104
  103 CALL REVIEW
  104 RETURN
C
      END
```

Figure 5-3 FORTRAN listing of subroutine EVNTS (Example 1).

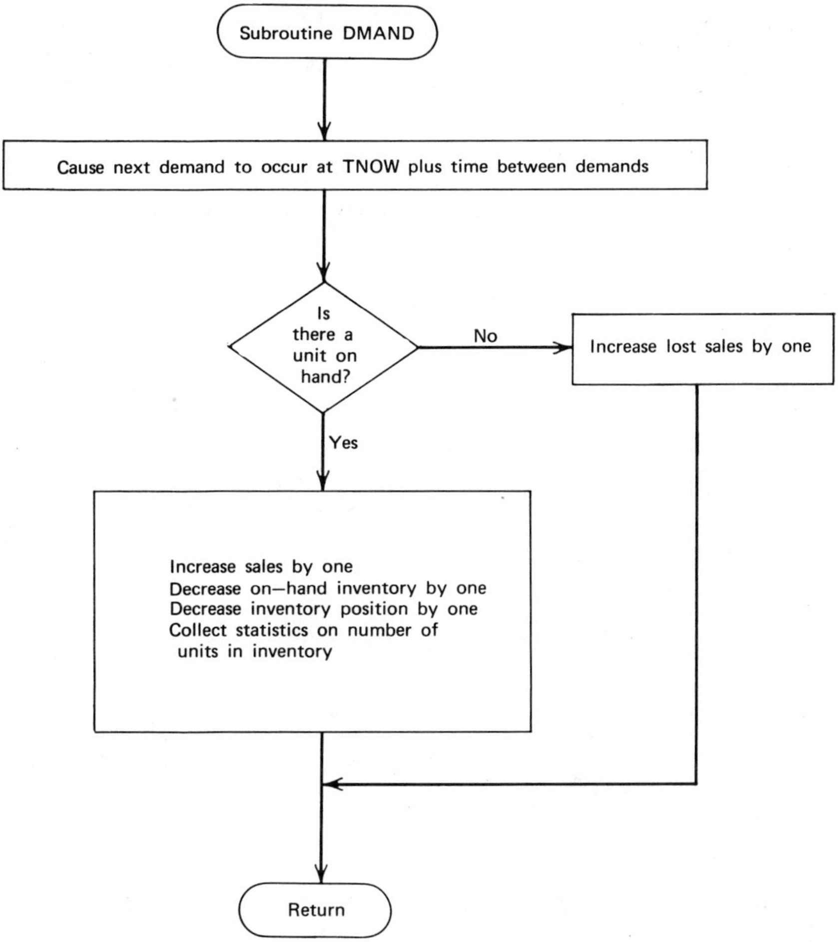

Figure 5-4 Flow chart of subroutine DMAND (Example 1).

scheduled at TNOW plus the lead time associated with orders. The number of units ordered is stored as attribute 3 for this event and the amount is added to the inventory position. The number of reviews performed is then increased by one and a return is made to the calling routine.

When a receipt event occurs, the inventory-on-hand is to be increased by the quantity ordered, which was stored as ATRIB(3). Before increasing the inventory-on-hand, statistics are collected on the inventory-on-hand at the time when an order is received, that is, the *safety stock level.* Statistics on the safety stock level are based on the number of observa-

```
      SUBROUTINE DMAND                                                  DMD      1
      COMMON /GCOM1/ ATRIB(25),JEVNT,MFA,MFE(100),MLE(100),MSTOP,NCRDR,NGCOM1    1
     1NAPO,NNAPT,NNATR,NNFIL,NNQ(100),NNTRY,NPRNT,PPARM(50,4),TNOW,TTBEGGCOM1    2
     2,TTCLR,TTFIN,TTRIB(25),TTSET                                      GCOM1    3
      COMMON /UCOM1/XL,POS,STOCK,TLEAD,CPO,CCHG,ULOSE,SLOST,TREV,TORD,SAUCOM1    1
     1LE, SPOU,PCOU,R,SCL,TBR,CPR                                       UCOM1    2
C                                                                       DMD      2
C*****CREATE AND CAUSE NEXT DEMAND                                      DMD      3
C                                                                       DMD      4
      ATRIB(1)=TNOW-XL*ALOG(DRAND(1))                                   DMD      5
      CALL FILEM (1)                                                    DMD      6
C                                                                       DMD      7
C*****TEST STOCK TO SEE IF CURRENT DEMAND CAN BE MET.  IT IS            DMD      8
C*****ASSUMED THAT ONE ITEM IS DEMANDED AT A TIME.  IF STOCK IS ZERO    DMD      9
C                                                                       DMD     10
      IF (STOCK) 101,101,102                                            DMD     11
C                                                                       DMD     12
C*****INCREASE  LOST SALES BY ONE.                                      DMD     13
C                                                                       DMD     14
  101 SLOST=SLOST+1.0                                                   DMD     15
      GO TO 103                                                         DMD     16
C                                                                       DMD     17
C*****IF STOCK IS GREATER THAN ZERO INCREASE  NUMBER OF SALES BY ONE    DMD     18
C*****AND DECREASE  THE STOCK LEVEL AND INVENTORY POSITIONS BY ONE.     DMD     19
C                                                                       DMD     20
  102 SALE=SALE+1.0                                                     DMD     21
      STOCK=STOCK-1.0                                                   DMD     22
      POS=POS-1.0                                                       DMD     23
C                                                                       DMD     24
C*****COLLECT STATISTICS ON THE NUMBER OF UNITS IN STOCK                DMD     25
C                                                                       DMD     26
      CALL TIMST (STOCK,TNOW,1)                                         DMD     27
  103 RETURN                                                            DMD     28
C                                                                       DMD     29
      END                                                               DMD     30
```

Figure 5-5 FORTRAN listing of subroutine DMAND (Example 1).

```
      SUBROUTINE REVIEW                                                 REV      1
      COMMON /GCOM1/ ATRIB(25),JEVNT,MFA,MFE(100),MLE(100),MSTOP,NCRDR,NGCOM1    1
     1NAPO,NNAPT,NNATR,NNFIL,NNQ(100),NNTRY,NPRNT,PPARM(50,4),TNOW,TTBEGGCOM1    2
     2,TTCLR,TTFIN,TTRIB(25),TTSET                                      GCOM1    3
      COMMON /UCOM1/XL,POS,STOCK,TLEAD,CPO,CCHG,ULOSE,SLOST,TREV,TORD,SAUCOM1    1
     1LE, SPOU,PCOU,R,SCL,TBR,CPR                                       UCOM1    2
C                                                                       REV      2
C*****CREATE AND CAUSE THE NEXT REVIEW EVENT                            REV      3
C                                                                       REV      4
      ATRIB(1)=TNOW+TBR                                                 REV      5
      CALL FILEM (1)                                                    REV      6
C                                                                       REV      7
C*****TEST INVENTORY POSITION AGAINST REORDER POINT.  IF INVENTORY      REV      8
C*****POSITION IS LESS THAN THE REORDER POINT, CREATE AND CAUSE A       REV      9
C*****RECEIPT EVENT AT THE CURRENT TIME PLUS THE LEAD TIME.             REV     10
C                                                                       REV     11
      IF (POS-R) 101,101,102                                            REV     12
  101 ATRIB(1)=TNOW+TLEAD                                               REV     13
      ATRIB(2)=2.0                                                      REV     14
      ATRIB(3)=SCL-POS                                                  REV     15
      CALL FILEM (1)                                                    REV     16
C                                                                       REV     17
C*****INCREMENT TOTAL ORDERS BY ONE AND INVENTORY POSITION AND          REV     18
C*****AMOUNT ON ORDER BY AMOUNT ORDERED                                 REV     19
C                                                                       REV     20
      POS=POS+ATRIB(3)                                                  REV     21
      TORD=TORD+1.0                                                     REV     22
C                                                                       REV     23
C*****INCREMENT COUNT OF NUMBER OF REVIEWS                              REV     24
C                                                                       REV     25
  102 TREV=TREV+1.0                                                     REV     26
      RETURN                                                            REV     27
C                                                                       REV     28
      END                                                               REV     29
```

Figure 5-6 FORTRAN listing of subroutine REVIEW (Example 1).

```
      SUBROUTINE RECPT
      COMMON /GCOM1/ ATRIB(25),JEVNT,MFA,MFE(100),MLE(100),MSTOP,NCRDR,N
     1NAPO,NNAPT,NNATR,NNFIL,NNQ(100),NNTRY,NPRNT,PPARM(50,4),TNOW,TTBEG
     2,TTCLR,TTFIN,TTRIB(25),TTSET
      COMMON /UCOM1/XL,POS,STOCK,TLEAD,CPO,CCHG,ULOSE,SLOST,TREV,TORD,SA
     1LE,SPOU,PCOU,R,SCL,TBR,CPR
C
C*****COLLECT STATISTICS ON THE NUMBER OF UNITS IN STOCK.
C*****INCREMENT NUMBER OF UNITS IN STOCK BY AMOUNT RECEIVED
C
      CALL COLCT (STOCK,1)
      STOCK=STOCK+ATRIB(3)
      CALL TIMST (STOCK,TNOW,1)
      RETURN
C
      END
```

Figure 5-7 FORTRAN listing of subroutine RECPT (Example 1).

tions, each observation occurring when an order is received. Thus GASP IV subroutine COLCT is used. Statistics concerning the inventory-on-hand are then collected by using subroutine TIMST. The FORTRAN listing for subroutine RECPT is given in Fig. 5-7.

When one simulation run is completed, that is, TNOW $\geq$ TTFIN, subroutine OTPUT is called. OTPUT computes and prints the averages associated with the simulation run. The FORTRAN listing for subroutine OTPUT is given in Fig. 5-8. The average safety stock is computed using the values collected when subroutine COLCT was called with code 1. The sum of all safety stock levels is stored in SSOBV(1,1) by subroutine COLCT. The number of observations of safety stock is stored in SSOBV(1,3). Thus the average safety stock (AVSS) is the ratio of

```
      SUBROUTINE OTPUT
      COMMON /GCOM1/ ATRIB(25),JEVNT,MFA,MFE(100),MLE(100),MSTOP,NCRDR,N
     1NAPO,NNAPT,NNATR,NNFIL,NNQ(100),NNTRY,NPRNT,PPARM(50,4),TNOW,TTBEG
     2,TTCLR,TTFIN,TTRIB(25),TTSET
      COMMON /GCOM6/ EENQ(100),IINN(100),KKRNK(100),MMAXQ(100),QQTIM(100
     1),SSOBV(25,5),SSTPV(25,6),VVNQ(100)
      COMMON /UCOM1/XL,POS,STOCK,TLEAD,CPO,CCHG,ULOSE,SLOST,TREV,TORD,SA
     1LE,SPOU,PCOU,R,SCL,TBR,CPR
C
C*****COLLECT STATISTICS AND COMPUTE EXPECTED PROFIT.
C
      AVSS=SSOBV(1,1)/SSOBV(1,3)
      CALL TIMST (STOCK,TNOW,1)
      AVIN=SSTPV(1,1)/SSTPV(1,3)
      AORD=TORD/TNOW
      ASAL=SALE/TNOW
      ALOST=SLOST/TNOW
      AREV=TREV/TNOW
      P=(SPOU-PCOU)*ASAL-CPO*AORD-CCHG*PCOU*AVIN-ULOSE*ALOST-CPR*AREV
C
C*****REPORT RESULTS
C
      WRITE (NPRNT,101) R,SCL,TBR,AORD,ALOST,ASAL,AVSS,AVIN,AREV,P
      RETURN
C
  101 FORMAT (39H    R    SCL    TBR        AORD         ALOST,55H        ASAL
     1       AVSS         AVIN          AREV              P/3(F5.0,1X),7(F10.4,1X)
     2)
C
      END
```

Figure 5-8 FORTRAN listing of subroutine OTPUT (Example 1).

these two quantities. As will be seen, this quantity is a normal output on the GASP IV summary report.

The average inventory can be calculated by dividing the integrated inventory-on-hand by the time period for the simulation. Since STOCK was integrated by calls to subroutine TIMST with code 1, the integrated inventory-on-hand is stored in SSTPV(1,1) and the time to which the integration is performed is SSTPV(1,3). In OTPUT the average inventory (AVIN) is computed as SSTPV(1,1)/SSTPV(1,3). Statistics on inventory-on-hand would also be part of the GASP IV summary report. In this case GASP IV would include the inventory level from the time of the last event to the end-of-simulation time. The value of the inventory-on-hand during this last interval is maintained as SSTPV(1,6); the calculation performed by GASP IV (in TIMST) for the average inventory is

$$\frac{\text{SSTPV(1,1)} + \text{SSTPV(1,6)} \star (\text{TNOW} - \text{SSTPV(1,3)}).}{\text{TNOW}}$$

This calculation could have been made in OTPUT.

A listing of the input data for one simulation run and the input printout produced by subroutine DATIN are given in Figs. 5-9 and 5-10.

Several values on the data cards bear discussion. The first card is read in the main program and initializes cost variables for the simulation. The last card sets the parameters for the inventory policy to be evaluated. It is read in subroutine INTLC. The maximum number of entries in the file NNTRY was set at 10. This number is an estimate. In this example it is known that there will always be one demand event and one review event. The number of receipt events is not known but certainly it is not expected to be more than eight at any one time. Therefore, NNTRY set at 10 should be sufficient. Since there are three attributes per entry and two pointers per entry, 50 cells should be allocated to NSET.

Card	Type
`  65.   40.   50.   0.2   20.   0.2    3.   30.`	USER
`PRITSKER              1     6    30 1973     1`	1
`     1     1     0     0     0     1    10     3     1 4000`	2
`3          1SFTYSTOK`	3
`4          1INVNTRY`	4
`     1`	7
`     1`	8
`     1     1     1     0           0.0        312.       165397`	11
`12         0`	12
`  18.   72.    4.`	USER

Figure 5-9 Listing of data input (Example 1).

```
                         SIMULATION PROJECT NUMBER   1  BY  PRITSKER

                         DATE  6/ 30/ 1973        RUN NUMBER    1 OF    1
                         LLSUP=0000000000000000   GASP IV VERSION 23JUN73

NNCLT=     1   NNSTA=     1   NNHIS=     0   NNPRM=     0   NNPLT=     0   NNSTR=     1   NNTRY=     10
NNATR=     3   NNFIL=     1   NNSET=  4000   NNEQD=    -0   NNEQS=    -0   NFLAG=    -0

COLCT NO.  1   LLABC=SFTYSTOK

TIMST NO.  1   LLABT=INVNTRY  I.C. =    -0.

KKRNK= (   1)

IINN = (   1)

MSTOP=     1   JJCLR=     1   JJBEG=     1   IICRD=     0   TTBEG=     0.            TTFIN=      3.1200E+02
JJFIL=     1
IISED= 65397
```

Figure 5-10 GASP IV echo check of input data (Example 1).

This is accomplished in the main program in the dimension statement and on data input by setting NNSET. In an extension to this example, NSET is used to store values for plotting. Because of this, NSET is dimensioned to 4000 and NNSET is set to 4000 on input. The initial value of stock-on-hand for statistics calculations is set on data card type 4. This only initializes SSTPV(1,6) and can also be accomplished by a call to TIMST in subroutine INTLC. This latter method would have been required if the initial stock level was read in subroutine INTLC. The value read on data card 4 *does not* initialize STOCK. In this example TIMST is called in INTLC to perform the initialization.

On data card type 11, MSTOP = 1 specifies that the simulation is to end at TTFIN = 312. JJCLR = 1 and JJFIL = 1 specifies that the statistical arrays and file array are to be initialized. JJBEG = 1 specifies that the random number generators and the variables associated with time are to be initialized. For only one run the IICRD value does not matter. As shown after the section on simulation results, IICRD does provide a convenient method for making multiple runs with only a few additional input cards. A type 12 data card with a zero in column 10 is required to indicate that there are no type 12 cards. Recall that initial events were established in subroutine INTLC.

Simulation Reports

Figure 5-11 presents the GASP IV summary report for the simulation of the inventory policy in which R = 18, SCL = 72, and TBR = 4. From subroutine OTPUT, the average profit per week using these values was found to be $87.77 over the 312 week period. The standard GASP IV summary report illustrates the output obtained from using COLCT and TIMST. The statistics for file 1 show that at most only three events were in the file. Thus only one receipt event was outstanding at a time. Clearly this is the case since for this run the time between reviews (four weeks) is greater than the lead time (three weeks).

Additional Runs for Example 1

Using the basic framework provided by Example 1, the use of GASP IV to perform multiple runs and to plot important variables is demonstrated. To perform multiple runs, with each run corresponding to an evaluation of the inventory policy with different values for R, SCL, and TBR, the following must be done at the end of a run, that is, at the beginning

```
                                          **GASP SUMMARY REPORT**

                              SIMULATION PROJECT NUMBER    1   BY   PRITSKER

                              DATE   6/ 30/ 1973        RUN NUMBER     1 OF     1

                              CURRENT TIME =   3.1200E+02

                             **STATISTICS FOR VARIABLES BASED ON OBSERVATION**
              MEAN          STD DEV        SD OF MEAN          CV            MINIMUM          MAXIMUM      OBS

SFTYSTOK   4.5455E-01     1.4050E+00     2.9955E-01      3.0910E+00      0.              6.0000E+00      22

                               **STATISTICS FOR TIME-PERSISTENT VARIABLES**
              MEAN          STD DEV        MINIMUM          MAXIMUM        TIME INTERVAL    CUR. VALUE

INVNTRY    2.8795E+01     2.0573E+01     0.               7.2000E+01      3.1200E+02      7.0000E+00

                             **GASP FILE STORAGE AREA DUMP AT TIME  3.1200E+02**


                             MAXIMUM NUMBER OF ENTRIES IN FILE STORAGE AREA =  3


                                        PRINTOUT OF FILE NUMBER   1
                                           TNOW =   3.1200E+02
                                           QQTIM=   3.1200E+02

                                  TIME PERIOD FOR STATISTICS 3.1200E+02
                                  AVERAGE NUMBER IN FILE         2.2115
                                  STANDARD DEVIATION              .4084
                                  MAXIMUM NUMBER IN FILE         3

                                              FILE CONTENTS
ENTRY   1    =     3.1206E+02     1.0000E+00     -0.
ENTRY   2    =     3.1500E+02     2.0000E+00      6.5000E+01
ENTRY   3    =     3.1600E+02     3.0000E+00     -0.
```

Figure 5-11 GASP IV summary report (Example 1).

of the next run (the method for accomplishing the reinitialization in this example is shown in parenthesis):

1. Set values for policy (read values in INTLC).
2. Reset statistical arrays and files (automatically done in DATIN when JJCLR = 1).
3. Reset time variables and random number seeds (automatically done in DATIN when JJBEG = 1).
4. Restart simulation with initial events (accomplished by DATIN calling INTLC).

In this example ten sequential runs are made. All values on data card types 1 through 12 are not changed, and no GASP IV data cards need be read for the subsequent runs. This is accomplished using data card type 0 with all LLSUP(·) equal to 2 and IICRD equal to 13. (Since TIMST is called in INTLC, the initial value of SSTPV(1,6) is reinitialized.)

Table 5-1 gives the final results for 10 simulation runs of the inventory system using five sets of values for the reorder point and stock control level and two values of the time between reviews. From this table, it is seen that a value of the average profit per week can be obtained through simulation, and that an economic evaluation of different parameter values for a given inventory policy can be made.

Another run was made for Example 1 to illustrate the plotting capability of GASP IV. In this run a plot of the inventory-on-hand, inventory position, and profit per week is obtained. This is accomplished through the writing of a new subroutine called RECRD, which records the

Table 5-1 Results of 10 Simulation Runs for Example 1

Decision Values			Average Values per Week					
Reorder Point	Stock Control Level	Time Between Reviews	Sales	Lost Sales	Orders	Inventory	Safety Stock	Profit
18	36	4	4.08	1.06	0.157	11.71	0.63	63.46
18	72	4	4.58	0.55	0.074	28.28	0.45	87.77
9	36	4	3.50	1.64	0.103	11.88	0.00	40.19
9	72	4	4.16	0.97	0.061	28.10	0.00	69.64
36	72	4	5.02	0.11	0.109	33.68	9.88	104.74
18	36	2	4.50	0.64	0.202	11.74	1.16	72.60
18	72	2	4.77	0.37	0.080	29.71	1.21	88.33
9	36	2	3.70	1.44	0.115	12.64	0.00	41.02
9	72	2	4.36	0.78	0.064	28.58	0.00	70.70
36	72	2	5.12	0.02	0.122	36.19	14.68	100.68

values of STOCK, POS, and profit per week for eventual plotting. The FORTRAN listing of subroutine RECRD is given in Fig. 5-12. The array PLOT(·) is used to transfer the values to be plotted to subroutine GPLOT. The statement CALL GPLOT(PLOT,TNOW,1) identifies PLOT(·) as the dependent variables, TNOW as the independent variable, and the code number for the plot as 1. Subroutine RECRD is called after each event. A convenient place to accomplish this is in subroutine EVNTS where the RETURN statement is replaced by the statement CALL RECRD (with statement number 4), which is then followed by a RETURN statement. The input data must then be changed to indicate that plots are to be made (NNPLT = 1) and data card type 6 must be prepared as shown below.

```
6A      1TIME                 0     3     0     2.
6B      1SSTOCK         1     1           0.          200.
6B      2PPOS           1     1           0.          200.
6B      3$PROFIT        1     1           0.          200.
```

Since only one plot is to be made, the tape number has been set equal to zero to indicate that the plot data is to be stored in NSET. The dimension of NSET, as discussed previously, was set to allow for storing the plot points. This is done in the dimension statement of the main program and on data card type 2 where NNSET is set equal to 4000. Since there are four values per plot point (three dependent and one independent value per point) this allows for the storage of approximately 1000 points. LLPLT is set at zero, which specifies that only a plot is desired and no table is to be printed. DTPLT is set at two, which indicates that points are to be plotted on two-week intervals. At each plot time, all values recorded

```
      SUBROUTINE RECRD                                                  REC     1
      DIMENSION PLOT(3)                                                 REC     2
      COMMON /GCOM1/ ATRIB(25),JEVNT,MFA,MFE(100),MLE(100),MSTOP,NCRDR,N GCOM1   1
     1NAPO,NNAPT,NNATR,NNFIL,NNQ(100),NNTRY,NPRNT,PPARM(50,4),TNOW,TTBEG GCOM1   2
     2,TTCLR,TTFIN,TTRIB(25),TTSET                                      GCOM1   3
      COMMON /GCOM6/ EENQ(100),IINN(100),KKRNK(100),MMAXQ(100),QQTIM(100 GCOM6   1
     1),SSOBV(25,5),SSTPV(25,6),VVNQ(100)                               GCOM6   2
      COMMON /UCOM1/XL,POS,STOCK,TLEAD,CPO,CCHG,ULOSE,SLOST,TREV,TORD,SA UCOM1   1
     1LE,SPOU,PCOU,R,SCL,TBR,CPR                                        UCOM1   2
      PLOT(1)=STOCK                                                     REC     3
      PLOT(2)=POS                                                       REC     4
      CALL TIMST(STOCK,TNOW,1)
      IF (TNOW) 102,102,101                                             REC     5
  101 PLOT(3)=((SPOU-PCOU)*SALE-(CPO*TORD+CPR*TREV+CCHG*PCOU*SSTPV(1,1)+ REC     6
     1ULOSE*SLOST))/TNOW                                                REC     7
      GO TO 103                                                         REC     8
  102 PLOT(3)=0.0                                                       REC     9
  103 CALL GPLOT (PLOT,TNOW,1)                                          REC    10
      RETURN                                                            REC    11
C                                                                       REC    12
      END                                                               REC    13
```

Figure 5-12 FORTRAN listing of subroutine RECRD (Example 1).

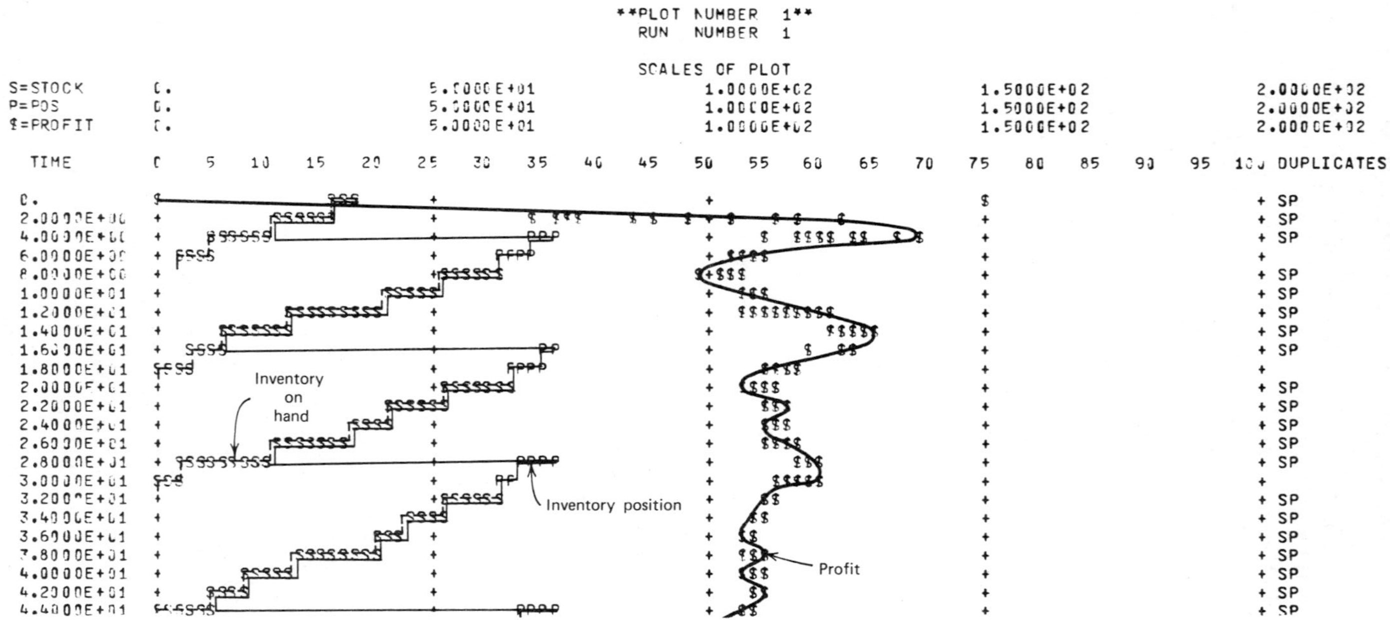
PLOT NUMBER 1
RUN NUMBER 1
SCALES OF PLOT
S=STOCK
P=POS
$=PROFIT
TIME
DUPLICATES
Inventory on hand
Inventory position
Profit

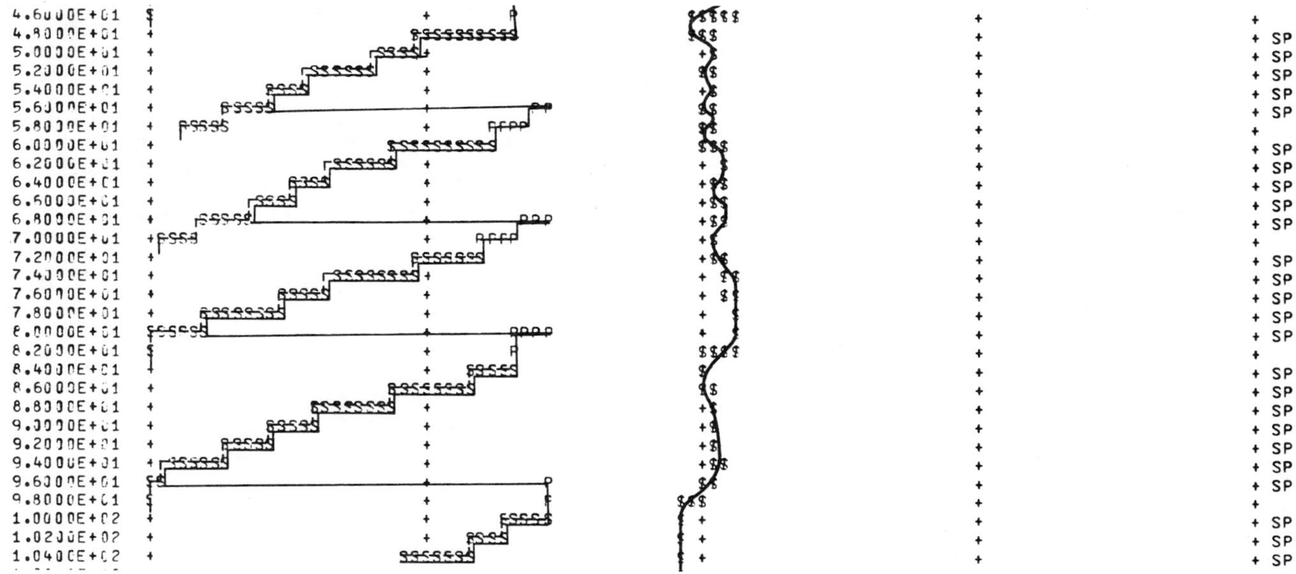

Figure 5-13 Plot output for inventory model (Example 1).

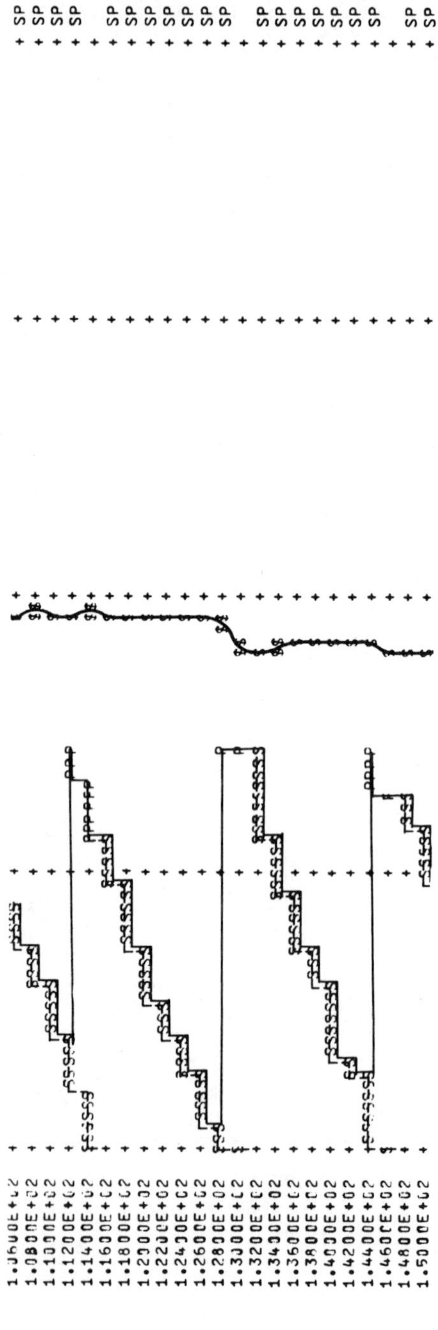
1.0600E+02
1.0800E+02
1.1000E+02
1.1200E+02
1.1400E+02
1.1600E+02
1.1800E+02
1.2000E+02
1.2200E+02
1.2400E+02
1.2600E+02
1.2800E+02
1.3000E+02
1.3200E+02
1.3400E+02
1.3600E+02
1.3800E+02
1.4000E+02
1.4200E+02
1.4400E+02
1.4600E+02
1.4800E+02
1.5000E+02

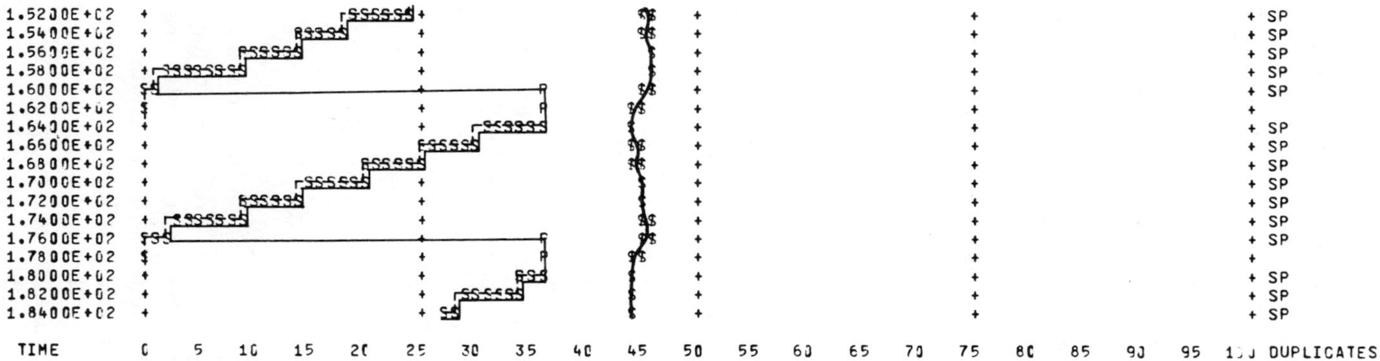


```
OUTPUT  CONSISTS  OF    987 POINT SETS (  2961 POINTS)
STORAGE ALLOCATED FOR   987 POINT SETS (  3948 WORDS )
STORAGE  NEEDED   FOR  1706 POINT SETS (  6824 WORDS )
```

Figure 5-13 *(continued)*

in the interval (T − 1.0, T + 1.0) are printed at T, where T = 0, DTPLT, 2 ⋆ DTPLT, ... A separate input card for each dependent variable is required specifying the plot symbol and variable name. The scale for the variable is then defined. In this example, the low and high values for the scale are to be specified as the PPLO and PPHI values. This is done by setting LLPLO and LLPHI equal to one for all variables. The plot resulting from the simulation run with R = 18, SCL = 72, and TBR = 4 is shown in Fig. 5-13. The dynamic behavior of the inventory-on-hand and the inventory position is easily seen from the plot. When the inventory-on-hand and the inventory position have the same value, only an "S" is plotted. The "SP" in the duplicates column indicates when this occurs. The average profit fluctuates significantly during the beginning of the simulation until it converges to a final steady state value. Plots can be extremely useful for observing the behavior of a model.

SIMULATION OF QUEUEING SITUATIONS

Queues consist of items waiting in line for service. Queueing situations arise frequently in business and private activities. Operations research, industrial engineering, and business administration literature is rich with examples of queueing situations involving production lines (26, 78, 97) job shops (5), traffic flow (120), fire departments (17), courts of justice, and so forth (99, 103). The basic elements of queueing situations are: (1) an arrival process, (2) a service mechanism, and (3) operating rules for the arrivals and the servers. When an arrival cannot be served immediately, it normally joins a queue and waits for service. Queueing situations involve uncertainty due to the stochastic nature of the times between arrivals and the time to serve an arrival.

In queueing situations, the servers and the items (people, jobs, cases, aircraft, etc.) seeking service are the primary entities of the system. The attributes that relate these entities to the status of the system are: number of items in the system, number of items in the queues of the servers, and status of the servers (busy or idle). The events that could change the status of the system involve the arrival of an item, the initiation of service on an item, and the completion of service on an item. When an item arrives, the number in the system is increased by one, which changes the status of the system. The item could possibly be put in a queue or if a server is available, service could be initiated. If there is a time delay before service can be initiated, the start-of-service event could be scheduled to occur after the delay time. A completion-of-service event changes the status of the system by possibly causing the item to leave the service system. In addition, if no item is waiting for the server, the server would be set to idle status. If an item is waiting, service could be initiated on the item waiting and another end-of-service event scheduled. The start-of-service event could be scheduled either from the arrival event or the end-of-service event. If there is no delay or set up involved in starting service for an item, the starting of service could be included in both the arrival and end-of-service events. This would reduce the number of the event routines required.

While programming the event routines of a queueing situation, the simulation analyst constantly asks the following two questions relating to the disposition of the item seeking service and the disposition of the server. What happens to the item on which service was just completed? And what happens to the server who just completed the service operation? In developing a simulation program that answers these questions, provisions must be made for maintaining entity status consistent with the event that is occurring by updating the attributes that define the entities when necessary. When an item arrives and is put in a queue, the attributes of that item are stored in a file representing the queue. When the item is removed from the queue and put in service, the attributes of the item must be maintained. Since the item is now in service, the GASP IV procedure is to associate the attributes of the item with the end-of-service event. Thus when the end-of-service event is taken from the event file, both the attributes of the item being served and the identification of the server who was performing the service become available through the user's coding of the attribute vector associated with the end-of-service event. By associating attributes with the item as it is flowing through the simulated system, no permanent storage need be allocated for items. The attributes of the item are stored in the filing array, QSET. Before the item arrives and after it departs, no information about the item is necessary and no information is stored in the computer about the item.

Two examples of queueing situations are presented. The first involves the simulation of a tanker fleet carrying crude oil. The second queueing example involves the simulation of a drive-in banking system.

EXAMPLE 2–DISCRETE SIMULATION OF A TANKER FLEET

Statement of the Problem

The system to be simulated consists of a fleet of 15 tankers. The tankers are loaded with crude oil in Valdez, Alaska and travel to Seattle, Washington where they are unloaded. Each tanker has a nominal carrying capacity of 150 tb (thousand barrels of crude). There are sufficient docks in Alaska so that all tankers can be loaded simultaneously. The average loading rate for a tanker is 50 tb/day. A tanker is loaded to its nominal carrying capacity ± 10 tb. The time to load a tanker is exponentially distributed with a mean equal to the amount loaded divided by the average loading rate. All the tankers unload at the same dock in Seattle with an average unloading rate of 200 tb/day. The amount left in the tanker after unloading is uniformly distributed between zero and 7.5 tb. The time to travel from Alaska to Washington when the tanker is loaded is normally distributed with a mean of five days and a standard deviation of 1.5 days. However, a tanker never takes less than 3.5 days or more than eight days in traveling from Alaska to Seattle. The time to travel from Seattle to Alaska unloaded is also normally distributed with a mean of four days, a standard deviation of one day with a minimum of three days and a maximum of seven days. The random variation in the travel time for the tankers is due to weather conditions and other uncertainties associated with ocean travel. It is desired to simulate the tanker fleet for 365 days to obtain estimates of the following quantities: dock utilization, tanker round trip time, tanker waiting time, and the number of tankers waiting for unloading.

The initial conditions for the simulation specify that the tankers are to arrive at their loading points at one-half day intervals starting with the first at time zero, the unloading dock is idle, and no tankers are waiting to be unloaded.

Simulation Objectives

A simulation model is to be developed to obtain the following statistics that describe the operation of the tanker fleet: dock utilization, tanker round trip time, tanker waiting time, and the number of tankers waiting for unloading.

Special Features

This example demonstrates the ease with which a simulation of a queueing problem can be obtained by using the event modeling philosophy. In the example the GASP IV subroutines for collecting statistical information are presented. Methods for processing events at the end of the simulation and for monitoring events during the simulation are demonstrated.

Procedure

To study this queueing situation, four events are modeled. These events listed by the code to be assigned to them are: (1) arrival of a tanker for loading, ARRL; (2) finish of tanker loading, FINL; (3) arrival of tanker for unloading, ARRUL; and (4) finish of tanker unloading, FINUL. To obtain a complete simulation of the tanker fleet the user must write a main program, subroutine EVNTS, the four event routines listed above, and subroutine OTPUT. In addition, it was decided to program the initial conditions and the initial events for the simulation in subroutine INTLC. Subroutine OTPUT wll be used to complete unloading for any tanker that has arrived at the unloading dock prior to the end-of-simulation time, TTFIN. Each of the subprograms written by the user are now described.

In the main program, as shown in Fig. 5-14, the card reader code (NCRDR) and the printer code (NPRNT) are established. Since the non-GASP variables will be initialized in subroutine INTLC, the main program's only other function is to call subroutine GASP to control the simulation.

Subroutine GASP first calls subroutine DATIN, which processes the data cards that initialize the GASP IV variables. Subroutine DATIN then calls subroutine INTLC to initialize non-GASP variables and initial entries in files not initialized through data input.

The FORTRAN listing for subroutine INTLC is given in Fig. 5-15. For this example, the non-GASP variables are:

Variable	Definition	Initial Value
ALIT	Amount left in tanker	Computed
ALR	Average loading rate	50 tb/day
AMTL	Amount loaded	Computed
AULR	Average unloading rate	200 tb/day
BUS	Unloading dock status: $0 \rightarrow$ idle; $1 \rightarrow$ busy	0
NTANK	Number of tankers	15
TCAP	Nominal carrying capacity of tanker	150 tb
TIFRT	Time for tanker round trip	Computed
WT	Waiting time for tanker at unloading dock	Computed
XL	Average loading time	Computed
XTBL	Number of tankers in loading docks	0

In subroutine INTLC the non-GASP variables are initialized through arithmetic statements. It was also decided to put the initial events into

```
      PROGRAM MAIN (INPUT,OUTPUT,TAPE5=INPUT,TAPE6=OUTPUT)              MX2       1
      DIMENSION NSET(140)                                                DIM       1
      COMMON QSET(140)                                                   COM       1
      COMMON /GCOM1/ ATRIB(25),JEVNT,MFA,MFE(100),MLE(100),MSTOP,NCRDR,NGCOM1     1
     1NAPO,NNAPT,NNATR,NNFIL,NNQ(100),NNTRY,NPRNT,PPARM(50,4),TNOW,TTBEGGCOM1     2
     2,TTCLR,TTFIN,TTRIB(25),TTSET                                       GCOM1     3
      EQUIVALENCE (NSET(1),QSET(1))                                      EQUIV     1
C                                                                        MX2       2
C*****SET CARD READER NUMBER AND PRINTER NUMBER.                         MX2       3
C                                                                        MX2       4
      NCRDR=5                                                            MX2       5
      NPRNT=6                                                            MX2       6
      CALL GASP                                                          MX2       7
      CALL EXIT                                                          MX2       8
C                                                                        MX2       9
      END                                                                MX2      10
```

Figure 5-14 FORTRAN listing of main program (Example 2).

the file in INTLC. For this simulation, two files are necessary; file 1 is the event file and file 2 is the queue of items waiting for unloading. Attributes 1 and 2 are the time of the event and the event code, which are the required definitions for the event file. Attributes 3 through 5 will be the same for both files and their definitions are:

Attribute 3—Start time of loading of tanker.
Attribute 4—Arrival time of tanker to unloading dock.
Attribute 5—Amount of crude in tanker.

```
      SUBROUTINE INTLC                                                   IC2       1
      COMMON /GCOM1/ ATRIB(25),JEVNT,MFA,MFE(100),MLE(100),MSTOP,NCRDR,NGCOM1     1
     1NAPO,NNAPT,NNATR,NNFIL,NNQ(100),NNTRY,NPRNT,PPARM(50,4),TNOW,TTBEGGCOM1     2
     2,TTCLR,TTFIN,TTRIB(25),TTSET                                       GCOM1     3
      COMMON /UCOM1/BUS,ALR,AULR,TCAP,XTBL                               UCOM1     1
C                                                                        IC2       2
C*****INITIALIZE NON-GASP VARIABLES.                                     IC2       3
C                                                                        IC2       4
      BUS=0.0                                                            IC2       5
      TCAP=150.                                                          IC2       6
      ALR=50.                                                            IC2       7
      AULR=200.                                                          IC2       8
      XTBL=0.0                                                           IC2       9
      NTANK=15                                                           IC2      10
      ATRIB(1)=0.                                                        IC2      11
      ATRIB(2)=1.0                                                       IC2      12
      ATRIB(3)=-1.0                                                      IC2      13
      ATRIB(4)=0.0                                                       IC2      14
      ATRIB(5)=0.0                                                       IC2      15
C                                                                        IC2      16
C*****ESTABLISH ARRIVAL AT LOADING DOCK FOR EACH TANKER.                 IC2      17
C                                                                        IC2      18
      DO 101 I=1,NTANK                                                   IC2      19
      CALL FILEM (1)                                                     IC2      20
  101 ATRIB(1)=ATRIB(1)+0.5                                              IC2      21
      WRITE (NPRNT,102) NTANK,ALR,AULR,TCAP                              IC2      22
      RETURN                                                             IC2      23
C                                                                        IC2      24
  102 FORMAT (1H1,19X,19HNUMBER OF TANKERS =,I5,/,20X,64HTRAVEL TIME LOAIC2      25
     1DED IS NORMALLY DISTRIBUTED USING PARAMETER SET 1,/,20X,66HTRAVEL IC2      26
     2TIME UNLOADED IS NORMALLY DISTRIBUTED USING PARAMETER SET 2,/,20X,IC2      27
     353HUNLOADING TIME IS EXPONENTIALLY DISTRIBUTED WITH MEAN,F6.1,6HTBIC2      28
     4/DAY,/,20X,16HUNLOADING RATE =,F6.1,6HTB/DAY,/,20X,17HTANKER CAPACIC2      29
     5ITY =,F6.1,2HTB)                                                   IC2      30
C                                                                        IC2      31
      END                                                                IC2      32
```

Figure 5-15 FORTRAN listing of subroutine INTLC (Example 2).

Attribute 3 is used to compute the round trip time for a tanker and attribute 4 is used to compute the waiting time for a tanker at the unloading dock. Attribute 5 is used to keep track of the amount of crude that is in the tanker since there is some variation in the nominal tanker capacity.

In subroutine INTLC initial arrival events are put into file 1, causing the arrival of the tankers to the loading docks at the appropriate time. ATRIB(1) is set at zero so that the first tanker arrives at its loading dock at time zero. ATRIB(2) is set equal to one to indicate that the event in the event file is the arrival event. ATRIB(3) is set equal to −1 to indicate that no round trip for this tanker is being completed and that this is just an initial event for the simulation. ATRIB(4) is arbitrarily set at zero, and ATRIB(5) is set at zero to indicate that the tanker is empty initially. Following the setting of these attributes, subroutine FILEM is called with an argument of one to insert the five attributes in the event file. Next, ATRIB(1) is increased by 0.5 so that the second tanker will arrive at its loading dock one-half day later. Through the DO LOOP, each tanker is given an arrival time and the arrival event is inserted into file 1. The last function performed by INTLC is the printing of the conditions for the simulation run.

After a return is made from subroutine INTLC, subroutine DATIN completes initialization and control is returned to subroutine GASP. In subroutine GASP, the first event is removed from the event file. For this simulation, the event is the arrival of a tanker to the loading dock at time zero. The current time, TNOW, is set equal to the time of the event. GASP IV then calls subroutine EVNTS with the event code argument set at the value that was stored in ATRIB(2) of the event just removed, which in this case is one. Subroutine EVNTS, through the use of a GO TO statement, deciphers the event code. The FORTRAN listing for subroutine EVNTS is shown in Fig. 5-16, which illustrates that event codes 1, 2, 3, and 4 correspond to ARRL, FINL, ARRUL, and FINUL.

The flow chart and FORTRAN listing for the arrival of tanker at the loading dock event are given in Figs. 5-17 and 5-18. The flow chart is

```
      SUBROUTINE EVNTS (IX)
      GO TO (101,102,103,104), IX
  101 CALL ARRL
      GO TO 105
  102 CALL FINL
      GO TO 105
  103 CALL ARRUL
      GO TO 105
  104 CALL FINUL
  105 RETURN
C
      END
```

Figure 5-16 FORTRAN listing of subroutine EVNTS (Example 2).

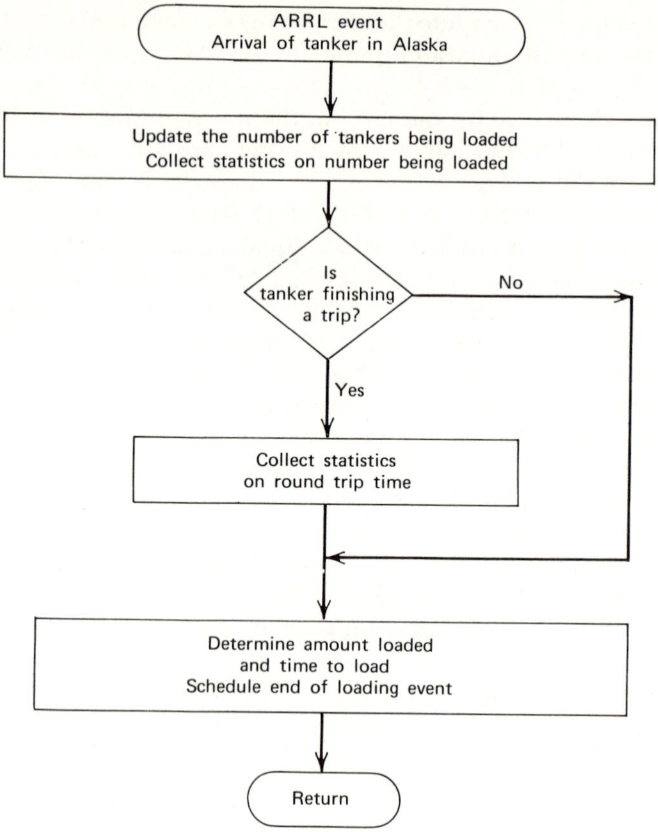

Figure 5-17 Flow chart of arrival event, ARRL (Example 2).

described first. The number of tankers in the loading docks is increased by one and statistics are computed on the number being loaded. A round trip for a tanker is considered to be the time it takes from the start of loading to the time the tanker arrives in Alaska for reloading. The tanker is finishing a trip if ATRIB(3), the start of loading time, has a positive value. Recall that in subroutine INTLC ATRIB(3) was given a negative value initially.

If the tanker is finishing a trip, statistics are collected on the round trip time. Next, the amount of crude to be loaded and the time required to load the crude on the tanker are determined. The time to load crude on the tanker is assumed to be exponentially distributed with a mean time equal to the amount to be loaded divided by the average loading rate. The amount to be loaded is the difference between the nominal carrying capacity of the tanker and the amount of crude in the tanker, plus a deviate drawn from the uniform distribution in the interval -10 to $+10$. An end-of-loading event FINL can then be scheduled to occur at the current time plus the time required for loading.

The FORTRAN listing presented in Fig. 5-18 illustrates how the GASP IV variables and GASP IV subprograms are used to implement the functions prescribed by the flow chart of the ARRL event. First, the number of tankers being loaded XTBL is increased by one and TIMST is called to maintain statistics on XTBL. A test is then made on ATRIB(3) to determine if this is the first arrival of the tanker for loading or whether the tanker is completing a round trip. The value for ATRIB(3) is associated with the last call to RMOVE. In this case, the last call to RMOVE occurred in subroutine GASP where the first event in the event file was removed. Therefore, ATRIB(3) is associated with the arriving tanker. If ATRIB(3) is negative, statistics will not be collected and a transfer is made to statement 101. Otherwise, the round trip time for the tanker is equal to the current time TNOW minus ATRIB(3). Subroutines COLCT and HISTO are then called to record the specific sample of the

```
      SUBROUTINE ARRL
      COMMON /GCOM1/ ATRIB(25),JEVNT,MFA,MFE(100),MLE(100),MSTOP,NCRDR,NPRNT
     1NAPO,NNAPT,NNATR,NNFIL,NNQ(100),NNTRY,NPRNT,PPARM(50,4),TNOW,TTBEG
     2,TTCLR,TTFIN,TTRIB(25),TTSET
      COMMON /UCOM1/BUS,ALR,AULR,TCAP,XTBL
      XTBL=XTBL+1.
      CALL TIMST (XTBL,TNOW,2)
C
C*****TEST TO SEE IF TANKER HAS MADE A ROUND TRIP.
C
      IF (ATRIB(3).LT.0.0) GO TO 101
C
C*****COMPUTE TIME FOR ROUND TRIP AND COLLECT STATISTICS.
C
      TIFRT=TNOW-ATRIB(3)
      CALL COLCT (TIFRT,2)
      CALL HISTO (TIFRT,2)
C
C*****COMPUTE AMOUNT TO BE LOADED AND AVERAGE TIME TO LOAD.
C
  101 AMTL=TCAP-ATRIB(5)+UNFRM(-10.0,10.0,1)
      XL=AMTL/ALR
      ATRIB(5)=AMTL+ATRIB(5)
C
C*****COMPUTE TIME OF FINISHING LOADING BASED ON EXPONENTIAL LOADING
C*****TIME.
C
      ATRIB(1)=TNOW-XL*ALOG(DRAND(2))
      ATRIB(2)=2.0
      ATRIB(3)=TNOW
C
C*****SCHEDULE THE COMPLETION OF LOADING EVENT.
C
      CALL FILEM (1)
      RETURN
C
      END
```

Figure 5-18 FORTRAN listing of subroutine ARRL (Example 2).

time for the round trip. The code assigned to these values is 2, indicating that the values in the second row of SSOBV and the second histogram are to be updated by the subroutine calls.

At statement 101, the amount to be loaded is determined. Here ATRIB(5) is associated with the tanker to be loaded and represents the current amount of crude in the tanker. A sample from the uniform distribution is obtained by the use of the function UNFRM, where the low and high values are given as arguments to the function and the third argument specifies that random number stream 1 is to be used. The average time to load the tanker is then determined as the amount to be loaded (AMTL) divided by the average loading rate (ALR). The amount in the tanker at the end of loading is stored as ATRIB(5) and is the amount to be loaded plus the amount that was in the tanker when it returned for loading. The time to load is then obtained as a sample from an exponential distribution, using the knowledge that the negative of the average loading time times the logarithm of a random number results in a deviate from the exponential distribution. ATRIB(1) is set equal to the current time plus the exponential deviate, and represents the time at which loading will be finished. ATRIB(2) is then set equal to 2, indicating that the event being filed in the event file is a "finish loading" event (FINL). ATRIB(3) is then set equal to TNOW to associate the time at which loading was initiated with the tanker. This value is used in computing the round trip time for the tanker. The event is filed in the event file by the statement CALL FILEM(1).

It is important to observe that in the coding of ARRL no specific mention of the tanker name or code number is used. The processing for each tanker as it arrives is written in a general form. Each tanker is only identified by the attribute values associated with it, that is, the start-of-loading time and the amount of crude currently in it. No identification is required for each tanker because statistics are being collected on tankers as a group instead of on individual tankers.

The next event to be considered is the finishing-of-loading event. The flow chart for this event is shown in Fig. 5-19. At the completion of loading, the tanker is ready to start its trip to Seattle. XTBL is reduced by one, and statistics are collected on the number of tankers being loaded XTBL using TIMST. The only function performed in subroutine FINL is the scheduling of the arrival of the tanker to the unloading dock. This involves setting the time of arrival and the event code for an arrival to the unloading dock event. The FORTRAN listing for subroutine FINL is shown in Fig. 5-20. The time of arrival at the unloading dock is set equal to the current time plus the deviate obtained from a normal distribution, which represents the travel time from Alaska to Washington.

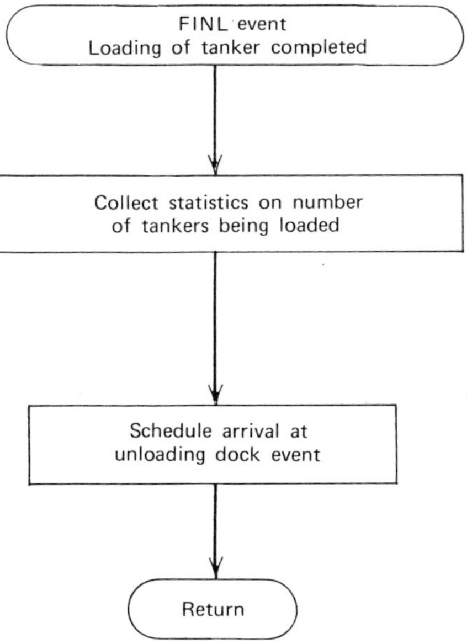

Figure 5-19 Flow chart of finish loading event, FINL (Example 2).

The parameters for the normal distribution are stored in the first parameter set, which is specified by the input data cards. Random number stream 4 is used when obtaining samples from this normal distribution.

The next event to be considered is ARRUL, which is the arrival of the tanker at the unloading dock. The flow chart of ARRUL is given in Fig. 5-21. First, the arrival time is recorded and stored as ATRIB(4). A test is then made to determine if the unloading dock is empty. If it is

```
      SUBROUTINE FINL                                                   FNL    1
      COMMON /GCOM1/ ATRIB(25),JEVNT,MFA,MFE(100),MLE(100),MSTOP,NCRDR,NGCOM1  1
     1NAPO,NNAPT,NNATR,NNFIL,NNQ(100),NNTRY,NPRNT,PPARM(50,4),TNOW,TTBEGGCOM1  2
     2,TTCLR,TTFIN,TTRIB(25),TTSET                                      GCOM1  3
      COMMON /UCOM1/BUS,ALR,AULR,TCAP,XTBL                              UCOM1  1
      XTBL=XTBL-1.                                                      FNL    2
      CALL TIMST (XTBL,TNOW,2)                                          FNL    3
C                                                                       FNL    4
C*****COMPUTE TIME FOR ARRIVAL AT UNLOADING DOCK USING A NORMALLY       FNL    5
C*****DISTRIBUTED TRAVEL TIME.                                          FNL    6
C                                                                       FNL    7
      ATRIB(1)=TNOW+RNORM(1,4)                                          FNL    8
      ATRIB(2)=3.0                                                      FNL    9
C                                                                       FNL   10
C*****SCHEDULE ARRIVAL AT UNLOADING DOCK.                               FNL   11
C                                                                       FNL   12
      CALL FILEM (1)                                                    FNL   13
      RETURN                                                            FNL   14
C                                                                       FNL   15
      END                                                               FNL   16
```

Figure 5-20 FORTRAN listing of subroutine FINL (Example 2).

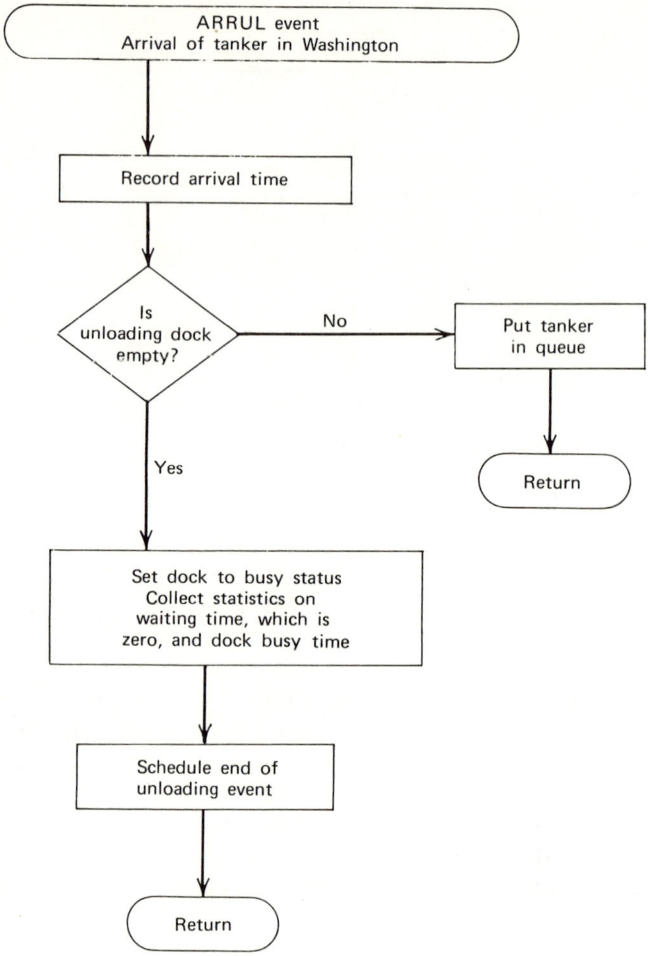

Figure 5-21 Flow chart of arrival at unloading dock, ARRUL (Example 2).

not, the arriving tanker is put in the queue of tankers waiting for the dock to become available. File 2 is used to store the tankers waiting in the queue. The priority system for file 2 is established through data input cards and, for this example, a FIFO rule was prescribed by setting IINN(2) = 3.

If the unloading dock is empty, the dock is then set to busy status. Statistics are collected on the waiting time for the new arrival, which is zero, and on the busy time of the unloading dock, which is a time persistent variable. A completion of unloading event is scheduled.

The FORTRAN listing for the ARRUL is given in Fig. 5-22. After

```
      SUBROUTINE ARRUL
      COMMON /GCOM1/ ATRIB(25),JEVNT,MFA,MFE(100),MLE(100),MSTOP,NCRDR,N
     1NAPO,NNAPT,NNATR,NNFIL,NNQ(100),NNTRY,NPRNT,PPARM(50,4),TNOW,TTBEG
     2,TTCLR,TTFIN,TTRIB(25),TTSET
      COMMON /UCOM1/BUS,ALR,AULR,TCAP,XTBL
C
C*****RECORD ARRIVAL TIME.
C
      ATRIB(4)=TNOW
C
C*****TEST TO SEE IF UNLOADING DOCK IS BUSY.
C
      IF (BUS.GT.0.0) GO TO 101
C
C*****COLLECT STATISTICS ON WAITING TIME.
C
      CALL COLCT (0.0,1)
      CALL HISTO (0.0,1)
C
C*****COLLECT STATISTICS ON BUSY STEPS.
C
      BUS=1.0
      CALL TIMST (BUS,TNOW,1)
      ALIT=UNFRM(0.0,7.5,3)
      ATRIB(1)=TNOW+(ATRIB(5)-ALIT)/AULR
      ATRIB(5)=ALIT
      ATRIB(2)=4.0
C
C*****SCHEDULE END OF UNLOADING EVENT.
C
      CALL FILEM (1)
      RETURN
C
C*****PUT TANKER IN QUEUE.
C
  101 CALL FILEM (2)
      RETURN
C
      END
```

Figure 5-22 FORTRAN listing of subroutine ARRUL (Example 2).

ATRIB(4) is set equal to the arrival time of the tanker, the busy status of the unloading dock is checked. If it is busy (BUS > 0), a transfer to statement 101 is made where the tanker is filed in the queue. If the unloading dock is empty, subroutines COLCT and HISTO are called with waiting times of zero. The second argument in the CALL statement specifies that the values are for the variable number 1, which the user has defined as the waiting time. Next, the status of the unloading dock is changed to busy by setting BUS = 1. A call is made to subroutine TIMST to collect statistics on the busy time of the unloading dock. This is a time persistent variable and is identified as time persistent variable number 1 by the third argument in the CALL statement. Note that the value of BUS is set before the call to subroutine TIMST. This establishes the value of BUS that should be used during the next time interval. When TIMST is called, integration is accomplished using the previous value, that is, the value stored in SSTPV(1,6). The end-of-unloading event is then scheduled. The amount left in the tanker is set equal to a sample from a uniform distribution in the interval [0,7.5]. The time to unload the tanker is equal to the amount of crude in the tanker, minus the amount left in the tanker, divided by the average unloading rate. This quantity is added to the current time to get the time for the completion of the unloading event. The amount left in the tanker is then stored as ATRIB(5). The event code for a completion-of-unloading event is established as ATRIB(2) and the event is put on the event calendar by the statement CALL FILEM(1).

The last event to consider is the completion-of-unloading event, FINUL. The flow chart for this event is shown in Fig. 5-23. First, the disposition of the tanker that completed unloading is determined. This is done by scheduling an arrival to the loading dock for the tanker. Next, the disposition of the server, that is, the unloading dock, is considered. If a tanker is waiting to be unloaded, it is removed from the queue of tankers and another unloading event is scheduled. If no tanker

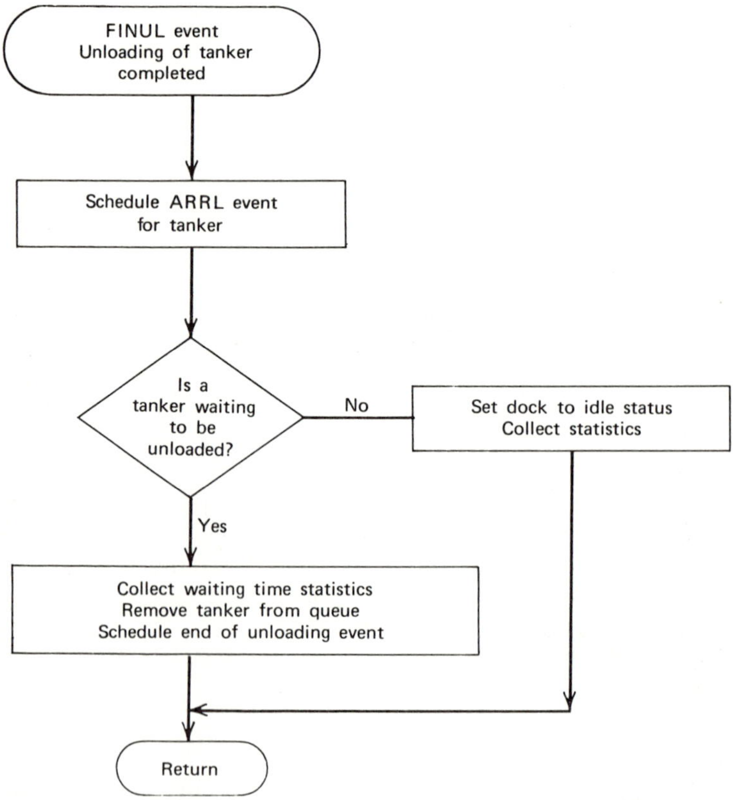

Figure 5-23 Flow chart of completion-of-unloading event, FINUL (Example 2).

is waiting to be unloaded, the unloading dock is set to idle status. The FORTRAN code to implement the FINUL event is shown in Fig. 5-24.

The scheduling of the arrival of the tanker to the loading dock is accomplished by setting the value of ATRIB(1) equal to the current time plus the transportation time. The transportation time is a sample from a normal distribution using the parameters stored in parameter set 2. The code for an ARRL event is 1, and this is the value given to ATRIB(2). The event is put on the event calendar by the statement CALL FILEM(1).

To determine if tankers are waiting for the unloading dock, the number of entries in file 2, NNQ(2), is tested. If NNQ(2) = 0, no tankers are waiting and a transfer to statement 20 is made where the unloading dock is set to idle status and statistics are collected on the busy status. If NNQ(2) is not zero, the first entry in file 2 is removed. This establishes the attributes for the tanker to be unloaded. The waiting time for the tanker is set equal to the current time minus the time the tanker entered the queue. Statistics are then collected on the waiting time, and the

```
      SUBROUTINE FINUL
      COMMON /GCOM1/ ATRIB(25),JEVNT,MFA,MFE(100),MLE(100),MSTOP,NCRDR,NGCOM1
     1NAPO,NNAPT,NNATR,NNFIL,NNQ(100),NNTRY,NPRNT,PPARM(50,4),TNOW,TTBEGGCOM1
     2,TTCLR,TTFIN,TTRIB(25),TTSET
      COMMON /UCOM1/BUS,ALR,AULR,TCAP,XTBL
      ATRIB(1)=TNOW+RNORM(2,4)
      ATRIB(2)=1.0
C
C*****SCHEDULE ARRL EVENT FOR TANKER.
C
      CALL FILEM (1)
C
C*****IS THERE A TANKER IN FILE 2.
C
      IF (NNQ(2).EQ.0) GO TO 101
C
C*****REMOVE FIRST TANKER FROM QUEUE AND COLLECT STATISTICS ON
C*****WAITING TIME.
C
      CALL RMOVE (MFE(2),2)
      WT= TNOW-ATRIB(4)
      CALL COLCT (WT,1)
      CALL HISTO (WT,1)
      ALIT=UNFRM(0.0,7.5,3)
      ATRIB(1)=TNOW+(ATRIB(5)-ALIT)/AULR
      ATRIB(5)=ALIT
      ATRIB(2)=4.0
C
C*****SCHEDULE END OF UNLOADING EVENT.
C
      CALL FILEM (1)
      RETURN
C
C*****COLLECT STATISTICS ON DOCK STATUS AND SET DOCK STATUS TO IDLE.
C
  101 BUS=0.0
      CALL TIMST (BUS,TNOW,1)
      RETURN
C
      END
```

Figure 5-24 FORTRAN listing of subroutine FINUL (Example 2).

attribute values associated with the FINUL event are established in a manner identical to that performed in subroutine ARRUL. The FINUL event is placed on the event calendar by the statement CALL FILEM(1). In FINUL the statements used in ARRUL for establishing another unloading event were repeated since only a few statements were involved. In general, a separate subroutine would be used to perform this function. Then calls to this subroutine from ARRUL and FINUL would be made to schedule the completion of the service event.

In subroutine FINUL, an arrival event to the loading dock is established and another completion-of-unloading event could be instituted. Both of these events were described previously, hence all events for the queueing model have been discussed.

Simulation of the queueing system proceeds over a period of time by advancing from event to event. In each event subroutine, statistics desired for analysis are updated. Statistics on the number in the queue are automatically collected by GASP IV as file statistics and, therefore, no reference is made to them in the event subroutines. When TNOW exceeds TTFIN, subroutine GASP calls subroutine OTPUT. The FORTRAN listing for subroutine OTPUT is shown in Fig. 5-25. In this simulation OTPUT is used to process those tankers that arrived to the unloading dock prior to the specified completion time for the simulation. The processing of events in the event file is accomplished by removing the first event, if there is one, and testing to see if the event is a FINUL event. If it is not, the event is discarded and another event is removed. If the event is a FINUL event, current time is updated to the

```
      SUBROUTINE OTPUT
      COMMON /GCOM1/ ATRIB(25),JEVNT,MFA,MFE(100),MLE(100),MSTOP,NCRDR,NG
     1NAPO,NNAPT,NNATR,NNFIL,NNQ(100),NNTRY,NPRNT,PPARM(50,4),TNOW,TTBEG
     2,TTCLR,TTFIN,TTRIB(25),TTSET
      COMMON /UCOM1/BUS,ALR,AULR,TCAP,XTBL
C
C*****TEST TO SEE IF THERE IS AN EVENT IN THE EVENT FILE.
C
  101 IF (NNQ(1).EQ.0) RETURN
C
C*****REMOVE FIRST EVENT FROM EVENT FILE.
C
      CALL RMOVE (MFE(1),1)
C
C*****TEST TO SEE IF THE EVENT IS A FINISHED UNLOADING EVENT.
C
      IF (ATRIB(2).NE.4.0) GO TO 101
C
C*****UPDATE TNOW TO TIME OF FINISHED UNLOADING EVENT.
C
      TNOW=ATRIB(1)
      CALL FINUL
      GO TO 101
C
      END
```

Figure 5-25 FORTRAN listing of subroutine OTPUT (Example 2).

time of the event, that is, TNOW = ATRIB(1). A call is then made to subroutine FINUL, which processes the tanker that completed unloading. In FINUL, if a tanker was waiting in the queue, another FINUL event would be scheduled. To process all such events, a return is made to statement 101, which continues to process events until there are no more entries in the event file. If it was desired to process only the tanker that was being unloaded at the end-of-simulation time, the statement after CALL FINUL would be a return statement.

Simulation Reports

Figures 5-26 and 5-27 present a listing of the input data and the input data echo check provided by subroutine DATIN. A careful comparison of Figs. 5-26 and 5-27 illustrates how the GASP IV input values are established. Figure 5-28 presents the printout of the files that is obtained at the end of subroutine DATIN. In file 1, note that monitor events (entries 16 and 17) with event code 0 were inserted into the file to print out the events occurring from day 150 to day 200. A partial printout of the event tracing, which is obtained from subroutine MONTR, is shown in Fig. 5-29.

Figure 5-30 is the GASP IV summary report for Example 2. After heading information is printed, along with the parameter set values, the statistics that were collected using subroutine COLCT are presented. It is seen that the waiting time (WAIT TIM) for a tanker at the unloading dock was, on the average, 0.74 days with a standard deviation of 0.74 days. These values were based on 399 observations and the minimum and maximum values observed for the waiting time were 0 and 3.76 days, respectively. The standard deviation of the mean and the coefficient of variation are given under columns SD OF MEAN and CV, respectively. The average round trip time (TRIP TIM) was 13.5 days, based on 393 observations. The next set of statistics on the summary report is for the data collected in subroutine TIMST. Here it is seen that the utilization of the unloading dock was 0.79 and the number of tankers being loaded was 3.19 over the total simulation time of 370 days.

Statistics regarding the use of files are shown at the bottom of Fig. 5-30. On the average, there were slightly over 15 events in file 1. A maximum of 17 events were stored in the event file corresponding to an event associated with each tanker and the two monitor events. The statistics for file 2 show that the average number of tankers waiting for unloading was approximately 0.80 and a maximum of 5 were in the queue at the same time.

```
PRITSKER             2     6    30 1973    1                     |  1
     2     2    ?    2     0       4   20  5      2  140         |  2
3          1WAIT TIM                                             |
3          2TRIP TIM                                             |  3
4          1UNL  UTIL         0.0                                |
4          2LDR  UTIL         0.0                                |  4
5          1WAIT TIM               100.0       0.5               |
5          2TRIP TIM               105.0       2.0               |  5
     1     3                                                     |
     1     3                                                     |  7
10         15.0        3.5          8.0        1.5               |  8
10         24.0        3.0          7.0        1.0               | 10
     1     1     1    00.0        365.0          1653974318319249452l2 | 11
12         1     150.          0.                                |
12         1     200.          0.                                | 12
12         0                                                     |
```

Figure 5-26 Listing of data input (Example 2).

```
                         SIMULATION PROJECT NUMBER    2   BY   PRITSKER

                         DATE   6/ 30/ 1973        RUN NUMBER     1 OF     1
                         LLSUP=0000000000000000    GASP IV VERSION 23JUN73

NNCLT=      2    NNSTA=      2    NNHIS=      2    NNPRM=      2    NNPLT=      0    NNSTR=      4    NNTRY=     20
NNATR=      5    NNFIL=      2    NNSET=    140    NNEQD=     -0    NNEQS=     -0    NFLAG=     -0

COLCT NO.   1    LLABC=WAIT TIM
COLCT NO.   2    LLABC=TRIP TIM

TIMST NO.   1    LLABT=UNL UTIL   I.C. =     0.
TIMST NO.   2    LLABT=LDR UTIL   I.C. =     0.

HISTO NO.   1    LLABH=WAIT TIM                     NNCEL=     10    HHLOW=     0.            HHWID=      5.0000E-01
HISTO NO.   2    LLABH=TRIP TIM                     NNCEL=     10    HHLOW=     5.0000E+00    HHWID=      2.0000E+00

KKRNK= (    1)       3

IINN = (    1)       3

PARAMETER SET        1 =      5.0000E+00     3.5000E+00     8.0000E+00     1.5000E+00
PARAMETER SET        2 =      4.0000E+00     3.0000E+00     7.0000E+00     1.0000E+00

MSTOP=      1    JJCLR=      1    JJBEG=      1    IICRD=      0    TTBEG=     0.            TTFIN=      3.6500E+02
JJFIL=      1
IISED= 65397           43183          19249          45212
```

Figure 5-27 GASP IV input echo check (Example 2).

```
                      **GASP FILE STORAGE AREA DUMP AT TIME  0.          **

                      MAXIMUM NUMBER OF ENTRIES IN FILE STORAGE AREA = 17

                               PRINTOUT OF FILE NUMBER    1
                                 TNOW =   0.
                                 QQTIM=   0.

                                       FILE CONTENTS
ENTRY  1   =   0.              1.0000E+00    -1.0000E+00      0.        0.
ENTRY  2   =   5.0000E-01      1.0000E+00    -1.0000E+00      0.        0.
ENTRY  3   =   1.0000E+00      1.0000E+00    -1.0000E+00      0.        0.
ENTRY  4   =   1.5000E+00      1.0000E+00    -1.0000E+00      0.        0.
ENTRY  5   =   2.0000E+00      1.0000E+00    -1.0000E+00      0.        0.
ENTRY  6   =   2.5000E+00      1.0000E+00    -1.0000E+00      0.        0.
ENTRY  7   =   3.0000E+00      1.0000E+00    -1.0000E+00      0.        0.
ENTRY  8   =   3.5000E+00      1.0000E+00    -1.0000E+00      0.        0.
ENTRY  9   =   4.0000E+00      1.0000E+00    -1.0000E+00      0.        0.
ENTRY 10   =   4.5000E+00      1.0000E+00    -1.0000E+00      0.        0.
ENTRY 11   =   5.0000E+00      1.0000E+00    -1.0000E+00      0.        0.
ENTRY 12   =   5.5000E+00      1.0000E+00    -1.0000E+00      0.        0.
ENTRY 13   =   6.0000E+00      1.0000E+00    -1.0000E+00      0.        0.
ENTRY 14   =   6.5000E+00      1.0000E+00    -1.0000E+00      0.        0.
ENTRY 15   =   7.0000E+00      1.0000E+00    -1.0000E+00      0.        0.
ENTRY 16   =   1.5000E+02      0.            -0.             -0.       -0.
ENTRY 17   =   2.0000E+02      0.            -0.             -0.       -0.

                               PRINTOUT OF FILE NUMBER    2
                                 TNOW =   0.
                                 QQTIM=   0.

                                 THE FILE IS EMPTY
```

Figure 5-28 File printout at time 0 (Example 2).

Histograms of the waiting time and the round trip time are shown in Fig. 5-31. It is seen that 92.7% or 361 tankers of the 399 observed had a waiting time less than or equal to two days. Each asterisk on the histogram plot represents a relative frequency of 2% rounded to the nearest multiple of 0.02. Thus the relative frequency of 0.036 is plotted with two asterisks. Capital C's are used to indicate the cumulative fre-

```
CURRENT EVENT.....TNOW= 1.5282E+02
   1.5282E+02      1.0000E+00     1.3602E+02     1.4873E+02     5.8750E+00
NEXT EVENT.......TTNEX= 1.5304E+02
   1.5304E+02      3.0000E+00     1.4563E+02     1.3873E+02     1.4154E+02

CURRENT EVENT.....TNOW= 1.5304E+02
   1.5304E+02      3.0000E+00     1.4563E+02     1.3873E+02     1.4154E+02
NEXT EVENT.......TTNEX= 1.5333E+02
   1.5333E+02      2.0000E+00     1.4912E+02     1.4374E+02     1.4397E+02

CURRENT EVENT.....TNOW= 1.5333E+02
   1.5333E+02      2.0000E+00     1.4912E+02     1.4374E+02     1.4397E+02
NEXT EVENT.......TTNEX= 1.5347E+02
   1.5347E+02      4.0000E+00     1.4405E+02     1.5048E+02     7.0887E+00

CURRENT EVENT.....TNOW= 1.5347E+02
   1.5347E+02      4.0000E+00     1.4405E+02     1.5048E+02     7.0887E+00
NEXT EVENT.......TTNEX= 1.5368E+02
   1.5368E+02      3.0000E+00     1.4698E+02     1.3910E+02     1.5677E+02
```

Figure 5-29 Output from subroutine MONTR showing event tracing (Example 2).

quency on the histogram plot. The histograms illustrate the exponential character of the waiting times and the normal character of the round trip times.

EXAMPLE 3—SIMULATION OF A DRIVE-IN BANK

Statement of the Problem

A drive-in bank has two windows, each manned by a teller and each with a separate drive-in lane. The drive-in lanes are adjacent. From previous observations it has been determined that the time interval between customer arrivals during rush hours is exponentially distributed with a mean time between arrivals of 0.5 time units. Congestion occurs only during rush hours, and only this period is to be analyzed. The service time is normally distributed for each teller with a mean service time of one time unit and a standard deviation of 0.3 time units. It has also been shown that customers have a preference for lane 1 if neither teller is busy or if the waiting lines are equal. At all other times, however, a customer chooses the shortest line. After a customer has entered the system, he may not leave until he is serviced. However, he may change lanes if he is the last customer in his lane and a difference of two customers exists between the two lanes. Because of parking space limitations, only three cars can wait in each lane. These cars, plus the car of the customer being serviced by each teller, allow a maximum of eight cars in the system. If the system is full when a customer arrives, he balks and is lost to the system.

The initial conditions are as follows:

1. Both drive-in windows are busy with end of services scheduled at time 1.
2. The first arrival is scheduled at 0.1 time unit.
3. Two customers are waiting in each queue.

Simulation Objectives

The objective is to develop a simulation model that can be used to analyze the banking situation in terms of the following statistics:

1. Teller utilization $= \dfrac{\text{total time performing service}}{\text{total simulation time}}$
2. Time integrated average number of customers in the system.

```
                              **GASP SUMMARY REPORT**

                    SIMULATION PROJECT NUMBER   2  BY  PRITSKER

                    DATE  6/ 30/ 1973       RUN NUMBER    1 OF    1

                    CURRENT TIME =  3.7036E+02

PARAMETER SET      1 =     5.0000E+00     3.5000E+00     8.0000E+00     1.5000E+00
PARAMETER SET      2 =     4.0000E+00     3.0000E+00     7.0000E+00     1.0000E+00

                   **STATISTICS FOR VARIABLES BASED ON OBSERVATION**
              MEAN          STD DEV        SD OF MEAN        CV           MINIMUM          MAXIMUM       OBS

WAIT TIM   7.3882E-01     7.4014E-01     3.7053E-02     1.0018E+00     0.               3.7627E+00     399
TRIP TIM   1.3521E+01     3.2319E+00     1.6303E-01     2.3904E-01     8.0140E+00       2.9502E+01     393

                      **STATISTICS FOR TIME-PERSISTENT VARIABLES**
              MEAN          STD DEV        MINIMUM          MAXIMUM       TIME INTERVAL   CUR. VALUE

UNL UTIL   7.8911E-01     4.0794E-01     0.               1.0000E+00     3.7036E+02     0.
LDR UTIL   3.1925E+00     1.3975E+00     0.               8.0000E+00     3.7036E+02     2.0000E+00
```

```
**GASP FILE STORAGE AREA DUMP AT TIME   3.7036E+02**

MAXIMUM NUMBER OF ENTRIES IN FILE STORAGE AREA = 17

           PRINTOUT OF FILE NUMBER    1
               TNOW =   3.7036E+02
               QQTIM=   3.7036E+02

     TIME PERIOD FOR STATISTICS 3.7036E+02
     AVERAGE NUMBER IN FILE        15.0404
     STANDARD DEVIATION             1.7697
     MAXIMUM NUMBER IN FILE        17

               THE FILE IS EMPTY


           PRINTOUT OF FILE NUMBER    2
               TNOW =   3.7036E+02
               QQTIM=   3.6549E+02

     TIME PERIOD FOR STATISTICS 3.7036E+02
     AVERAGE NUMBER IN FILE          .7960
     STANDARD DEVIATION             1.0269
     MAXIMUM NUMBER IN FILE         5

               THE FILE IS EMPTY
```

Figure 5-30 GASP IV summary report (Example 2).

```
                                   **HISTOGRAM NUMBER  1**

                                          WAIT TIM

OBSV     RELA     CUML       UPPER
FREQ     FREQ     FREQ     CELL LIMIT     0         20        40        60        60       100
                                          +    +    +    +    +    +    +    +    +    +    +
  97     .243     .243     0.             +************                                   +
  86     .216     .459     5.0000E-01     +***********            C                       +
  94     .236     .694     1.0000E+00     +************                       C           +
  64     .160     .855     1.5000E+00     +********                                   C   +
  29     .073     .927     2.0000E+00     +****                                          C +
  19     .048     .975     2.5000E+00     +**                                            C+
   6     .015     .990     3.0000E+00     +*                                             C+
   1     .003     .992     3.5000E+00     +                                               C
   3     .008    1.000     4.0000E+00     +                                               C
   0    0.000    1.000     4.5000E+00     +                                               C
   0    0.000    1.000     5.0000E+00     +                                               C
   0    0.000    1.000        INF         +                                               C
 ---                                      +    +    +    +    +    +    +    +    +    +    +
 399                                      0         20        40        60        80       100
```

```
                                        **HISTOGRAM NUMBER  2**

                                               TRIP TIM

 OBSV      RELA      CUML         UPPER
 FREQ      FREQ      FREQ       CELL LIMIT      0        20        40        60        80       100
                                                +    +    +    +    +    +    +    +    +    +    +
    0     0.000     0.000       5.0000E+00      +                                                 +
    0     0.000     0.000       7.0000E+00      +                                                 +
   14      .036      .036       9.0000E+00      +**                                               +
   71      .181      .216       1.1000E+01      +********* C                                      +
  110      .280      .496       1.3000E+01      +**************          C                        +
   94      .239      .735       1.5000E+01      +************                        C            +
   54      .137      .873       1.7000E+01      +*******                                    C     +
   24      .061      .934       1.9000E+01      +***                                           C  +
   14      .036      .969       2.1000E+01      +**                                             C +
    8      .020      .990       2.3000E+01      +*                                               C+
    2      .005      .995       2.5000E+01      +                                                 C
    2      .005     1.000          INF          +                                                 C
  ---                                           +    +    +    +    +    +    +    +    +    +    +
  393                                           0        20        40        60        80       100
```

Figure 5-31 Histogram outputs for Example 2.

3. Time between departures from the drive-in windows.
4. Average time a customer is in the system.
5. Average number of customers in each queue.
6. Percent of arriving customers who balk.

A simulated time period of 1000 time units will be used.*

Special Features

This example illustrates the facility with which complex queueing problems can be analyzed by simulation using GASP IV. Difficult aspects of a queueing situation, such as balking and jockeying, are simulated with little additional effort. In addition, it is shown that the basic simulation concepts presented in the introduction to this section provide a good background for modeling complex queueing situations. Subroutine MONTR is used to reset (CLEAR) statistical calculations and to obtain periodic summary reports.

Procedure

The events used to model the banking system are (1) customer arrival to the system (ARRVL) and (2) customer exit from the system (ENDSV). Three files are used; file 1 is the event file. Attributes of customers waiting for tellers 1 and 2 are stored in files 2 and 3, respectively. The attributes for each file are shown below:

File 1	Attribute 1:	Scheduled time of event
	Attribute 2:	Event code
	Attribute 3:	Time customer entered system
	Attribute 4:	Not used
Files 2 and 3	Attributes 1 and 2:	Not used
	Attribute 3:	Time customer entered system
	Attribute 4:	Time customer entered queue This may be different from the time he entered system if the customer has changed lanes

* If the rush period is 100 time units, either a 1000 time unit simulation or ten 100 time unit simulations could be performed. The choice depends on whether the initial starting conditions are prescribed each time, or the ending conditions at time 100 are acceptable starting conditions.

The definitions of the non-GASP variables are given below:

Non-GASP Variables	Definition	Initial Value
XBUZ(J)	0 if teller J is idle; 1 if teller J is busy	(1.0,1.0)
XISYS	Number of items in the system	6.0
CBALK	Number of customers balking	0.0
TCUST	Number of customers arriving	0.0
XL	Mean time between arrivals	0.5
TLD	Time of last departure from the system	0.0
TBD	Time between departures from the system	Computed
TISYS	Time spent in the system by each customer	Computed
XMAXS	Maximum number of cars allowed in the system	8.0

The parameters for the service time of the tellers is stored in the GASP IV array, PPARM. It is assumed that the service time for both tellers is normally distributed with the same parameter values, which are: PPARM(1,1) = mean = 1; PPARM(1,2) = minimum service time = .2; PPARM(1,3) = maximum service time = 1.8; and PPARM(1,4) = standard deviation = 0.3.

In the main program the card reader and printer numbers and the non-GASP variables are initialized. Subroutine GASP is then called. Since only one run is to be made, execution is terminated when a return is made to the main program. The FORTRAN listing of the main program is given in Fig. 5-32.

The standard format for subroutine EVNTS is used as seen in Fig. 5-33. Event code 1 signifies an arrival event; event codes 2 and 3 signify end of services for tellers 1 and 2, respectively.

Consider first the event "arrival at the bank," which is flow charted in Fig. 5-34, and the corresponding listing given in Fig. 5-35. When an arrival occurs, the next arrival is scheduled by generating the time between arrivals. Rather than use the function ERLNG to generate a sample from an exponential distribution, the expression − XL ⋆ ALOG (DRAND(1)) is used, where XL is the mean time between arrivals. The total number of arrivals is then increased by 1. The number in the system, XISYS, is checked and if equal to XMAXS, the customer balks (CBALK is increased by 1). If XISYS < XMAXS, XISYS is increased

```
      PROGRAM MAIN(INPUT,OUTPUT,TAPE7,TAPE5=INPUT,TAPE6=OUTPUT)
      DIMENSION NSET(240)
      COMMON QSET(240)
      COMMON /GCOM1/ ATRIB(25),JEVNT,MFA,MFE(100),MLE(100),MSTOP,NCRDR,N
     1NAPO,NNAPT,NNATR,NNFIL,NNQ(100),NNTRY,NPRNT,PPARM(50,4),TNOW,TTBEG
     2,TTCLR,TTFIN,TTRIB(25),TTSET
      COMMON /UCOM1/ XL,XBUZ(2),XISYS,CBALK,TCUST,TLD,XMAXS
      EQUIVALENCE (NSET(1),QSET(1))
C
C*****MAIN PROGRAM
C
      NCRDR=5
      NPRNT=6
      READ (NCRDR,101) XL,XBUZ,XISYS,XMAXS
C
C*****INITIALIZE NUMBER OF CUSTOMERS BALKING (CBALK), TOTAL CUSTOMERS
C*****ARRIVING (TCUST), AND TIME LAST DEPARTURE (TLD) AT 0.
C
      CBALK=0.
      TCUST=XISYS
      TLD=0.
      CALL GASP
      STOP
C
  101 FORMAT (5F10.2)
C
      END
```

Figure 5-32 FORTRAN listing of the main program (Example 3).

by 1 and statistics are collected on XISYS by the statement CALL TIMST(XISYS,TNOW,3). The number 3 in the call statement indicates XISYS is the third variable collected in TIMST.

The tellers are checked to see if either is idle, that is, if XBUZ(J) = 0. If both are busy, the shorter queue is determined by comparing NNQ(2) with NNQ(3), and the customer is put in the appropriate queue. Recall that file 2 is the queue for teller 1; file 3 is the queue for teller 2; and NNQ(J) is a GASP IV variable specifying the number in file J. If a teller is free, a service time is generated, and an end-of-service event is scheduled. The teller is set to busy status and statistics on his busy time are collected. The normally distributed service time is obtained by using the function RNORM(1,2), where the first argument specifies the parameter set to be used and the second argument specifies the random number stream. Since both tellers have the same service time parameters, parameter set 1 is used for both (if they were different, parameter set J could be used). A different random number stream is

```
      SUBROUTINE EVNTS (I)
      GO TO (101,102,102), I
  101 CALL ARRVL
      GO TO 103
  102 CALL ENDSV
  103 RETURN
C
      END
```

Figure 5-33 FORTRAN listing of subroutine EVNTS (Example 3).

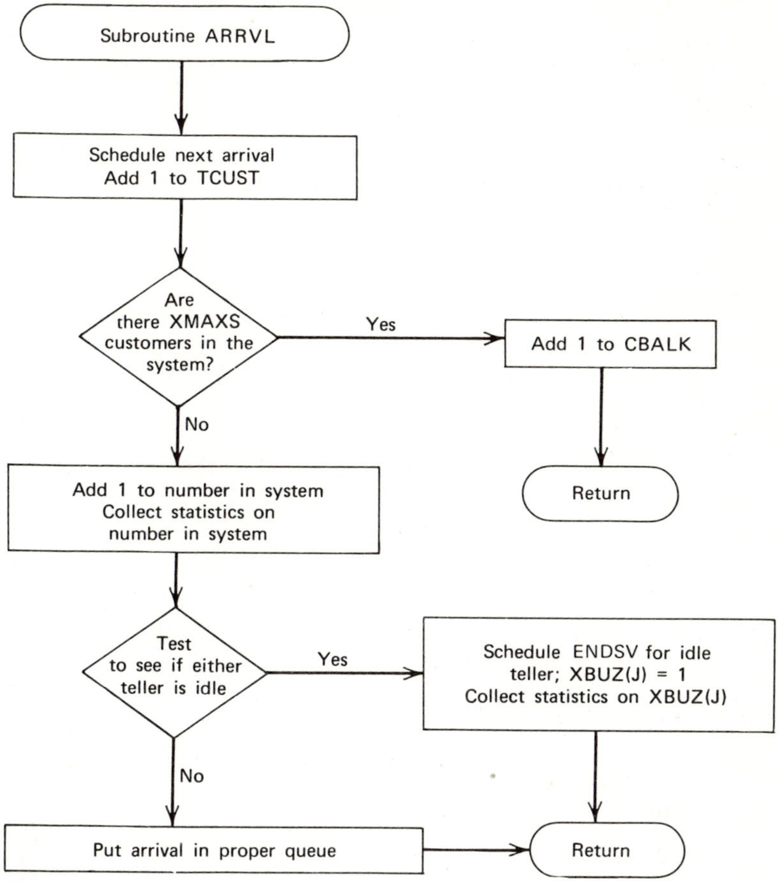

Figure 5-34 Flow chart of the event "arrival at bank."

used for obtaining service time values than was used to obtain interarrival times. This is normally a good practice since the arrival times can be kept fixed and different service patterns evaluated or vice versa. A return to GASP IV is made through EVNTS.

The end-of-service event has been assigned event codes of 2 and 3. This event is flow charted in Fig. 5-36. When an end-of-service event (ENDSV) occurs, XISYS is decreased by one, and statistics are updated on XISYS, TISYS, and TBD. If a customer is waiting for either teller, a service is scheduled after the customer is removed from the appropriate queue. If the queues differ by two or more, the last customer of the longer queue switches queues. This is done by removing the last entry (the entry stored starting in cell MLE) of the longer queue and putting

```
      SUBROUTINE ARRVL
      COMMON /GCOM1/ ATRIB(25),JEVNT,MFA,MFE(100),MLE(100),MSTOP,NCRDR,N
     1NAPO,NNAPT,NNATR,NNFIL,NNQ(100),NNTRY,NPRNT,PPARM(50,4),TNOW,TTBEG
     2,TTCLR,TTFIN,TTRIB(25),TTSET
      COMMON /UCOM1/ XL,XBUZ(2),XISYS,CBALK,TCUST,TLD,XMAXS
C
C*****CAUSE NEXT ARRIVAL TO OCCUR.
C
      ATRIB(1)=TNOW-XL*ALOG(DRAND(1))
      ATRIB(3)=ATRIB(1)
      ATRIB(2)=1.
      CALL FILEM (1)
C
C*****INCREASE  TOTAL CUSTOMERS ARRIVING.
C
      TCUST=TCUST+1.
C
C*****TEST TO SEE IF SYSTEM IF FULL.
C
      IF (XISYS-XMAXS) 102,101,101
C
C*****SYSTEM IS FULL.  INCREASE  NUMBER OF BALKERS.
C
  101 CBALK=CBALK+1.
      RETURN
C
C*****INCREASE  NUMBER IN SYSTEM AND COLLECT STATISTICS ON IT.
C
  102 XISYS=XISYS+1.
      CALL TIMST (XISYS,TNOW,3)
C
C*****SET ARRIVAL TIME OF THIS CUSTOMER TO TNOW.
C
      ATRIB(3)=TNOW
C
C*****TEST TO SEE IF EITHER SERVER IS FREE.
C
      IF (XBUZ(1)) 111,104,103
  103 IF (XBUZ(2)) 111,105,107
  104 M=1
      GO TO 106
  105 M=2
C
C*****ASSIGN ARRIVING CUSTOMER TO FREE SERVER.  CAUSE END OF SERVICE
C*****EVENT.
C
  106 ATRIB(1)=TNOW+RNORM(1,2)
      ATRIB(2)=M+1
      CALL FILEM (1)
C
C*****SET ASSIGNED SERVER TO BUSY STATUS.
C
      XBUZ(M)=1.
      CALL TIMST (XBUZ(M),TNOW,M)
      RETURN
C
C*****BOTH SERVERS ARE BUSY.  PUT CUSTOMER IN SHORTER QUEUE.
C
  107 ATRIB(4)=TNOW
      IF (NNQ(2)-NNQ(3)) 108,109,109
  108 CALL FILEM (2)
      GO TO 110
  109 CALL FILEM (3)
  110 RETURN
  111 CALL ERROR (87)
      CALL EXIT
      RETURN
C
      END
```

Figure 5-35 FORTRAN listing of subroutine ARRVL (Example 3).

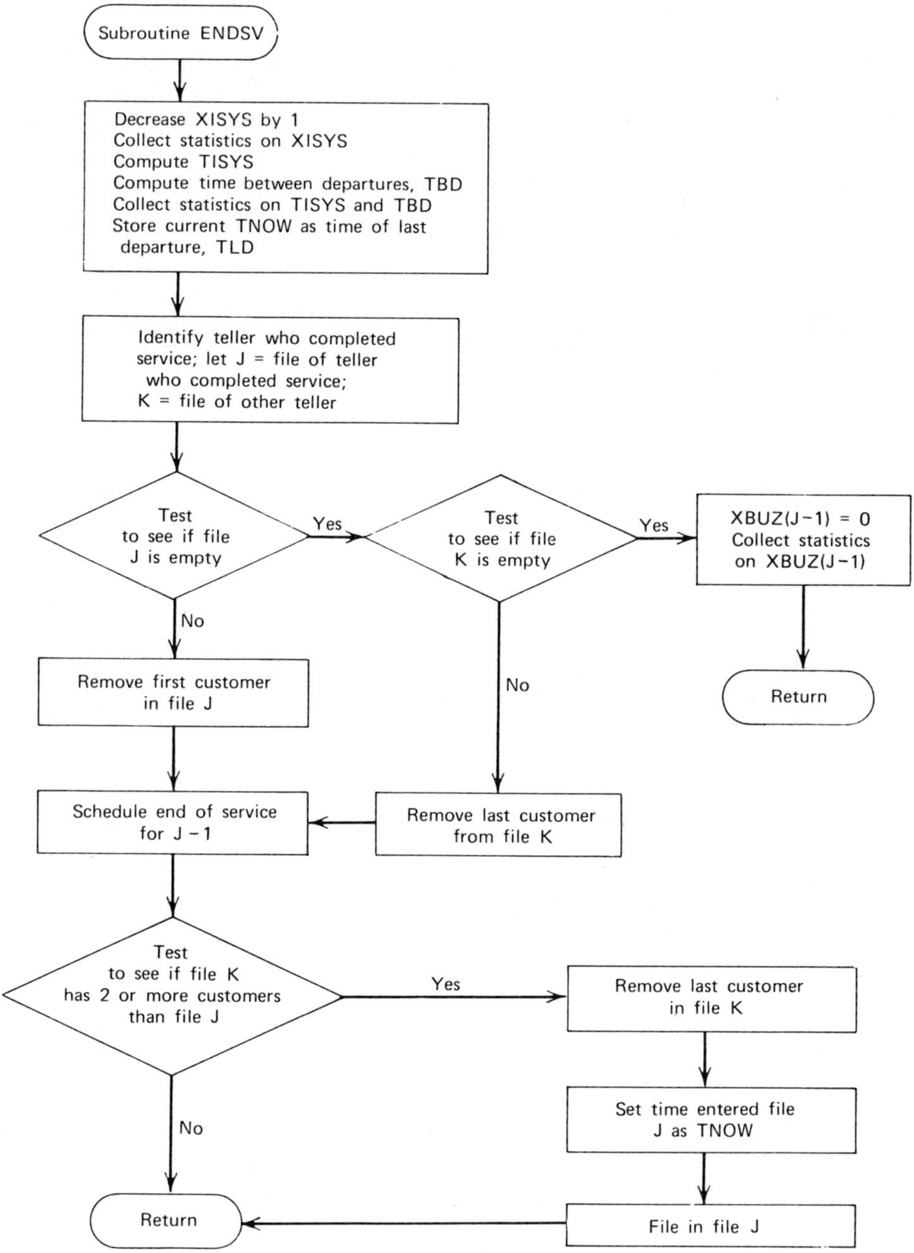

Figure 5-36 Flow chart of the event "end of customer service."

it in the file of the shorter queue. A return to GASP IV is then made. The FORTRAN listing for event ENDSV is given in Fig. 5-37. Comment cards are inserted into the listing to define the purpose of each group of statements. The event code for an end-of-service event is defined as either 2 or 3, which corresponds to the file number in which customers are stored when waiting for the teller. By setting J = JEVNT, the

```
      SUBROUTINE ENDSV
      COMMON /GCOM1/ ATRIB(25),JEVNT,MFA,MFE(100),MLE(100),MSTOP,NCRDR,N
     1NAPO,NNAPT,NNATR,NNFIL,NNQ(100),NNTRY,NPRNT,PPARM(50,4),TNOW,TTBEG
     2,TTCLR,TTFIN,TTRIB(25),TTSET
      COMMON /UCOM1/ XL,XBUZ(2),XISYS,CBALK,TCUST,TLD,XMAXS
C
C*****SERVICE IS COMPLETED.  DECREMENT NUMBER IN SYSTEM.  COLLECT
C*****STATISTICS ON CUSTOMER TIME IN SYSTEM AND TIME BETWEEN DEPARTURES.
C
      XISYS=XISYS-1.
      CALL TIMST (XISYS,TNOW,3)
      TISYS=TNOW-ATRIB(3)
      CALL COLCT (TISYS,1)
      TBD=TNOW-TLD
      TLD=TNOW
      CALL COLCT (TBD,2)
C
C*****J = NUMBER OF QUEUE OF SERVER WITH COMPLETED SERVICE.  M = SERVER
C*****NUMBER, K = NUMBER OF QUEUE OF THE OTHER SERVER.
C
      J=JEVNT
      M=J-1
      IF (J-2) 111,101,102
  101 K=3
      GO TO 103
  102 K=2
  103 IF (NNQ(J)) 111,104,106
  104 IF (NNQ(K)) 111,105,110
  105 XBUZ(M)=0.
      CALL TIMST (XBUZ(M),TNOW,M)
      RETURN
C
C*****PUT FIRST CUSTOMER OF QUEUE J IN SERVICE.
C
  106 CALL RMOVE (MFE(J),J)
C
C*****CAUSE END OF SERVICE EVENT.
C
  107 ATRIB(1)=TNOW+RNORM(1,2)
      ATRIB(2)=J
      CALL FILEM (1)
C
C*****TEST DIFFERENCE IN QUEUE LENGTHS TO DETERMINE IF JOCKEYING IS TO
C*****TAKE PLACE.
C
      IF (NNQ(K)-NNQ(J)-2) 108,109,109
  108 RETURN
  109 CALL RMOVE (MLE(K),K)
      ATRIB(4)=TNOW
      CALL FILEM (J)
      RETURN
C
C*****SINCE QUEUE OF SERVER M IS EMPTY, LAST CUSTOMER IN QUEUE OF OTHER
C*****SERVER IS SERVED BY M.
C
  110 CALL RMOVE (MLE(K),K)
      GO TO 107
  111 CALL ERROR (86)
      CALL EXIT
C
      END
```

Figure 5-37 FORTRAN listing of subroutine ENDSV (Example 3).

appropriate file for the teller that completed a service is established. Letting M = J − 1 establishes M as the teller number. K is then set equal to the file of the other teller. If both files are empty (NNQ(J) = 0 and NNQ(K) = 0), teller M is set idle. If teller M has a customer waiting in his queue (file J), the customer is removed from file J (statement 106) and an end-of-service event for teller M is scheduled to occur.

Next, a test on the difference in the number of customers in the queues is made. If the difference is two or more, jockeying occurs. To accomplish this the last entry in file K is removed and is filed in file J.

When TNOW equals TTFIN, the simulation is completed and subroutine GASP calls OTPUT. The average number of customers balking is calculated and printed in OTPUT. Figure 5-38 gives the FORTRAN listing for subroutine OTPUT. OTPUT returns control to GASP, which calls SUMRY to print the summary report. Only one run will be made at the end of which a return to the main program is made, thereby completing the program execution.

A listing of the input data cards and the GASP IV echo check are presented in Fig. 5-39. The values up to data card type 12 are defined by the echo check. Data card types 5, 6, and 9 are not required since there are no histograms, plots, or continuous variables. For data card types 3, 4, 10, and 12, the first five columns of the card are used for identifying the card type. This is only done when there can be multiple cards of a given type. The data on the programmer's card is read in the main program. On data card type 11, the ending conditions for the simulation are specified. Since MSTOP = 1, the simulation will end at time TTFIN, which is 1000 for this example. Initialization of the file structure is specified by setting JJFIL = 1.

Data card type 12 specifies the initial entries for the files. The GASP IV printout of these entries is shown in Fig. 5-40. In file 1, entry 1 is the arrival event (ATRIB(2) = 1.), entry 2 is the end-of-service event for

```
      SUBROUTINE OTPUT                                                  OT3     1
      COMMON /GCOM1/ ATRIB(25),JEVNT,MFA,MFE(100),MLE(100),MSTOP,NCRDR,NGCOM1   1
     1NAPO,NNAPT,NNATR,NNFIL,NNQ(100),NNTRY,NPRNT,PPARM(50,4),TNOW,TTBEGGCOM1   2
     2,TTCLR,TTFIN,TTRIB(25),TTSET                                      GCOM1   3
      COMMON /UCOM1/ XL,XBUZ(2),XISYS,CBALK,TCUST,TLD,XMAXS             UCOM1   1
      WRITE (NPRNT,101) XL,PPARM(1,1)                                   OT3     2
      YBALK=CBALK*100./TCUST                                            OT3     3
      WRITE (NPRNT,102) YBALK,CBALK,TCUST                               OT3     4
      RETURN                                                            OT3     5
C                                                                       OT3     6
  101 FORMAT (/35X,32HMEAN TIME BETWEEN ARRIVALS     = F5.2/,35X,32HMEAN OT3     7
     1SERVICE TIME FOR TELLERS = F5.2)                                  OT3     8
  102 FORMAT (35X,31HPERCENT OF CUSTOMERS BALKING = F6.2/,35X,30HNUMBER OT3     9
     1OF CUSTOMERS BALKING = F6.2/,35X,15HTOTAL CUSTOMERS,14X,2H= F7.2) OT3    10
C                                                                       OT3    11
      END                                                               OT3    12
```

Figure 5-38 FORTRAN listing of subroutine OTPUT (Example 3).

```
0.5          1.0          1.0          6.0          8.0                      USER
PRITSKER                  3     6     30 1973     1                          1
      2    3    0     1     0     2   30     4     3  240                    2
3          1TISYS
3          2TBD                                                              3
4          1XBUZ(1)            1.0
4          2XBUZ(2)            1.0                                           4
4          3XISYS              6.0
      1    4    4                                                            7
      1    3    3                                                            8
10         11.0         0.2          1.8          0.3                        10
      1    1    1     00.0         1000.             13095170446            11
12         1       0.1          1.0
12         1       1.0          2.0          0.0
12         1       1.0          3.0          0.0
12         2                    0.0          0.0
12         2                    0.0          0.0                             12
12         3                    0.0          0.0
12         3                    0.0          0.0
12         1     100.0         -2.0
12         1     200.0         -5.0        100.0
12         0
```

Figure 5-39 Input data descriptions for Example 3.

```
                              SIMULATION PROJECT NUMBER   3  BY  PRITSKER

                              DATE  6/ 30/ 1973         RUN NUMBER     1 OF     1
                              LLSUP=0000000000000000    GASP IV VERSION 23JUN73

NNCLT=      2    NNSTA=      3    NNHIS=      0    NNPRM=      1    NNPLT=      0    NNSTR=      2    NNTRY=     30
NNATR=      4    NNFIL=      3    NNSET=    240    NNEQD=     -0    NNEQS=     -0    NFLAG=     -0

COLCT NO.   1    LLABC=TISYS
COLCT NO.   2    LLABC=TBD

TIMST NO.   1    LLABT=XBUZ(1)    I.C. =      1.0000E+00
TIMST NO.   2    LLABT=XBUZ(2)    I.C. =      1.0000E+00
TIMST NO.   3    LLABT=XISYS      I.C. =      6.0000E+00

KKRNK= (    1)       4        4

IINN = (    1)       3        3

PARAMETER SET        1 =      1.0000E+00      2.0000E-01      1.8000E+00      3.0000E-01

MSTOP=      1    JJCLR=      1    JJBEG=      1    IICRD=      0    TTBEG=      0.              TTFIN=      1.0000E+03
JJFIL=      1
IISED= 30951              70445
```

Figure 5-39 *(continued)*

```
                                        **GASP FILE STORAGE AREA DUMP AT TIME  0.              **

                                        MAXIMUM NUMBER OF ENTRIES IN FILE STORAGE AREA =   9

                                                    PRINTOUT OF FILE NUMBER     1
                                                        TNOW =  0.
                                                        OOTIM=  0.

                                                         FILE CONTENTS
ENTRY   1    =       1.0000E-01        1.0000E+00        -0.                    -0.
ENTRY   2    =       1.0000E+00        2.0000E+00         0.                    -0.
ENTRY   3    =       1.0000E+00        3.0000E+00         0.                    -0.
ENTRY   4    =       1.0000E+02       -2.0000E+00        -0.                    -0.
ENTRY   5    =       2.0000E+02       -5.0000E+00          1.0000E+02           -0.

                                                    PRINTOUT OF FILE NUMBER     2
                                                        TNOW =  0.
                                                        OOTIM=  0.

                                                         FILE CONTENTS
ENTRY   1    =   -0.               0.                 0.                    -0.
ENTRY   2    =   -0.               0.                 0.                    -0.

                                                    PRINTOUT OF FILE NUMBER     3
                                                        TNOW =  0.
                                                        OOTIM=  0.

                                                         FILE CONTENTS
ENTRY   1    =   -0.               0.                 0.                    -0.
ENTRY   2    =   -0.               0.                 0.                    -0.
```

Figure 5-40 File storage area dump at time 0 (Example 3).

teller 1 (ATRIB(2) = 2.), and entry 3 is the end-of-service event for teller 2 (ATRIB(2) = 3.). Two monitor events are included in file 1.

At time 100., the statistical arrays are to be cleared. This is accomplished by a monitor event with a code of -2. This event reinitializes the SSOBV, SSTPV, and queue statistics arrays (also histogram cells (JJCEL) when necessary). This event is shown as entry 4 of file 1 in Fig. 5-40. For this example, summary reports are desired every 100 time units, starting at time 200. This is accomplished with a monitor event having code -5 with ATRIB(1) = 200 and ATRIB(3) = 100. Entry 5 of file 1 represents this monitor event. The entries in files 2 and 3 represent the initial customers in the queues. All their attributes are zero since they are presumed to have arrived and joined their queues at time 0. The GASP IV echo check identifies the complete initialization of the GASP IV variables.

Simulation Reports

Through the use of MONTR, summary reports were obtained at times 200, 300, . . . , 1000. Each report contains statistics starting from time 100 since the statistical arrays were cleared at time 100 through the use of MONTR with code −2. The average values printed in the summary reports are given in Table 5-2.

Table 5-2. Average Values from Periodic Summary Reports

Calculation Time	Time in System (TISYS)	Time between Departures (TBD)	Busy Fraction Teller 1 (XBUZ(1))	Busy Fraction Teller 2 (XBUZ(2))	Number in System (XISYS)
200	2.47	0.54	0.95	0.91	4.56
300	2.25	0.56	0.91	0.85	4.04
400	2.25	0.55	0.92	0.88	4.13
500	2.33	0.54	0.93	0.90	4.32
600	2.37	0.54	0.93	0.90	4.37
700	2.38	0.54	0.94	0.91	4.41
800	2.41	0.54	0.94	0.91	4.48
900	2.38	0.54	0.93	0.90	4.39
1000	2.42	0.54	0.94	0.91	4.49

From Table 5-2 it is evident that at time 300 all the averages are within 10% of the value calculated at time 1000.

The information printed in subroutine OTPUT is shown in Fig. 5-41.

Mean time between arrivals	=	.50
Mean service time for tellers	=	1.00
Percent of customers balking	=	9.37
Number of customers balking	=	192.00
Total customers	=	2050.00

Figure 5-41 Output from subroutine OTPUT (Example 3).

This output shows that 2050 customers sought service in the 1000 time units, and that 9.37% or 192 balked. The expected number of customers in 1000 time units, based on the mean time between customers of 0.5, is 2000. Note that the clearing of statistics at time 100 only applies to GASP IV generated statistics and not those obtained by the user.

The GASP IV summary report obtained at time 1000 is presented in Fig. 5-42. It shows that the statistics are based on 1675 customers processed by the tellers in the time period 100 to 1000. The average time in the system for a customer was 2.42, and one customer spent over 5.36 time units obtaining service. The large fraction of customers balking and

```
                               **GASP SUMMARY REPORT**

                     SIMULATION PROJECT NUMBER   3  BY  PRITSKER

                     DATE  6/ 30/ 1973       RUN NUMBER    1 OF    1

                     CURRENT TIME =  1.0000E+03

PARAMETER SET      1 =    1.0000E+00      2.0000E-01      1.8000E+00      3.0000E-01

                      **STATISTICS FOR VARIABLES BASED ON OBSERVATION**
              MEAN          STD DEV       SD OF MEAN        CV           MINIMUM         MAXIMUM      OBS

TISYS      2.4170E+00     1.0548E+00     2.5773E-02     4.3640E-01     3.9943E-01     5.3642E+00    1675
TBD        5.3765E-01     3.6047E-01     8.8076E-03     6.7045E-01     4.1598E-04     3.3623E+00    1675

                        **STATISTICS FOR TIME-PERSISTENT VARIABLES**
              MEAN          STD DEV       MINIMUM        MAXIMUM       TIME INTERVAL   CUR. VALUE

XBUZ(1)    9.3835E-01     2.4051E-01     0.             1.0000E+00     9.0000E+02     0.
XBUZ(2)    9.1405E-01     2.8029E-01     0.             1.0000E+00     9.0000E+02     1.0000E+00
XISYS      4.4850E+00     2.2471E+00     0.             8.0000E+00     9.0000E+02     1.0000E+00
```

```
**GASP FILE STORAGE AREA DUMP AT TIME  1.0000E+03**

MAXIMUM NUMBER CF ENTRIES IN FILE STORAGE AREA = 11

                                          PRINTOUT OF FILE NUMBER   1
                                              TNOW =  1.0000E+03
                                              QQTIM=  1.0000E+03

                                   TIME PERIOD FOR STATISTICS 9.0000E+02
                                   AVERAGE NUMBER IN FILE         3.8524
                                   STANDARD DEVIATION              .4290
                                   MAXIMUM NUMBER IN FILE         4

                                                FILE CONTENTS
ENTRY  1   =    1.0001E+03     1.0C00E+00      1.0001E+03     -0.
ENTRY  2   =    1.0004E+03     3.0000E+00      9.9952E+02     -0.
ENTRY  3   =    1.1000E+03    -5.0000E+00      1.0000E+02     -0.

                                          PRINTOUT OF FILE NUMBER   2
                                              TNOW =  1.0000E+03
                                              QQTIM=  9.9822E+02

                                   TIME PERIOD FOR STATISTICS 9.0000E+02
                                   AVERAGE NUMBER IN FILE         1.4024
                                   STANDARD DEVIATION             1.0814
                                   MAXIMUM NUMBER IN FILE         3

                                              THE FILE IS EMPTY

                                          PRINTOUT OF FILE NUMBER   3
                                              TNOW =  1.0000E+03
                                              QQTIM=  9.9808E+02

                                   TIME PERIOD FOR STATISTICS 9.0000E+02
                                   AVERAGE NUMBER IN FILE         1.2302
                                   STANDARD DEVIATION             1.0286
                                   MAXIMUM NUMBER IN FILE         3

                                              THE FILE IS EMPTY
```

Figure 5-42 GASP IV summary report at time 1000 (Example 3).

the high utilization of the tellers (94% and 91% of the time) indicates that the bank system is overloaded. The average number of customers in the system is 4.49. The file printouts for files 2 and 3 give the statistics for the number in the queues of tellers 1 and 2, respectively. Here the decision of the customers to select teller 1 over teller 2, when a choice exists, is indicated by the higher average number in the queue of teller 1 (1.40 versus 1.23). Another indication that the system is overloaded is that the waiting time on the average is greater than the service time, that is, average time in system is 2.42 and average service time is 1.00. Another statistic of interest is the average time between departure of customers, which is 0.54 time units. This indicates a potential bottleneck on the output side of the system and could cause a severe congestion problem for customers attempting to return to street traffic. It may also serve as an indication that the system definition may have to be enlarged to include street traffic, which could result in the blocking of the tellers.

SIMULATION OF NETWORKS

Networks and network analyses are playing an increasingly important role in the description and improvement of systems. The Critical Path Method (CPM), the Program Evaluation and Review Technique (PERT), and the Graphical Evaluation and Review Technique (GERT), for example, are widely used by business organizations (21, 49, 83, 92, 104, 105, 108, 138).

This chapter discusses the use of simulation to study and analyze networks that are models of systems. These networks consist of a collection of *branches* and *nodes*. The branches usually represent activities and the nodes milestones. The nodes are the end points of the branches and represent the starting and ending times of activities.* The emphasis of this chapter is placed on the methods for *simulating* such networks.

The entities associated with a network structure are the activities of the network and the resources used to perform the activities (when resources are included in the analysis). The status of the system represented by the network is reflected by the status of the activities (not performed, ongoing, completed) and the number of resources being used for the ongoing activities. An interesting observation is that a change in the status of these entities can only occur when an activity is completed. Therefore, under the next event philosophy, only an end-of-activity event is necessary to obtain a complete simulation of a network. The end-of-activity event could cause new activities to be started, which occurs

* Simulation of activity-on-node or precedence networks follows the same pattern as presented in this chapter (112).

when all predecessor activities for that activity have been completed. When an activity is completed, the resources working on the activity are made available. Availability of these resources can allow other activities to be started. Resources are allocated to the activities that are started, but again this occurs only when some other activity was completed.

The basic approach discussed above has led to the development of the GERT and SMOOTH network simulation languages (110, 111, 127), which are written in GASP II and GASP IV, respectively. These network simulation languages allow a user to describe the nodes and branches of the network and to obtain a simulation of the network without writing any computer code. In the next section, two examples that demonstrate how networks can be simulated using GASP IV are presented. The procedures used in these examples are similar to those used in the network simulation languages mentioned above.

In the first network example a PERT network is simulated to obtain an estimate of the frequency distribution of the time needed to complete the project represented by the network (81). In this example activity times are sampled from the different distributions. In addition, specified probability mass functions are used to describe activity times. A criticality index for each activity included in the PERT network is also computed. The criticality index is the fraction of the time an activity is on a critical path of the network, that is, the number of simulations in which the activity was on the critical path divided by the total number of simulations (134).

The second example involves a network model that represents the activities performed in a maintenance facility. It is assumed that the maintenance facility has limited resources and that each activity may require as many as three different types of resources (24). Each activity also requires a fixed amount of time. Simulation is used to study the effect of dispatching rules on the project duration when dispatching of the activities is limited by the available resources. This example demonstrates the use of simulation for the study of decision-making.

EXAMPLE 4—SIMULATION OF A PERT NETWORK

Statement of the Problem

PERT is a technique for evaluating and reviewing a program consisting of interdependent activities (83). A PERT network is a graphical illustration of the relations between the activities of a program.

A PERT network consists of branches and nodes, where the branches represent the activities and the nodes represent milestones or events associated with the program. Each activity emanates from a node and terminates at a node. A node is *realized* when *all* activities terminating at the node have been completed. When a node is realized, all activities emanating from that node are *released* and can be scheduled. If a node has no branches terminating at it, the node is called a *source* node. If a node has no branches emanating from it, the node is called a *sink* node. Every network can be converted to a network with one source node and one sink node through the use of "dummy" branches. A *path* of the network is a sequence of branches from the source node to the sink node for which no branch of the network is included in the sequence more than once.

The PERT approach to analyzing networks of activities is based on several assumptions. One of these assumptions involves the characterization of the time to complete a program (the time to realize the network's sink node) as the time to complete the path of longest expected duration. This path is called the *critical* path. If the times associated with the activities of a program are random variables, the path with the longest duration depends on the specific samples drawn to represent the activity times. If a program is performed many times, the critical path, therefore, will not always be the same. Van Slyke (134) has used simulation as a method for studying PERT networks. In this example, GASP IV is used to simulate a PERT network. Figure 5-43 illustrates the PERT network to be simulated and the activity numbers for each of the branches of the network. The activity descriptions for each branch of the network are given in Table 5-3.

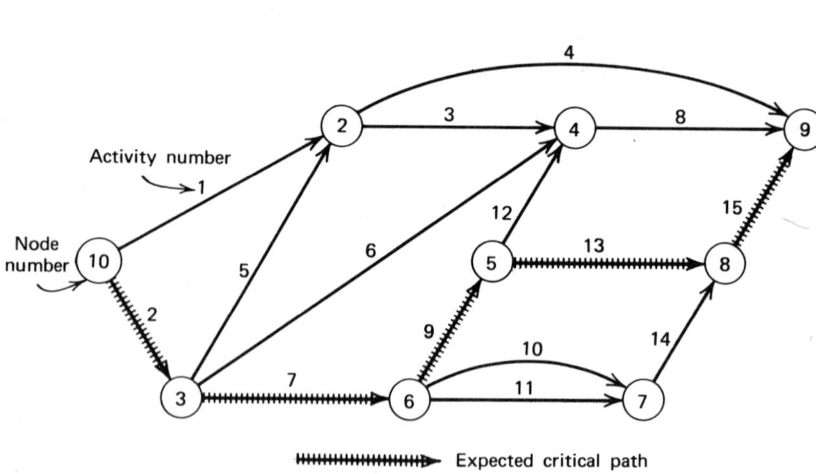

Figure 5-43 PERT network to be simulated.

Table 5-3. Activity Descriptions* for PERT Network Given in Fig. 5-43

Activity Number (NA)	Start Node	End Node	Distribution Code and Type	Parameter Values† PPARM(NA,J) 1	2	3	4	Mean	Variance
1	10	2	5. Lognormal	2.228	−999.0	100.0	0.198	10	4.00
2	10	3	4. Exponential	6.000	0.0	100.0	1.000	6	36.00
3	2	4	3. Uniform	—	4.0	10.0	—	7	3.00
4	2	9	6. Gamma	1.500	0.0	100.0	9.330	14	21.00
5	3	2	7. Beta	4.000	0.0	12.0	2.000	8	4.71
6	3	4	3. Uniform	—	0.0	17.0	—	13	5.33
7	3	6	2. Normal	5.000	0.0	100.0	1.000	5	1.00
8	4	9	4. Erlang	4.000	0.0	100.0	2.000	8	32.00
9	6	5	1. Constant	7.000	—	—	—	7	0.00
10	6	7	8. Triangular	3.000	1.0	8.0	—	4	2.16
11	6	7	9. Discrete	(.1,1)	(.5,3)	(.4,6)	—	4	3.00
12	5	4	9. Discrete	(.15,0)	(.7,2)	(.15,4)	—	2	1.20
13	5	8	9. Discrete	(.2,2)	(.4,4)	(.4,10)	—	6	10.40
14	7	8	9. Discrete	(.4,2)	(.3,10)	(.3,14)	—	8	26.40
15	8	9	9. Discrete	(.25.3)	(.5,5)	(.25,7)	—	5	2.00

* The computation of the parameter values for each distribution type, based on values of the mean and variance, is described in Chapter 4.

† For discrete densities the parameters are stored in the non-GASP IV arrays CPROB(NA,J) and ACTME(NA,J). On input, CPROB(NA,J) is the probability that activity NA takes on the time value ACTME(NA,J). For discrete distributions, the vector (CPROB(NA,J), ACTME(NA,J)) is listed under the parameter values for each J value.

Simulation Objectives

The objective of this problem is to perform a simulation of a PERT-type network to obtain the following statistics based on 400 simulations of the network:

1. Average time at which each node is realized.
2. Minimum time at which each node is realized.
3. Maximum time at which each node is realized.
4. Standard deviation of the time each node is realized.
5. Histograms of the time to realize nodes.
6. Percentage of the simulation runs in which an activity was on the critical path (the criticality index).

Special Features

In this example the methods used for simulating networks are described. Sampling from different distribution types and from a probability mass function are presented. The use of subroutine COPY and a method for obtaining multiple simulation runs without returning to subroutine DATIN are illustrated.

Sampling from a Probability Mass Function

Before presenting the procedure for simulating networks, the method for sampling from a probability mass function is discussed. Sampling from a prescribed probability mass function requires the use of a discrete version of the probability-integral-transformation (see Chapter 4). First, the cumulative distribution function associated with the discrete random variable is obtained. A random variable with a probability mass function and its associated cumulative distribution function are illustrated in Fig. 5-44. From the probability mass function presented in this diagram, it is seen that the probability of the random variable X equaling 10 is 0.3; of X equaling 20 is 0.4; of X equaling 30 is 0.2; and of X equaling 50 is 0.1. All other values of X have a zero probability of occurring. To obtain samples of X, one must select in a random fashion 10, 20, 30, and 50 with relative frequencies represented by the probabilities.

The distribution function reveals how this may be done in a method analogous to the probability integral transformation. A random number can be used as a value for the distribution function and can be transformed to obtain a value of X. The random number defines an ordinate value from which a value of X can be obtained.

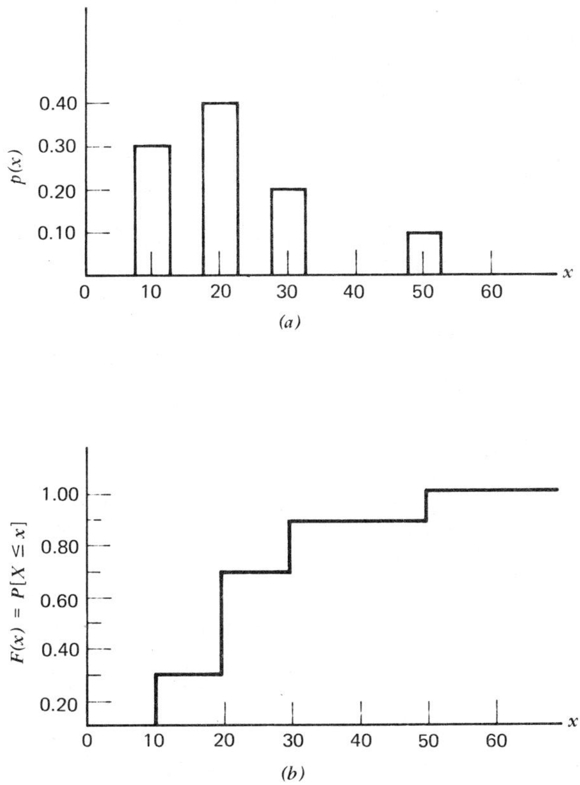

Figure 5-44 Illustration of the (*a*) probability mass function and (*b*) distribution function of a discrete random variable.

The validity of this approach is predicated on the theory that the probability of obtaining a random number in the interval (0,.3) is 0.3; thus 30% of the time the value of 10 will be assigned to X. Furthermore, the probability that the random number is in the interval (.3,.7) is 0.4; hence 40% of the time the value assigned to X will be 20. Continuing in this fashion, it is seen that this procedure generates random samples of the variable X distributed according to the probability mass function.

The function DISCR was written for Example 4 to generate samples for a random variable described by a probability mass function. The FORTRAN listing is given in Fig. 5-45. DISCR is used to obtain the times for activities 11–15 of the PERT network given in Fig. 5-43. The sampling procedure generates a random number and tests it against the break points in the distribution function, until the cumulative probability is greater than or equal to the random number. (In the main program, the probability mass function is converted to the distribution function

```
      FUNCTION DISCR(K)
      COMMON /UCOM1/ NREL(25),NRELP(25),NUMC(25),NCN(25),NCA(25),
     1CPROB(25,3),ACTME(25,3),LNODE,LACT,NSORC,NSINK
      RN=DRAND(1)
      DO 101 I=1,3
      IF (CPROB(K,I)-RN) 101,102,102
  101 CONTINUE
      CALL ERROR (17)
      CALL EXIT
  102 DISCR=ACTME(K,I)
      RETURN
C
      END
```

Figure 5-45. FORTRAN listing of function DISCR.

and stored in the array CPROB.) When this occurs, the activity time associated with the cumulative probability value is selected as the sample value.

It is possible to include a general subprogram in GASP IV to sample from a probability mass function. However, such a program has not been provided since the storage requirements for sampling from general probability mass functions can become excessive. A programmer can conveniently include a function similar to DISCR in simulation problems requiring sampling from probability mass functions. In this way, the subprogram can be tailored to meet the particular requirements of the simulation.

Simulation Procedure

Simulation of a PERT network is accomplished with the use of one type of event, an end-of-an-activity event. Each node of the network is an entity of the network model and has an attribute called the *number of releases*. The number of releases is the number of activities ending at the node. Each time an end-of-activity event occurs, the number of releases of the end node of the activity is decreased by one. When the number of releases for an end node is reduced to zero, the node is *realized*. All activities emanating from a node are scheduled to occur upon node realization. Since activities can be started only when some other activity ends, there is no need to have a separate event to start activities. When a node is realized, statistics are collected on the node. In addition, the activity and starting node of the activity that caused the node to be realized are recorded. These values are used to determine the critical path for a simulation run.

A file is used for each node of the network. File 1 is the event file, which contains the end-of-activity events. File J is used to store all activities emanating from node J. (Note that node numbers must be greater than 1.) When node J is released, the attributes of activities emanating from J are obtained using subroutine COPY. End-of-activity events are placed in the event file to occur at TNOW plus a sample drawn from the distribution type associated with the activity. Subroutine SAMPL is used to decode the distribution types. The attributes associated with each file are:

Attributes	File 1	File J (J = 2,L NODE)
1	End-of-activity time	Distribution type
2	Activity number*	Activity number
3	End node	End node
4	Start node	Start node

The non-GASP variables for this example are defined below:

Variable	Definition	Initial Values
ACTME(K,J)	The values for the time to perform activity K	See Table 5-3
CPROB(K,J)	Probability of obtaining Jth value of time to perform activity K on input; converted to the distribution function in the main program	See Table 5-3
J	Node number; J = 2,3 . . . ,LNODE	—
LACT	Largest activity number for the network	15
LNODE	Largest node number for the network	10
NCA(J)	Activity that is critical to node J in a given simulation run	0
NCN(J)	Node that is critical to node J in a given simulation run	0
NREL(J)	Number of releases remaining for node J	(2,1,3,1,1,2,2,3,0)
NRELP(J)	Initial number of releases for node J	(2,1,3,1,1,2,2,3,0)
NSORC	Source node number	10
NSINK	Sink node number	9
NUMC(K)	Number of times activity K is critical	0

* Since there is only one event type, an event code is not necessary. Therefore, the end-of-activity event is coded in subroutine EVNTS.

In the main program the source and sink node numbers and the largest node and activity numbers are defined. The number of releases for each node is then read into the array NREL and placed into NRELP. The probability mass functions are then read into the arrays CPROB and ACTME. CPROB is then converted to the distribution function. The number of times activity K is on the critical path NUMC(K) is initialized to zero. The program then calls GASP, which controls the simulation. Figure 5-46 gives the FORTRAN listing for the main program.

Simulation of the PERT network is started by inserting an initial event into the event file with an ending node equal to the source node of the network. No other initial events are stored in the event file. Attributes of activities emanating from node J are stored in file J. The initial file entries are established in subroutine DATIN through the reading of data cards.

Subroutine GASP starts the simulation by removing the first entry from the event file, which is the end-of-activity event with the source node as its end node. In subroutine EVNTS all activities having the source

```
      PROGRAM MAIN (INPUT,OUTPUT,TAPE5=INPUT,TAPE6=OUTPUT)
      DIMENSION NSET(200)
      COMMON QSET(200)
      COMMON /GCOM1/ ATRIB(25),JEVNT,MFA,MFE(100),MLE(100),MSTOP,NCRDR,N
     1NAPO,NNAPT,NNATR,NNFIL,NNQ(100),NNTRY,NPRNT,PPARM(50,4),TNOW,TTBEG
     2,TTCLR,TTFIN,TTRIB(25),TTSET
      COMMON /UCOM1/ NREL(25),NRELP(25),NUMC(25),NCN(25),NCA(25),
     1CPROB(25,3),ACTME(25,3),LNODE,LACT,NSORC,NSINK
      EQUIVALENCE (NSET(1),QSET(1))
C
C*****MAIN PROGRAM
C
      NCRDR=5
      NPRNT=6
      READ (NCRDR,105) LNODE,LACT,NSORC,NSINK
C
C*****READ THE NUMBER OF RELEASES (ACTIVITIES INCIDENT) ON EACH NODE.
C
      READ (NCRDR,105) (NREL(N),N=2,LNODE)
      DO 101 I=2,LNODE
C
C*****NRELP IS THE PERMANENT NUMBER OF RELEASES.
C
  101 NRELP(I)=NREL(I)
      DO 102 K=1,LACT
      READ (NCRDR,106) NACT,(CPROB(NACT,I),ACTME(NACT,I),I=1,3)
      IF (NACT.EQ.0) GO TO 103
      DO 102 I=2,3
      IM1=I-1
  102 CPROB(NACT,I)=CPROB(NACT,IM1)+CPROB(NACT,I)
  103 DO 104 K=1,LACT
  104 NUMC(K)=0
C
C*****NUMC(K) = NUMBER OF TIMES ACTIVITY K IS CRITICAL.
C
      CALL GASP
      CALL EXIT
C
  105 FORMAT (40I2)
  106 FORMAT (5X,I5,6F10.3)
C
      END
```

Figure 5-46 FORTRAN listing of the main program (Example 4).

node as their start node are given end-of-activity event times. The completion times for the activities are computed as the current time plus a value drawn from the appropriate distribution type. When this is accomplished, control is returned to subroutine GASP, and the next event is removed from the event file.

An activity that has just been completed has its end node stored in ATRIB(3). In subroutine EVNTS the number of releases for this end node is decreased by 1. A test is made to see if the end node is realized, which would permit more activities to be scheduled. If the end node is not realized, control is returned to subroutine GASP. This process of (1) scheduling activities, (2) testing to see if nodes are realized when end-of-activity events occur, and (3) scheduling more activities, is continued until the sink node of the network is realized. At this point, the entire network has been simulated, and statistics for one simulation run can be computed. Specific details involved in this process are given below in the description of the subroutines.

The flow chart and FORTRAN listing for subroutine EVNTS are given in Figs. 5-47 and 5-48, respectively. EVNTS is called each time an activity is completed. First, J is set as the end node of the completed activity. A test is made to see if J is the source node. If J is the source node, all activities emanating from it are released and subsequently scheduled by causing an end-of-activity event for each. After all released activities are scheduled, control is returned to the calling routine (GASP). If J is not the source node, the number of releases for node J is decreased by one. A test is made to determine if node J is realized. If node J is not realized, control is returned to GASP. If node J is realized, statistics are collected on node J including histogram information. Next, the critical activity and the node that was critical to node J are determined. These are the activity just completed and the starting node of the activity just completed.

A test is then made to see if the node released is the sink node, NSINK. If J is not the sink node, all activities emanating from it are released by copying their attributes and scheduling end-of-activity events. Function SAMPL(JDIST,JPRAM) is used to obtain the time to perform the activity. COLCT and HISTO are used to keep statistics on the activity durations. Control is then returned to GASP. If node J is the sink node, the critical path is determined and the counters associated with the activities on the critical path are increased by one. The critical path is determined by finding both the activity and the node that are critical to the sink node. The critical node is the starting node of the critical activity. The variables defining the critical activity and critical node are LCA and LCN, respectively. If LCN is not the source node, the activity

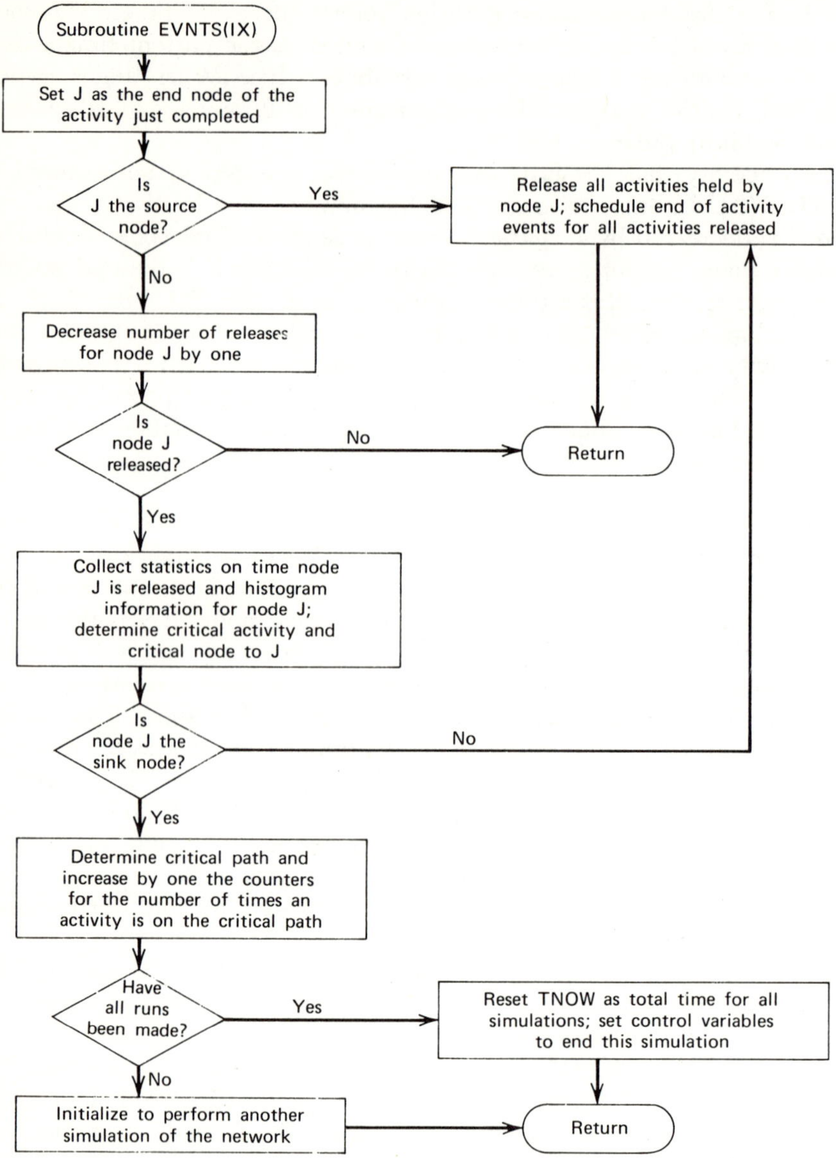

Figure 5-47 Flow chart of an end-of-activity event (Example 4).

critical to the critical node is determined and the counter for this new critical activity is increased by one. This weaving back through the network is continued until the source node is reached. Statements accomplishing the weaving procedure are given in Fig. 5-48, starting with statement 107.

In Example 4, NNRNS, is used as the number of times the network is to be simulated. Since no reports are desired until all 400 runs have been made, TNOW is set as the total time for all simulations so that statistics on the files calculated in subroutine PRNTQ will be accurate. The GASP IV control variables for obtaining GASP IV summary reports are set, and control is returned to GASP.

If all the runs have not been made, the number of runs is decreased by one. TNOW and the QQTIM vector are initialized to zero. The number of releases for each node is set to the initial number of releases for each node. An initial event that realizes the source node is put into the event file. Control is then returned to subroutine GASP, which starts a new simulation run.

The function SAMPL is given in Fig. 5-49. As can be seen, SAMPL decodes the distribution type and calls the appropriate random deviate generator to obtain an activity duration time. In Fig. 5-50 subroutine OTPUT is shown. Here the proportion of times an activity is critical, divided by the number of simulation runs, is computed. This information is printed in subroutine OTPUT.

A listing of the input data for the GASP IV simulation of the PERT network of Fig. 5-43 is shown in Fig. 5-51.

Simulation Reports

The GASP IV summary report for this example is given in Fig. 5-52.

A comparison of the average time to realize a node and the PERT expected times is given below:

Node	PERT Expected Time	Simulated Average Time
2	14	14.98
3	6	6.20
4	21	22.70
5	18	18.21
6	11	11.20
7	15	16.06
8	24	26.67
9	29	34.69

```
      SUBROUTINE EVNTS (IX)                                             EV4
      DIMENSION NSET(1)
      COMMON QSET(1)
      COMMON /GCOM1/ ATRIB(25),JEVNT,MFA,MFE(100),MLE(100),MSTOP,NCRDR,NGCOM1
     1NAPO,NNAPT,NNATR,NNFIL,NNQ(100),NNTRY,NPRNT,PPARM(50,4),TNOW,TTBEGGCOM1
     2,TTCLR,TTFIN,TTRIB(25),TTSET                                      GCOM1
      COMMON /GCOM5/ IIEVT,IISED(6),JJBEG,JJCLR,MMNIT,MMON,NNAME(3),NNCFGCOM5
     1I,NNDAY,NNPT,NNSET,NNPRJ,NNPRM,NNRNS,NNRUN,NNSTR,NNYR,SSEED(6)    GCOM5
      COMMON /GCOM6/ EENQ(100),IINN(100),KKRNK(100),MMAXQ(100),QQTIM(100GCOM6
     1),SSOBV(25,5),SSTPV(25,6),VVNQ(100)                               GCOM6
      COMMON /UCOM1/ NREL(25),NRELP(25),NUMC(25),NCN(25),NCA(25),       UCOM
     1CPROB(25,3),ACTME(25,3),LNODE,LACT,NSORC,NSINK                    UCOM
      EQUIVALENCE (NSET(1),QSET(1))                                     EQUIV
C                                                                       EV4
C*****SET J = TO THE END NODE OF THE ACTIVITY JUST COMPLETED.           EV4
C                                                                       EV4
      J=ATRIB(3)                                                        EV4
      IF (J-NSORC) 101,104,101                                          EV4
C                                                                       EV4
C*****FOR J NOT EQUAL TO NSORC, DECREMENT NUMBER OF RELEASES FOR NODE J.EV4
C                                                                       EV4
  101 NREL(J)=NREL(J)-1                                                 EV4
C                                                                       EV4
C*****TEST TO SEE IF J IS RELEASED.                                     EV4
C                                                                       EV4
      IF (NREL(J)) 103,103,102                                          EV4
  102 RETURN                                                            EV4
C                                                                       EV4
C*****J IS RELEASED. COLLECT STATISTICS ON THE TIME NODE J WAS RELEASED.EV4
C                                                                       EV4
  103 JM1=J-1                                                           EV4
      CALL COLCT (TNOW,JM1)                                             EV4
      CALL HISTO (TNOW,JM1)                                             EV4
C                                                                       EV4
C*****SET CRITICAL ACTIVITY TO J AS THE ACTIVITY JUST COMPLETED AND     EV4
C*****SET CRITICAL NODE TO J AS THE STARTING NODE OF THE ACTIVITY JUST  EV4
C*****COMPLETED.                                                        EV4
C                                                                       EV4
      NCA(J)=ATRIB(2)                                                   EV4
      NCN(J)=ATRIB(4)                                                   EV4
C                                                                       EV4
C*****DETERMINE IF J IS THE SINK NODE.                                  EV4
C                                                                       EV4
      IF (J-NSINK) 104,107,104                                          EV4
C                                                                       EV4
C*****RELEASE ALL ACTIVITIES HELD BY NODE J                             EV4
C                                                                       EV4
  104 NEXT=MFE(J)                                                       EV4
  105 IF (NEXT.EQ.0) GO TO 102                                          EV4
      CALL COPY (NEXT)                                                  EV4
      ISUC=NEXT+NNAPO                                                   EV4
      NEXT=NSET(ISUC)                                                   EV4
      JDIST=ATRIB(1)                                                    EV4
      JPRAM=ATRIB(2)                                                    EV4
      DEV=SAMPL(JDIST,JPRAM)                                            EV4
      NCC=LNODE-2+JPRAM                                                 EV4
      IF (NCC.GT.25) GO TO 106                                          EV4
      CALL COLCT (DEV,NCC)                                              EV4
      CALL HISTO (DEV,NCC)                                              EV4
      ATRIB(1)=TNOW+DEV                                                 EV4
  106 CALL FILEM (1)                                                    EV4
      GO TO 105                                                         EV4
C                                                                       EV4
C*****END OF 1 NETWORK SIMULATION CHECK END OF RUN                      EV4
C*****TRACE BACK THROUGH NETWORK TO DETERMINE CRITICAL ACTIVITIES.      EV4
C                                                                       EV4
  107 LCN=NSINK                                                         EV4
      LCA=NCA(NSINK)                                                    EV4
  108 NUMC(LCA)=NUMC(LCA)+1                                             EV4
      LCN=NCN(LCN)                                                      EV4
      IF (LCN-NSORC) 109,110,109                                        EV4
  109 LCA=NCA(LCN)                                                      EV4
```

Figure 5-48 FORTRAN listing of subroutine EVNTS (Example 4).

```
      GO TO 108
C
C*****TEST NUMBER OF TIMES THE NETWORK HAS BEEN SIMULATED.
C
  110 IF (NNRNS-1) 114,114,111
  111 NNRNS=NNRNS-1
C
C*****REVERSE FILE NUMBERS SO THAT ACTIVITIES SCHEDULED FOR PRECEEDING
C*****RUN ARE NOW ACTIVITIES TO BE SCHEDULED.
C
      TNOW=0.
      DO 112 IJ=1,LNODE
  112 QQTIM(IJ)=0.
C
C*****INSERT INITIAL EVENT.
C
      ATRIB(1)=0.
      ATRIB(2)=1.
      ATRIB(3)=NSORC
      CALL FILEM (1)
C
C*****RESET NUMBER OF RELEASES FOR EACH NODE.
C
      DO 113 I=2,LNODE
  113 NREL(I)=NRELP(I)
      RETURN
C
C*****END OF ALL SIMULATION RUNS.
C
  114 MSTOP=-1
C
C*****SINCE ALL STATISTICS WERE GATHERED FOR NRUNS TO OBTAIN APPROPRIATE
C*****VALUES FOR THE QUEUE STATISTICS, TNOW MUST BE SET = TO TOTAL TIME
C*****FOR ALL SIMULATIONS.  THIS VALUE IS IN SUMA(9,1).
C
      TNOW=SSOBV(NSINK-1,1)
      DO 115 K=1,NNFIL
  115 QQTIM(K)=TNOW
      RETURN
C
      END
```

Figure 5-48 (*continued*)

```
      FUNCTION SAMPL(JD,JP)
      COMMON /GCOM1/ ATRIB(25),JEVNT,MFA,MFE(100),MLE(100),MSTOP,NCRDR,NGCOM1
     1NAPO,NNAPT,NNATR,NNFIL,NNQ(100),NNTRY,NPRNT,PPARM(50,4),TNOW,TTBEGGCOM1
     2,TTCLR,TTFIN,TTRIB(25),TTSET
      GO TO (101,102,103,104,105,106,107,108,109), JD
  101 SAMPL=PPARM(JP,1)
      GO TO 110
  102 SAMPL=RNORM(JP,1)
      GO TO 110
  103 A=PPARM(JP,2)
      B=PPARM(JP,3)
      SAMPL=UNFRM(A,B,1)
      GO TO 110
  104 SAMPL=ERLNG(JP,1)
      GO TO 110
  105 SAMPL=RLOGN(JP,1)
      GO TO 110
  106 SAMPL=GAMA(JP,1)
      GO TO 110
  107 SAMPL=BETA(JP,1)
      GO TO 110
  108 SAMPL=TRIAG(JP,1)
      GO TO 110
  109 SAMPL=DISCR(JP)
  110 RETURN
C
      END
```

Figure 5-49 FORTRAN listing of function SAMPL (Example 4).

```
      SUBROUTINE OTPUT                                                  OT4    1
      COMMON /GCOM1/ ATRIB(25),JEVNT,MFA,MFE(100),MLE(100),MSTOP,NCRDR,NGCOM1  1
     1NAPO,NNAPT,NNATR,NNFIL,NNQ(100),NNTRY,NPRNT,PPARM(50,4),TNOW,TTBEGGCOM1  2
     2,TTCLR,TTFIN,TTRIB(25),TTSET                                      GCOM1  3
      COMMON /GCOM6/ EENQ(100),IINN(100),KKRNK(100),MMAXQ(100),QQTIM(100GCOM6  1
     1),SSOBV(25,5),SSTPV(25,6),VVNQ(100)                               GCOM6  2
      COMMON /UCOM1/ NREL(25),NRELP(25),NUMC(25),NCN(25),NCA(25),       UCOM   1
     1CPROB(25,3),ACTME(25,3),LNODE,LACT,NSORC,NSINK                    UCOM   2
C                                                                       OT4    2
C*****LET Y BE THE NUMBER OF SIMULATION RUNS.                           OT4    3
C                                                                       OT4    4
      NSM1=NSINK-1                                                      OT4    5
      Y=SSOBV(NSM1,3)                                                   OT4    6
C                                                                       OT4    7
C*****COMPUTE PROPORTION OF TIME ACTIVITY I WAS CRITICAL.               OT4    8
C                                                                       OT4    9
      DO 101 I=1,LACT                                                   OT4   10
      XNUM=NUMC(I)                                                      OT4   11
      XNUM=XNUM/Y                                                       OT4   12
  101 WRITE (NPRNT,102) I,XNUM                                          OT4   13
      RETURN                                                            OT4   14
C                                                                       OT4   15
  102 FORMAT (27X,35H THE CRITICALITY INDEX FOR ACTIVITY,I4,3H IS,F10.6)OT4   16
C                                                                       OT4   17
      END                                                               OT4   18
```

Figure 5-50 FORTRAN listing of subroutine OTPUT (Example 4).

For those nodes that are on a serial path and do not require parallel activities to be performed, the PERT estimates are good. This is the case for nodes 3, 5, and 6. In all other cases the average times from the simulation are greater than the expected times obtained from the PERT calculations. These figures were anticipated since the PERT calculations for the expected times take into account only the longest expected path to a node. Because other paths may have a time greater than that of the longest expected path, the PERT calculation is optimistic. The time to complete the project represented by the network is given by the time to realize node 9. The histogram for the realization time of node 9 is graphed in Fig. 5-53 with a histogram computed from the normal distribution assumed for node 9 by the PERT method. From the histogram, the estimate of the probability of completing the project by the PERT expected time of 29 is approximately 0.19.

The file printout information of the GASP IV summary report revealed an average of 3.08 entries in file 1. This means that on the average 3.08 activities were simultaneously performed. Also recorded was that, at most, six activities were being performed at one time in any simulation run.

In Fig. 5-54 the criticality index for each activity is shown. It is seen that there is more than one critical path for the PERT network, depending on the actual activity times.

In this example statistical estimates of the parameters and histograms for the times to perform each activity were obtained. A comparison of the values given in Table 5-3 with values presented in Fig. 5-52 indicate

```
10151009
020103010 1020203
        11    .10       1.00        .50       3.00        .40      6.0
        12    .15       0.00        .70       2.00        .15      4.00
        13    .20       2.00        .40       4.00        .40     10.00      USER
        14    .40       2.00        .30      10.00        .30     14.00
        15    .25       3.00        .50       5.00        .25      7.00
---------------------------------------------------------------------------
PRITSKER            4       6    30 1973   400                               1
---------------------------------------------------------------------------
   23      0   23    10     0     1    25     4     10   150                 2
---------------------------------------------------------------------------
3          1NODE 2
3          2NODE 3
3          3NODE 4
3          4NODE 5
3          5NODE 6
3          6NODE 7
3          7NODE 8                                                           3
3          8NODE 9
3           9 1 RLOGN
3          10 2 ERLNG
3          11 3 UNFRM
3          12 4 GAMA
3          13 5 BETA
3          14 6 UNFRM
3          15 7 RNORM
3          16 8 ERLNG
3          17 9 CONST
3          1810 TRIAG
3          1911 DISCR
3          2012 DISCR
3          2113 DISCR
3          2214 DISCR
3          2315 DISCR
---------------------------------------------------------------------------
5          1NODE 2               10 8.0      2.0
5          2NODE 3               10 1.0      2.0
5          3NODE 4               1016.0      2.0
5          4NODE 5               1012.0      2.0
5          5NODE 6               10 5.0      2.0
5          6NODE 7               1010.0      2.0
5          7NODE 8               1016.0      2.0
5          8NODE 9               2022.0      2.0
5           9 1 RLOGN            10 6.5       .50
5          10 2 ERLNG            10 0.0      1.50                            5
5          11 3 UNFRM            10 4.0      1.0
5          12 4 GAMA             10 7.0      2.0
5          13 5 BETA             10 4.0      1.0
5          14 6 UNFRM            10 9.0      1.0
5          15 7 RNORM            10 3.0       .50
5          16 8 ERLNG            10 0.0      2.0
5          17 9 CONST             5 6.0       .50
5          1810 TRIAG            10 1.25     1.0
5          1911 DISCR            10 0.0      1.0
5          2012 DISCR            10 0.0      0.5
5          2113 DISCR            10 1.0      1.0
5          2214 DISCR            10 3.0      1.0
5          2315 DISCR            10 0.0      1.0
---------------------------------------------------------------------------
     1     1     1     1     1     1     1     1     1     1                 6
---------------------------------------------------------------------------
     1     1     1     1     1     1     1     1     1     1                 7
---------------------------------------------------------------------------
10         1      2.283      -999.       100.      0.198
10         2      6.000         0.       100.      1.000                     10
10         3      0.000         4.        10.      0.000
10         4      1.500         0.       100.      9.333
10         5      4.000         0.        12.      2.000
10         6      0.000         9.        17.      0.000
10         7      5.000         0.       100.      1.000
10         8      4.000         0.       100.      2.000
10         9      7.000         0.         0.      0.000
10        10      3.000         1.         8.      0.000
---------------------------------------------------------------------------
     0     1     1     1           0           0 163157                      11
---------------------------------------------------------------------------
12         1        0.0        1.0       10.0
12        10        5.0        1.0        2.0       10.0
12        10        4.0        2.0        3.0       10.0
12         2        6.0        4.0        9.0        2.0
12         2        3.0        3.0        4.0        2.0
12         3        7.0        5.0        2.0        3.0
12         3        3.0        6.0        4.0        3.0
12         3        2.0        7.0        6.0        3.0
12         4        4.0        8.0        9.0        4.0
12         6        1.0        9.0        5.0        6.0
12         6        8.0       10.0        7.0        6.0
12         6        9.0       11.0        7.0        6.0                     12
12         5        9.0       12.0        4.0        5.0
12         5        9.0       13.0        8.0        5.0
12         7        9.0       14.0        8.0        7.0
12         8        9.0       15.0        9.0        9.0
12         0
```

Figure 5-51 Listing of data cards for Example 4.

GASP SUMMARY REPORT

SIMULATION PROJECT NUMBER 4 BY PRITSKER

DATE 6/ 30/ 1973 RUN NUMBER 1 OF 1

CURRENT TIME = 1.3878E+04

PARAMETER SET	1 =	2.2830E+00	-9.9900E+02	1.0000E+02	1.9800E-01
PARAMETER SET	2 =	6.0000E+00	0.	1.0000E+02	1.0000E+00
PARAMETER SET	3 =	0.	4.0000E+00	1.0000E+01	0.
PARAMETER SET	4 =	1.5000E+00	0.	1.0000E+02	9.3330E+00
PARAMETER SET	5 =	4.0000E+00	0.	1.2000E+01	2.0000E+00
PARAMETER SET	6 =	0.	9.0000E+00	1.7000E+01	0.
PARAMETER SET	7 =	5.0000E+00	0.	1.0000E+02	1.0000E+00
PARAMETER SET	8 =	4.0000E+00	0.	1.0000E+02	2.0000E+00
PARAMETER SET	9 =	7.0000E+00	0.	0.	0.
PARAMETER SET	10 =	3.0000E+00	1.0000E+00	8.0000E+00	0.

STATISTICS FOR VARIABLES BASED ON OBSERVATION

	MEAN	STD DEV	SD OF MEAN	CV	MINIMUM	MAXIMUM	OBS
NODE 2	1.4985E+01	6.6327E+00	3.3163E-01	4.4262E-01	7.3763E+00	6.2517E+01	400
NODE 3	6.1973E+00	6.7208E+00	3.3604E-01	1.0844E+00	6.8207E-03	5.3738E+01	400
NODE 4	2.2698E+01	6.6873E+00	3.3436E-01	2.9462E-01	1.2842E+01	6.9173E+01	400
NODE 5	1.8208E+01	6.7619E+00	3.3810E-01	3.7137E-01	9.7624E+00	6.5871E+01	400
NODE 6	1.1208E+01	6.7619E+00	3.3810E-01	6.0331E-01	2.7624E+00	5.8871E+01	400
NODE 7	1.6060E+01	6.8337E+00	3.4168E-01	4.2551E-01	5.1700E+00	6.1871E+01	400
NODE 8	2.6672E+01	7.3761E+00	3.6881E-01	2.7655E-01	1.3817E+01	7.0968E+01	400
NODE 9	3.4694E+01	7.4005E+00	3.7003E-01	2.1331E-01	2.2215E+01	7.6871E+01	400
1 RLOGN	1.0089E+01	1.9805E+00	9.9025E-02	1.9631E-01	6.1515E+00	1.8043E+01	400
2 ERLNG	6.1979E+00	6.7208E+00	3.3604E-01	1.0844E+00	6.8207E-03	5.3738E+01	400
3 UNFRM	6.9628E+00	1.7575E+00	8.7876E-02	2.5242E-01	4.0216E+00	9.9954E+00	400
4 GAMA	1.3903E+01	4.2471E+00	2.1235E-01	3.0548E-01	5.6023E+00	2.8278E+01	400
5 BETA	8.0763E+00	2.1643E+00	1.0822E-01	2.6799E-01	1.4743E+00	1.1788E+01	400
6 UNFRM	1.2993E+01	2.3332E+00	1.1665E-01	1.7957E-01	9.0165E+00	1.6987E+01	400
7 RNORM	5.0101E+00	1.0814E+00	5.4069E-02	2.1584E-01	2.0361E+00	9.1611E+00	400
8 ERLNG	7.7641E+00	5.1449E+00	2.5720E-01	6.6254E-01	1.3620E-01	3.2607E+01	400
9 CONST	7.0000E+00	0.	0.	0.	7.0000E+00	7.0000E+00	400
10 TRIAG	3.9713E+00	1.5147E+00	7.5737E-02	3.8142E-01	1.1514E+00	7.8631E+00	400
11 DISCR	3.9075E+00	1.6974E+00	8.4870E-02	4.3439E-01	1.0000E+00	6.0000E+00	400
12 DISCR	1.9250E+00	1.0897E+00	5.4483E-02	5.6605E-01	0.	4.0000E+00	400
13 DISCR	5.9550E+00	3.3370E+00	1.6685E-01	5.6038E-01	2.0000E+00	1.0000E+01	400
14 DISCR	7.8000E+00	5.2649E+00	2.6320E-01	6.7487E-01	2.0000E+00	1.4000E+01	400
15 DISCR	5.1200E+00	1.3304E+00	6.6521E-02	2.5985E-01	3.0000E+00	7.0000E+00	400

Figure 5-52 GASP IV summary report for PERT network simulation.

HISTOGRAM NUMBER 8

NODE 9

OBSV FREQ	RELA FREQ	CUML FREQ	UPPER CELL LIMIT
0	0.000	0.000	2.2000E+01
7	.017	.017	2.4000E+01
18	.045	.062	2.6000E+01
28	.070	.132	2.8000E+01
42	.105	.237	3.0000E+01
67	.167	.405	3.2000E+01
65	.162	.567	3.4000E+01
44	.110	.677	3.6000E+01
29	.072	.750	3.8000E+01
30	.075	.825	4.0000E+01
17	.042	.867	4.2000E+01
16	.040	.907	4.4000E+01
7	.017	.925	4.6000E+01
7	.017	.942	4.8000E+01
9	.022	.965	5.0000E+01
5	.012	.977	5.2000E+01
3	.007	.985	5.4000E+01
0	0.000	.985	5.6000E+01
0	0.000	.985	5.8000E+01
0	0.000	.985	6.0000E+01
1	.002	.987	6.2000E+01
5	.012	1.000	INF

400			

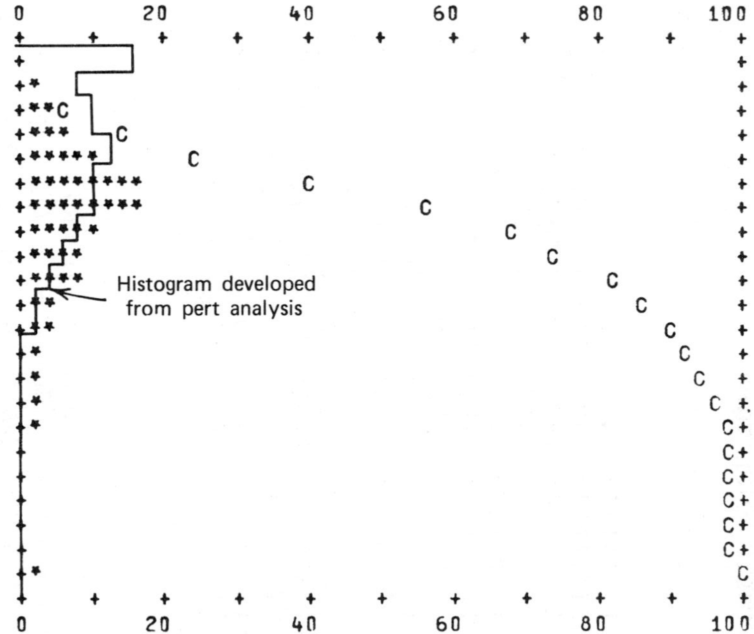

Figure 5-53 Histogram of time to complete PERT network and PERT assumed distribution.

```
                    **INTERMEDIATE RESULTS**

THE CRITICALITY INDEX FOR ACTIVITY   1 IS   .115000
THE CRITICALITY INDEX FOR ACTIVITY   2 IS   .885000
THE CRITICALITY INDEX FOR ACTIVITY   3 IS   .215000
THE CRITICALITY INDEX FOR ACTIVITY   4 IS   .187500
THE CRITICALITY INDEX FOR ACTIVITY   5 IS   .287500
THE CRITICALITY INDEX FOR ACTIVITY   6 IS   .037500
THE CRITICALITY INDEX FOR ACTIVITY   7 IS   .560000
THE CRITICALITY INDEX FOR ACTIVITY   8 IS   .295000
THE CRITICALITY INDEX FOR ACTIVITY   9 IS   .262500
THE CRITICALITY INDEX FOR ACTIVITY  10 IS   .175000
THE CRITICALITY INDEX FOR ACTIVITY  11 IS   .122500
THE CRITICALITY INDEX FOR ACTIVITY  12 IS   .042500
THE CRITICALITY INDEX FOR ACTIVITY  13 IS   .220000
THE CRITICALITY INDEX FOR ACTIVITY  14 IS   .237500
THE CRITICALITY INDEX FOR ACTIVITY  15 IS   .517500
```

Figure 5-54 Criticality indices for activities in PERT network simulation.

that the GASP IV random deviate generators yield the parameters desired for the various distribution types. Figure 5-55 presents selected histograms to indicate that the shape of the distribution of the samples is as expected.

EXAMPLE 5—SIMULATION OF DECISION RULES FOR SCHEDULING ACTIVITIES WHEN RESOURCES ARE LIMITED

Statement of the Problem

As shown in Example 4, activities and their sequence in a particular project can be represented in network form. In this example each activity requires a specified constant amount of time. However, to perform an activity requires the use of one or more of the following three resource types: workspace, mechanics, and technicians.

Problems of this type are called *resource allocation problems under limited resources.* A large amount of research has been devoted to these problems (24,92). One aspect of resource allocation research is the development of rules for determining the order to perform the activities when limited resources restrict the number of activities that can be performed at one time. Example 5 presents a GASP IV simulation approach to this problem.

The network to be analyzed is presented in Fig. 5-56 and is adapted from an example presented in the reference manual on ASTRA(6). A tabular description of each activity and its resource requirements is presented in Table 5-4. Resources are assumed to be required for the complete duration of an activity. One workspace, four mechanics, and two technicians are available to perform the activities.

Simulation Objectives

The objective of this example is to determine the relative effectiveness of rules for dispatching activities that require multiple resources when resources are limited.

For each dispatching rule, the following statistics will be obtained: (1) duration of the total project, (2) utilization of each resource type, and (3) a schedule of the start times for each activity of the project.

Special Features

In this example the use of simulation to gain familiarity with the effect of different dispatching rules in resource allocation problems is featured. No random variables are generated; the problem is completely deter-

Table 5-4 Resource Requirements for a Network of Activities Describing a Maintenance Problem

Activity Number	Start Node	End Node	Workspace	Mechanics	Technicians	Duration
1	2	3	1	3	0	3
2	2	4	0	0	2	9
3	2	5	1	2	0	2
4	2	6	0	1	0	1
5	2	7	1	2	0	2
6	3	8	0	4	1	4
7	4	9	0	0	2	8
8	5	12	0	2	0	1
9 (Dummy)	6	7	0	0	0	0
10	6	11	0	1	0	1
11	7	11	1	1	0	2
12	8	9	1	3	0	5
13	9	10	0	1	1	1
14	9	10	1	1	2	2
15	11	9	0	1	1	1
16	12	9	0	2	0	3

```
                                  **HISTOGRAM NUMBER 11**

                                         3 UNFRM

OBSV    RELA     CUML        UPPER
FREQ    FREQ     FREQ      CELL LIMIT     0         20        40        60        80        100
                                          +    +    +    +    +    +    +    +    +    +    +
   0   0.000    0.000      4.0000E+00     +                                                 +
  73    .182     .182      5.0000E+00     +*********                                        +
  69    .172     .355      6.0000E+00     +*********        C                               +
  67    .167     .522      7.0000E+00     +********                 C                       +
  61    .152     .675      8.0000E+00     +********                         C               +
  60    .150     .825      9.0000E+00     +*******                                 C        +
  70    .175    1.000      1.0000E+01     +*********                                        C
   0   0.000    1.000      1.1000E+01     +                                                 C
   0   0.000    1.000      1.2000E+01     +                                                 C
   0   0.000    1.000      1.3000E+01     +                                                 C
   0   0.000    1.000      1.4000E+01     +                                                 C
   0   0.000    1.000         INF         +                                                 C
 ---                                      +    +    +    +    +    +    +    +    +    +    +
 400                                      0         20        40        60        80        100
```

```
                                         **HISTOGRAM NUMBER 13**

                                                5 BETA

OBSV      RELA      CUML        UPPER
FREQ      FREQ      FREQ     CELL LIMIT      0         20        40        60        80        100
                                             +    +    +    +    +    +    +    +    +    +    +
  18      .045      .045     4.0000E+00      +**                                               +
  18      .045      .090     5.0000E+00      +** C                                             +
  31      .077      .167     6.0000E+00      +****   C                                         +
  57      .142      .310     7.0000E+00      +*******      C                                   +
  54      .135      .445     8.0000E+00      +*******             C                            +
  70      .175      .620     9.0000E+00      +*********                    C                   +
  65      .162      .782     1.0000E+01      +********                             C           +
  54      .135      .917     1.1000E+01      +*******                                     C    +
  33      .082     1.000     1.2000E+01      +****                                             C
   0     0.000     1.000     1.3000E+01      +                                                 C
   0     0.000     1.000     1.4000E+01      +                                                 C
   0     0.000     1.000        INF          +                                                 C
 ---                                         +    +    +    +    +    +    +    +    +    +    +
 400                                         0         20        40        60        80        100
```

Figure 5-55 Histograms of selected activity durations obtained in Example 4.

```
                         **HISTOGRAM NUMBER 15**

                                7 RNORM

OBSV     RELA    CUML       UPPER     
FREQ     FREQ    FREQ     CELL LIMIT    0        20        40        60        80       100
                                        +    +    +    +    +    +    +    +    +    +    +
  14     .035     .035    3.0000E+00    +**                                               +
  22     .055     .090    3.5000E+00    +***C                                             +
  33     .082     .172    4.0000E+00    +****    C                                        +
  55     .137     .310    4.5000E+00    +*******       C                                  +
  71     .177     .487    5.0000E+00    +*********              C                         +
  77     .192     .680    5.5000E+00    +**********                       C               +
  56     .140     .820    6.0000E+00    +*******                                 C        +
  45     .112     .932    6.5000E+00    +******                                        C  +
  18     .045     .977    7.0000E+00    +**                                              C+
   5     .012     .990    7.5000E+00    +*                                               C+
   1     .002     .992    8.0000E+00    +                                                 C
   3     .007    1.000       INF        +                                                 C
 ---                                    +    +    +    +    +    +    +    +    +    +    +
 400                                    0        20        40        60        80       100
```

```
                                  **HISTOGRAM NUMBER 16**

                                         8 ERLNG

OBSV     RELA     CUML       UPPER
FREQ     FREQ     FREQ    CELL LIMIT    0        20        40        60        80        100
                                        +    +    +    +    +    +    +    +    +    +    +
   0    0.000    0.000    0.            +                                                 +
  31     .077     .077    2.0000E+00    +****                                             +
  73     .182     .260    4.0000E+00    +*********    C                                   +
  77     .192     .452    6.0000E+00    +**********             C                         +
  66     .165     .617    8.0000E+00    +********                       C                 +
  46     .115     .732    1.0000E+01    +******                               C           +
  31     .077     .810    1.2000E+01    +****                                    C        +
  27     .067     .877    1.4000E+01    +***                                         C    +
  15     .037     .915    1.6000E+01    +**                                            C  +
  13     .032     .947    1.8000E+01    +**                                             C +
  10     .025     .972    2.0000E+01    +*                                               C+
  11     .027    1.000       INF        +*                                                C
 ---                                    +    +    +    +    +    +    +    +    +    +    +
 400                                    0        20        40        60        80        100
```

Figure 5-55 *(continued)*

HISTOGRAM NUMBER 18

10 TRIAG

```
OBSV    RELA    CUML       UPPER
FREQ    FREQ    FREQ    CELL LIMIT    0        20        40        60        80       100
                                      +    +    +    +    +    +    +    +    +    +    +
   2    .005    .005    1.2500E+00    +                                                 +
  49    .122    .127    2.2500E+00    +******                                           +
  94    .235    .362    3.2500E+00    +************     C                               +
 101    .252    .615    4.2500E+00    +*************                 C                  +
  71    .177    .792    5.2500E+00    +*********                              C         +
  42    .105    .897    6.2500E+00    +*****                                       C    +
  33    .082    .980    7.2500E+00    +****                                            C+
   8    .020   1.000    8.2500E+00    +*                                                C
   0   0.000   1.000    9.2500E+00    +                                                 C
   0   0.000   1.000    1.0250E+01    +                                                 C
   0   0.000   1.000    1.1250E+01    +                                                 C
   0   0.000   1.000       INF        +                                                 C
 ---                                  +    +    +    +    +    +    +    +    +    +    +
 400                                  0        20        40        60        80       100
```

```
                                      **HISTOGRAM NUMBER 21**

                                            13 DISCR

OBSV     RELA      CUML        UPPER
FREQ     FREQ      FREQ     CELL LIMIT      0        20        40        60        80       100
                                            +    +    +    +    +    +    +    +    +    +    +
   0    0.000     0.000     1.0000E+00      +                                                  +
  80     .200      .200     2.0000E+00      +**********                                        +
   0    0.000      .200     3.0000E+00      +          C                                       +
 163     .407      .607     4.0000E+00      +********************         C                    +
   0    0.000      .607     5.0000E+00      +                              C                   +
   0    0.000      .607     6.0000E+00      +                              C                   +
   0    0.000      .607     7.0000E+00      +                              C                   +
   0    0.000      .607     8.0000E+00      +                              C                   +
   0    0.000      .607     9.0000E+00      +                              C                   +
 157     .392     1.000     1.0000E+01      +********************                              C
   0    0.000     1.000     1.1000E+01      +                                                  C
   0    0.000     1.000        INF          +                                                  C
 ---                                        +    +    +    +    +    +    +    +    +    +    +
 400                                        0        20        40        60        80       100
```

Figure 5-55 *(continued)*

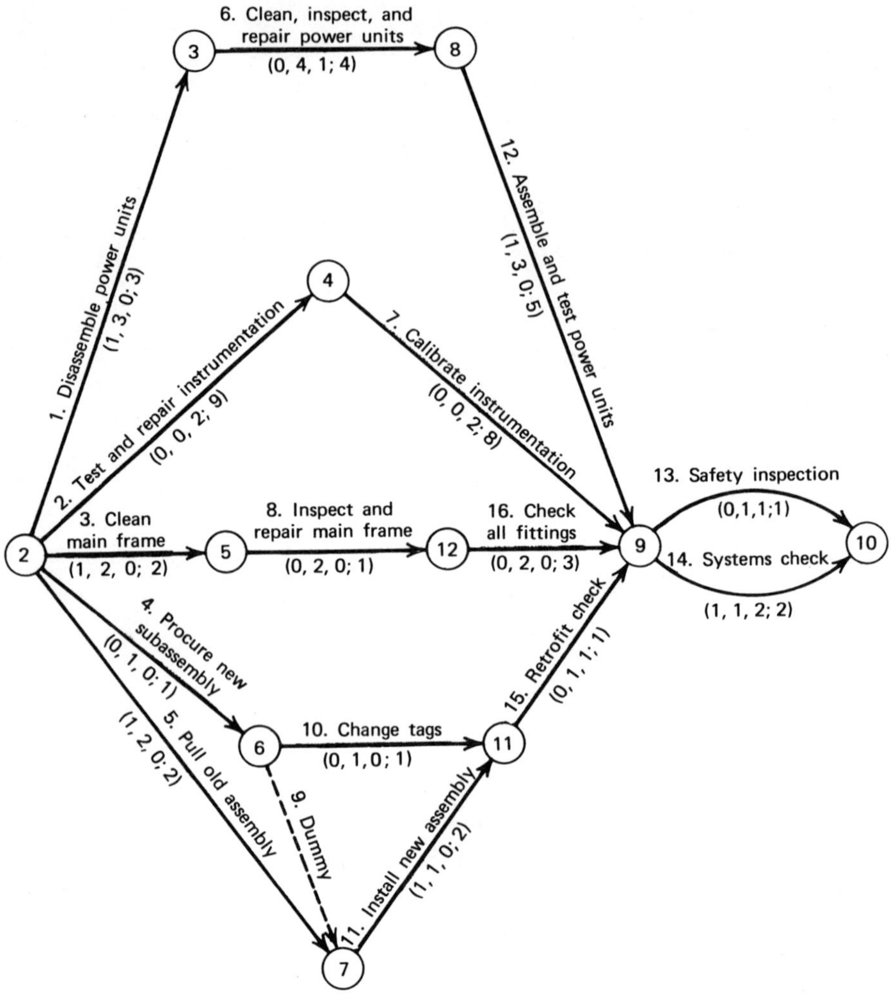

Figure 5-56 Network of activities describing a maintenance problem. The vector (w,m,t;d) specifies that the activity requires "w" work spaces, "m" mechanics, "t" technicians, and "d" time units. Reprinted by permission of the General Electric Company from "GE-400 Series Resource Allocation (ASTRA)," General Electric Company, © 1965.

ministic. Simulation is used to dispatch the activities in a manner dictated by various decision rules. Another feature is a special routine that locates an entry in a file if three of its attributes are less than three specified values. The use of the array PPARM for storing attributes is also illustrated.

Simulation Procedure

The simulation of a network for studying dispatching rules is accomplished with only one event. Therefore, subroutine EVNTS is used as the event routine.

The network aspects of this problem are similar to those described in Example 4. Each node, N, of the network has a variable NREL(N) associated with it that defines the number of releases associated with the node. Each time an end-of-activity event occurs, the number of releases at the end node is decreased by one. If the number of releases for the node is zero, the node is realized, and any activities emanating from the node can be started. Whether or not an activity is actually started depends on the resources available and the resources required to perform the activity. Recall that in PERT networks, as soon as all predecessors to an activity are completed, the activity is started. In resource problems an additional constraint due to limited resources may delay the starting of activities even though all of its predecessors are completed.

The resources available for use on activities are changed at two times. First, when an activity is scheduled to begin the resources available are decreased by the amount needed for the activity. Second, when an activity is completed the resources available are increased by the amount that was used in performing the activity. The array RESA(I) is used to store the amount of resource type I available for dispatching. RESA(I) is changed accordingly at the above two points in time.

Activities emanating from node N are stored in file N. Since file 1 is the event file, a node number of 1 is prohibited. A file is used to store the activities that have been released and are waiting for resources to be scheduled. The number of the file for released activities, NFRA, is the largest node number plus one (MNODE + 1).

When node N is released, the activities stored in file N are copied into file NFRA. A comparison of the activities in file NFRA is then made in accordance with a dispatching priority method, and the activity with the highest priority is dispatched. Dispatching continues until insufficient resources are available to perform any activity. When this occurs, another end-of-activity event is processed, which makes resources available and the dispatching process is repeated.

When the sink node of the network is realized, one dispatching rule has been evaluated. Since the simulation is deterministic, the same results would be obtained if the simulation were repeated. However, changing the priority rule changes the dispatching of activities. This is accomplished in subroutine EVNTS after each complete simulation of the network.

The duration and the resources required for activity I are stored in row I of the array PPARM as shown below:

PPARM(I,1) = number of workspaces required for activity I.
PPARM(I,2) = number of mechanics required for activity I.
PPARM(I,3) = number of technicians required for activity I.
PPARM(I,4) = duration of activity I.

This illustrates that the PPARM array can be used for purposes other than storing parameters of distributions from which samples are to be obtained. An advantage to using PPARM is that input and output is automatically provided for the PPARM array.

The definitions of the non-GASP and their initial values as used in Example 5 are:

Variable	Definition	Initial Value
BESTP	Best priority computed	0
DRULE(IP)	Description of priority rule IP	Input
HORL(IP)	Indicator to specify if priority rule is low-value-first or high-value-first: −1 low-values-first; +1 high-values-first	Input
I	Resource type; I = 1,2,3	—
IP	Code for scheduling priority rule	1
LOCBA	Location of the best activity in file NFRA	0
MACT	Largest activity number	16
MNODE	Largest node number	13
N	End node number	—
NFRA	Number of the file of released activities	MNODE + 1 = 14
NREL(N)	Number of releases remaining for node N; N = 2, . . . , 12.	(1,1,1,1,1,2,1,4,2,1)
NRELP(N)	Initial number of releases for node N; N = 2, . . . , 12.	(1,1,1,1,1,2,1,4,2,1)

NRESC	Number of resources	3
NSINK	Number of the sink node	10
NSORC	Number of the source node	2
PRITY	Calculated value of priority	—
RESA(I)	Number of units of resource I available during the simulation	(1,4,2)
RESAP(I)	Initial number of units of resource I available	(1,4,2)
REUSE(I)	Time integrated utilization of resource I	(0,0,0)

In file 1, attribute 1 is the event time, attribute 2 is the end node of the activity (an event code is not necessary since there is only one event), and attribute 3 is the parameter set (row of PPARM) where the duration and resource requirements for the activities are stored. All other files in Example 5 use attributes 2 and 3 only. Note that the attribute definitions for Example 5 are different than those presented in Example 4 to emphasize that attribute definitions are both problem and user oriented.

The FORTRAN listing for the main program of Example 5 is given in Fig. 5-57. It initializes the non-GASP variables and calls subroutine GASP. In this example NNRNS is used as the number of decision rules to be tested. The decision rules are changed in the end-of-activity event where NNRNS is updated. In this manner, multiple runs for different decision rules can be obtained without returning to subroutine GASP or subroutine DATIN. Direct calls to subroutine INTLC are used to initialize non-GASP variables between simulations of the network. The FORTRAN listing of subroutine INTLC is given in Fig. 5-58.

Since there is only one event type associated with this simulation, subroutine EVNTS is used as the event routine. Subroutine EVNTS performs all operations required when (1) the end of an activity event occurs and (2) a simulation of the network is completed. This latter task involves establishing a new decision rule and initializing the variables to start a new simulation. The decision rules to be tested are:

1. Dispatch activity with the shortest duration time first.
2. Dispatch activity with the longest duration time first.
3. Dispatch activity with the smallest requirement for workspace first.
4. Dispatch activity with the lowest requirement for mechanics first.
5. Dispatch activity with the lowest requirement for technicians first.
6. Dispatch activity whose end node has the least number of releases first.

```
      PROGRAM MAIN (INPUT,OUTPUT,TAPE5=INPUT,TAPE6=OUTPUT)              MX5      1
      DIMENSION NSET(1000)                                              DIM      1
      COMMON QSET(1000)                                                 COM      1
      COMMON /GCOM1/ ATRIB(25),JEVNT,MFA,MFE(100),MLE(100),MSTOP,NCRDR,NGCOM1    1
     1NAPO,NNAPT,NNATR,NNFIL,NNQ(100),NNTRY,NPRNT,PPARM(50,4),TNOW,TTBEGGCOM1    2
     2,TTCLR,TTFIN,TTRIB(25),TTSET                                      GCOM1    3
      COMMON /UCOM1/NREL(25),NRELP(25),RESA(3),RESAP(3),REUSE(3),IP,    UCOM1    1
     1 NRULE,NFRA,NSORC,NSINK,MACT,MNODE,NRESC,HORL(10),DRULE(10,3)     UCOM1    2
      EQUIVALENCE(NSET(1),QSET(1))                                      EQUIV    1
      NCRDR=5                                                           MX5      2
      NPRNT=6                                                           MX5      3
C                                                                       MX5      4
C*****READ THE SOURCE AND SINK NODE NUMBERS, AND THE NUMBER OF          MX5      5
C*****RESOURCES, NODES, AND ACTIVITIES.                                 MX5      6
C                                                                       MX5      7
      READ (NCRDR,101) NSORC,NSINK,MACT,MNODE,NRESC                     MX5      8
      WRITE (NPRNT,102) NSORC,NSINK,MACT,MNODE,NRESC                    MX5      9
      NFRA=MNODE+1                                                      MX5     10
      IP=1                                                              MX5     11
C                                                                       MX5     12
C*****READ NUMBER OF RELEASES FOR NODES, RESOURCE AVAILABILITIES AND    MX5     13
C*****DECISION RULE DESCRIPTORS.                                        MX5     14
C                                                                       MX5     15
      READ (NCRDR,104) (NRELP(I),I=1,MNODE)                             MX5     16
      WRITE (NPRNT,103) (NRELP(I),I=1,MNODE)                            MX5     17
      READ (NCRDR,106) (RESAP(I),I=1,NRESC)                             MX5     18
      WRITE (NPRNT,105) (RESAP(I),I=1,NRESC)                            MX5     19
      READ (NCRDR,101) NRULE                                            MX5     20
      READ (NCRDR,107) ((HORL(I),(DRULE(I,J),J=1,3)),I=1,NRULE)         MX5     21
      WRITE (NPRNT,108) NRULE,((HORL(I),(DRULE(I,J),J=1,3)),I=1,NRULE)  MX5     22
      CALL GASP                                                         MX5     23
C                                                                       MX5     24
  101 FORMAT (5I10)                                                     MX5     25
  102 FORMAT (51H      NSORC      NSINK       MACT      MNODE      NRESC/1X,MX5     26
     15I10)                                                             MX5     27
  103 FORMAT (21H (NRELP(I),I=1,MNODE)/(10I5))                          MX5     28
  104 FORMAT (15I5)                                                     MX5     29
  105 FORMAT (21H (RESAP(I),I=1,NRESC)/(10F5.0))                        MX5     30
  106 FORMAT (3F5.2)                                                    MX5     31
  107 FORMAT (F5.0,3A4)                                                 MX5     32
  108 FORMAT (7H NRULE=,I5/12H HORL  DRULE/(1X,F5.0,2X,3A4))            MX5     33
C                                                                       MX5     34
      END                                                               MX5     35
```

Figure 5-57 FORTRAN listing of the main program (Example 5).

```
      SUBROUTINE INTLC                                                  IC5      1
      COMMON /UCOM1/NREL(25),NRELP(25),RESA(3),RESAP(3),REUSE(3),IP,    UCOM1    1
     1 NRULE,NFRA,NSORC,NSINK,MACT,MNODE,NRESC,HORL(10),DRULE(10,3)     UCOM1    2
C                                                                       IC5      2
C*****RESET RESOURCE AVAILABILITY AND USAGE AND NODE RELEASES.          IC5      3
C                                                                       IC5      4
      DO 101 I=1,NRESC                                                  IC5      5
      RESA(I)=RESAP(I)                                                  IC5      6
  101 REUSE(I)=0.0                                                      IC5      7
C                                                                       IC5      8
C     RESET NODE RELEASES                                               IC5      9
C                                                                       IC5     10
      DO 102 I=1,MNODE                                                  IC5     11
  102 NREL(I)=NRELP(I)                                                  IC5     12
      RETURN                                                            IC5     13
C                                                                       IC5     14
      END                                                               IC5     15
```

Figure 5-58 FORTRAN listing of subroutine INTLC (Example 5).

7. Dispatch activity whose end node has the greatest number of releases first.

Since these dispatching rules can result in ties, a tie-breaking procedure is required. Ties in Example 5 are broken by selecting the activity that has been waiting the longest for dispatching; that is, the one that was released earliest.

The flow chart and FORTRAN listing for subroutine EVNTS are given in Figs. 5-59 and 5-60. Since an event code is not necessary, the argument N of subroutine EVNTS is used as the end node of the activity being completed. In subroutine GASP, the argument for EVNTS is always set equal to ATRIB(2), which, in this example, is the end node number of an activity.

If the end node is the source node (NSORC), or if the end node is released and is not the sink node (NSINK), all activities emanating from the node are copied from file N to file NFRA. Activities are transferred in the order in which they are filed in file N.

After the activities that can be scheduled are inserted into file NFRA, the file is searched to find the activity with the highest priority for which resources are available. This is accomplished in subroutine LOCBA, which tests, in order, each entry in file NFRA until an entry is found for which resources are available. If none exists, a zero value is returned. When an entry is found it is compared, using the priority rule, against the best entry located previously and the better one is retained as the current best entry. A return from LOCBA is made to subroutine EVNTS. When LOCBA returns a zero value, no activities can be dispatched and subroutine EVNTS returns control to GASP.

If an entry is located in file NFRA that can be dispatched, the activity corresponding to the entry is dispatched. When an activity is dispatched, the resources used by the activity are subtracted from the resources available and an end-of-activity event is scheduled to occur at TNOW plus the duration time of the activity. The function LOCBA is called again to determine whether another activity can be scheduled.

When an activity is completed, the resources that have been used on the completed activity are now made available for processing other activities. The number of releases for the end node of the activtiy is decreased by one and a test is made to determine whether there are activities waiting to be scheduled. (Are there entries in file NFRA?) If not, control is returned to subroutine GASP. If activities are available for dispatching, function LOCBA is called and the procedure described above is followed.

When the sink node is released, the final statistics associated with the simulation run are computed and printed. A test is then made to deter-

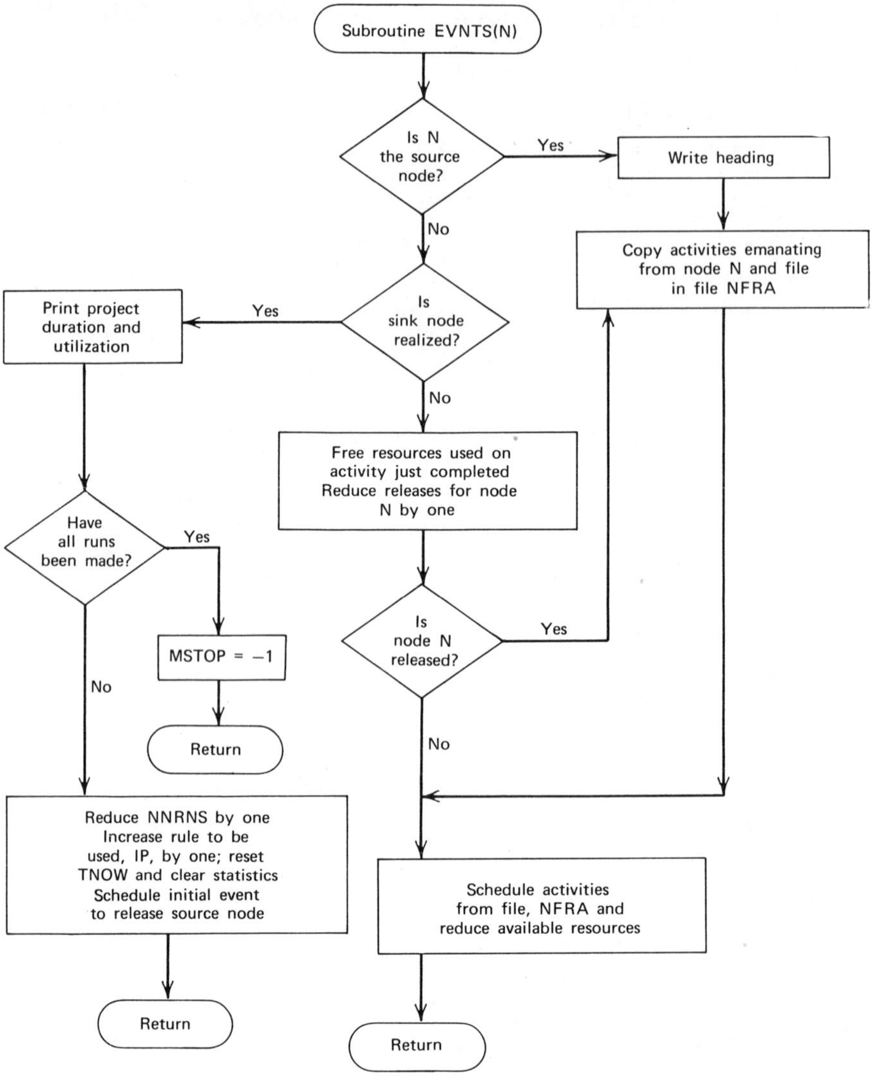

Figure 5-59 Flow chart of subroutine EVNTS (Example 5).

mine if all rules have been tested. If they have, the simulation is completed and the GASP IV control variable MSTOP is set equal to −1. Subroutine GASP returns control to the main program since NNRNS has been reduced to one and the program is stopped.

If all dispatching rules have not been tested, the next rule is established. The variables are initialized so that another simulation run can be made by calling subroutine INTLC and subroutine MONTR with JEVNT = −2. This call to subroutine MONTR resets file statistics and clears statistical storage arrays. The startup event that causes the source node to be released is inserted into file 1. Control is then returned to GASP.

The flow chart for subroutine LOCBA is given in Fig. 5-61 and the FORTRAN listing in Fig. 5-62.

```
72/03/17 VINTAGE RUM - 18:25 02/13/75.

                  SUBROUTINE EVNTS (N)
000003            DIMENSION NSET(1)
000003            COMMON QSET(1)
000003            COMMON /GCOM1/ ATRIB(25),JEVNT,MFA,MFE(100),MLE(100),MSTOP,NCRDR,N
                 1NAPO,NNAPT,NNATR,NNFIL,NNQ(100),NNTRY,NPRNT,PPARM(50,4),TNOW,TTBEG
                 2,TTCLR,TTFIN,TTRIB(25),TTSET
000003            COMMON /GCOM5/ IIEVT,IISED(6),JJBEG,JJCLR,MMNIT,MMON,NNAME(3),NNCF
                 1I,NNDAY,NNPT,NNSET,NNPRJ,NNPRM,NNRNS,NNRUN,NNSTR,NNYR,SSEED(6)
000003            COMMON /UCOM1/NREL(25),NRELP(25),RESA(3),RESAP(3),REUSE(3),IP,
                 1 NRULE,NFRA,NSORC,NSINK,MACT,MNODE,NRESC,HCRL(10),DRULE(10,3)
000003            EQUIVALENCE(NSET(1),QSET(1))
            C
            C*****TEST THE END NODE TO DETERMINE IF IT IS THE SOURCE NODE
            C*****OF THE NETWORK (N=NSORC).
            C
000003            IF (N-NSORC) 105,101,105
            C
            C*****IT IS THE SOURCE NODE
            C
000005        101 WRITE (NPRNT,114) (DRULE(IP,I),I=1,3)
000020        102 NEXT=MFE(N)
            C
            C*****COPY EVENTS RELEASED FROM FILE N TO FILE NFRA.
            C
000023        103 IF (NEXT) 107,108,104
000025        104 CALL COPY (NEXT)
000027            CALL FILEM (NFRA)
000031            ICS=NEXT+NNAPO
000033            NEXT=NSET(ICS)
000034            GO TO 103
            C
            C*****TEST FOR RUN COMPLETION.
            C
000036        105 IF (N.EQ.NSINK.AND.NREL(NSINK).EQ.1) GO TO 110
            C
            C*****RELEASE RESOURCES USED BY THE ACTIVITY COMPLETION AND TEST IF
            C*****END NODE IS REALIZED.
            C
000045            NPN=ATRIB(3)
000046            DO 106 J=1,NRESC
000050        106 RESA(J)=RESA(J)+PPARM(NPN,J)
000061            NREL(N)=NREL(N)-1
000063            IF (NREL(N)) 107,102,108
000065        107 CALL ERROR (3)
            C
            C*****SCHEDULE ACTIVITIES FROM FILE NFRA.
            C
000067        108 NTRY=LOCBA(X)
000072            IF (NTRY.EQ.0) RETURN
000074            CALL RMOVE (NTRY,NFRA)
000076            NPN=ATRIB(3)
000100            DO 109 J=1,NRESC
000102            RESA(J)=RESA(J)-PPARM(NPN,J)
000106        109 REUSE(J)=REUSE(J)+PPARM(NPN,J)*PPARM(NPN,4)
000115            WRITE (NPRNT,115) NPN,TNOW,(PPARM(NPN,J),J=1,4)
```

Figure 5-60 FORTRAN listing of subroutine EVNTS (Example 5).

```
72/03/17 VINTAGE RUM - 18:25 02/13/75.

000134          ATRIB(1)=TNOW+PPARM(NPN,4)
000137          CALL FILEM (1)
000140          GO TO 108
          C
          C*****END OF ONE SIMULATION RUN OF THE NETWORK.
          C
000142      110 DO 111 J=1,NRESC
000144      111 REUSE(J)=REUSE(J)/(TNOW*RESAP(J))
000151          WRITE (NPRNT,116) TNOW,(REUSE(J),J=1,NRESC)
          C
          C*****ARE ALL RUNS COMPLETED.
          C
000166          IF (NNRNS-1) 107,112,113
          C
          C*****YES
          C
000172      112 MSTOP=-1
000173          RETURN
          C
          C*****NO -- RESET THE SYSTEM
          C
000174      113 NNRNS=NNRNS-1
000176          IP=IP+1
000177          CALL INTLC
000200          TNOW=0.0
000201          JEVNT=-2
000202          CALL MONTR
          C
          C     SCHEDULE SOURCE NODE COMPLETION
          C
000203          ATRIB(1)=0.0
000204          ATRIB(2)=NSORC
000206          CALL FILEM (1)
000207          RETURN
          C
000210      114 FORMAT (///18H SCHEDULE USING A ,3A4,16H PRIORITY SCHEME//61H    AC
               1TIVITY    RELEASED          RESOURCES UTILIZED          DURATION)
000210      115 FORMAT (1X,I10,5F10.4)
000210      116 FORMAT (/14X,32HDURATION     RESOURCE UTILIZATION/11X,5F10.4)
          C
000210          END
```

Figure 5-60 *(continued)*

Function LOCBA locates the best activity to be dispatched according to the dispatching rule employed during the run. When LOCBA is called, file NFRA contains all activities that have been released and are ready to be scheduled. For each activity in file NFRA, it is determined whether resources are available to perform the activity and a comparison based on the priority defined by the dispatching rule is performed. IP is the number of the dispatching rule being tested and HORL(IP) indicates whether high values or low values are preferred.

The first statement in function LOCBA establishes a low value for the best priority, BESTP. LOCBA is set at zero to indicate that no activity has been located which requires less resources than those available. The variable NEXT is used as a pointer to the activities in file NFRA. It is initially set to the first entry in file NFRA. If NEXT is zero, there are no entries in NFRA and a return is made. The activity number (which is also the parameter set number) is then determined as the third attribute for the entry. This is obtained by setting NPN equal to QSET(NEXT + 3). Since an attribute value is desired in this statement,

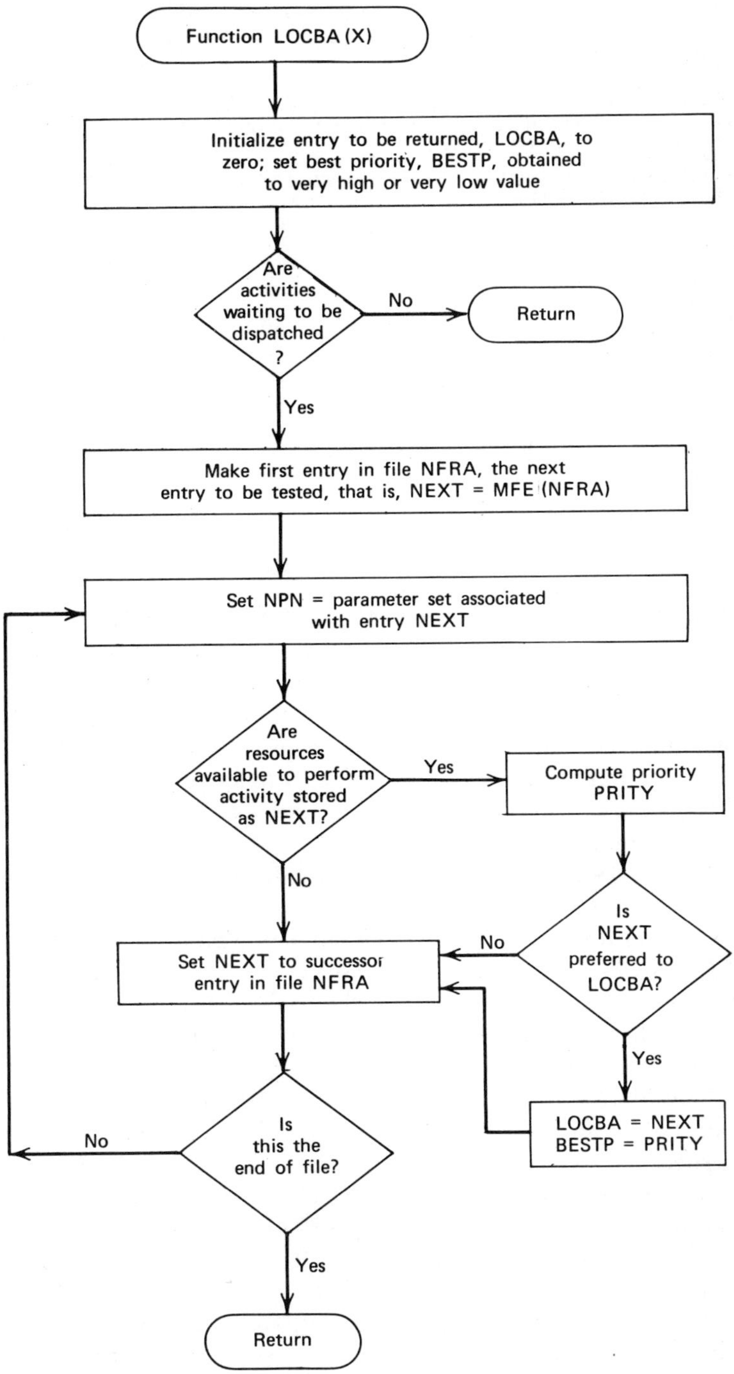

Figure 5-61 Flow chart of function locate best activity, LOCBA (Example 5).

```
      FUNCTION LOCBA(X)
      DIMENSION NSET(1)
      COMMON QSET(1)
      COMMON /GCOM1/ ATRIB(25),JEVNT,MFA,MFE(100),MLE(100),MSTOP,NCRDR,NG
     1NAPO,NNAPT,NNATR,NNFIL,NNQ(100),NNTRY,NPRNT,PPARM(50,4),TNOW,TTBEG
     2,TTCLR,TTFIN,TTRIB(25),TTSET
      COMMON /UCOM1/NREL(25),NRELP(25),RESA(3),RESAP(3),REUSE(3),IF,
     1 NRULE,NFRA,NSORC,NSINK,MACT,MNODE,NRESC,HORL(10),DRULE(10,3)
      EQUIVALENCE(NSET(1),QSET(1))
C
C*****FUNCTION TO RETURN WITH CELL LOCATION OF NEXT ACTIVITY IN FILE
C*****NFRA TO SCHEDULE.
C
      BESTP=-HORL(IP)*10.0E20
      LOCBA=0
      NEXT=MFE(NFRA)
  101 IF (NEXT.EQ.0) RETURN
      NPN=QSET(NEXT+3)
      DO 102 J=1,NRESC
      IF (RESA(J).LT.PPARM(NPN,J)) GO TO 104
  102 CONTINUE
      PRITY=PRIRTY(NEXT)
      IF ((PRITY-BESTP)*HORL(IP)) 104,104,103
  103 BESTP=PRITY
      LOCBA=NEXT
  104 ICS=NEXT+NNAPO
      NEXT=NSET(ICS)
      GO TO 101
C
      END
```

Figure 5-62 FORTRAN listing of subroutine LOCBA (Example 5).

the array QSET must be referenced even though NSET and QSET are equivalenced. The internal computer representations for NSET and QSET are for integer and real variables, respectively. Thus *NSET must be used when referring to the pointers and QSET must be used when obtaining attribute values.*

The activity is a candidate for dispatching if the resources available exceed the resource requirements for each resource type. If this is not the case, a transfer is made to statement 104 where the next activity in file NFRA is determined. If the activity is a candidate, the priority for the activity is determined through the use of function PRIRTY. The priority for the activity is compared against the best priority value. If the candidate activity has a higher priority, it is established as the best activity considered to this time by resetting BESTP and LOCBA.

The next entry in file NFRA is established by defining the cell number for the successor activity, ICS, as the first cell number, NEXT, plus the number of attributes plus one, NNAPO. The first cell number for the successor activity is the value stored in NSET(ICS). This value is assigned to the variable NEXT. A transfer back to statement 101 to repeat the above process is then performed.

The FORTRAN listing for function PRIRTY is given in Fig. 5-63. First, the attributes for the activity on which priority is desired are copied into ATRIB through the use of subroutine COPY. The priority variable is then established through a computed GO TO statement. The seven

```
      FUNCTION PRIRTY(NEXT)
      COMMON /GCOM1/ ATRIB(25),JEVNT,MFA,MFE(100),MLE(100),MSTOP,NCRDR,N
     1NAPO,NNAPT,NNATR,NNFIL,NNQ(100),NNTRY,NPRNT,PPARM(50,4),TNOW,TTBEG
     2,TTCLR,TTFIN,TTRIB(25),TTSET
      COMMON /UCOM1/NREL(25),NRELP(25),RESA(3),RESAP(3),REUSE(3),IP,
     1 NRULE,NFRA,NSORC,NSINK,MACT,MNODE,NRESC,HORL(10),DRULE(10,3)
C
C*****FUNCTION TO RETURN VALUE OF PRIORITY OF ENTRY $NEXT$ ACCORDING
C*****TO PRIORITY SCHEME $IP$.
C
      CALL COPY (NEXT)
      NPN=ATRIB(3)
      I=IP
      GO TO (101,101,102,103,104,105,105), I
C
C*****DURATION TIME
C
  101 PRIRTY=PPARM(NPN,4)
      RETURN
C
C*****WORK SPACE REQUIREMENT
C
  102 PRIRTY=PPARM(NPN,1)
      RETURN
C
C*****MECHANIC REQUIREMENT
C
  103 PRIRTY=PPARM(NPN,2)
      RETURN
C
C*****TECHNICIAN REQUIREMENT
C
  104 PRIRTY=PPARM(NPN,3)
      RETURN
C
C*****END NODE RELEASES
C
  105 NPN=ATRIB(2)
      PRIRTY=NREL(NPN)
      RETURN
C
      END
```

Figure 5-63 FORTRAN listing of subroutine PRIRTY (Example 5).

dispatching rules to be tested involve five parameters on which priority is based. Except for the case where the number of releases establishes priority, each of the rules involves a value stored in the array PPARM. As shown in the FORTRAN listing, these are easily obtained and set equal to the priority to be returned, PRIRTY. In the case where the remaining number of releases is used to set priority, the end node number is established in statement 105 by setting NPN equal to the second attribute for the activity. The number of releases remaining is then NREL(NPN), and this is set equal to the PRIRTY value. If it is desired to test other dispatching rules, function PRIRTY can easily be modified.

The input values for Example 5 are presented in Fig. 5-64.

Simulation Reports

Figure 5-65 presents a summary of the results obtained for the seven dispatching rules tested. For this example, the priority rule, dispatch

```
                                                                                     USER
       2         10         16         12         3
       1    1    1    1    1    2    1    4    2    2    1
  1.   4.   2.
       7
  -1SHORT DUR.
   1LONG DUR.
  -1LFAST SPACE
  -1LEAST MECH.
  -1LEAST TECH.
  -1MIN RELEASES
   1MAX RELEASES
PRITSKER            5    6   30 1973     7000000000000202                             1
   0    0    0   16    0    1  100    3   13 1000                                     2
   1    1    1    1    1    1    1    1    1    1    1    1    3                      7
   1    1    1    1    1    1    1    1    1    1    1    1    1                      8
10         1         1.         3.         0.         3.
10         2         0.         0.         2.         9.
10         3         1.         ?.         0.         2.
10         4         0.         1.         0.         1.
10         5         1.         2.         0.         2.                               10
10         6         0.         4.         1.         4.
10         7         0.         0.         2.         8.
10         8         0.         2.         0.         1.
10         9         0.         0.         0.         0.
10        10         0.         1.         0.         1.
```

```
10       11          1.         1.         0.         2.
10       12          1.         3.         0.         5.
10       13          0.         1.         1.         1.
10       14          1.         1.         2.         2.
10       15          0.         1.         1.         1.
10       16          0.         2.         0.         3.
```

`     0     1       1     1                         195207`	11

```
12        1          0.         2.
12        2          0.         3.         1.
12        2          0.         4.         2.
12        2          0.         5.         3.
12        2          0.         6.         4.
12        2          0.         7.         5.
12        3          0.         8.         6.
12        4          0.         9.         7.
12        5          0.        12.         8.
12        6          0.         7.         9.
12        6          0.        11.        10.
12        7          0.        11.        11.
12        8          0.         9.        12.
12        9          0.        10.        13.
12        9          0.        10.        14.
12       11          0.         9.        15.
12       12          0.         9.        16.
12        0
```

12

Figure 5-64 Listing of input data cards and GASP IV echo check of input data (Example 5).

```
                              SIMULATION PROJECT NUMBER   5  BY  PRITSKER

                              DATE   6/ 30/ 1973          RUN NUMBER    1 OF    7
                              LLSUP=000000000000202       GASP IV VERSION 23JUN73

NNCLT=      0   NNSTA=      0   NNHIS=     0   NNPRM=     16   NNPLT=     0   NNSTR=     1   NNTRY=   100
NNATR=      3   NNFIL=     13   NNSET=  1000   NNEQD=     -0   NNEQS=    -0   NFLAG=    -0

KKRNK= (   1)      1      1      1      1      1      1      1      1      1      1      1      3

IINN = (   1)      1      1      1      1      1      1      1      1      1      1      1      1

PARAMETER SET    1 =   1.0000E+00    3.0000E+00    0.            3.0000E+00
PARAMETER SET    2 =   0.            0.            2.0000E+00    9.0000E+00
PARAMETER SET    3 =   1.0000E+00    2.0000E+00    0.            2.0000E+00
PARAMETER SET    4 =   0.            1.0000E+00    0.            1.0000E+00
PARAMETER SET    5 =   1.0000E+00    2.0000E+00    0.            2.0000E+00
PARAMETER SET    6 =   0.            4.0000E+00    1.0000E+00    4.0000E+00
PARAMETER SET    7 =   0.            0.            2.0000E+00    8.0000E+00
PARAMETER SET    8 =   0.            2.0000E+00    0.            1.0000E+00
PARAMETER SET    9 =   0.            0.            0.            0.
PARAMETER SET   10 =   0.            1.0000E+00    0.            1.0000E+00
PARAMETER SET   11 =   1.0000E+00    1.0000E+00    0.            1.0000E+00
PARAMETER SET   12 =   1.0000E+00    3.0000E+00    0.            2.0000E+00
PARAMETER SET   13 =   0.            1.0000E+00    0.            5.0000E+00
PARAMETER SET   14 =   1.0000E+00    1.0000E+00    1.0000E+00    1.0000E+00
PARAMETER SET   15 =   0.            1.0000E+00    2.0000E+00    2.0000E+00
PARAMETER SET   16 =   0.            2.0000E+00    1.0000E+00    1.0000E+00
```

Figure 5-64 *(continued)*

the activity with the shortest duration time first, produced the shortest project duration time of 25 days. If resources are unlimited, it takes 19 days to complete the project. Thus the effect of limiting resources is to increase the time required to complete the project by six days.

The utilization of the three resources is also presented in Fig. 5-65. For a given project duration, the utilization of the resources is the same since a fixed amount of resources is required to complete the project. Thus keeping track of utilization during the simulation is done only to demonstrate the method used to obtain resource utilization statistics. Other than noting the interesting pattern of the results, no general statements can be made from this small simulation example for one particular network.

A sample of the output, which includes the project duration, the resource utilization, and the schedule of activities is given in Fig. 5-66. This output was printed in subroutine EVNTS. The results are for run number 1, which employs the dispatch rule that activities having the shortest duration are dispatched first. A paper-and-pencil simulation of this dispatching rule can be used to verify the results.

Run Number	Dispatching Priority Rule	Project Duration	Resource Utilization 1	2	3
1	Shortest duration	25	0.64	0.64	0.88
2	Longest duration	29	0.55	0.55	0.76
3	Smallest requirement for work stations	29	0.55	0.55	0.76
4	Smallest requirement for mechanics	30	0.53	0.53	0.73
5	Smallest requirement for technicians	29	0.55	0.55	0.76
6	End node with least number of releases	29	0.55	0.55	0.76
7	End node with greatest number of releases	30	0.53	0.53	0.73

Figure 5-65 Summary of results for different rules for dispatching resources to activities.

EXERCISES

5-1. Change the lead time in Example 1 to be Erlang-distributed with $\beta = 1.5$ and $\alpha = 2$, that is, a mean of 3. Compare the results with the constant lead time results.

INTERMEDIATE RESULTS

SCHEDULE USING A SHORT DUR. PRIORITY SCHEME

ACTIVITY	RELEASED	RESOURCES UTILIZED			DURATION
4	0.0000	0.0000	1.0000	0.0000	1.0000
3	0.0000	1.0000	2.0000	0.0000	2.0000
2	0.0000	0.0000	0.0000	2.0000	9.0000
9	1.0000	0.0000	0.0000	0.0000	0.0000
10	1.0000	0.0000	1.0000	0.0000	1.0000
8	2.0000	0.0000	2.0000	0.0000	1.0000
5	2.0000	1.0000	2.0000	0.0000	2.0000
16	3.0000	0.0000	2.0000	0.0000	3.0000
11	4.0000	1.0000	1.0000	0.0000	2.0000
1	6.0000	1.0000	3.0000	0.0000	3.0000
15	9.0000	0.0000	1.0000	1.0000	1.0000
6	10.0000	0.0000	4.0000	1.0000	4.0000
12	14.0000	1.0000	3.0000	0.0000	5.0000
7	14.0000	0.0000	0.0000	2.0000	8.0000
13	22.0000	0.0000	1.0000	1.0000	1.0000
14	23.0000	1.0000	1.0000	2.0000	2.0000

DURATION	RESOURCE UTILIZATION		
25.0000	.6400	.6400	.8800

Figure 5-66 Schedule of activities, project duration, and resource utilization for shortest duration priority dispatching.

5-2. Develop a search procedure to locate the best values of reorder point, stock control level and review period for the inventory situation of Example 1.

5-3. Rewrite Example 1 so that the same quantity is ordered at each reorder time.

5-4. If the discount store of Example 1 decides to install a transactions recording system, how much should they be willing to invest in such a system?

5-5. Perform a sensitivity analysis on the expected profit for the situation described in Example 1 when the cost of goodwill is considered to be between \$10.00 and \$20.00.

5-6. Simulate a single server queueing system where service is exponentially distributed with a mean service time of one hour and there are two types of arrivals. Arrival type 1 is an item of high priority and waits only for the processing of other high priority items. The time intervals between arrivals of high priority items is exponentially distributed with a mean time between arrivals of four hours. The time between arrivals of low priority items is also exponentially distributed, but has a mean time between arrivals of two hours. Obtain statistics regarding server utilization and information concerning the time in the system and in the queue for high and low priority items. Assume that service on low priority items is not interrupted to process high priority items.

5-7. Repeat the simulation given in Exercise 5-6 with the assumption that high priority items interrupt the servicing of low priority items. Interrupted items are inserted at the beginning of the queue of low priority items. Show that the time remaining for those items interrupted is exponentially distributed with a mean time equal to the mean service time.

5-8. Jobs arrive at a job shop so that the interarrival time is exponentially distributed with a mean time between arrivals of 1.25 hours. The time to process a job is uniformly distributed in the interval 0.75 to 1.25 hours. The time to process the jobs is estimated prior to the time the job is performed. Simulate the processing of jobs in the order of shortest processing time first. Obtain statistics describing the average time jobs are in the shop, the variation of the time the jobs are in the shop, and the utilization of the server. Assume that the *actual* processing times for the jobs are equal to the *estimates* of the processing times. Repeat the simulation with jobs with the longest processing time performed first. Then carry out the simulation with the jobs processed in order of their arrival time. Compare the results.

5-9. Repeat Exercise 5-8 for a situation in which the actual processing time is equal to the estimated processing time plus a sample drawn from a normal distribution with a mean of zero and a standard deviation of 0.2.

5-10. A conveyor system involves five servers stationed along a conveyor belt. Items to be processed by the servers arrive at the first server at a constant rate of four per minute. Service time for each server is one minute, and is exponentially distributed. No storage is provided before each server; therefore, the server must be idle if he is to remove the item from the conveyor belt. If the first server is idle, the item is processed by that server. At the end-of-service time, the item is removed from the system. If the first server is busy when the item arrives, it continues down the conveyor belt until it arrives at the second server. The delay time between servers is one minute. If an item encounters a situation in which all servers are busy, it is recycled to the first server with a time delay of five minutes. Simulate the above conveyor system to determine statistics concerning the time spent in the system by an item, the percentage of time each server is busy, and the number of busy servers (103).

5-11. Repeat the simulation of Exercise 5-10 with a time delay of two minutes between servers. Is there an effect on the utilization of the servers because of a change in the time delay between servers, that is, the speed of the conveyor?

5-12. Consider the conveyor situation described in Exercise 5-10, except that the last server has sufficient space for storage so that all items passing servers 1, 2, 3, and 4 are processed by server 5. Simulate this situation to obtain the statistics requested in Exercise 5-10.

5-13. Let the storage space before each server for the conveyor system described in Exercise 5-10 be two units. When storage exists before each server of a conveyor system, decisions regarding the removal of items must be established. Propose decision rules for determining whether items should be removed from the conveyor belt and placed in storage before a particular server. Simulate the decision rules to obtain the statistics requested in Exercise 5-10.

5-14. The maintenance facility of a large manufacturer performs two operations. These operations must be performed in series; operation 2 always follows operation 1. Only eight units, including the two units that can be worked on, can be handled at one time. Current company policy subcontracts the maintenance of a unit if it cannot gain access to the in-house facility. Allocate the six spaces to the queues of the work stations to minimize subcontracting subject to the restriction that down time be less than three days on the average. The time interval between requests for maintenance is exponentially distributed with a mean of 0.4 days. Service times are approximately exponentially distributed, with the first station requiring, on the average, 0.25 days and the second service station 0.5 days. If the queue of the second station is full, the first work station is blocked and a unit cannot leave that station. A blocked work station cannot serve other units. Initial conditions are:

(*a*) Both work stations are busy with end of services scheduled at time 1.

(*b*) The first arrival is scheduled to arrive at the maintenance shop at time 0.1.

(c) No units in the queues of the work stations.

The maintenance facility is to be simulated for one year.

5-15. For the network simulation of Example 4, determine the number of simulations that would be required to obtain a 95% probability that (*a*) the estimate of the project duration is within 0.1 of a standard deviation of the theoretical project duration, (*b*) the estimate of the variance of the project duration is within 10% of the theoretical variance of the project duration, and (*c*) the difference between the observed and theoretical criticality indices is less than or equal to 0.005 (134).

5-16. The use of antithetical variates (13,14,90) for simulating PERT networks has been performed by Burt and Gaver. In this application, the simulations of the network would be performed in pairs where the time for an activity is first obtained based on a random number r_j, and in the second of the pair the activity time is based on $(1 - r_j)$. This variance reduction method should reduce the number of runs required to achieve desired confidence levels. Rewrite the PERT simulation of Example 4 to incorporate the use of antithetical variates.

5-17. Develop and test different dispatching rules for the network presented in Example 5.

5-18. Test dispatching rules for the conditions given in Example 5 when the times to perform the activities are random variables. Assume each activity time is lognormally distributed, with the mean as given, and variances equal to 0.2 times the mean.

5-19. Suppose that two ways of performing each activity given in Example 5 exist. The requirements for the alternative procedure are given below:

Activity Number	Workspace	Mechanics	Technicians	Duration
1	0	4	0	5
2	1	1	1	5
3	0	2	0	5
4	0	0	1	1
5	1	4	0	1
6	0	3	2	4
7	0	0	1	12
8	0	1	0	3
9	0	0	0	0
10	0	0	1	2
11	1	1	1	1
12	1	3	1	4
13	1	0	1	1
14	0	2	1	2
15	0	1	0	2
15	0	1	0	8

Test different dispatching rules by randomly selecting which of the two alternatives to include in the network, that is, by drawing a random number arbitrarily specify the alternative to be included in the network. Repetitive runs for the same dispatching rule will then be required (110). (Note: the probability assigned to an alternative can be used as an intuitive judgment as to the preferred alternative.)

5-20. A company has six retail outlets in a given city. The distribution of demand for a particular item at these particular outlets is Poisson-distributed with a mean of 10 units per day. These retail outlets are serviced by a distribution warehouse. It takes one day for an order to be received at the distribution warehouse from a retail outlet. Orders can be delivered from the distribution warehouse to each retail outlet in five days on the average. The distribution of this time is lognormal with variance of one. The distribution warehouse places orders on the factory every fourteen days. The time for the distribution warehouse to obtain a shipment from the factory is normally distributed with a mean of 90 days and a standard deviation of ten days; however, orders never are received in either less than 60 days or more than 120 days. Simulate the problem to determine the variation in inventory levels for a given inventory policy at the retail outlets and the distribution warehouse for a three year period, with each year consisting of 240 days. Print yearly summary reports.

The initial conditions for the simulation are: first demand at time 0: stock at each outlet, 70 units; inventory position at each outlet, 70 units; stock at warehouse, 1,920; three procurements from factory are in process, each for 1,800 units, one due to be received at day 30, one at day 60 and one at day 90; and first review of warehouse inventory position will be at day 30.

5.21. (For installations that have a time-share computer capability.) Convert Example 1 to a time-share simulation by incorporating a decision maker into the simulation. The decision maker must decide at each review event whether to place an order and the amount to be ordered. Displays of past status and current values should be available to the decision maker upon request (113).

Chapter Six

GASP IV

Continuous Simulation

This chapter presents two examples of GASP IV programs that analyze situations that are modeled using continuous concepts. In using GASP IV to model continuous systems, there are no time-events; hence no events are scheduled into the future. The models involve state variables and the definition of state-events based on the conditions of state variables. Time is advanced through the time step mechanism of the executive subroutine (GASP) using a step size consistent with input specifications. The state variables are computed at the end of each step.

The development of a GASP IV continuous simulation program requires only the writing of a main program and subroutines STATE, SCOND, SSAVE, EVNTS, and INTLC. The last two of these subprograms may not be required for a particular application. Of course, all of the GASP IV subprograms are available for use.

In writing a continuous simulation program, it has been found expeditious to code subroutine STATE first. In STATE, the equations governing the behavior of the system model are written. To do this, the state variables are defined and the model relating these variables is coded. The conditions that define state-events are then written in subroutine SCOND. The consequences of the occurrence of a state-event are coded in subroutine EVNTS, which is called whenever the conditions defining a state-event are satisfied. The main program and subroutine INTLC are used for initializing the state variables and the non-GASP variables associated with the application. Subroutine SSAVE is used to record the values of the variables throughout the simulation for eventual output. The main program, INTLC and SSAVE, are normally easy to write and often require only a few statements.

The two examples included in this chapter illustrate the procedures used in developing a continuous simulation program. Example 6 involves the analysis of a pilot ejection system of an aircraft. The example illustrates how different termination conditions can be used to stop a simulation run. In addition, sequential simulation runs are made with multiple plots prepared for each run.

Example 7 involves the analysis of a slip clutch commonly used in business machines. In this example, the programming of higher order differential equations is illustrated. A method for changing the equations describing a system model based on the occurrence of state-events is included.

In both examples the features available for plotting information are described and illustrated. Tabular output of the important variables involved in the simulations are presented. Complete descriptions of Examples 6 and 7 follow.

EXAMPLE 6–PILOT EJECTION

Statement of the Problem

A pilot ejection system of an aircraft that is flying level and at a constant velocity is to be simulated. This example is frequently cited in the literature and is referred to as the pilot ejection model. The specific version described here is extracted from Reference 23.

The pilot ejection system, when activated, causes the pilot and his seat to travel along rails at a specified exit velocity V_E at an angle Θ_E backward from vertical. After traveling a vertical distance Y_1, the seat becomes disengaged from its mounting rails and at this point the pilot is considered out of the cockpit. When this occurs, a second phase of operation begins during which the pilot's trajectory is influenced by the force of gravity and atmospheric drag. A critical aspect of this phase is whether the pilot will clear the vertical stabilizer of the aircraft. The vertical stabilizer is 60 ft behind and 12 ft above the cockpit. A graphical and mathematical description of the two phases are shown in Fig. 6-1, with a legend for the variables of the model.

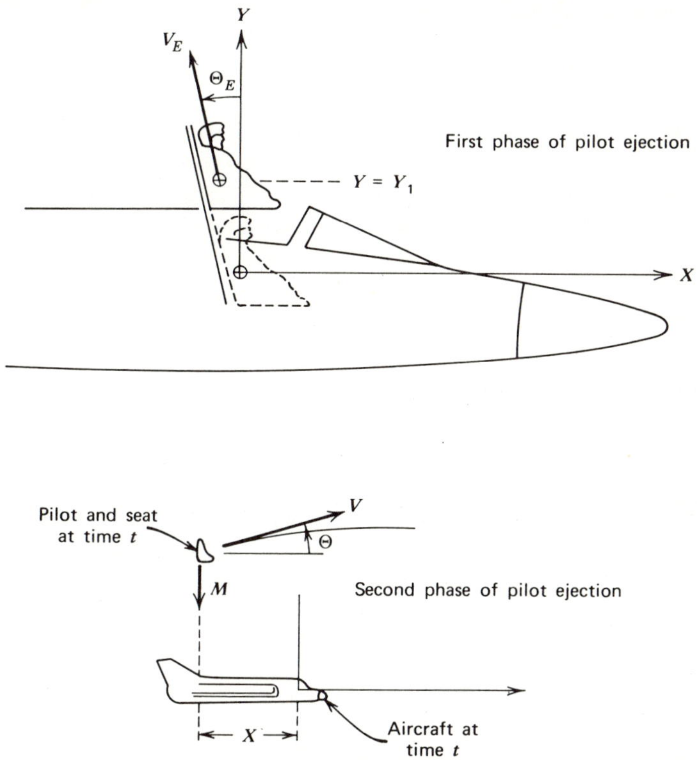

Figure 6-1 Graphical and mathematical description of a pilot ejection model.

Variable	Definition	Equations
X	Horizontal distance from point of ejection	$\frac{dX}{dt} = V \cos \Theta - V_A$
Y	Vertical distance from point of ejection	$\frac{dY}{dt} = V \sin \Theta$
Y_1	Vertical distance above point of ejection where first phase ends	$\frac{dV}{dt} = 0, \quad 0 \leq Y < Y_1$
V_A	Velocity of aircraft	$\frac{d\Theta}{dt} = 0, \quad 0 \leq Y < Y_1$
V	Pilot and seat velocity	
Θ	Angle for pilot and seat movement	
V_E	Ejection velocity	
Θ_E	Angle of ejection	$D = \frac{1}{2}\rho \; C_d S V^2$
M	Mass of pilot and seat	$\frac{dV}{dt} = -\frac{D}{M} - g \sin \Theta, \quad Y \geq Y_1$
ρ, c_d, S	Parameters of the model	$\frac{d\Theta}{dt} = -\frac{(g \cos \Theta)}{V}, \quad Y \geq Y_1$

Simulation Objectives

The objective of this simulation is to determine the trajectory of a pilot ejected from an aircraft to assess whether he would hit the vertical stabilizer of the aircraft. This information is desired for a fixed ejection velocity and angle for two aircraft velocities, 900 ft/sec and 500 ft/sec.

Special Features

The purpose of this example is to introduce the use of GASP IV for the preparation of a continuous simulation model. For the first time, the user written subroutines STATE, SCOND, and SSAVE are illustrated. The procedures for programming different run termination conditions within a run and for making multiple runs are demonstrated. On each run two plots are prepared and printed. On one of the plots, altitude versus distance, is graphed to illustrate the plotting of a state variable against an independent variable other than time.

Simulation Procedure

The pilot ejection model is simulated using continuous variables. The equations describing the state variables and their derivatives are programmed in subroutine STATE. The conditions defining state-events are coded in subroutine SCOND. Since this is a continuous model, no time-events are involved. Since multiple runs will be made, the main program will only initialize those non-GASP variables, which are constant for all runs. Other non-GASP variables and the initial conditions for the simulation will be set in subroutine INTLC. Subroutine SSAVE will be used to collect the data required to portray the trajectory of the pilot as he leaves the aircraft. It will also be used to plot the pilot's relative position from the aircraft over time, and his speed and direction over time.

As discussed above, the main program is only used to initialize the card reader number and printer number and those non-GASP variables that remain constant over all runs. After this is done, subroutine GASP is called to control the running of the simulation. The FORTRAN listing for the main program is shown in Fig. 6-2.

The major programming effort for this example is expended in writing subroutine STATE where the equations describing the pilot ejection model are coded. Table 6-1 presents a listing of the GASP IV variables that are equivalent to the variables presented in Fig. 6-1 and discussed

```
      PROGRAM MAIN (INPUT,OUTPUT,TAPE1,TAPE2,TAPE5=INPUT,TAPE6=OUTPUT)     MX6     1
      DIMENSION NSET(20000)                                                DIM     1
      COMMON QSET(20000)                                                   COM     1
      COMMON /GCOM1/ ATRIB(25),JEVNT,MFA,MFE(100),MLE(100),MSTOP,NCRDR,NGCOM1  1
     1NAPO,NNAPT,NNATR,NNFIL,NNQ(100),NNTRY,NPRNT,PPARM(50,4),TNOW,TTBEGGCOM1  2
     2,TTCLR,TTFIN,TTRIB(25),TTSET                                         GCOM1   3
      COMMON /UCOM1/ CD,G,RHO,THED,VA,VE,XM,XS,Y1                          UCOM    1
      EQUIVALENCE(NSET(1),QSET(1))                                         EQUIV   1
      NCRDR=5                                                              MX6     2
      NPRNT=6                                                              MX6     3
      READ (NCRDR,101) XM,G,CD,XS,Y1,VE,THED,RHO                           MX6     4
      CALL GASP                                                            MX6     5
      CALL EXIT                                                            MX6     6
C                                                                          MX6     7
  101 FORMAT (7F5.0,E10.4)                                                 MX6     8
C                                                                          MX6     9
      END                                                                  MX6    10
```

Figure 6-2 FORTRAN listing of main program (Example 6).

Table 6-1 Variables for Pilot Ejection Model

Problem Statement	GASP IV	Initial Value
X	SS(1)	0.0
dX/dt	DD(1)	Computed
Y	SS(2)	0.0
dY/dt	DD(2)	Computed
V	SS(3)	Computed
dV/dt	DD(3)	0.0
Θ	SS(4)	Computed
$d\Theta/dt$	DD(4)	0.0
C_d	CD	1.0
g	G	32.2 ft/sec^2
ρ	RHO	2.3769×10^{-3} slugs/ft^3
Θ_E(rad)	THE	15./57.3
Θ_E(deg)	THED	15.0
V_A	VA	Input
V_E	VE	40.0 ft/sec
M	XM	7 slugs
S	XS	10.0 ft^2
Y_1	Y1	4.0 ft

in the problem statement. As can be seen from Table 6-1, there is a direct mnemonic relationship between the GASP IV variables and the variables included in the model. The coding of the equations presented in Fig. 6-1 using the GASP IV variables is shown below.

```
DD(1) = SS(3) * COS(SS(4)) - VA
DD(2) = SS(3) * SIN(SS(4))
DD(3) = 0.                              SS(2) < Y1
```

$$\begin{aligned} DD(4) &= 0. && SS(2) < Y1 \\ DD(3) &= -XD/XM - G \star SIN(SS(4)) && SS(2) \geq Y1 \\ DD(4) &= -G \star COS(SS(4))/SS(3) && SS(2) \geq Y1 \end{aligned}$$

where

$$XD = 0.5 \star RHO \star CD \star XS \star SS(3) \star SS(3)$$

When SS(2) $\geq$ Y1, the pilot is released from the cockpit and the second set of equations for DD(3) and DD(4) are used. Since the relative position of the pilot during the simulated period of interest will always exceed Y1 after he is released, the test of whether SS(2) is greater than Y1 can be used for specifying when the equations for DD(3) and DD(4) are to be used.

These derivative equations are coded in subroutine STATE. The FORTRAN listing for subroutine STATE is shown in Fig. 6-3. It should be noted that DD(1), DD(2), DD(3), and DD(4) are functions of both SS(3) and SS(4). The RKE integration algorithm of GASP IV simultaneously solves for the desired SS($\cdot$) values and the multiple dependence is taken into account. The order of coding the DD($\cdot$) equations will not affect the results obtained in this example.

Three conditions define state-events. A state-event occurs when the pilot achieves a relative height of Y1 with respect to the aircraft. When this occurs the equations governing the pilot's movement are altered. The other two state-events are for stopping the simulation. When the pilot is 60 ft behind the airplane, he will be beyond the vertical stabilizer. When the pilot is 30 ft above the airplane, he is well above the 12 ft high tail. In either case, the simulation is halted. In terms of the GASP IV variables, these conditions are SS(1) ≤ -60 and SS(2) ≥ 30. The other condition for stopping involves time exceeding 4 sec. This is accomplished through the input data by setting TTFIN = 4.

The FORTRAN listing for subroutine SCOND is given in Fig. 6-4. In this subroutine, the conditions associated with the state-events of the model are coded. The first statement is associated with the event of the pilot leaving the cockpit. The statement causes GASP to locate

```
      SUBROUTINE STATE                                                  ST6      1
      COMMON /GCOM2/ DD(100),DDL(100),DTFUL,DTNOW,ISEES,LFLAG(50),NFLAG,GCOM2   1
     1NNEQD,NNEQS,NNEQT,SS(100),SSL(100),TTNEX                          GCOM2    2
      COMMON /UCOM1/ CD,G,RHO,THED,VA,VE,XM,XS,Y1                       UCOM     1
      DD(1)=SS(3)*COS(SS(4))-VA                                         ST6      2
      DD(2)=SS(3)*SIN(SS(4))                                            ST6      3
      IF (SS(2)-Y1) 102,101,101                                         ST6      4
  101 XD=.5*RHO*CD*XS*SS(3)*SS(3)                                       ST6      5
      DD(3)=-XD/XM-G*SIN(SS(4))                                         ST6      6
      DD(4)=-G*COS(SS(4))/SS(3)                                         ST6      7
  102 RETURN                                                            ST6      8
C                                                                       ST6      9
      END                                                               ST6     10
```

Figure 6-3 FORTRAN listing of subroutine STATE (Example 6).

```
      SUBROUTINE SCOND                                                  SC6      1
      COMMON /GCOM1/ ATRIB(25),JEVNT,MFA,MFE(100),MLE(100),MSTOP,NCRDR,NGCOM1    1
     1NAPO,NNAPT,NNATR,NNFIL,NNQ(100),NNTRY,NPRNT,PPARM(50,4),TNOW,TTBEGGCOM1    2
     2,TTCLR,TTFIN,TTRIB(25),TTSET                                      GCOM1    3
      COMMON /UCOM1/ CD,G,RHO,THED,VA,VE,XM,XS,Y1                       UCOM     1
      I=KROSS(2,0,0.,Y1,1,0.)                                           SC6      2
      MSTOP=KROSS(1,0,0.,-60.,-1,0.)                                    SC6      3
      IF (MSTOP) 102,101,101                                            SC6      4
  101 MSTOP=-KROSS(2,0,0.,30.,1,0.)                                     SC6      5
  102 RETURN                                                            SC6      6
C                                                                       SC6      7
      END                                                               SC6      8
```

Figure 6-4 FORTRAN listing of subroutine SCOND (Example 6).

the time at which SS(2) increases from less than to greater than Y1. A tolerance of zero is specified indicating that the event is to be located within a minimum time step DTMIN specified on input. In this example, DTMIN = 0.0001 sec. Function KROSS is equated to the local variable I, which is not used because there is no further action necessary. The purpose of this statement is to make sure the step size is reduced when a crossing of Y1 by SS(2) occurs. This statement causes the event time to be located with sufficient precision by specifying an ISEES < 0 until DTMIN is used by subroutine GASP. When the event occurs, the state variables are computed and saved in SSAVE for later plot and tabular output.

The actual model changes associated with the seat leaving the rail are coded in subroutine STATE where the derivative equations for DD(3) and DD(4) are employed as soon as SS(2) $>$ Y1. An alternative method would be to set an indicator when the value of I, as computed in SCOND, indicates a crossing. If other changes were required these would be coded in subroutine EVNTS, which is called at the state-event time.

The state-event for stopping a run can occur if SS(1) becomes less than -60 or SS(2) becomes greater than 30. These conditions are two of the three conditions specified for run termination. One method for communicating to subroutine GASP that a run is completed is to set MSTOP < 0. In this instance, MSTOP can be used as the state-event flag indicator. On input MSTOP is set equal to one.

Letting MSTOP = KROSS$(1,0,0.0,-60.0,-1,0.0)$ causes MSTOP to be set negative when SS(1) ≤ -60.0. Similarly MSTOP = $-$ KROSS $(2,0,0.0,30.0,+1,0.0)$ causes MSTOP to be set negative when SS(2) ≥ 30.0. The first of these conditions to occur will cause a termination of the run. If MSTOP remains equal to one, the run terminates when simulated time TNOW reached TTFIN = 4.

Subroutine SSAVE calls GPLOT to save the data required for two plots. In this example, the data is written onto auxiliary tape units 1 and 2 by subroutine GPLOT. Although it is much faster and more convenient to save plot data in core, whenever more than one plot or table is required per run, GASP IV requires that they must *all* be stored on auxiliary tape units. The FORTRAN listing of subroutine SSAVE is given in Fig. 6-5. The statement CALL GPLOT(SS(2),SS(1),1) will collect values of SS(2) for eventual plotting against SS(1). This plot will give the trajectory of the ejected pilot relative to the position of the aircraft. On data input, SS(1) is specified as the independent variable and only one dependent variable is to be plotted. For GPLOT to print a meaningful plot the values of SS(1) (the independent variable in this plot) must be monotonically nonincreasing or nondecreasing throughout the simulation.

The second call to GPLOT, that is, CALL GPLOT(SS(1),TNOW,2), is used to plot SS(1), SS(2), SS(3), and SS(4) against time. On data input, four dependent variables are specified. Therefore, only the first four values of SS(·) are plotted. Other characteristics of the plots are discussed when describing the data input and output.

Subroutine INTLC is used to initialize those state variables, derivatives, and non-GASP variables that require initialization prior to each run. For this example, INTLC is written to allow the aircraft velocity to be initialized through data input prior to every run. In the FORTRAN listing of INTLC given in Fig. 6-6, the first statement performs this reading operation. The initial values of the state variables and their derivatives are then established for a run. The initial position of the pilot relative to the aircraft is at the origin, that is, SS(1) = 0.0 and SS(2) = 0.0. The initial values of DD(1) and DD(2) are set by a call to subroutine STATE in subroutine DATIN.

The initial values of V and Θ (pilot's initial velocity vector) are given by

$$V_{\text{initial}} = \sqrt{(V_A - V_E \sin \Theta_E)^2 + (V_E \cos \Theta_E)^2}$$

and

$$\Theta_{\text{initial}} = \tan^{-1}\left(\frac{V_E \cos \Theta_E}{V_A - V_E \sin \Theta_E}\right)$$

These initial values are made equal to SS(3) and SS(4) at the beginning of the simulation since ejection is initiated at time 0.

```
      SUBROUTINE SSAVE                                                  SV6    1
      COMMON /GCOM1/ ATRIB(25),JEVNT,MFA,MFE(100),MLE(100),MSTOP,NCRDR,NGCOM1  1
     1NAPO,NNAPT,NNATR,NNFIL,NNQ(100),NNTRY,NPRNT,PPARM(50,4),TNOW,TTBEGGCOM1  2
     2,TTCLR,TTFIN,TTRIB(25),TTSET                                      GCOM1  3
      COMMON /GCOM2/ DD(100),DDL(100),DTFUL,DTNOW,ISEES,LFLAG(50),NFLAG,GCOM2  1
     1NNEQD,NNEQS,NNEQT,SS(100),SSL(100),TTNEX                          GCOM2  2
      CALL GPLOT (SS(2),SS(1),1)                                        SV6    2
      CALL GPLOT (SS(1),TNOW,2)                                         SV6    3
      RETURN                                                            SV6    4
C                                                                       SV6    5
      END                                                               SV6    6
```

Figure 6-5 FORTRAN listing of subroutine SSAVE (Example 6).

```
      SUBROUTINE INTLC                                                  IC6      1
      COMMON /GCOM1/ ATRIB(25),JEVNT,MFA,MFE(100),MLE(100),MSTOP,NCRDR,NGCCM1    1
     1NAPO,NNAPT,NNATR,NNFIL,NNQ(100),NNTRY,NPRNT,PPARM(50,4),TNOW,TTBEGGCOM1    2
     2,TTCLR,TTFIN,TTRIB(25),TTSET                                      GCOM1    3
      COMMON /GCOM2/ DD(100),DDL(100),DTFUL,DTNOW,ISEES,LFLAG(50),NFLAG,GCOM2    1
     1NNEQD,NNEQS,NNEQT,SS(100),SSL(100),TTNEX                          GCOM2    2
      COMMON /UCOM1/ CD,G,RHO,THED,VA,VE,XM,XS,Y1                       UCOM     1
      READ (NCRDR,101) VA                                               IC6      2
      THE=THED/57.3                                                     IC6      3
      VX= VA-VE*SIN(THE)                                                IC6      4
      VY= VE*COS(THE)                                                   IC6      5
      SS(1)=0.                                                          IC6      6
      SS(2)=0.                                                          IC6      7
      SS(3)=SQRT(VX*VX+VY*VY)                                           IC6      8
      SS(4)=ATAN(VY/VX)                                                 IC6      9
      DD(3)=0.                                                          IC6     10
      DD(4)=0.                                                          IC6     11
      RETURN                                                            IC6     12
C                                                                       IC6     13
  101 FORMAT (1F10.0)                                                   IC6     14
C                                                                       IC6     15
      END                                                               IC6     16
```

Figure 6-6 FORTRAN listing of subroutine INTLC (Example 6).

In this example the only nontermination event occurs when the pilot leaves the cockpit. Because of the simplicity of this event, it has been coded directly into subroutine STATE. Therefore, subroutine EVNTS is not required for this example. The dummy routine EVNTS included in the GASP IV package would be used under these conditions.

The procedure for initializing the GASP IV and non-GASP variables is now described. The main program initializes NCRDR and NPRNT and reads one card to initialize selected non-GASP variables. Subroutine DATIN (called by subroutine GASP) initializes the GASP IV variables. Part of this initialization involves reading the GASP IV input data cards. A listing of the input data cards and the GASP IV echo check of these cards is given in Fig. 6-7. There are 14 data cards required in this example, consisting of (1) a data card read by the main program, (2) GASP IV data card types 1, 2, 6, 9, and 11, and (3) one data card for each run read by subroutine INTLC. Prior to execution of the first run, the first 13 data cards are read. After completion of the first run, the 14th data card is read during initialization for the second run. All values from the first 12 cards are retained unless changed in a user written subroutine.* Because the GASP IV variable IICRD is set equal to 13 on data card type 11, no GASP IV data cards are read for the second run.

In this example several of the options related to the use of GPLOT are illustrated. The echo check of the input data for data card type 6

* An exception to this rule is for the variable MSTOP. If MSTOP is changed during program execution, it is reset to its input value (in subroutine GASP) to allow for multiple runs with the same stopping conditions, even if data card type 11 is bypassed.

```
    7.  32.2    1.  10.    4.   40.   15.   .0023769                                         USER
PRITSKER                6     6     30 1973    2                                            1
     0       0     0    0     2     0     0     0     0     0     4     0     0             2
6A           1X POS.                1     1    -1          -1.
6B           1YY POS.         1     1           0.          20.
6B           2TIME                  2     4     2          .01                              6
6B           1XX POS.         1     1         -70.          30.
6B           2YY POS.         1     0           0.          20.
6B           3VSPEED          2     2         100.         100.
6B           4TTHETA          0     0
     0       0          0.      5.E-6           0.         .01         .01         TEST     9
     1       1     1   13           0.          4.     0                                    11
        900.                                                                                USER
        500.
```

Figure 6-7 Input data cards and GASP IV echo check (Example 6).

```
                         SIMULATION PROJECT NUMBER  6  BY  PRITSKER

                         DATE  6/ 30/ 1973          RUN NUMBER    1 OF    2
                         LLSUP=0000000000000000     GASP IV VERSION 23JUN73

NNCLT=     0    NNSTA=     0    NNHIS=     0    NNPRN=     0    NNPLT=     2    NNSTR=     1    NNTRY=     0
NNATR=     0    NNFIL=     0    NNSET=     0    NNEQD=     4    NNEQS=     0    NFLAG=     0

GPLOT NO.  1    LLABP=X POS.    IITAP=     1    NNVAR=     1    LLPLT=    -1                   DTPLT=   -1.0000E+00
  VAR NO.  1         Y=Y POS.   LLPLO=     1    LLPHI=     1    PPLO =     0.                 PPHI =    2.0000E+01
GPLOT NO.  2    LLABP=TIME      IITAP=     2    NNVAR=     4    LLPLT=     2                   DTPLT=    1.0000E-02
  VAR NO.  1         X=X POS.   LLPLO=     1    LLPHI=     1    PPLO =    -7.0000E+01         PPHI =    3.0000E+01
  VAR NO.  2         Y=Y POS.   LLPLO=     1    LLPHI=     1    PPLO =     0.                 PPHI =    2.0000E+01
  VAR NO.  3         V=SPEED    LLPLO=     2    LLPHI=     2    PPLO =     1.0000E+02         PPHI =    1.0000E+02
  VAR NO.  4         T=THETA    LLPLO=     0    LLPHI=     0    PPLO =    -0.                 PPHI =   -0.

IIEVT=     0    LLEPR=     0    AAERR=     0.                   RRERR=     5.0000E-06
DTMIN=     1.0000E-04           DTMAX=     1.0000E-02           DTSAV=     1.0000E-02

MSTOP=     1    JJCLR=     1    JJBEG=     1    IICRD=    13    TTBEG=     0.                  TTFIN=    4.0000E+00
JJFIL=     0
IISED=    -0
```

Figure 6-7 *(continued)*

given in Fig. 6-7 indicates that the first plot uses logical tape 1 (IITAP(1) = 1). A quick plot is to be obtained (LLPLT = −1), which means that no table is prepared, maxima and minima are not found, and the user must specify the maximum and minimum ordinate values for each of the plotted variables. Since the independent variable for the first plot decreases during the simulation, the plotting interval must decrease. This is specified by making DTPLT < 0. In this example DTPLT = −1.0, which specifies that all values recorded in the interval (X + 0.5, X − 0.5) will be plotted at X.

For the second plot, both a table and plot are requested (LLPLT = 2). The plotting interval is 0.01, which in this case corresponds to the communications interval (DTSAV = 0.01). Points will be plotted at every 0.02 seconds and at event times. For variable number 1 of plot 2, the LLPLO value is one, specifying that the value of PPLO of −70. is to be used as the smallest ordinate value on the plot, that is, the value corresponding to the left most axis. For variable 3, LLPLO is 2 and PPLO is 100.0. This specifies that rounding down to the nearest 100 is desired. For example, if the smallest observed value of variable 3 is 593.0, the left hand axis would be set at 500.0. If LLPHI = 3, PPHI = 100.0, and the largest observed value is 890.0, the right hand axis would be set at 900.0. For variable 4, LLPLO and LLPHI are zero and the minimum and maximum values observed are to be used.

The sequence in which the subprograms are executed is now described. Subroutine GASP is called by the main program and immediately calls subroutine DATIN. DATIN reads in the data cards, initializes GASP IV variables, calls subroutines INTLC and STATE, and then returns to subroutine GASP. Subroutine GASP now controls the simulation by advancing time in steps. During each step advance, the RKE algorithm integrates the DD($\cdot$) equations using subroutine STATE to evaluate DD($\cdot$) at select time points within the step.

When a step is acceptable, based on consideration of accuracy, subroutine GASP calls subroutine SCOND to test if any state-events occurred because of the updating of the state variables. If a state-event was passed, the step size is reduced and the above process is repeated with a new step size. If a state-event ends the step, subroutine EVNTS is called. If the state-event is one that ends the simulation, MSTOP is set at −1 and subroutine GASP ends the run by calling OTPUT and SUMRY. When MSTOP = 1, subroutine GASP checks TNOW against TTFIN; if TNOW $\geq$ TTFIN, the simulation run is also ended.

In this example two runs were requested by reading in a value of two for NNRNS. Following the completion of the first run, subroutine GASP calls DATIN, which bypasses the reading of data cards since IICRD > 12. DATIN does reset GASP IV variables internally and calls INTLC and

```
**GASP STATE STORAGE AREA DUMP AT TIME  0.                     **

          (I)          SS(I)               DD(I)
           1           0.                 -1.0352E+01
           2           0.                  3.8637E+01
           3           8.9049E+02          0.
           4           4.3403E-02          0.
```

Figure 6-8 GASP IV printout of initial values of state variables and their derivatives (Example 6).

STATE as in the first run. Control is then returned to subroutine GASP to perform the second simulation run.

Simulation Reports

After printing the input values for a simulation, subroutine GASP prints the initial values of the state variables and their derivatives. These are shown in Fig. 6-8. Intermediate results for the first simulation in which the aircraft velocity was 900 ft/sec are shown in Fig. 6-9. Because a zero tolerance was specified for detecting a crossing in subroutine SCOND, diagnostic messages that tolerances on the state-events could not be met were expected. The messages could have been suppressed by setting the GASP IV variable LLERR = −1, but it was decided to retain the diagnostics to clearly indicate the occurrence of the specified state conditions. The messages indicate that the pilot left the cockpit at time 0.10359 and the simulation ended at time 0.43052. Since DTMIN was set at 0.0001, these results indicate that the pilot left the cockpit in the time interval, 0.10349–0.10359, and that the conditions for ending the simulation occurred in the interval 0.43042–0.43052.

Figure 6-10 is the plot of the pilot's position relative to the aircraft resulting from the first run. Note that the independent variable on the first plot is not time. The independent variable is, however, a monotonically nonincreasing variable. With GASP IV, the independent variable must be monotonically nonincreasing if DTPLT <0 and monotonically

```
                                              **INTERMEDIATE RESULTS**


SPECIFIED  TOLERANCE  EXCEEDED FOR SS(  2) AT TIME   1.0359E-01

SPECIFIED  TOLERANCE  EXCEEDED FOR SS(  1) AT TIME   4.3052E-01
```

Figure 6-9 Intermediate results showing diagnostic messages for Example 6.

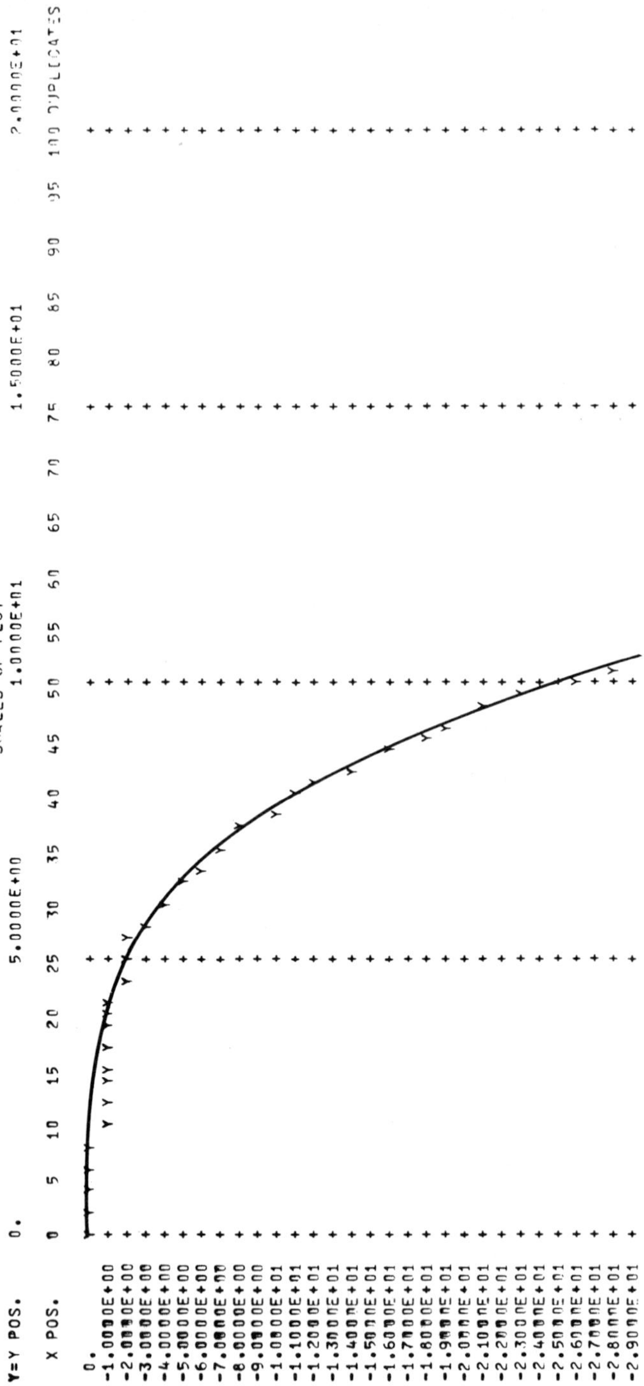

PLOT NUMBER 1
RUN NUMBER 1
SCALES OF PLOT
Y=Y POS.
X POS.
0.
5.0000E+00
1.0000E+01
1.5000E+01
2.0000E+01
DUPLICATES

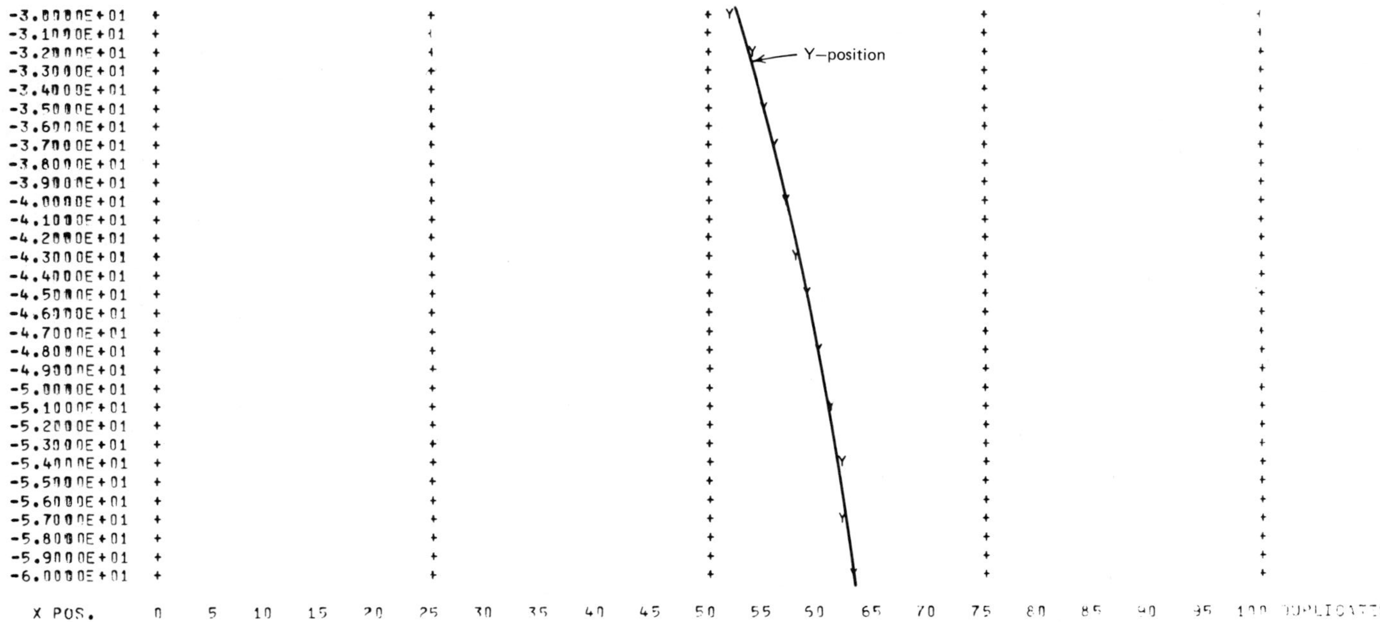

OUTPUT CONSISTS OF 49 POINT SETS (49 POINTS)

Figure 6-10 Plot of pilot's position relative to aircraft for aircraft velocity of 900 ft/sec.

nondecreasing if DTPLT > 0. From the first plot, it is seen that the pilot clears the cockpit (Y = 4.0) at about X = −1.0. At X = −30.0, Y is approximately 10.4 and at X = −60.0, Y is approximately 12.8. Clearly, problems exist with the ejection system if aircraft velocity is 900 ft/sec. If desired, the precise values for X and Y could have been obtained by requesting a table. Since they are printed out for plot 2, this was not done.

The table for plot 2 is labeled ** TABLE NUMBER 2 ** and is presented in Fig. 6-11. In this table, the state variables are given as a function of time. The state-event representing the pilot leaving the cockpit is seen at time 0.10359. At this time, two sets of values are shown in the table since GASP IV records the values at the end of the step before the event and immediately after the event occurs. This second set of values is recorded in case the event causes a discrete change in the variables. At the end of the table, minimum and maximum values are printed.

The plot corresponding to the table is presented in Fig. 6-12. At the top of the plot, the symbols representing the variables are defined with the scales for each variable. The scales used correspond to the input conditions specified. The plots illustrate how the state variables change with time.

The form of the output of the second run is similar to the output of the first run. Figure 6-13 presents the plot of the state variables over time, when the aircraft is traveling at 500 ft/sec. In this case, the pilot is above the 12 ft level at 0.37 sec, at which time he is 16.8 ft behind the cockpit.

EXAMPLE 7—ANALYSIS OF A SLIP CLUTCH

Statement of the Problem

The system to be modeled involves a slip clutch commonly used in business machines. It consists of an electric motor, a slip clutch, a 50:1 gear transmission, a cam, and an arresting spring. The presentation is based on a model developed by Tramposch and Jones (133), who modified 1130 CSMP in order to code the model.

The motor of the system drives the cam through the transmission and clutch. The operational sequence begins with the entire system at rest. The motor is turned on and drives the system until the cam has almost completed one revolution. The motor is turned off when the motor shaft displacement is 306 rad, which corresponds to a cam displacement of

TABLE NUMBER 2
RUN NUMBER 1

TIME	X POS.	Y POS.	SPEED	THETA
0.	0.	0.	8.9049E+02	4.3403E-02
0.	0.	0.	8.9049E+02	4.3403E-02
1.0000E-02	-1.0352E-01	3.8637E-01	8.9049E+02	4.3403E-02
2.0000E-02	-2.0704E-01	7.7274E-01	8.9049E+02	4.3403E-02
3.0000E-02	-3.1056E-01	1.1591E+00	8.9049E+02	4.3403E-02
4.0000E-02	-4.1408E-01	1.5455E+00	8.9049E+02	4.3403E-02
5.0000E-02	-5.1760E-01	1.9319E+00	8.9049E+02	4.3403E-02
6.0000E-02	-6.2112E-01	2.3182E+00	8.9049E+02	4.3403E-02
7.0000E-02	-7.2464E-01	2.7046E+00	8.9049E+02	4.3403E-02
8.0000E-02	-8.2816E-01	3.0910E+00	8.9049E+02	4.3403E-02
9.0000E-02	-9.3168E-01	3.4774E+00	8.9049E+02	4.3403E-02
1.0000E-01	-1.0352E+00	3.8637E+00	8.9049E+02	4.3403E-02
1.0359E-01	-1.0809E+00	4.0019E+00	8.8570E+02	4.3274E-02
1.0359E-01	-1.0809E+00	4.0019E+00	8.8570E+02	4.3274E-02
1.1000E-01	-1.2050E+00	4.2456E+00	8.7723E+02	4.3040E-02
1.2000E-01	-1.5054E+00	4.6187E+00	8.6435E+02	4.2670E-02
1.3000E-01	-1.9326E+00	4.9831E+00	8.5183E+02	4.2295E-02
1.4000E-01	-2.4828E+00	5.3391E+00	8.3968E+02	4.1915E-02
1.5000E-01	-3.1527E+00	5.6869E+00	8.2786E+02	4.1529E-02
1.6000E-01	-3.9388E+00	6.0266E+00	8.1637E+02	4.1138E-02
1.7000E-01	-4.8380E+00	6.3584E+00	8.0520E+02	4.0741E-02
1.8000E-01	-5.8472E+00	6.6825E+00	7.9433E+02	4.0338E-02
1.9000E-01	-6.9634E+00	6.9991E+00	7.8375E+02	3.9931E-02
2.0000E-01	-8.1838E+00	7.3083E+00	7.7344E+02	3.9517E-02
2.1000E-01	-9.5058E+00	7.6103E+00	7.6340E+02	3.9099E-02
2.2000E-01	-1.0927E+01	7.9052E+00	7.5362E+02	3.8674E-02
2.3000E-01	-1.2444E+01	8.1931E+00	7.4409E+02	3.8245E-02
2.4000E-01	-1.4055E+01	8.4742E+00	7.3480E+02	3.7810E-02
2.5000E-01	-1.5758E+01	8.7487E+00	7.2573E+02	3.7369E-02
2.6000E-01	-1.7550E+01	9.0165E+00	7.1688E+02	3.6923E-02
2.7000E-01	-1.9429E+01	9.2780E+00	7.0825E+02	3.6471E-02
2.8000E-01	-2.1393E+01	9.5331E+00	6.9983E+02	3.6014E-02
2.9000E-01	-2.3441E+01	9.7820E+00	6.9160E+02	3.5552E-02
3.0000E-01	-2.5569E+01	1.0025E+01	6.8356E+02	3.5084E-02
3.1000E-01	-2.7777E+01	1.0262E+01	6.7571E+02	3.4610E-02
3.2000E-01	-3.0063E+01	1.0492E+01	6.6803E+02	3.4131E-02
3.3000E-01	-3.2424E+01	1.0718E+01	6.6053E+02	3.3647E-02
3.4000E-01	-3.4859E+01	1.0937E+01	6.5319E+02	3.3157E-02
3.5000E-01	-3.7367E+01	1.1151E+01	6.4602E+02	3.2661E-02
3.6000E-01	-3.9945E+01	1.1359E+01	6.3900E+02	3.2160E-02
3.7000E-01	-4.2593E+01	1.1562E+01	6.3213E+02	3.1654E-02
3.8000E-01	-4.5308E+01	1.1759E+01	6.2541E+02	3.1142E-02
3.9000E-01	-4.8090E+01	1.1951E+01	6.1883E+02	3.0625E-02
4.0000E-01	-5.0937E+01	1.2138E+01	6.1238E+02	3.0102E-02
4.1000E-01	-5.3848E+01	1.2320E+01	6.0607E+02	2.9574E-02
4.2000E-01	-5.6821E+01	1.2496E+01	5.9989E+02	2.9040E-02
4.3000E-01	-5.9855E+01	1.2668E+01	5.9383E+02	2.8500E-02
4.3052E-01	-6.0014E+01	1.2677E+01	5.9352E+02	2.8472E-02
4.3052E-01	-6.0014E+01	1.2677E+01	5.9352E+02	2.8472E-02
MINIMUM	-6.0014E+01	0.	5.9352E+02	2.8472E-02
MAXIMUM	0.	1.2677E+01	8.9049E+02	4.3403E-02

Figure 6-11 Table of values for plot 2 of pilot ejection model with aircraft velocity of 900 ft/sec.

PLOT NUMBER 2
RUN NUMBER 1

SCALES OF PLOT

X=X POS.	-7.0000E+01	-4.5000E+01	-2.0000E+01	5.0000E+00	3.0000E+01
Y=Y POS.	0.	5.0000E+00	1.0000E+01	1.5000E+01	2.0000E+01
V=SPEED	5.0000E+02	6.0000E+02	7.0000E+02	8.0000E+02	9.0000E+02
T=THETA	2.8472E-02	3.2205E-02	3.5937E-02	3.9670E-02	4.3403E-02

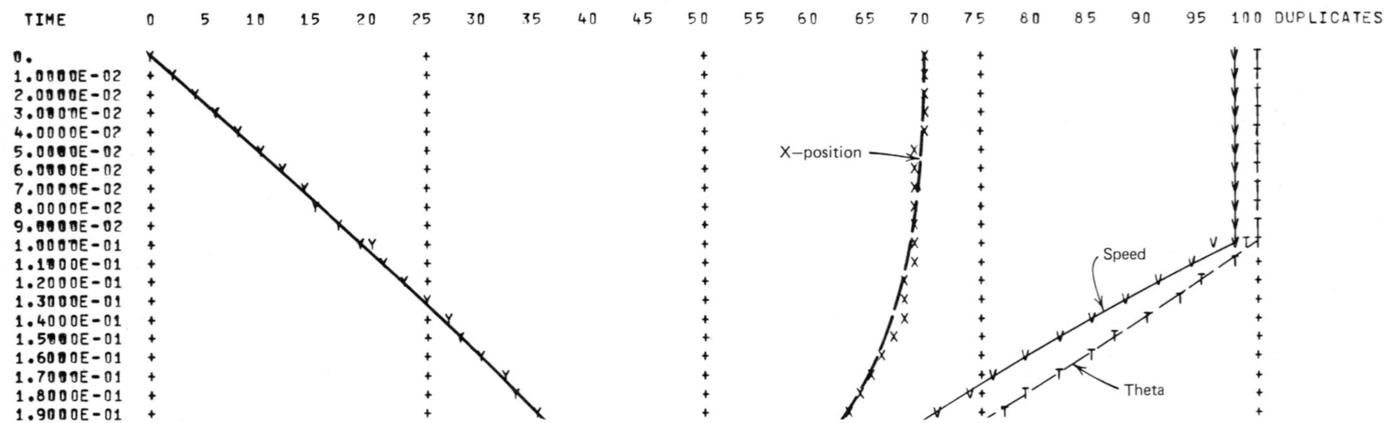

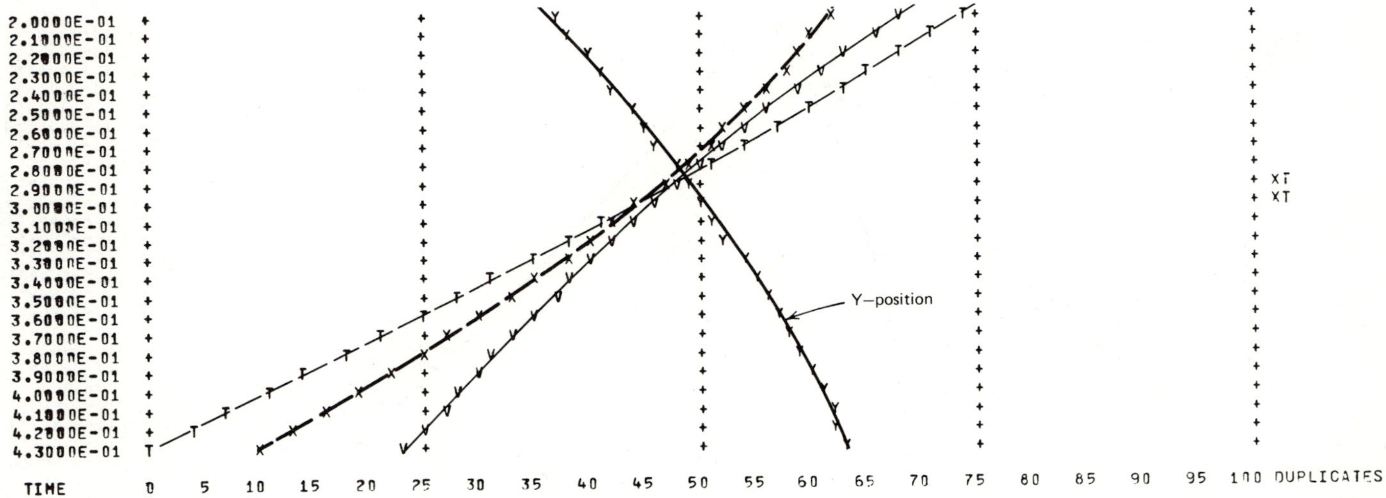

OUTPUT CONSISTS OF 49 POINT SETS (135 POINTS)

Figure 6-12 Plot of pilot position and velocity over time for pilot ejection model with aircraft velocity of 900 ft/sec.

PLOT NUMBER 2
RUN NUMBER 2

SCALES OF PLOT

X=X POS.	-7.0000E+01	-4.5000E+01	-2.0000E+01	5.0000E+00	3.0000E+01
Y=Y POS.	0.	5.0000E+00	1.0000E+01	1.5000E+01	2.0000E+01
V=SPEED	3.0000E+02	3.5000E+02	4.0000E+02	4.5000E+02	5.0000E+02
T=THETA	3.1168E-02	4.3063E-02	5.4957E-02	6.6851E-02	7.8745E-02

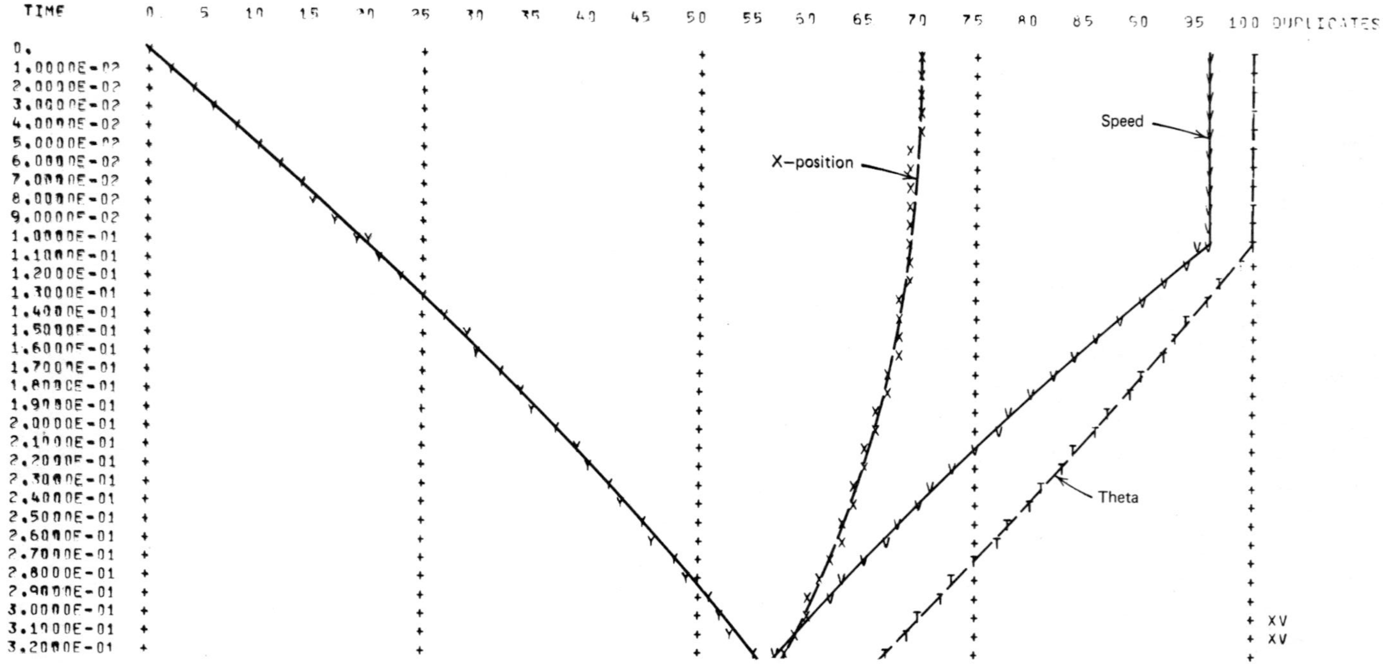

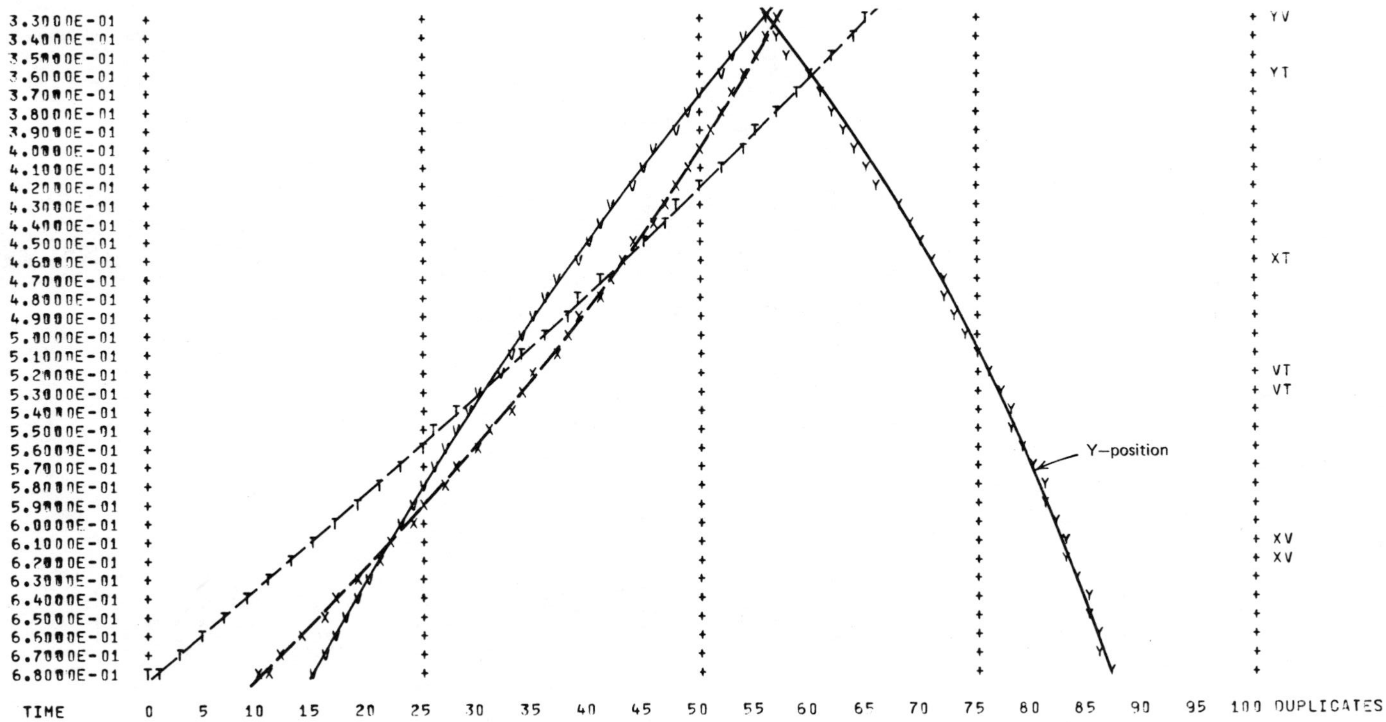

OUTPUT CONSISTS OF 74 POINT SETS (295 POINTS)

Figure 6-13 Plot of pilot position and velocity over time for pilot ejection model with aircraft velocity of 500 ft/sec.

Table 6-2 Motor Torque as a Function of Motor Velocity

Motor Velocity	Motor Torque
0.00	0.525
126.00	0.413
252.00	0.356
378.00	0.300
504.00	0.244
630.00	0.187
756.00	0.144
882.00	0.109
1008.00	0.070
1134.00	0.030
1260.00	0.000

306/50 = 6.12 rad. The system then coasts until the cam displacement reaches 314/50 rad at which time the arresting spring is engaged. Following engagement of the arresting spring (causing a very high arresting torque on the cam), impact conditions prevail as the system is slowed. As a result of the relatively high moment of inertia of the motor and the maximum torque that can be transmitted across the clutch, the system oscillates several times between a slip and a nonslip mode as the motor is slowed down.

The characteristics of the motor are given by its moment of inertia and an empirically determined torque, as presented in Table 6-2. The slip clutch is described by the maximum torque it can transmit. The cam is characterized by its moment of inertia and an empirically determined torque, as presented in Table 6-3. The arresting spring is described by the resultant arresting torque associated with it.

Table 6-3 Cam Torque as a Function of Cam Displacement

Cam Displacement	Cam Torque
0.0	0.125
31.4	0.505
62.8	0.016
94.4	0.344
125.6	0.090
157.0	0.060
188.4	0.070
251.2	0.078
282.6	0.562
314.0	0.090

Simulation Objectives

The objective of this example is to use GASP IV to analyze the Tramposch and Jones model for the slip clutch. The desired outputs from the simulation analysis are:

1. Motor shaft velocity as a function of time.
2. Cam shaft velocity as a function of time.
3. Cam shaft displacement as a function of time.
4. Impact torque as a function of time.

Special Features

This example demonstrates the use of state-events to change the equations describing a model. The method for describing a set of higher order (second order in this case) differential equations is applied. An EQUIVALENCE statement is used in subroutine STATE to allow for better mnemonic description of the equations for state variables.

Simulation Procedure

Since the model to be simulated is given, only the procedures required to use GASP IV to code the model are presented.

In the model equations, the gear transmission is effectively eliminated by adjusting the torque across it and writing all equations in terms of motor shaft displacement, velocity, and acceleration. Thus the model cam displacement, velocity, or acceleration must be divided by 50 to obtain their equivalent actual values. The equations for the model that are derived based on the equations of motion for the system are as follows.

MODE = 1. No Clutch Slip

$$\ddot{\Theta}_M = [\mathrm{ON} \star T_1(\dot{\Theta}_M) - \mathrm{SPRNG} \star (\Theta_c - \mathrm{THTAS}) - T_2(\Theta_c)]/(\mathrm{XIM} + \mathrm{XIC})$$

$$\ddot{\Theta}_c = \ddot{\Theta}_M$$

MODE = 2. Clutch Slip

$$\ddot{\Theta}_M = [\mathrm{ON} \star T_1(\dot{\Theta}_M) - \mathrm{TORQS}]/\mathrm{XIM}$$

$$\ddot{\Theta}_c = [\mathrm{TORQS} - \mathrm{SPRNG} \star (\Theta_c - \mathrm{THTAS}) - T_2(\Theta_c)]/\mathrm{XIC}$$

where Θ_M and Θ_c are the angular displacements of the motor and cam, respectively (dots above a variable are used to indicate time derivatives), $T_i(\cdot)$ is table look-up function i, and the other variables are as defined in Table 6-4.

Table 6-4 Definitions of State Variables and Non-GASP Variables

Variable	Initial Value	Definition
ACCC = DD(4)	Computed	Angular acceleration of the cam shaft
ACCM = DD(2)	Computed	Angular acceleration of the motor shaft
DISC = SS(3)	0.0	Angular displacement of the cam shaft
DISM = SS(1)	0.0	Angular displacement of the motor shaft
MODE	1	Indicator showing which set of state equations applies
ON	1.0	Indicator showing if motor is on (1.0) or off (0.0)
SPRNG	0.0	Spring constant of arresting spring if spring is engaged; zero otherwise
THTAM	306.0	Angular displacement of motor shaft at which motor is turned off or on
THTAS	314.0	Angular displacement of cam shaft at which arresting spring is engaged
TORQC	Computed	Cam torque
TORQI = SS(5)	Computed	Impact torque; torque caused by arresting spring
TORQM = SS(6)	Computed	Motor torque
TORQS	0.876	Slip torque; maximum torque transmitted by clutch
VELC = SS(4) = DD(3)	0.0	Angular velocity of the cam shaft
VELM = SS(2) = DD(1)	0.0	Angular velocity of the motor shaft
XIC	1./245000.0	Moment of inertia of cam
XIM	1./10500.0	Moment of inertia of motor

Transforming the model into GASP IV terms involves two steps. First, the equations must be converted to a set of first order differential equations using the procedures described in Chapter 3. Second, the GASP IV state variable arrays SS(·) and DD(·) must be used.

For j = M and c, let $\dot{\Theta}_{j1} = \Theta_{j2} = \dot{\Theta}_j$. This specifies that $\dot{\Theta}_{j2} = \ddot{\Theta}_j$ and $\Theta_{j1} = \Theta_j$. Using these variables, the equations for the model become as follows.

MODE = 1. No Clutch Slip

$$\dot{\Theta}_{M2} = [\text{ON} \star T_1(\Theta_{M2}) - \text{SPRNG} \star (\Theta_{c1} - \text{THTAS}) - T_2(\Theta_{c1})]/(\text{XIM} + \text{XIC})$$

$$\dot{\Theta}_{M1} = \Theta_{M2}$$

$$\Theta_{c2} = \Theta_{M2}$$

$$\dot{\Theta}_{c1} = \Theta_{c2}$$

MODE = 2. Clutch Slip

$$\dot{\Theta}_{M2} = [\text{ON} \star T_1(\Theta_{M2}) - \text{TORQS})/\text{XIM}$$

$$\dot{\Theta}_{M1} = \Theta_{M2}$$

$$\dot{\Theta}_{c2} = [\text{TORQS} - \text{SPRNG} \star (\Theta_{c1} - \text{THTAS}) - T_2(\Theta_{c1})]/\text{XIC}$$

$$\dot{\Theta}_{c1} = \Theta_{c2}$$

This completes the first step in the transformation.

Transforming the equations into the GASP IV variables is now a direct substitution by equating the following variables: DISM = SS(1) = Θ_{M1}, DD(1) = $\dot{\Theta}_{M1}$, VELM = SS(2) = Θ_{M2}, ACCM = DD(2) = $\dot{\Theta}_{M2}$, DISC = SS(3) = Θ_{c1}, DD(3) = $\dot{\Theta}_{c1}$, VELC = SS(4) = Θ_{c2}, and ACCC = DD(4) = $\dot{\Theta}_{c2}$.

In this example it is desired to plot impact torque. SS(5) will represent this quantity, that is, SS(5) = SPRNG ★ (Θ_{c1} − THTAS). Also, a state condition is defined on the motor torque. To facilitate the use of the function KROSS, SS(6) is defined as the motor torque, that is, SS(6) = ON ★ $T_1(\Theta_{M2})$.

For documentation purposes, the SS(·) and DD(·) arrays were equivalenced to more recognizable names, as defined in Table 6-4, through the following FORTRAN EQUIVALENCE statement:

```
EQUIVALENCE (DISM,SS(1)),(VELM,SS(2)),(ACCM,DD(2)),(DISC,SS
(3)),(VELC,SS(4)),(ACCC,DD(4)),(TORQI,SS(5)),(TORQM,SS(6))
```

The cam torque is defined as TORQC = $T_2(\Theta_{c1})$. The equations of the model using the new variable names are as follows.

MODE = 1. No Clutch Slip

```
ACCM = [ON ★ TORQM − TORQI − TORQC]/(XIM + XIC)
DD(1) = VELM
ACCC = ACCM
DD(3) = VELC
```

MODE = 2. Clutch Slip

```
ACCM = (ON ★ TORQM − TORQS)/XIM
```

DD(1) = VELM
ACCC = (TORQS − TORQC − TORQI)/XIC
DD(3) = VELC

The coding of these equations is given in subroutine STATE. The FORTRAN listing of STATE is given in Fig. 6-14. The coding is taken directly from the derived model with the variable MODE used to determine the set of equations to be used. The GASP IV table-look-up function GTABL is used to obtain the motor torque and cam torque.

The tables providing the functional relationships for motor torque and cam torque are initialized in the main program along with the other variables defined in Table 6-4. The FORTRAN listing of the main program is given in Fig. 6-15.

In this example QSET is used only for the storage of plot data and must be dimensioned greater than the amount of data to be saved. The dimension should be greater than the number of variables to be plotted on a line, plus one (for the independent variable), times the number of point sets to be saved. The user must also remember to set NNSET on data card type 2 to a value equal to the dimension of QSET.

The state-events defined for this model are: (1) turn on motor; (2) turn off motor; (3) engage arresting spring; (4) disengage arresting spring; (5) begin clutch slip; (6) end clutch slip; and (7) save minimum cam velocity.* Subroutine SCOND performs the dual function of causing GASP to search for specified state conditions defining these state-

```
      SUBROUTINE STATE                                                  ST7      1
      COMMON /GCOM2/ DD(100),DDL(100),DTFUL,DTNOW,ISEES,LFLAG(50),NFLAG,GCOM2    1
     1NNEQD,NNEQS,NNEQT,SS(100),SSL(100),TTNEX                          GCOM2    2
      COMMON /UCOM1/ MODE,ON,SPRNG,THTAM,THTAS,TORQS,XIC,XIM,TORQCT(11),UCOM1    1
     1TORQMT(11)                                                        UCOM1    2
      EQUIVALENCE (DISM,SS(1)),(VELM,SS(2)),(ACCM,DD(2)),(DISC,SS(3)),(VUSEQV    1
     1ELC,SS(4)),(ACCC,DD(4)),(TORQI,SS(5)),(TORQM,SS(6))              USEQV    2
      TORQM=GTABL(TORQMT,VELM,0.,1250.0002,126.00002)*ON               ST7      2
      TORQI=SPRNG*(DISC-THTAS)                                          ST7      3
      TORQC=GTABL(TORQCT,DISC,0.,314.,31.4)                            ST7      4
      GO TO (101,102), MODE                                             ST7      5
  101 ACCM=(TORQM-TORQC-TORQI)/(XIM+XIC)                                ST7      6
      ACCC=ACCM                                                         ST7      7
      GO TO 103                                                         ST7      8
  102 ACCM=(TORQM-TORQS)/XIM                                            ST7      9
      ACCC=(TORQS-TORQC-TORQI)/XIC                                      ST7     10
  103 DD(1)=VELM                                                        ST7     11
      DD(3)=VELC                                                        ST7     12
      RETURN                                                            ST7     13
C                                                                       ST7     14
      END                                                               ST7     15
```

Figure 6-14 FORTRAN listing of subroutine STATE (Example 7).

* The occurrence of minimum cam velocity can be thought of as an information-gathering event.

```
      PROGRAM MAIN (INPUT,OUTPUT,TAPE5=INPUT,TAPE6=OUTPUT)               MX7
      DIMENSION NSET(10000)                                              DIM
      COMMON QSET(10000)                                                 COM
      COMMON /GCOM1/ ATRIB(25),JEVNT,MFA,MFE(100),MLE(100),MSTOP,NCRDR,NGCOM1
     1NAPO,NNAPT,NNATR,NNFIL,NNQ(100),NNTRY,NPRNT,PPARM(50,4),TNOW,TTBEGGCOM1
     2,TTCLR,TTFIN,TTRIB(25),TTSET                                       GCOM1
      COMMON /GCOM2/ DD(100),DDL(100),DTFUL,DTNOW,ISEES,LFLAG(50),NFLAG,GCOM2
     1NNEQD,NNEQS,NNEQT,SS(100),SSL(100),TTNEX                           GCOM2
      COMMON /UCOM1/ MODE,ON,SPRNG,THTAM,THTAS,TORQS,XIC,XIM,TORQCT(11),UCOM1
     1TORQMT(11)                                                         UCOM1
      EQUIVALENCE (DISM,SS(1)),(VELM,SS(2)),(ACCM,DD(2)),(DISC,SS(3)),(VUSEQV
     1ELC,SS(4)),(ACCC,DD(4)),(TORQI,SS(5)),(TORQM,SS(6))                USEQV
      EQUIVALENCE(NSET(1),QSET(1))                                       EQUIV
      NCRDR=5                                                            MX7
      NPRNT=6                                                            MX7
      DO 101 I=1,4                                                       MX7
  101 SS(I)=0.                                                           MX7
      XIM=1./10500.                                                      MX7
      XIC=1./245000.                                                     MX7
      TORQS=.876                                                         MX7
      ON=1.                                                              MX7
      SPRNG=0.                                                           MX7
      MODE=1                                                             MX7
      THTAM=306.                                                         MX7
      THTAS=314.                                                         MX7
      READ (NCRDR,102) TORQCT                                            MX7
      READ (NCRDR,102) TORQMT                                            MX7
      CALL GASP                                                          MX7
      CALL EXIT                                                          MX7
C                                                                        MX7
  102 FORMAT (11F5.3)                                                    MX7
C                                                                        MX7
      END                                                                MX7
```

Figure 6-15 FORTRAN listing of main program (Example 7).

events and to mark the occurrence of those conditions. The FORTRAN listing for subroutine SCOND is given in Fig. 6-16. LFLAG(1) is used to define state-events 1 and 2, which occur when the motor displacement (SS(1) = DISM) crosses THTAM in either direction. LFLAG(2) is used to define state-events 3 and 4, which occur when the cam displacement (SS(3) = DISM) crosses THTAS in either direction.

LFLAG(3) is used to define state-event 5 where the clutch begins to slip. This occurs when the motor torque (SS(6) = TORQM) exceeds ACCM ⋆ XIM + TORQS in the positive direction. The specified condition of TORQM crossing ACCM ⋆ XIM + TORQS in the positive direc-

```
      SUBROUTINE SCOND                                                   SC7
      COMMON /GCOM2/ DD(100),DDL(100),DTFUL,DTNOW,ISEES,LFLAG(50),NFLAG,GCOM2
     1NNEQD,NNEQS,NNEQT,SS(100),SSL(100),TTNEX                           GCOM2
      COMMON /UCOM1/ MODE,ON,SPRNG,THTAM,THTAS,TORQS,XIC,XIM,TORQCT(11),UCOM1
     1TORQMT(11)                                                         UCOM1
      LFLAG(1)=KROSS(1,0,0.,THTAM,0,.1)                                  SC7
      LFLAG(2)=KROSS(3,0,0.,THTAS,0,.1)                                  SC7
      LFLAG(3)=KROSS(6,-2,XIM,TORQS,1,.001)                              SC7
      LFLAG(4)=KROSS(4,2,1.,0.,1,.2)                                     SC7
      LFLAG(5)=KROSS(-4,0,0.,0.,1,1.)                                    SC7
      RETURN                                                             SC7
C                                                                        SC7
      END                                                                SC7
```

Figure 6-16 FORTRAN listing of subroutine SCOND (Example 7).

tion is equivalent to TORQM − ACCM ⋆ XIM crossing TORQS in the positive direction. This is the condition for the beginning of slip because the torque exerted by the motor on the slip clutch exceeds the torque that the clutch can transmit.

LFLAG(4) is used to define state-event 6, the ending of clutch slip. This occurs when the cam velocity (SS(4) = VELC) crosses the motor velosity (SS(2) = VELM) in the positive direction. LFLAG(5) is used to define the times at which the cam velocity goes from a negative value to a positive value. This occurs when the cam acceleration (SS(6) = ACCC) crosses zero in the positive direction.

The state conditions to be detected as a result of the coding of subroutine SCOND, presented in Fig. 6-16, are summarized on page 313 where XDPT = XIM ⋆ DD(2) + TORQS. Note that LFLAG(1) and LFLAG(2) can have values of +2, +1, 0, −1, or −2 because they flag crossings in both directions. However, LFLAG(3), LFLAG(4), and LFLAG(5) can only have values of +2, +1, or 0 because they only flag crossings in the positive direction. Also, the values of LFLAG(I), I = 1, NFLAG are reset to zero after subroutine EVNTS is called. Thus LFLAG(I) specifies the point of achievement of the state conditions, not the continued existence of conditions. The LFLAG vector is used in subroutine EVNTS to cause the model changes required when state-events occur.

Figure 6-17 presents the FORTRAN listing of subroutine EVNTS. In this example no separate event subroutines are used and all state-events are coded in EVNTS. Subroutine EVNTS consists of sequential testing of the flagged state conditions. If LFLAG(1) < 0, the motor is turned on.

```
      SUBROUTINE EVNTS (IX)                                             EV7      1
      COMMON /GCOM2/ DD(100),DDL(100),DTFUL,DTNOW,ISEES,LFLAG(50),NFLAG,GCOM2    1
     1NNEQD,NNEQS,NNEQT,SS(100),SSL(100),TTNEX                          GCOM2    2
      COMMON /UCOM1/ MODE,ON,SPRNG,THTAM,THTAS,TORQS,XIC,XIM,TORQCT(11),UCOM1    1
     1TORQMT(11)                                                        UCOM1    2
      EQUIVALENCE (DISM,SS(1)),(VELM,SS(2)),(ACCM,DD(2)),(DISC,SS(3)),(VUSEQV    1
     1ELC,SS(4)),(ACCC,DD(4)),(TORQI,SS(5)),(TORQM,SS(6))               USEQV    2
      IF (LFLAG(1)) 101,103,102                                         EV7      2
  101 ON=1.                                                             EV7      3
      GO TO 103                                                         EV7      4
  102 ON=0.                                                             EV7      5
  103 IF (LFLAG(2)) 105,106,104                                         EV7      6
  104 SPRNG=2.2                                                         EV7      7
      GO TO 106                                                         EV7      8
  105 SPRNG=0.                                                          EV7      9
  106 IF (LFLAG(3)) 108,108,107                                         EV7     10
  107 MODE=2                                                            EV7     11
  108 IF (LFLAG(4)) 110,110,109                                         EV7     12
  109 MODE=1                                                            EV7     13
      VELC=VELM                                                         EV7     14
  110 RETURN                                                            EV7     15
C                                                                       EV7     16
      END                                                               EV7     17
```

Figure 6-17 FORTRAN listing of subroutine EVNTS (Example 7).

State Variable	Equivalent Variable	Flag Value	Crossing Condition	Tolerance Interval Defining State-Event
SS(1)	DISM	LFLAG(1) = +1	↑THTAM	THTAM ≤ SS(1) ≤ THTAM + 0.1
SS(1)	DISM	LFLAG(1) = −1	↓THTAM	THTAM − 0.1 ≤ SS(1) ≤ THTAM
SS(3)	DISC	LFLAG(2) = +1	↑THTAS	THTAS ≤ SS(3) ≤ THTAS + 0.1
SS(3)	DISC	LFLAG(2) = −1	↓THTAS	THTAS − 0.1 ≤ SS(3) ≤ THTAS
SS(6)	TORQM	LFLAG(3) = +1	↑XDPT	XDPT ≤ SS(6) ≤ XDPT + .001
SS(4)	VELC	LFLAG(4) = +1	↑SS(2)	SS(2) ≤ SS(4) ≤ SS(2) + 0.2
DD(4)	ACCC	LFLAG(5) = +1	↑0.0	0.0 ≤ DD(4) ≤ 1.0

If LFLAG(1) > 0, the motor is turned off. If LFLAG(2) < 0, the spring is disengaged. If LFLAG(2) > 0, the spring is engaged. If LFLAG(3) > 0, the MODE $= 2$ set of equations are used. If LFLAG(4) > 0, the MODE $= 1$ set of equations are used. Simply stated, when the velocity of both sides of the clutch is the same, slip has ceased. Because there is a tolerance associated with the location of state-events, when LFLAG(4) > 0 the velocity of the motor will not be exactly equal to the velocity of the cam. They may differ by 0.2 rad/sec if the crossing is within tolerance, by more if it is not. To compensate for this, cam velocity is equated to motor velocity whenever LFLAG(4) $= 1$. This causes no computational difficulties since it occurs only at event times. Note that LFLAG(5) is not used in subroutine EVNTS; in fact, on input NFLAG is set at four, indicating that there are only four state condition indicator flags being used. In this case, LFLAG(5) is being used as a dummy variable. The same can be done with any of the GASP IV variables that are dimensioned to a value greater than that which is used in a given simulation. The state condition associated with LFLAG(5) is defined only to assure that all local minima of cam velocity will appear in the output.

The FORTRAN listing of subroutine SSAVE is given in Fig. 6-18. In this example it serves only to save data for a table and plot.

The input data and the GASP IV echo check are shown in Fig. 6-19. The first two data cards are non-GASP data cards read by the main program. Subsequent input are GASP IV data cards: one type 1, one type 2, five type 6, one type 9, and one type 11.

Simulation Reports

The motor and cam start at rest and their velocities and displacements gradually increase. The plot of motor velocity, cam displacement, cam

```
      SUBROUTINE SSAVE                                                  SV7       1
      COMMON /GCOM1/ ATRIB(25),JEVNT,MFA,MFE(100),MLE(100),MSTOP,NCRDR,NGCOM1     1
     1NAPO,NNAPT,NNATR,NNFIL,NNQ(100),NNTRY,NPRNT,PPARM(50,4),TNOW,TTBEGGCOM1     2
     2,TTCLR,TTFIN,TTRIB(25),TTSET                                      GCOM1     3
      COMMON /GCOM2/ DD(100),DDL(100),DTFUL,DTNOW,ISEES,LFLAG(50),NFLAG,GCOM2     1
     1NNEQD,NNEQS,NNEQT,SS(100),SSL(100),TTNEX                          GCOM2     2
      COMMON /UCOM1/ MODE,ON,SPRNG,THTAM,THTAS,TORQS,XIC,XIM,TORQCT(11),UCOM1     1
     1TOROMT(11)                                                        UCOM1     2
      EQUIVALENCE (DISM,SS(1)),(VELM,SS(2)),(ACCM,DD(2)),(DISC,SS(3)),(VUSEQV     1
     1ELC,SS(4)),(ACCC,DD(4)),(TORQI,SS(5)),(TORQM,SS(6))               USEQV     2
      CALL GPLOT (SS(2),TNOW,1)                                         SV7       2
      RETURN                                                            SV7       3
C                                                                       SV7       4
      END                                                               SV7       5
```

Figure 6-18 FORTRAN listing of subroutine SSAVE (Example 7).

velocity, and impact torque, starting at time 0.590 sec is shown in Fig. 6-20. From the plot, impact starts at approximately 0.775 sec and lasts until 0.85 sec. The details of the impact region can be obtained by examining the values in the table corresponding to this region, which is shown in Fig. 6-21.

From Fig. 6-21 it is seen that the cam shaft displacement (and, therefore, the motor shaft displacement) exceeds 306 rad at time 0.76075 causing a state-event to occur. In subroutine EVNTS the motor is turned off. Cam displacement continues until it exceeds 314 rad at time 0.77487. This state-event causes the arresting spring to be engaged. Note that in the table state-events can be identified since two lines are provided for each state-event occurrence. Both the values before and after the event are tabulated. The initial slip occurs at time 0.77544. At time 0.78050, the arresting spring is disengaged since the cam shaft displacement decreased below 314 rad. At time 0.78535 slip ceases as the cam shaft velocity (469.86) exceeds the motor shaft velocity (464.82). The difference in the velocities is greater than the tolerance (0.2) prescribed for the state-event in subroutine SCOND. This results in a message indicating that the tolerance is too tight or that DTMIN is too large. The warning messages for this example, showing all the cases in which tolerances could not be met, are illustrated in Fig. 6-22.

At the ending of slip condition at time 0.78535, the motor and cam shaft velocities are equated as described previously. Although not illustrated in Fig. 6-21, the slip-nonslip operation repeated until time 0.84850 when impact was completed.

The simulation is completed at time 1.0, which was the TTFIN value specified. At the end of the table the minimum and maximum values observed for the tabled variables are printed.

EXERCISES

6-1. In the pilot ejection model described in Example 6, include a state-event that occurs when the pilot leaves the cockpit. When this state-event occurs, a uniformly distributed disturbance of 0 to 10 ft/sec affects the velocity of the pilot and the seat. Simulate the pilot ejection system under these conditions.

6-2. Modify the pilot ejection model of Example 6 to allow for a two-pilot aircraft. The second pilot ejects from the aircraft 1 sec after the first pilot. The second pilot is located 7 ft behind the first pilot. Simulate the system for an aircraft speed of 500 ft/sec to determine if the pilots maintain a separation of 5 ft and if the pilots clear the aircraft. Assume all parameters used in Example 6 hold for the two pilot situation.

Input cards	USER
.125 .505 .016 .344 .090 .060 .070 .070 .078 .562 .090 .525 .413 .356 .300 .244 .187 .144 .109 .070 .030 0.00	
PRITSKER 7 6 30 1973 1	1
0 0 0 0 1 0 0 0 010000 4 2 4	2
6A 1TIME 0 4 2 .005 6B 12M VEL 1 1 -1000. 1000. 6B 23C DIS 1 1 0. 500. 6B 34C VEL 1 1 -1000. 1000. 6B 4TTORQI 1 1 0. 50.	6
1 0 0. 5.E-6 .0001 .001 .001	9
1 0 1 0 0. 1.	11

Figure 6-19 Listing of input cards and GASP IV echo check printout (Example 7).

```
                                  SIMULATION PROJECT NUMBER   7   BY   PRITSKER

                                  DATE  6/ 30/ 1973          RUN NUMBER     1 OF     1
                                  LLSUP=0000000000000000     GASP IV VERSION 23JUN73

NNCLT=       0     NNSTA=       0    NNHIS=      0    NNPRM=      0    NNPLT=      1    NNSTR=      1    NNTRY=      0
NNATR=       0     NNFIL=       0    NNSET= 10000     NNEQD=      4    NNEQS=      2    NFLAG=      4

GPLOT NO.  1       LLABP=TIME        TTTAP=      0    NNVAR=      4    LLPLT=      2                DTPLT=      5.0000E-03
  VAR NO.  1             2=M VEL     LLPLO=      1    LLPHI=      1    PPLO =     -1.0000E+03       PPHI =      1.0000E+03
  VAR NO.  2             3=C DIS     LLPLO=      1    LLPHI=      1    PPLO =      0.               PPHI =      5.0000E+02
  VAR NO.  3             4=C VEL     LLPLO=      1    LLPHI=      1    PPLO =     -1.0000E+03       PPHI =      1.0000E+03
  VAR NO.  4             T=TORQI     LLPLO=      1    LLPHI=      1    PPLO =      0.               PPHI =      5.0000E+01

IIEVT=       1     LLERR=       0    AAERR=      0.                    RRERR=      5.0000E-06
DTMIN=       1.0000E-04              DTMAX=      1.0000E-03            DTSAV=      1.0000E-03

MSTOP=       1     JJCLR=       0    JJBEG=      1    IICRD=      0    TTBEG=      0.               TTFIN=      1.0000E+00
JJFIL=      -0
IISED=      -0
```

Figure 6-19 *(continued)*

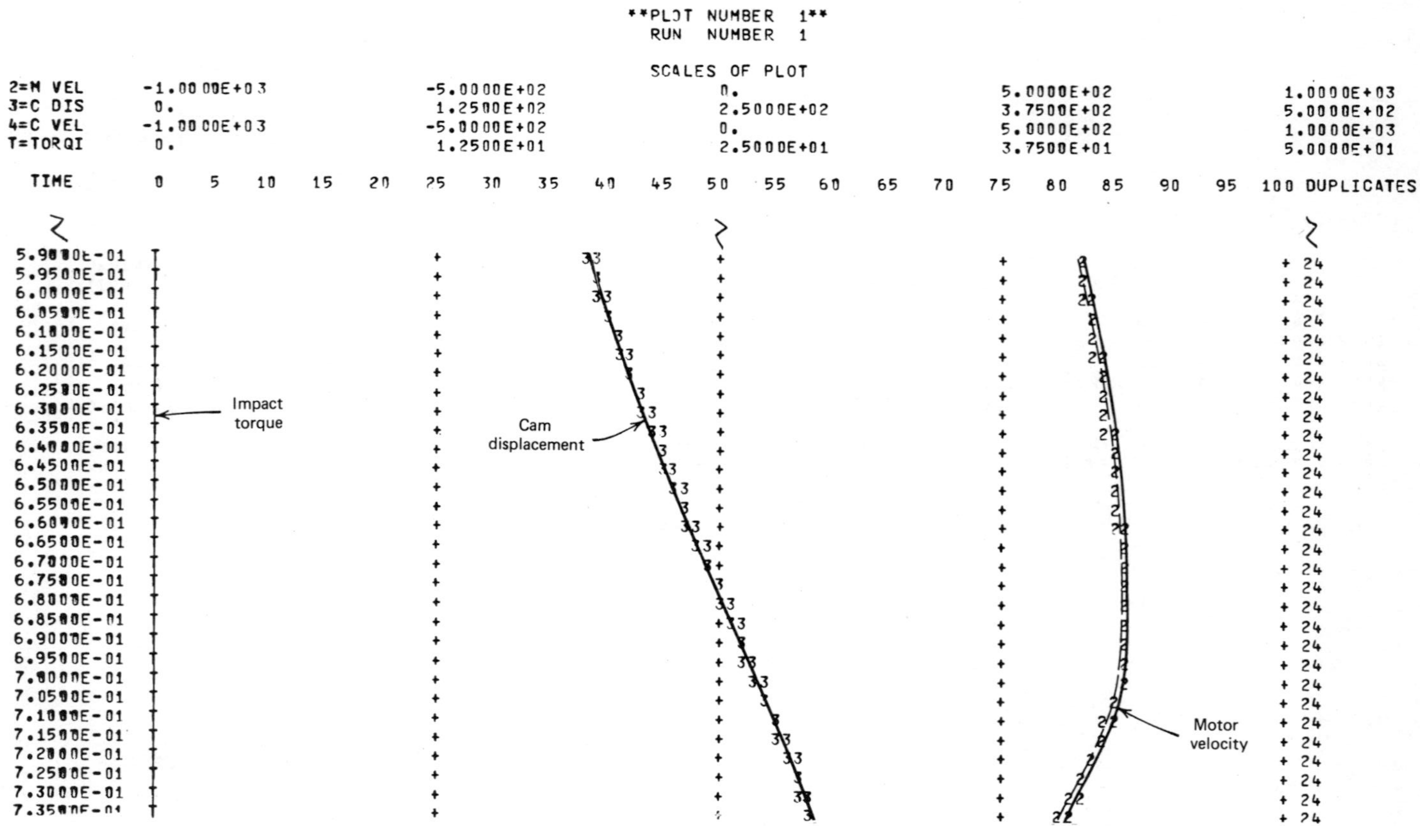
PLOT NUMBER 1
RUN NUMBER 1
SCALES OF PLOT
2=M VEL -1.0000E+03 -5.0000E+02 0. 5.0000E+02 1.0000E+03
3=C DIS 0. 1.2500E+02 2.5000E+02 3.7500E+02 5.0000E+02
4=C VEL -1.0000E+03 -5.0000E+02 0. 5.0000E+02 1.0000E+03
T=TORQI 0. 1.2500E+01 2.5000E+01 3.7500E+01 5.0000E+01
TIME 0 5 10 15 20 25 30 35 40 45 50 55 60 65 70 75 80 85 90 95 100 DUPLICATES
Impact torque
Cam displacement
Motor velocity

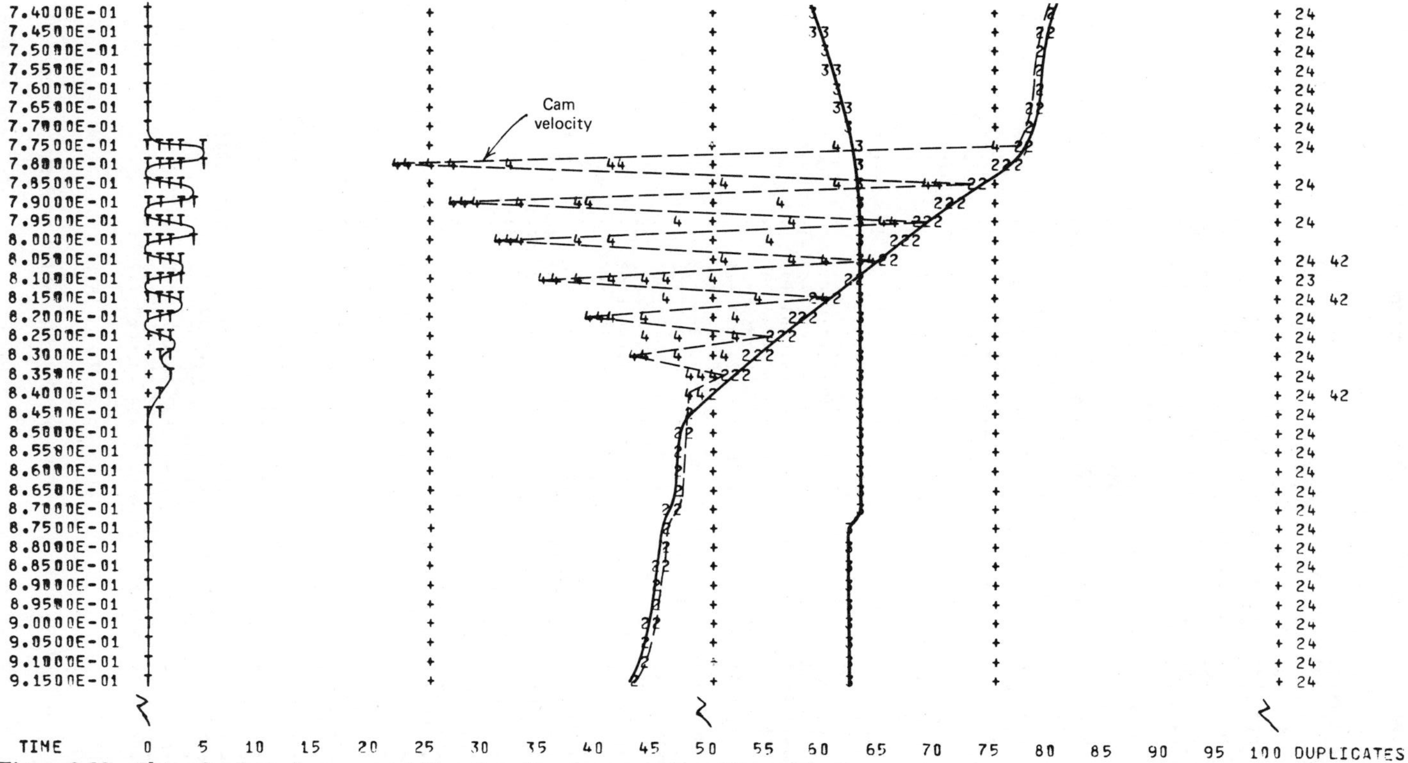

Figure 6-20 Plot of selected state variables for slip clutch analysis (Example 7).

TIME	VELM	DISC	VELC	TORQI
7.6000E-01	5.8054E+02	3.0560E+02	5.8054E+02	0.
7.6075E-01	5.8051E+02	3.0604E+02	5.8051E+02	0.
7.6075E-01	5.8051E+02	3.0604E+02	5.8051E+02	0.
7.6100E-01	5.7998E+02	3.0618E+02	5.7998E+02	0.
7.6200E-01	5.7794E+02	3.0676E+02	5.7794E+02	0.
7.6300E-01	5.7598E+02	3.0734E+02	5.7598E+02	0.
7.6400E-01	5.7411E+02	3.0792E+02	5.7411E+02	0.
7.6500E-01	5.7233E+02	3.0849E+02	5.7233E+02	0.
7.6600E-01	5.7063E+02	3.0906E+02	5.7063E+02	0.
7.6700E-01	5.6902E+02	3.0963E+02	5.6902E+02	0.
7.6800E-01	5.6750E+02	3.1020E+02	5.6750E+02	0.
7.6900E-01	5.6606E+02	3.1076E+02	5.6605E+02	0.
7.7000E-01	5.6470E+02	3.1133E+02	5.6470E+02	0.
7.7100E-01	5.6344E+02	3.1189E+02	5.6344E+02	0.
7.7200E-01	5.6225E+02	3.1246E+02	5.6225E+02	0.
7.7300E-01	5.6116E+02	3.1302E+02	5.6116E+02	0.
7.7400E-01	5.6014E+02	3.1358E+02	5.6014E+02	0.
7.7488E-01	5.5933E+02	3.1407E+02	5.5933E+02	0.
7.7488E-01	5.5933E+02	3.1407E+02	5.5933E+02	1.5212E-01
7.7500E-01	5.5893E+02	3.1414E+02	5.5893E+02	3.0589E-01
7.7544E-01	5.5594E+02	3.1439E+02	5.5594E+02	8.5028E-01
7.7544E-01	5.5594E+02	3.1439E+02	5.5594E+02	8.5028E-01
7.7600E-01	5.5082E+02	3.1468E+02	5.0170E+02	1.5066E+00
7.7700E-01	5.4163E+02	3.1506E+02	2.1136E+02	2.3282E+00
7.7800E-01	5.3243E+02	3.1507E+02	-1.8788E+02	2.3542E+00
7.7900E-01	5.2323E+02	3.1472E+02	-4.9032E+02	1.5738E+00
7.7968E-01	5.1702E+02	3.1435E+02	-5.5635E+02	7.8035E-01
7.7968E-01	5.1702E+02	3.1435E+02	-5.5635E+02	7.8034E-01
7.8000E-01	5.1403E+02	3.1418E+02	-5.4014E+02	3.8647E-01
7.8050E-01	5.0943E+02	3.1392E+02	-4.5633E+02	-1.6781E-01
7.8050E-01	5.0943E+02	3.1392E+02	-4.5633E+02	0.
7.8100E-01	5.0483E+02	3.1372E+02	-3.6038E+02	0.
7.8200E-01	4.9564E+02	3.1345E+02	-1.6939E+02	0.
7.8300E-01	4.8644E+02	3.1338E+02	2.0979E+01	0.
7.8400E-01	4.7724E+02	3.1350E+02	2.1142E+02	0.
7.8500E-01	4.6804E+02	3.1380E+02	4.0265E+02	0.
7.8535E-01	4.6482E+02	3.1396E+02	4.6989E+02	0.
7.8535E-01	4.6482E+02	3.1396E+02	4.6482E+02	0.
7.8551E-01	4.6467E+02	3.1403E+02	4.6467E+02	0.
7.8551E-01	4.6467E+02	3.1403E+02	4.6467E+02	7.0167E-02
7.8600E-01	4.6267E+02	3.1426E+02	4.6267E+02	5.6767E-01
7.8630E-01	4.6022E+02	3.1440E+02	4.6022E+02	8.7227E-01
7.8630E-01	4.6022E+02	3.1440E+02	4.6022E+02	8.7227E-01
7.8700E-01	4.5378E+02	3.1470E+02	3.8662E+02	1.5391E+00
7.8800E-01	4.4458E+02	3.1496E+02	1.1866E+02	2.1212E+00
7.8900E-01	4.3539E+02	3.1492E+02	-2.1044E+02	2.0155E+00
7.9000E-01	4.2619E+02	3.1458E+02	-4.3111E+02	1.2763E+00
7.9054E-01	4.2124E+02	3.1434E+02	-4.6088E+02	7.4194E-01
7.9054E-01	4.2124E+02	3.1434E+02	-4.6088E+02	7.4194E-01
7.9100E-01	4.1699E+02	3.1413E+02	-4.2967E+02	2.8447E-01
7.9150E-01	4.1239E+02	3.1393E+02	-3.4100E+02	-1.4421E-01
7.9150E-01	4.1239E+02	3.1393E+02	-3.4100E+02	0.
7.9200E-01	4.0779E+02	3.1379E+02	-2.4498E+02	0.
7.9300E-01	3.9859E+02	3.1364E+02	-5.3525E+01	0.
7.9400E-01	3.8940E+02	3.1368E+02	1.3773E+02	0.
7.9500E-01	3.8020E+02	3.1391E+02	3.2950E+02	0.
7.9525E-01	3.7790E+02	3.1400E+02	3.7760E+02	0.
7.9525E-01	3.7790E+02	3.1400E+02	3.7760E+02	6.1137E-03
7.9530E-01	3.7744E+02	3.1402E+02	3.8690E+02	4.8161E-02
7.9530E-01	3.7744E+02	3.1402E+02	3.7744E+02	4.8166E-02
7.9600E-01	3.7442E+02	3.1429E+02	3.7442E+02	6.2762E-01
7.9629E-01	3.7200E+02	3.1439E+02	3.7200E+02	8.6371E-01
7.9629E-01	3.7200E+02	3.1439E+02	3.7200E+02	8.6371E-01
7.9700E-01	3.6546E+02	3.1464E+02	3.0930E+02	1.4102E+00
7.9800E-01	3.5625E+02	3.1485E+02	9.0073E+01	1.8703E+00
7.9900E-01	3.4705E+02	3.1481E+02	-1.7556E+02	1.7718E+00
8.0000E-01	3.3785E+02	3.1453E+02	-3.5073E+02	1.1654E+00

Figure 6-21 Table of selected state variables for slip clutch analysis (Example 7).

```
                                    **INTERMEDIATE RESULTS**

SPECIFIED  TOLERANCE  EXCEEDED  FOR  SS(  6)  AT  TIME   7.7544E-01
SPECIFIED  TOLERANCE  EXCEEDED  FOR  DD(  4)  AT  TIME   7.7968E-01
SPECIFIED  TOLERANCE  EXCEEDED  FOR  SS(  4)  AT  TIME   7.8535E-01
SPECIFIED  TOLERANCE  EXCEEDED  FOR  SS(  6)  AT  TIME   7.8630E-01
SPECIFIED  TOLERANCE  EXCEEDED  FOR  DD(  4)  AT  TIME   7.9054E-01
SPECIFIED  TOLERANCE  EXCEEDED  FOR  SS(  4)  AT  TIME   7.9530E-01
SPECIFIED  TOLERANCE  EXCEEDED  FOR  SS(  6)  AT  TIME   7.9629E-01
SPECIFIED  TOLERANCE  EXCEEDED  FOR  DD(  4)  AT  TIME   8.0049E-01
SPECIFIED  TOLERANCE  EXCEEDED  FOR  SS(  4)  AT  TIME   8.0448E-01
SPECIFIED  TOLERANCE  EXCEEDED  FOR  SS(  6)  AT  TIME   8.0555E-01
SPECIFIED  TOLERANCE  EXCEEDED  FOR  DD(  4)  AT  TIME   8.0980E-01
SPECIFIED  TOLERANCE  EXCEEDED  FOR  SS(  4)  AT  TIME   8.1315E-01
SPECIFIED  TOLERANCE  EXCEEDED  FOR  SS(  6)  AT  TIME   8.1444E-01
SPECIFIED  TOLERANCE  EXCEEDED  FOR  DD(  4)  AT  TIME   8.1866E-01
SPECIFIED  TOLERANCE  EXCEEDED  FOR  SS(  4)  AT  TIME   8.2180E-01
SPECIFIED  TOLERANCE  EXCEEDED  FOR  SS(  6)  AT  TIME   8.2344E-01
SPECIFIED  TOLERANCE  EXCEEDED  FOR  DD(  4)  AT  TIME   8.2761E-01
SPECIFIED  TOLERANCE  EXCEEDED  FOR  SS(  4)  AT  TIME   8.3049E-01
SPECIFIED  TOLERANCE  EXCEEDED  FOR  SS(  6)  AT  TIME   8.3339E-01
SPECIFIED  TOLERANCE  EXCEEDED  FOR  DD(  4)  AT  TIME   8.3735E-01
SPECIFIED  TOLERANCE  EXCEEDED  FOR  SS(  4)  AT  TIME   8.3930E-01
```

Figure 6-22 Warning messages regarding exceeding of tolerances defining state-events (Example 7).

6-3. It is desired to make ten runs for the pilot ejection model where the velocity of the aircraft is uniformly distributed between 500 and 900 ft/sec. Show the program coding and input changes that would be required to make these ten runs.

6-4. In the model of a slip clutch in Example 7, determine the approximate value of DTMIN that would be required in order that tolerances on the state-events would not be exceeded.

6-5. Determine if the equations for the state variables for Example 7 could be written in SS(·) form.

6-6. Rewrite Example 7 so that a step size during the impact period is reduced to make more frequent evaluations during the impact region. Also rewrite the simulation so that the plot during the impact region will better illustrate the dynamic behavior of the system.

6-7. SERENDIPITY is a deterministic model to simulate tree biomass dynamics of a closed-canopy, forested watershed (45). Trees are divided into three size classes: 1.3–8.8, 8.9–23.8, and greater than 23.8 cm dbh (diameter at breast height). The live above ground biomasses of the three classes are designated x_1, x_2, and x_3, respectively. There are three variables, x_4, x_5, and x_6 for the threc size classes of standing dead material, and x_7 is the total live root biomass in all dbh classes. The equations defining the rate of change of these variables are:

$$\frac{dx_i}{dt} = [\lambda_i - \sigma_i (1 - \delta_{i3})]\, x_i \left(1 - \frac{x}{y}\right) - m_i x_i \left(1 + \frac{x}{y}\right) +$$

$$[\sigma_{i-1} (1 - \delta_{i1})\, x_{i-1} + \beta(x_2^\star + x_3^\star)\, \delta_{i1}] \left(1 - \frac{x}{y}\right), \qquad i = 1, 2, 3;$$

$$\frac{dx_i}{dt} = m_{i-3} x_{i-3} \left(1 + \frac{x}{y}\right) - (\gamma_{i-3} + \mu_{i-3}) x_i, \; i = 4, 5, 6;$$

and

$$\frac{dx_7}{dt} = \varepsilon \left[\sum_{i=1}^{3} \lambda_i x_i + \beta(x_2^\star + x_3^\star) \left(1 - \frac{x}{y}\right)\right] - \left(\sum_{i=1}^{3} m_i x_i\right) \left(1 + \frac{x}{y}\right) \left(\frac{x_7}{x}\right) - \eta x_7$$

where

$$\delta_{ij} = \begin{cases} 0 \text{ if } i \neq j \\ 1 \text{ if } i = j; \end{cases}$$

$$x = \sum_{i=1}^{3} x_i;$$

$\lambda_i x_i \left(1 - \frac{x}{y}\right)$ = net production of group i;

$\sigma_i x_i \left(1 - \frac{x}{y}\right)$ = transfer rate of biomass from group i to group $i + 1$ (outgrowth)

$m_i x_i \left(1 + \frac{x}{y}\right)$ = rate at which biomass is lost from group i due to mortality;

$\beta (x_2^\star + x_3^\star) \left(1 - \frac{x}{y}\right)$ = rate at which biomass is added to group 1 because of saplings reaching 1.25 cm dbh (ingrowth).

$x_2^\star$ and $x_3^\star$ are values of x_2 and x_3 obtained at time $t^\star = t - 3$.

A convenient form for delaying state variables is to use a smoothing function. In this case, let $x_8 = x_2^\star$ and $x_9 = x_3^\star$ and let

$$\frac{dx_8}{dt} = \frac{(x_2 - x_8)}{3}$$

and

$$\frac{dx_9}{dt} = \frac{(x_3 - x_9)}{3.}$$

The parameter values employed in implementing SERENDIPITY on Walker Branch Watershed are specified below.

Model Parameters	Definition	Value
λ_1	Production rate, small size class	0.12/yr
λ_2	Production rate, medium size class	0.05/yr
λ_3	Production rate, large size class	0.03/yr
σ_1	Outgrowth rate from small size class	0.10/yr
σ_2	Outgrowth rate from medium size class	0.025/yr
m_1	Mortality rate from small size class	0.02/yr
m_2	Mortality rate from medium size class	0.01/yr
m_3	Mortality rate from large size class	0.005/yr
β	Ingrowth rate	0.001/yr
γ_1	Microbial decay rate, small standing dead	0.0001/yr
γ_2	Microbial decay rate, medium standing dead	0.0001/yr
γ_3	Microbial decay rate, large standing dead	0.0001/yr
μ_1	Movement rate, small standing dead to forest floor	0.2/yr
μ_2	Movement rate, medium standing dead to forest floor	0.2/yr
μ_3	Movement rate, large standing dead to forest floor	0.2/yr
η	Root turnover rate	0.266/yr
y	Maximum aboveground live biomass density	400,000 kg/ha
ε	Ratio of biomass translocated to the roots to above ground production	2.0

Perform a simulation to observe the tree biomass dynamics for a 300-year period if the initial conditions for the x_i sector are: 10,000, 30,000, 60,000, 2,500, 2,000, 2,000, and 32,000 (measured in kilograms per hectare).

6-8. In Exercise 6-7 let the production rates, λ_i, be normally distributed random variables with mean equal to the rate given and standard deviation equal to one-tenth of the mean. Perform a simulation for the tree system when these random elements are incorporated.

6-9. Determine the effects of a 20% increase in the production parameters for the problem presented in Exercise 6-7.

6-10. The following differential equations (23) yield values of x and y such that $x^2 + y^2 \to 1$ as time $\to$ infinity, no matter what the initial conditions are for x and y (except $x = y = 0$).

$$\frac{dx}{dt} = y + kx(1 - x^2 - y^2)/\sqrt{x^2 + y^2}, \qquad x(0) = A$$

and

$$\frac{dy}{dt} = -x + ky(1 - x^2 - y^2)/\sqrt{x^2 + y^2}, \qquad y(0) = B.$$

Obtain time histories of x and y for $t = 0$ to 10 in steps of 0.2 for the following two cases:

Case 1. $A = 0.5$, $B = 1.0$, and $k = 2$.
Case 2. $A = 0.0$, $B = 0.8$, and $k = 2$.

6-11. Cedar Bog Lake, Minnesota, has been modeled by Williams and is representative of a lake ecosystem model (139). The model includes three species, a solar energy supply (x_s), and the organic matter that forms a sediment on the lake bottom (x_o). These lake entities are modeled in terms of their energy content (cal/cm^2) and the energy transfers between the various lake entities and losses to the environment (x_e). The three species are plants (x_p), herbivores (x_h), and carnivores (x_c). The differential equations relating these species to the sediment and the solar energy source are shown below.

$$\frac{dx_p}{dt} = x_s - (1.00 + 2.55 + 0.48)x_p.$$

$$\frac{dx_h}{dt} = 0.48x_p - (6.90 + 6.12 + 4.85)x_h.$$

$$\frac{dx_c}{dt} = 4.85x_h - (2.70 + 1.95)x_c.$$

$$\frac{dx_o}{dt} = 2.55x_p + 6.12x_h + 1.95x_c.$$

$$\frac{dx_e}{dt} = 1.00x_p + 6.90x_h + 2.70x_c.$$

The values of the variables at time zero are: $x_p(0) = 0.83$, $x_h(0) = 0.003$, and $x_c(0) = 0.0001$.

The annual cycle in solar radiation is simulated using the following equation:

$$x_s = 95.9\ (1 + 0.635 \sin t)$$

where t is time in radians and a year equals 2π rad. These equations represent such processes as the predation of one species by another, plant photosynthesis, and the decaying of dead species. Energy transfers between lake entities and its environment are due to respiration and migration.

Perform a simulation of the lake ecosystem represented by the above equations for a two-year period.

6-12. Superimpose a normally distributed random variation on the solar energy supplied to the lake ecosystem presented in Exercise 6-11.

6-13. Determine the effects of a step increase of 20% in the solar energy input to the lake ecosystem described in Exercise 6-11.

6-14. Suppose that 20% of the energy losses to the lake sediment of Exercise 6-11 are returned in some fashion as input to plants. Determine the effect of this change in lake ecosystem structure on the behavior of the model.

6-15. A nonlinear, eight species model of Cedar Bog Lake is also presented by Williams (139). Review this model and use GASP IV to analyze it.

Chapter Seven

GASP IV

Combined Simulation

This chapter presents two examples of GASP IV programs that analyze situations that are modeled using combined discrete-continuous concepts. In developing a combined simulation program, four phases can be identified. First, it is efficient to start the modeling process with the state variables. These are normally more easily modeled because there is a direct correspondence between the physical aspects of a system and the equations governing the dynamic behavior of the state variables. Second, the conditions defining state-events are enumerated. This leads naturally to a third phase, the consideration of the time-events and the flow charting of decision processes and status changes that occur at each time-event. Fourth, the effects of the time-events on the state variables are developed and modeled. Iterations of these four phases are then performed until the user is satisfied with the combined simulation model developed. Within each phase, the amount of detail included is dependent on the objective of the simulation. The statistics to be collected and the method of collection also relate to the analysis objective.

The two examples included in this chapter illustrate the versatility of GASP IV in modeling combined problems and also demonstrate the commonality involved in combined simulations. Example 8 of this chapter is an elaboration of Example 2 presented in Chapter 5 and involves the simulation of a tanker fleet that provides crude oil to a refinery. In Example 8 the unloading of tankers is presumed to be a continuous process.

The crude oil is transferred from tankers to a storage tank that serves as the input to a refinery. State variables are used to represent the amount of crude in the tanker being unloaded and the amount in the storage tank. The input to the storage tank (the input from the tanker) and the output from the storage tank (the input to the refinery) are represented by continuous variables. The level of crude in the storage tank represents an inventory of crude that is used to supply the refinery. The refinery demand is assumed to be constant. When the storage tank cannot supply crude for the refinery, the situation is analogous to the stock-out situation in inventory studies. The discussion in Example 8 concentrates on the procedures to model the combined tanker-storage tank situation. The example is representative of a wide class of queueing-inventory situations in which the service time is dependent on the status of the system and can vary in a continuous manner.

Example 9 involves the simulation of a chemical reaction process. Four reactors are simulated, each of which processes a reactant until a prescribed concentration level is reached. After completing the processing of a batch, a reactor must be discharged, cleaned, and recharged. The time to perform these maintenance operations is described statistically and can be scheduled to occur in the future. However, the completion of a batch cannot be scheduled since this depends on the reaction rate of the reactor. The rate of reaction is described by a differential equation. All reactors are driven by a compressor through a surge tank. Based on the surge tank pressure, reactors can be shut down or allowed to start. Thus the surge tank pressure couples the reactors into an operating system. This example illustrates the simulation of a chemical process involving state variables and discrete events.

The similarity between Examples 8 and 9 is not apparent at first. After reviewing the GASP IV models, it becomes evident that the tanker entities of Example 8 are similar to the reactor entities of Example 9. Tankers are unloaded continuously and after completing unloading, travel a prescribed distance, are loaded, and then travel back to the unloading dock. Each of these activities is described statistically and is scheduled to occur discretely. At the unloading dock the tankers are either put in a queue waiting for service or unloading is initiated. Unloading is completed when the amount of crude in the tanker falls below a prescribed level.

In the chemical reaction process, after completing the processing of a batch the reactors go through maintenance activities involving discharge cleanup, and charging. These activities are described statistically and can be scheduled to occur discretely. After completing the maintenance operations, a new batch for the reactor is started, if possible. If pressure is too low, the reactor cannot be started and must wait. Thus it is put in a queue waiting until the surge tank pressure builds up. Completion of processing occurs when the concentration of the reactants falls below a prescribed level.

With this brief comparison, the analogous nature of the tankers and reactors and of the crude oil and the reactant can be identified.

GASP IV has been used for modeling and analyzing a diversity of combined problems. These include global climate modification due to air pollution (135); the flow of cadmium in an electroplating process (126); the flow of cadmium in an ecosystem (116); the energy consumption of elevators in tall buildings (128); the throughput of a soaking pit furnace; the growth of alfalfa; the harvesting of hay; the control of the human menstrual cycle; and filtering and scheduling in a refinery system. Furthermore, a general simulation program (SMOOTH), to analyze continuous-discrete networks, has been developed using GASP IV as its base (127). The analysis of systems using combined simulation techniques is a fertile area for research and development.

Complete descriptions of Examples 8 and 9 are now presented. The discussion emphasizes the interaction between the discrete and continuous aspects of the models and the procedures used to develop a combined simulation program written in GASP IV.

EXAMPLE 8—SIMULATION OF A TANKER FLEET

Statement of the Problem

Example 8 is an extension of Example 2 with the representation of the unloading of a tanker as a continuous process. The simulation involves a fleet of 15 tankers. The tankers are loaded in Valdez, Alaska and travel to Seattle, Washington. It is assumed that all tankers can be loaded simultaneously, if necessary. In Seattle there is only one unloading dock, which supplies a storage tank, which feeds a refinery through a pipeline. The storage tank receives crude from a tanker at the dock at a constant rate of 300 tb/day*. The storage tank supplies crude to the refinery continuously at a constant rate of 150 tb/day. A two shift day is used for the unloading dock operation, and the dock is closed at 8 p.m. and opens at 4 a.m. Safety considerations require the stopping of unloading of the crude when the dock is shut down.

The storage tank has a capacity of 2000 tb. When it is full, unloading is halted until the amount in the tank decreases to 80% of capacity. When the storage tank is empty, supply to the refinery is halted until 50 tb is

* tb=thousand barrels.

reached to avoid the possibility of frequent refinery start-ups and shut-downs. The characteristics associated with thc tankers are listed below:

1. Nominal carrying capacity is 150 tb.
2. Travel time loaded is normally distributed with a mean of 5.0 days and a standard deviation of 1.5 days.
3. Travel time unloaded is normally distributed with a mean of 4.0 days and a standard deviation of 1 day.
4. Time to load is $(150 + x)/50$ days, where x is uniformly distributed in the interval $(-10,10)$.
5. Unloading rate is 300 tb/day.

The initial conditions for the simulation are that the storage tank is half full and the tankers are to arrive at their loading points at 1/2 day intervals, starting with the first at time 0.

Simulation Objective

The objective of this example is to simulate the above system for 365 days to obtain estimates of the following quantities:

1. Unloading dock utilization.
2. Loading dock utilization.
3. Time refinery has a crude input available.
4. Amount of crude in the storage tank.
5. Tanker round trip time.
6. Tanker waiting time.
7. Number of tankers waiting for unloading.

Special Features

The use of state-events and time-events to control the unloading process is a special feature of this example. For example, the time-events, shut-down and start-up of the unloading dock, change the unloading rate discretely. The state-event, storage tank at capacity, also stops unloading. These interactions between entities and state variables are demonstrated throughout this example.

Simulation Procedure

The simulation procedure for Example 8 is similar to the procedure presented for Example 2. The discussion here emphasizes the continuous processes included in the model and the interaction between discrete events and the state variables.

Two state variables are used in this simulation: SS(1), amount of crude in a tanker at the unloading dock, and SS(2), amount of crude in the storage tank. The state variable SS(1) represents the amount of crude ready to be unloaded. SS(1) will be zero when no tanker is in the unloading dock and it will be equal to the amount of crude in the tanker when a tanker is in the unloading dock. When a tanker leaves the unloading dock, SS(1) either becomes zero or is set equal to the amount of crude in the next tanker to be unloaded.

There are five possible conditions that would result in a state-event and each is identified by the GASP IV indicator variable LFLAG as shown below.

Flag Indicator Used	Definition of Condition
LFLAG(1)	Completion of tanker unloading that occurs when tanker has less than 5% of its load remaining
LFLAG(2)	Storage tank has decreased to less than 5 tb, therefore, stop supply to refinery
LFLAG(3)	Storage tank has increased to 50 tb, therefore, start supplying refinery again
LFLAG(4)	Storage tank has reached its capacity, therefore, stop the unloading of the tanker
LFLAG(5)	Storage tank amount has decreased to 80% of capacity therefore, tanker unloading can begin again

The events for the simulation are:

Event Code	Definition
1	Arrival of tanker for loading, ARRL
2	Finish of tanker loading, FINL
3	Arrival of tanker for unloading, ARRUL
4	State-event involving one or more of the five conditions described above
5	Shutdown of unloading dock, SHUTD
6	Start-up of unloading dock, STARU

In addition to the event file, a file is used for the tankers waiting to be unloaded and another is used to store the attributes of the tanker being unloaded. Since no time-event is scheduled when the tanker is being unloaded, the tanker's attributes are stored in file 3, a special file used here only for this purpose. The attribute definitions for entries in the files are given below.

Attribute Value	Definition
ATRIB(1)	Time of event
ATRIB(2)	Event code
ATRIB(3)	Start time of loading of tanker
ATRIB(4)	Arrival time to unloading
ATRIB(5)	Amount of crude in tanker

File 1 is ranked on attribute 1 with a LVF priority. Secondary ranking is arbitrary. For file 2, the queue of tankers at the unloading dock, priority will be FIFO and the ranking attribute is arbitrary. File 3, when used, contains the one tanker being unloaded and priority is arbitrarily set to be FIFO.

Definitions of the non-GASP variables and their initial values are:

Variable	Initial Value	Definition
ALR	50.0	Average loading rate (tb/day)
BCAP	1600.0	Level in storage tank at which unloading can begin again
BUS	0.0	Indicator that a tanker is in unloading dock: $0 \rightarrow$ no; $1 \rightarrow$ yes
FKT	1.0	Storage tank indicator: $1 \rightarrow$ accepting input; $0 \rightarrow$ not accepting input
AMTL	—	Amount to be loaded
FPCT	0.05	Fraction of tanker capacity allowed to remain after unloading
KS	1.0	Shift indicator: $0 \rightarrow$ working; $1 \rightarrow$ not working
RATEI	300.0	Nominal input rate to storage tank
RATEO	150.0	Nominal output rate from storage tank
RATIN	0.0	Actual input rate to storage tank
RATOUT	150.0	Actual output rate from storage tank
SCAP	2000.0	Capacity of storage tank
SFIN	—	Level of crude in tanker to indicate end of unloading
TCAP	150.0	Tanker capacity
TIFRT	—	Time for tanker round trip
WT	—	Waiting time for tanker
XTBL	0.0	Number of tankers being loaded

Equations for the two state variables are defined in subroutine STATE by the two difference equations:

$$\text{SS}(1) = \text{SSL}(1) - \text{DTNOW} \star \text{RATIN}$$
$$\text{SS}(2) = \text{SSL}(2) + \text{DTNOW} \star (\text{RATIN} - \text{RATOUT})$$

The FORTRAN listing of subroutine STATE is given in Fig. 7-1.

```
      SUBROUTINE STATE                                                  ST8    1
      COMMON /GCOM2/ DD(100),DDL(100),DTFUL,DTNOW,ISEES,LFLAG(50),NFLAG,GCOM2  1
     1NNEQD,NNEQS,NNEQT,SS(100),SSL(100),TTNEX                          GCOM2  2
      COMMON /UCOM1/BUS,KS,START,ALR,RATEI,RATEO,RATIN,RATOUT,SFIN      UCOM1  1
     1,SCAP,BCAP,TCAP,FPCT,FKT,NTANK,XTBL                               UCOM1  2
      SS(1)=SSL(1)-DTNOW*RATIN                                          ST8    2
      SS(2)=SSL(2)+DTNOW*(RATIN-RATOUT)                                 ST8    3
      RETURN                                                            ST8    4
C                                                                       ST8    5
      END                                                               ST8    6
```

Figure 7-1 FORTRAN listing of subroutine STATE (Example 8).

The above equations appear relatively simple but are deceptive since RATIN and RATOUT have different values during the simulation because of the status of the system. These equations could easily be made more complex by making them functions of the type of crude and their own levels.

Five conditions were specified on the state variables that could alter the dynamics of the system. These are coded in subroutine SCOND, which is shown in Fig. 7-2. The values for the LFLAG vector resulting from the prescribed conditions are shown below.

State Variable	Flag Value	Crossing Condition	Tolerance Interval
SS(1)	LFLAG(1) = −1	↓SFIN	$0 \leq \text{SS}(1) \leq \text{SFIN}$
SS(2)	LFLAG(2) = −1	↓ 5.0	$0 \leq \text{SS}(2) \leq 5.0$
SS(2)	LFLAG(3) = +1	↑50.0	$50 \leq \text{SS}(2) \leq 65.0$
SS(2)	LFLAG(4) = +1	↑SCAP	$\text{SCAP} \leq \text{SS}(2) \leq \text{SCAP} + 15.0$
SS(2)	LFLAG(5) = −1	↓BCAP	$\text{BCAP} - 5.0 \leq \text{SS}(2) \leq \text{BCAP}$

The crossing condition specifies the threshold that defines the state-event and the direction of the crossing required to cause the state-event. Thus LFLAG(5) will be set at −1 when SS(2) decreases below BCAP but not below BCAP − 5. When this occurs subroutine GASP automatically calls subroutine EVNTS with event code IIEVT, which is set equal to four for this example. If SS(2) also crossed BCAP − 5 at the same time, the step size would be reduced.

```
      SUBROUTINE SCOND                                                   SC8     1
      COMMON /GCOM2/ DD(100),DDL(100),DTFUL,DTNOW,ISEES,LFLAG(50),NFLAG,GCOM2   1
     1NNEQD,NNEQS,NNEQT,SS(100),SSL(100),TTNEX                          GCOM2   2
      COMMON /UCOM1/BUS,KS,START,ALR,RATEI,RATEO,RATIN,RATOUT,SFIN      UCOM1   1
     1,SCAP,BCAP,TCAP,FPCT,FKT,NTANK,XTBL                               UCOM1   2
      LFLAG(1)=KROSS(1,0,0.,SFIN,-1,SFIN)                               SC8     2
      LFLAG(2)=KROSS(2,0,0.,5.,-1,5.)                                   SC8     3
      LFLAG(3)=KROSS(2,0,0.,50.,1,15.)                                  SC8     4
      LFLAG(4)=KROSS(2,0,0.,SCAP,1,15.)                                 SC8     5
      LFLAG(5)=KROSS(2,0,0.,BCAP,-1,5.)                                 SC8     6
      RETURN                                                            SC8     7
C                                                                       SC8     8
      END                                                               SC8     9
```

Figure 7-2 FORTRAN listing of subroutine SCOND (Example 8).

The state-event or events that occur are determined by testing LFLAG(·) in subroutine EVNTS. The FORTRAN listing for subroutine EVNTS is shown in Fig. 7-3. When the event code IX is 4, a state-event has occurred. The coding for the processing of state-events begins at statement 4 in subroutine EVNTS. A check is made to determine if the amount of crude in the storage tank has decreased below the BCAP level. If this has just occurred, LFLAG(5) will have a negative value. When LFLAG(5) has a negative value, the storage tank can start accepting input again. The indicator FKT is set to the value 1.0 to indicate this. If a tanker is in the unloading dock (BUS = 1.0) and the current time is during a working shift (KS = 0), the rate of input to the storage tank RATIN is set equal to the nominal input rate RATEI. Otherwise RATIN maintains a zero value.

At statement 105, LFLAG(1) is tested to determine if the tanker in the unloading dock has just completed unloading. If it has, the finish unloading event is simulated by a call to subroutine FINUL. FINUL is described later. Next, a test is made to determine if the crude in the storage tank has just exceeded the capacity of the storage tank. If it has, the input rate is set at zero and the indicator FKT is set at zero to indicate that no further inputs can be made to the storage tank until the level of crude has decreased below BCAP.

At statement 106, a test is made to determine if the amount of crude in the storage tank has just been fully depleted. If it has, a transfer is made to statement 107 where the output from the storage tank is set at zero. Subroutine TIMST is called to compute the amount of time the refinery is operating. The first argument to TIMST is 0.0 since down time is to be accumulated during the next interval. To determine if the amount of crude in the storage tank just exceeded the 50.0 tb required to start the refinery, LFLAG(3) is tested. If LFLAG(3) is greater than zero, the output rate RATOUT from the storage tank is set equal to the nominal output rate RATEO. When this occurs, the refinery is being turned on and, therefore, statistics on refinery operating time need to be collected. This is accomplished by calling TIMST with a value of 1.0 to

```
      SUBROUTINE EVNTS (IX)
      COMMON /GCOM1/ ATRIB(25),JEVNT,MFA,MFE(100),MLE(100),MSTOP,NCRDR,N
     1NAPO,NNAPT,NNATR,NNFIL,NNQ(100),NNTRY,NPRNT,PPARM(50,4),TNOW,TTBEG
     2,TTCLR,TTFIN,TTRIB(25),TTSET
      COMMON /GCOM2/ DD(100),DDL(100),DTFUL,DTNOW,ISEES,LFLAG(50),NFLAG,
     1NNEQD,NNEQS,NNEQT,SS(100),SSL(100),TTNEX
      COMMON /UCOM1/BUS,KS,START,ALR,RATEI,RATEO,RATIN,RATOUT,SFIN
     1,SCAP,BCAP,TCAP,FPCT,FKT,NTANK,XTBL
      GO TO (101,102,103,104,108,109), IX
  101 CALL ARRL
      GO TO 110
  102 CALL FINL
      GO TO 110
  103 CALL ARRUL
      GO TO 110
C
C*****STORAGE TANK CAN START ACCEPTING INPUT IF LFLAG(5).LT.0.
C
  104 IF (LFLAG(5).GE.0) GO TO 105
      FKT=1.0
      IF (BUS.EQ.0.0) GO TO 105
C
C*****RATE INTO TANK SET TO RATEI IF A TANKER IS IN UNLOADING DOCK
C*****(BUS=1.0), INPUT IS ALLOWED (FKT=1.0) AND TIME IS WITHIN WORKING
C*****SHIFT(KS=0)
C
      RATIN=RATEI*FLOAT(1-KS)
C
C*****CALL FINUL IF TANKER IS UNLOADED (LFLAG(1).LT.0).
C
  105 IF (LFLAG(1).LT.0) CALL FINUL
C
C*****STOP INPUT TO STORAGE TANK IF IT IS AT SCAP (LFLAG(4).GT.0).
C
      IF (LFLAG(4).LE.0) GO TO 106
      RATIN=0.0
      FKT=0.0
C
C*****SHUT DOWN REFINERY IF STORAGE TANK IS EMPTY (LFLAG(2).LT.0).
C
  106 IF (LFLAG(2).LT.0) GO TO 107
C
C*****SUFFICIENT CRUDE IN STORAGE TANK TO START REFINERY (LFLAG(3)
C*****IS GREATER THAN ZERO.)
C
      IF (LFLAG(3).LE.0) RETURN
      RATOUT=RATEO
C
C*****COLLECT STATISTICS - SPECIFY REFINERY WILL BE UP DURING NEXT TIME
C*****INTERVAL.
C
      CALL TIMST (1.0,TNOW,3)
      RETURN
  107 RATOUT=0.0
C
C*****COLLECT STATISTICS - SPECIFY REFINERY WILL BE DOWN DURING NEXT
C*****TIME INTERVAL.
C
      CALL TIMST (0.0,TNOW,3)
      GO TO 110
  108 CALL SHUTD
      GO TO 110
  109 CALL STARU
  110 RETURN
C
      END
```

Figure 7-3 FORTRAN listing of subroutine EVNTS (Example 8).

indicate that refinery operating time should accrue during the next time interval. This completes the description of the testing for state-events in subroutine EVNTS.

The events that simulate the arrival of the tanker to the loader (ARRL), the finishing of loading of a tanker (FINL), and the arrival of a tanker to the unloading dock (ARRUL), follow the description provided for these events in Example 2. The FORTRAN listing for these events as used in Example 8 are shown in Figs. 7-4, 7-5, and 7-6, respectively. In subroutine ARRUL, a change is made since the finishing-of-unloading event cannot be scheduled. When a tanker is put in the unloading dock, the input rate to the storage tank is appropriately set, based on the values of the shift indicator KS and the storage tank indicator FKT. The amount of crude to be unloaded is established as state variable 1, that is SS(1). The threshold variable to indicate when unloading is finished (SFIN) is set equal to a fraction of SS(1). The attributes of the tanker being unloaded are then maintained by storing them in file 3. This is required since no event regarding the tanker has been put in file 1.

The finish unloading event FINUL for the tanker is a state-event and

```
      SUBROUTINE ARRL
      COMMON /GCOM1/ ATRIB(25),JEVNT,MFA,MFE(100),MLE(100),MSTOP,NCRDR,N
     1NAPO,NNAPT,NNATR,NNFIL,NNQ(100),NNTRY,NPRNT,PPARM(50,4),TNOW,TTBEG
     2,TTCLR,TTFIN,TTRIB(25),TTSET
      COMMON /UCOM1/BUS,KS,START,ALR,RATEI,RATEO,RATIN,RATOUT,SFIN
     1,SCAP,BCAP,TCAP,FPCT,FKT,NTANK,XTBL
      XTBL=XTBL+1.0
      CALL TIMST (XTBL,TNOW,2)
C
C*****TEST TO SEE IF TANKER HAS MADE A ROUND TRIP.
C
      IF (ATRIB(3).LT.0.0) GO TO 101
      TIFRT=TNOW-ATRIB(3)
      CALL COLCT (TIFRT,2)
      CALL HISTO (TIFRT,2)
C
C*****COMPUTE TIME FOR ROUND TRIP AND COLLECT STATISTICS.
C
C
C*****COMPUTE AMOUNT TO BE LOADED AND AVERAGE TIME TO LOAD.
C
  101 AMTL=TCAP-ATRIB(5)+UNFRM(-10.0,10.0,1)
      XL=AMTL/ALR
      ATRIB(5)=AMTL+ATRIB(5)
C
C*****COMPUTE TIME OF FINISHING LOADING BASED ON EXPONENTIAL LOADING
C*****TIME.
C
      ATRIB(1)=TNOW-XL*ALOG(DRAND(2))
C
C*****SCHEDULE THE COMPLETION OF LOADING EVENT.
C
      ATRIB(2)=2.0
      ATRIB(3)=TNOW
      CALL FILEM (1)
      RETURN
C
      END
```

Figure 7-4 FORTRAN listing of subroutine ARRL (Example 8).

```
      SUBROUTINE FINL
      COMMON /GCOM1/ ATRIB(25),JEVNT,MFA,MFE(100),MLE(100),MSTOP,NCRDR,N
     1NAPO,NNAPT,NNATR,NNFIL,NNQ(100),NNTRY,NPRNT,PPARM(50,4),TNOW,TTBEG
     2,TTCLR,TTFIN,TTRIB(25),TTSET
      COMMON /UCOM1/BUS,KS,START,ALR,RATEI,RATEO,RATIN,RATOUT,SFIN
     1,SCAP,BCAP,TCAP,FPCT,FKT,NTANK,XTBL
      XTBL=XTBL-1.
      CALL TIMST (XTBL,TNOW,2)
C
C*****COMPUTE TIME FOR ARRIVAL AT UNLOADING DOCK USING A NORMALLY
C*****DISTRIBUTED TRAVEL TIME.
C
      ATRIB(1)=TNOW+RNORM(1,4)
      ATRIB(2)=3.0
C
C*****SCHEDULE ARRIVAL AT UNLOADING DOCK.
C
      CALL FILEM (1)
      RETURN
C
      END
```

Figure 7-5 FORTRAN listing of subroutine FINL (Example 8).

```
      SUBROUTINE ARRUL
      COMMON /GCOM1/ ATRIB(25),JEVNT,MFA,MFE(100),MLE(100),MSTOP,NCRDR,N
     1NAPO,NNAPT,NNATR,NNFIL,NNQ(100),NNTRY,NPRNT,PPARM(50,4),TNOW,TTBEG
     2,TTCLR,TTFIN,TTRIB(25),TTSET
      COMMON /GCOM2/ DD(100),DDL(100),DTFUL,DTNOW,ISEES,LFLAG(50),NFLAG,
     1NNEQD,NNEQS,NNEQT,SS(100),SSL(100),TTNEX
      COMMON /UCOM1/BUS,KS,START,ALR,RATEI,RATEO,RATIN,RATOUT,SFIN
     1,SCAP,BCAP,TCAP,FPCT,FKT,NTANK,XTBL
C
C*****RECORD ARRIVAL TIME.
C
      ATRIB(4)=TNOW
C
C*****TEST TO SEE IF UNLOADING DOCK IS BUSY.
C
      IF (BUS.GT.0.0) GO TO 101
C
C*****COLLECT STATISTICS ON WAITING TIME.
C
      CALL COLCT (0.0,1)
      CALL HISTO (0.0,1)
C
C*****COLLECT STATISTICS ON BUSY STEPS.
C
      BUS=1.0
      CALL TIMST (BUS,TNOW,1)
C
C*****SCHEDULE END OF UNLOADING EVENT.
C
      CALL FILEM (3)
      SS(1)=ATRIB(5)
      SFIN=FPCT*SS(1)
      IF (KS.EQ.0) RATIN=RATEI*FKT
      RETURN
C
C*****PUT TANKER IN QUEUE.
C
  101 CALL FILEM (2)
      RETURN
C
      END
```

Figure 7-6 FORTRAN listing of subroutine ARRUL (Example 8).

is called when LFLAG(1) is detected to be less than zero in subroutine EVNTS. When this occurs, the tanker can be removed from the unloading dock, which is accomplished by a call to subroutine RMOVE to remove the first entry in file 3. Scheduling of the tanker to arrive at the loading dock is then performed. The amount of crude left in the tanker at this time is the value of SS(1). If another tanker is to be unloaded, the process described above for initiating the unloading of a tanker is repeated. If no tanker was waiting to be unloaded, the unloading dock is set idle, the rate into the storage tank is set at zero, and state variable 1 is given a zero value. The FORTRAN listing for subroutine FINUL is given in Fig. 7-7.

The shutdown and startup of the unloading dock due to a change in shift are coded in subroutines SHUTD and STARU respectively. The

```
      SUBROUTINE FINUL                                                  FUL
      COMMON /GCOM1/ ATRIB(25),JEVNT,MFA,MFE(100),MLE(100),MSTOP,NCRDR,NGCOM1
     1NAPO,NNAPT,NNATR,NNFIL,NNQ(100),NNTRY,NPRNT,PPARM(50,4),TNOW,TTBEGGCOM1
     2,TTCLR,TTFIN,TTRIB(25),TTSET                                      GCOM1
      COMMON /GCOM2/ DD(100),DDL(100),DTFUL,DTNOW,ISEES,LFLAG(50),NFLAG,GCOM2
     1NNEQD,NNEQS,NNEQT,SS(100),SSL(100),TTNEX                          GCOM2
      COMMON /UCOM1/BUS,KS,START,ALR,RATEI,RATEO,RATIN,RATOUT,SFIN      UCOM1
     1,SCAP,BCAP,TCAP,FPCT,FKT,NTANK,XTBL                               UCOM1
C                                                                       FUL
C*****SCHEDULE ARRL EVENT FOR TANKER.                                   FUL
C                                                                       FUL
      CALL RMOVE (MFE(3),3)                                             FUL
      ATRIB(1)=TNOW+RNORM(2,4)                                          FUL
      ATRIB(2)=1.0                                                      FUL
      ATRIB(5)=SS(1)                                                    FUL
      CALL FILEM (1)                                                    FUL
C                                                                       FUL
C*****IS THERE A TANKER IN FILE 2.                                      FUL
C                                                                       FUL
      IF (NNQ(2).EQ.0) GO TO 101                                        FUL
C                                                                       FUL
C*****REMOVE FIRST TANKER FROM QUEUE AND COLLECT STATISTICS ON          FUL
C*****WAITING TIME.                                                     FUL
C                                                                       FUL
      CALL RMOVE (MFE(2),2)                                             FUL
      WT=TNOW-ATRIB(4)                                                  FUL
      CALL COLCT (WT,1)                                                 FUL
      CALL HISTO (WT,1)                                                 FUL
C                                                                       FUL
C*****SCHEDULE END OF UNLOADING EVENT.                                  FUL
C                                                                       FUL
      RATIN=RATEI*FKT                                                   FUL
      CALL FILEM (3)                                                    FUL
      SS(1)=ATRIB(5)                                                    FUL
      SFIN=FPCT*SS(1)                                                   FUL
      RETURN                                                            FUL
C                                                                       FUL
C*****COLLECT STATISTICS ON DOCK STATUS AND SET DOCK STATUS TO IDLE.    FUL
C                                                                       FUL
  101 BUS=0.0                                                           FUL
      CALL TIMST (BUS,TNOW,1)                                           FUL
      RATIN=0.0                                                         FUL
      SS(1)=0.0                                                         FUL
      RETURN                                                            FUL
C                                                                       FUL
      END                                                               FUL
```

Figure 7-7 FORTRAN listing of subroutine FINUL (Example 8).

```
      SUBROUTINE SHUTD
      COMMON /GCOM1/ ATRIB(25),JEVNT,MFA,MFE(100),MLE(100),MSTOP,NCRDR,N
     1NAPO,NNAPT,NNATR,NNFIL,NNQ(100),NNTRY,NPRNT,PPARM(50,4),TNOW,TTBEG
     2,TTCLR,TTFIN,TTRIB(25),TTSET
      COMMON /UCOM1/BUS,KS,START,ALR,RATEI,RATEO,RATIN,RATOUT,SFIN
     1,SCAP,BCAP,TCAP,FPCT,FKT,NTANK,XTBL
      KS=1
      ATRIB(1)=TNOW+(1./3.)
      ATRIB(2)=6.0
      CALL FILEM (1)
      IF (BUS.EQ.0.0) RETURN
      CALL TIMST (0.0,TNOW,1)
      RATIN=0.0
      RETURN
C
      END
```

Figure 7-8 FORTRAN listing of subroutine SHUTD (Example 8).

FORTRAN listings for these routines are given in Figs. 7-8 and 7-9. When the unloading dock is shut down, the indicator KS is set at one. A startup event is scheduled to occur in one-third of a day. If no tanker is at the unloading dock (BUS = 0.0), no changes are required to the system status. If a tanker is in the unloading dock (BUS = 1.0), statistics are collected on the busy time and the input rate into the storage tank is set at zero. The indicator BUS is not changed since it is used in the start-up event to determine if a tanker is in the unloading dock.

When a shift is to be started, the shift indicator KS is set at zero to indicate that a working shift is in progress. The next shutdown is then scheduled to occur in two-thirds of a day. If the unloading dock does not have a tanker in it, no further change is required to the system status. If the unloading dock is occupied, statistics are collected on the unloading dock's busy time, and the input rate to the storage tank is then set equal to the nominal rate times the indicator reflecting the storage tank's ability to accept input. This completes the description of all the time- and state-events associated with the tanker-storage tank simulation.

```
      SUBROUTINE STARU
      COMMON /GCOM1/ ATRIB(25),JEVNT,MFA,MFE(100),MLE(100),MSTOP,NCRDR,N
     1NAPO,NNAPT,NNATR,NNFIL,NNQ(100),NNTRY,NPRNT,PPARM(50,4),TNOW,TTBEG
     2,TTCLR,TTFIN,TTRIB(25),TTSET
      COMMON /UCOM1/BUS,KS,START,ALR,RATEI,RATEO,RATIN,RATOUT,SFIN
     1,SCAP,BCAP,TCAP,FPCT,FKT,NTANK,XTBL
      KS=0
      ATRIB(1)=TNOW+(2./3.)
      ATRIB(2)=5.0
      CALL FILEM (1)
      IF (BUS.EQ.0.0) RETURN
      CALL TIMST (1.0,TNOW,1)
      IF (NNQ(3).EQ.0) CALL ERROR (6)
      RATIN=RATEI*FKT
      RETURN
C
      END
```

Figure 7-9 FORTRAN listing of subroutine STARU (Example 8).

```
      PROGRAM MAIN (INPUT,OUTPUT,TAPE5=INPUT,TAPE6=OUTPUT)              MX8      1
      DIMENSION NSET(20000)                                             DIM      1
      COMMON QSET(20000)                                                COM      1
      COMMON /GCOM1/ ATRIB(25),JEVNT,MFA,MFE(100),MLE(100),MSTOP,NCRDR,NGCOM1    1
     1NAPO,NNAPT,NNATR,NNFIL,NNQ(100),NNTRY,NPRNT,PPARM(50,4),TNOW,TTBEGGCOM1    2
     2,TTCLR,TTFIN,TTRIB(25),TTSET                                      GCOM1    3
      EQUIVALENCE (NSET(1),QSET(1))                                     EQUIV    1
C                                                                       MX8      2
C*****SET CARD READER NUMBER AND PRINTER NUMBER.                        MX8      3
C                                                                       MX8      4
      NCRDR=5                                                           MX8      5
      NPRNT=6                                                           MX8      6
      CALL GASP                                                         MX8      7
      CALL EXIT                                                         MX8      8
C                                                                       MX8      9
      END                                                               MX8     10
```

Figure 7-10 FORTRAN listing of main program (Example 8).

The main program and subroutine INTLC are shown in Figs. 7-10 and 7-11. These subroutines are in standard GASP IV form. In the main program NSET is dimensioned to 20,000 since plot data will be stored in it. In this example all values of the state variables will be recorded every 0.25 day by setting DTSAV equal to this value on input. Subroutine SSAVE is then called every 0.25 day in addition to being called at every

```
      SUBROUTINE INTLC                                                  IC8      1
      COMMON /GCOM1/ ATRIB(25),JEVNT,MFA,MFE(100),MLE(100),MSTOP,NCRDR,N GCOM1    1
     1NAPO,NNAPT,NNATR,NNFIL,NNQ(100),NNTRY,NPRNT,PPARM(50,4),TNOW,TTBEG GCOM1    2
     2,TTCLR,TTFIN,TTRIB(25),TTSET                                      GCOM1    3
      COMMON /GCOM2/ DD(100),DDL(100),DTFUL,DTNOW,ISEES,LFLAG(50),NFLAG, GCOM2    1
     1NNEQD,NNEQS,NNEQT,SS(100),SSL(100),TTNEX                          GCOM2    2
      COMMON /UCOM1/BUS,KS,START,ALR,RATEI,RATEO,RATIN,RATOUT,SFIN      UCOM1    1
     1,SCAP,BCAP,TCAP,FPCT,FKT,NTANK,XTBL                               UCOM1    2
C                                                                       IC8      2
C*****INITIALIZE NON-GASP VARIABLES.                                    IC8      3
C                                                                       IC8      4
      SFIN=0.0                                                          IC8      5
      KS=1                                                              IC8      6
      FKT=1.0                                                           IC8      7
      BUS=0.0                                                           IC8      8
      NTANK=15                                                          IC8      9
      TCAP=150.                                                         IC8     10
      SCAP=2000.                                                        IC8     11
      BCAP=0.8*SCAP                                                     IC8     12
      RATEO=150.                                                        IC8     13
      ALR=50.                                                           IC8     14
      XTBL=0.0                                                          IC8     15
      RATEI=300.                                                        IC8     16
      FPCT=0.05                                                         IC8     17
      SS(1)=0.                                                          IC8     18
      RATIN=0.                                                          IC8     19
      SS(2)=0.5*SCAP                                                    IC8     20
      RATOUT=RATEO                                                      IC8     21
C                                                                       IC8     22
C*****ESTABLISH ARRIVAL AT LOADING DOCK FOR EACH TANKER.                IC8     23
C                                                                       IC8     24
      ATRIB(1)=0.                                                       IC8     25
      ATRIB(2)=1.0                                                      IC8     26
      ATRIB(3)=-1.0                                                     IC8     27
      ATRIB(4)=0.0                                                      IC8     28
      ATRIB(5)=0.0                                                      IC8     29
      DO 101 I=1,NTANK                                                  IC8     30
      CALL FILEM (1)                                                    IC8     31
  101 ATRIB(1)=ATRIB(1)+0.5                                             IC8     32
      RETURN                                                            IC8     33
C                                                                       IC8     34
      END
```

Figure 7-11 FORTRAN listing of subroutine INTLC (Example 8).

event time. In subroutine SSAVE the values of SS(1) and SS(2) are recorded through a call to subroutine GPLOT. The GASP IV summary report will then provide a printed record of the values of these state variables. The FORTRAN listing for subroutine SSAVE is given in Fig. 7-12.

```
      SUBROUTINE SSAVE                                                  SV8     1
      COMMON /GCOM1/ ATRIB(25),JEVNT,MFA,MFE(100),MLE(100),MSTOP,NCRDR,NGCOM1   1
     1NAPO,NNAPT,NNATR,NNFIL,NNQ(100),NNTRY,NPRNT,PPARM(50,4),TNOW,TTBEGGCOM1   2
     2,TTCLR,TTFIN,TTRIB(25),TTSET                                      GCOM1   3
      COMMON /GCOM2/ DD(100),DDL(100),DTFUL,DTNOW,ISEES,LFLAG(50),NFLAG,GCOM2   1
     1NNEQD,NNEQS,NNEQT,SS(100),SSL(100),TTNEX                          GCOM2   2
      COMMON /UCOM1/BUS,KS,START,ALR,RATEI,RATEO,RATIN,RATOUT,SFIN      UCOM1   1
     1,SCAP,BCAP,TCAP,FPCT,FKT,NTANK,XTBL                               UCOM1   2
      CALL GPLOT (SS(1),TNOW,1)                                         SV8     2
      CALL TIMSA (SS(2),TNOW,4)                                         SV8     3
      RETURN                                                            SV8     4
C                                                                       SV8     5
      END                                                               SV8     6
```

Figure 7-12 FORTRAN listing of subroutine SSAVE (Example 8).

A listing of the input data cards for this example is given in Fig. 7-13.

Simulation Reports

Figure 7-14 presents a printout of the input data provided by the GASP IV echo check. Most of the input information is standard and only special information is discussed. Note that NNSET is set at 20,000 so that QSET can store the data collected in subroutine GPLOT. The number of entries in the file is set at 30, which will allow a simulation involving up to 28 tankers. An entry is required for each tanker and for each start-up and

```
PRITSKER            8    6   30 1973    1                                    1
    2    4    2    9    1    5   30    5    320000    0    2    5              2
3        1WAIT TIM                                                           3
3        2TRIP TIM
4        1UNL UTIL       0.0                                                 4
4        2LDR UTIL       0.0
4        3REFIN UP       1.0
4        4AMTINSTR    1000.0
5        1WAIT TIM             10    0.0      .25                            5
5        2TRIP TIM             10  6.0      2.0
6A       1TIME                  0    2    0   .25                            6
6B       1TTANKER        1      1   0.0      300.
6B       2SSTORAGE       1      1  0.0       2000.
    1    1    3                                                              7
    1    1    3                                                              8
    4       .00001    .00001              .25        .25                     9
10       1  5.0      3.5       8.0      1.5                                 10
10       2  4.0      3.0       7.0      1.0
    1    1    1      0.0       365.0       16539743183192494521215893       11
12       1   0.       0.                                                    12
12       1 0.16666    6.
12       1    5.0     0.
12       0
```

Figure 7-13 Listing of input data cards (Example 8).

```
                         SIMULATION PROJECT NUMBER    8  BY  PRITSKER

                         DATE   6/ 30/ 1973          RUN NUMBER     1 OF     1
                         LLSUP=000000000000000000    GASP IV VERSION 23JUN73

NNCLT=     2   NNSTA=     4   NNHIS=     2   NNPRM=     2   NNPLT=     1   NNSTR=     0   NNTRY=    30
NNATR=     5   NNFIL=     3   NNSET= 23000   NNEQD=     0   NNEQS=     2   NFLAG=     3

COLCT NO.  1   LLABC=WAIT TIM
COLCT NO.  2   LLABC=TRIP TIM

TIMST NO.  1   LLABT=UNL UTIL  I.C. =    0.
TIMST NO.  2   LLABT=LDR UTIL  I.C. =    0.
TIMST NO.  3   LLABT=REFIN UP  I.C. =    1.0000E+00
TIMST NO.  4   LLABT=AMTINSTR  I.C. =    1.0000E+03

HISTC NO.  1   LLABH=WAIT TIM                NNCEL=    10   HHLOW=    0.             HHWID=    2.5000E-01
HISTC NO.  2   LLABH=TRIP TIM                NNCEL=    10   HHLOW=    6.0000E+00     HHWID=    2.0000E+00

GPLOT NO.  1   LLABP=TIME      IITAP=     0  NNVAR=     2   LLPLT=    2              DTPLT=    2.5000E-01
  VAR NO.  1        T=TANKER   LLPLO=     1  LLPHI=     1   PPLO =    0.             PPHI =    3.0000E+02
  VAR NO.  2        S=STORAGE  LLPLO=     1  LLPHI=     1   PPLO =    0.             PPHI =    2.0000E+03

KKRNK= (   1)      1      3

IINN = (   1)      1      3

IIEVT=     4   LLERR=    -0   AAERR=    1.0000E-03             RRERR=    1.0000E-03
DTMIN=     2.5000E-03         DTMAX=    2.5000E-01             DTSAV=    2.5000E-01

PARAMETER SET    1 =    5.0000E+00   3.5000E+00   8.0000E+00   1.5000E+00
PARAMETER SET    2 =    4.0000E+00   3.0000E+00   7.0000E+00   1.0000E+00

MSTOP=     1   JJCLR=     1   JJBEG=     1   IICRD=    -0   TTBEG=    0.             TTFIN=    3.6500E+02
JJFIL=     1
IISED= 65397          43183          19249          45212          15893
```

Figure 7-14 GASP IV echo check of input data (Example 8).

```
                        **GASP SUMMARY REPORT**

              SIMULATION PROJECT NUMBER   8  BY  PRITSKER

              DATE  6/ 30/ 1973       RUN NUMBER   1 OF   1

              CURRENT TIME =  3.6500E+02


PARAMETER SET      1 =    5.0000E+00    3.5000E+00    8.0000E+00    1.5000E+00
PARAMETER SET      2 =    4.0000E+00    3.0000E+00    7.0000E+00    1.0000E+00


                 **STATISTICS FOR VARIABLES BASED ON OBSERVATION**
               MEAN        STD DEV      SD OF MEAN        CV          MINIMUM        MAXIMUM      OBS

WAIT TIM    1.2923E+00    1.1938E+00    6.1323E-02    3.2339E-01    0.            5.3657E+00    379
TRIP TIM    1.4182E+01    3.2398E+00    1.6797E-01    2.2845E-01    7.7653E+00    2.7213E+01    372

                   **STATISTICS FOR TIME-PERSISTENT VARIABLES**
               MEAN        STD DEV       MINIMUM       MAXIMUM     TIME INTERVAL  CUR. VALUE

UNL UTIL    5.9259E-01    4.9135E-01    0.            1.0000E+00    3.6500E+02    0.
LDR UTIL    3.0688E+00    1.4335E+00    0.            8.0000E+00    3.6500E+02    4.0000E+00
REFIN UP    9.9830E-01    4.1245E-02    0.            1.0000E+00    3.6500E+02    1.0000E+00
AMTINSTR    1.4874E+03    4.8153E+02    2.6731E+00    2.0140E+03    3.6500E+02    1.8287E+03
```

```
**GASP FILE STORAGE AREA DUMP AT TIME   3.6500E+02**

MAXIMUM NUMBER OF ENTRIES IN FILE STORAGE AREA = 18

                    PRINTOUT OF FILE NUMBER    1
                        TNOW =   3.6500E+02
                        QQTIM=   3.6483E+02

                TIME PERIOD FOR STATISTICS 3.6500E+02
                AVERAGE NUMBER IN FILE        13.7959
                STANDARD DEVIATION             1.5012
                MAXIMUM NUMBER IN FILE        18

                                   FILE CONTENTS
ENTRY   1   =   3.6517E+02   6.0000E+00   -0.          -0.          -0.
ENTRY   2   =   3.6532E+02   1.0000E+00   3.4875E+02   3.5646E+02   5.5129E+00
ENTRY   3   =   3.6556E+02   1.0000E+00   3.5272E+02   3.5789E+02   3.3364E+00
ENTRY   4   =   3.6567E+02   3.0000E+00   3.6127E+02   3.5493E+02   1.5446E+02
ENTRY   5   =   3.6608E+02   3.0000E+00   3.6011E+02   3.5361E+02   1.4004E+02
ENTRY   6   =   3.6651E+02   2.0000E+00   3.5851E+02   3.5366E+02   1.5873E+02
ENTRY   7   =   3.6683E+02   2.0000E+00   3.5739E+02   3.5147E+02   1.5848E+02
ENTRY   8   =   3.6752E+02   3.0000E+00   3.5985E+02   3.5482E+02   1.5710E+02
ENTRY   9   =   3.6755E+02   1.0000E+00   3.4857E+02   3.6030E+02   1.0908E+00
ENTRY  10   =   3.6776E+02   1.0000E+00   3.5088E+02   3.5923E+02   2.3373E+00
ENTRY  11   =   3.6781E+02   2.0000E+00   3.5671E+02   3.4885E+02   1.4491E+02
ENTRY  12   =   3.6807E+02   1.0000E+00   3.4825E+02   3.5836E+02   4.2313E+00
ENTRY  13   =   3.6827E+02   2.0000E+00   3.5996E+02   3.5419E+02   1.5401E+02
ENTRY  14   =   3.6879E+02   1.0000E+00   3.5356E+02   3.5967E+02   6.8704E+00
```

Figure 7-15 GASP IV summary report (Example 8).

```
                                        PRINTOUT OF FILE NUMBER    2
                                            TNOW =   3.6500E+02
                                            DDTIM=   3.6444E+02

                                    TIME PERIOD FOR STATISTICS 3.6500E+02
                                    AVERAGE NUMBER IN FILE            1.3463
                                    STANDARD DEVIATION                1.3121
                                    MAXIMUM NUMBER IN FILE            6

                                              FILE CONTENTS
ENTRY   1   =      3.6362E+02      3.0000E+00      3.5642E+02      3.6362E+02      1.5961E+02

                                        PRINTOUT OF FILE NUMBER    3
                                            TNOW =   3.6500E+02
                                            DDTIM=   3.6444E+02

                                    TIME PERIOD FOR STATISTICS 3.6500E+02
                                    AVERAGE NUMBER IN FILE             .8716
                                    STANDARD DEVIATION                 .3346
                                    MAXIMUM NUMBER IN FILE            1

                                              FILE CONTENTS
ENTRY   1   =      3.6187E+02      3.0000E+00      3.5511E+02      3.6187E+02      1.5700E+02




                              **GASP STATE STORAGE AREA DUMP AT TIME  3.6500E+02**

                                      (I)          SS(I)            DD(I)
                                       1         3.8254E+01        0.
                                       2         1.8287E+03        0.
```

Figure 7-15 *(continued)*

shutdown event. Since events store the information for a tanker, the number of entries can at most be the number of tankers plus two. Since there are five attributes plus two pointers per entry, 210 cells of NSET are allocated to the filing system. This leaves 19,790 cells of NSET for storing the values to be plotted.

By setting IITAP(1) = 0, core storage is specified for the plot data. With LLPLT = 2, both a table and plot are to be provided by the GASP IV summary report. The plotting interval DTPLT is set equal to 0.25 days. This specifies that all data points in the interval (T − 0.125, T + 0.125) will be plotted at the time point T. Specification of a large DTPLT value will result in many points being plotted on the same line. If DTPLT is small in comparison with DTSAV, one point at most can be expected per line. LLPLO and LLPHI values are set at one to indicate that the PPLO and PPHI values are to be used for the smallest and largest values on the plot. The other input data shown in Fig. 7-14 is similar to that provided by other examples.

The GASP summary report for example 8 is presented in Fig. 7-15.

As can be seen from the output statistics, the unloading dock is in use almost 60% of a day. This represents over 14 of the 16 hours it is being operated. The system appears to have been designed to insure little or no refinery down time. The fraction of time the refinery is operating is 0.998; it would have been 1.00 if the initial conditions were not so adverse. This high fraction of refinery operating time occurs at the expense of the tankers, which have a waiting time of 1.29 days. This is further illustrated by the printout for file 2, which indicates that the average number waiting for the unloading dock is 1.35, and that as many as six tankers were waiting at one time. The statistics regarding file 3 indicate that there was a tanker in the unloading dock 87% of the time. This statistic includes all shifts since a tanker is in file 3 regardless of whether the unloading dock is unloading or not.

The final values of the state variables and their derivatives are printed under the heading "GASP State Storage Area Dump at Time 3.6500E + 02." The two histograms collected during this simulation are shown in Fig. 7-16. From histogram 2, the probability that a round trip takes less than a given number of days can be estimated. For example, the estimate of the probability that a tanker completes a round trip in 16 days or less is 0.745.

A portion of the tabular output obtained from subroutine GPLOT is shown in Fig. 7-17. Throughout the table sets of values are repeated. This occurs because at each event time the state variables are recorded at the end of the step that is before the event, and then again after the event. This is necessary to record discrete changes in the variables if they occur at event times. An example of this can be seen at time 6.1667; a STARU event occurred but the state variable values were not changed. At the end of the table minimum and maximum values that occurred during the simulation are printed.

A plot of the tabular information is shown in Fig. 7-18. At the start of the simulation, all of the tankers were scheduled to arrive at the loading dock. Thus there were no tankers at the unloading dock and the amount to be unloaded represented by the letter T is at the zero point on the plot. Note that the scales for each variable are different and that T is plotted from zero to 300, whereas S, the level in the storage tank, is plotted from zero to 2000. Cursors are provided at the 0, 25, 50, 75, and 100% levels.

Since there are no tankers at the unloading dock, the amount in the storage tank is depleted by the amount being sent to the refinery. From the plot, this depletion continues until time 6.25. At time 5.75 the first tanker arrived. The tanker arrival according to the plot could have occurred anywhere between 5.625 and 5.875. The exact time of tanker arrival can be determined by referring to the table output. (In this case it was 5.8689.) Since shutdown (third shift) starts at 5.833, unloading of the tanker does not commence. At time 6.1667 the first shift begins and tanker unloading is initiated. This is plotted at time 6.25. Since the input

```
                              **HISTOGRAM NUMBER  1**

                                    WAIT TIM

OBSV     RELA     CUML       UPPER
FREQ     FREQ     FREQ    CELL LIMIT    0         20        40        60        80        100
                                        +    +    +    +    +    +    +    +    +    +    +
  63     .166     .166    0.            +********                                         +
  26     .069     .235    2.5000E-01    +***        C                                     +
  25     .066     .301    5.0000E-01    +***           C                                  +
  35     .092     .393    7.5000E-01    +*****              C                             +
  39     .103     .496    1.0000E+00    +*****                   C                        +
  30     .079     .575    1.2500E+00    +****                        C                    +
  27     .071     .646    1.5000E+00    +****                           C                 +
  30     .079     .726    1.7500E+00    +****                               C             +
  19     .050     .776    2.0000E+00    +***                                   C          +
  11     .029     .805    2.2500E+00    +*                                      C         +
   8     .021     .826    2.5000E+00    +*                                       C        +
  66     .174    1.000       INF        +*********                                        C
 ---                                    +    +    +    +    +    +    +    +    +    +    +
 379                                    0         20        40        60        80        100
```

```
                                 **HISTOGRAM NUMBER  2**

                                       TRIP TIM

OBSV   RELA    CUML       UPPER
FREQ   FREQ    FREQ    CELL LIMIT    0         20        40        60        80       100
                                     +    +    +    +    +    +    +    +    +    +    +
   0  0.000   0.000   6.0000E+00     +                                                 +
   1   .003    .003   8.0000E+00     +                                                 +
  29   .078    .081   1.0000E+01     +****                                             +
  66   .177    .258   1.2000E+01     +*********   C                                    +
  99   .266    .524   1.4000E+01     +*************            C                       +
  82   .220    .745   1.6000E+01     +***********                         C            +
  52   .140    .884   1.8000E+01     +*******                                    C     +
  21   .056    .941   2.0000E+01     +***                                           C  +
  12   .032    .973   2.2000E+01     +**                                              C+
   9   .024    .997   2.4000E+01     +*                                                C
   0  0.000    .997   2.6000E+01     +                                                 C
   1   .003   1.000      INF         +                                                 C
 ---                                 +    +    +    +    +    +    +    +    +    +    +
 372                                 0         20        40        60        80       100
```

Figure 7-16   Histogram output (Example 8).

TABLE NUMBER 1
RUN NUMBER 1

TIME	TANKER	STORAGE
4.7500E+00	0.	2.8750E+02
4.8333E+00	0.	2.7500E+02
4.8333E+00	0.	2.7500E+02
5.0000E+00	0.	2.5000E+02
5.0000E+00	0.	2.5000E+02
5.1667E+00	0.	2.2500E+02
5.1667E+00	0.	2.2500E+02
5.2500E+00	0.	2.1250E+02
5.5000E+00	0.	1.7500E+02
5.5000E+00	0.	1.7500E+02
5.7500E+00	0.	1.3750E+02
5.8333E+00	0.	1.2500E+02
5.8333E+00	0.	1.2500E+02
5.9945E+00	0.	1.0082E+02
5.9945E+00	0.	1.0082E+02
6.0000E+00	0.	1.0000E+02
6.0000E+00	0.	1.0000E+02
6.0295E+00	0.	9.5579E+01
6.0295E+00	0.	9.5579E+01
6.1667E+00	0.	7.5001E+01
6.1667E+00	0.	7.5001E+01
6.1887E+00	0.	7.1688E+01
6.1887E+00	0.	7.1688E+01
6.2386E+00	0.	6.4204E+01
6.2386E+00	0.	6.4204E+01
6.2500E+00	0.	6.2500E+01
6.5000E+00	0.	2.5000E+01
6.5000E+00	0.	2.5000E+01
6.5377E+00	0.	1.9350E+01
6.5377E+00	0.	1.9350E+01
6.6438E+00	0.	3.4252E+00
6.6438E+00	0.	3.4252E+00
6.7500E+00	0.	3.4252E+00
6.8333E+00	0.	3.4252E+00
6.8333E+00	0.	3.4252E+00
7.0000E+00	0.	3.4252E+00
7.0000E+00	0.	3.4252E+00
7.0357E+00	0.	3.4252E+00
7.0357E+00	1.4807E+02	3.4252E+00
7.1667E+00	1.4807E+02	3.4252E+00
7.1667E+00	1.4807E+02	3.4252E+00
7.2500E+00	1.2306E+02	2.8427E+01
7.2594E+00	1.2026E+02	3.1236E+01
7.2594E+00	1.2026E+02	3.1236E+01
7.3056E+00	1.0639E+02	4.5102E+01
7.3056E+00	1.0639E+02	4.5102E+01
7.3655E+00	8.8406E+01	6.3085E+01
7.3655E+00	8.8406E+01	6.3085E+01
7.4255E+00	7.0423E+01	7.2076E+01
7.4255E+00	7.0423E+01	7.2076E+01
7.5000E+00	4.8064E+01	8.3236E+01
7.6234E+00	1.1033E+01	1.0177E+02
7.6234E+00	1.1033E+01	1.0177E+02
7.6551E+00	1.5410E+00	1.0652E+02
7.6551E+00	1.4850E+02	1.0652E+02
7.7500E+00	1.2002E+02	1.2076E+02
7.7861E+00	1.0918E+02	1.2618E+02
7.7861E+00	1.0918E+02	1.2618E+02
7.8333E+00	9.5026E+01	1.3326E+02
7.8333E+00	9.5026E+01	1.3326E+02
8.0000E+00	9.5026E+01	1.0823E+02
8.1667E+00	9.5026E+01	8.3255E+01
8.1667E+00	9.5026E+01	8.3255E+01
8.2500E+00	7.0024E+01	9.5736E+01
8.3611E+00	3.6685E+01	1.1243E+02
8.3611E+00	3.6685E+01	1.1243E+02
8.4653E+00	5.4390E+00	1.2805E+02
8.4653E+00	1.5125E+02	1.2805E+02
8.5000E+00	1.4083E+02	1.3326E+02
8.7500E+00	6.5831E+01	1.7076E+02
MINIMUM	0.	3.4252E+00
MAXIMUM	1.6000E+02	2.0149E+03

Figure 7-17 Tabular output of state variables (Example 8).

rate for the storage tank is greater than its output rate, the amount of crude in the storage tank increases momentarily as the tanker is being unloaded. The amount of crude in the tanker decreases until the tanker is unloaded at time 6.75. At time 7.50 the refinery is shut down since the storage tank is empty. The next tanker arrives at 7.75. At time 8.31 the refinery begins operation again as there are 50 tb in the storage tank. As can be seen, the plot illustrates the combined discrete-continuous nature of the simulation. The second part of the plot illustrates the steady-state behavior of the system. The amount in the storage tank oscillates between SCAP and BCAP, and tankers are in the unloading dock waiting for storage space to become available in order to unload their crude.

EXAMPLE 9–SIMULATION OF A CHEMICAL REACTION PROCESS (55)

Statement of the Problem

A hydrogenation reaction is conducted in four reactors operating in parallel. Each reactor may be started, stopped, discharged, or cleaned independently of the others. A compressor with a constant molal flow rate provides a supply of hydrogen gas to the reactors through a surge pressure tank and individual valves for each reactor. The valve connecting each reactor to the surge tank is adjusted by controls that make the effective pressure in each reactor the minimum of surge tank pressure and critical pressure (100 psia).

Initially the surge tank pressure is equal to 500 psia. Each reactor is charged with a fresh batch of reactant and the four reactors are scheduled to be turned on at half hour intervals beginning with reactor 1 at time 0. As a reaction proceeds, the concentration of the reactant (and the demand for hydrogen for that reactor) decreases. As long as surge tank pressure remains above the critical pressure of 100 psia, the decrease in concentration is exponential. The concentration of each reactant is monitored until it decreases to 10% of its initial value at which time the reactor is considered to have completed a batch. At this time the reactor is turned off, discharged, cleaned, and recharged. The time to discharge a reactor is known to be exponentially distributed with a mean time of one hour. The time to clean and recharge a reactor is known to be approximately normally distributed with a mean of one hour and a standard deviation of one-half hour.

The operating policy for the system prescribes that the last reactor started will be immediately turned off whenever surge tank pressure falls below the critical value of 100 psia. All other reactors that are on at that

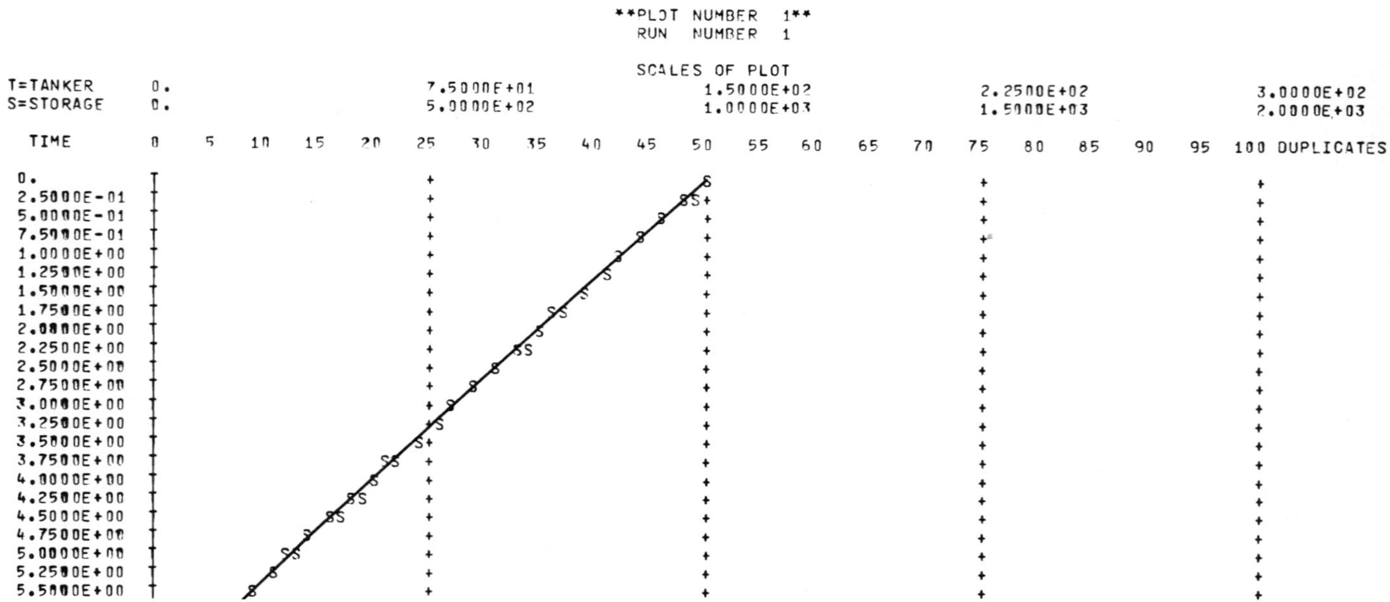
PLOT NUMBER 1
RUN NUMBER 1
SCALES OF PLOT
T=TANKER 0. 7.5000E+01 1.5000E+02 2.2500E+02 3.0000E+02
S=STORAGE 0. 5.0000E+02 1.0000E+03 1.5000E+03 2.0000E+03
TIME 0 5 10 15 20 25 30 35 40 45 50 55 60 65 70 75 80 85 90 95 100 DUPLICATES
0.
2.5000E-01
5.0000E-01
7.5000E-01
1.0000E+00
1.2500E+00
1.5000E+00
1.7500E+00
2.0000E+00
2.2500E+00
2.5000E+00
2.7500E+00
3.0000E+00
3.2500E+00
3.5000E+00
3.7500E+00
4.0000E+00
4.2500E+00
4.5000E+00
4.7500E+00
5.0000E+00
5.2500E+00
5.5000E+00

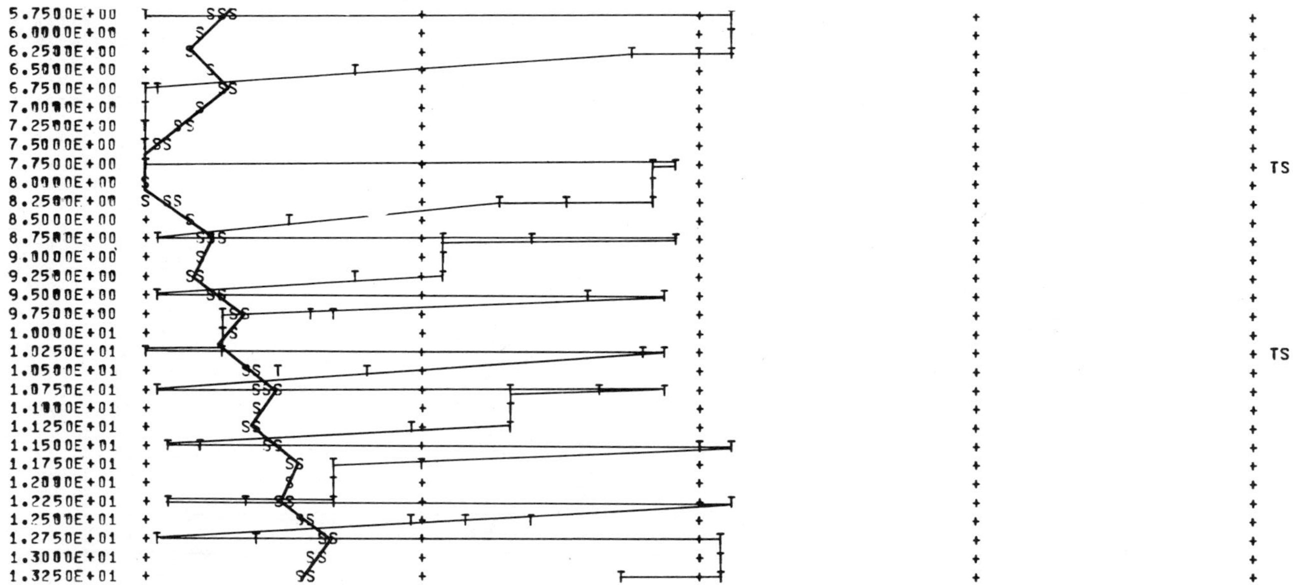

Figure 7-18 Plot of state variables (Example 8).

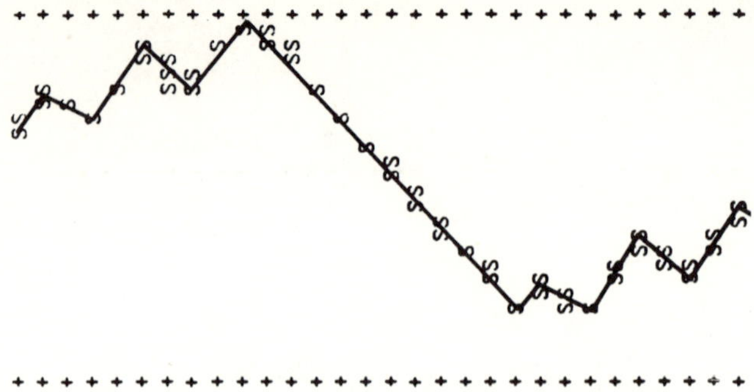

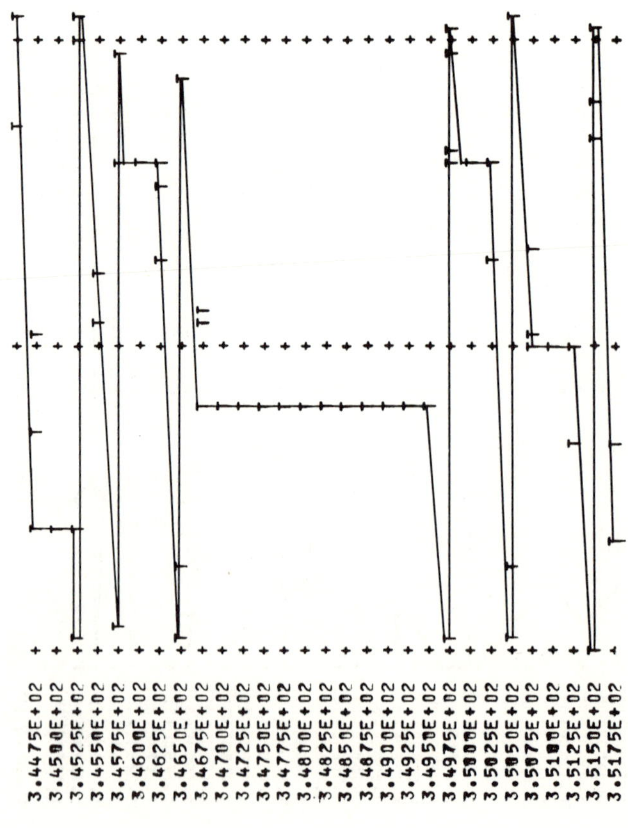
3.4475E+02
3.4500E+02
3.4525E+02
3.4550E+02
3.4575E+02
3.4600E+02
3.4625E+02
3.4650E+02
3.4675E+02
3.4700E+02
3.4725E+02
3.4750E+02
3.4775E+02
3.4800E+02
3.4825E+02
3.4850E+02
3.4875E+02
3.4900E+02
3.4925E+02
3.4950E+02
3.4975E+02
3.5000E+02
3.5025E+02
3.5050E+02
3.5075E+02
3.5100E+02
3.5125E+02
3.5150E+02
3.5175E+02

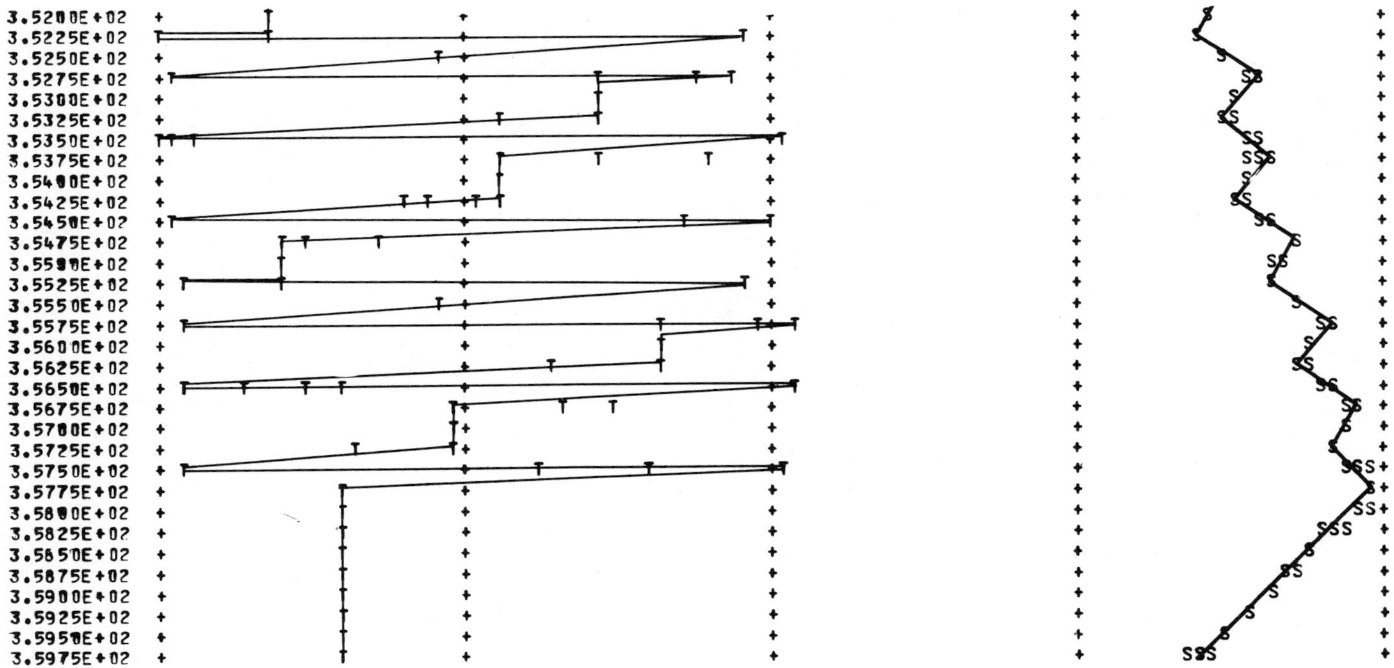

Figure 7-18 *(continued)*

time will continue, but no reactor will be started if surge tank pressure is below a nominal pressure of 150 psia.

Simulation Objective

The objective of this simulation is to model and analyze a chemical reaction process that involves a continuous batch process subject to controls imposed by surge tank pressure. In addition to a plot of the operation of the process, statistics on the maintenance time, the number of reactors on, and the surge tank pressure are to be obtained.

Special Features

In this example the subroutine used to model state-events makes calls to the subroutines used to model time-events. This further demonstrates the interaction between discrete and continuous processes. First order differential equations are modeled and the RKE algorithm is used for integration. The use of files to store the attributes of reactors and for categorizing reactor status is also demonstrated.

Simulation Procedure

Figure 7-19 provides a schematic representation of the compressor, surge tank, valves, and reactors. The definitions of the parameters and variables of the model are given in Table 7-1.

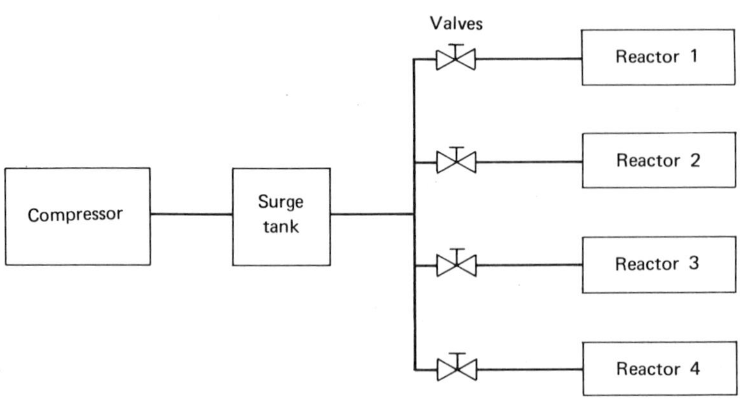

Figure 7-19 Schematic diagram for reactor example.

Table 7-1 Parameters and Variables for Chemical Reaction Model

Model Parameters	Initial Value	Definition
RK(1)	0.03466	Reaction constant for product 1
RK(2)	0.00866	Reaction constant for product 2
RK(3)	0.01155	Reaction constant for product 3
RK(4)	0.00770	Reaction constant for product 4
V(1)	10.0	Volume of reactor 1
V(2)	15.0	Volume of reactor 2
V(3)	20.0	Volume of reactor 3
V(4)	25.0	Volume of reactor 4
VS	50.0	Volume of surge tank
RR	10.73	Gas constant
TEMP	550.0	System operating temperature
FC	0.19	Flow constant of compressor; FC ★ SUMFO is compressor molal flow rate
PNOM	150.0	Nominal pressure
PCRIT	100.0	Critical pressure
SUMFO	Calculated	Maximum possible molal flow of hydrogen to all reactors
ATDIS	1.0	Average time to discharge a reactor
RTV	RR ★ TEMP/VS	Composite reaction constant
FCOMP	FC ★ SUMFO	Compressor molal flow rate
Model Variables		
SS(1)	SO(1) = 0.1	Concentration of reactor 1
SS(2)	SO(2) = 0.4	Concentration of reactor 2
SS(3)	SO(3) = 0.2	Concentration of reactor 3
SS(4)	SO(4) = 0.5	Concentration of reactor 4
SS(5)	SO(5) = 500.0	Surge tank pressure
DD(I), I = 1,4	0.0	Derivative of SS(I) with respect to time
F(I), I = 1,4	0.0	Molal flow rate of hydrogen to reactor I
SUMF	0.0	Total molal flow of hydrogen to all reactors
XRON	0.0	Number of reactors on
RON(I), I = 1,4	0.0	A flag indicating whether reactor I is on (1.0) or off (0.0)

The basic equation for the change in concentration of reactor I, SS(I), is

$$\frac{dSS(I)}{dt} = -RK(I) \star PEFF \star SS(I), \qquad I = 1,4$$

where RK(I) is the reaction constant for reaction I and PEFF is the effective surge tank pressure. The GASP IV coding of this differential equation is directly obtained by substituting DD(I) for dSS(I)/dt. SS(5) is the state variable used to represent surge tank pressure. Using the definitions provided by Table 7-1, the model's state equations describing the chemical reactor system are:

$$\begin{aligned}
PEFF &= \text{Minimum of } (PCRIT, SS(5)) \\
DD(I) &= \begin{cases} -RK(I) \star SS(I) \star PEFF & \text{if reactor I is on.} \\ 0 & \text{if reactor I is off.} \end{cases} \\
F(I) &= -DD(I) \star V(I) \\
SUMF &= F(1) + F(2) + F(3) + F(4) \\
DD(5) &= (RR \star TEMP/VS) \star ((FC \star SUMFO) - SUMF) \\
&= RTV \star (FCOMP - SUMF)
\end{aligned}$$

The events for the simulation are:

Event Code	Definition and Name
1	Starting of reaction process, START
2	Stopping of reaction process, STOPP
3	State-events that involve starting and stopping reaction process, SEVNT

The conditions for state-events and flags used in the simulation to indicate these conditions are:

Flag Indicator Used	Definition of Condition
LFLAG(I), I = 1,4	Concentration of batch has decreased below the level prescribed for batch completion
LFLAG(5)	Surge tank pressure has increased above nominal pressure and reactors waiting can be started or restarted
LFLAG(6)	Surge tank pressure has decreased below critical pressure and last reactor started must be stopped

Three files are used in this example. File 1 is the event file. An entry in file 2 consists of the attributes of the reactors waiting to be started. A reactor is put in file 2 if, after completing maintenance, the surge tank pressure is below the nominal value. Also, if a reactor is stopped because pressure has fallen below the critical value, it is filed in file 2. An entry in file 3 consists of the attributes of reactors that are processing a batch. The attribute definitions for entries in the files are:

Attribute Variable	Definition
ATRIB(1)	Event time
ATRIB(2)	Event code
ATRIB(3)	Reactor number
ATRIB(4)	Accumulated batch processing time
ATRIB(5)	Last time reactor was started or stopped

As always, file 1 is ranked on attribute 1 with LVF priority. Secondary ranking for file 1 is arbitrary. Entries in file 1 are the time-events of the model. Each time-event has the attributes of a reactor being maintained associated with it. For file 2, the reactors waiting to be started or restarted are ranked on the highest value of accumulated batch processing time (KKRNK(2) = 4, IINN(2) = 2). When the reactors are started, the first entry in file 2 is removed. Using this procedure, the last reactor started of a group of reactors is the one with the smallest accumulated processing time. File 3 is a LIFO file and contains reactors that are processing a batch. Thus removal of the last reactor started when pressure drops below the critical level amounts to removing the first entry in file 3.

The subprograms written for this example are: a main program, subroutine STATE; subroutine SCOND; subroutine EVNTS, two time-event subroutines (START and STOPP); one state-event subroutine, SEVNT; and subroutine SSAVE. Each of these is described below.

The main program performs the functions of dimensioning NSET, setting the card reader and printer values, initializing non-GASP variables, initializing state variables, and calling GASP. The FORTRAN listing is given in Fig. 7-20. Throughout all listings, comment cards have been used to describe the functions performed by sets of statements. Definitions of variables are the same as those given in Table 7-1. The variables SS(6) and SS(7) are used to plot the values of PCRIT and PNOM and are not used in any other way during the simulation. This illustrates a use of SS(I) for I > NNEQT.

Subroutine STATE is shown in Fig. 7-21. The definition of the deriva-

```
      PROGRAM MAIN(INPUT,OUTPUT,TAPE7,TAPE5=INPUT,TAPE6=OUTPUT)
      DIMENSION NSET(20000)                                             DIM     1
      COMMON QSET(20000)                                                COM     1
      COMMON /GCOM1/ ATRIB(25),JEVNT,MFA,MFE(100),MLE(100),MSTOP,NCRDR,N GCOM1   1
     1NAPO,NNAPT,NNATR,NNFIL,NNQ(100),NNTRY,NPRNT,PPARM(50,4),TNOW,TTBEG GCOM1   2
     2,TTCLR,TTFIN,TTRIB(25),TTSET                                      GCOM1   3
      COMMON /GCOM2/ DD(100),DDL(100),DTFUL,DTNOW,ISEES,LFLAG(50),NFLAG, GCOM2   1
     1NNEQD,NNEQS,NNEQT,SS(100),SSL(100),TTNEX                          GCOM2   2
      COMMON /UCOM1/ ATDIS,FCOMP,PCRIT,PNOM,RTV,F(4),RK(4),RON(4),SO(5), UCOM1   1
     1V(4),XRON(1)                                                      UCOM1   2
      EQUIVALENCE(NSET(1),QSET(1))                                      EQUIV   1
      NCRDR=5                                                           MX9     2
      NPRNT=6                                                           MX9     3
C                                                                       MX9     4
C*****READ INITIAL VALUES OF USER DEFINED VARIABLES AND PARAMETERS.     MX9     5
C                                                                       MX9     6
      READ (NCRDR,102) SO                                               MX9     7
      READ (NCRDR,102) RK                                               MX9     8
      READ (NCRDR,102) V,VS                                             MX9     9
      READ (NCRDR,102) RR,TEMP,ATDIS,FC,PNOM,PCRIT                      MX9    10
C                                                                       MX9    29
C*****CALL GASP EXECUTIVE.                                              MX9    30
C                                                                       MX9    31
      CALL GASP                                                         MX9    32
      CALL EXIT                                                         MX9    33
C                                                                       MX9    34
  102 FORMAT (6F10.4)                                                   MX9    35
C                                                                       MX9    36
      END                                                               MX9    37
```

```
      SUBROUTINE INTLC                                                  IC9     1
      COMMON /GCOM2/ DD(100),DDL(100),DTFUL,DTNOW,ISEES,LFLAG(50),NFLAG, GCOM2   1
     1NNEQD,NNEQS,NNEQT,SS(100),SSL(100),TTNEX                          GCOM2   2
      COMMON /UCOM1/ ATDIS,FCOMP,PCRIT,PNOM,RTV,F(4),RK(4),RON(4),SO(5), UCOM1   1
     1V(4),XRON(1)                                                      UCOM1   2
C                                                                       IC9     2
C*****SET INITIAL CONDITIONS FOR THIS RUN.                              IC9     3
C                                                                       IC9     4
      RTV=RR*TEMP/VS                                                    IC9     5
      XRON(1)=0.                                                        IC9     6
      SUMFO=0.                                                          IC9     7
      DO 101 I=1,4                                                      IC9     8
      RON(I)=0.                                                         IC9     9
      SS(I)=SO(I)                                                       IC9    10
  101 SUMFO=SUMFO+(RK(I)*SO(I)*V(I)*PCRIT)                              IC9    11
      FCOMP=FC*SUMFO                                                    IC9    12
      SS(5)=SO(5)                                                       IC9    13
C                                                                       IC9    14
C*****S(6) AND S(7) WILL BE USED FOR PLOTTING PURPOSES ONLY.  NO STATE  IC9    15
C*****EQUATIONS ARE INVOLVED.                                           IC9    16
C                                                                       IC9    17
      SS(6)=PNOM                                                        IC9    18
      SS(7)=PCRIT                                                       IC9    19
      RETURN                                                            IC9    20
C                                                                       IC9    21
      END                                                               IC9    22
```

Figure 7-20 FORTRAN listing of main program and subroutine INTLC (Example 9).

tive equations is taken directly from the equations given above. Specifying the equations in terms of the DD(·) variables indicates that the RKE integration package is to be used.

To use an Euler type of integration, an equation for the concentration level would be written directly. For this example, such an alternative is available. The GASP IV statement for concentration I would be

$$\text{SS(I)} = \text{SSL(I)} \star (1.0 - \text{DTNOW} \star \text{RK(I)} \star \text{PEFF} \star \text{RON(I)}).$$

As discussed in Chapter 3, DTNOW is automatically determined to allow for time-events and/or state-events to occur during the integration process, that is, when events intervene the fixed step size is reduced to

```
      SUBROUTINE STATE                                                  ST9     1
      COMMON /GCOM2/ DD(100),DDL(100),DTFUL,DTNOW,ISEES,LFLAG(50),NFLAG,GCOM2   1
     1NNEQD,NNEQS,NNEQT,SS(100),SSL(100),TTNEX                          GCOM2   2
      COMMON /UCOM1/ ATDIS,FCOMP,PCRIT,PNOM,RTV,F(4),RK(4),RON(4),SO(5),UCOM1   1
     1V(4),XRON(1)                                                      UCOM1   2
      SUMF=0.                                                           ST9     2
C                                                                       ST9     3
C*****DEFINE THE STATE EQUATIONS.                                       ST9     4
C                                                                       ST9     5
      PEFF=AMIN1(SS(5),PCRIT)                                           ST9     6
      DO 101 I=1,4                                                      ST9     7
      DD(I)=-RK(I)*SS(I)*RON(I)*PEFF                                    ST9     8
      F(I)=-DD(I)*V(I)                                                  ST9     9
  101 SUMF=SUMF+F(I)                                                    ST9    10
      DD(5)=RTV*(FCOMP-SUMF)                                            ST9    11
      RETURN                                                            ST9    12
C                                                                       ST9    13
      END                                                               ST9    14
```

Figure 7-21 FORTRAN listing of subroutine STATE (Example 9).

allow events to occur at the end of or within the prescribed step size. The above represents only two of the possible ways to code subroutine STATE for this example. Throughout the remainder of this example it is assumed that the equations for DD(·) are provided in subroutine STATE.

The FORTRAN listing for subroutine SCOND is given in Fig. 7-22. SCOND locates specified state conditions and flags the occurrence of those conditions. In this example, the program tests for six state conditions. These are the conditions in which the concentration of reactant in any of the four reactors crosses its batch-completion concentration in the negative direction (LFLAG(I), I = 1,4)), surge tank pressure crosses the critical pressure in the negative direction (LFLAG(5)), and surge tank pressure crosses the nominal pressure in the positive direction

```
      SUBROUTINE SCOND                                                  SC9     1
      COMMON /GCOM2/ DD(100),DDL(100),DTFUL,DTNOW,ISEES,LFLAG(50),NFLAG,GCOM2   1
     1NNEQD,NNEQS,NNEQT,SS(100),SSL(100),TTNEX                          GCOM2   2
      COMMON /UCOM1/ ATDIS,FCOMP,PCRIT,PNOM,RTV,F(4),RK(4),RON(4),SO(5),UCOM1   1
     1V(4),XRON(1)                                                      UCOM1   2
C                                                                       SC9     2
C*****DEFINE A STATE-EVENT WHENEVER A REACTOR CONCENTRATION FALLS       SC9     3
C*****BELOW A SPECIFIED COMPLETION CONCENTRATION.                       SC9     4
C                                                                       SC9     5
      DO 101 I=1,4                                                      SC9     6
      SOIC=.1*SO(I)                                                     SC9     7
      LFLAG(I)=KROSS(I,0,0.,SOIC,-1,.001)                               SC9     8
  101 CONTINUE                                                          SC9     9
C                                                                       SC9    10
C*****DEFINE A STATE-EVENT WHENEVER PRESSURE CROSSES NOMINAL IN THE     SC9    11
C*****POSITIVE DIRECTION OR CRITICAL IN THE NEGATIVE DIRECTION.         SC9    12
C                                                                       SC9    13
      LFLAG(5)=KROSS(5,0,0.,PNOM,1,1.)                                  SC9    14
      LFLAG(6)=KROSS(5,0,0.,PCRIT,-1,1.)                                SC9    15
      RETURN                                                            SC9    16
C                                                                       SC9    17
      END                                                               SC9    18
```

Figure 7-22 FORTRAN listing of subroutine SCOND (Example 9).

(LFLAG(6)). The values of the LFLAG vector resulting from the prescribed conditions are shown below:

State Variable	Flag Value	Crossing Condition	Tolerance Interval
SS(I), I=1,4	LFLAG(I)=−1	↓ SOIC = 0.1 ★ SO(I)	SOIC − 0.001 ≤ SS(I) ≤ SOIC
SS(5)	LFLAG(5)=+1	↑ PNOM	PNOM ≤ SS(5) ≤ PNOM + 1.
SS(6)	LFLAG(6)=−1	↓ PCRIT	PCRIT − 1. ≤ SS(6) ≤ PCRIT

The FORTRAN listing of subroutine EVNTS is given in Fig. 7-23. EVNTS calls one of the three events associated with the reactor process. For this example a separate state-event subroutine is used. The option is always available to code the processing of any or all events in subroutine EVNTS. The trade-off is between computational efficiency and documentation and debugging ease.

A flow chart for subroutine START is presented in Fig. 7-24. START is called at the point in time at which it is desired to start a reaction process. If surge tank pressure is below nominal, it causes the entity representing the associated reactor to be put in file 2, awaiting conditions enabling the reactor to be started. If surge tank pressure is above nominal, the appropriate counters, flags, and attributes are set and the entry is put in file 3 awaiting conditions causing it to be stopped. The FORTRAN listing for subroutine START is given in Fig. 7-25.

The flow chart for subroutine STOPP is presented in Fig. 7-26. STOPP is called at the point in time at which a reaction process is either completed or must be stopped because of low pressure. First, the reactor is set to off status by the statement RON(NR) = 0. Next, the number of

```
      SUBROUTINE EVNTS (IX)
C
C*****CALL THE EVENT SUBROUTINE WHICH DEFINES THE EVENT CURRENTLY
C*****BEING PROCESSED.
C
      GO TO (101,102,103), IX
  101 CALL START
      RETURN
  102 CALL STOPP
      RETURN
  103 CALL SEVNT
      RETURN
C
      END
```

Figure 7-23 FORTRAN listing of subroutine EVNTS (Example 9).

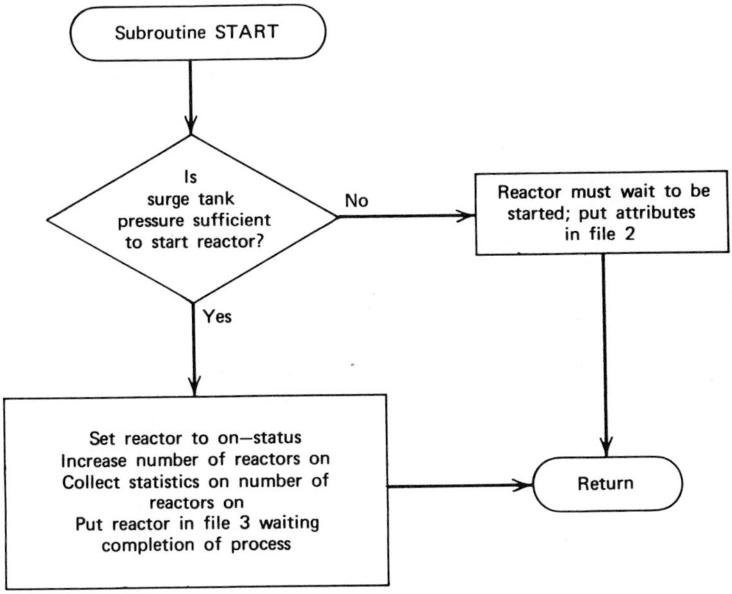

Figure 7-24 Flow chart of subroutine START (Example 9).

```
      SUBROUTINE START
      COMMON /GCOM1/ ATRIB(25),JEVNT,MFA,MFE(100),MLE(100),MSTOP,NCRDR,N
     1NAPO,NNAPT,NNATR,NNFIL,NNQ(100),NNTRY,NPRNT,PPARM(50,4),TNOW,TTBEG
     2,TTCLR,TTFIN,TTRIB(25),TTSET
      COMMON /GCOM2/ DD(100),DDL(100),DTFUL,DTNOW,ISEES,LFLAG(50),NFLAG,
     1NNEQD,NNEQS,NNEQT,SS(100),SSL(100),TTNEX
      COMMON /UCOM1/ ATDIS,FCOMP,PCRIT,PNOM,RTV,F(4),RK(4),RON(4),SO(5),
     1V(4),XRON(1)
C
C*****CHECK TO SEE IF THE SYSTEM PRESSURE IS GREATER THAN NOMINAL.
C
      IF (SS(5).GE.PNOM) GO TO 101
C
C*****PRESSURE IS BELOW NOMINAL. SINCE NO REACTORS CAN BE STARTED AT
C*****THIS TIME, FILE ENTITY IN FILE AWAITING SUFFICIENT PRESSURE.
C
      CALL FILEM (2)
      GO TO 102
C
C*****PRESSURE IS ABOVE NOMINAL. DETERMINE REACTOR NUMBER. SET FLAG
C*****INDICATING REACTOR IS ON. COLLECT STATISTICS ON THE NUMBER OF
C*****REACTORS ON. INCREMENT THE NUMBER OF REACTORS ON. SET ATTRIBUTES
C*****AND FILE AWAITING CONDITIONS FOR A STOPP EVENT.
C
  101 NR=ATRIB(3)
      RON(NR)=1.
      XRON(1)=XRON(1)+1.
      CALL TIMST (XRON(1),TNOW,1)
      ATRIB(2)=2.
      ATRIB(5)=TNOW
      CALL FILEM (3)
  102 RETURN
C
      END
```

Figure 7-25 FORTRAN listing of subroutine START (Example 9).

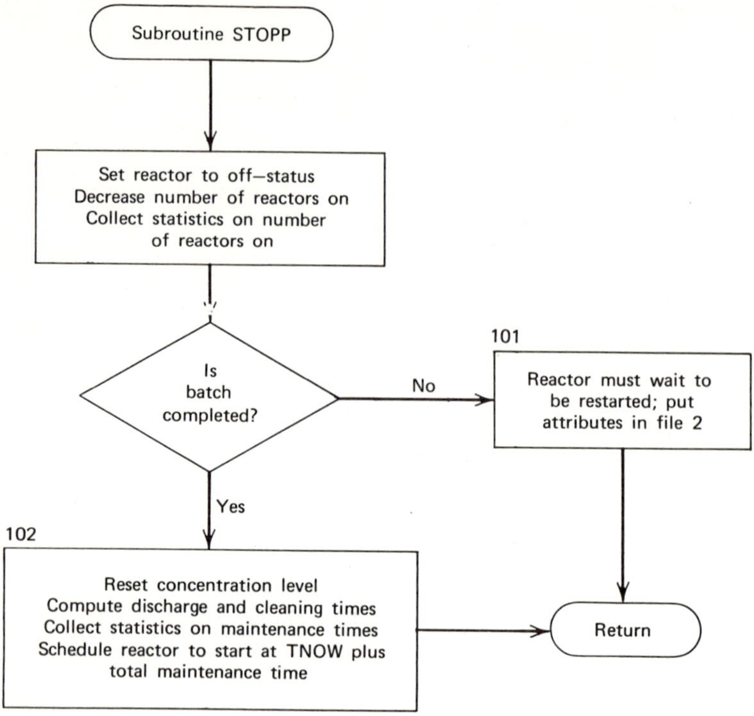

Figure 7-26 Flow chart of subroutine STOPP (Example 9).

reactors on is reduced by one and statistics are collected on the number of reactors on. A check is then made to determine if the STOPP event is caused by batch completion or low pressure. If it is caused by low pressure, attributes are set and the entity is filed awaiting sufficient pressure to start. If it is caused by batch completion, concentration is initialized for the next batch. The total maintenance time, which involves a discharge, clean, and recharge time, is determined. Statistics are collected on these times using the GASP IV subroutines COLCT and HISTO. The desired start of the next batch for this reactor is scheduled to occur at the current time plus the maintenance time. The FORTRAN listing for subroutine STOPP is given in Fig. 7-27.

The flow chart for subroutine SEVNT is presented in Fig. 7-28. SEVNT tests for all state-events by checking the LFLAG values set in subroutine SCOND. For I = 1,4 a negative LFLAG(I) value indicates that reactor I has completed its processing and needs to be stopped. The reactor is removed from file 3 to obtain its attributes. Subroutine STOPP is then called to stop the process. If LFLAG(5) is positive, pressure has increased

```
      SUBROUTINE STOPP
      DIMENSION TDIS(1), TTCL(1), TTDN(1)
      COMMON /GCOM1/ ATRIB(25),JEVNT,MFA,MFE(100),MLE(100),MSTOP,NCRDR,N
     1NAPO,NNAPT,NNATR,NNFIL,NNQ(100),NNTRY,NPRNT,PPARM(50,4),TNOW,TTBEG
     2,TTCLR,TTFIN,TTRIB(25),TTSET
      COMMON /GCOM2/ DD(100),DDL(100),DTFUL,DTNOW,ISEES,LFLAG(50),NFLAG,
     1NNEQD,NNEQS,NNEQT,SS(100),SSL(100),TTNEX
      COMMON /UCOM1/ ATDIS,FCOMP,PCRIT,PNOM,RTV,F(4),RK(4),RON(4),SO(5),
     1V(4),XRON(1)
C
C*****DETERMINE REACTOR NUMBER. SET FLAG TO OFF. COLLECT STATISTICS ON
C*****NUMBER OF REACTORS ON. DECREMENT NUMBER OF REACTORS ON.
C
      NR=ATRIB(3)
      RON(NR)=0.
      XRON(1)=XRON(1)-1.
      CALL TIMST (XRON(1),TNOW,1)
C
C*****DETERMINE IF STOPP EVENT IS DUE TO BATCH COMPLETION OR LOW
C*****PRESSURE.
C
      IF (LFLAG(NR)) 102,101,101
C
C*****STOPP IS DUE TO LOW PRESSURE. SET ATTRIBUTES AND FILE AWAITING
C*****CONDITIONS FOR START EVENT.
C
  101 ATRIB(2)=1.
      ATRIB(4)=ATRIB(4)+TNOW-ATRIB(5)
      ATRIB(5)=TNOW
      CALL FILEM (2)
      GO TO 103
C
C*****STOPP IS DUE TO COMPLETION OF A BATCH. SET CONCENTRATION FOR
C*****START OF NEW BATCH. GENERATE RANDOM DEVIATES DESCRIBING TIME TO
C*****DISCHARGE AND TIME TO CLEAN.  COLLECT STATISTICS AND HISTOGRAMS
C*****ON TOTAL DOWN TIME, TIME TO DISCHARGE, AND TIME TO CLEAN.
C*****SET ATTRIBUTES AND FILE IN EVENT FILE AWAITING TIME FOR START
C*****EVENT.
C
  102 SS(NR)=SO(NR)
      TDIS(1)=-ATDIS*ALOG(DRAND(NR))
      TTCL(1)=RNORM(1,NR)
      TTDN(1)=TDIS(1)+TTCL(1)
      CALL COLCT (TTDN(1),1)
      CALL COLCT (TDIS(1),2)
      CALL COLCT (TTCL(1),3)
      CALL HISTO (TTDN(1),1)
      CALL HISTO (TDIS(1),2)
      CALL HISTO (TTCL(1),3)
      ATRIB(1)=TNOW+TTDN(1)
      ATRIB(2)=1.
      ATRIB(4)=0.
      ATRIB(5)=0.
      CALL FILEM (1)
  103 RETURN
C
      END
```

Figure 7-27 FORTRAN listing of subroutine STOPP (Example 9).

above the nominal value and all waiting reactors may be started. The attributes associated with these reactors, if any, are obtained by removing them from file 2. If there are any, the reaction process is started by calling subroutine START. If LFLAG(6) is negative, pressure has decreased below the critical value and the last reactor started is stopped. This involves removing the last entry inserted into file 3. The FORTRAN listing for subroutine SEVNT is given in Fig. 7-29.

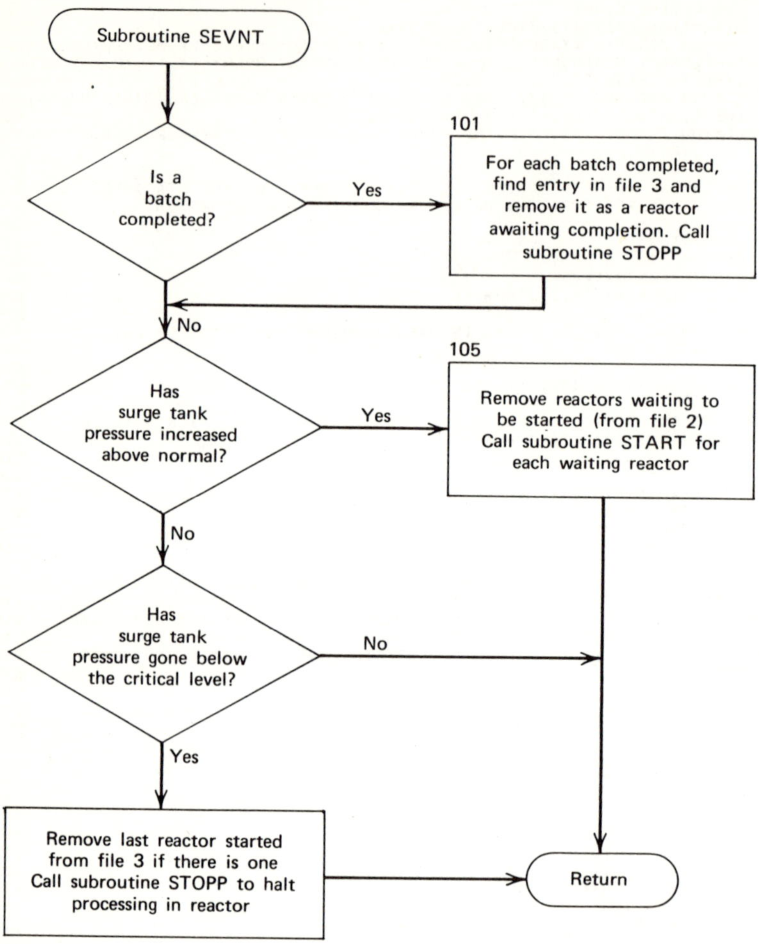

Figure 7-28 Flow chart of subroutine SEVNT (Example 9).

In subroutine SSAVE, subroutines GPLOT and TIMSA are called to collect data. The FORTRAN listing of SSAVE is given in Fig. 7-30. GPLOT is used to store the state variable values for future printing and plotting. On input, seven variables are specified for the plot. By passing the vector SS(·), SS(1) through SS(7) are passed to GPLOT even though NNEQT specifies there are only five state variables. In the main program, SS(6) and SS(7) were set as PNOM and PCRIT. By this procedure, cursors at these values are plotted by GPLOT. Subroutine TIMSA collects statistics on the surge tank pressure SS(5) over time.

```
      SUBROUTINE SEVNT                                                  SVT    1
      COMMON /GCOM1/ ATRIB(25),JEVNT,MFA,MFE(100),MLE(100),MSTOP,NCRDR,NGCOM1  1
     1NAPO,NNAPT,NNATR,NNFIL,NNQ(100),NNTRY,NPRNT,PPARM(50,4),TNOW,TTBEGGCOM1  2
     2,TTCLR,TTFIN,TTRIB(25),TTSET                                      GCOM1  3
      COMMON /GCOM2/ DD(100),DDL(100),DTFUL,DTNOW,ISEES,LFLAG(50),NFLAG,GCOM2  1
     1NNEQD,NNEQS,NNEQT,SS(100),SSL(100),TTNEX                          GCOM2  2
      COMMON /UCOM1/ ATDIS,FCOMP,PCRIT,PNOM,RTV,F(4),RK(4),RON(4),SO(5),UCOM1  1
     1V(4),XRON(1)                                                      UCOM1  2
C                                                                       SVT    2
C*****CHECK TO SEE IF ANY REACTOR COMPLETED PROCESSING A BATCH AT THE   SVT    3
C*****PRESENT TIME.                                                     SVT    4
C                                                                       SVT    5
      DO 102 I=1,4                                                      SVT    6
      IF (LFLAG(I)) 101,102,102                                         SVT    7
C                                                                       SVT    8
C*****A REACTOR DID COMPLETE A BATCH AT THE PRESENT TIME. FIND THE      SVT    9
C*****ENTRY DESCRIBING THAT ENTITY. REMOVE IT FROM THE FILE AWAITING    SVT   10
C*****STOPP. SET ATTRIBUTES AND CALL STOPP TO PROCESS EVENT.            SVT   11
C                                                                       SVT   12
  101 X=I                                                               SVT   13
      NTRY=NFIND(X,5,3,3,.00001)                                        SVT   14
      CALL RMOVE (NTRY,3)                                               SVT   15
      ATRIB(1)=TNOW                                                     SVT   16
      ATRIB(4)=ATRIB(4)+TNOW-ATRIB(5)                                   SVT   17
      CALL STOPP                                                        SVT   18
  102 CONTINUE                                                          SVT   19
C                                                                       SVT   20
C*****CHECK TO SEE IF PRESSURE WENT FROM LESS THAN TO GREATER THAN      SVT   21
C*****NOMINAL AT THE PRESENT TIME.                                      SVT   22
C                                                                       SVT   23
      IF (LFLAG(5)) 103,103,105                                         SVT   24
C                                                                       SVT   25
C*****CHECK TO SEE IF PRESSURE WENT FROM GREATER THAN TO LESS THAN      SVT   26
C*****CRITICAL AT THE PRESENT TIME.                                     SVT   27
C                                                                       SVT   28
  103 IF (LFLAG(6)) 104,108,108                                         SVT   29
C                                                                       SVT   30
C*****CHECK TO SEE IF THERE ARE ANY REACTORS CURRENTLY AWAITING STOPP.  SVT   31
C                                                                       SVT   32
  104 IF (NNQ(3)) 108,108,107                                           SVT   33
C                                                                       SVT   34
C*****CHECK TO SEE IF THERE ARE ANY REACTORS CURRENTLY AWAITING START.  SVT   35
C                                                                       SVT   36
  105 IF (NNQ(2)) 108,108,106                                           SVT   37
C                                                                       SVT   38
C*****PRESSURE HAS JUST CROSSED NOMINAL IN THE POSITIVE DIRECTION.      SVT   39
C*****REMOVE ALL ENTRIES AWAITING START. SET ATTRIBUTES AND CALL START  SVT   40
C*****TO PROCESS EVENT(S).                                              SVT   41
C                                                                       SVT   42
  106 CALL RMOVE (MFE(2),2)                                             SVT   43
      ATRIB(1)=TNOW                                                     SVT   44
      CALL START                                                        SVT   45
      GO TO 105                                                         SVT   46
C                                                                       SVT   47
C*****PRESSURE HAS JUST CROSSED CRITICAL IN THE NEGATIVE DIRECTION.     SVT   48
C*****REMOVE LAST ENTRY STARTED. CALL STOPP TO PROCESS EVENT.           SVT   49
C                                                                       SVT   50
  107 CALL RMOVE (MFE(3),3)                                             SVT   51
      ATRIB(1)=TNOW                                                     SVT   52
      CALL STOPP                                                        SVT   53
  108 RETURN                                                            SVT   54
C                                                                       SVT   55
      END                                                               SVT   56
```

Figure 7-29 FORTRAN listing of subroutine SEVNT (Example 9).

```
      SUBROUTINE SSAVE                                                  SV9     1
      COMMON /GCOM1/ ATRIB(25),JEVNT,MFA,MFE(100),MLE(100),MSTOP,NCRDR,NGCOM1   1
     1NAPO,NNAPT,NNATR,NNFIL,NNQ(100),NNTRY,NPPNT,PPARM(50,4),TNOW,TTBEGGCOM1   2
     2,TTCLR,TTFIN,TTRIB(25),TTSET                                      GCOM1   3
      COMMON /GCOM2/ DD(100),DDL(100),DTFUL,DTNOW,ISEES,LFLAG(50),NFLAG,GCOM2   1
     1NNEQD,NNEQS,NNEQT,SS(100),SSL(100),TTNEX                          GCOM2   2
C                                                                       SV9     2
C*****SAVE VALUES OF STATE VARIABLES FOR PLOT.                          SV9     3
C                                                                       SV9     4
      CALL GPLOT (SS,TNOW,1)                                            SV9     5
      CALL TIMSA (SS(5),TNOW,2)                                         SV9     6
      RETURN                                                            SV9     7
C                                                                       SV9     8
      END                                                               SV9     9
```

Figure 7-30 FORTRAN listing of subroutine SSAVE (Example 9).

Simulation Reports

A listing of the input data cards and the GASP IV echo check for Example 9 is given in Fig. 7-31. Only selected output reports are presented for this example. In Fig. 7-32 a statistical summary of those variables for which calls were made to subroutines COLCT, TIMST, and TIMSA is presented. The output shows that the time to maintain a reactor (DOWN TIM) is on the average 1.85 hours, based on 136 observations. The statistics on time persistent variables show that on the average only 1.86

```
0.1       0.4       0.2       0.5       500.                                |
0.03466   0.00866   0.01155   0.00770                                       | USER
10.       15.       20.       25.       50.                                 |
10.73     550.      1.        .19       150.      100.                      |
PRITSKER            9     6   30 1973   1                                   | 1
    3     2     3   1     1     5     5     5   320000    5     0     6     | 2
3         1DOWN TIM                                                         |
3         2DISCH T                                                          | 3
3         3CLEAN T                                                          |
4         1REACT ON     0.0                                                 | 4
4         2PRESSURE  1000.0                                                 |
5         1DOWN TIM           10        0.00       0.50                     |
5         2DISCH T            10        0.00       0.25                     | 5
5         3CLEAN T            10        0.00       0.25                     |
6A        1TIME                0     7    -1         .1                     |
6B        11CONC 1       1     1          0.         .5                     |
6B        22CONC 2       1     1          0.         .5                     |
6B        33CONC 3       1     1          0.         .5                     | 6
6B        44CONC 4       1     1          0.         .5                     |
6B        5PPRESSURE     1     1          0.       1000.                    |
6B        6.PNOM         1     1          0.       1000.                    |
6B        7.PCRIT        1     1          0.       1000.                    |
    1     4     5                                                           | 7
    1     2     4                                                           | 8
    3     0         0.        0.        .001        .1        .1            | 9
10        1         1.        0.        2.          .5                      | 10
    1     1     1    0        0.        150.      171717727277373774747757 57 | 11
12        1         0.        1.        1.         0.                       |
12        1         .5        1.        2.         0.                       |
12        1         1.        1.        3.         0.                       | 12
12        1        1.5        1.        4.         0.                       |
12        0                                                                 |
```

Figure 7-31 Listing of input data cards and GASP IV echo check of input data cards (Example 9).

```
                          SIMULATION PROJECT NUMBER   9  BY  PRITSKER

                          DATE  6/ 30/ 1973        RUN NUMBER    1 OF    1
                          LLSUP=0000000000000000   GASP IV VERSION 23JUN73

NNCLT=     3   NNSTA=     2   NNHIS=     3   NNPRM=     1   NNPLT=     1   NNSTR=     5   NNTRY=     5
NNATR=     5   NNFIL=     3   NNSET= 20000   NNEQD=     5   NNEQS=     0   NFLAG=     6

COLCT NO.  1   LLABC=DOWN TIM
COLCT NO.  2   LLABC=DISCH T
COLCT NO.  3   LLABC=CLEAN T

TIMST NO.  1   LLABT=REACT ON  I.C. =     0.
TIMST NO.  2   LLABT=PRESSURE  I.C. =     1.0000E+03

HISTO NO.  1   LLABH=DOWN TIM                NNCEL=    10   HHLOW=     0.            HHWID=     5.0000E-01
HISTO NO.  2   LLABH=DISCH T                 NNCEL=    10   HHLOW=     0.            HHWID=     2.5000E-01
HISTO NO.  3   LLABH=CLEAN T                 NNCEL=    10   HHLOW=     0.            HHWID=     2.5000E-01

GPLOT NO.  1   LLABP=TIME      IITAP=     0  NNVAR=     7   LLPLT=    -1             DTPLT=     1.0000E-01
  VAR NO.  1        1=CONC 1   LLPLO=     1  LLPHI=     1   PPLO =     0.            PPHI =     5.0000E-01
  VAR NO.  2        2=CONC 2   LLPLO=     1  LLPHI=     1   PPLO =     0.            PPHI =     5.0000E-01
  VAR NO.  3        3=CONC 3   LLPLO=     1  LLPHI=     1   PPLO =     0.            PPHI =     5.0000E-01
  VAR NO.  4        4=CONC 4   LLPLO=     1  LLPHI=     1   PPLO =     0.            PPHI =     5.0000E-01
  VAR NO.  5        P=PRESSURE LLPLO=     1  LLPHI=     1   PPLO =     0.            PPHI =     1.0000E+03
  VAR NO.  6        .=PNOM     LLPLO=     1  LLPHI=     1   PPLO =     0.            PPHI =     1.0000E+03
  VAR NO.  7        .=PCRIT    LLPLO=     1  LLPHI=     1   PPLO =     0.            PPHI =     1.0000E+03

KKRNK= (    1)      4      5

IINN = (    1)      2      4

IIEVT=     3   LLERR=     0   AAERR=     1.0000E-05          RRERR=     1.0000E-05
DTMIN=     1.0000E-03         DTMAX=     1.0000E-01          DTSAV=     1.0000E-01

PARAMETER SET     1 =     1.0000E+00     0.            2.0000E+00     5.0000E-01

MSTOP=     1   JJCLR=     1   JJBEG=     1   IICRD=     0   TTBEG=     0.            TTFIN=     1.5000E+02
JJFIL=     1
IISED= 71717          72727          73737          74747          75757
```

Figure 7-31 *(continued)*

```
                               **GASP SUMMARY REPORT**

                        SIMULATION PROJECT NUMBER   9  BY  PRITSKER

                        DATE  6/ 30/ 1973        RUN NUMBER    1 OF    1

                        CURRENT TIME  =  1.5000E+02


PARAMETER SET      1 =     1.0000E+00     0.              2.0000E+00     5.0000E-01


                        **STATISTICS FOR VARIABLES BASED ON OBSERVATION**
             MEAN          STD DEV        SD OF MEAN         CV           MINIMUM          MAXIMUM       OBS

DOWN TIM   1.8503E+00     1.0438E+00     8.9506E-02     5.6399E-01     7.6947E-02     6.0620E+00    136
DISCH T    8.7102E-01     3.0762E-01     7.7828E-02     1.0420E+00     2.6797E-04     4.6214E+00    136
CLEAN T    9.7975E-01     4.6829E-01     4.0155E-02     4.7796E-01     0.             2.0000E+00    136

                          **STATISTICS FOR TIME-PERSISTENT VARIABLES**
             MEAN          STD DEV        MINIMUM         MAXIMUM      TIME INTERVAL    CUR. VALUE

REACT ON   1.8592E+00     8.3323E-01     0.             4.0000E+00     1.5000E+02     2.0000E+00
PRESSURE   2.7719E+02     2.3708E+02     4.7624E+01     1.2832E+03     1.5000E+02     3.1496E+02


                       **GASP FILE STORAGE AREA DUMP AT TIME  1.5000E+02**


                       MAXIMUM NUMBER OF ENTRIES IN FILE STORAGE AREA =  4


                               PRINTOUT OF FILE NUMBER   1
                                   TNOW =  1.5000E+02
                                   QQTIM=  1.4973E+02
```

```
                    TIME PERIOD FOR STATISTICS 1.5000E+02
                    AVERAGE NUMBER IN FILE          1.6809
                    STANDARD DEVIATION              1.0488
                    MAXIMUM NUMBER IN FILE          4

                              FILE CONTENTS
ENTRY  1  =  1.5110E+02   1.0000E+00   4.0000E+00   0.          0.
ENTRY  2  =  1.5146E+02   1.0000E+00   1.0000E+00   0.          0.

                      PRINTOUT OF FILE NUMBER   2
                           TNOW =  1.5000E+02
                           QQTIM=  1.4848E+02

                    TIME PERIOD FOR STATISTICS 1.5000E+02
                    AVERAGE NUMBER IN FILE           .4599
                    STANDARD DEVIATION               .6688
                    MAXIMUM NUMBER IN FILE          3

                           THE FILE IS EMPTY


                      PRINTOUT OF FILE NUMBER   3
                           TNOW =  1.5000E+02
                           QQTIM=  1.4973E+02

                    TIME PERIOD FOR STATISTICS 1.5000E+02
                    AVERAGE NUMBER IN FILE          1.8592
                    STANDARD DEVIATION               .8332
                    MAXIMUM NUMBER IN FILE          4

                              FILE CONTENTS
ENTRY  1  =  1.4973E+02   2.0000E+00   3.0000E+00   0.          1.4973E+02
ENTRY  2  =  1.4848E+02   2.0000E+00   2.0000E+00   3.3723E-01  1.4848E+02
```

Figure 7-32 GASP IV summary report (Example 9).

```
**GASP STATE STORAGE AREA DUMP AT TIME  1.5000E+02**

        (I)          SS(I)             DD(I)
         1         1.0000E-01        -0.
         2         8.0173E-02        -6.9429E-02
         3         1.4622E-01        -1.6888E-01
         4         5.0000E-01        -0.
         5         3.1496E+02        -7.8686E+00
```

Figure 7-32 *(continued)*

reactors are on simultaneously, and the average surge tank pressure is 277 psia. The former value is also obtained from file 3 statistics since it contains the reactors while they are processing a batch. The standard GASP IV histogram for the DOWN TIM variable is shown in Fig. 7-33.

Figure 7-34 is a plot of the concentration levels for each reactor and the surge tank. The heading lists the user specified plot symbol and associated identifier as well as the scale for each variable to be plotted. Thus the plot symbol "P" represents the system pressure on a scale ranging from 0 to 1000 psia. The symbol "·" is used, in this case, to represent critical pressure (100 psia) and nominal pressure (150 psia). The dynamic behavior of the system can be seen in Fig. 7-34. Initially, only reactor 1 was on, and pressure rose rapidly until reactor 2 was turned on at time 0.5. Reactor 1 was turned off because of batch completion (a state-event) at about 0.7 hours. For display purposes, the concentration levels are plotted at their initial values while the reactors are off. Beginning with the start of reactor 3 at time 1.0, pressure fell rapidly. There is an obvious discontinuity in the pressure curve at time 1.5 when reactor 4 was started. Pressure first went critical at about 1.9 hours, causing reactor 1 to be stopped since it was the last one started. From 1.9 until 3.9 hours pressure slowly increased from the critical to the nominal value.

This simulation further illustrates the concepts involved in a combined discrete-continuous simulation. The summary reports and plots demonstrate the different types of information that can be obtained from a simulation of combined systems.

EXERCISES

7-1. For the tanker refinery presented in Example 8, rewrite subroutine STATE so that the state variables are defined in terms of DD(·) equations. Write an equation to determine the total amount of crude passing through the storage tank.

HISTOGRAM NUMBER 1

DOWN TIM

OBSV FREQ	RELA FREQ	CUML FREQ	UPPER CELL LIMIT
0	0.000	0.000	0.
3	.022	.022	5.0000E-01
27	.197	.219	1.0000E+00
29	.212	.431	1.5000E+00
27	.197	.628	2.0000E+00
18	.131	.759	2.5000E+00
15	.109	.869	3.0000E+00
8	.058	.927	3.5000E+00
5	.036	.964	4.0000E+00
1	.007	.971	4.5000E+00
1	.007	.978	5.0000E+00
3	.022	1.000	INF

137			

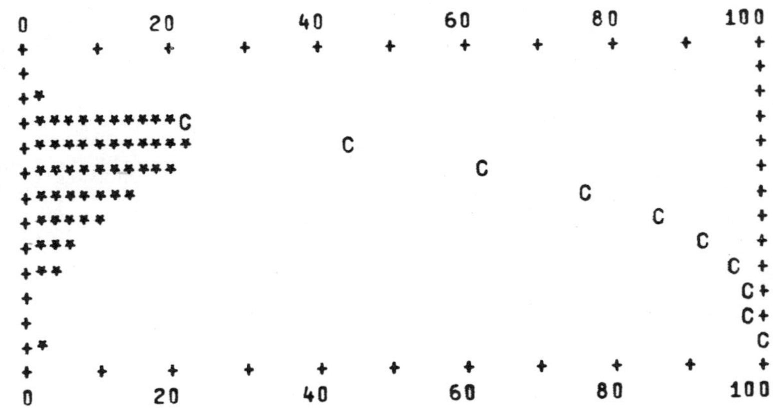

Figure 7-33 Histogram of down time (Example 9).

PLOT NUMBER 1
RUN NUMBER 1

SCALES OF PLOT

1=CONC 1	0.	1.2500E-01	2.5000E-01	3.7500E-01	5.0000E-01
2=CONC 2	0.	1.2500E-01	2.5000E-01	3.7500E-01	5.0000E-01
3=CONC 3	0.	1.2500E-01	2.5000E-01	3.7500E-01	5.0000E-01
4=CONC 4	0.	1.2500E-01	2.5000E-01	3.7500E-01	5.0000E-01
P=PRESSURE	0.	2.5000E+02	5.0000E+02	7.5000E+02	1.0000E+03
.=PNOM	0.	2.5000E+02	5.0000E+02	7.5000E+02	1.0000E+03
.=PCRIT	0.	2.5000E+02	5.0000E+02	7.5000E+02	1.0000E+03

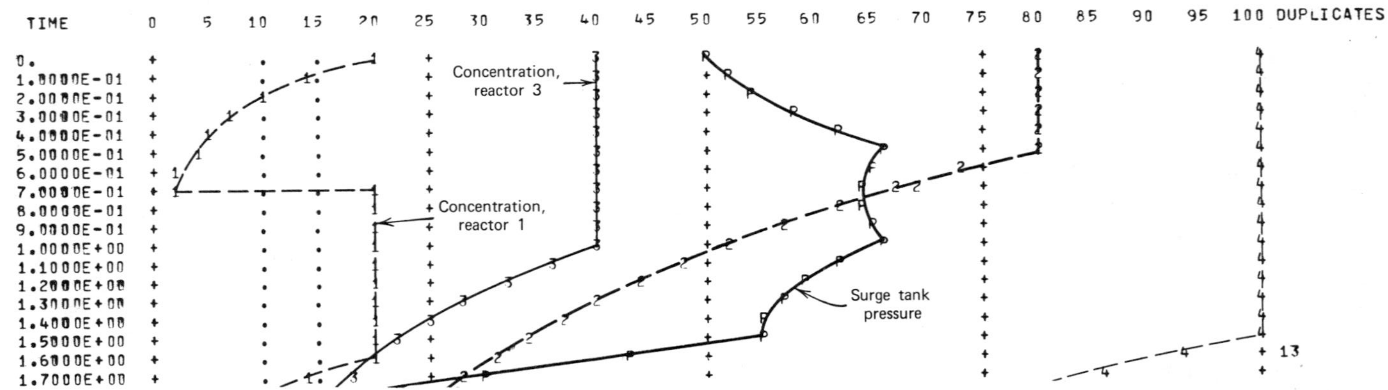

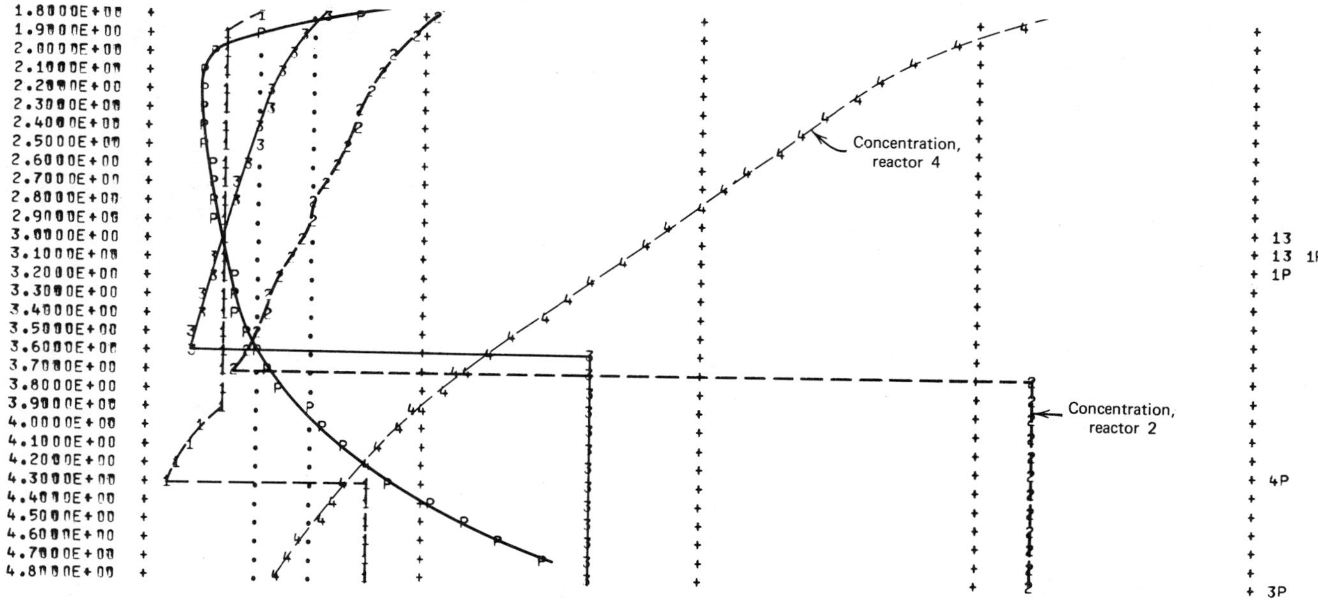

Figure 7-34 Plot of state variables (Example 9)

7-2. For the tanker refinery problem, assume that the rate of input to the storage tank decreases exponentially from the nominal value by the factor $1 - e^{-x/5}$ where x = SS(1)/TCAP. Determine the effects on the system due to this change in flow rate.

7-3. Develop equations that make the flow rate from tanker to storage tank a function of the level of crude in the tanker, storage tank, and the viscosity of the crude in the tanker. Develop the code for subroutine STATE to simulate the developed flow equations.

7-4. It has been proposed that offshore unloading docks be built for unloading tankers at Seattle. Three such docks have been proposed, each of which can process at a rate two-thirds that of the current dock. Compare system operation between the three offshore unloading docks versus the current unloading dock operated on a three shift basis.

7-5. For the problem stated in Example 8, an elaboration of the refinery is to be made. Consider that the refinery consists of four phases, the first of which is processing. Crude is taken from the initial storage tank and processed in a processing unit at a rate of 150 tb/day. After processing, the material is stored in an intermediate storage tank (phase 2), after which it goes through a filtering unit (phase 3). The rate of filtering is dependent on the condition of the filter. A filter has an expected life of 30 days. Initially, when the filter is new, the filter rate is 200 tb/day. The rate of flow through the filter decreases linearly until it is 100 tb/day after 30 days. The time to replace a filter is exponentially distributed with a mean of 0.5 days. The fourth phase of the refinery is a finished product storage tank. The finished product is removed from the tank according to the demand for the product, which is cyclic over an approximately 90 day period with a mean of 150 tb/day. All other characteristics of the system are identical to those presented in Example 8, except that the unloading dock works on a 24 hour schedule. Simulate the above system for 200 days, using different filter replacement policies to obtain the output requested in Example 8 and the following quantities: processor utilization, filter utilization, amount in intermediate storage tank, amount in final storage tank, and percentage of time demand is lost. Initial conditions for the simulation are that the raw material storage tank is 50% full, the intermediate tank is 60% full, and the final storage tank is 40% full. The capacity of each storage tank is 2000 lb.

7-6. For the chemical reaction process of Example 9, show the programming changes required if the conditions under which reactors may be started when the surge tank pressure exceeds 150 psia are changed to allow only one reactor to start for each increase of 50 psia above the critical pressure.

7-7. In Example 9, suppose that it is required to have a maintenance man available to clean the reactor. Rewrite the program under the condition that only one maintenance man is available and reactors requiring cleaning and recharging must wait if the maintenance man is busy. Determine the effect on throughput of the requirements to have a maintenance man to perform the cleaning and recharging.

7-8. For Example 9, solve the differential equations in terms of the initial conditions and rewrite the simulation program to use the derived solution.

7-9. Steel ingots arrive at a soaking pit furnace in a steel plant (4,43) with an interarrival time that is exponentially distributed with a mean of 1.25 hours. The soaking pit furnace heats an ingot so that it may be economically rolled in the next stage of the process. The temperature change of an ingot in the soaking pit furnace is described by the following differential equation:

$$\frac{dh_i}{dt} = (H - h_i) \star c$$

where h_i is the temperature of the ith ingot in the soaking pit; c is the heating time coefficient of an ingot and is equal to $0.10 + X$, where X is normally distributed with a mean of 0.05 and a standard deviation of 0.01 (a minimum of 0.0 and maximum of 0.10 is assumed); and H is the furnace temperature which is heated towards 2000°F with a heating rate constant of 0.2, that is,

$$\frac{dH}{dt} = (2000 - H) \star 0.2.$$

The ingots interact with one another in that adding a "cold" ingot to the furnace reduces the temperature of the furnace and thus changes the heating time for all ingots in the furnace. The temperature reduction is equal to the differences in furnace and ingot temperature, divided by the number of ingots in the furnace. There are 10 soaking pits in the furnace. When a cold ingot arrives and the furnace is full, it is stored in a cold ingot bank. It is assumed that the initial temperature of an arriving ingot is uniformly distributed in the interval from 100 to 200°F. All ingots put in the cold ingot bank are assumed to have a temperature of 100°F upon insertion into the soaking pit. The desired temperature of an ingot coming out of the soaking pit is specified for a set of ingots. The specification is that ingots are to be uniformly distributed in the interval from 800 to 1000°F. It is desired to simulate the above system for 1000 hours to obtain estimates of the following quantities:

(*a*) Heating time of the ingots.
(*b*) Final temperature distribution of the ingots.
(*c*) Waiting time of the ingots in the cold storage bank.
(*d*) Utilization of the soaking pit furnace.

The initial conditions are that there are six ingots in the furnace which have initial temperatures of 550, 600, . . . , 800°F respectively. Temperature of the furnace is 650°F and an ingot is due to arrive at time 0.

7-10. Suppose that in Exercise 7-9 the number of ingots in the soaking pit is restricted by the temperature in the soaking pit as follows:

Temperature (°F)	Maximum Number
800	5
1100	8

Assuming that ingots in the furnace are not removed when the conditions occur, perform the simulation requested in Exercise 7-9 to include these conditions.

7-11. Change Exercise 7-10 so that ingots are removed from the furnace if the maximum number permitted is exceeded. Develop equations for the cooling of ingots when they are removed. Perform the simulation specified in Exercise 7-9 for these conditions.

7-12. Determine the effect of maintaining ingot temperature in a warming pit instead of the cold storage bank.

7-13. Formulate a discrete-continuous model and analyze it using GASP IV.

7-14. Perform a simulation to determine the dynamic behavior of the tree biomass system (45) of Exercise 6-7 with the following events superimposed:

(*a*) The planting of small trees every six years; the biomass of small trees planted is equal to 15% of the small trees existing at the time of planting.

(*b*) The occurrence of a catastrophic event that reduces the biomass of large trees by 30% and that of medium sized trees by 15%. The time between catastrophic events is exponentially distributed with a mean of 10 years.

(*c*) When the amount of biomass for small trees decreases below 65,000 kg/ha, schedule a planting of 15,000 kg/ha of small trees. The biomass for small trees planted is considered to be included in the model one year after the condition is detected.

(*d*) When the biomass of large trees is less than 1.3 times greater than the biomass for medium trees, 15% of the medium trees are harvested.

7-15. Develop the performance indices and control strategies for maintaining an ecologically stable tree biomass system, given the model presented in Exercise 6-7 and using the information contained in Exercise 7-14.

7-16. Simulate the model of Cedar Bog Lake (139) presented in Exercise 6-11 when the following control policies are superimposd on the natural environment: stock the lake with carnivores by 0.3 cal/cm^2 every tenth of a year; replenish the lake with herbivores when the population of carnivores increases above 0.6 cal/cm^2; and spray the lake to reduce the plant population by 70% every 0.5 years. Simulate Cedar Bog Lake under the above control strategies (127).

7-17. Develop performance measures and control strategies for modifying the lake ecosystem model described in Exercise 6-11. Simulate the lake ecosystem in order to evaluate your proposed control strategies (see Exercise 6-15 and 7-16).

Chapter Eight

GASP IV

Systems Dynamics Analysis

Systems Dynamics, as developed by Forrester, is a problem solving approach to complex problems which emphasizes the structural aspects of models of systems (36,39). Systems are defined and modeled based on *defined* causal relations. The state variables included in a model are those variables perceived by the analyst as contributing significantly to the fundamental behavior of the system under study. Through this modeling approach, a high level of aggregation can be obtained in a model since the state variables are defined by the modeler. The causal relations are developed by the modeler based on experience, intuition, data sources, inferences, heroic assumptions, and any other means available. Scientists and engineers trying to resolve ecological, environmental, and societal problems require new fundamental approaches (47,96,98,136). Systems Dynamics is one of these approaches. While others are being developed, the widespread use of Systems Dynamics for modeling at an aggregate level is anticipated.

The Systems Dynamics modeling philosophy is basically a continuous one (100). State variables, called *levels,* are defined in difference equation-like form and may be nonlinear. Nonlinearities are also included in the model through the use of table functions, delays, and clipping operations. The DYNAMO programming language (115) was developed to provide a language for analyzing Systems Dynamics models to obtain the dynamic behavior of the model. DYNAMO uses a fixed step size, Euler-type integration to evaluate the level variables over time.

GASP IV is an alternative language for analyzing Systems Dynamics models. In addition, GASP IV provides two areas of extended capabilities. First, GASP IV furnishes additional modeling capabilities through the concept of state-events. Second, GASP IV supports discrete-continuous modeling interaction, which opens a new dimension for Systems Dynamics models.* As described in Chapter 1, GASP IV has numerous advantages over special simulation languages like DYNAMO in terms of availability and flexibility.

This chapter demonstrates the use of GASP IV for performing Systems Dynamics modeling and analysis. To accomplish this, two well-documented models, World Dynamics (38, 86) and Industrial Dynamics (36) are coded. In this way, the extensive amount of background information regarding the development of the model can be eliminated from this book to allow concentration on the use of GASP IV in these areas. This approach, although efficient, does not demonstrate the capabilities mentioned above that are available in GASP IV for extending Systems Dynamics models. These capabilities will be illustrated in another publication on applications of GASP IV.

In addition to the world model and the industrial dynamics model presented in this chapter, GASP IV has been used to analyze the following Systems Dynamics oriented models: a model of DDT flow in the environment (87), a cadmium ecosystem model (116), a water resources systems dynamics model, and a global climate dynamics model (135).

Before proceeding with the two examples, sections are presented on modeling concepts and computational sequence and on equation types and functions for Systems Dynamics.

MODELING CONCEPTS AND COMPUTATIONAL SEQUENCES

In Systems Dynamics there are three fundamental equation forms for defining level, rate, and auxiliary variables. A *level* in Systems Dynamics corresponds to a state variable. *Rates* specify the values by which levels change over time. *Auxiliaries* are used to evaluate the components of rate equations and to avoid the interdependence between levels and rates.

* Principle 4.3-3 of Principles of Systems (39), on which Systems Dynamics is based, states that "Levels are changed only by the rates." The author disagrees with a strict interpretation of this principle since there are numerous situations in which the achievement of one level causes a discrete change in another level.

They are also used to simplify equation forms so that fundamental relations are not buried in complex equations.

In GASP IV the specification of an equation form, such as a level, rate, or auxiliary equation, is not necessary. Any type of equation consistent with FORTRAN practices is allowed. Thus the equation form when using GASP IV becomes a modeling construct to help the user build a model of the system under study.

Equations defining the dynamic behavior of the system would be coded in subroutine STATE. When subroutine STATE is called, the status of the system has been established at time TTLAS, and subroutine STATE is being called to determine the values of state variables at time TNOW. After computing values of the variables defined by the equations coded in subroutine STATE, subroutine GASP evaluates these values to determine if they are acceptable. They may not be acceptable for two reasons: (1) time was advanced too far and a state-event occurred within the projected time interval, and (2) accuracy requirements when using numerical integration were exceeded. In either of these cases, subroutine GASP would reduce the step size, return the status to that established for time TTLAS, and then recall subroutine STATE in an attempt to project the status of the system for a smaller time increment. By projecting status and then evaluating it before advancing time, GASP IV allows for the inclusion of time-events and state-events in the model and permits the modeling of the system in terms of state variables or derivatives of state variables or both.

Consider first that all levels are modeled in terms of equations for the state variables, that is, the SS(·) vector. This corresponds to the procedure employed by DYNAMO. In this situation, the time advance interval, DTNOW, is always equal to the full step size, DTFUL, which is set equal to the maximum step size allowed, DTMAX, unless an event occurs during the interval from TTLAS to TNOW where TNOW = TTLAS + DTNOW. If an event is within the interval, DTNOW is reduced so that the intervening event is not passed. In this manner the values of SS(·) are projected and evaluated. If the values of SS(·) are accepted, status is updated by setting TTLAS = TNOW and SSL(I) = SS(I) for all I. If an intervening event occurs within a step, the step size is reduced so that TNOW is the time the event occurs and subroutine STATE is called to update SS(·) corresponding to this value of TNOW. TTLAS is then updated to TNOW.

The appropriate event routine, which can discretely change SS(·), is then called. After performing the computations programmed in the event routines, GASP updates SSL(·) by setting SSL(I) = SS(I) for all I. Thus for models involving equations written only in terms of SS(·), the values of SS(·) and SSL(·) will always be the same when subroutine STATE is called. Therefore, if there are no derivative equations in subroutine STATE, the following two statements are equivalent: SS(I) = SSL(I) + DTNOW ⋆ RATE and SS(I) = SS(I) + DTNOW ⋆ RATE. This information can be useful when equivalenced variables are defined. For example, if P is equivalenced to SS(1), then the statement P = P + DTNOW ⋆ RATE is sufficient to define P without defining a variable that is equivalenced to SSL(1).

There is a basic difference in the computational sequences used by GASP IV and DYNAMO. In a GASP IV simulation, time is projected from TTLAS to TNOW. When subroutine STATE is called, the status of the system has been accepted at time TTLAS, that is, the levels at the beginning of a step have been accepted. Subroutine STATE attempts to project new values for the levels that are to be evaluated by subroutine GASP. The rates of change for the levels for the next step have not been computed when STATE is called. Thus in subroutine STATE, the computation of rates must be done prior to a projection of new level values for time TNOW. This is in contrast to the procedure used in DYNAMO in which the rates of change during a step are computed at the end of the previous step and assumed to be constant for the next step. The DYNAMO method of computation presumes no discrete changes due to events. Since rates are normally functions of levels, and since the level values at the end of a step may be different from the level values at the beginning of the next step (i.e., a discrete change due to an event may have taken place), the rates by which levels are to be changed must be computed first in subroutine STATE. Figure 8-1 illustrates the calculations at times TTLAS and TNOW.

GASP IV allows the flexibility to model a system directly in terms of derivatives of state variables, that is, the DD(·) variables.* The DD(·) variables represent the *rates* by which levels are changed. To avoid confusion with the definition of rates as used in Systems Dynamics and DYNAMO, the latter are referred to as rate components and the DD(·) variables as rates. Clearly, rate components can be used in the equations for either SS(·) or DD(·).

When equations are written in terms of the DD(·) variables, subrou-

* Although the author basically agrees with Forrester's observation that "Representing a system in terms of integral equations gives a more immediate and evident equivalence between the model and the real system" (39), there are situations where a system is conceived in terms of differential equations or a combination of differential and integral equations. Since modeling is an individualistic process, the vehicle that provides the framework for modeling and eventual analysis should be flexible and should not restrict the modeler.

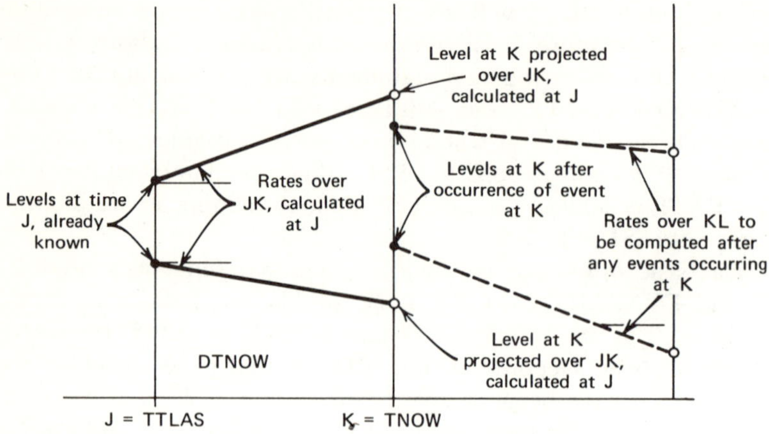

Figure 8-1 Calculations at times TTLAS and TNOW.

tine STATE is called at intermediate points within a step. After each return from subroutine STATE, subroutine GASP computes new values of SS(·) based on the equations defining DD(·). Subroutine STATE is then called again at another intermediate point within the step so that the DD(·) variables can be recomputed with these new values for the SS(·) variables. In this manner, state variables that simultaneously depend on the SS(·) variables can be evaluated. That is, GASP IV allows a model whose equations are defined as a set of simultaneous differential equations. Recall that a step is used to project the levels to the end of the step. The values of the levels at the beginning of the step are the last accepted values. These must be maintained in order that values be available if the projected values are not acceptable. The last accepted rates and levels are maintained by the arrays DDL(·) and SSL(·), respectively. Because of the intermediate calls to subroutine STATE when derivative equations are involved, DD(·) and SS(·) are not necessarily equal to DDL(·) and SSL(·) when subroutine STATE is called.

Whenever subroutine STATE is called, DTNOW is the time increment by which GASP is attempting to project the status of the system. Immediately following an event in which a discrete change could have been made to a level, subroutine STATE can be called with a DTNOW = 0.0. This call to STATE is to update status of the system at the current time based on discrete changes. *Because DTNOW may be zero, it should not be used as the denominator in computing a rate component.*

By using a variable step size, GASP updates values at the points in time at which a condition is satisfied. For example, if a level is to be restricted to be less than or equal to the value 10, in GASP the point in time at which the level crosses the value 10 could be located within a specified tolerance by using function KROSS in subroutine SCOND. Time would only be advanced to this specific point. In DYNAMO, a "clip" function would be used and as soon as the variable exceeded the value 10 at the end of a step, the level would be set at 10. This clipping operation can lead to inaccurate results. If a fixed step size is required when using GASP IV and no events are defined, it can be specified by setting the minimum step size DTMIN equal to the maximum step size DTMAX.

The initial conditions for a GASP IV simulation of a Systems Dynamics model are established in the main program or in subroutine INTLC. Subroutine DATIN calls STATE to initialize state variables. All GASP IV subroutines for information storage and retrieval, random deviate generation, and so forth are available for use in Systems Dynamics modeling in their usual manner. The Systems Dynamics modeler can use subroutine SCOND for defining the conditions for state-events based on level or rate values, subroutine SSAVE for recording system status for future output, and subroutine EVNTS for decoding events of the model and performing any computations at event times. If state-events and time-events are not included in the Systems Dynamics model, subroutines SCOND and EVNTS are not required.

EQUATION TYPES AND FUNCTIONS

The translation of DYNAMO type statements into GASP IV or FORTRAN is a straightforward process (80). A comparison of statement forms is shown in Table 8-1. In DYNAMO variables that are functions of time are so indicated by a period following the variable name and subscripts denoting time following the period. Single letters indicate points in time and double letters denote that the value holds for the interval. Three points in time are used, which are represented by J, K, and L. The interval between these points is represented by JK and KL. The length of the interval is fixed and defined by the variable DT.

In GASP IV time is normally implied and not included in the variable description. Exceptions to this rule are SSL(·) and DDL(·), which are the values of SS(·) and DD(·) at TTLAS. Only two time points are considered in GASP IV, TTLAS and TNOW, with the time interval between them defined as DTNOW. In general, TTLAS corresponds to time J and TNOW corresponds to time K. When values at TNOW are accepted, TTLAS is updated to TNOW and another projection is initiated.

Table 8-1 Comparison of DYNAMO and GASP IV Statement Forms

DYNAMO Statement	GASP IV Statement
1. PER = 52	1. PER = 52.
2. AID = 6	2. AID = 6.
3. ALF = (1000) (RRI)	3. ALF = 1000. ★ RRI
4. TIS.K = IAR.K + IAD.K + IAF.K	4. TIS = IAR + IAD + IAF
5. SNE.K = (SIH) SIN((2PI) (TIME.K)/PER)	5. SNE = SIH ★ SIN(6.28318 ★ TNOW/PER)
6. UOR.K = UOR.J + (DT) (RRR.JK − SSR.JK)	6a. SS(1) = SSL(1) + DTNOW ★ (RRR − SSR)
	6b. SS(1) = SS(1) + DTNOW ★ (RRR − SSR) if NNEQD = 0
	6c. DD(1) = RRR − SSR
7. RSR.K = RSR.J + (DT) (1/DRR) (RRR.JK − RSR.J)	7a. DD(3) = (1./DRR) ★ (RRR − RSR)
	7b. SS(3) = SSL(3) + DTNOW ★ (RRR − RSR)/DDR
8. STP.K = STEP(STH,STT)	8. IF(TNOW.GT.STT) STP = STH
9. SSR.KL = CLIP(STR.K,NIR.K, NIR.K,STR.K)	9. SSR = STR IF (NIR.LT.STR) SSR = NIR
10. Y.K = SMOOTH(Q.JK,SMTM)	10a. CALL GDLAY (10,10,Q,SMTM)
	10b. SS(10) = SSL(10) + DTNOW ★ (Q − SSL(10))/ SMTM and Y = SS(10)
11. Y.K = DLINF1(X.K,TRX)	11a. CALL GDLAY (11,11,X,TRX)
	11b. DD(11) = (X − S(11))/TRX
	11c. SS(11) = SSL(11) + DTNOW ★ (X − SSL(11))/ TRX and Y = SS(11)
12. PSR.KL = DELAY3 (PDR.JK,DCR)	12. CALL GDLAY (18,20,PDR, DCR) and PSR = SS(20)
13. Y.K = DLINF3(X.K,TRX)	13. CALL GDLAY (15,17,X,TRX) and Y = SS(17)

In Table 8-1 statements 1, 2, and 3 illustrate the similarity between replacement statement types. Statements 4 and 5 illustrate the implied time dependence of the GASP IV statements. The equations for TIS and SNE would be included in subroutine STATE, which would be called at time TNOW, and hence would be associated with TNOW without so indicating. Statements 6 and 7 represent level equations in DYNAMO.

The alternative forms for writing these equations in GASP IV are shown. (The subscripts for SS(·) and DD(·) would be selected by the user.) For statement 6, if SS(1) was equivalenced to UOR, the statement could have been written as

```
UOR = UOR + DTNOW * (RRR - SSR)
```

(assuming no derivative equations were included in the model).

The STEP function in DYNAMO establishes a time at which a variable is to be set at a given value. Thus statement 8 specifies that STP is to be set at STH when time becomes greater than STT. The GASP/FORTRAN equivalent is direct.

Statement 9 illustrates a CLIP function that performs the following operations:

$$\text{SSR.KL} = \begin{cases} \text{STR.K if NIR.K} \geq \text{STR.K} \\ \text{NIR.K if NIR.K} < \text{STR.K} \end{cases}$$

In the GASP IV equivalent, it is assumed that NIR was declared as a real variable in a REAL statement.

In statement 10, the SMOOTH function of DYNAMO averages a rate of flow for use at a specific point in time. The DYNAMO equations resulting from the statement Y.K = SMOOTH(Q.JK,SMTM) are:

$$\text{Y.K} = \text{L.K/SMTM}$$

where

$$\text{L.K} = \text{L.J} + (\text{DT})(\text{Q.JK} - \text{Y.J}).$$

Replacing L.K and L.J in the above difference equation yields

$$(\text{Y.K})(\text{SMTM}) = (\text{Y.J})(\text{SMTM}) + (\text{DT})(\text{Q.JK} - \text{Y.J})$$

or

$$\text{Y.K} = \text{Y.J} + (\text{DT/SMTM})(\text{Q.JK} - \text{Y.J}).$$

The exponential smoothing nature of this equation is seen by rewriting it as

$$\text{Y.K} = (\text{Y.J})(1 - \text{DT/SMTM}) + (\text{Q.JK})(\text{DT/SMTM})$$
$$\text{Y.K} = (\text{Y.J})(1 - \alpha) + (\text{Q.JK})(\alpha)$$

where α = DT/SMTM and can be considered as a smoothing constant. In GASP IV the SMOOTH function can be accomplished by subroutine GDLAY or direct coding of the user. The statement GDLAY(10,10,Q, SMTM) results in the following code

```
DD(10) = (Q - SS(10))/SMTM
```

where state variable 10 has been assigned to model level Y. GASP IV automatically integrates DD(10) to provide a value for SS(10) and the user should set Y = SS(10).

The user could obtain the above result directly, using the above statement in place of the call to GDLAY. If only a level value was desired, as in the case of the DYNAMO SMOOTH function, the following statements could be used

```
SS(10) = SSL(10) + DTNOW * (Q - SSL(10))/SMTM
```

and

```
Y = SS(10).
```

In this case DD(10) is not computed. In this equation the variable SS(10) could be used to replace SSL(10) on the right hand side if NNEQD = 0 since no intermediate calls to STATE between TTLAS and TNOW would be made.

In statement 11 DLINF1, the first order delay of a level, is presented. The computation performed by this function is

```
Y.K = Y.J + (DT)(X.K - Y.J)/TRX
```

where X.K is the input at time K and TRX is the time to recognize the difference between level Y.J and the input X.K. The similarity of the functional form between DLINF1 and SMOOTH is apparent. The corresponding GASP IV statement would be

```
DD(11) = (X - SS(11))/TRX
```

or, equivalently,

```
SS(11) = SSL(11) + DTNOW * (X - SSL(11))/TRX.
```

The GASP IV statement CALL GDLAY(11,11,X,TRX) would result in the statement given for DD(11) presented above. In all three of the GASP IV codings, the value of Y is obtained as SS(11).

Statement 12, PSR.KL = DELAY3(PDR.JK,DCR), is the DYNAMO function for a third order delay DELAY3 with input PDR.JK and delay time DCR. The equivalent DYNAMO statements for function DELAY3 are:

```
 R1.KL = R1.JK + (DT)(PDR.JK − R1.JK)/(DCR/3)
 R2.KL = R2.JK + (DT)(R1.JK − R2.JK)/(DCR/3)
PSR.KL = PSR.JK + (DT)(R2.JK − PSR.JK)/(DCR/3)
```

From these equations, it is seen that the difference equations are for rates and (PSR.KL − PSR.JK)/DT is essentially a rate of change of a rate.

The GASP IV statement CALL GDLAY(18,20,PDR,DCR) processes the following code:

```
DD(18) = (DORD/DCR) ⋆ (PDR − SS(18))
DD(19) = (DORD/DCR) ⋆ (SS(18) − SS(19))
DD(20) = (DORD/DCR) ⋆ (SS(19) − SS(20))
```

where SS(20) is the value of PSR desired and DORD, the order of the delay, equals $20 - 18 + 1 = 3$.

The coding of GDLAY permits a variable order delay as the value of DORD is computed as a function of the first two arguments of GDLAY. The comment made regarding the user's writing his own delay subroutine is equally appropriate in this case and the one that follows.

Statement 13 is the DYNAMO function for a third order information delay DLINF3 with input X.K and time to recognize the difference TRX. The equations for DLINF3 are similar to those for DELAY3 with the exception that the difference equations are for level variables. The GASP IV statement equivalent to statement 13 is CALL GDLAY(15,17, X,TRX), which processes the following code:

```
DD(15) = (DORD/TRX) ⋆ (X − SS(15))
DD(16) = (DORD/TRX) ⋆ (SS(15) − SS(16))
DD(17) = (DORD/TRX) ⋆ (SS(16) − SS(17))
```

where SS(17) is the value Y desired, DD(17) is the derivative of SS(17), and DORD, the order of the delay, equals $17 - 15 + 1 = 3$. This completes the comparison of DYNAMO and GASP IV statement forms.

The translation of two existing and well-documented Systems Dynamics models is now presented. The first is a world model. In this example level equations are used. The ease with which multiple runs can be made using GASP IV is demonstrated. The second example involves a

Table 8-2 Definition of Variables for World Dynamics Model

Variable*	Definition
BR	Birth rate
BRCM	Birth-rate-from-crowding multiplier
BRFM	Birth-rate-from-food multiplier
BRMM	Birth-rate-from-material multiplier
BRPM	Birth-rate-from-pollution multiplier
CFIFR	Capital fraction indicated by food ratio
CI	Capital investment
CIAF	Capital-investment-in-agriculture fraction
CID	Capital-investment discard
CIG	Capital-investment generation
CIM	Capital-investment multiplier
CIQR	Capital-investment-from-quality ratio
CIR	Capital-investment ratio
CIRA	Capital-investment ratio in agriculture
CR	Crowding ratio
DR	Death rate
DRCM	Death-rate-from-crowding multiplier
DRFM	Death-rate-from-food multiplier
DRMM	Death-rate-from-material multiplier
DRPM	Death-rate-from-pollution multiplier
ECIR	Effective-capital-investment ratio

* The letters I, N, and T when added to the variable name respectively denote initial, normal, and table, for example, BRN is birth rate normal.

model of a factory, distributor, and retail system. In this example rate equations are used to define the system variables.

EXAMPLE 10—A WORLD DYNAMICS MODEL

Statement of the Problem

The world model analyzed in this example was defined by Forrester and has been described by him in detail (38). An extensive analysis of an extended version* of this model has been reported by Meadows et al. (86). For readers interested in the model development and use, these books are highly recommended. World Dynamics is an aggregate model of world interactions to illustrate the behavior of a set of defined variables depending on whether population growth is eventually suppressed by a

* These extensions are easily coded in GASP IV. For explanation purposes, the basic model was selected for presentation.

Table 8-2 *(continued)*

Variable*	Definition
F	Food
FC	Food coefficient
FCM	Food-from-crowding multiplier
FPCI	Food potential from capital investment
FPM	Food-from-pollution multiplier
FR	Food ratio
MSL	Material standard of living
NR	Natural Resources
NREM	Natural-resource-extraction multiplier
NRFR	Natural-resources-fraction remaining
NRI	Natural resources, initial
NRMM	Natural-resources-from material multiplier
NRUR	Natural-resources-usage rate
P	Population
PD	Population density
POL	Pollution
POLA	Pollution absorption
POLCM	Pollution-from-capital multiplier
POLG	Pollution generation
POLR	Pollution ratio
POLS	Pollution standard
QL	Quality of life
QLC	Quality of life from crowding
QLF	Quality of life from food
QLM	Quality of life from material
QLP	Quality of life from pollution
QLS	Quality of life standard

shortage of natural resources, pollution, over-crowding, or an insufficient food supply. The model portrays the world interactions by designating five interrelated variables as levels: population P, natural resources NR, capital-investment CI, capital investment-in-agriculture fraction CIAF, and pollution POL. Table 8-2 defines the variables that are used in this example. The equations for the model are presented in the discussion of subroutine STATE.

Simulation Objectives

The primary objective of this example is to investigate the response of a World Dynamics model to five different initial values of BRN (Birth Rate Normal).

Special Features

Difference equations are used to define the state variables (levels). Multiple runs are performed using data card type 0. Subroutine OTPUT is written to obtain a final report to eliminate the need for a full summary report.

Simulation Procedure

The major GASP IV coding required for Systems Dynamics problems is for subroutine STATE. Each level equation is essentially an equation for a state variable. The rate components and the "auxiliary" values required for the computation of the rate components must be evaluated prior to the evaluation of the levels. Using the definitions of Table 8-2, the statements for the rate components are:

```
BR = P ⋆ BRN ⋆ BRFM ⋆ BRMM ⋆ BRCM ⋆ BRPM
DR = P ⋆ DRN ⋆ DRMM ⋆ DRPM ⋆ DRFM ⋆ DRCM
NRUR = P ⋆ XNRUN ⋆ NRMM
CIG = P ⋆ CIM ⋆ CIGN
CID = CI ⋆ CIDN
POLG = P ⋆ POLN ⋆ POLCM
POLA = POL/POLAT
```

where all variables on the right hand side are previous values of levels or values already obtained in subroutine STATE.

The above equations illustrate that Forrester hypothesized multiplicative relationships in the computation of rate components. For example, birth rate, which is a component rate to be used in the computation of population, is equal to the product of the current population, birth rate normal, birth-rate-from-food multiplier, birth-rate-from-material multiplier, birth-rate-from-crowding multiplier and birth-rate-from-pollution multiplier. Each of the multipliers are in turn computed from other variables. For example, BRFM, birth-rate-from-food multiplier, is obtained from a table function with the independent variable being the food ratio, FR. FR in turn is equal to a product of terms divided by food normal. Each of these relations is included in subroutine STATE.

With the above rate components, new values for the levels can be computed using the following statements:

```
P = P + DTNOW ⋆ (BR − DR)
```

```
NR = NR + DTNOW ★ (− NRUR)
CI = CI + DTNOW ★ (CIG − CID)
POL = POL + DTNOW ★ (POLG − POLA)
CIAF = CIAF + DTNOW ★ (CFIFR ★ CIQR − CIAF)/CIAFT
QL = QLS ★ QLM ★ QLC ★ QLF ★ QLP
```

The equation for population P indicates that the population projected to time TNOW is equal to the population at TTLAS, plus the time interval times the rate of change of population. The time interval is DTNOW = TNOW − TTLAS and the rate of change of population is equal to the birth rate, BR, minus the death rate, DR. The above equations are coded directly in subroutine STATE and together with the statements for evaluating the "auxiliaries" comprise the World Dynamics model. The FORTRAN listing of subroutine STATE is given in Fig. 8-2. In this example the level variables are equivalenced to the SS(·) variables and SSL(·) are not required because no discrete changes were made to SS(·) and no events were based on SS(·) values.

The FORTRAN listing of the main program for this example is given in Fig. 8-3. In the main program the card reader and printer numbers are set and the table functions are read. Subroutine GASP is then called to control the simulation.

Subroutine INTLC initializes the non-GASP variables that specify the starting conditions for each run. The birth rate normal, BRN, is read to allow it to vary from run to run based on data input. The FORTRAN listing for subroutine INTLC is given in Fig. 8-4.

Subroutine SSAVE calls subroutine GPLOT to record the values to be plotted. The array PLOT is used to pass the values to GPLOT. An EQUIVALENCE statement is used to define the levels in terms of the SS(·) variables since only the latter are in COMMON storage. The FORTRAN listing of subroutine SSAVE is given in Fig. 8-5. Subroutine OTPUT prints a table and plots the values recorded in SSAVE by calling subroutine GPLOT with a code of 0. The FORTRAN listing of subroutine OTPUT is given in Fig. 8-6.

A listing of input data cards for Example 10 is shown in Fig. 8-7. The first 26 cards are read in the main program to define the needed table functions. The next 15 cards are GASP IV data cards types 1, 2, 6, 9, and 11. In this case, because NNRNS > 1 and IICRD = 0, a type 0 data card is used. This permits the user to redefine LLSUP(·) and IICRD to suppress the storage area dumps for the first run (LLSUP(13) = 2, LLSUP (14) = 2), to bypass the reading of all GASP IV data cards for subse-

```
      SUBROUTINE STATE
      REAL MSL,NREM,NRFR,NRMM,NR,NRI,NRUR,NREMT,NRMMT,LA
      COMMON /GCOM2/ DD(100),DDL(100),DTFUL,DTNOW,ISEES,LFLAG(50),NFLAG,
     1NNEOD,NNEQS,NNEQT,SS(100),SSL(100),TTNEX
      COMMON /UCOM1/ BR,BRCM,BRFM,BRMM,BRN,BRPM,CFIFR,CIAFI,CIAFN,CIAFT,
     1CID,CIDN,CIG,CIGN,CII,CIM,CIQR,CIR,CIRA,CR,DR,DRCM,DRFM,DRMM,DRN,DU
     2PPM,ECIR,ECIRN,FC,FCM,FN,FPCI,FPM,FR,LA,MSL,NREM,NRFR,NRI,NRMM,NRU
     3R,PDN,PI,POLA,POLAT,POLCM,POLG,POLI,POLN,POLR,POLS,QL,QLC,QLF,QLM,
     4QLP,QLS,XNRUN
      COMMON /UCOM2/ BRCMT(6),BRFMT(5),BRMMT(6),BRPMT(7),CFIFRT(5),CIMT
     1(6),CIQRT(5),DRCMT(6),DRFMT(9),DRMMT(11),DRPMT(7),FCMT(6),FPCIT(7)
     2,FPMT(7),NREMT(5),NRMMT(11),POLATT(7),POLCMT(6),QLCT(11),QLFT(5),Q
     3LMT(6),QLPT(7)
      EQUIVALENCE (P,SS(1)),(NR,SS(2)),(CI,SS(3)),(POL,SS(4)),(CIAF,SS(5
     1))
C
C*****AUXILIARIES.
C
      NRFR=NR/NRI
      CR=P/(LA*PDN)
      CIR=CI/P
      NREM=GTABL(NREMT,NRFR,0.,1.,.25)
      ECIR=CIR*(1.-CIAF)*NREM/(1.-CIAFN)
      MSL=ECIR/ECIRN
      BRMM=GTABL(BRMMT,MSL,0.,5.,1.)
      DRMM=GTABL(DRMMT,MSL,0.,5.,.5)
      DRCM=GTABL(DRCMT,CR,0.,5.,1.)
      BRCM=GTABL(BRCMT,CR,0.,5.,1.)
      CIRA=CIR*CIAF/CIAFN
      FPCI=GTABL(FPCIT,CIRA,0.,6.,1.)
      FCM=GTABL(FCMT,CR,0.,5.,1.)
      POLR=POL/POLS
      FPM=GTABL(FPMT,POLR,0.,60.,10.)
      FR=FPCI*FCM*FPM*FC/FN
      CIM=GTABL(CIMT,MSL,0.,5.,1.)
      POLCM=GTABL(POLCMT,CIR,0.,5.,1.)
      POLAT=GTABL(POLATT,POLR,0.,60.,10.)
      CFIFR=GTABL(CFIFRT,FR,0.,2.,.5)
      QLM=GTABL(QLMT,MSL,0.,5.,1.)
      QLC=GTABL(QLCT,CR,0.,5.,.5)
      QLF=GTABL(QLFT,FR,0.,4.,1.)
      QLP=GTABL(QLPT,POLR,0.,60.,10.)
      NRMM=GTABL(NRMMT,MSL,0.,10.,1.)
      CIQR=GTABL(CIQRT,QLM/QLF,0.,2.,.5)
      DRPM=GTABL(DRPMT,POLR,0.,60.,10.)
      DRFM=GTABL(DRFMT,FR,0.,2.,.25)
      BRFM=GTABL(BRFMT,FR,0.,4.,1.)
      BRPM=GTABL(BRPMT,POLR,0.,60.,10.)
C
C*****RATE COMPONENTS.
C
      BR=P*BRN*BRFM*BRMM*BRCM*BRPM
      DR=P*DRN*DRMM*DRPM*DRFM*DRCM
      NRUR=P*XNRUN*NRMM
      CIG=P*CIM*CIGN
      CID=CI*CIDN
      POLG=P*POLN*POLCM
      POLA=POL/POLAT
C
C*****LEVELS.
C
      QL=QLS*QLM*QLC*QLF*QLP
      P=P+DTNOW*(BR-DR)
      NR=NR-DTNOW*NRUR
      CI=CI+DTNOW*(CIG-CID)
      POL=POL+DTNOW*(POLG-POLA)
      CIAF=CIAF+DTNOW*(CFIFR*CIQR-CIAF)/CIAFT
      RETURN
C
      END
```

Figure 8-2 FORTRAN listing of subroutine STATE (Example 10).

```
      PROGRAM MAIN (INPUT,OUTPUT,TAPE5=INPUT,TAPE6=OUTPUT)                MXA    1
      REAL NSL,NREM,NRFR,NRMM,NR,NRI,NRUR,NREMT,NRMMT,LA                   REAL   1
      DIMENSION NSET(310)                                                  DIM    1
      COMMON QSET(310)                                                     COM    1
      COMMON /GCOM1/ ATRIB(25),JEVNT,MFA,MFE(100),MLE(100),MSTOP,NCRDR,NGCOM1   1
     1NAPO,NNAPT,NNATR,NNFIL,NNQ(100),NNTRY,NPRNT,PPARM(50,4),TNOW,TTBEGGCOM1   2
     2,TTCLR,TTFIN,TTRIB(25),TTSET                                         GCOM1  3
      COMMON /UCOM2/ BRCMT(6),BRFMT(5),BRMMT(6),BRPMT(7),CFIFRT(5),CIMT UCOM2   1
     1(6),CIQRT(5),DRCMT(6),DRFMT(9),DRMMT(11),DRPMT(7),FCMT(6),FPCIT(7)UCOM2   2
     2,FPMT(7),NREMT(5),NRMMT(11),POLATT(7),POLCMT(6),QLCT(11),QLFT(5),QUCOM2   3
     3LMT(6),QLPT(7)                                                       UCOM2  4
      EQUIVALENCE(NSET(1),QSET(1))                                         EQUIV  1
      NCRDR=5                                                              MXA    2
      NPRNT=6                                                              MXA    3
      READ (NCRDR,101) BRCMT                                               MXA    4
      READ (NCRDR,101) BRFMT                                               MXA    5
      READ (NCRDR,101) BRMMT                                               MXA    6
      READ (NCRDR,101) BRPMT                                               MXA    7
      READ (NCRDR,101) CFIFRT                                              MXA    8
      READ (NCRDR,101) CIMT                                                MXA    9
      READ (NCRDR,101) CIQRT                                               MXA   10
      READ (NCRDR,101) DRCMT                                               MXA   11
      READ (NCRDR,101) DRFMT                                               MXA   12
      READ (NCRDR,101) DRMMT                                               MXA   13
      READ (NCRDR,101) DRPMT                                               MXA   14
      READ (NCRDR,101) FCMT                                                MXA   15
      READ (NCRDR,101) FPCIT                                               MXA   16
      READ (NCRDR,101) FPMT                                                MXA   17
      READ (NCRDR,101) NREMT                                               MXA   18
      READ (NCRDR,101) NRMMT                                               MXA   19
      READ (NCRDR,101) POLATT                                              MXA   20
      READ (NCRDR,101) POLCMT                                              MXA   21
      READ (NCRDR,101) QLCT                                                MXA   22
      READ (NCRDR,101) QLFT                                                MXA   23
      READ (NCRDR,101) QLMT                                                MXA   24
      READ (NCRDR,101) QLPT                                                MXA   25
      CALL GASP                                                            MXA   26
      CALL EXIT                                                            MXA   27
C                                                                          MXA   28
  101 FORMAT (7F10.4)                                                      MXA   29
C                                                                          MXA   30
      END                                                                  MXA   31
```

Figure 8-3 FORTRAN listing of main program (Example 10).

quent runs (IICRD = 13), and to suppress the GASP IV summary report for all runs (LLSUP(15) = 2). In this case, all user defined data input cards read in subroutine INTLC can directly follow the GASP IV type 0 card.

Because the GASP IV summary report is suppressed, the programmer must provide for any required simulation reports. This was done by having subroutine OTPUT call subroutine GPLOT to prepare and print the data that was collected in subroutine SSAVE.

Simulation Reports

The GASP IV echo check is shown in Fig. 8-8. Note that AAERR and RRERR are defined (to their default values) even though they are not

```
      SUBROUTINE INTLC                                                  ICA      1
      REAL MSL,NREM,NRFR,NRMM,NR,NRI,NRUR,NREMT,NRMMT,LA                REAL     1
      COMMON /GCOM1/ ATRIB(25),JEVNT,MFA,MFE(100),MLE(100),MSTOP,NCRDR,NGCOM1    1
     1NAPO,NNAPT,NNATR,NNFIL,NNQ(100),NNTRY,NPRNT,PPARM(50,4),TNOW,TTBEGGCOM1    2
     2,TTCLR,TTFIN,TTRIB(25),TTSET                                      GCOM1    3
      COMMON /GCOM2/ DD(100),DDL(100),DTFUL,DTNOW,ISEES,LFLAG(50),NFLAG,GCOM2    1
     1NNEQD,NNEQS,NNEQT,SS(100),SSL(100),TTNEX                          GCOM2    2
      COMMON /UCOM1/ BR,BRCM,BRFM,BRMM,BRN,BRPM,CFIFR,CIAFI,CIAFN,CIAFT,UCOM1    1
     1CID,CIDN,CIG,CIGN,CII,CIM,CIQR,CIR,CIRA,CR,DR,DRCM,DRFM,DRMM,DRN,DUCOM1    2
     2RPM,ECIR,ECIRN,FC,FCM,FN,FPCI,FPM,FR,LA,MSL,NREM,NRFR,NRI,NRMM,NRUUCOM1    3
     3R,PDN,PI,POLA,POLAT,POLCM,POLG,POLI,POLN,POLR,POLS,QL,QLC,QLF,QLM,UCOM1    4
     4QLP,QLS,XNRUN                                                     UCOM1    5
      COMMON /UCOM2/ BRCMT(6),BRFMT(5),BRMMT(6),BRPMT(7),CFIFRT(5),CIMT UCOM2    1
     1(6),CIQRT(5),DRCMT(6),DRFMT(9),DRMMT(11),DRPMT(7),FCMT(6),FPCIT(7)UCOM2    2
     2,FPMT(7),NREMT(5),NRMMT(11),POLATT(7),POLCMT(6),QLCT(11),QLFT(5),QUCOM2    3
     3LMT(6),QLPT(7)                                                    UCOM2    4
      EQUIVALENCE (P,SS(1)),(NR,SS(2)),(CI,SS(3)),(POL,SS(4)),(CIAF,SS(5USEQV    1
     1))                                                                USEQV    2
C                                                                       ICA      2
C*****INITIAL CONDITIONS.                                               ICA      3
C                                                                       ICA      4
      PI=1.65E9                                                         ICA      5
      READ (NCRDR,101) BRN                                              ICA      6
      ECIRN=1.                                                          ICA      7
      NRI =900.E9                                                       ICA      8
      XNRUN=1.                                                          ICA      9
      DRN=.028                                                          ICA     10
      LA=135.E6                                                         ICA     11
      PDN=26.5                                                          ICA     12
      FC=1.                                                             ICA     13
      FN=1.                                                             ICA     14
      CIAFN=.3                                                          ICA     15
      CII=.4E9                                                          ICA     16
      CIGN=.05                                                          ICA     17
      CIDN=.025                                                         ICA     18
      POLS=3.6E9                                                        ICA     19
      POLI=.2E9                                                         ICA     20
      POLN=1.                                                           ICA     21
      CIAFI=.2                                                          ICA     22
      CIAFT=15.                                                         ICA     23
      QLS=1.                                                            ICA     24
      P=PI                                                              ICA     25
      NR=NRI                                                            ICA     26
      CI=CII                                                            ICA     27
      POL=POLI                                                          ICA     28
      CIAF=CIAFI                                                        ICA     29
      RETURN                                                            ICA     30
C                                                                       ICA     31
  101 FORMAT (F5.0)                                                     ICA     32
C                                                                       ICA     33
      END                                                               ICA     34
```

Figure 8-4 FORTRAN listing of subroutine INTLC (Example 10).

used when NNEQD = 0. Because GASP IV permits the user to change the value of NNEQD during the execution of a simulation run, these default values are established. In this example DTMAX was set to DTMIN, which causes a fixed step to be used. Because NNEQD = 0 and no events are included in the model, the step size for this example will always be DTMAX.

The plotted output for the first (BRN = 0.04) and last (BRN = 0.02) of the five runs are shown in Figs. 8-9 and 8-10. By properly selecting the limits for the plots, five variables can be plotted primarily in the

```
      SUBROUTINE SSAVE                                                  SVA      1
      REAL MSL,NREM,NRFR,NRMM,NR,NRI,NRUR,NREMT,NRMMT,LA                REAL     1
      DIMENSION PLOT(10)                                                SVA      2
      COMMON /GCOM1/ ATRIB(25),JEVNT,MFA,MFE(100),MLE(100),MSTOP,NCRDR,NGCOM1   1
     1NAPO,NNAPT,NNATR,NNFIL,NNQ(100),NNTRY,NPRNT,PPARM(50,4),TNOW,TTBEGGCOM1   2
     2,TTCLR,TTFIN,TTRIB(25),TTSET                                      GCOM1    3
      COMMON /GCOM2/ DD(100),DDL(100),DTFUL,DTNOW,ISEES,LFLAG(50),NFLAG,GCOM2   1
     1NNEQD,NNEQS,NNEQT,SS(100),SSL(100),TTNEX                          GCOM2    2
      COMMON /UCOM1/ BR,BRCM,BRFM,BRMM,BRN,BRPM,CFIFR,CIAFI,CIAFN,CIAFT,UCOM1   1
     1CID,CIDN,CIG,CIGN,CII,CIM,CIQR,CIR,CIRA,CR,DR,DRCM,DRFM,DRMM,DRN,DUCOM1   2
     2RPM,ECIR,ECIRN,FC,FCM,FN,FPCI,FPM,FR,LA,MSL,NREM,NRFR,NRI,NRMM,NRUUCOM1   3
     3R,PDN,PI,POLA,POLAT,POLCM,POLG,POLI,POLN,POLR,POLS,QL,QLC,QLF,QLM,UCOM1   4
     4QLP,QLS,XNRUN                                                     UCOM1    5
      COMMON /UCOM2/ BRCMT(6),BRFMT(5),BRMMT(6),BRPMT(7),CFIFRT(5),CIMT UCOM2    1
     1(6),CIQRT(5),DRCMT(6),DRFMT(9),DRMMT(11),DRPMT(7),FCMT(6),FPCIT(7)UCOM2    2
     2,FPMT(7),NREMT(5),NRMMT(11),POLATT(7),POLCMT(6),QLCT(11),QLFT(5),QUCOM2   3
     3LMT(6),QLPT(7)                                                    UCOM2    4
      EQUIVALENCE (P,SS(1)),(NR,SS(2)),(CI,SS(3)),(POL,SS(4)),(CIAF,SS(5USEQV   1
     1))                                                                USEQV    2
      PLOT(1)=P                                                         SVA      3
      PLOT(2)=POLR                                                      SVA      4
      PLOT(3)=CI                                                        SVA      5
      PLOT(4)=QL                                                        SVA      6
      PLOT(5)=NR                                                        SVA      7
      PLOT(6)=FR                                                        SVA      8
      PLOT(7)=MSL                                                       SVA      9
      PLOT(8)=QLC                                                       SVA     10
      PLOT(9)=QLP                                                       SVA     11
      PLOT(10)=CIAF                                                     SVA     12
      CALL GPLOT (PLOT,TNOW,1)                                          SVA     13
      RETURN                                                            SVA     14
C                                                                       SVA     15
      END                                                               SVA     16
```

Figure 8-5 FORTRAN listing of subroutine SSAVE (Example 10).

0–50% range and five in the 50–100% range. Each plot then consists of a top half and a bottom half and the possible confusion from having 10 variables on a plot is decreased. Two plots per run could have been obtained but this would have increased execution time as the core plot option is not available when more than 1 plot is requested. The change in the dynamic behavior of the model by a halving of the birth rate normal (from 0.04 to 0.02) can be seen by comparing Figs. 8-9 and 8-10.

In running this simulation no external excitation of the system is introduced. For stable systems the dynamic behavior exhibited is due to the transients of the model. When the model is simulated for a longer period of time, all levels reach their steady state values.

```
      SUBROUTINE OTPUT                                                  OTA      1
      DIMENSION X(10)                                                   OTA      2
      CALL GPLOT (X,XX,0)                                               OTA      3
      RETURN                                                            OTA      4
C                                                                       OTA      5
      END                                                               OTA      6
```

Figure 8-6 FORTRAN listing of subroutine OTPUT (Example 10).

```
1.05      1.        .9        .7        .6        .55                        
0.        1.        1.6       1.9       2.                                   
1.2       1.        .85       .75       .7        .7                         
1.02      .9        .7        .4        .25       .15       .1               
1.        .6        .3        .15       .1                                   
.1        1.        1.8       2.4       2.8       3.                         
.7        .8        1.        1.5        2.                                  
.9        1.        1.2       1.5       1.9       3.                         
30.       3.        2.        1.4       1.        .7        .6         USER
.5        .5                                                                 
3.        1.8       1.        .8        .7        .6        .53              
.5        .5        .5        .5                                             
.92       1.3       2.        3.2       4.8       6.8       9.2              
2.4       1.        .6        .4        .3        .2                         
.5        1.        1.4       1.7       1.9       2.05      2.2              
1.02      .9        .65       .35       .2        .1        .05              
0.        .15       .5        .85       1.                                   
0.        1.        1.8       2.4       2.9       3.3       3.6              
3.8       3.9       3.95      4.                                             
.6        2.5       5.        8.        11.5      15.5      20.              
.05       1.        3.        5.4       7.4       8.                         
2.        1.3       1.        .75       .55       .45       .38              
.3        .25       .22       .2                                             
0.        1.        1.8       2.4       2.7                                  
.2        1.        1.7       2.3       2.7       2.9                        
1.04      .85       .6        .3        .15       .05       .02              
PRITSKER          10    6    30 1973    5                               1
    0    0    0    0    1    5    0    0    0  310    0    5    0       2
6A        1TIME                  0   10   -1         8.                     
6B        1PP           1    1        0.        16.E9                       
6B        22POLR        1    1        0.          80.                       
6B        3CCI          1    1        0.        40.E9                       
6B        4QQL          1    1        0.           4.                   6
6B        5NNR          1    1        0.      2000.E9                       
6B        6FFR          1    1       -2.           2.                       
6B        7MMSL         1    1       -2.           2.                       
6B        84QLC         1    1       -2.           2.                       
6B        95QLP         1    1       -2.           2.                       
6B       10ACIAF        1    1       -.2          .6                        
    0    0       0.        0.        .2        .2        8.             9
    1    1    1    0        1900.       2100.    0    0    0    0    0    0  11
2222222222 222222 13                                                    0
  .04                                                                       
 .035                                                                       
  .03                                                              USER
 .025                                                                       
  .02                                                                       
```

Figure 8-7 Listing of input data cards (Example 10).

EXAMPLE 11—SYSTEMS DYNAMICS MODEL OF A FACTORY, DISTRIBUTOR, AND RETAILER SYSTEM

Statement of the Problem

A factory, distributor, and retailer model developed by Forrester is to be simulated using GASP IV. The model is representative of the Systems Dynamics approach to problem solving and has been fully described by Forrester. A DYNAMO source listing has been published and is used as the model definition (36). A definition of the variables included in the model are given in Table 8-3. The equations defining the model are extensive. To avoid duplication, the description of the equations is only given in terms of the GASP IV coding of subroutine STATE. Table 8-3,

```
                              SIMULATION PROJECT NUMBER  10  BY  PRITSKER

                              DATE   6/ 30/ 1973         RUN NUMBER    1 OF    5
                              LLSUP=00000000000000       GASP IV VERSION 23JUN73

NNCLT=      0    NNSTA=     0    NNHIS=     0    NNPRM=     0    NNPLT=     1         NNSTR=     5    NNTRY=     0
NNATR=      0    NNFIL=     0    NNSET=   310    NNEQD=     0    NNEQS=     5         NFLAG=     0

GPLOT NO.   1    LLABP=TIME      IITAP=     0    NNVAR=    10    LLPLT=    -1              DTPLT=     8.0000E+00
  VAR NO.   1         P=P        LLPLO=     1    LLPHI=     1    PPLO =    0.              PPHI =     1.6000E+10
  VAR NO.   2         2=POLR     LLPLO=     1    LLPHI=     1    PPLO =    0.              PPHI =     8.0000E+01
  VAR NO.   3         C=CI       LLPLO=     1    LLPHI=     1    PPLO =    0.              PPHI =     4.0000E+10
  VAR NO.   4         Q=QL       LLPLO=     1    LLPHI=     1    PPLO =    0.              PPHI =     4.0000E+00
  VAR NO.   5         N=NR       LLPLO=     1    LLPHI=     1    PPLO =    0.              PPHI =     2.0000E+12
  VAR NO.   6         F=FR       LLPLO=     1    LLPHI=     1    PPLO =   -2.0000E+00      PPHI =     2.0000E+00
  VAR NO.   7         M=MSL      LLPLO=     1    LLPHI=     1    PPLO =   -2.0000E+00      PPHI =     2.0000E+00
  VAR NO.   8         4=QLC      LLPLO=     1    LLPHI=     1    PPLO =   -2.0000E+00      PPHI =     2.0000E+00
  VAR NO.   9         5=QLP      LLPLO=     1    LLPHI=     1    PPLO =   -2.0000E+00      PPHI =     2.0000E+00
  VAR NO.  10         A=CIAF     LLPLO=     1    LLPHI=     1    PPLO =   -2.0000E-01      PPHI =     6.0000E-01

IIEVT=      0    LLERR=     0    AAERR=    1.0000E-05          RRERR=    1.0000E-05
DTMIN=      2.0000E-01           DTMAX=    2.0000E-01          DTSAV=    8.0000E+00

MSTOP=      1    JJCLR=     1    JJBEG=     1    IICRD=     0    TTBEG=    1.9000E+03      TTFIN=     2.1000E+03
JJFIL=      0
IISED=      0               0               0               0              0

LLSUP=      22222222222222       IICRD=    13
```

Figure 8-8 GASP IV echo check of input (Example 10).

```
**PLOT NUMBER  1**
  RUN  NUMBER  1

              SCALES OF PLOT
P=P       0.            4.0000E+09   8.0000E+09   1.2000E+10   1.6000E+10
2=POLR    0.            2.0000E+01   4.0000E+01   6.0000E+01   8.0000E+01
C=CI      0.            1.0000E+10   2.0000E+10   3.0000E+10   4.0000E+10
Q=QL      0.            1.0000E+00   2.0000E+00   3.0000E+00   4.0000E+00
N=NR      0.            5.0000E+11   1.0000E+12   1.5000E+12   2.0000E+12
F=FR     -2.0000E+00   -1.0000E+00   0.           1.0000E+00   2.0000E+00
M=MSL    -2.0000E+00   -1.0000E+00   0.           1.0000E+00   2.0000E+00
4=QLC    -2.0000E+00   -1.0000E+00   0.           1.0000E+00   2.0000E+00
5=QLP    -2.0000E+00   -1.0000E+00   0.           1.0000E+00   2.0000E+00
A=CIAF   -2.0000E-01    0.           2.0000E-01   4.0000E-01   6.0000E-01
```

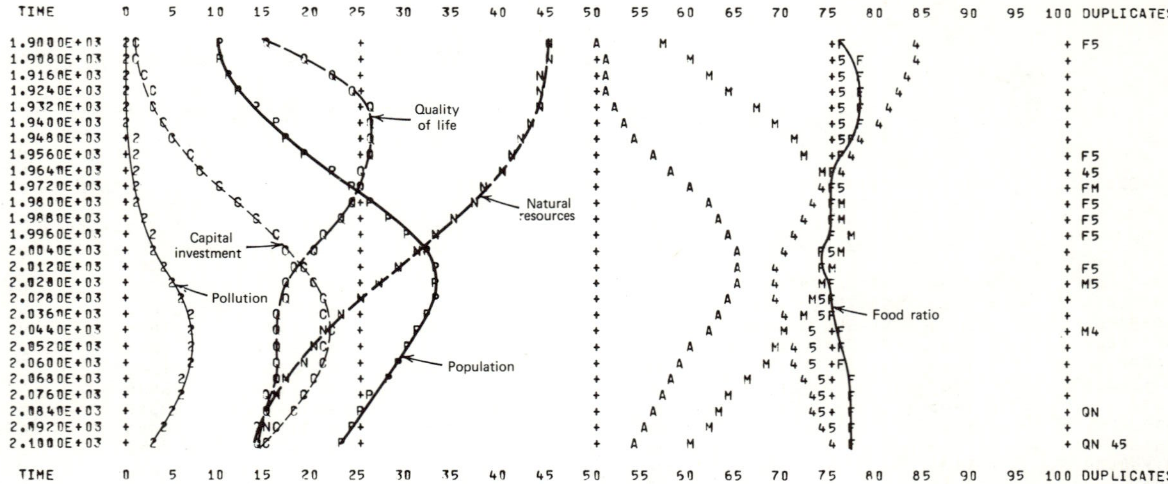


```
OUTPUT   CONSISTS  OF     28 POINT SETS (   239 POINTS)
STORAGE ALLOCATED FOR     28 POINT SETS (   308 WORDS )
STORAGE  NEEDED   FOR     28 POINT SETS (   308 WORDS )
```

Figure 8-9 Plot of dynamic behavior of world model for a birth rate normal value of 0.04.

PLOT NUMBER 1
RUN NUMBER 5

SCALES OF PLOT

P=P	0.	4.0000E+09	8.0000E+09	1.2000E+10	1.6000E+10
2=POLR	0.	2.0000E+01	4.0000E+01	6.0000E+01	8.0000E+01
C=CI	0.	1.0000E+10	2.0000E+10	3.0000E+10	4.0000E+10
Q=QL	0.	1.0000E+00	2.0000E+00	3.0000E+00	4.0000E+00
N=NR	0.	5.0000E+11	1.0000E+12	1.5000E+12	2.0000E+12
F=FR	-2.0000E+00	-1.0000E+00	0.	1.0000E+00	2.0000E+00
M=MSL	-2.0000E+00	-1.0000E+00	0.	1.0000E+00	2.0000E+00
4=QLC	-2.0000E+00	-1.0000E+00	0.	1.0000E+00	2.0000E+00
5=QLP	-2.0000E+00	-1.0000E+00	0.	1.0000E+00	2.0000E+00
A=CIAF	-2.0000E-01	0.	2.0000E-01	4.0000E-01	6.0000E-01

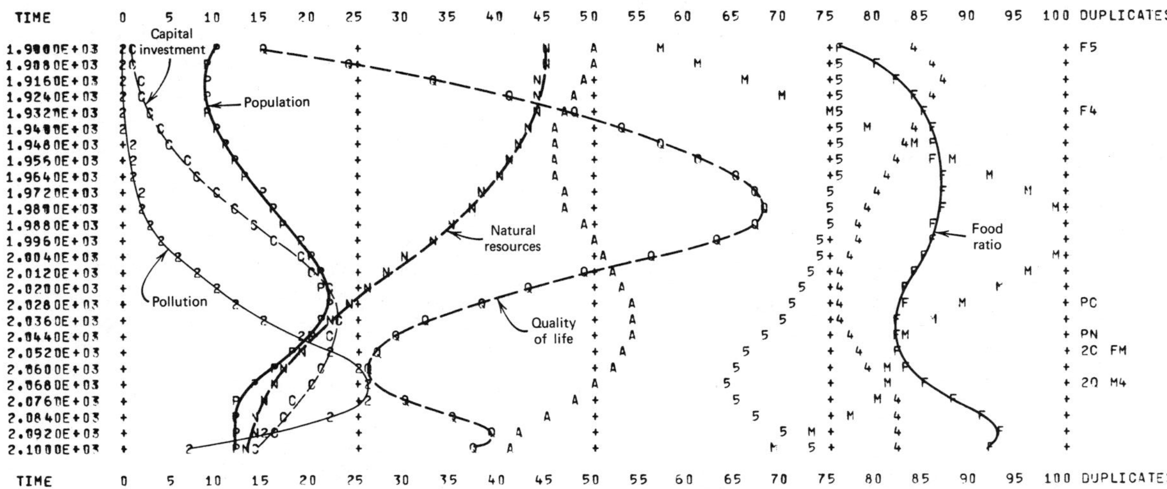

OUTPUT CONSISTS OF 28 POINT SETS (280 POINTS)
STORAGE ALLOCATED FOR 28 POINT SETS (308 WORDS)
STORAGE NEEDED FOR 28 POINT SETS (308 WORDS)

Figure 8-10 Plot of dynamic behavior of world model for a birth rate normal value of 0.02.

Table 8-3 Definition of Variables for Factory, Distributor, and Retail System

Variable	Definition	Initial Values*		
		$j = R$	$j = D$	$j = F$
AIj	Proportionality constant between inventory and average sales at j	8.0	6.0	4.0
CPj	Clerical in-process orders at j	DCR ★ RRI	DCD ★ RRI	DCF ★ RRI
DCj	Delay in clerical order processing at j	3.0	2.0	1.0
DFj	Delay in filling orders at j	a	a	a
DHj	Delay due to minimum handling time required at j	1.0	1.0	1.0
DIj	Delay in inventory adjustment at j	4.0	4.0	4.0
DMj	Delay in order mailing from j	5.0	5.0	6.0
DRj	Delay in smoothing requisitions at j	8.0	8.0	8.0
DTj	Delay in transportation of goods to j	1.0	2.0	—
DUj	Average delay in unfilled orders at j caused by out-of-stock items	0.4	0.6	1.0
IAj	Inventory actual at j	AIR ★ RRI	AID ★ RRI	AIF ★ RRI
IDj	Inventory desired at j	a	a	a
LAj	Pipeline orders actual from j	a	a	a
LDj	Pipeline orders desired in transit to j	a	a	a
MOj	Manufacturing orders per week into factory	—	a	MDF
MTj	Material in transit to j	DTR ★ RRI	DTD ★ RRI	na
NIj	Negative inventory limit rate at j	a	a	a
PDj	Purchasing rate decision at j	r	RRD	—
PMj	Purchase orders in mail from j	DMF ★ RRI	DMD ★ RRI	—
PSj	Purchase orders sent per week from j	PDR	PDD	na
RRj	Requisitions received per week at j	RRI	PSR	PSD

RSj	Requisitions per week smoothed at j (average sales/week)	RRR	RRI	RRI
SRj	Shipments received per week at j	SSD	SSF	MOF
SSj	Shipments sent per week from j	r	RRD	RRF
STj	Shipping rate to be tried at j	a	a	a
UNj	Unfilled orders, normal, at j	a	a	a
UOj	Unfilled orders at j	1.4 ★ RRI	1.6 ★ RRI	2.0 ★ RRI
ALF	Constant specifying manufacturing capacity limit per week at factory	—	—	1000 ★ RRI
DPF	Delay in production lead time at factory	—	—	6.0
MDF	Manufacturing rate decision at factory	—	—	RRF
MWF	Manufacturing rate wanted at factory	—	—	a
OPF	Orders in production at the factory	—	—	DPF ★ RRI

* a = initial value set by auxiliary equation;
r = initial value set by rate component equation;
na = not applicable;
— = not used.

in conjunction with the description of the GASP IV coding, provides the specification of the model of the factory, distributor, and retailer system.

Simulation Objectives

The objective of this example is to analyze a previously developed model to obtain information about its dynamic and extreme behavior.

Special Features

This example further demonstrates that GASP IV is a language that can be used for the coding of Systems Dynamics models. The use of the GASP IV subroutines GDLAY and GTABL are illustrated. GASP IV derivative equations are used to obtain level variables. The computational sequence for this problem, as coded in subroutine STATE, is auxiliaries, rate components, and rates. Levels are automatically obtained by integrating the rates using the RKE integration package. Integration accuracy requirements for the level variables are prescribed.

Simulation Procedure

The coding for this example is, for all practical purposes, a statement-by-statement translation of DYNAMO code to GASP IV code. All the types of statements used in the coding of the factory, distributor, retailer model were presented in Table 8-1. The FORTRAN listing for subroutine STATE is shown in Fig. 8-11. For comparison purposes, the coding in subroutine STATE is divided into sections corresponding to auxiliary equations, rate component equations, and rate (derivative) equations. Throughout this example the variable names defined by Forrester are used. Table 8-4 presents the equivalence between the SS(·) variables and these names. A REAL statement is used in order that implicit integer names need not be changed.

Selected portions of subroutine STATE are now described. The sequence number of statements, as given in Fig. 8-11, is used to identify the location of a statement. When simulated time is greater than zero, the requisitions received at retail is increased by 10% (S-5).

The next set of statements are auxiliary equations dealing with the factory sector. The number of unfilled orders, normal, at factory (UNF) is equal to the estimate of the number of requisitions per week at factory

```
      SUBROUTINE STATE                                                  STB    1
      REAL IAD,IAF,IAR,IDD,IDF,IDR,LAD,LAF,LAR,LDD,LDF,LDR,MDF,MNR,MOD,MREALID 1
     1OF,MTD,MTR,MWF,NID,NIF,NIR,MPF                                    REALID 2
      COMMON /GCOM1/ ATRIB(25),JEVNT,MFA,MFE(100),MLE(100),MSTOP,NCRDR,NGCOM1  1
     1NAPO,NNAPT,NNATR,NNFIL,NNQ(100),NNTRY,NPRNT,PPARM(50,4),TNOW,TTBEGGCOM1  2
     2,TTCLR,TTFIN,TTRIB(25),TTSET                                      GCOM1  3
      COMMON /GCOM2/ DD(100),DDL(100),DTFUL,DTNOW,ISEES,LFLAG(50),NFLAG,GCOM2  1
     1NNEQD,NNEQS,NNEQT,SS(100),SSL(100),TTNEX                          GCOM2  2
      COMMON /UCOM1/ AID,AIF,AIR,ALF,DCD,DCF,DCR,DFD,DFF,DFR,DHD,DHF,DHRUCOM1  1
     1,DID,DIF,DIR,DMD,DMR,DPF,DRD,DRF,DRR,DTD,DTR,DUD,DUF,DUR,IDD,IDF,IUCOM1  2
     2DR,LAD,LAF,LAR,LDD,LDF,LDR,MDF,MNR,MOD,MWF,NID,NIF,NIR,PDD,PDR,RDRUCOM1  3
     3,SSD,SSF,SSR,STD,STF,STR,UND,UNF,UNR,RRR,RRI,DMF                  UCOM1  4
      EQUIVALENCE (UOR,SS(1)),(IAR,SS(2)),(RSR,SS(3)),(CPR,SS(4)),(PMR,SUSEQV  1
     1S(5)),(MTR,SS(6)),(UOD,SS(7)),(IAD,SS(8)),(RSD,SS(9)),(CPD,SS(10))USEQV  2
     2,(PMD,SS(11)),(MTD,SS(12)),(UOF,SS(13)),(IAF,SS(14)),(RSF,SS(15)),USEQV  3
     3(CPF,SS(16)),(OPF,SS(17)),(PSR,SS(20)),(RRD,SS(23)),(SRR,SS(26)),(USEQV  4
     4PSD,SS(29)),(RRF,SS(32)),(SRD,SS(35)),(MOF,SS(38)),(SRF,SS(41))   USEQV  5
C                                                                       STB    2
C*****INPUT TEST FUNCTIONS                                              STB    3
C                                                                       STB    4
      IF (TNOW.GT.0.0) RRR=1.1*RRI                                      STB    5
C                                                                       STB    6
C*****AUXILIARY EQUATIONS                                               STB    7
C                                                                       STB    8
      UNF=RSF*(DHF+DUF)                                                 STB    9
      LAF=CPF+OPF                                                       STB   10
      LDF=RSF*(DCF+DPF)                                                 STB   11
      IDF=AIF*RSF                                                       STB   12
      MWF=RRF+(1./DIF)*(IDF-IAF+LDF-LAF+UOF-UNF)                        STB   13
      DFF=DUF*IDF/IAF+DHF                                               STB   14
      NIF=IAF/DTFUL                                                     STB   15
      STF=UOF/DFF                                                       STB   16
      UND=RSD*(DHD+DUD)                                                 STB   17
      LAD=CPD+PMD+UOF+MTD                                               STB   18
      LDD=RSD*(DCD+DMD+DFF+DTD)                                         STB   19
      IDD=AID*RSD                                                       STB   20
      MPF=DUF*IDF                                                       STB   21
      DFF=(MPF/IAF)+DHF                                                 STB   22
      MOD=DUD*IDD                                                       STB   23
      DFD=(MOD/IAD)+DHD                                                 STB   24
      NID=IAD/DTFUL                                                     STB   25
      STD=UOD/DFD                                                       STB   26
      UNR=RSR*(DHR+DUR)                                                 STB   27
      LAR=CPR+PMR+UOD+MTR                                               STB   28
      LDR=RSR*(DCR+DMR+DFD+DTR)                                         STB   29
      IDR=AIR*RSR                                                       STB   30
      DFR=DUR*IDR/IAR+DHR                                               STB   31
      NIR=IAR/DTFUL                                                     STB   32
      STR=UOR/DFR                                                       STB   33
```

Figure 8-11 FORTRAN listing of subroutine STATE (Example 11).

(smoothed), times the sum of the minimum handling delay at the factory, and the average delay in unfilled orders at the factory caused by out-of-stock items (S-9). The actual pipeline orders from the factory (LAF) is set equal to the sum of the clerical in-process orders at the factory (CPF) and the orders in production at the factory (OPF) (S-10). The pipeline orders desired in transit to the factory (LDF) is the product of the requisitions per week smoothed at the factory (RSF) and the sum of the delays due to clerical order processing at factory (DCF) and the production lead time at the factory (DPF) (S-11). The inventory desired at the factory (IDF) is the product of the proportionality constant between inventory and average sales at the factory (AIF)

```
C
C*****RATE COMPONENTS.
C
      SSR=STR
      IF (NIR.LT.STR) SSR=NIR
      PDR=RRR+(1./DIR)*(IDR-IAR+LDR-LAR+UOR-UNR)
      CALL GDLAY (18,20,PDR,DCR)
      CALL GDLAY (21,23,PSR,DMR)
      PDD=RRD+(1./DID)*(IDD-IAD+LDD-LAD+UOD-UND)
      SSD=STD
      IF (NID.LT.STD) SSD=NID
      CALL GDLAY (24,26,SSD,DTR)
      CALL GDLAY (27,29,PDD,DCD)
      CALL GDLAY (30,32,PSD,DMD)
      SSF=STF
      IF (NIF.LT.STF) SSF=NIF
      CALL GDLAY (33,35,SSF,DTD)
      MDF=MWF
      IF (ALF.LT.MWF) MDF=ALF
      CALL GDLAY (36,38,MDF,DCF)
      CALL GDLAY (39,41,MOF,DPF)
C
C*****RATE EQUATIONS.
C
      DD( 1)=RRR-SSR
      DD( 2)=SRR-SSR
      DD( 3)=(1./DRR)*(RPR-RSR)
      DD( 4)=PDR-PSR
      DD( 5)=PSR-RRD
      DD( 6)=SSD-SRR
      DD( 7)=RRD-SSD
      DD( 8)=SRD-SSD
      DD( 9)=(1./DRD)*(RRD-RSD)
      DD( 10)=PDD-PSD
      DD( 11)=PSD-RRF
      DD( 12)=SSF-SRD
      DD( 13)=RRF-SSF
      DD( 14)=SRF-SSF
      DD( 15)=(1./DRF)*(RRF-RSF)
      DD( 16)=MDF-MOF
      DD( 17)=MOF-SRF
      RETURN
C
      END
```

Figure 8-11 *(continued)*

and the requisitions per week smoothed at the factory (RSF) (S-12). The manufacturing rate wanted at the factory (MWF) is equal to the requisitions received at the factory (RRF) plus the sum of the differences between desired levels and actual levels of inventory at the factory, in transit to the factory, or on order by the factory, divided by the delay in inventory adjustment at the factory (DIF) (S-13). The delay in filling orders at the factory (DFF) is the sum of the delay caused by out of stock items (DUF) and delay due to minimum handling time (DHF) with the former quantity adjusted by the ratio of the inventory desired to the inventory actual (IDF/IAF) (S-14).

The negative inventory limit rate at the factory is set equal to the inventory actual at the factory divided by a full step size (S-15). Since DTNOW can be zero, it is necessary to use DTFUL rather than DTNOW to obtain a rate over an interval. The shipping rate to be tried at the

Table 8-4 Definition and Equivalence of Variable Names (Example 11)

Variables	Equivalenced Variables	Definition
UOR	SS(1)	Unfilled Orders at Retail
IAR	SS(2)	Inventory Actual at Retail
RSR	SS(3)	Requisitions Smoothed at Retail
CPR	SS(4)	Clerical in-Process orders at Retail
PMR	SS(5)	Purchase orders in Mail from Retail
MTR	SS(6)	Material in Transit to Retail
UOD	SS(7)	Unfilled Orders at Distributor
IAD	SS(8)	Inventory Actual at Distributor
RSD	SS(9)	Requisitions Smoothed at Distributor
CPD	SS(10)	Clerical in-Process orders at Distributor
PMD	SS(11)	Purchase orders in Mail from Distributor
MTD	SS(12)	Material in Transit to Distributor
UOF	SS(13)	Unfilled Orders at Factory
IAF	SS(14)	Inventory Actual at Factory
RSF	SS(15)	Requisitions Smoothed at Factory
CPF	SS(16)	Clerical in-Process orders at Factory
OPF	SS(17)	Orders in Production at Factory
PSR	SS(20)	Purchase orders Sent from Retail
RRD	SS(23)	Requisitions Received at Distributor
SRR	SS(26)	Shipments Received at Retail
PSD	SS(29)	Purchase orders Sent from Distributor
RRF	SS(32)	Requisitions Received at Factory
SRD	SS(35)	Shipments Received at Distributor
MOF	SS(38)	Manufacturing Orders at Factory
SRF	SS(41)	Shipments Received at Factory

factory (STF) is equal to the ratio of the unfilled orders at the factory and the delay in filling orders at the factory (S-16). This completes the description of the auxiliary equations for the factory sector. The auxiliary equations for the distributor and retail sector follow along the same lines as those presented above. Since the intent is not to explain how the model was developed, but to present the equations of the model, the description of the distributor and retail section is bypassed.

The next section of subroutine STATE involves the calculation of rate components. There are three basic types of equations contained in the rate component section for this model: (1) rate components that are limited to prescribed maximum values when specified conditions are exceeded; (2) rate components that are set equal to a basic rate plus a correction factor because of the difference between desired and actual levels; and (3) rate components that are determined as delayed values of other rate components.

The first two statements of the rate components section of subroutine STATE illustrate the calculation of a rate component that is limited in value. If the negative inventory rate at retail NIR is less than the rate to be tried at retail STR, the shipments sent per week from retail SSR is set equal to the negative inventory rate at retail. If this is not the case, SSR is set equal to STR. Two GASP IV statements (S-37) and (S-38) are used to represent the DYNAMO "CLIP function" described above. The purchase rate decision at retail PDR is then set equal to the requisitions received at retail, plus differences between desired and actual inventory and pipeline values, divided by the delay in inventory adjustment at retail DIR (S-39). A rate component computed as a delayed value of another rate component is obtained through the use of the GASP IV variable order delay, subroutine GDLAY.

GDLAY is equivalent to the DYNAMO function DELAY3 when delay times are constant. Consider the delay caused by the statement (S-40): CALL GDLAY (18,20,PDR,DCR). The input to the delay is PDR and the delay constant is DCR. SS(18) and SS(19) correspond to the first and second delay stages and SS(20) is the third stage, which is the output of the delay. Through an EQUIVALENCE statement, PSR = SS(20) and it represents the purchase orders sent from retail, which is related to PDR, the purchase rate decision at retail, through the third order delay. The value of PSR is then used in the computation of the rate of change in purchase orders in mail from retail, PMR, which is calculated in the equation for DD(5).

The equations shown in the rate component section of subroutine STATE involve the three types of calculations described above.

The last section of subroutine STATE involves the calculation of the rate equations based on the rate components. The rate equations are written for the DD(·) variables that prescribe the rate of change of the levels for the system. An equivalence statement relates the model variables to the state variables SS(·). Thus UOR, unfilled orders at retail, is equivalent to SS(1), and DD(1) is the rate of change of unfilled orders at retail. The equation for DD(1) specifies that the rate of change of unfilled orders at retail is equal to the difference between requisitions received at retail per week (RRR) and shipments sent from retail per week (SSR). Rate equations are computed either as algebraic differences of component rates or as differences between levels, which are converted to rates by dividing by a smoothing or averaging time. The rate equations coded in subroutine STATE follow this pattern. The integration of the DD(·) to obtain values for the levels (SS(·)) is automatically accomplished by GASP.

The main program shown in Fig. 8-12 dimensions QSET, sets the card reader and printer numbers, and calls subroutine GASP. Initialization of the non-GASP variables is performed in subroutine INTLC. All of the initial conditions and constants (all DYNAMO type N and C equations) are coded as shown in the FORTRAN listing for subroutine INTLC in Fig. 8-13.

The output for this example is a plot of selected variables over time. The 10 variables to be plotted are recorded in subroutine SSAVE through a call to subroutine GPLOT. The FORTRAN listing for subroutine SSAVE is presented in Fig. 8-14. The input data and GASP IV echo check for this example are shown in Fig. 8-15. The input data consists of one data card type 1, one data card type 2, 11 data cards type 6, one data card type 9, and one data card type 11. No special features are included in the data input for this example.

Simulation Reports

The only outputs illustrated for this example are the table and associated plot for the variables collected in GPLOT. The table output is shown in Fig. 8-16. These values are plotted in Fig. 8-17.

The situation modeled involves an increase in requisitions received at retail, RRR, of 10% after time 0. The dynamic behavior of the other variables of the model is then observed. Because of the increase in RRR, the inventory at retail, IAR (represented by a B on the plot), drops slightly but then increases to a value higher than its initial value. This increase is due to the higher demand rate, which results in more orders from the retail outlet.

The increased demand has an effect on the inventory at the factory,

```
      PROGRAM MAIN (INPUT,OUTPUT,TAPE5=INPUT,TAPE6=OUTPUT)              MXB    1
      DIMENSION NSET(1000)                                              DIM    1
      COMMON QSET(1000)                                                 COM    1
      COMMON /GCOM1/ ATRIB(25),JEVNT,MFA,MFE(100),MLE(100),MSTOP,NCRDR,NGCOM1  1
     1NAPO,NNAPT,NNATR,NNFIL,NNQ(100),NNTRY,NPRNT,PPARM(50,4),TNOW,TTBEGGCOM1  2
     2,TTCLR,TTFIN,TTRIB(25),TTSET                                      GCOM1  3
      EQUIVALENCE(NSET(1),QSET(1))                                      EQUIV  1
      NCRDR=5                                                           MXB    2
      NPRNT=6                                                           MXB    3
      CALL GASP                                                         MXB    4
      CALL EXIT                                                         MXB    5
C                                                                       MXB    6
      END                                                               MXB    7
```

Figure 8-12 FORTRAN listing of main program (Example 11).

```
      SUBROUTINE INTLC                                                  ICB    1
      REAL IAD,IAF,IAR,IDD,IDF,IDR,LAD,LAF,LAR,LDD,LDF,LDR,MDF,MNR,MOD,MREALID 1
     1OF,MTD,MTR,MWF,NID,NIF,NIR,MPF                                    REALID 2
      COMMON /GCOM2/ DD(100),DDL(100),DTFUL,DTNOW,ISEES,LFLAG(50),NFLAG,GCOM2  1
     1NNEQD,NNEQS,NNEQT,SS(100),SSL(100),TTNEX                          GCOM2  2
      COMMON /UCOM1/ AID,AIF,AIR,ALF,DCD,DCF,DCR,DFD,DFF,DFR,DHD,DHF,DHRUCOM1  1
     1,DID,DIF,DIR,DMD,DMR,DPF,DRD,DRF,DRR,DTD,DTR,DUD,DUF,DUR,IDD,IDF,IUCOM1  2
     2DR,LAD,LAF,LAR,LDD,LDF,LDR,MDF,MNR,MOD,MWF,NID,NIF,NIR,PDD,PDR,RDRUCOM1  3
     3,SSD,SSF,SSR,STD,STF,STR,UND,UNF,UNR,RRR,RRI,DMF                  UCOM1  4
      EQUIVALENCE (UOR,SS(1)),(IAR,SS(2)),(RSR,SS(3)),(CPR,SS(4)),(PMR,SUSEQV  1
     1S(5)),(MTR,SS(6)),(UOD,SS(7)),(IAD,SS(8)),(RSD,SS(9)),(CPD,SS(10))USEQV  2
     2,(PMD,SS(11)),(MTD,SS(12)),(UOF,SS(13)),(IAF,SS(14)),(RSF,SS(15)),USEQV  3
     3(CPF,SS(16)),(OPF,SS(17)),(PSR,SS(20)),(RRD,SS(23)),(SRR,SS(26)),(USEQV  4
     4PSD,SS(29)),(RRF,SS(32)),(SRD,SS(35)),(MOF,SS(38)),(SRF,SS(41))   USEQV  5
C                                                                       ICB    2
C*****TEST INPUT CONDITIONS                                             ICB    3
C                                                                       ICB    4
      RRI=1000.                                                         ICB    5
C                                                                       ICB    6
C*****PARAMETERS                                                        ICB    7
C                                                                       ICB    8
      AID=6.                                                            ICB    9
      AIF=4.                                                            ICB   10
      AIR=8.                                                            ICB   11
      ALF=1000.*RRI                                                     ICB   12
      DCD=2.                                                            ICB   13
      DCF=1.                                                            ICB   14
      DCR=3.                                                            ICB   15
      DHD=1.                                                            ICB   16
      DHF=1.                                                            ICB   17
      DHR=1.                                                            ICB   18
      DID=4.                                                            ICB   19
      DIF=4.                                                            ICB   20
      DIR=4.                                                            ICB   21
      DMD=.5                                                            ICB   22
      DMR=.5                                                            ICB   23
      DPF=6.                                                            ICB   24
      DRD=8.                                                            ICB   25
      DRF=8.                                                            ICB   26
      DRR=8.                                                            ICB   27
      DTD=2.                                                            ICB   28
      DTR=1.                                                            ICB   29
      DUD=.6                                                            ICB   30
      DUF=1.                                                            ICB   31
      DUR=.4                                                            ICB   32
C                                                                       ICB   33
C*****INITIAL CONDITIONS                                                ICB   34
C                                                                       ICB   35
      RRR=RRI                                                           ICB   36
      UOR=RRI*(DHR+DUR)                                                 ICB   37
      IAR=AIR*RRI                                                       ICB   38
      RSR=RRR                                                           ICB   39
      CPR=DCR*RRI                                                       ICB   40
      PDR=RRR                                                           ICB   41
      PSR=PDR                                                           ICB   42
      RRD=PSR                                                           ICB   43
      PMR=DMR*RRI                                                       ICB   44
      MTR=DTR*RRI                                                       ICB   45
      SSD=RRD                                                           ICB   46
      UOD=RRI*(DHD+DUD)                                                 ICB   47
      IAD=AID*RRI                                                       ICB   48
      RSD=RRI                                                           ICB   49
      CPD=DCD*RRI                                                       ICB   50
      PDD=RRD                                                           ICB   51
      PSD=PDD                                                           ICB   52
      RRF=PSD                                                           ICB   53
      PMD=DMD*RRI                                                       ICB   54
      MTD=DTD*RRI                                                       ICB   55
      SSF=RRF                                                           ICB   56
      MDF=RRF                                                           ICB   57
      UOF=RRI*(DHF+DUF)                                                 ICB   58
      IAF=AIF*RRI                                                       ICB   59
```

Figure 8-13 FORTRAN listing of subroutine INTLC (Example 11).

```
      RSF=RRI                                                           ICB   60
      CPF=DCF*RRI                                                       ICB   61
      OPF=DPF*RRI                                                       ICB   62
      SSR=RRR                                                           ICB   63
      SRR=SSD                                                           ICB   64
      SRD=SSF                                                           ICB   65
      MOF=MDF                                                           ICB   66
      SRF=MOF                                                           ICB   67
      RETURN                                                            ICB   68
C                                                                       ICB   69
      END                                                               ICB   70
```

Figure 8-13 *(continued)*

```
      SUBROUTINE SSAVE                                                  SVB    1
      REAL IAD,IAF,IAR,IDD,IDF,IDR,LAD,LAF,LAR,LDD,LDF,LDR,MDF,MNR,MOD,MREALID 1
     1OF,MTD,MTR,MWF,NID,NIF,NIR,MPF                                    REALID 2
      DIMENSION PLOT(10)                                                SVB    2
      COMMON /GCOM1/ ATRIB(25),JEVNT,MFA,MFE(100),MLE(100),MSTOP,NCRDR,NGCOM1  1
     1NAPO,NNAPT,NNATR,NNFIL,NNQ(100),NNTRY,NPRNT,PPARM(50,4),TNOW,TTBEGGCOM1  2
     2,TTCLR,TTFIN,TTRIB(25),TTSET                                      GCOM1  3
      COMMON /GCOM2/ DD(100),DDL(100),DTFUL,DTNOW,ISEES,LFLAG(50),NFLAG,GCOM2  1
     1NNEQD,NNEQS,NNEQT,SS(100),SSL(100),TTNEX                          GCOM2  2
      COMMON /UCOM1/ AID,AIF,AIR,ALF,DCD,DCF,DCR,DFD,DFF,DFR,DHD,DHF,DHRUCOM1  1
     1,DID,DIF,DIR,DMD,DMR,DPF,DRD,DRF,DRR,DTD,DTR,DUD,DUF,DUR,IDD,IDF,IUCOM1  2
     2DR,LAD,LAF,LAR,LDD,LDF,LDR,MDF,MNR,MOD,MWF,NID,NIF,NIR,PDD,PDR,RDRUCOM1  3
     3,SSD,SSF,SSR,STD,STF,STR,UND,UNF,UNR,RRR,RRI,DMF                  UCOM1  4
      EQUIVALENCE (UDR,SS(1)),(IAR,SS(2)),(RSR,SS(3)),(CPR,SS(4)),(PMR,SUSEQV  1
     1S(5)),(MTR,SS(6)),(UOD,SS(7)),(IAD,SS(8)),(RSD,SS(9)),(CPD,SS(10))USEQV  2
     2,(PMD,SS(11)),(MTD,SS(12)),(UOF,SS(13)),(IAF,SS(14)),(RSF,SS(15)),USEQV  3
     3(CPF,SS(16)),(OPF,SS(17)),(PSR,SS(20)),(RRD,SS(23)),(SRR,SS(26)),(USEQV  4
     4PSD,SS(29)),(RRF,SS(32)),(SRD,SS(35)),(MOF,SS(38)),(SRF,SS(41))   USEQV  5
      PLOT(1)=RRR                                                       SVB    3
      PLOT(2)=RRD                                                       SVB    4
      PLOT(3)=RRF                                                       SVB    5
      PLOT(4)=MOF                                                       SVB    6
      PLOT(5)=SRF                                                       SVB    7
      PLOT(6)=IAF                                                       SVB    8
      PLOT(7)=UOF                                                       SVB    9
      PLOT(8)=IAD                                                       SVB   10
      PLOT(9)=IAR                                                       SVB   11
      PLOT(10)=DFF                                                      SVB   12
      CALL GPLOT (PLOT,TNOW,1)                                          SVB   13
      RETURN                                                            SVB   14
C                                                                       SVB   15
      END                                                               SVB   16
```

Figure 8-14 FORTRAN listing of subroutine SSAVE (Example 11).

IAF (represented by an A on the plot), which is delayed as a result of the delay time in requisitions reaching the factory. Again the inventory at the factory attains a value greater than the initial inventory at the factory because of the increased demand. The other variables illustrated in the plot of Fig. 8-17 reflect the dynamic behavior of the system in response to an increase in demand. The plots agree with those obtained by DYNAMO as presented by Forrester (36).

Table 8-5 illustrates the type of statistical information that can be extracted from the table and plot. It shows that the model behavior reflects a 44% increase in factory output, 21 weeks after a 10% increase in demand occurs. Table 8-6 presents minimum and maximum inventory levels following the 10% increase in demand. As can be seen, small input changes can result in significant changes in the dynamic behavior of the model.

```
PRITSKER          11     6    30 1973     1                                   |  1
     0     0     0     0     1     5     0     0     0 1000    41     0     0       |  2
6A          1TIME                  0    10     2        1.                         |
6B          1RRRR           1      1          0.     2000.                         |
6B          2DRRD           1      1          0.     2000.                         |
6B          3FRRF           1      1          0.     2000.                         |
6B          4MMOF           1      1          0.     2000.                         |  6
6B          5SSRF           1      1          0.     2000.                         |
6B          6AIAF           1      1          0.    10000.                         |
6B          7UUOF           1      1          0.    10000.                         |
6B          8CIAD           1      1          0.    10000.                         |
6B          9BIAR           1      1          0.    10000.                         |
6B         1 0WDFF          1      1          0.       10.                         |
     0     0          0.           0.        .01        1.          1.             |  9
     1     1     1     0          -4.        75.     0     0     0     0     0     0  | 11
```

Figure 8-15 Listing of data input cards and GASP IV echo check (Example 11).

```
                         SIMULATION PROJECT NUMBER  11  BY  PRITSKER

                         DATE  6/ 30/ 1973        RUN NUMBER    1 OF    1
                         LLSUP=00000000000000     GASP IV VERSION 23JUN73

NNCLT=     0    NNSTA=     0    NNHIS=     0    NNPRM=     0    NNPLT=     1    NNSTR=     5    NNTRY=     0
NNATR=     0    NNFIL=     0    NNSET=  1000    NNEQD=    41    NNEQS=     0    NFLAG=     0

GPLOT NO.  1    LLABP=TIME      IITAP=     0    NNVAR=    10    LLPLT=     2              DTPLT=     1.0000E+00
  VAR NO.  1         R=RRR      LLPLO=     1    LLPHI=     1    PPLO =     0.             PPHI =     2.0000E+03
  VAR NO.  2         D=PRD      LLPLO=     1    LLPHI=     1    PPLO =     0.             PPHI =     2.0000E+03
  VAR NO.  3         F=RRF      LLPLO=     1    LLPHI=     1    PPLO =     0.             PPHI =     2.0000E+03
  VAR NO.  4         M=MOF      LLPLO=     1    LLPHI=     1    PPLO =     0.             PPHI =     2.0000E+03
  VAR NO.  5         S=SRF      LLPLO=     1    LLPHI=     1    PPLO =     0.             PPHI =     2.0000E+03
  VAR NO.  6         A=IAF      LLPLO=     1    LLPHI=     1    PPLO =     0.             PPHI =     1.0000E+04
  VAR NO.  7         U=UOF      LLPLO=     1    LLPHI=     1    PPLO =     0.             PPHI =     1.0000E+04
  VAR NO.  8         C=IAD      LLPLO=     1    LLPHI=     1    PPLO =     0.             PPHI =     1.0000E+04
  VAR NO.  9         B=IAR      LLPLO=     1    LLPHI=     1    PPLO =     0.             PPHI =     1.0000E+04
  VAR NO. 10         W=DFF      LLPLO=     1    LLPHI=     1    PPLO =     0.             PPHI =     1.0000E+01

IIEVT=     0    LLFRR=     0    AAERR=     1.0000E-05          RRERR=     1.0000E-05
DTMIN=     1.0000E-02           DTMAX=     1.0000E+00          DTSAV=     1.0000E+00

MSTOP=     1    JJCLR=     1    JJBEG=     1    IICRD=     0    TTBEG=    -4.0000E+00    TTFIN=     7.5000E+01
JJFIL=     0
IISED=     0               0               0               0               0
```

Figure 8-15 *(continued)*

TABLE NUMBER 1
RUN NUMBER 1

TIME	PPR	RRD	RRF	MOF	SRF	IAF	UOF	IAD	IAR	DFF
-4.0000E+00	1.0000E+03	1.0000E+03	1.0000E+03	1.0000E+03	1.0000E+03	4.0000E+03	2.0000E+03	6.0000E+03	8.0000E+03	2.0000E+00
-4.0000E+00	1.0000E+03	1.0000E+03	1.0000E+03	1.0000E+03	1.0000E+03	4.0000E+03	2.0000E+03	6.0000E+03	8.0000E+03	2.0000E+00
-3.0000E+00	1.0000E+03	1.0000E+03	1.0000E+03	1.0000E+03	1.0000E+03	4.0000E+03	2.0000E+03	6.0000E+03	8.0000E+03	2.0000E+00
-2.0000E+00	1.0000E+03	1.0000E+03	1.0000E+03	1.0000E+03	1.0000E+03	4.0000E+03	2.0000E+03	6.0000E+03	8.0000E+03	2.0000E+00
-1.0000E+00	1.0000E+03	1.0000E+03	1.0000E+03	1.0000E+03	1.0000E+03	4.0000E+03	2.0000E+03	6.0000E+03	8.0000E+03	2.0000E+00
0.	1.0000E+03	1.0000E+03	1.0000E+03	1.0000E+03	1.0000E+03	4.0000E+03	2.0000E+03	6.0000E+03	8.0000E+03	2.0000E+00
1.0000E+00	1.1000E+03	1.0024E+03	1.0000E+03	1.0000E+03	1.0000E+03	4.0000E+03	2.0000E+03	6.0000E+03	8.0000E+03	2.0000E+00
2.0000E+00	1.1000E+03	1.0229E+03	1.0004E+03	1.0000E+03	1.0000E+03	4.0000E+03	2.0001E+03	6.0000E+03	7.9732E+03	2.0000E+00
3.0000E+00	1.1000E+03	1.0587E+03	1.0058E+03	1.0011E+03	1.0000E+03	3.9997E+03	2.0022E+03	5.9980E+03	7.9131E+03	2.0000E+00
4.0000E+00	1.1000E+03	1.0954E+03	1.0245E+03	1.0087E+03	1.0001E+03	3.9970E+03	2.0133E+03	5.9861E+03	7.8398E+03	2.0004E+00
5.0000E+00	1.1000E+03	1.1259E+03	1.0591E+03	1.0317E+03	1.0005E+03	3.9869E+03	2.0435E+03	5.9548E+03	7.7690E+03	2.0027E+00
6.0000E+00	1.1000E+03	1.1485E+03	1.1046E+03	1.0744E+03	1.0022E+03	3.9621E+03	2.0988E+03	5.8398E+03	7.7130E+03	2.0098E+00
7.0000E+00	1.1000E+03	1.1642E+03	1.1536E+03	1.1338E+03	1.0071E+03	3.9173E+03	2.1788E+03	5.8239E+03	7.6781E+03	2.0250E+00
8.0000E+00	1.1000E+03	1.1744E+03	1.2002E+03	1.2023E+03	1.0173E+03	3.8517E+03	2.2789E+03	5.7354E+03	7.6653E+03	2.0505E+00
9.0000E+00	1.1000E+03	1.1805E+03	1.2410E+03	1.2721E+03	1.0350E+03	3.7699E+03	2.3928E+03	5.6448E+03	7.6724E+03	2.0866E+00
1.0000E+01	1.1000E+03	1.1836E+03	1.2747E+03	1.3373E+03	1.0610E+03	3.6802E+03	2.5143E+03	5.5622E+03	7.6957E+03	2.1320E+00
1.1000E+01	1.1000E+03	1.1842E+03	1.3008E+03	1.3939E+03	1.0954E+03	3.5930E+03	2.6378E+03	5.4949E+03	7.7320E+03	2.1841E+00
1.2000E+01	1.1000E+03	1.1829E+03	1.3196E+03	1.4397E+03	1.1367E+03	3.5177E+03	2.7578E+03	5.4473E+03	7.7783E+03	2.2389E+00
1.3000E+01	1.1000E+03	1.1801E+03	1.3311E+03	1.4735E+03	1.1828E+03	3.4620E+03	2.8686E+03	5.4215E+03	7.8325E+03	2.2919E+00
1.4000E+01	1.1000E+03	1.1760E+03	1.3355E+03	1.4949E+03	1.2312E+03	3.4312E+03	2.9647E+03	5.4181E+03	7.8927E+03	2.3384E+00
1.5000E+01	1.1000E+03	1.1709E+03	1.3331E+03	1.5036E+03	1.2790E+03	3.4277E+03	3.0409E+03	5.4370E+03	7.9575E+03	2.3745E+00
1.6000E+01	1.1000E+03	1.1650E+03	1.3242E+03	1.5000E+03	1.3238E+03	3.4521E+03	3.0927E+03	5.4780E+03	8.0255E+03	2.3973E+00
1.7000E+01	1.1000E+03	1.1586E+03	1.3093E+03	1.4845E+03	1.3634E+03	3.5033E+03	3.1170E+03	5.5405E+03	8.0954E+03	2.4053E+00

1.8000E+01	1.1000E+03	1.1520E+03	1.2893E+03	1.4582E+03	1.3960E+03	3.5793E+03	3.1123E+03	5.7270E+03	8.2364E+03	2.3789E+00
1.9000E+01	1.1000E+03	1.1452E+03	1.2654E+03	1.4225E+03	1.4202E+03	3.6776E+03	3.0795E+03	5.8472E+03	8.3054E+03	2.3476E+00
2.0000E+01	1.1000E+03	1.1384E+03	1.2388E+03	1.3792E+03	1.4353E+03	3.7951E+03	3.0208E+03	5.9816E+03	8.3721E+03	2.3074E+00
2.1000E+01	1.1000E+03	1.1318E+03	1.2108E+03	1.3305E+03	1.4407E+03	3.9286E+03	2.9404E+03	6.1260E+03	8.4355E+03	2.2611E+00
2.2000E+01	1.1000E+03	1.1256E+03	1.1827E+03	1.2787E+03	1.4365E+03	4.0743E+03	2.8435E+03	6.2757E+03	8.4947E+03	2.2112E+00
2.3000E+01	1.1000E+03	1.1199E+03	1.1555E+03	1.2258E+03	1.4231E+03	4.2282E+03	2.7358E+03	6.4255E+03	8.5491E+03	2.1599E+00
2.4000E+01	1.1000E+03	1.1148E+03	1.1302E+03	1.1742E+03	1.4015E+03	4.3858E+03	2.6231E+03	6.5702E+03	8.5979E+03	2.1092E+00
2.5000E+01	1.1000E+03	1.1103E+03	1.1075E+03	1.1254E+03	1.3728E+03	4.5424E+03	2.5106E+03	6.7049E+03	8.6408E+03	2.0609E+00
2.6000E+01	1.1000E+03	1.1065E+03	1.0877E+03	1.0811E+03	1.3384E+03	4.6933E+03	2.4029E+03	6.8255E+03	8.6776E+03	2.0160E+00
2.7000E+01	1.1000E+03	1.1035E+03	1.0713E+03	1.0424E+03	1.2998E+03	4.8339E+03	2.3033E+03	6.9289E+03	8.7082E+03	1.9754E+00
2.8000E+01	1.1000E+03	1.1011E+03	1.0583E+03	1.0099E+03	1.2588E+03	4.9598E+03	2.2143E+03	7.0129E+03	8.7330E+03	1.9398E+00
2.9000E+01	1.1000E+03	1.0994E+03	1.0487E+03	9.8399E+02	1.2168E+03	5.0674E+03	2.1373E+03	7.0768E+03	8.7523E+03	1.9095E+00
3.0000E+01	1.1000E+03	1.0982E+03	1.0422E+03	9.6479E+02	1.1754E+03	5.1540E+03	2.0731E+03	7.1205E+03	8.7668E+03	1.8844E+00
3.1000E+01	1.1000E+03	1.0976E+03	1.0387E+03	9.5206E+02	1.1360E+03	5.2176E+03	2.0215E+03	7.1454E+03	8.7769E+03	1.8647E+00
3.2000E+01	1.1000E+03	1.0974E+03	1.0377E+03	9.4536E+02	1.0996E+03	5.2577E+03	1.9820E+03	7.1530E+03	8.7834E+03	1.8501E+00
3.3000E+01	1.1000E+03	1.0975E+03	1.0388E+03	9.4407E+02	1.0670E+03	5.2744E+03	1.9538E+03	7.1456E+03	8.7869E+03	1.8403E+00
3.4000E+01	1.1000E+03	1.0979E+03	1.0418E+03	9.4750E+02	1.0391E+03	5.2690E+03	1.9359E+03	7.1258E+03	8.7881E+03	1.8351E+00
3.5000E+01	1.1000E+03	1.0985E+03	1.0462E+03	9.5488E+02	1.0161E+03	5.2435E+03	1.9272E+03	7.0960E+03	8.7875E+03	1.8341E+00
3.6000E+01	1.1000E+03	1.0992E+03	1.0516E+03	9.6541E+02	9.9815E+02	5.2006E+03	1.9265E+03	7.0588E+03	8.7857E+03	1.8370E+00
3.7000E+01	1.1000E+03	1.0999E+03	1.0578E+03	9.7833E+02	9.8527E+02	5.1435E+03	1.9327E+03	7.0163E+03	8.7831E+03	1.8432E+00
3.8000E+01	1.1000E+03	1.1007E+03	1.0645E+03	9.9290E+02	9.7721E+02	5.0753E+03	1.9447E+03	6.9707E+03	8.7800E+03	1.8524E+00
3.9000E+01	1.1000E+03	1.1014E+03	1.0713E+03	1.0085E+03	9.7361E+02	4.9993E+03	1.9616E+03	6.9236E+03	8.7769E+03	1.8641E+00
4.0000E+01	1.1000E+03	1.1021E+03	1.0780E+03	1.0244E+03	9.7400E+02	4.9189E+03	1.9823E+03	6.8766E+03	8.7739E+03	1.8777E+00
		⋮			⋮			⋮		
MINIMUM	1.0000E+03	1.0000E+03	1.0000E+03	9.4407E+02	9.7361E+02	3.4277E+03	1.9265E+03	5.4181E+03	7.6653E+03	1.8341E+00
MAXIMUM	1.1000E+03	1.1842E+03	1.3355E+03	1.5036E+03	1.4407E+03	5.2744E+03	3.1170E+03	7.1530E+03	8.8031E+03	2.4053E+00

Figure 8-16 Tabular output of state variables for retailer, warehouse, and factory model.

PLOT NUMBER 1
RUN NUMBER 1

SCALES OF PLOT

R=RRR	0.	5.0000E+02	1.0000E+03	1.5000E+03	2.0000E+03
D=RRD	0.	5.0000E+02	1.0000E+03	1.5000E+03	2.0000E+03
F=RRF	0.	5.0000E+02	1.0000E+03	1.5000E+03	2.0000E+03
M=MOF	0.	5.0000E+02	1.0000E+03	1.5000E+03	2.0000E+03
S=SRF	0.	5.0000E+02	1.0000E+03	1.5000E+03	2.0000E+03
A=IAF	0.	2.5000E+03	5.0000E+03	7.5000E+03	1.0000E+04
U=UOF	0.	2.5000E+03	5.0000E+03	7.5000E+03	1.0000E+04
C=IAD	0.	2.5000E+03	5.0000E+03	7.5000E+03	1.0000E+04
B=IAR	0.	2.5000E+03	5.0000E+03	7.5000E+03	1.0000E+04
W=DFF	0.	2.5000E+00	5.0000E+00	7.5000E+00	1.0000E+01

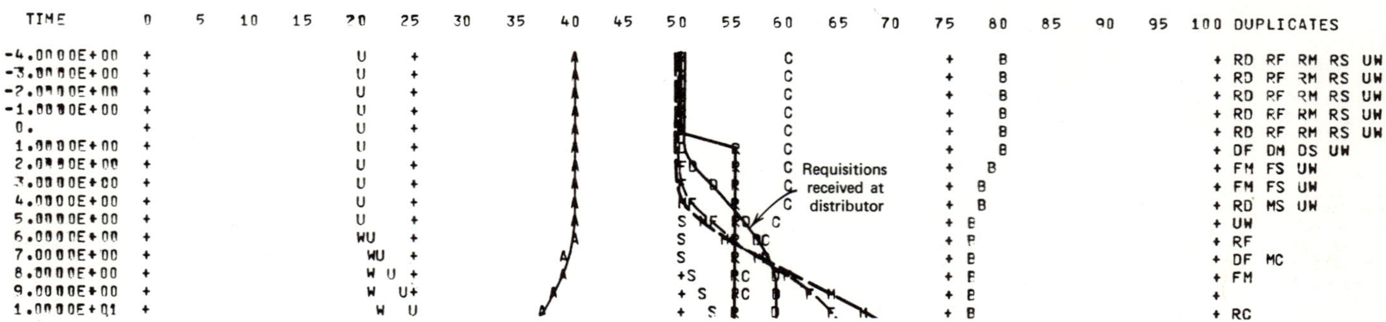

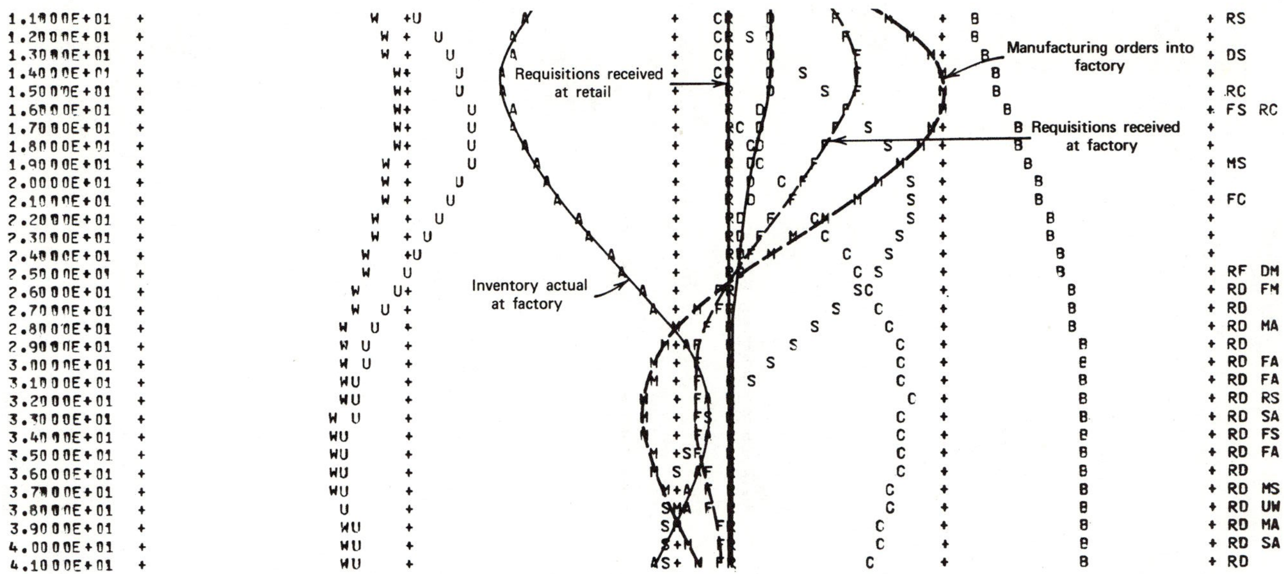

Figure 8-17. Plot of dynamic behavior of state variables for retailer, warehouse, factory model.

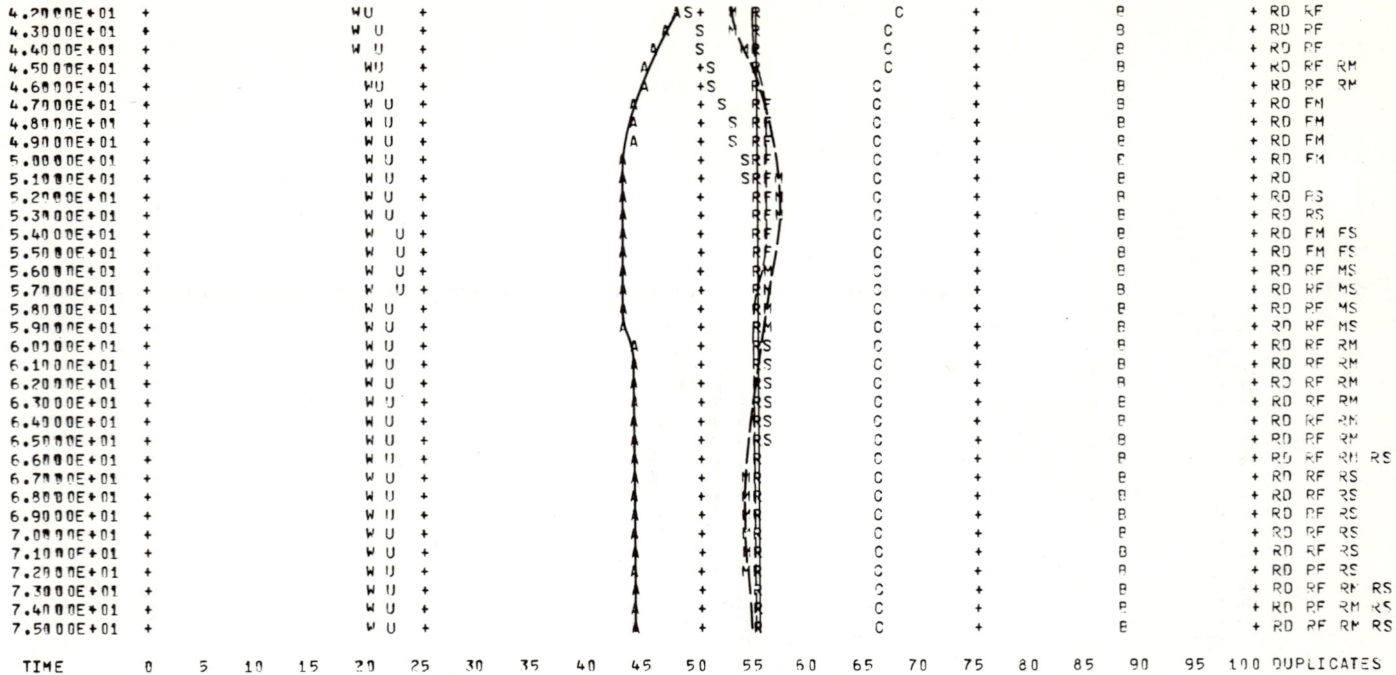


```
OUTPUT   CONSISTS   OF      82 POINT SETS (   820 POINTS)
STORAGE  ALLOCATED  FOR     90 POINT SETS (   990 WORDS )
STORAGE  NEEDED     FOR     82 POINT SETS (   902 WORDS )
```

Figure 8-17 *(continued)*

Table 8-5 Peak Order and Production Rates Following 10% Demand Increase

Variable	Initial Value	Peak Value	Percentage Change	Time of Peak Value Occurrence
Retail Demand, RRR	1000	1100	10.0	Constant
Distributor Demand, RRD	1000	1336	33.6	14
Factory Demand, RRF	1000	1180	11.8	11
Manufacturing orders, MOF	1000	1504	50.4	15
Manufacturing output, SRF	1000	1441	44.1	21

Table 8-6 Minimum, Maximum, and Final Inventory Levels Following 10% Demand Increase

Variable	Initial Value	Minimum Value	Percentage Change	Maximum Value	Percentage Change
Retail Inventory, IAR	8000	7665	4.2	8803	10.4
Distributor Inventory, IAD	6000	5418	9.7	7153	19.2
Factory Inventory, IAF	4000	3428	14.3	5274	31.8

EXERCISES

8-1. Run the World Dynamics model for 500 years to determine if steady state conditions are reached.

8-2. In the world model of Example 10, consider the inclusion of wars that occur every 30 years on the average. The time between wars is exponentially distributed. The length of the war is uniformly distributed between 0 and 10 years. For each ongoing war, the death rate is increased by 2% and the birth rate is decreased by 1%. The yearly depletion of natural resources is increased by 20%. Following a war, the birth rate is increased by 5% for the first 5 years following the war. Examine the behavior of the model for a 200 year period.

8-3. Use GASP IV to analyze Forrester's model of urban dynamics (37).

8-4. Convert Exercise 5-20 to a Systems Dynamics format. Use GASP IV to obtain the dynamic behavior of the converted model.

8-5. For the Industrial Dynamics model, Example 11, assume that the requisitions at retail are normally distributed about the initial value with a standard deviation of 10% of the initial value. Perform the simulation to assess the dynamic behavior of the model.

8-6. For the industrial dynamics example, assume that the demand rate is a function of the unfilled orders at retail as shown in the following table:

Unfilled Orders at Retail, UOR	Increase in Requisitions Received at Retail, RRR (%)
1200	30.00
1250	15.00
1300	10.00
1350	5.00
1400	0.00
1450	−5.00
1500	−10.00
1550	−15.00
1600	−30.00

When the inventory at the factory warehouse exceeds the initial inventory at the factory warehouse by 25%, production at the factory is stopped. Production at the factory does not start again until the inventory at the factory warehouse drops to a value that is 10% above its initial inventory level. If the inventory at the factory warehouse drops to 80% of its initial value, an order is subcontracted to an alternate producer for 1000 units. The time required to obtain these units is Gamma-distributed with the following parameters: mean = 10 weeks and standard deviation of 2 weeks. Simulate the industrial dynamics situation as presented in Example 11 with the new features presented above. Collect statistics on the number of times production is halted, the number of times subcontracting was required, and any other statistical measures that will help you analyze the system.

8-7. Select a problem from *Problems in Industrial Dynamics* (60) and perform a simulation for the problem using GASP IV.

8-8. Select one of the papers in *Toward Global Equilibrium: Collected Papers* (87) and perform a simulation using GASP IV.

References and Bibliography

1. Abramowitz, M., and I. A. Stegun, Eds., *Handbook of Mathematical Functions,* Applied Mathematics Series 55, Washington, D.C.: National Bureau of Standards, 1964.
2. American National Standards Institute, *American National Standard Basic FORTRAN,* ANSI X3.10-1966.
3. American National Standards Institute, *American National Standard FORTRAN,* ANSI X3.9-1966.
4. Ashour, S., and S. G. Bindingnavle, "An Optimal Design of a Soaking Pit Rolling Mill System," *SIMULATION,* Vol. 19, June 1972, pp. 207–214.
5. Ashour, S., and S. D. Vaswani, "A GASP Simulation Study of Job-Shop Scheduling," *SIMULATION,* Vol. 19, January 1972, pp. 1–10.
6. *ASTRA, GE-400 Series Resource Allocation, Reference Manual,* CPB 1157, November 1965.
7. Berman, M. B., "Generating Random Variates from Gamma Distributions with Non-Integer Shape Parameters," The Rand Corporation, R-641-PR, Santa Monica, Calif., November 1970.
8. *Bibliography on Simulation,* New York: IBM Corp., 320-0924-0, 1966.
9. Box, G. E. P., and M. E. Muller, "A Note on the Generation of Random Normal Deviates," *Am. Math. Stat.,* Vol. 29, 1958, pp. 610–611.
10. Brennan, R. D., and R. N. Linebarger. "A Survey of Digital Simulation: Digital Analog Simulator Programs," *SIMULATION,* Vol. 3, No. 6, December 1964, pp. 22–36.
11. Buchan, J., and E. Koenigsburg, *Scientific Inventory Management,* Englewood Cliffs, N.J.: Prentice-Hall, Inc., 1963.
12. Burr, I. W., "A Useful Approximation to the Normal Distribution Function, with Application to Simulation," *Technometrics,* Vol. 9, November 1967, pp. 647–651.
13. Burt, J. M., Jr., and M. Garman, "Monte Carlo Techniques for Stochastic Network Analysis," *Fourth Conference on the Applications of Simulation,* December 9–11, 1970, pp. 146–153.
14. Burt, J. M., Jr., D. P. Gaver, and M. Perlas, 'Simple Stochastic Networks: Some Problems and Procedures," *Nav. Res. Logist. Quart.,* Vol. 17, December 1970, pp. 439–460.

15. Buxton, J. N., *Simulation Programming Languages*, Amsterdam: North-Holland Publishing Company, 1968.

16. Carnahan, B., H. A. Luther, and J. O. Wilkes, *Applied Numerical Methods*, New York: John Wiley and Sons, Inc., 1969.

17. Carter, G., and E. Ignall, "A Simulation Model of Fire Department Operations," *IEEE-SSC*, Vol. 6, October 1970, pp. 282–292.

18. Chai, A. S., "A Fifth-Order Modified Runge-Kutta Integration Algorithm," *SIMULATION*, Vol. 18, January 1972, pp. 21–27.

19. Chorafas, D. N., *Systems and Simulation*, New York: Academic Press, 1965.

20. Chu, Y., *Digital Simulation of Continuous Systems*, New York: McGraw-Hill Book Company, 1969.

21. Clayton, E. R., and L. J. Moore, "GERT vs. PERT," *J. Syst. Management*, Vol. 23, February 1972, pp. 18–19.

22. Clymer, A. B., "The Modeling of Hierarchical Systems," *Conference on Applications of Continuous System Simulation Languages*, June 30th and July 1st, 1969, pp. 1–16.

23. *CONTROL DATA MIMIC—A Digital Simulation Language Reference Manual*, Publication No. 44610400, Revision D, Control Data Corporation, Minneapolis, Minn., 1970.

24. Davis, E. W., "Resource Allocation in Project Networks Models—A Survey," *J. Ind. Eng.*, Vol. XVII, April 1966, pp. 177–88.

25. Easton, A. T., *BASIC T COMPILER*, NASA-Goddard Space Flight Center, Greenbelt, Md., February 1971.

26. Elmaghraby, E. E., *The Design of Production Systems*, New York: Reinhold Publishing Corp., 1966.

27. Emshoff, J. R., and R. L. Sisson, *Design and Use of Computer Simulation Models*, New York: The Macmillan Company, 1970.

28. England, R., "Error Estimates for Runge-Kutta Type Solutions to Systems of Ordinary Differential Equations," *Comput. J.*, Vol. 12, May 1969, pp. 166–170.

29. Evans, G. W., II, G. F. Wallace, and G. L. Sutherland, *Simulation Using Digital Computers*, Englewood Cliffs, N.J.; Prentice-Hall, Inc., 1967.

30. Fahrland, D. A., *Combined Discrete Event/Continuous Systems Simulation*, SRC-68-16, Systems Research Center, Case Western Reserve University, Ohio, July 1968.

31. Fahrland, D. A., "Combined Discrete Event/Continuous Systems Simulation," *SIMULATION*, Vol. 14, February 1970, pp. 61–72.

32. Fishman, G. S., "Estimating Sample Size in Computer Simulation Experiments," *Manage. Sci.*, Vol. 18, September 1971, pp. 21–38.

33. Fishman, G. S., *Concepts and Methods in Discrete Event Digital Simulation*, New York: John Wiley and Sons, Inc., 1973.

34. Fishman, G. S., "Problems in the Statistical Analysis of Simulation Experiments: The Comparison of Means and the Length of Sample Records," *Comm. ACM*, Vol. 10, February 1967, pp. 91–99.

35. Fishman, G. S., and P. J. Kiviat, "The Analysis of Simulation-Generated Time Series," *Manage. Sci.*, Vol. 13, March 1967, pp. 525–557.

36. Forrester, J. W., *Industrial Dynamics*, New York: John Wiley and Sons, Inc., 1961.

37. Forrester, J. W., *Urban Dynamics,* Cambridge, Mass.: The M.I.T. Press, 1969.

38. Forrester, J. W., *World Dynamics,* Cambridge, Mass.: Wright-Allen Press, Inc., 1972.

39. Forrester, J. W., *Principles of Systems,* Cambridge, Mass.: Wright-Allen Press, Inc., 1971.

40. Fox, B. L., "Generation of Random Samples from the Beta and F Distributions," *Technometrics,* Vol. 5, 1963, pp. 269–270.

41. Fox, B. L., *Notes on Operations Research—5.* Operations Research Center, University of California, ORC 66-13, Berkeley, Calif., 1966.

42. Golden, D. G., *A Generalized Language for Discrete/Continuous Simulation,* unpublished Ph.D. Thesis, Case Western Reserve University, Ohio, January, 1972.

43. Golden, D. G., and J. D. Schoeffler, "GSL-A Combined Continuous and Discrete Simulation Language," *SIMULATION,* Vol. 20, January 1973, pp. 1–8.

44. Golden, D. G., and J. D. Schoeffler, "Implementation Problems of a Combined Continuous-Discrete Simulation Language," *SIMULATION,* Vol. 20, February 1973, pp. 49–52.

45. Goldstein, R. A., and W. F. Harris, "SERENDIPITY—A Watershed Level Simulation Model of Tree Biomass Dynamics," *Proceedings of the 1973 Summer Computer Simulation Conference,* July 1973, pp. 691–696.

46. Gordon, G., *System Simulation,* Englewood Cliffs, N.J.: Prentice-Hall, Inc. 1969.

47. Guetzkow, H., P., Kotler, and R. L. Schultz, *Simulation in Social and Administrative Science,* Englewood Cliffs, N.J.: Prentice-Hall, Inc., 1972.

48. Hadley, G., and T. M. Whiten, *Analysis of Inventory Systems,* Englewood Cliffs, N.J.: Prentice-Hall, Inc., 1963.

49. Halpin, D. W., and W. W. Happ, "Digital Simulation of Equipment Allocation for Corps of Engineer Construction Planning," U.S. Army, CERL, Champaign, Ill., 1971.

50. Hammersley, J. M., and D. C. Handscomb, *Monte Carlo Methods,* London: Methuen and Company, Ltd., 1964.

51. Hixson, H. G., "CLASS Composite Language Approach for System Simulation (A Tutorial)," *Fifth Conference on Applications of Simulation,* December 8–10, 1971, pp. 94–109.

52. Hixson, H. G., "Equipment Maintenance Studies Using a Combination of Discrete Event and Continuous System Simulation," *Third Conference on Applications of Simulation,* December 5–7, 1969, pp. 209–219.

53. Hunter, J. S., and T. H. Naylor, "Experimental Design for Computer Simulation Experiments," *Manage. Sci.,* Vol. 16, March 1970, pp. 422–435.

54. Hurst, N. R., *GASP IV: A Combined Continuous/Discrete FORTRAN based Simulation Language,* unpublished Ph.D. Thesis, Purdue University, Indiana, 1973.

55. Hurst, N. R., and A. A. B. Pritsker, "Simulation of a Chemical Reaction Process Using GASP IV," *SIMULATION,* Vol. 21, September 1973, pp. 71–75.

56. Ignall, E. J., "On Experimental Designs for Computer Simulation Experiments," *Manage. Sci.,* Vol. 18, March 1972, pp. 384–389.

57. IBM Corporation, *Continuous System Simulation for the Management Scientist,* Form GE20-0349-0, White Plains, N.Y., 1971.

58. IBM Corporation, *Introduction to 1130 Systems Modeling Program II (CSMP II)*, GH20-0848-1, White Plains, N.Y., 1970.

59. IBM Corporation, *General Purpose Simulation System/360 OS and DO5 Version 2 User's Manual,* SH20-0694-0, White Plains, N.Y., 1969.

60. Jarmain, W. E., Ed., *Problems in Industrial Dynamics,* Cambridge, Mass.: The M.I.T. Press, 1963.

61. Jöhnk, M. D., "Erzeugung von Betaverteilten und Gammaverteilten Zufallszahien," *Metrika,* Vol. 8, 1964, pp. 5–15.

62. Jones, R. E., *RUNKUT: Runge-Kutta Integrator of Systems of First Order Ordinary Differential Equations,* Sandia Laboratories, SC-M-70-724, November 1970.

63. Kamins, M., *Two Notes on the Lognormal Distribution,* RM-3781-PR (DDC No. AD 415360), The Rand Corporation, Santa Monica, Calif., August 1963.

64. Kaplan, M., R. C. Wentworth, and L. D. Bryson, "Interactive Simulation, An Answer to What Is the Question," *Society of Petroleum Engineers of AIME,* Paper Number SPE 3870, 1972.

65. Kay, Ira M., 'An Over-the-Shoulder Look at Discrete Simulation Languages," *AFIPS Conference Proceedings 40,* Spring 1972, pp. 791–798.

66. Kiviat, P. J., *GASP—A General Activity Simulation Program,* Monroeville, Pa.: Applied Research Laboratory, U.S. Steel Corporation, July 8, 1963.

67. Kiviat, P. J., "Development of Discrete Digital Simulation Languages," *SIMULATION,* Vol. 8, February 1967, pp. 65–70.

68. Kiviat, P. J., *Digital Event Simulation: Modeling Concepts,* The Rand Corporation, RM-5378-PR, Santa Monica, Calif., 1967.

69. Kiviat, P. J., *Digital Computer Simulation: Computer Programming Languages,* The Rand Corporation, RM-5883-PR, Santa Monica, Calif., 1969.

70. Kiviat, P. J., "System Simulation," *International Symposium on System Engineering,* Vol. 1, Purdue University, Indiana, October 23–27, 1972, pp. 85–90.

71. Kiviat, P. J., R. Villanueva, and H. Markowitz, *The SIMSCRIPT II Programming Language,* Englewood Cliffs, N.J.: Prentice-Hall, Inc., 1969.

72. Knuth, D. E., *The Art of Computer Programming, Vol. 1: Fundamental Algorithms,* Reading, Pa.: Addison-Wesley, 1969.

73. Knuth, D. E., *The Art of Computer Programming: Vol. 2, Seminumerical Algorithms,* Reading, Pa.: Addison-Wesley, 1969.

74. Krasnow, H. S., "Computer Languages for System Simulation," in *Digital Computer User's Handbook,* Melvin Klerer and Granino A. Korn, Eds., New York: McGraw-Hill Book Company, 1967, pp. 258–277.

75. Kunz, K. S., *Numerical Analysis,* New York: McGraw-Hill Book Company, 1957.

76. Larson, C., "The Efficient Use of FORTRAN," *DATAMATION,* August 1, 1971, pp. 25–31.

77. Lehmer, D. H., "Mathematical Methods in Large-Scale Computing Units," *Ann. Comp. Laboratory,* Vol. 26, Harvard University, 1951, pp. 141–146.

78. Lewin, D. E., *In-Process Manufacturing Quality Control,* unpublished Ph.D. Thesis, The Massachusetts Institute of Technology, Massachusetts, 1971.

79. Lewis, P. A. W., A. S. Goodman, and J. M. Miller, "A Pseudo Random Number Generator for the System/360," *IBM Systems J.*, Vol. 8, 1969, pp. 136–146.

80. Llewellyn, R. W., *FORDYN: An Industrial Dynamics Simulator,* Raleigh, N.C.: privately printed, 1965.

81. MacCrimmon, K. R., and C. A. Ryavec, "An Analytical Study of the PERT Assumptions," *Oper. Res.*, Vol. 12, 1964, pp. 16–38.

82. MacLaren, M. D., and G. Marsaglia, "Uniform Random Number Generators," *J. ACM,* Vol. 12, January 1965, pp. 83–89.

83. Malcolm, D. G., J. H. Rosenbloom, C. E. Clark, and W. Fazer, "Application of a Technique for Research and Development Program Evaluation," *Oper. Res.*, Vol. 7, 1959, pp. 616–669.

84. Markowitz, H. M., H. W. Karr, and B. Hausner, *SIMSCRIPT: A Simulation Programming Language,* Englewood Cliffs, N.J.: Prentice-Hall, 1963.

84. Martin, F. F., *Computer Modeling and Simulation,* New York: John Wiley and Sons, Inc., 1968.

86. Meadows, D. H., D. L. Meadows, J. Randers, and W. W. Behrens, III, *The Limits to Growth,* Washington, D.C.: Potomac Associates, 1972.

87. Meadows, D. L., and D. H. Meadows, Eds., *Toward Global Equilibrium: Collected Papers,* Cambridge, Mass.: Wright-Allen Press, Inc., 1973.

88. Meier, R. C., W. T. Newell, and H. L. Pazer, *Simulation in Business and Economics,* Englewood Cliffs, N.J. Prentice-Hall, Inc., 1969.

89. Mihram, G. A., *Simulation: Statistical Foundations and Methodology.* New York: Academic Press, 1972.

90. Mihram, G. A., "On Antithetic Variates," *Proceedings of the 1973 Summer Computer Simulation Conference,* Montreal: July 17–19, 1973, pp. 91–95.

91. Mize, J. H., and J. G. Cox, *Essentials of Simulation,* Englewood Cliffs, N.J.: Prentice-Hall, Inc., 1968.

92. Moder, J. J., and C. R. Phillips, *Project Management with CPM and PERT,* New York: Prinhold Publishing Corp., 1964.

93. Nance, R. E., "On Time Flow Mechanisms for Discrete System Simulation," *Manage. Sci.*, Vol. 18, September 1971, pp. 59–73.

94. Naylor, T. H., "Bibliography 19: Simulation and Gaming," *Comput. Revs.*, January 1969, pp. 61–69.

95. Naylor, T. H., J. L. Balintfy, D. S. Burdick, and K. Chu, *Computer Simulation Techniques,* New York: John Wiley & Sons, Inc., 1965.

96. Orcutt, G. H., M. Greenberger, J. Korbel, and A. M. Rivlin, *Microanalysis of Socioeconomic Systems: A Simulation Study,* New York: Harper and Row, 1961.

97. Pai, A. R., and K. L. McRoberts, "Simulation Research in Interchargeable Part Manufacturing," *Manage. Sci.*, Vol. 17, August 1971, pp. B732–B743.

98. Patten, B. C., Ed., *Systems Analysis and Simulation in Ecology,* New York: Academic Press, 1971.

99. Petersen, C. C., "Multivariable Problem solving by Simulation," *Ind. Eng.*, Vol. 5, June 1973.

100. Petersen, N. D., "MIMIC, An Alternative Programming Language for Industrial Dynamics," *J. Socio-Economic Plann. Sci.*, Vol. 6, June 1972, pp. 319–327.

101. Phillips, D. T., and C. S. Beightler, 'Procedures for Generating Gamma Variates with Non-Integer Parameter Sets," *J. Stat. Comput. Simul.*, Vol. 1, 1972, pp. 197–208.

102. Phillips, D. T., *Applied Goodness of Fit Testing*, AIIE Monograph Series, AIIE-OR-72-1, Atlanta, Georgia, 1972.

103. Pritsker, A. A. B., "Applications of Multichannel Queueing Results to the Analysis of Conveyor Systems," *J. Ind. Eng.*, Vol. XVII, January, 1966, pp. 14–21.

104. Pritsker, A. A. B., *GERT: Graphical Evaluation and Review Technique*, The Rand Corporation, RM-4973-NASA, Santa Monica, Calif., April 1966.

105. Pritsker, A. A. B., and W. W. Happ, "GERT: Part I, Development," *J. Ind. Eng.*, Vol. XVII, May, 1966, pp. 267–74.

106. Pritsker, A. A. B., and N. R. Hurst, "GASP IV: A Combined Continuous-Discrete FORTRAN based Simulation Language," *SIMULATION*, Vol. 21, September 1973, pp. 65–70.

107. Pritsker, A. A. B., and P. J. Kiviat, *Simulation with GASP II*, Englewood Cliffs, N.J.: Prentice-Hall, Inc., 1969.

108. Pritsker, A. A. B., and G. E. Whitehouse, "GERT: Part II, Applications," *J. Ind. Eng.*, Vol. XVII, June 1966, 293–301.

109. Pritsker, A. A. B., *The GASP IV User's Manual*, Pritsker & Associates, Inc., 1201 Wiley Drive, West Lafayette, Ind., September, 1973.

110. Pritsker, A. A. B., *New GERT Concepts and a GERT Network Simulation Program*, RM 71-8, Purdue University, Indiana, May 1971.

111. Pritsker, A. A. B., *Q-GERT: GERT Networks with Queueing Capabilities*, RM 72-7, Purdue University, Indiana, December 1972.

112. Pritsker, A. A. B., *Precedence GERT*, RM 71-14, School of Industrial Engineering, Purdue University, Indiana, December 1971.

113. Pritsker, A. A. B., *JASP: A Simulation Language for a Time-Shared System*, The Rand Corporation, RM-6279-PR, Santa Monica, Calif., June 1970.

114. Prothero, A., "Local-Error Estimates for Variable-Step Runge-Kutta Methods," in *Lecture Notes in Mathematics*, J. L. Morris, Ed., New York: Springer-Verlag, 1969, pp. 228–233.

115. Pugh, A. L., III, *DYNAMO II User's Manual*, Cambridge, Mass.: The M.I.T. Press, 1970.

116. Purdue University, "Environmental Flow of Cadmium and Other Trace Metals," West Lafayette, Indiana, July 1973.

117. Rand Corporation, *A Million Random Digits with 1,000,000 Normal Deviates*, New York: Free Press, 1955.

118. Reitman, J., *Computer Simulation Applications*, New York: John Wiley and Sons, Inc., 1971.

119. Robinson, L. F., "How GASP, SIMULA, and DYNAMO View a Problem," in *Progress in Simulation*, Ira M. Kay and John McLeod, Eds., New York: Gordon and Breach, 1972, pp. 167–214.

120. Sakai, T., and N. Nagao, "Simulation of Traffic Flows in a Network," *Comm. ACM*, Vol. 12, June 1969, pp. 311–318.

121. Schmidt, J. W., and R. E. Taylor, *Simulation and Analysis of Industrial Systems,* Homewood, Ill. Richard D. Irwin, Inc., 1970.

122. Schriber, T., *A GPSS Primer* (preliminary printing), Ulrich's Books, Inc., 549 East University, Ann Arbor, Mich., 1972.

123. SCi Simulation Software Committee, "The SCi Continuous System Simulation Language (CSSL)," *SIMULATION,* Vol. 9, December 1967, pp. 281–303.

124. Shampine, L. F., and H. A. Watts, *Efficient Runge-Kutta Codes,* Sandia Laboratories, SC-RR-70-615, September 1970.

125. Shampine, L. F., and H. A. Watts, "Comparing Error Estimators for Runge-Kutta Methods," *Math. Comput.,* Vol. 25, July 1971, pp. 445–455.

126. Sigal, C. E., "Designing a Production System with Environmental Considerations," *Proceedings of the AIIE Fall Institute Conference,* New York: 1973.

127. Sigal, C. E., and A. A. B. Pritsker, "SMOOTH: A Combined Continuous-Discrete Network Simulation Language," *SIMULATION,* Vol. 21, March 1974.

128. Sweet, A., and S. Duket, "A Simulation Study of Energy Consumption by Elevators in Tall Buildings," unpublished Report, Purdue University, Indiana, 1973.

129. Teichrow, D., J. Lubin, and D. Truitt, "Discussion of Computer Simulation Techniques and Comparison of Languages," *SIMULATION,* Vol. 9, October 1967, pp. 181–190.

130. Taha, H. A., *Operations Research: An Introduction,* New York: The Macmillan Company, 1971 .

131. Tocher, K. D., "Review of Computer Simulation Languages," *Oper. Res. Quart.,* Vol. 16, June 1965, pp. 189–217.

132. Tognetti, P., "Discrete Simulation Languages with Reference to a Bio-simulation—A User's Impressions," *Fourth Australian Computer Conference,* Adelaide, 1969, pp. 377–382.

133. Tramposch, H., and H. A. Jones, Jr. "Impact Problems Efficiently Solved With 1130 CSMP," *SIMULATION,* Vol. 14, February 1970, pp. 73–79.

134. Van Slyke, R. M., "Monte Carlo Methods and the PERT Problem," *Oper. Res.,* Vol. XI, September-October 1963, pp. 839–860.

135. Warden, D. E., "Dynamic Model for Evaluating Man's Impact on Global Climate," unpublished M.S. Thesis, Purdue University, Indiana, May 1973.

136. Watt, K. E. F., *Ecology and Resource Management,* New York: McGraw-Hill Book Company, 1968.

137. Weinert, E., "A SIMSCRIPT FORTAN-Case Study," *Comm. ACM,* Vol. 10, December 1967, pp. 784–792.

138. Whitehouse, G. E., *Systems Analysis and Design Using Network Techniques,* Englewood Cliffs, N.J.: Prentice-Hall, Inc., 1973.

139. Williams, R. B., "Computer Simulation of Energy Flow in Cedar Bog Lake, Minnesota Based on the Classical Studies of Lindeman," in *Systems Analysis and Simulation in Ecology,* B. C. Patten, Ed., New York: Academic Press, 1971.

140. Wyman, F., *Simulation Modeling: A Guide to Using SIMSCRIPT.* New York: John Wiley & Sons, Inc., 1970.

Appendix One

GASP IV

Runge-Kutta-England Integration*

The integration method provided by GASP IV is a fourth order, variable step size Runge-Kutta routine for integrating systems of first order ordinary differential equations with initial values. The particular constants and error estimation used are from England (28), as further described by Shampine and Watts (124).

Runge-Kutta integration has three advantages that make it the method of choice for GASP IV. First, it is widely used and well-documented. For example, MIMIC and CSMP provide Runge-Kutta integration. Second, it is easy to change the step size with a Runge-Kutta routine. Because of the need for variable step size in a combined simulation (events are not normally spaced uniformly in time) this is very important, particularly in a combined simulation having many time events. The third advantage is closely related to the second. Runge-Kutta integration is self-starting, thus there is no loss of efficiency when restarting from an event. This is of critical importance in a combined simulation.

There are two disadvantages of Runge-Kutta. First, it requires more derivative evaluations per step than some other methods of equivalent accuracy. For example, a fourth order Runge-Kutta method requires four derivative evaluations per step whereas a predictor-corrector method of the same accuracy may require as few as two. A second disad-

* Much of this appendix is taken directly from Hurst (54).

vantage of a Runge-Kutta method is that it is difficult and expensive to find suitable truncation error estimates. This factor is somewhat mitigated by the use of the England method for estimation of truncation error. This method requires fewer derivative evaluations than the more common dual mesh methods, and it also permits the step size to be changed by any amount with no computational penalty. A derivation and description of Runge-Kutta methods are contained in most books on numerical analysis (16,75).

The Runge-Kutta-England method provides the specific capability of numerically integrating a system of first order ordinary differential equations of the form

$$y'(t) = f(y(t); t)$$

with initial condition $y(t_0)$ *where* $y'(t) = dy(t)/dt$. If $y(t)$ is a vector, the above equation represents a system of first order simultaneous differential equations. It is assumed in the equations given below that $y(t)$ is a vector.

The RKE algorithm is a two step procedure involving nine function evaluations over the two steps. Let $t_1 = t_0 + h$ and $t_2 = t_1 + h = t_0 + 2h$. The procedure as implemented in GASP IV for computing $y(t_1)$ and $y(t_2)$ involves the evaluation of the following equations:

$$\begin{aligned}
a_1 &= hf(y(t_0); t_0)\\
a_2 &= hf(y(t_0) + 0.5a_1; t_0 + 0.5h)\\
a_3 &= hf(y(t_0) + 0.25(a_1 + a_2); t_0 + 0.5h)\\
a_4 &= hf(y(t_0) - a_2 + 2a_3; t_0 + h)\\
y(t_1) &= y(t_0) + \frac{1}{6}(a_1 + 4a_3 + a_4)\\
a_5 &= hf(y(t_1); t_1)\\
a_6 &= hf(y(t_1) + 0.5a_5; t_1 + 0.5h)\\
a_7 &= hf(y(t_1) + 0.25(a_5 + a_6); t_1 + 0.5h)\\
\text{EERR} &= \frac{1}{90}(-a_1 + 4a_3 + 17a_4 - 23a_5 + 4a_7 - b) + 0(h^6)
\end{aligned}$$

where* $$b = hf(y(t_0) + \frac{1}{6}(-a_1 - 96a_2 + 92a_3 - 121a_4 + 144a_5 + 6a_6 - 12a_7); t_2).$$

* The symbol b is used in the above since b is only used in the computation of EERR and need not be stored. Each a_j value is stored and thus there must be NNEQD ★ 7 storage locations available for storing the a_j values. GASP IV allows NNEQD ≤ 100, therefore, 700 storage locations are allocated to storing the a_j values.

If EERR $\leq$ AAERR + RRERR $\star$ $y(t_1)$

then

$$y(t_2) = y(t_1) + \frac{1}{6}(a_5 + 4a_7 + hf(y_1(t) - a_6 + 2a_7; t_2)).$$

In the above procedure a_j is a vector and EERR is computed for each state variable. Only if the error estimate is allowable for all the state variables will the $y(t_2)$ values be computed.

The implementation of the above procedure is contained in subroutine GASP. The function evaluations are obtained through calls to subroutine STATE with the appropriate values for SS($\cdot$) and TNOW representing the two arguments, that is, $f(\mu;v)$ is evaluated by a call to STATE with μ = SS($\cdot$) and v = TNOW. The value of the function is the value of the derivative of SS($\cdot$) and is stored as DD($\cdot$), which is then available to compute the values of a_j. The two step procedure is performed over the interval DTFUL so that the half step h is equal to 0.5 $\star$ DTFUL. The time interval for specific evaluations is made available as DTNOW. The values of the state variables at t_1 are maintained in the variables SI($\cdot$) and DI($\cdot$).

The actual coding of the Runge-Kutta-England procedure is shown in Fig. 4-2 beginning at statement 126. First, a variable (LDBL) is set to indicate that the current step has not failed an accuracy test. Next, values for the length of a half step (DTHLF) and a quarter step (DTQRT) are calculated. The initial values for the state variables and their derivatives are available as SSL(I) and DDL(I). The succeeding statements, through 130, sequentially calculate the appropriate Runge-Kutta constants (A1(I), A2(I), A3(I), or A4(I)), revise the values of the state variables, revise the value of time, and calculate revised values for the derivatives of the state variables (by a CALL STATE statement.) At statement 130 the calculated values for the state variables are for a half step point so that a check is made to determine if a state-event has occurred. (Note, however, that the accuracy of the half step values has not yet been verified.) If a state-event has occurred, or been passed, the appropriate action is taken. If not, the half step values of the state variables and their derivatives are stored as SI(I) and DI(I). The procedure then continues as before until, at statement GSP 127, the estimated local truncation error for the entire step is calculated. This estimate (EERR) is compared to the total allowable error (TERR = AAERR + ABS (RRERR $\star$ SI(I))) to determine if accuracy is acceptable. If not, the step size is reduced and the step is restarted from TTLAS, unless DTFUL = DTMIN, in which case the step is accepted or a fatal error is caused, based on the value of LLERR. If accuracy is acceptable, any state-event that occurred at the half step is processed. If none, the final portion of the Runge-Kutta procedure continues as before from statement 150. The end-of-step values for the state variables are calculated in statement 153. This concludes a full Runge-Kutta step.

It is important to note that the procedure just described permits the integration of sets of simultaneous differential equations, however, equations of the form $y = f(y;t)$, in which f is not the integration operator, usually require an iterative method of solution. GASP IV does not provide such a method; however, it is possible for the user to code such a method in subroutine STATE. The MIMIC Implicit Function (23) gives an example of an iterative technique that could be used in such a case.

Appendix Two

GASP IV

Glossary of Variables

Variable	Definition
AAERR	Absolute local truncation error allowed in Runge-Kutta integration. Used with RRERR to control accuracy; not used when NNEQD = 0.
ATRIB(I)	Buffer for attribute values being stored in or retrieved from QSET.
DD(I)	If I $\leq$ NNEQD, the value of the derivative of SS(I) at TNOW. If NNEQD $<$ I $\leq$ NNEQT, the value of the state variable DD(I) at TNOW.
DDL(I)	If I $\leq$ NNEQD, the value of the derivative of SS(I) at TTLAS. If NNEQD $<$ I $\leq$ NNEQT, the value of the state variable DD(I) at TTLAS.
DTACC	Maximum next step size permitted based on accuracy requirements.
DTFUL	Step size of the full time step currently being executed if NNEQT $>$ 0; undefined if NNEQT = 0.
DTMAX	Maximum allowable step size; user specified; not used if NNEQT = 0.
DTMIN	Minimum allowable step size; user specified; not used if NNEQD = 0.
DTNOW	TNOW − TTLAS; undefined if NNEQT = 0.

Variable	Definition
DTPLT(I)	Increment of the independent variable between successive plot sets for plot I; user specified.
DTSAV	Increment of the independent variable between successive save times if NNEQT > 0; undefined if NNEQT = 0; user specified.
EENQ(I)	Time integrated number of entries in file I.
HHLOW(I)	Upper limit of the first cell of histogram I.
HHWID(I)	Width of each cell (excluding the first and last cells) of histogram I.
IICRD	Indicator used in DATIN for initialization; specifies the data card type at which reading of data cards is to begin for the next simulation run.
IIEVT	Code for state-events; read in initially; undefined if NNEQT is zero.
IINN(I)	Priority ranking indicator for file I. If IINN(I) = 1, entries in file I are ordered by attribute KKRNK(I) from lowest to highest value (LFV). If IINN(I) = 2, the entries in file I are ordered by attribute KKRNK(I) from highest to lowest value (HVF). If IINN(I) = 3, the entries in file I are ordered first-in-first-out (FIFO). If IINN(I) = 4, the entries in file I are ordered last-in-first-out (LIFO). IINN(1) specifies secondary, tie-breaking ranking for file 1 (primary ranking for file 1 is always LVF); for all other files IINN(I) specifies primary ranking.
IISED(I)	Integer seed for the Ith stream of the random number generator (DRAND).
IITAP(I)	Index of the tape on which data for plot I are stored. If IITAP(I) = 0, data are stored in QSET.
IITES	Internal indicator that a time-event ends the current step. Undefined in NNEQT = 0.
ISEES	Indicator that a state-event ends the current step. ISEES > 0 indicates at least one state-event within tolerance and none exceeding tolerance. First such state event is associated with SS(ISEES) if ISEES < 1001 or DD(ISEES − 1000) if ISEES > 1000. ISEES < 0 indicates at least one state-event exceeding tolerance. First such state-event is associated with SS(ISEES) if ISEES < 1000 or DD(ISEES − 1000) if ISEES > 1000. ISEES = 0 indicates no state-event.
JEVNT	Code of time-event that is the second attribute of an

Variable	Definition
	event equal to ATRIB(2) to be processed. Also used as a control in subroutine MONTR when set equal to 0, −1, −2, −3, −4, −5, or −6.
JJBEG	Variable used to control initialization; nonzero only during initialization. For JJBEG nonzero: DRAND initialized, TNOW = TTBEG, TTLAS = TNOW, TTNEX = TTFIN, and save interval initialized. For JJBEG positive, in addition to above: subroutine INTLC called, DTFUL = DTMAX, DTNOW = 0, subroutine STATE called, and state variables initialized.
JJCEL(I)	Storage array for histograms.
JJCLR	Variable used to control initialization of statistical storage arrays SSOBV, SSTPV, and JJCEL. For JJCLR positive, arrays are initialized.
JJFIL	Variable used to control initialization of files. For JJFIL positive, initialization is performed.
KKRNK(I)	Attribute on which file I is ranked.
LFLAG(I)	State condition flags. For I ≤ NFLAG, reset to zero immediately following the processing of an event.
LLABC(I)	Label associated with Ith variable used in COLCT.
LLABH(I)	Label associated with Ith histogram.
LLABP(IJ)	Label associated with variable IJ of plot I. LLABP(11) associated with the independent variable.
LLABT(I)	Label associated with Ith variable used in TIMST or TIMSA.
LLERR	Indicates type of error check in Runge-Kutta integration. For LLERR = 1, step size will be reduced until DTNOW = DTMIN, then fatal error. For LLERR = 0, step size reduced until DTNOW = DTMIN, then warning only and proceed. For LLERR = −1, step size reduced until DTNOW = DTMIN, then proceed with no warning.
LLPHI(IJ)	Control variable; user specified. LLPHI(IJ) = 0 indicates that the maximum ordinate value for plotted variable IJ is the maximum value of the variable. LLPHI(IJ) = 1 specifies that maximum as PPHI(IJ). LLPHI(IJ) = 2 specifies that it is the maximum value of the variable rounded up to the nearest PPHI(IJ).
LLPLO(IJ)	Control variable; user specified. LLPLO(IJ) = 0 indicates that the minimum ordinate value for plotted variable IJ is the minimum value of the variable.

Variable	Definition
	LLPLO(IJ) = 1 specifies minimum as PPLO(IJ). LLPLO(IJ) = 2 specifies that it is the minimum value of the variable rounded down to the nearest PPLO(IJ).
LLPLT	Control variable; user specified. LLPLT $<$ 0 indicates quick plot. LLPLO and LLPHI must both be equal to one, and PPLO and PPHI must be used. LLPLT = 0 indicates normal plot only. LLPLT = 1 indicates normal table only. LLPLT $>$ 1 indicates normal table and plot.
LLSAV	An internal control variable associated with the save interval.
LLSUP(I)	Control variable; user specified. Used to suppress reading and/or echo checking of input data.
LLSYM(IJ)	Plot symbol for variable IJ.
MFA	Relative address of the first cell of NSET available for storing a new entry.
MFE(I)	Relative address of the first entry in file I.
MLE(I)	Relative address of the last entry in file I.
MMAXQ(I)	Maximum number of entries in file I.
MMPTS	Maximum number of point sets for which there is storage allocated in NSET. Defined only if there is a plot or table using core storage.
MMON	Month label for report heading.
MSTOP	Indicator for specifying method of ending the simulation. If MSTOP = 0, a statement must be included in which MSTOP is made negative to stop the simulation. If MSTOP $>$ 0, simulation is ended when TNOW $\geq$ TTFIN.
NCRDR	Number of the card reader.
NFLAG	Number of state condition flags (LFLAG) being used.
NNAME	Label for user's name for heading.
NNAPO	Number of attributes plus one (NNAPO = NNATR + 1).
NNAPT	Number of attributes plus two (NNAPT = NNATR + 2).
NNATR	Number of attributes per entry in QSET.
NNCEL(I)	Number of cells (not including end cells) in histogram I when input by user. Changed in DATIN to be the index of the last cell associated with histogram I.
NNCFI	Number of cells of the file storage array NSET allocated for the assignment of files. NNCFI = NNTRY ⋆ NNAPT.

Variable	Definition
NNCLT	Number of sets of statistics collected by COLCT.
NNDAY	Label for date for heading.
NNEQD	Largest subscript for DD(·) when defined by a derivative equation. (For efficiency, NNEQD should be the number of derivative equations.)
NNEQS	Number of state variables that can be defined by state equations.
NNEQT	Largest subscript used for state variables. Normally, equal to the number of state and derivative equations, NNEQT = NNEQD + NNEQS.
NNFIL	Number of files in NSET.
NNHIS	Number of histograms.
NNPLT	Number of plots and/or tables.
NNPRJ	Label for project number for heading.
NNPRM	Number of parameter sets.
NNPT	Number of point sets for which there is insufficient storage allocated in NSET. Defined only if there is a plot or table using core storage.
NNPTS(I)	Number of point sets for plot/table I that have been saved.
NNQ(I)	Current number of entries in file I.
NNRNS	Number of runs remaining, including the one being processed.
NNRUN	Number of current simulation run.
NNSET	Dimension of NSET; set by user in GASP IV data card type 2; used to compute amount of storage available in NSET. (Note, this variable is not a GASP COMMON variable.)
NNSTA	Number of sets of statistics that can be collected by TIMST and TIMSA.
NNSTR	Number of random number streams.
NNTRY	Maximum allowable number of entries in NSET.
NNVAR(IJ)	Number of variables to be plotted/tabled in plot/table IJ.
NNYR	Label for year for date in heading.
NPRNT	Number of printer.
NSET(I)	Integer representation of filing array. Used for pointers only.
PPARM(J,I)	Array for storing parameter values.
PPHI(I)	Value associated with plot ordinate. See LLPHI(I).
PPLO(I)	Value associated with plot ordinate. See LLPLO(I).
QQTIM(I)	Time of last use of file I.

Variable	Definition
QSET(I)	Real valued representation of the file storage area. Used for all attribute values.
RRERR	Relative local truncation error allowed in Runge-Kutta integration. Used with AAERR to control accuracy.
SS(I)	Value of the state variables SS(I) at TNOW.
SSEED(I)	Seed for the Ith stream of the random number generator.
SSL(I)	Value of the state variable SS(I) at TTLAS.
SSOBV(I,J)	Array for storing statistics generated by COLCT.
SSTPV(I,J)	Array for storing statistics generated by TIMST.
TNOW	Current time of simulation. When a step advance is in progress, TNOW is the time to which GASP IV is trying to advance.
TTBEG	Initial value of TNOW (if JJBEG > 0).
TTCLR	Time at which subroutine CLEAR was last called.
TTFIN	Time to end simulation if MSTOP > 0.
TTLAS	Last time at which an event could have occurred.
TTNEX	Scheduled time of occurrence of the most imminent time-event. (TTNEX = TTFIN if there are no scheduled time-events.)
TTRIB(I)	Storage area the same size as ATRIB. Used by subroutine PRNTQ.
TTSAV	Next save time; undefined if NNEQT = 0.
TTSET	Time at which subroutine SET was last called.
VVNQ(I)	Time integrated square of the number of entries in file I.

Appendix Three

GASP IV

Error Codes

Error Code	Error Condition	Location of Error Condition
101*	TTNEX < TNOW	GASP 20
102	NNEQT < 0	GASP 21
103	NNEQD < 0	GASP 61
104	Failed accuracy test and LLERR > 0	GASP 146
105	Failed tolerance test and LLERR > 0	GASP 196
106	NNQ(1) < 0	GASP 278
107	NNRNS < 1	GASP 320
196	Requested number of cells for histograms greater than dimension for JJCEL	DATIN 106
197	Requested number of random number streams, NNSTR, exceeds allowable	DATIN 195
198	Requested number of state variables, NNEQT, exceeds allowable	DATIN 55
199	Requested number of parameter sets, NNPRM, exceeds allowable	DATIN 50
200	Requested number of flags, NFLAG, exceeds allowable	DATIN 49

* This error can be caused by the use of blank COMMON by the user.

Error Code	Error Condition	Er
201	IICRD < 0	DAT
202	Number of cells for file entries, NNSET, set too small	DAT
203	Attempted to read too many initial entries or initial entries not ended with IFILE = 0.	DAT
204	Requested number of variables for which statistics are to be collected based on observations, NNCLT, exceeds allowable	DAT
205	Requested number of variables for which time persistent statistics requested, NNSTA, exceeds allowable	DATIN 44
206	Requested number of histograms, NNHIS, exceeds allowable	DATIN 45
207	Requested number of plots, NNPLT, exceeds allowable	DATIN 46
208	Requested number of attributes per entry, NNATR, exceeds allowable	DATIN 47
209	Requested number of files, NNFIL, exceeds allowable	DATIN 48
211	NNCLT <0	CLEAR 4
212	NNSTA < 0	CLEAR 12
213	NNHIS < 0	CLEAR 20
221	NNTRY ≤ 0	SET 2
301	Attempted to file more than allowable number of entries, NNTRY, in NSET(MFA ≤ 0).	FILEM 6
302	NNQ(IFILE) < 0 or IFILE < 1	FILEM 21,47,63,91
311	NNTRY ≤ 0 or IFILE $= 0$	RMOVE 5,13
312*	NEXTE $<$ or IFILE < 1	RMOVE 57,61
313	NTRY ≤ 0	COPY 5
411	MFE(IFILE) < 0	NFIND 12
412	KBEST < 0	NFIND 47
501	ICLCT $>$ NNCLT	COLCT 10
502	SSOBV(J,3) < 0	COLCT 22

* This error can be caused by the use of blank COMMON by the user.

Error Code	Error Condition	Location of Error Condition
511	ISTAT > NNSTA	TIMST 10 or TIMSA 5
512	SSTPV(J,3) < TTCLR	TIMST 26
521	IHIST > NNHIS	HISTO 14
531	Independent variable of plot is not monotonic	GPLOT 120,175
541	Incorrect file pointers	PRNTQ 49
551	NNEQT < 0	PRNTS 3
561	NNPRM < 0	SUMRY 11
562	NNCLT < 0	SUMRY 18
563	NNSTA < 0	SUMRY 26
564	NNFIL < 0	SUMRY 32
565	NNEQT < 0	SUMRY 38
566	NNHIS < 0	SUMRY 44
567	NNPLT < 0	SUMRY 50
601	JEVNT = −6	MONTR 9
602	MFE(1) < 0	MONTR 10
701	ISTRM = 0 or ISTRM > NNSTR	DRAND 10
741	PPARM(IPAR,4) < 1	ERLNG 3
801	IFILE > NNFIL	SUMQ 3
811	IFILE > NNFIL	PRODQ 3
831	ILS < IFS	GDLAY 4,8

INDEX